Cruelty to Animals and Interpersonal Violence

Cruelty to Animals and Interpersonal Violence

READINGS IN RESEARCH AND APPLICATION

EDITED BY
RANDALL LOCKWOOD AND FRANK R. ASCIONE

Purdue University Press / West Lafayette, Indiana

02   01   00   99   98   5   4   3   2   1

♾ The paper used in this book meets the minimum requirements of American National Standard for Information Sciences—Permanence of Paper for Printed Library Materials, ANSI Z39.48-1992.

Printed in the United States of America

Library of Congress Cataloging-in-Publication Data
Cruelty to animals and interpersonal violence : readings in research and application / edited by Randall Lockwood and Frank R. Ascione.
       p.   cm.
   Includes bibliographical references and index.
   ISBN 1-55753-105-6 (cloth : alk. paper). — ISBN 1-55753-106-4 (pbk. : alk. paper)
   1. Animal welfare. 2. Animals, Treatment of. 3. Cruelty. 4. Violence—Psychological aspects. 5. Human-animal relationships. I. Lockwood, Randall, 1948–   . II. Ascione, Frank R.

   HV4708.C78   1997
   616.85'8—dc21   97–41462
                              CIP

CONTENTS

ACKNOWLEDGMENTS

I wish to thank Paul Irwin, president of the Humane Society of the United States, and Patricia Forkan, executive vice president, for their support of this project and their commitment to shaping a truly humane society through the protection of all potential victims of violence. I would also like to thank Debbie Duel, HSUS program manager, for her assistance in keeping so many people in touch and informed.

To my wife, Julie, and daughter, Susan, I wish to express my thanks for their tolerance and understanding of my frequent absences as I have attempted to help others translate the ideas in this book into practice. They have helped me realize the importance of striving for a world where all members of the family can feel loved, safe, and secure. Finally, to my mother I express the deepest appreciation for her ability to teach wonder at, and respect for, the other creatures and cultures we encounter.

RANDALL LOCKWOOD

This book would not have been possible without the dedicated assistance of Teresa M. Thompson. Teresa was an undergraduate at Utah State University during the time the seeds of this project began to germinate. Although she, no doubt, considered our relationship as one of student and mentor, I consider her a valued colleague. She did most of the tedious library work required to assemble the materials in this book. Teresa has gone on to complete graduate study and is now a school counselor. Many children will be touched by her empathy, kindness, sensitivity, and professional dedication.

Tolerance, patience, encouragement, excitement, and gently critical editing—I have been wrapped in these qualities provided by my wife and dear friend, Debbie, during this project and many others. She and my children, Matthew, Catherine, and David have taught me so beautifully that no man is an island. Being anchored in their lives has facilitated my work and provided me with abundant gifts of caring. My deepest thanks to each of you.

FRANK R. ASCIONE

INTRODUCTION

The landscapes of violence have become too familiar, too close to home. Despite decades of scientific research, we are only beginning to understand the roots of violence that underlie child maltreatment, spouse and partner abuse, and aggression in our schools, neighborhoods, and communities. Cruelty to animals is often a part of these landscapes of violence and at times shows a strong link to destructive interpersonal relationships.

Collectively, we have spent nearly fifty years examining the factors involved in the humane and inhumane treatment of animals. We both bring our respective backgrounds in experimental and developmental psychology to our attempts to understand the human capacity for kindness and cruelty. As we began our collaboration in this area of inquiry, we lamented a common frustration: research on the association between animal maltreatment and interpersonal violence is scattered throughout journals of diverse scientific disciplines, and information about animal cruelty specifically is often hidden in periodicals and monographs in that abstracts and indices sometimes fail to mention animal abuse, even though its significance is referred to in the articles themselves.

We have both, at different times, reviewed the literature on animal cruelty and interpersonal violence (Ascione 1993; DeViney, Dickert, and Lockwood 1983—both included in section 2). Our survey of past research has been both enlightening and frustrating, since information on the subject often lies buried, like treasure, in these reports. We have been impressed by the depth and breadth of scholarship devoted to this topic and by the diversity of disciplines—from anthropology to biochemistry to criminology—that have considered the subject worthy of study.

We share the concern that much of this material has not been integrated into the training or thinking of those who might benefit most from a better understanding of the interconnectedness of all forms of violence against innocent victims of many different kinds. Many of our colleagues in psychology are unaware of the majority of the research collected here, as are many professionals in the fields of psychiatry, social work, law enforcement, criminal justice, and veterinary medicine. These are the people in the best position to apply the concepts and data in this book to improve the protection of people and animals, and perhaps to more readily identify the perpetrators of violence.

Over the years we have frequently been contacted by such professionals, as well as students, the media, and animal-protection advocates seeking scientific references on this subject. It became clear that the literature we had uncovered as background to our own research would be of benefit to others interested in violence against animals and people. We sought to compile as much of this literature as possible in a single readily available resource. This volume represents our best efforts in achieving this goal.

This book was designed to appeal to a diverse audience. For the layperson fascinated with benevolent and malevolent human-animal interactions, we have prefaced each section of readings with a brief introduction to the issues addressed by the articles included in that section and the reasons for their inclusion. Although most of the articles are from professional publications, we have selected papers that are readable and do not require extensive or technical background knowledge. The articles included in sections 1 and 2 provide broad overviews of the topic, and the lay reader would be well served to begin with these sections.

We also hope that professionals on the front lines of the interface between cruelty to animals and interpersonal violence will find this compilation useful. Legislators, animal-control officers, law-enforcement personnel and supervisors, prosecutors and members of the judiciary, and workers in child welfare and domestic violence should find information and ideas relevant to their respective professional interests and programs.

One of the dilemmas we faced early in this project was deciding which articles from our overflowing files to include in this book. Although research in this area is scattered, it is still extensive. Had we included all of the references on our wish lists, readers would be holding a volume many times thicker and more expensive. Clearly this compilation could not be exhaustive or comprehensive—selectivity was a necessary evil with which we had to deal. We apologize to authors whose work could not be included in this book for any of a variety of reasons.

We chose articles that could be considered classics in the field, as well as others that are representative of work in specific disciplines, such as criminology or psychiatry. Our concern that our selectivity might prevent readers from appreciating the depth and breadth of the literature on this topic was allayed when we examined the list of references cited in each article. We believe that the papers collected here, along with their reference sections, constitute one of the most extensive listings yet compiled of research on animal maltreatment and interpersonal violence.

Our professional activities have often taken us into the landscapes of violence in which people and animals suffer. We strongly believe that the wounds in human relationships and human-animal relationships are preventable and that empathy and compassion for all fellow creatures, human and nonhuman, must be nurtured and sustained. We hope that by highlighting the connections between cruelty to animals and interpersonal violence, the potential for violence in all its forms will be reduced.

SECTION 1: PHILOSOPHICAL AND HISTORICAL BACKGROUND

This section explores the philosophical and historical foundations of concern about the connections between animal cruelty and societal violence. It is fitting that we begin this collection with an excerpt from John Locke's 1705 essay "Some Thoughts concerning Education." Many of the central themes and questions of this book are addressed here with elegant simplicity and a modern sensitivity to the key questions of the origins of violence.

For Locke, the empiricist notion of a "blank slate" of human experience meant that when we are confronted by violence in an individual, we must look for the experiences and influences that might have produced such violence and have led that person away from humanity's natural state of goodness, independence, and equality. For Locke, as for many psychologists and sociologists today, the answer lies in the impact of "contrary teaching," experiences that deaden the sensibilities and allow cruelty to become a pleasure. He sees the far-reaching consequences of teaching children to laugh when they hurt another living thing or see harm come to others. Like many of the modern authors in this volume, he suggests that this can initiate a progressive escalation of cruelty.

In the eighteenth century Locke's writing had significant influence on people's awareness of the need for fostering a child's sensitivity and compassion at an early stage. His suggestions for intervention and prevention also have a modern tone. In many ways we should consider him an early proponent of humane and environmental education in his insistence that "people should be accustomed, from their cradles, to be tender to all sensible creatures and to spoil or waste nothing at all." Likewise, his recommendations for dealing with children for whom cruelty has become a pleasure parallels much modern thought in its emphasis on correction through proper role models rather than through physical punishment and harm.

The entry by Sandor Ferenczi moves us from the philosophical to the psychological realm. While Locke spoke in generalities, several early psychoanalytic writers explored individual case histories in depth, setting the stage for the more detailed retrospective and prospective studies we see with larger samples later on. This particular case history is included because of its focus on the young boy's "pleasure in fantasy about the cruel torture of poultry" and on the coexistence in this child of violence against animals and people. Unfortunately Ferenczi gives us no insights into his patient's later development, and we do not know if his problems proved to be predictive of adolescent or adult violence. The psychoanalytic emphasis on sexual events and attitudes, seen in this piece and in Sigmund Freud's discussion of the classic case of Little Hans and his fear of horses, has been ignored in much of the more modern literature on animal cruelty. Only recently have researchers begun to rediscover the potential role that animal cruelty may play in the eroticization of violence, as reflected in the 1986 essay of Robert K. Ressler and his colleagues (included in section 5). Although much of the orientation of Ferenczi's analysis may seem quaint and archaic, the interconnectedness of sex, violence, and experiences with animals continues to deserve close attention.

Like Locke, Margaret Mead was concerned with the process by which children become full human beings, but her view of human nature is different from that of Locke. Her focus in this piece is on how societies teach children not to commit murder rather than on the violent childhood experiences that might influence aggressive behavior. Like Temple Grandin (1988—included in section 9), she points out the problems posed by the ambiguity of a society's attitude toward the killing of animals and people. Animals and people are killed in many socially sanctioned contexts—for food or sport in the case of animals and in warfare and criminal justice in the case of humans. A child's socialization must include instruction in maneuvering through these moral complexities to form perceptions of violence that fit the individual's culture. Mead concludes that failure to correct the perception of malicious killing of animals is one significant pattern in the development of violence that violates societal norms. She provides one of the earliest suggestions that societies should watch for and record evidence of children's and adolescents' killing and torture of animals and institute carefully planned programs of empathy and animal care to prevent the escalation of violence.

This section concludes with David Favre and Vivien Tsang's 1993 "archaeological" analysis of the development of anticruelty laws in the 1800s. They document an intriguing evolutionary process whereby animals are first treated as property that is not to be "damaged" by someone other than the owner; this attitude shifted to protection of animals from suffering without regard to their ownership or commercial value. Society's actions on these issues have been complicated by the fact that animals can be viewed as sentient creatures capable of suffering and, at the same time, as objects with commercial value. As the authors note, pain and suffering was not a legal concern until quite recently, but even in the early stages of animal-protection laws there was a sensitivity to the moral impact of animal abuse on human perpetrators and witnesses. The authors note that awareness of the connections between animal cruelty and violence against humans was reflected in the positioning of animal-cruelty statutes in chapters dealing with "offenses against chastity, decency and morality."

Favre and Tsang end with the sobering analysis that animal-protection laws have remained largely unchanged for one hundred years and conclude that our legal relationship with animals will remain rooted in the philosophy of the 1870s until society at large can be convinced that a new perspective is justified. Perhaps such a shift in perspective may be helped by the recognition that animals become victims of violence for many of the same reasons, and at the hands of the same perpetrators, as the human victims of such abuse.

"CRUELTY," §116 (SOME THOUGHTS CONCERNING EDUCATION)

One thing I have frequently observed in children, that, when they have got possession of any poor creature, they are apt to use it ill; they often torment and treat very roughly young birds, butterflies, and such other poor animals, which fall into their hands, and that with a seeming kind of pleasure. This, I think, should be watched in them; and if they incline to any such cruelty, they should be taught the contrary usage; for the custom of tormenting and killing of beasts will, by degrees, harden their minds even towards men; and they who delight in the suffering and destruction of inferior creatures, will not be apt to be very compassionate or benign to those of their own kind. Our practice takes notice of this, in the exclusion of butchers from juries of life and death. Children should from the beginning be bred up in an abhorrence of killing or tormenting any living creature, and be taught not to spoil or destroy any thing unless it be for the preservation or advantage of some other that is nobler. And truly, if the preservation of all mankind, as much as in him lies, were every one's persuasion, as indeed it is every one's duty, and the true principle to regulate our religion, politics, and morality by, the world would be much quieter, and better-natured, than it is. But to return to our present business; I cannot but commend both the kindness and prudence of a mother I knew, who was wont always to indulge her daughters, when any of them desired dogs, squirrels, birds, or any such things, as young girls use to be delighted with: but then, when they had them, they must be sure to keep them well, and look diligently after them, that they wanted nothing, or were not ill used; for, if they were negligent in their care of them, it was counted a great fault, which often forfeited their possession; or at least they failed not to be rebuked for it, whereby they were early taught diligence and good-nature. And indeed I think

people should be accustomed, from their cradles, to be tender to all sensible creatures, and to spoil or waste nothing at all.

This delight they take in doing of mischief (whereby I mean spoiling of any thing to no purpose, but more especially the pleasure they take to put any thing in pain that is capable of it) I cannot persuade myself to be any other than a foreign and introduced disposition, an habit borrowed from custom and conversation. People teach children to strike, and laugh when they hurt, or see harm come to others; and they have the examples of most about them to confirm them in it. All the entertainment of talk and history is of nothing almost but fighting and killing; and the honour and renown that is bestowed on conquerors (who for the most part are but the great butchers of mankind) farther mislead growing youths, who by this means come to think slaughter the laudable business of mankind, and the most heroic of virtues. By these steps unnatural cruelty is planted in us; and what humanity abhors, custom reconciles and recommends to us, by laying it in the way to honour. Thus, by fashion and opinion, that comes to be a pleasure, which in itself neither is, nor can be any. This ought carefully to be watched, and early remedied, so as to settle and cherish the contrary and more natural temper of benignity and compassion in the room of it; but still by the same gentle methods, which are to be applied to the other two faults before mentioned. It may not perhaps be unreasonable here to add this farther caution, viz. that the mischiefs or harms that come by play, inadvertency, or ignorance, and were not known to be harms, or designed for mischief's sake, though they may perhaps be sometimes of considerable damage, yet are not at all, or but very gently, to be taken notice of. For this, I think, I cannot too often inculcate, that whatever miscarriage a child is guilty of, and whatever be

John Locke, "Cruelty," §116 of *Some Thoughts concerning Education,* in *The Works of John Locke in Nine Volumes.* 12th ed. (London: C. & J. Rivington), 8:112–14.

the consequence of it, the thing to be regarded in taking notice of it, is only what root it springs from, and what habit it is like to establish; and to that the correction ought to be directed, and the child not to suffer any punishment for any harm which may have come by his play or inadvertency. The faults to be amended lie in the mind; and if they are such as either age will cure, or no ill habits will follow from, the present action, whatever displeasing circumstances it may have, is to be passed by without any animadversion.

A LITTLE CHANT'CLEER [1]

A LADY a former patient of mine who had retained her interest in psycho-analysis, called my attention to the case of a little boy, which she surmised would be of general interest.

The case was that of a five-year-old boy, Árpád by name, who according to the unanimous reports of all his relatives had developed up to the age of three and a half in quite a regular way both mentally and physically, and was said to have been a perfectly normal child; he spoke fluently and shewed considerable intelligence.

All at once he became quite different. In the summer of 1910 the family went to an Austrian spa, where they had also spent the previous summer, and took rooms in the same house as in the year before. Immediately after the arrival the child's demeanour changed in a curious way. Hitherto he had taken an interest in all the goings on, both indoors and out of doors, that might attract the attention of a child; from now on he was interested in only one

[1] Published in the Internat. Zeitschr. f. arztl. Psychoanalyse, 1913.

Reprinted from Sandor Ferenczi, *Sex in Psychoanalysis: Contributions to Psychoanalysis* (Boston: Gorham Press, 1916), 240–52.

thing, and that was the fowl-house in the courtyard of the dwelling. Early in the morning he hastened to the poultry, watched them with tireless interest, imitated their sounds and movements, and cried when he was forcibly removed from the fowl-run. But even when he was away from it he did nothing else but crow and cackle. He did this unintermittingly for hours at a time, and answered to questions only with these animal cries, so that his mother was seriously concerned lest her child would lose his power of speech.

This peculiar behaviour of little Árpád lasted throughout the whole duration of the summer stay. When the family returned to Budapest he began once more to speak in a human way, but his talk was almost exclusively of cocks, hens, and chickens, at the most with geese and ducks besides. His usual game, repeated endlessly every day, was as follows: He crumpled up newspaper into the shape of cocks and hens, and offered them for sale; then he would take some object (generally a small flat brush), call it a knife, carry his "fowl" to the sink (where the cook really used to kill the poultry, and cut the throat of his paper hen. He shewed how the fowl bled, and with his voice and gestures gave an excellent imitation of its death agony. Whenever fowls were offered for sale in the courtyard little Árpád got restless, ran in and out of the door, and gave no peace until his mother bought some. He wanted to witness their slaughter. Of live cocks, however, he was not a little afraid.

The parents asked the child endless times why he was so afraid of cocks, and Árpád always related the same story: He had once gone out to the hen-coop, had micturated into it, whereupon a fowl or capon with yellow feathers (sometimes he said with brown) came and bit his penis, and Ilona, the servant, had dressed the wound. Then they cut the cock's throat, so that he died.

Now, as a matter of fact, the parents remembered this occurrence, which had happened in the *first* summer spent in the spa, when Árpád was only two and a half years old. One day the mother had heard the little one shrieking fearfully, and learnt from the servant that he was frightened of a cock which had snapped at his penis. Since Ilona was no longer in the family's service it could not be ascertained whether on that occasion Árpád had really been hurt or (as the mother's memory went) had merely been bandaged by Ilona to calm him.

The curious part of the matter was that the psychical after-effect of this experience had set in with the child after a latent period of a whole year, on the second visit to the summer residence, without anything having happened in the meanwhile to which the relatives could ascribe this sudden recurrence of the fear of fowls and the interest in them. I did not, however, let the negative nature of this evidence restrain me from putting a question to the child's *entourage*, one sufficiently justified by psycho-analytical experience, namely, whether in the course of the latent period the child had not been threatened—as so often happens—with the cutting off of his penis on account of voluptuous playing with his genitals. The answer, given unwillingly, was to the effect that at the present time, it was true, the boy was fond of playing with his member, for which he often got punished, that it was also "not impossible" that someone might have "jokingly" threatened to cut it off, further that Árpád had had this bad habit "for a long time," but whether he already had it in the latent year was no longer known.

In what comes presently it will be seen that in fact Árpád had not been spared this threat at a later date, so that we are entitled to regard the assumption as probable that it was the threat experienced in between which had so greatly excited the child on re-visiting the scene of the first terrifying experience, in which the well-being of his member had similarly been endangered. A second possibility is of course not to be excluded, namely, that the first fright already had been exaggerated by a still earlier threat of castration, and that the excitement on re-visiting the hen-coop is to be ascribed to the increase of "sexual hunger" that had come about in the meantime. Unfortunately it was no longer possible to reconstruct these time relationships, and we have to be content with the probability of the casual connection.

Personal investigation of the boy yielded nothing striking or abnormal. Immediately on entering my room his attention was attracted by a small bronze mountain cock among the numerous other objects lying about; he brought it to me and asked "will you give it to me?" I gave him some paper and a pencil and he immediately drew a cock (not unskilfully). Then I got him to tell me the story about the cock. But he was already bored and wanted to get back to his toys. Direct psycho-analytic investigation was therefore impossible, and I had to confine myself to getting the lady who was interested in the case and, being a neighbour and friend of the family, could watch him for hours at a time, to note down his curious remarks and gestures. I was able to establish so much for myself, however, that Árpád was mentally very alert and also not untalented; his mental interest and his talent were, it is true, peculiarly centered round the feathered folk of the fowl-run. He clucked and crowed in a masterly way. Early in the morning he woke the family—a true Chanticleer—with a lusty crow. He was musical, but sang only popular songs in which cock, fowl, or the like came, being especially fond of the song:

"To Debreczen I must run,
  There to buy a turkey-cock."

then the songs: "Chicken, chicken, come, come, come," and

"Under the window are two chickens,
Two little cocks and a hen."

He could draw, as was remarked above, but he confined himself exclusively to birds with a large beak, drawing these with considerable skill. One thus sees the directions in which he was seeking to sublimate his pathologically strong interest in these creatures. The parents had finally to put up with his hobbies, seeing that their interdictions did no good, and bought for him various toy birds made of unbreakable material with which he carried out all sorts of fanciful games.

Árpád was in general a pleasant little fellow, but very defiant whenever he was reprimanded or beaten. He hardly ever cried, and never begged for forgiveness. Apart from these character traits, however, there were no traces of true neurotic traits to be recognised. He was easily frightened, dreamt a great deal (of fowls, of course) and often slept badly (*Pavor nocturnus*).

Árpád's curious sayings and actions, which were noted down by the lady observer, mostly display an unusual pleasure in phantasies about the cruel torturing of poultry. His typical game, imitating the slaughter of fowls, I have already mentioned; to this should be added that even in his bird dreams it was mostly "killed" cocks and hens that he saw. I will here give a literal translation of some of his characteristic sayings:

"I should like to have a live plucked cock," he once said quite spontaneously. "He must have no wings, no feathers, and no tail, only a comb, and he must be able to walk like that."

He was playing in the kitchen with a fowl that had just been slaughtered by the cook. All of a sudden he went into the next room, fetched a curling-tongs out of a drawer, and cried: "Now I will stick this dead fowl's blind eyes." The slaughtering of poultry was quite a festival for him. He could dance round the animals' bodies for hours at a time in a state of intense excitement.

Someone, pointing to the slaughtered fowl, asked him: "Would you like it to wake again?" "The devil I would; I would knock it down again at once myself."

He often played with potatoes or carrots (which he said were fowls), slicing them into small pieces with a knife. He could hardly be restrained from throwing to the ground a vase that had fowls painted on it.

The affects displayed in regard to fowls, however, were by no means simply those of hate and cruelty, but were plainly ambivalent. Very often he would kiss and stroke the slaughtered animal, or he would "feed" his wooden goose with maize, as he had seen the cook do; in doing this he clucked and peeped continuously. Once he threw his unbreakable doll (a fowl) in the oven because he could not tear it, but then pulled it out again at once, cleansed it and caressed it. The animal figures in his picture book, however, had a worse time of it; he tore them in pieces, was then naturally unable to bring them back to life, and got very upset.

If such symptoms were observed in an adult insane patient, the psycho-analyst would not hesitate to interpret the excessive love and hate concerning poultry as a transference of unconscious affects that really referred to human beings, probably near relatives, but which were repressed and could only manifest themselves in this displaced, distorted way. He would further interpret the desire to pluck and blind the animals as symbolising castration intentions, and regard the whole syndrome as a reaction to the patient's fear of the idea of his own castration. The ambivalent attitude would then arouse in the analyst the suspicion that mutually contradictory feelings in the patient's mind were balancing each other, and on the basis of numerous experiential facts he would have to surmise that this ambivalence probably referred to the father, who—although otherwise honoured and loved—had at the same time to be also hated on account of the sexual restrictions sternly imposed by him. In a word, the analytic interpretation would run: The cock signified in the syndrome the father.[2]

In little Árpád's case we can spare ourselves the trouble of making any interpretation. The work of repression was not yet able entirely to conceal the significance of his peculiarities; the original thing, the repressed tendencies, could still be discerned in his talk, and indeed it became evident at times with a startling openness and crudity.

His cruelty was often displayed in regard to human beings also, and was strikingly often directed against the genital region of adults. "I'll give you one in the faeces, in your behind," he was fond of saying to a boy somewhat older than himself. Once he said, still more plainly, "I'll cut your middle out." The idea of blinding occupied him pretty often. He once asked his neighbour: "Can one make a person blind with fire or with water?" (He was also highly interested in the genitals of poultry. With every fowl that was slaughtered they had to enlighten him about the sex—whether it was a cock, a hen, or a capon.)

He ran to the bed of a grown-up girl and called out: "I'll cut your head off, lay it on your belly,

---

[2] In a very large number of analyses of dreams and neuroses the figure of the father is discovered behind that of an animal. See Freud, Schriften, etc. Ch. 1, and Internat. Zeitschr. f. Psychoanalyse, Jahrg. I, Heft 2.—Professor Freud tells me that one of his next works in "Imago" will make use of this identity to explain totemism. (This has since appeared in book form under the title "Totem und Tabu." Transl.)

and eat it up." Once he said quite suddenly: "I should like to eat a potted mother (by analogy: potted fowl); my mother must be put in a pot and cooked, then there would be a potted mother and I could eat her." (He grunted and danced the while). "I would cut her head off and eat it this way" (making movements as if eating something with a knife and fork).

After cannibalistic desires of this sort he would at once get an attack of remorse, in which he masochistically yearned for cruel punishments. "I want to be burnt," he would then call out: "Break off my foot and put it in the fire." "I'll cut my head off. I should like to cut my mouth up so that I didn't have any."

There can be no doubt that by fowl, cock, chicken he meant his own family, for he said once quite spontaneously: "My father is the cock!" On another occasion: "Now I am small, now I am a chicken. When I get bigger I shall be a fowl. When I am bigger still I shall be a cock. When I am biggest of all I shall be a coachman." (The coachman who drove their carriage seemed to impress him even more than did his father).

After this independent and uninfluenced admission of the boy we can better understand the enormous excitement with which he was never tired of watching the goings on in the fowl-yard. He could conveniently observe in the hen-coop all the secrets of his own family about which no information was vouchsafed to him at home; the "helpful animals" shewed him in an unconcealed way everything he wanted to see, especially the continual sexual activity between cock and hen, the laying of eggs, and the creeping out of the young brood. The dwelling conditions at Árpád's are such that he had beyond all question been an ear-witness to similar proceedings (between the parents). The curiosity in this way aroused he then had to satisfy by insatiable gazing at animals.

We are also indebted to Árpád for the last confirmation of my assumption that the morbid dread of cocks was ultimately to be traced to the threat of castration for onanism.

One morning he asked the neighbour: "Tell me, why do people die?" (Answer: Because they get old and grow tired). "Hm! So my grandmother was also old? No! She wasn't old, and yet she died. Oh, when there's a God why does he always let me fall down? And why does he make people have to die?" Then he began to get interested in angels and souls, upon which he was given the explanation that they are only fairy-tales. At this he got quite rigid with fright and said: "No! That's not true! There are angels. I have seen one who carries the dead children to heaven." Then he asked, horrified: "Why do children die?" "How long can one live?"

It was only with great difficulty that he calmed down.

It turned out then that early on the same day the chamber-maid had suddenly lifted his bed-clothes and found him manipulating his penis, whereupon she threatened to cut it off. The neighbour tried to quiet him and told him that no harm would be done to him; every child did things of that sort. Upon which Árpád cried out indignantly: "That's not true! Not every child! My papa has never done anything like that."

Now we understand better his unquenchable rage towards the cock who wanted to do with his member what the grown-ups threatened to do, and his awe for this sexual animal which dared to do everything that filled him with terror; we also understand the cruel punishments that he pronounced on himself (on account of the onanism and the sadistic phantasies).

To complete the picture, so to speak, he began later on to occupy himself greatly with religious thoughts. Old, bearded Jews filled him with great respect, mixed with dread. He begged his mother to invite these beggars into the house. When one actually came, however, he would hide and watch him from a respectable distance; as one of these was going away the boy let his head hang down and said, "Now I am a beggar-fowl." Old Jews interested him, so he said, because they come "from God" (out of the temple).

In conclusion another utterance of Árpád's may be given which shews that he had not watched the goings on of the fowls so long for nothing. He told his neighbour one day in all seriousness: "I shall marry you and your sister and my three cousins and the cook; no, instead of the cook rather my mother." He wanted, therefore, to be a real "cock of the roost."

CULTURAL FACTORS IN THE CAUSE AND PREVENTION OF PATHOLOGICAL HOMICIDE*

MARGARET MEAD, Ph.D†

Every human society faces the task of turning all of the children born to its members into full human beings, who will walk and talk, think and feel and act like that particular society's version of our common human nature—like Eskimos or Frenchmen, Iranians or Russians, Samoans or Americans. No society of which we have any record has ever fully succeeded with every child that is born. Even where life is so rigorous and methods of medicine so little developed that most defective and vulnerable children die, some will grow to manhood and womanhood with imperfect enculturation, with an incomplete or deviant understanding of the culture within which they were born.

Such deviations may, of course, be both positive and negative—the man who somehow attains a divine discontent will become the prophet and the innovator; the man who fails to learn to handle his impulses in socially approved ways may resort to rape and theft, murder and arson. Such failures occur in even the simplest societies and it is important to know to what degree we can attribute their failure to accept or improve upon the norms of their society to genetic factors, to the way in which they were reared, to special traumatic circumstances (being orphaned, seeing a parent slain, being alone with a dying grandfather, watching a ceremonial post-mortem caesarian operation), or to the institutionalized ways in which a culture selects from each generation those who are to carry the burden of antisocial behavior—the thieves and the fences, the killers, the kidnappers, the skid row alcoholics, the narcotic addicts and professional arsonists, who by their behavior, point a moral and adorn a tale, and even, in counterpoint fashion, contribute to the stability of the social system.

All of these factors are important. Studies of pathological murderers without motives, who show clouded states of consciousness, suggest constitutional factors; studies of psychopathic children with unusual amounts of energy also suggest constitutional factors. In minute analysis of the form of some pathological killings, thematic elements related to earlier trauma can be found. In the criminal areas of the great cities,

* Read at the 16th annual meeting of the Midcontinent Psychiatric Meeting, Sept. 14, 1963, under the title "Problems of Criminology and Law in Different Cultures."
† Visiting Sloan Professor April through June 1959, and Visiting Professor of Anthropology May through June 1962, in the Menninger School of Psychiatry, Topeka, Kansas.

Reprinted from the *Bulletin in the Menninger Clinic* 28 (1964): 11–22, with kind permission of the Guilford Press.

there are schools of crime, with continuity through generations, which select for entrance some of the children born in the slums, and some of those who drift down through the upper strata of society.

In cities like Hong Kong it is possible to trace both traditional and socially supported delinquency—traditional, in the boys who are attached to temples of thieves, and modern forms of delinquency among the children of newcomers to the middle class. We know that in every great city, old or new, occidental or oriental, within the domain of the communists, in neutralist areas and among those countries that ally themselves with the values of western Europe and the English speaking world—there are an enormous number of individuals who fall by the wayside, fail to adapt to the expectations of their society, and find institutionalized niches waiting for them, the criminal quarter, the underworld of smuggling, dope, and drink and crime, the gray world of illegal gambling, betting and prostitution, the armed centers of resistance of the rackets, the gangsters, the thugs, the professional killers and arsonists. The larger and more heterogeneous and anonymous the society, the larger the proportion of those who are unable to function within its usual norms.

The identification and description of the particular constitution of the individuals who are least able to function within the accepted forms of education is a task for physical anthropologists, geneticists, physiologists, neurologists. The identification of the psychic make-up of such individuals is the particular realm of psychiatry. Sociology and anthropology are concerned with the identification of the social and cultural conditions within which these individuals, initially vulnerable, traumatized and brutalized in childhood, or simply unfortunately located in the wrong part of the city, grow up.

In selecting the cultural factors in pathological homicide for discussion here, I wish to use this as an illustration of the way in which the kind of interchange that is possible within the widening boundaries of the psychiatric community in Topeka can lead to new insights and new research problems.

When I first came to the Menninger School of Psychiatry as a Sloan Visiting Professor in the spring of 1959, I was working on my Freud lecture on adolescence,[1] and I asked to be told about any interesting case conferences on adolescents. One of the first I attended dealt with a boy who presented signs of dangerous destructiveness; he had been in the habit of killing cats by banging their heads against an alley wall and had accidentally injured the eye of a school mate with a knife. During the discussion of the case, the psychiatrist mentioned a study of cases of homicide by Rosen, Satten, Mayman and Karl Menninger.[2] Alerted to their study, I discussed with them the occurrence of apparently unmotivated murderous violence against strangers as it was institutionalized as *amok* among Malay peoples.

The authors of the homicide study described the cases of four men who had killed with great violence, and apparently no provocation, individuals who simply happened to be on the scene. In one of these cases, Ehrenreich[3] had conducted a number of hypnotic sessions in which the thematic plot had been elicited—an episode in which the patient's uncle, enraged at catching his wife in bed with a lover, had seized the patient and started to choke him. "When the patient screamed for help, the uncle put him in a coffin and closed it." Thereafter, the boy had frequent convulsive seizures for which his uncle beat him. He was frightened badly when he was seduced by an older woman, suffered the loss of a girl, for whose death he blamed himself, and whom he had an obsessive desire to follow into the grave. His later history includes necrophiliac attacks on women killed during the European war and the murder and mutilation of a prostitute whom he was driving home from a party. In this detailed case, and the three other less detailed cases, the same story was repeated—uncontrollable violence unleashed against victims who, however they might fit into the picture of the murderer's past, were almost random choices at the actual moment of killing.

After reading the homicide study, I came upon the following passages from a taped interview with an old southern Negro singer in Alan Lomax's *The Rainbow Sign*:[4]

> . . . Joe Tripp has cut up about twenty people and he's walkin the streets a free man right today in Livingston. Joe gambles and sells whiskey and hustles around for a livin and nobody has ever known him to work, except when Judge Pentland got him out of jail.
>
> Judge Pentland was short of hands that time and so he called up the jail Monday mornin, told them to turn Joe out, and so they turned him out and he went on out to the judge's place and plowed. Plowed *good* all week till Saturday night. Then he told Judge Pentland, said, "I know you don't owe me nothin, but I'm goin on to town tonight and I would like to have a little change, please sir, to put in my pocket."
>
> Judge said, "Joe, you gonna get drunk and get in a fight. You ain't gonna be here Monday to help me." "Give you my word, captain, I'll be

here Monday. I don't know what I might have done, but I'll be here plowin Monday."

"Well, Joe, I'm not goin to give you but just two dollars."

"Just anything you give me I'll thank you for it. You don't owe me nothin anyway."

So the judge give him two dollars and, sure enough, Joe went to town and got into a fight and the judge said, "Put him back in jail. I can't make nothin out of him. If it wasn't for weekends, Joe would be one of the best workers down here. It's just weekends mess him up."

Joe don't pick no fights, but he'll sho fight if anybody bother him any way. See, he gambles, practically gambles all the time he's not in prison. Happen to make a payday, he'll go down in Tin Cup where they gamblin and he'll get him a big glass of whisky. He'll be there in the yard awhile, drunk, eyes half shut, woofin around, and then he'll go inside the house.

"You all move. Move now and let *me* get down there."

"Throw down, man, throw down."

Joe will pull *all* his money and throw it down. Everybody else got two dollars down, but Joe will put down all he got—maybe three or four dollars. He's not payin any attention until somebody tell him, "Joe, you got too much money down there. Them folks ain't bettin but two dollars."

One of *them* say, "Man, what *you* talkin for? You ain't in this game. Let the man bet."

Well, an argument will start up and Joe will sort of wake up to himself and say, "I'll just take my money back."

"No, you can't . . . It's already down."

Old Joe will show them where he *can* take it up. He'll reach out and take his and some of theirs, too. Then he'll back up in the corner of the house, ram his hand down in his pocket, open up that little-bitty knife he carry, and wait. Some of them may not know him and they say, "I'm gonna have *my* money."

Joe say, "Well, *git* it then."

So that person who don't know Joe will fly into him and Joe will go to cuttin and everybody else in the house will leave. Just them two will be in there fightin and pretty soon you can hear that man hollerin, "Somebody come here, please, and take this man offa me." But nobody will come till the police come to take Joe to jail and the other guy to the hospital.

Joe won't never kill nobody. I been knowin about him twenty years and I ain't never heard nobody say he's killed nobody yet. See, he won't carry a good knife. Anybody try to give him a long, stout knife, he won't have it. He'll get him a two-bit pocketknife and the blade won't be longer than your little finger, not long enough to reach the heart. Joe don't *want* to reach the heart. He cuts um through the stomach, on the back, the arms, and on the legs—anywhere the fleshiest places at.

He jobs straight in. Then he rips down with the end of his knife. Just sticks straight in and pulls down. And continually go on like that. If the man should fall or somebody be partin um, Joe won't stop, he just keep right on jobbin and rippin until the man really boogied up for true. By the time he get to the hospital, that man'll be just solid blood. The doctor will look at him and say, "Where's the worst place on him? This man bleedin *all* over. I declare I don't know where to start sewin him up."

I don't know, but some of them *say* Joe has got tempers. He drinks whisky and he gets don't-carish. "I don't care if I do. . . ." He just go on and *do*. He say to himself, "I know they gonna put me in jail, so I'm gonna fix up a good job of it. Then I won't be worried if they put me in there. If you have to do anything like fightin, don't just touch your man, don't just shove him around. *Mommick* him up good, because you've got to go to jail anyhow."

. . . Sis say he was a mighty mean and disobedient boy and she always told him he wouldn't come to no good end. He'd kill folks' hogs and chickens. If he wouldn't kill a hog, he'd cut both ears off and cook that for his fresh meat. Sis would beat him to death one day and tomorrow she'd go way down in the field, choppin, and when she'd come back, somebody would be at the house tellin her what Joe had done.

"Joe done killed two of my chickens . . . Joe done milked my cows . . . Joe done killed my best rooster . . ." He'd do just anything. One time he got mad at a lady comin over and tellin how he'd cut her hog's ears off and he went into her garden—he went in there and pulled up every one of her greens, row by row. The sheriff came and carried him in there and measured his feet in the tracks and it was *his* foot all right.

He's still livin out in the country with his mother. He calls that home. He was married once but he beat his wife so much till finally she died, just kinda weaklied away. In the summer time, when it's real hot, he comes over to town and sleeps on people's porches. Sundays, when folks pass by where he is on their way to church, he'll holler, "You all goin to church?"

"Yeah, Joe, you better come on and go with us today."

"No, I won't go up there. You all just give God my love. Tell him I'm still here."

. . . Never even thinks about all those mean things he's done. And he's nice to people. *He* treats everybody right. But just don't fight him, just don't work him up, or you gonna get cut!

The likeness to the four cases was striking; there was the blurring of consciousness, the random and unpremeditated violence, and the death of the wife after repeated maltreatment came close to murder. But there was one great difference: Joe remained a member of his small community; they accepted him, and the worst trouble came only when, for example, in a gambling game, "Some of them may not know him, and they say, 'I'm gonna have *my* money.' "[4] Then the trouble would start.

Although Joe showed all of the general sorts of behavior reported for the other cases, violent behavior and violent reprisals in childhood, easily and irrationally triggered violence, blurring of consciousness, an inability to stop an impulsive act once it had started, he did not in fact become a murderer.

His case was like that of a man, Nang Darmi, in the Balinese village of Bajoeng Gede who sometimes, but not always, might slash at a man who asked to borrow his machete. People knew about it, they were somewhat wary, but they didn't stop casually borrowing his machete. Once in a while somebody got badly cut. But the man was not punished in any way, his wife did not leave him; he remained a member of the village community where everyone knew and accepted his peculiarity.

The next week, I was being shown around the occupational therapy section in one of the hospitals and my psychiatrist guide pointed out a man who had been extraordinarily paranoid and violent. He had been permitted to work in occupational therapy, but the psychiatrist, who had been reared in a small southeastern town, had alerted everyone to give him a wide berth in any narrow space. The crisis had come when the patient had invited a group of visitors to come up close to where he was working with a large chisel on a piece of wood. When they approached him, the patient smiled and laid the chisel down, and from then on his recovery began.

Another case conference concerned a boy with a low impulse control, and a record of disproportionate attacks of nonstop violence at home, who had wrung the neck of his canary. And a little later, in a conference on children's coping behavior, there was a reported incident of a well-adjusted little farm boy who related proudly how he had killed an enormous mouse singlehanded, with his shoe.

Then far away from Topeka, there was a singularly shocking murder of a little three-year-old girl by a teen-age neighbor boy who had been a quiet, model student. The little girl, sunsuit strap fallen off her shoulder, had wandered in, the boy had seized her, carried her downstairs and killed her.

This then was the sequence of events—a case conference in which the invitation was in response to my stated interest; an encounter with the authors of a research paper about which I had heard, and to which I could contribute cross-cultural material; the accidental sequence in which I read *The Rainbow Sign* and the extraordinary fit in its material, which also reiterated the theme of killed animals; the report on the handling of a violent patient by a psychiatrist who had grown up in a small southeastern town and was accustomed to treating violence with respect; the second case of a violent boy who strangled his canary; the child in the coping project who could report with pride his valor in the culturally approved slaughter of the farmer's enemy, a mouse; and finally the inexplicable murder of a friendly child by a quiet, studious boy.

It is upon sequences of this sort that the development of anthropological insights depends, as month after month one follows, attentively, a stream of events within some primitive village until a pattern emerges. It is upon behavioral sequences—as a patient relates them, in combination with carefully reported episodes in the hospital, in recreation, in occupational therapy—that the psychiatrist depends for his knowledge of an emerging pattern in individual patients. Finally it is from the sequence of case conferences, research papers, reading, and the consultations with colleagues which are such an outstanding aspect of life in The Menninger Foundation, that theoretical insights develop. It is because there are so many levels of relevant experience available, almost simultaneously, that work in a setting like this is so meaningful to a behavioral scientist, perhaps particularly so to the field worker who has learned to watch for constant meaningful cross-referencing within his material.

In their paper, Rosen, Satten, Mayman and Karl Menninger[2] reported that the four men all had a "long standing, sometimes lifelong, history of erratic control over aggressive impulses" and "in the historical background of all the cases was the occurrence of extreme parental violence during childhood," and "evidence of severe emotional deprivation in early life." They further defined the four men as having "ego-images of themselves as physically inferior, weak, and inadequate" and that "these individuals brought to the scene [of the murder] a potential readiness to kill which was activated by the unconscious perception of the victim as representing a key figure in some past network of trauma. In these cases, the act of murder can be understood theoretically as resulting from the interplay of the following factors: (a) a strong surcharge of aggressive and hostile impulses; (b) relative weakness or lack of flexibility in the delaying mechanisms of the ego; (c) somewhat impaired reality perception; (d) disturbed capacity for positive emotional investment in people; and (e) the various unconscious meanings to the murderer of the victim." They concluded their paper with the hope: "Out of a greater understanding of this syndrome as representing psychopathology and an appropriate concern of the psychiatrist and clinical psychologist can perhaps arise some ideas about the prevention of murder by such individuals as well as an approach to the possibility of their treatment."

In carrying out this expressed hope, the anthropologist and sociologist have a part to play. Beyond the widely recognized need for establishing living conditions within our entire society so that the areas of poverty, slums, and social deprivation which are generally responsible for the conditions of emotional deprivation found in many of such cases, lies the need to identify the specific conditions which either prevent or facilitate the development of this particular kind of murderer. It seemed clear, from our knowledge of small primitive societies, from cases like Joe, that in small communities, where everyone knew everyone else, although such personalities were found, the more terrible social consequences could often be averted. The great contrast between Joe, or Nang Darmi of the Balinese village, Bajoeng Gede, and the four reported killers, was that Joe and Nang Darmi were lifelong members of a community while the four killers roamed anonymously over continents without close ties. In the case of the little girl murdered by a neighbor, it was in a city where the families of the two children were worlds apart in the way they had reared their children; the little girl's whole outgoing warmth was not something with which the inhibited, overdisciplined boy had ever been prepared to cope. In a kind of world where encounters with strangers become commoner than encounters with those one knows, all of the old protections, knowledge of the temper of a fellow villager, of the cues that are appropriate between people if provocation is to be avoided are vanishing.

At the same time, lonely, withdrawn children, with "ego-images of themselves as physically inferior, weak and inadequate"[2] may spend many hours a week in a half trance, alone before a television set, soaking in images of violence and murder. With no other viewer there to correct their perceptions, their reality perceptions between what has happened, might happen, what is day dream, nightmare, or past or future deeds, become blurred."[5] Children in urban communities are taught to fear the stranger and told in a booklet with brightly colored illustrations from the Los Angeles Sheriff's office:[6]

> Most people love a little child
>   some grown ups, though, are bad.
> The bad ones look like good ones
>   like any Mom or Dad.
> So that is why you must not talk
>   to strangers that you meet;
>   don't let them give you any toys,
>   or anything to eat.
> If someone that you do not know
>   should offer you a treat,
>   remember how he looks and talks,
>   but run fast, up the street.
> Don't go away with him at all,
>   although he asks you to;
>   If he should grab you, scream so
>   loud, that help will come to you.
> If someone in a motor car
>   should offer you a ride,
>   scream loudly as you run away
>   but do not get inside.

Compare here the report of Ehrenreich's patient; before he killed and mutilated the woman whom he hardly knew: "The more she yelled, the more I felt like everything happened to me in my life come down. I felt bad . . . suddenly I felt myself like I was falling and I saw something, a strange face. And I saw a coffin and somebody was trying to put me in that coffin . . . Then I was grabbing something . . . I heard her scream, when she screamed it sounded like something I heard once before, it was screaming, scaring me, and I remember fighting. I was screaming and frightened like I was trying to get away from something . . . didn't remember seeing her anymore. . . ."[3]

The admonitions from the sheriff's department to the children of Los Angeles County[6] ends:

> It's never safe in alleys
>   or empty buildings too.
> It's always best to travel
>   where Mother tells you to.

> Remember how The Cautious Twins
> make Mother feel so proud;
> she knows they won't go off alone—
> *they play with their own crowd.*   (italics mine)

And so in the modern world, the circle within which more pathologically killing-prone, frightened, impulse-ridden individuals wander, among strangers who give them false cues, or who by fleeing invite pursuit, becomes wider and more dangerous. The old controls of the face-to-face community, despite which such killings sometimes occurred, are gone and it becomes more urgent to identify early the children who may grow up to kill anyone who happens to be on the scene. Fritz Peters[7] in his novel, *Descent,* has vividly dramatized in fiction the terror that may lurk at any point in a modern community.

I now want to bring together these cross-referencing materials in another way and ask: How do human societies teach their children not to commit murder—that is, not to kill in forbidden ways? We know of no human society that does not distinguish between permissible and impermissible killing. To kill a human being in forbidden ways is *murder;* to kill the trespasser, the enemy, is approved, or even enjoined. But most human children do not have demonstrations during childhood of the distinctions between murder and the enjoined, approved brave killing of other human beings. How do they learn? Here we can go back to the cases and notice the recurrence of killing and torture of living things. We have the adolescent boy who swings cats by their tails and smashes their heads against the wall and then wounds a schoolmate.

The boy who strangles his canary, on the Word Association Test, "blocked on the word 'snake,' for a time was unable to give any verbal response, but instead reported a memory of the time that he was caring for some baby birds in a nest. Visiting the nest one day he discovered a snake, which had just killed the birds. Without thinking further, he ran into the house, got the loaded rifle which he always kept by his bedside and emptied a fully loaded magazine into the snake."[2]

And Joe "He'd kill folks' hogs and chickens. If he couldn't kill a hog he'd cut both ears off and cook that for his fresh meat. Sis would beat him to death one day and tomorrow she'd go way down in the field, choppin, and when she'd come back, somebody would be at the house tellin her what Joe had done."[4]

In every culture children are taught which creatures they may and may not kill and how. English parents rely heavily on teaching a child to control a presumedly innate cruelty by admonitions not to torture animals. In his wide survey of English parental attitudes Geoffrey Gorer asked: "What is the worst thing that a child can do?" Thirteen per cent answered "Torture an animal."[8] A fly may be swatted but it is cruel to pull off its wings. A chicken may be killed for eating, but this must be done quickly and "mercifully." Ants that get into the kitchen may be killed with spray; but to tread on an ant hill for no reason, is disapproved. Cats may be kept to kill mice—and a very small boy who kills a mouse is a good boy, a brave boy—but children are discouraged from watching a cat "torture" a half dead mouse or bird. Fish below a certain size must be thrown back into the stream. Deer can only be killed in season, however much they eat the young vegetables. Then there are ambiguities, a porcupine that gets under the house—should or should not Daddy kill it? Delicately, precisely, carefully, within each subculture, in the country, in the city, on the farm, by the sea, the lines are drawn. Pests to be killed, food to be eaten, pets to be loved, are discriminated for the growing child.

Here when the original lines are drawn, occur, I suggest, the first episodes which prefigure the murder of the anonymous human victim. The child with weak impulse control, prone to attacks of aggression and hostility, violates one of these tabus. The adult, who was himself trained by requirements that he keep the tabu, reacts violently to the child's transgression. "Sis would beat him to death one day and tomorrow . . ." in an endless cycle. Here is one set of predisposing conditions which fits very well with the tales of abuse and violence in the life histories. "They was trying to scare me, and screaming at me. Tried to scare me out of those fits. My uncle caught a rattlesnake and brought it to the house. He tied a piece of cloth on his head and put it in a box and put me in the room in the middle of the floor. I used to couldn't talk, I was dumb, I was always sick after that coffin incident with fits. Grandmother said I had devils in my head. She said the devil had taken possession of me and I was a bad thing in the family."[3]

And there is a second set of conditions—when the child who kills or tortures in a tabued way is not caught, or if caught is not punished. A failure of punishment here, where there is a cultural reliance on teaching and learning, can be as fatal or possibly even more fatal, than too violent punishment. The temptation to try it again, try something bigger, kill a cat instead of a bird, wring a dog's neck instead of a canary's, can take possession of the child. Success in the next symbolic murder intensifies the predilection toward a landslide impulsive act of greater aggressive magnitude. In the words of Satten, *et al.*, "the hostility once aroused and finding overt motoric expression did not spend itself until he had exhausted all the destructive potential. . . ."[2]

In many parts of the present day world of great mobility, from class to class, region to region, country to city, the tabus about killing and torturing living creatures are no longer reliable. Parents no longer can teach, without conscious thought, by their admonitions, looks of horror or repulsion, quick slaps and retaliations, the difference between murder and permitted self-protection or patriotic defense. We may expect that for more and more children, the culturally expected cues will be missing, and they will inadvertantly stumble on forms of behavior that will arouse irrational rage in the adults around them, and invite reprisals and severe punishment or find a way in which secretly to act out their hostile fantasies that are daily fed on television.

It would, therefore, seem wise to include a more carefully planned handling of behavior toward living creatures in our school curriculum on the one hand, and to alert all child therapists to watch for any record of killing or torturing a living thing. It may well be that this could prove a diagnostic sign, and that such children, diagnosed early, could be helped instead of being allowed to embark on a long career of episodic violence and murder.

REFERENCES

1. MEAD, MARGARET: Cultural Contexts of Puberty and Adolescence. *Bull. Philadelphia Assn. Psa.* 9:59–79, 1959.
2. SATTEN, JOSEPH, MENNINGER, KARL, ROSEN, IRWIN AND MAYMAN, MARTIN: Murder Without Apparent Motive. *Amer. J. Psychiat.* 117:48–53, 1960.
3. EHRENREICH, GERALD A.: Headache, Necrophilia, and Murder. *Bull. Menninger Clin.* 24:273–287, 1960.
4. LOMAX, ALAN: *The Rainbow Sign.* New York, Duell, Sloan, Pierce, 1959.
5. MEAD, MARGARET: Violence and Your Child. *TV Guide*, March 21–27, 1959, pp. 17–19.
6. SHERIFF'S DEPARTMENT, LOS ANGELES COUNTY: *The Cautious Twins.* Los Angeles, Calif., Lincoln Saving and Loan Association.
7. PETERS, A. A.: *Descent.* New York, Farrar, Straus, 1952.
8. GORER, GEOFFREY: *Exploring English Character.* New York, Criterion, 1955.

THE DEVELOPMENT OF ANTI-CRUELTY LAWS DURING THE 1800's

Professor David Favre†
Vivien Tsang

"[L]aws and the enforcement or observance of laws for the protection of dumb brutes from cruelty are, in my judgment, among the best evidences of the justice and benevolence of men."[1]

TABLE OF CONTENTS

INTRODUCTION

The nineteenth century saw a significant transformation of society's attitude toward animals,[2] which was reflected in the

---

† Professor David Favre of the Detroit College of Law is a board member of the Animal Legal Defense Fund and has written a number of books and articles on animal issues over the past twelve years.

Vivien Tsang graduated from The Detroit College of Law in 1993.

1. Stephens v. State, 3 So. 458 (Miss. 1887) (Arnold, J., plurality).

2. Access to nineteenth century writing on the topic of animals is limited. There is almost no discussion from the legal perspective. *See* CHARLES R. MAGEL, A BIBLIOGRAPHY ON ANIMAL RIGHTS AND RELATED MATTERS 51-451 (1981).

Reprinted from the *Detroit College of Law Review* 1 (1993): 1–35, with permission of the Detroit College of Law at Michigan State University Law Review.

legal system. The legal system began the century viewing animals as items of personal property not much different than a shovel or plow. During the first half of the century, lawmakers began to recognize that an animal's potential for pain and suffering was real and deserving of protection against its unnecessary infliction.

The last half of the nineteenth century saw the adoption of anti-cruelty laws which became the solid foundation upon which today's laws still stand. As will be discussed, during the 1860's and 1870's Henry Bergh of New York City was a primary force in the adoption, distribution, and enforcement of these laws in the United States. Underlying the changes of the law were parallel changes of social attitude toward animals. This Article will explore the changes within the legal world during the nineteenth century.

I. THE BRITISH SET THE STAGE

Notwithstanding the political independence that the United States obtained from Great Britain during the late 1700's and early 1800's, there was still a considerable transfer of ideas from the intellectually mature mother country to the newly formed and basically frontier United States. The first articulations of concern for the moral and legal status of animals appeared in British writing.[3] Reverend Humphrey Primatt in *A Dissertation on the Duty of Mercy and Sin of Cruelty to Brute Animals,* written in 1776, pleaded for the care of animals.

> See that no brute of any kind . . . whether intrusted to thy care, or coming in thy way, suffer thy neglect or abuse. Let no views of profit, no compliance with custom, and no fear of ridicule of the world, ever tempt thee to the least act of cruelty or injustice to any creature whatsoever. But let this be your invariable rule, everywhere, and at all times, to do unto others as, in their condition, you would be done unto.[4]

---

3. For a fuller discussion of the English debate about duty toward animals, see RODERICK F. NASH, THE RIGHTS OF NATURE 16-25 (1989); JAMES TURNER, RECKONING WITH THE BEAST: ANIMALS, PAIN AND HUMANITY IN THE VICTORIAN MIND (1980).

4. SYDNEY H. COLEMAN, HUMANE SOCIETY LEADERS IN AMERICA 18 (1924) (quoting REV. HUMPHREY PRIMATT, A DISSERTATION ON THE DUTY OF MERCY AND SIN OF CRUELTY TO BRUTE ANIMALS (1776)).

Jeremy Bentham, an English barrister, was one of the few legal writers who addressed the issue of animals and the legal system. His *Introduction to the Principles of Morals and Legislation*[5] was closely studied at the time by a large number of individuals, some of whom went on to propose legislation for the protection of animals.[6] Bentham argued that there was no reason why animals should not be accorded protection under the law. Bentham pointed out that animals, "on account of their interests having been neglected by the insensibility of the ancient jurists, stand degraded into the class of *things*."[7] Within a footnote entitled "Interests of the inferior animals improperly neglected in legislation,"[8] Bentham argued that the capacity for suffering is the vital characteristic that gives a being the right to legal consideration.[9] The final sentence of the footnote is often used today as a rallying cry for those seeking to promote the cause of animal rights: "The question is not, Can they *reason*? nor, Can they *talk*? but *Can they suffer*."[10]

Having made intellectual arguments for concern about animals, the British followed up with changes in the legal system. On May 15, 1809, Lord Erskine addressed Parliament in support of the bill which he had introduced for the protection

---

5. JEREMY BENTHAM, AN INTRODUCTION TO THE PRINCIPLES OF MORALS AND LEGISLATION (Oxford, Clarendon Press 1781).

6. *See* COLEMAN, *supra* note 4, at 14-15; NASH, *supra* note 3, at 25.

7. BENTHAM, *supra* note 5, at 310.

8. *Id.* at 310-11 n.1.

9. *Id.*

10. *Id.* The following is a more extensive portion of the footnote:
The day has been, I grieve to say in many places it is not yet past, in which the greater part of the species, under the denomination of slaves, have been treated by the law exactly upon the same footing as, in England for example, the inferior races of animals are still. The day *may* come, when the rest of the animal creation may acquire those rights which never could have been withholden from them but by the hand of tyranny. . . . It may come one day to be recognized, that the number of legs, the villosity of the skin, or the termination of the *os sacrum*, are reasons equally insufficient for abandoning a sensitive being to the same fate. What else is it that should trace the insuperable line? Is it the faculty of reason, or, perhaps, the faculty of discourse? But a full-grown horse or dog is beyond a comparison a more rational, as well as a more conversable animal, than an infant of a day, or a week, or even a month old. But suppose the case were otherwise, what would it avail? the question is not, Can they *reason*? nor, Can they *talk*? but *Can they suffer*?
Id. at 311.

of animals.[11] This date may represent the first time animal protection was seriously debated by a full legislative body. In his address, Lord Erskine stated:

> They (animals) are created, indeed, for our use, but not for our abuse. Their freedom and enjoyment, when they cease to be consistent with our just dominions and enjoyment, can be no part of their natures; but whilst they are consistent I say their rights, subservient as they are, ought to be as sacred as our own . . . the bill I propose to you, if it shall receive the sanction of Parliament, will not only be an honor to the country, but an era in the history of the world.[12]

The bill passed the House of Lords, but was defeated in the House of Commons.[13]

Some thirteen years later the battle was taken up again, this time by Richard Martin. On June 10, 1822, Martin succeeded in obtaining passage of a law known as "Dick Martin's Act . . . An Act to Prevent the Cruel and Improper Treatment of Cattle."[14] As compromise was necessary for its passage, it was a limited first step. It was made illegal for any person to "wantonly and cruelly beat or ill-treat[] [any] horse, mare, gelding, mule, ass, ox, cow, heifer, steer, sheep or other cattle . . . ."[15] The law imposed a "fine of not more than five pounds or less than ten shillings, or imprisonment not exceeding three months."[16] It was during this period of time that an organization was formed in London that would become the Royal Society for the Protection of Animals and be an inspiration for Henry Bergh.[17]

II. THE LEGAL FRAMEWORK IN THE UNITED STATES

Under the legal system of the United States there are two primary sources of law which govern the conduct of individuals.

---

11. COLEMAN, *supra* note 4, at 20-21.

12. *Id.* at 21-22 (quoting LORD ERSKINE, ADDRESS TO PARLIAMENT (1809)). For a few more details see RICHARD D. RYDER, ANIMAL REVOLUTION 81-88 (1989).

13. COLEMAN, *supra* note 4, at 21.

14. *Id.* at 26, 29.

15. *Id.* at 29.

16. *Id.* For a full discussion of the English law with quotes and references, see Davis v. American Soc'y for the Prevention of Cruelty to Animals, 75 N.Y. 362 (1873) [hereinafter Davis v. A.S.P.C.A.].

17. RYDER, *supra* note 12, at 89-92.

The first is legislation. While the first half of the 1800's saw tentative attempts at the adoption of anti-cruelty legislation, the real legislative effort would not occur until the 1860's and beyond.[18] The second source of law is the cumulative result of court decisions. For centuries legal concepts had been developed and applied within the English court system. These were transferred to the colonies and slowly became modified as the United States legal system developed independent of the English system. The concepts that arise out of this tradition are generally referred to as the common law.[19]

It is doubtful whether cruelty to animals was a criminal offense in England in the early common law period before 1800.[20] There are no recorded cases which resulted in criminal penalties.[21] When an animal was the property of someone, then there was no doubt as to the ability of the owner to bring a civil action for the loss under the concept of trespass.[22] However, acts against animals might be indictable as other offenses.[23]

Between 1800 and 1850 in the United States there were a handful of cases which allowed criminal prosecution for harm to animals under an assortment of theories.[24] One legal theory

---

18. *See infra* notes 65-83 and accompanying text.

19. *See* SIR WILLIAM BLACKSTONE, COMMENTARIES ON THE LAWS OF ENGLAND (Oxford, Clarendon Press 1765) (setting forth the first encyclopedic treatment of the common law. It is a four volume set which attempts to set out the entire system of law in England. During the colonial days in the United States it was the portable library used by many horse riding lawyers and judges).

20. The Chief Justice of the New Jersey Supreme Court in 1858 stated: "The general rule is that no injuries of a private nature [to animals], unless they some way concern the king or effect the public, are indictable at common law." State v. Beekman, 27 N.J.L. 124, 125 (1858) (giving a full discussion of the English law). "The offense charged [of cruelly beating a horse] was not a crime or misdemeanor at common law . . . ." McCausland v. People, 145 P. 685, 686 (Colo. 1914).

21. Davis v. A.S.P.C.A., 75 N.Y. 362 (1873).

22. In a Mississippi case, a man shot some hogs that had invaded his field after several attempts at hearding them out failed. The court noted that this would not violate the cruelty law but might nevertheless give rise to a civil action of trespass. Stephens v. State, 3 So. 458 (Miss. 1888).

23. "In England, at Common Law, acts of cruelty perpetrated upon animals in public, constituted a common nuisance and were indictable as such." *Davis*, 75 N.Y. at 370.

24. See *Davis*, 75 N.Y. 362 for a list of 13 cases.

utilized was that of malicious mischief. As explained by one court:

> There is a well-defined difference between the offense of malicious or mischievous injury to property, and that of cruelty to animals. The former constituted an indictable offense at common law, while the latter did not. The former has ever been recognized as an indictable offense as a measure of protection to the owner of property liable to be maliciously or mischievously injured. The latter has, in more recent years, been made punishable as a scheme for the protection of animals without regard to their ownership.[25]

Another early case made the distinction clear when the court stated that an indictment for malicious mischief would lie only if it could be proved that the animal killed was the property of another.[26]

In addition to this approach, courts could fashion a cause of action under the concepts of public nuisance; that is, a breach of the public peace.[27] The pain and suffering of the animal was not as much of a legal concern during this time as was the moral impact of the action on humans.[28] What a man did in the privacy of his home to his animals, his children, and sometimes even his wife, was his concern alone, not that of the legal system. To make cruelty to animals a crime would require legislation.

A. Early American Legislation

Statutory language expressly adopted by a legislative process usually reflects the broader societal attitudes which in essence the legislature represents. The evolution of statutory language concerning animals during the nineteenth century paralleled the

---

25. State v. Bruner, 12 N.E. 103, 104 (Ind. 1887). *See also* State v. Beekman, 27 N.J.L. 124 (1858).

26. State v. Pierce, 7 Ala. 728 (1845).

27. In an action for "maliciously, wilfully and wickedly killing a horse," the offense was held to amount to a public wrong. Republica v. Teischer, 1 Dall. 335 (Penn. 1788).

28. Lord Campbell thought that, while the brutes had no legal rights, to inflict cruelty on animals in the public "injur[es] the moral charcter of those who witness it—and may therefore be treated as a crime." Elbrige T. Gerry, The Law of Cruelty to Animals, Address Before the Bar of Delaware County (August 16, 1875) (quoting Lord Campbell, 9 Lives Lord Chancellors 22-23).

evolution of society's attitude toward animals. Nowhere in the legislative examples set out below do we have any contemporaneous records about the debate in the legislature: We do not know the submitter of the legislation, the nature of the debate, or who supported the measures as adopted. This analysis is limited to the actual language adopted. Indeed, there is a dearth of both legal and nonlegal writing dealing with animal issues during that century. Indirect evidence of their concerns is the best available. However, if the words chosen have the same meaning today, the rather terse legalistic language, once taken apart and examined closely, should reveal much about the attitudes of the day. Insight is available to those willing to be legal archaeologists; to those willing to dig into the dark recesses of law library basements.

An example of a statute that reflects the strict property concept of animals, which existed at the beginning of the nineteenth century, is found in Vermont legislative law.[29] Section 1 made it illegal to steal a horse, but not a cow or dog. Section 2 stated in part:

> Every person who shall wilfully and maliciously kill, wound, maim or disfigure any horse, or horses, or horse kind, cattle, sheep, or swine, of another person, or shall wilfully or maliciously administer poison to any such animal . . . shall be punished by imprisonment [of] . . . not more that five years, or fined not exceeding five hundred dollars . . . .[30]

The statute contained no provision prohibiting the cruel treatment of the animals, the word not being found in the statute. The list of animals protected was limited to commercially valuable animals. Pets or wild animals were excluded. The purpose of this law was to protect commercially valuable property from the interference of others, not to protect animals from pain and suffering.[31]

---

29. 1846 Vt. Laws 34.

30. *Id.* at 34.2.

31. Nearly identical language was adopted in 1857 in the Michigan Criminal Code chapter entitled: Offenses Against Property, MICH. COMP. LAWS § 181.45 (1857) which read as follows:

> Every person who shall willfully and maliciously kill, maim or disfigure any horses, cattle, or other beasts of another, or shall willfully and maliciously administer poison to any such horses, cattle or other beasts . . . shall be punished by imprisonment . . . not more than five years, or by fine not exceeding one thousand dollars. . . .

Under the statute a crime was committed only if the harmed animal was owned by someone else, thus the language "of another."[32] Therefore, if a person maimed his own animal it would not be a crime. Nor was it a crime to harm a wild or ownerless domestic animal. Actions had to constitute wilful and malicious conduct before they were deemed illegal. Finally, since the penalty was for up to five years of jail time, a violation of this law was a felony. It appears the legislature sought to control humans harming valuable property of another, not to stop the unnecessary infliction of pain upon animals.

The next step in the legal evolution is represented by the earliest statute yet uncovered; the Maine statute considered in 1821. This tentative law provided:

> § 7. *Be it Further enacted*, That if any person shall cruelly beat any horse or cattle, and be thereof convicted, . . . he shall be punished by fine not less than two dollars nor more than five dollars, or by imprisonment in the common gaol for a term not exceeding thirty days, according to the aggravation of the offence.[33]

In this statute, the operative phrase was "cruelly beat." This phrase encompasses an extremely narrow range of conduct. The common sense definition of the term "cruelly" is assumed to be that only a cruel beating is illegal, not killing, cutting, maiming, or one of a hundred other actions. Like the previously discussed statute, the Maine statute applied only to commercially valuable animals: horses and cattle.[34]

The Maine statute represented a new, tentative step forward because, in this case, no distinction was made as to who owns the animal. It was illegal to cruelly beat your own horse or cattle, as well as that of another. Since common law criminal law concepts did not limit what a person did with their own property, this law suggested a new societal interest: concern for the animal itself. While the motivation and purpose of

---

32. This author's interpretation of the Vermont Statute is that if Mr. *X* got mad at neighbor Mr. *Y* and shot three of *Y*'s sheep, killing one and wounding two, he would have been found in violation of this law. If Mr. *X* shot Mr. *Y*'s dog, no violation of the law could have been claimed. If Mr. *X* shot one of his own sheep in the leg and watched it slowly die over the next three days, again, no violation of this law.

33. Me. Laws ch. IV, § 7 (1821).

34. *Id.*

this statute is not known to us, the limited nature of its coverage suggests a modest motivation. Perhaps some member of the legislature may have observed an "unnecessary"[35] beating of a horse or a cow that was outrageous enough to trigger the drafting of this law. This provision did not contain the language which we will later see as reflective of the thoughtful legislative process and broad considerations of social policy.

Finally, note the level of punishment contained in the Maine statute: a two to five dollar fine and/or up to thirty days in jail.[36] One of the best ways to gauge the seriousness with which the legislature views an issue is to examine the level of punishment provided. Unlike the felonious horse-maiming statute set out above,[37] the penalties provided here suggest the bare threshold of criminality. While the legislature thought the cruel beating of cattle and horses was wrong, they were not so sure there should be a criminal punishment for committing the wrong.

The first known anti-cruelty law in the United States was passed the year *before* the first such law was passed in England. However, there is no record that this law was followed by the creation of any public organization to help enforce the law or compel change in public conduct, as was the case in England at this time or in New York in the 1860's. It marked the initiation of concern, but not the birth of a social movement.

More representative of the first wave of anti-cruelty laws in the United States was the New York law of 1829:

> § 26 Every person who [part one] shall maliciously kill, maim or wound any horse, ox or other cattle, or any sheep, belonging to another, or [part two] shall maliciously and cruelly beat or torture any such animals, whether belonging to himself or another, shall upon conviction, be adjudged guilty of a misdemeanor.[38]

The criminal prohibitions consisted of two distinct parts. The first part was qualified with the phrase "belonging to another"

---

35. *See infra* text accompanying notes 133-38.

36. Me. Laws ch. IV, § 7 (1821).

37. 1846 Vt. Laws 34.

38. N.Y. Rᴇᴠ. Sᴛᴀᴛ. tit. 6, § 26 (1829). The key phrase "maliciously kill, maim or wound . . ." was also used in the 1823 act adopted by the English Parliament. 3 Geo. IV ch. 54 (1823). The phrase "cruelly beat, abuse or ill treating . . . ." had been part of the first English law. It is not known whether or not the New York Legislature was aware of these English laws when it adopted the 1829 law. *See* Davis v. A.S.P.C.A., 75 N.Y. 362 (1873).

while the second was qualified "belonging to himself or another."[39] The purpose of the first part was to provide protection for private property, while the second dealt with cruelty to animal regardless of ownership. The two parts prohibit very different actions. In the first part, the legislature made criminal those actions which would most likely interfere with the commercial value of the animal: killing, maiming, or wounding. In the second part, the legislature focused upon that which might be perceived as causing pain and suffering to the animal: beatings and torture. One result of the different language was that it was not illegal to maliciously kill or maim your own animal. The legislature most likely presumed that financial self-interest would protect against this possibility. However, if you killed your own horse by beating it to death, the beating, but not the killing, was illegal.

Both parts of this legislation attempted to stop the affirmative acts of individuals. Under neither parts of the legislation would it have been illegal to kill a horse by starvation. Requiring a person to care for an animal, imposing an affirmative act, had always been considered more burdensome than prohibiting an action. The affirmative duty of care would be added later as the concern for the well-being of animals became stronger.[40]

In the New York statute, the level of crime was denoted as a mere misdemeanor, with jail time of no more than one year. The New York legislature took this issue more seriously than Maine as judged by the punishment, but New York still defined violations as a misdemeanor rather than a felony. Some additional insight on legislative attitude can be obtained from observing other crimes of that time period and the level of punishments that were set by the legislature. Under a Pennsylvania statute, it was a misdemeanor with a maximum fine of two hundred dollars to cruelly beat a horse.[41] To expose and abandon your own child under the age of seven was also a misdemeanor, but with a maximum fine of one hundred dollars.[42]

---

39. N.Y. Rev. Stat. tit. 6, § 26 (1829).
40. *See infra* notes 75-78 and accompanying text.
41. Pa. Laws tit. IV, § 46 (1860).
42. *Id.* § 45.

The most serious limitation of the New York legislation was the limited list of protected animals. It was not yet illegal to torture a dog or a bear. The limited list set forth in both parts was most likely utilized because this was the list with which the legislature was familiar. The legislature had not yet made the conceptual bridge that, if it was wrong to cruelly torture a cow, it should also have been wrong to torture a cat or dog. The critical factor ought not be the value of the animal to the owner, but the ability of the animal to suffer.[43]

Initially, the societal concern about cruelty to animals contained mixed motives. While some did not believe moral duties were owed to animals, they did accept that cruelty to animals was potentially harmful to the human actor, as it might lead to cruel acts against humans. Thus, the concern was for the moral state of the human actor, rather than the suffering of the non-human animal. This focus of concern was reflected in the early state laws by the location of the anti-cruelty provision within the criminal code. In many states, these provisions were found in chapters of the criminal code entitled, "Of Offenses Against Chastity, Decency and Morality."[44] This was the case in New Hampshire,[45] Minnesota,[46] Michigan,[47] and Pennsylvania[48] among others.[49]

---

43. Because of the incremental nature of the legislative development process, it is not unusual for laws to progress in small steps even though the result may be, in part, logically inconsistent.

44. *See infra* notes 45-48.

45. N.H. Rev. Stat. § 219.12 (1843).

46. Minn. Stat. § 96.18 (1858).

47. Mich. Rev. Stat. § 8.22 (1838).

48. Pa. Laws tit. IV, § 46 (1860).

49. In addition to prohibiting cruelty to animals, these chapters made an assortment of morally reprehensible acts illegal. Consider the list of section titles found in chapter 219 of New Hampshire's law. *See supra* note 45. All are under the heading "Of Offences Against Chastity, Decency and Morality." This contained provisions concerning adultery, lewdness, fornication, cohabiting, incest, blasphemy, profane swearing, digging up dead bodies, injuring tombs, and cruelty to animals. In Minnesota's equivalent chapter, the section after the cruelty to animals section prohibited performing labor or attending a dance on the Lords Day. Minn. Stat. § 96.19 (1858). Anyone convicted of the "abominable and detestable crime against nature with any beast," (presumably this language referred to the crime of bestiality) received 20 years in jail. Mich. Rev. Stat. § 8.14 (1838). Eight sections below this the cruel torture of a horse had a maximum sentence of one year. *Id.* at § 8.22. One is left with the clear impression that for many of the legislatures before 1860 this was an issue predominately of human morality.

The ideas contained in the 1829 Act were replicated by many state legislatures over the following thirty years. Michigan's 1838 law,[50] Connecticut's 1854 law,[51] Minnesota's 1858 law,[52] and Vermont's 1854 law[53] adopted part two of the New York law. All of these laws were broader than New York's law, as they applied to acts against, not only horses and oxen, but to other animals, so long as the animals were owned by someone. In 1843, New Hampshire adopted a law that only used the language from part one of the New York law.[54] Tennessee adopted a law in 1858 about animal cruelty, which was drafted distinctly different from New York's law.[55] Pennsylvania's law of 1860 used both portions from the 1829 New York law. But like Michigan, Pennsylvania expanded the scope to include "other domestic animals."[56]

One case under the Minnesota law demonstrates the continued confusion about the purpose of the these cruelty laws. A defendant was indicted for the shooting of a dog under the criminal statue which provided that "[e]very person who shall wilfully and maliciously kill, maim or disfigure any horses, cattle or other beasts of another person . . . shall be punished."[57] The court decided that the indictment failed as a dog could not be considered a beast.

> [I]t seems to me, that all [animals] such as have, in law, no value, were not intended to be included in that general term. . . . The term beasts may well be intended to include asses, mules, sheep and swine, and perhaps, some other domesticated animals, but it would be going quite too far to hold that dogs were intended.[58]

This was reflective of the continued confusion about the intended purpose of the law: to protect valuable personal property or to restrict the pain and suffering inflicted upon animals.

---

50. MICH. REV. STAT. § 8.22 (1838).
51. CONN. STAT. tit. V, ch. X, § 142 (1854).
52. MINN. STAT. § 96.18 (1858).
53. 1854 Vt. Laws 51.1.
54. N.H. REV. STAT. § 219.12 (1843).
55. TENN. CODE §§ 1668-1672 (1858). This statute is structured to allow a private law suit and recovery of a fine for the person bringing the cause of action. If the offense is committed by a slave, the punishment is 39 stripes (lashes). To jail a slave would be to punish the master who loses the services of the slave. *Id.*
56. Pa. Laws tit. IV, § 46 (1860).
57. United States v. Gideon, 1 Minn. 292, 296 (1856).
58. *Gideon*, 1 Minn. at 296.

B. The Bergh Era Begins

The life of Henry Bergh is set out elsewhere and will not be repeated here.[59] His impact on the legal world began in 1866. After his return from a trip to Europe, where he observed both the cruelty inflicted upon animals and the efforts of the Royal Society for the Protection of Animals on behalf of animals, he became focused on the animal cruelty issue.[60] Because of his social and political connections, it was not difficult for him to approach the New York legislature in Albany.

Although not a lawyer, Henry Bergh was able to direct the drafting of substantially different legislation.[61] He also understood that the mere passage of legislation was insufficient— without dedicated enforcement, the laws would never actually reach out and touch the lives of the animals about which he was concerned. Therefore, beside the drafting and passage of new criminal laws, Bergh sought the charter of an organization which, like the Royal Society of London, would be dedicated to the implementation of the law.[62] He asked the New York Legislature for a state-wide charter for the American Society for the Prevention of Cruelty to Animals ("A.S.P.C.A."), whose purpose, as set forth in its constitution, was "[t]o provide effective means for the prevention of cruelty to animals throughout the United States, to enforce all laws which are now or may hereafter be enacted for the protection of animals and to secure, by lawful means, the arrest and conviction of all persons violating such laws."[63] The charter was granted on April 10, 1866. Henry Bergh was unanimously elected as the A.S.P.C.A.'s first president, a position he continued to hold until his death in 1888.[64]

---

59. Materials on the early events of Bergh's life are set out in Sydney H. Coleman, Humane Society Leaders In America 33-35 (1924).

60. *Id.* at 35-36.

61. *Id.* at 38.

62. *Id.*

63. *Id.* at 39-40 (quoting American Society for the Prevention of Cruelty to Animals, Constitution (1866)).

64. *Id.* at 40.

III. NEW LEGISLATION

Henry Bergh realized the short comings of the existing New York law, and therefore sought strengthening amendments. His first attempt was in 1866 when the prior language of 1829 was amended to read: "Every person who shall, by his act or neglect, maliciously kill, maim, wound, injure, torture, or cruelly beat any horse, mule, ox, cattle, sheep, or other animal, belonging to himself or another, shall, upon conviction, be adjudged guilty of a misdemeanor."[65]

This law represented several significant steps forward for animals. First, the provisions applied regardless of the ownership of an animal. Second, the negligent act, as well as the intentional act, of an individual could lead to criminal liability. Third, the list of illegal actions was expanded. Note that the word "cruelly" modified only the word "beat."

While this law was a step forward, it was still in the mold of the early anti-cruelty statutes and contained two significant shortcomings when enforcement was sought. First, and most obviously, the list of animals was still limited to those that were commercially valuable. Certainly Mr. Bergh's vision would not have been limited by such categorization. The second shortcoming, and even more significant from a legal perspective, was the continued use of the qualifying term "maliciously." No action of a human against an animal was illegal unless the state could prove, under the criminal law standard of beyond a reasonable doubt, that the defendant acted with malicious intent.[66] This was difficult to do as it required the reading of an individual's mind. If one were to whip the back of a horse to make it move a wagon to which it was attached, it would not normally be considered malicious. Such an act may not be done out of feeling of ill will toward the horse, rather it may be out of a desire to get on with a job. So long as some excuse could be presented to the court, it was difficult to prove malice.[67] If an individual were to approach

---

65. N.Y. REV. STAT. ch. 682, § 26 (1881) (amending N.Y. PENAL LAW § 26 (1866)).

66. *Id.*

67. State v. Avery, 44 N.H. 392 (1862). According to the court, when the defendant is charged with an offense to "willfully kill, maim, beat or wound"

a horse in a field and whip it out of hate of the owner, or hate of the horse, this clearly satisfied the requirement of malice.

The 1866 New York Act included a second section. This was a first attempt to address a special problem which did not fit within the words of the first section. It stated: "Every owner, driver or possessor of an old, maimed or diseased horse or mule, turned loose or left disabled in any street, lane or place of any city in this state . . . for more than three hours . . . shall . . . be adjudged guilty of a misdemeanor."[68] Apparently, in the City of New York it was often the case that, when a work animal reached a point of age, disease, or exhaustion, so as to no longer have economic value, it was simply abandoned in the streets.[69] This was the first law in the United States adopted to deal with the issue of animal abandonment.

With the adoption of the A.S.P.C.A. charter and the passage of the above law, Henry Bergh went to work and was immediately active in enforcing the law. However, he clearly wanted more because within months, drafts for a new law were created. By the first anniversary of the A.S.P.C.A., a new, restructured, and greatly expanded law was passed by the New York Legislature.[70] The following paragraphs set out a summary of the key points of the law. Section 1 provided

---

certain animals, an instruction is proper which informs the jury that

> malice [is] not limited to ill-will to an animal, or its owner, or to wanton cruelty but [that an] act will be malicious if it results from any bad or evil motive [such as] cruelty of disposition, violent passion, a design to give pain to others, or a determination [by the owner of an animal] to show that he will do what he will with his own property without regard to the remonstrances of others.

Avery, 44 N.H. at 396. Defendant, who was convicted of cruelly whipping his horse, could not complain of these instructions, for "if the beating was wrongful . . . and without just cause or excuse, the law would regard it as malicious and therefore, [if] it was done from any of the motives enumerated in the instructions malice would be implied." *Id.* "Punishment administered to an animal in an honest and good faith effort to train it is not without justification" and not an offense. *Id.* The court equated criminal intent with evil intent, demonstrating that it was the actor's moral sense that was at issue. *Id.*

68. N.Y. Rev. Stat. § 682.2 (1866). "An Act better to prevent cruelty to animals." *Id.*

69. Remember all transportation of commerce at this point was either by man or beast.

70. N.Y. Rev. Stat. §§ 375.2-.9 (1867). *See* app. A.

for the law to apply to "any living creature." This marvelously sweeping statement finally eliminated the limitation that protection was only for animals of commercial value.[71] All provisions of this section applied regardless of the issue of ownership of the animal.[72] The list of illegal acts was greatly expanded to include: overdriving and overloading; torturing and tormenting; depriving of necessary sustenance; unnecessarily or cruelly beating; and needlessly mutilating or killing.[73] Yet, note that none of the acts were qualified by the term "maliciously." The focus changed from the mind set of the individual to objective evidence of what happened to the animal.

To address the ongoing problems of animals being forced to fight each other, often to their death, for the owners and spectators delight, section 2 of the New York Act made animal fighting illegal. While specifically identifying bull, bear, dog and cock fighting, it applied to any living creature. The ownership and keeping of fighting animals as well as the management of the fights themselves was illegal.[74]

For the first time the law imposed a duty to provide "sufficient quality of good and wholesome food and water" upon anyone who kept (impounded) an animal.[75] Just as important from a practical enforcement perspective, the new law allowed any persons, even the A.S.P.C.A., to enter private premises and care for the animal's needs. This was a very practical provision which allowed immediate help to the animals regardless of the criminal action which might or might not be brought later against the owner or keeper.[76]

Another first for this legislation was its concern about the transportation of animals. Section 5 made it illegal to transport "any creature in a cruel or inhuman manner." Again with an eye to helping the animal, the law allowed the taking away by officials, such as A.S.P.C.A. officers, of any animal being transported cruelly so that they might be given the proper care.[77]

---

71. *Id.* § 375.1.
72. *Id.*
73. *Id.*
74. *Id.* § 375.2.
75. *Id.* §§ 375.3-.4.
76. *Id.* § 375.4.
77. *Id.* § 375.5.

Section 6 was a curious provision requiring the registration of dogs, but no other animal, used by businesses for the pulling of loads. The registration number was to be placed on the vehicle being pulled by the dog.[78] Perhaps this was to make identification of owners easier, but little explanation of this section is found in the sources of the time.

As a follow up to the second section of the 1866 Act, section 7 of the 1867 Act made illegal the abandonment of any "maimed, sick, infirm or disabled creature." Under the previous law it was not at all clear what could be done with an abandoned animal. Under the 1867 Act, a magistrate or the captain of the police could authorize the destruction of such a creature.[79]

Focusing on the issue of enforcement, Mr. Bergh must have realized that normal police forces could not be counted upon to seriously and vigorously enforce this new law. Therefore, section 8 specifically provided that agents of the A.S.P.C.A. could be given the power to arrest violators of the adopted law.[80] This delegation of state criminal authority to a private organization was, and is, truly extraordinary. This, more than any other aspect of the 1867 Act, reflected the political power and trust that Bergh must have had within the city of New York and in the state capital. Another unusual provision was the requirement that all collected fines would be given to the A.S.P.C.A.; the pragmatic Bergh again at work.[81]

---

78. *Id.* § 375.6.

79. *Id.* § 375.7.

80. *Id.* § 375.8. This power was further expanded in a later Act:
Any officer, agent or member of said Society may lawfully interfere to prevent the perpetration of any act of cruelty upon any animal in his presence. Any person who shall interfere with or obstruct any such officer, agent or member in the discharge of his duty, shall be guilty of a misdemeanor.
N.Y. Rev. Stat. § 12.3 (1874).

81. For the first twelve months of the society's existence, 66 convictions were secured out of 119 prosecutions, and more than $7400 was received for support of the society, including $296 from criminal fines. American Society for the Prevention of Cruelty to Animals, 1867 Annual Report 47-54 (1867) [hereinafter Report 1867]. By 1889 the income of the A.S.P.C.A. had increased to over $100,000 for the year, but money from fines amounted to only $2126. American Society for the Prevention of Cruelty to Animals, 1890 Annual Report 11 (1890).

With the threat of actual enforcement of meaningful anti-cruelty statutes came the first lobbying for an exemption from the law. Section 10 of the Act provided an exemption for "properly conducted scientific experiments or investigations," at a medical college or university of the State of New York.[82] Thus, one of the more heated debates of today must have been carried out over 120 years ago in the New York Legislature.[83]

With the 1867 Act, an ethical concern for the plight of animals was transformed for the first time into comprehensive legislation. The focus of social concern was on the animals themselves. While it is not known who drafted the specific words used, the language was visionary in scope while addressing a number of specific, pragmatic points.

A.   Enforcement on the Streets of New York

A law is meaningless unless it directs or controls the conduct of individuals. For this to happen the laws must be enforced. This is normally the responsibility of the government, but Henry Bergh realized early on that if the law was to have any meaning in the streets of New York, where the animals lived and suffered, that it was up to him and his newly formed A.S.P.C.A.[84] He had the power to arrest law breakers, normally reserved for the police, and was appointed a prosecutor in New York so that he could argue for the conviction of the offenders before a judge.[85] It is a testament to the character of Henry Bergh that this extraordinary power of the state, vested in one private individual, was apparently never abused. It was, however, aggressively used.[86]

---

82. N.Y. REV. STAT. § 375.10 (1867).

83. In 1991 when the federal government proposed regulations dealing with the use of animals in research laboratories over 10,000 comments were received from the general public. *See generally* 56 Fed. Reg. 6426 (1991).

84. SYDNEY H. COLEMAN, HUMANE SOCIETY LEADERS IN AMERICA 38 (1924).

85. *Id.* at 48.

86. *Id.* at 42-46. He and his men were so aggressive that the Broadway and East Side Stage Company sought and obtained an injunction against the A.S.P.C.A. The courts said that the A.S.P.C.A. had no right to stop a stage unless its inspectors could see that the cruelty law was being broken. The State House Cases, 15 Abb. Pr. (n.s.) 51 (N.Y. 1873).

The first case for which Mr. Bergh obtained a successful prosecution under the new statute dealt with the method by which sheep and calves were transported to the "shambles" (slaughter houses). The animals had their four feet tied together and were put into carts on top of one another like sacks. The A.S.P.C.A. brought charges, obtaining a conviction and ten dollar fine.[87]

A landmark case which brought the A.S.P.C.A. and Mr. Bergh to the attention of the general public in its first year was the "turtle case."[88] As described by Sydney Coleman:

> But the general public was still apathetic and Mr. Bergh longed for some case that would turn the spotlight on the society and give it space on the front page of the newspapers. The discovery of a boatload of live turtles that had been shipped from Florida on their backs, with their flippers pierced and tied together with strings, offered this opportunity. When the captain of the vessel refused to turn the turtles over, Mr. Bergh caused his arrest, together with the members of his crew. They were taken to the Tombs, but were later acquitted of cruelty by the court . . . . The judge, before whom the case was tried, told Bergh to go home and mind his own business. Some of the newspapers charged him with being overzealous and many abused him roundly. A lengthy satire in the *New York Herald*, a few days later, set all New York talking. For a time James Gordon Bennett continued to systematically ridicule Bergh and his society, but later the two men became personal friends and the *Herald* one of the staunchest supporters of the movement. The final outcome of the turtle case was to greatly increase the number of supporters and friends of the new society.[89]

During the first year, a number of different types of cruelty were addressed by Mr. Bergh. One of the most abusive situations dealt with the horses used to pull the omnibuses and street railways of the time.[90] Other topics included concern about

---

87. REPORT 1867, *supra* note 81, at 4, 47; *see* COLEMAN, *supra* note 84, at 42.

88. REPORT 1867, *supra* note 81, at 5.

89. COLEMAN, *supra* note 84, at 42-43 (citing People v. Tinsdale, 10 Abb. Pr. (n.s.) 374 (N.Y. 1868)). After the case, the Captain of the ship sued Bergh for false arrest, but this action was dismissed on the grounds of lack of malice. REPORT 1867, *supra* note 81, at 48.

90. People v. Tinsdale, 10 Abb. Pr. (n.s.) 374 (N.Y. 1868).
Nothing did more for the advancement of the [A.S.P.C.A.] than this campaign. Mr. Bergh would station himself at the junction of two or

adulterated food for horses and cattle,[91] and transportation of cattle by railroad.[92] Bergh also fought to eliminate dog and cock fights. Bergh opened a vigorous fight against these cruelties, even instigating raids.[93]

B. The Ripple Effect

While the New York law would not have happened but for the energy and drive of Henry Bergh,[94] his actions clearly struck a responsive cord in a number of individuals around the country. Evidence of the societal readiness for animal

---

more lines and examine the team and load of every car that passed. If the load was too heavy he would compel some of the passengers to alight, or if one or both of the horses were unfit for service he suspended them from work.

COLEMAN, *supra* note 84, at 44.

A legal battle ensued when a driver and conductor were arrested for the overloading of the horse cars. The defendants were tried by a jury, and both were convicted and fined $250. On appeal, the supreme court sustained the verdict—this decision was a great victory for the A.S.P.C.A. and Bergh. *Id.*

91. COLEMAN, *supra* note 84, at 44-45.
92. REPORT 1867, *supra* note 81, at 10.
93. *Id.* at 12.
94. One contempory author sought to understand the nature of his personality and the motivation for Bergh's work:

I have inquired from those who worked at his side, of those who to-day splendidly head the now powerful Society, and they know no more of that mysterious "why" than I do.

He was a cool, calm man. He did not love horses; he disliked dogs. Affection, then, was not the moving cause. He was a healthy, clean-living man, whose perfect self-control showed steady nerves that did not shrink sickeningly from sights of physical pain; therefore he was not moved by self-pity or hysterical sympathy. One can only conclude that he was born for his work. He was meant to be the Moses of the domestic animal, meant to receive the "table of the law" for their protection, and to coax, drive, or teach the people to respect and obey those laws.

How else can you explain that large, calm, impersonal sort of justice, that far-seeing pity that was not confined to the sufferers of the city's streets, but sent forth agents to protect the tormented mules and horses of the tow-path; to search out the ignorant cruelties of the rustic, whose neglect of stock caused animal martyrdom—the incredible horrors of stabling in cellars and roofless shanties. Good God! the hair rises at the thought of the flood of anguish that man tried to stem and stop.

No warm, loving, tender, nervous nature could have borne to face it for an hour, and he faced and fought it for a lifetime. His coldness was his armor, and its protection was sorely needed.

Clara Morris, *Riddle of the Nineteenth Century: Mr. Henry Bergh, in* 18 McCLURE 414, 422 (1902).

protection legislation was found in the rapid adoption of the legislation and the creation of animal protection societies around the country. Bergh was the catalyst, but the actions in many other states required the work and support of others outside the political power and influence of Bergh. Beside the drafting of the laws, Bergh's other major contribution was the generation of publicity about the issues. Because of the force of his personality and the visible way in which he ran his campaigns against animal cruelty, he was able to generate a large volume of newspaper coverage, first in New York and then around the country.[95]

Within a few years Massachusetts,[96] Pennsylvania,[97] Illinois,[98] New Hampshire[99] and New Jersey[100] had adopted the same pattern of legislation as in New York with both new criminal laws and the charted creations of state Societies for the Prevention of Cruelty to Animals ("S.P.C.A.").[101] One exception to the pattern was Maryland which did not adopt any statute until 1890 and then adopted a very short provision clearly not based on New York's statute.[102] One legally significant addition to the New York model was a clause used by a number of states which imposed a specific duty on the owner or keeper of an animal and required that the animal be provided with appropriate shelter or protection from the weather.[103] Also, these statutes tended to use slightly different

---

95.   REPORT 1867, *supra* note 81, at 19, 52. *See* COLEMAN, *supra* note 84, at 48.

96.   "An Act for the More Effectual Prevention of Cruelty to Animals." MASS. GEN. L. ch. 344 (1869).

97.   XXIV PA. STAT. §§ 7770-7783 (1920).

98.   Prevention of Cruelty to Animals Act, 1869 Ill. Laws § 3.

99.   1878 N.H. Laws 281.

100.   N.J. REV. STAT. §§ 64-82 (1873).

101.   As of 1890, 31 states had some level of organized Society for the Prevention of Cruelty to Animals. AMERICAN SOCIETY FOR THE PREVENTION OF CRUELTY TO ANIMALS, 1890 ANNUAL REPORT 36. *See generally*, RICHARD D. RYDER, ANIMAL REVOLUTION 171-75 (1989).

102.   1890 Md. Laws 198.

103.   For example, Massachusetts adopted the following language: "[W]hoever having the charge or custody of any animal, either as owner or otherwise, inflicts unnecessary cruelty upon the same, or unnecessarily fails to provide the same with proper food, drink, shelter or protection from the weather . . . ." MASS. GEN. L. ch. 344, § 1 (1869).

terminology. While the New York statute consistently referred to "any living creature" other states used the term "animal" and then went on to define the term animal to include "all brute creatures."[104] Levels of punishment also varied between the states. While New Hampshire and Massachusetts both provided penalties of up to one year in jail and a $250 fine, Michigan provided a maximum of three months in jail and a $100 fine,[105] Illinois had no jail time and a fine of $50 to $100,[106] and Nebraska, whose law protected only domestic animals, had a fine of $5 to $50.[107]

Apparently, the legislation was lost on the wagon trains heading for California. It did not adopt any legislation until 1872 when the California Legislature adopted a law similar to the 1829 New York legislation.[108] It was not until 1900 that California passed the more comprehensive legislation adopted thirty years earlier in New York.[109]

IV. Taking the Laws to Court

First comes the legislation, then the police enforcement and prosecution, but the judges have the final authority to mold and shape a law. Regardless of what the legislature and police say, a criminal conviction can not be obtained unless a judge agrees. The one thing Bergh could not do was get himself appointed as a judge over cruelty cases. The attitude and workings of the courts are harder to discern at this distance of time than that of the legislature. This is true because there are two levels of courts: trial courts and appeals courts. Trial courts, where the evidence is heard and the verdict is given, leave almost no trace of their activities at the distance of one hundred years. Except for the records of the A.S.P.C.A. itself, there are almost no official written records about who was charged with what crime, what evidence was presented, or what result occurred.

---

104. New Hampshire defined animals as "all brute creatures and birds." N.H. Rev. Stat. § 281.31 (1878).
105. Mich. Comp. Laws § 285.1 (1929).
106. Ill. Stat. §§ 5a.6-.7 (1869).
107. Neb. Stat. § 67d (1887).
108. Cal. Penal Code § 597 (1872).
109. 1900 Cal. Stat. § 154 (amending Cal. Penal Code § 597 (1872)).

Appeals courts leave a better record. Since appeals courts do their work by drafting opinions which are organized and reprinted for future use, these opinions are accessible. In the area of cruelty law, however, because of the limited number of appeals, the window through which we can view the judicial process is very limited. When a person is found innocent at the trial court level, the verdict is almost never appealed by the state. Additionally, given that the offense is a misdemeanor, often only a modest fine is levied. Since most offenders have little money of their own, few guilty defendants are willing to pay a lawyer to appeal the case to the next level. Each state has only a handful of decisions prior to 1900, and some have no reported decisions concerning cruelty laws.

We will move from one state court opinion to another state without pause because the laws are so similar in nature and the issues so fundamental that there is very little variation in judicial outlook around the country. Court opinions give shape and scope to the words of the legislature. They place the issues in the broader social and legal context. Judges, like legislators, usually reflect the attitudes of the times, and bring their personal attitudes and beliefs with them when they make decisions. One judge set forth his attitude in one of the early cases:

> It is not correct to assert that the policy of this kind of legislation, especially that which has for its purpose the prevention of cruelty to brutes, is a regulation of the dominion of the private citizen over his own private property merely. It truly has its origin in the intent to save a just standard of humane feeling from being debased by pernicious effects of bad example—the human heart from being hardened by public and frequent exhibitions of cruelty to dumb creatures, committed to the care and which were created for the beneficial use of man.[110]

One of the functions of the court is to simply confirm the language of the legislature. The courts agreed that the language of the new statutes imposed liability without regard to the issue of ownership, that the provisions apply to one's own

---

110. Christie v. Bergh, 15 Abb. Pr. (n.s.) 51 (N.Y. 1873) (this case has been referred to as "*The Stage Horse Cases*").

animals, as well as those of other owners, unknown owners, or no owners. In *State v. Bruner*,[111] where a man poured turpentine on a live goose and set it afire, the court clarified that under the statute, "a man may be guilty of cruelty to his own animal, or to an animal without any known owner, or to an animal which has in fact no owner."[112] The court also had to clarify that the list of protected animals was, in fact, as broad as the legislature stated. In *Grise v. State*,[113] the court provided one of the first opinions which discussed the cruelty statute with a view toward assessing the types of animals to be afforded protection by the law: animal statutes "embrace all living creatures" and the "abstract rights in all animal creation . . . from the largest and noblest to the smallest and most insignificant."[114]

Another function of the courts is to provide key definitions of words used in statutes but left undefined by the legislature. An obviously important term is "cruelty." Although used frequently in every day conversation, its definition, particularly for criminal law purposes, is not so obvious.[115] Combining the opinions of a number of cases, one useful definition of cruelty is: (1) human conduct, by act or omission; (2) which inflicts pain and suffering on a nonhuman animal; and (3) which occurs without legally acceptable justifiable conduct (legislative language or socially acceptable custom).[116]

Both at common law and under the statutes adopted, the mere killing of an animal, without more, was not "cruelty." Before the killing of an animal can support a conviction under a cruelty statute, it must be found that the killing was done

---

111. 104 N.E. 103 (Ind. 1887).
112. *Bruner*, 104 N.E. at 104.
113. 37 Ark. 456 (1881).
114. *Grise*, 37 Ark. at 458. *See* Freel v. Down, 136 N.Y.S. 440 (1911) (holding sea turtles are animals within the criminal law); State v. Claiborne, 505 P.2d 732 (Kan. 1973) (holding that game cocks are not animals); State *ex rel* Del Monto v. Woodmansee, 72 N.E.2d 789 (Ohio 1956) (holding that chickens are not within the animal slaughter act).
115. *See generally* DAVID FAVRE & MURRAY LORING, ANIMAL LAW ch. 9 (1983).
116. *Down*, 136 N.Y.S. 440. (Is pain inflicted during transportation process justifiable?) "What constitutes cruelty is a question of fact on all the evidence in a prosecution for cruelty to animals." *Id*. at 446.

116. *Down*, 136 N.Y.S. 440. (Is pain inflicted during transportation process justifiable?) "What constitutes cruelty is a question of fact on all the evidence in a prosecution for cruelty to animals." *Id*. at 446.

in a cruel manner.[117] The court in *Horton v. State*[118] held: "[T]he mere act of killing an animal, without more, is not cruelty, otherwise one could not slaughter a pig or ox for the market, and man could eat no more meat."[119] Thus, the shooting and almost instant killing of a dog was not a violation of the statute making it an offense to cruelly kill any domestic animal.[120] The court said that the purpose of the statute was not to punish for an offense against property but to prevent cruelty to animals.[121] To them, the word "cruelly," when considered with other offenses proscribed by the statute—as torturing, tormenting, mutilating, or cruelly beating—"as well as . . . the manifest purpose of the statute, evidently mean[t] something more than to kill."[122] Likewise, the court in *State v. Neal*[123] defined cruelty to "include every act etc., whereby unjustifiable physical pain, suffering, or death is caused."[124]

One of Bergh's cases in New York brought him face-to-face with the definition of cruelty. In the case where the sea turtles were being shipped on their backs, the court and much of the public did not believe the law had been violated because they did not believe that sea turtles could feel pain or suffer from lack of food and water.[125] Without proof of suffering the court dismissed the action.[126] But, forty years later a court did sustain a cruelty conviction concerning the shipment of sea turtles.[127]

---

117. *See* Horton v. State, 27 So. 468 (Ala. 1900); State v. Neal, 27 S.E. 81 (N.C. 1897).

118. 27 So. 468 (Ala. 1900).

119. *Horton*, 27 So. at 468.

120. *Id.*

121. *Id.*

122. *Id.*

123. 27 S.E. 81 (N.C. 1897).

124. *Neal*, 27 S.E. at 85.

125. Allegedly, the Magistrate who dismissed the action stated "No greater pain was inflicted than by the bite of a mosquito." AMERICAN SOCIETY FOR THE PREVENTION OF CRUELTY TO ANIMALS, 1867 ANNUAL REPORT 48 (1867) [hereinafter REPORT 1867].

126. *Neal*, 27 S.E. at 81.

127. Freel v. Downs, 136 N.Y.S. 440 (1911), involved a trial of a master of a steamship and the consignee of a shipment of 65 green turtles, commonly used for food, on charges of cruelty to animals. It was charged that both defendants,

Courts have construed "cruelty" to include beating horses;[128] burning a goose;[129] pouring acid on hooves;[130] overworking;[131] starving or depriving a horse of proper shelter;[132] freeing a captive fox in the presence of a pack of hounds and allowing the hounds to tear the fox apart;[133] and passively permitting a dog to attack or kill other dogs.[134] In most criminal cases, the actions or inactions of the human are a given. The question then becomes whether the act violated the existing standard of cruelty. It is also the case that, generally, the courts accept that the animal experiences pain or suffering. Many cases revolve around the third part of the definition, whether or not the action is justifiable. Under certain circumstances, cruelty and even torture, are not considered "cruelty" in the legal sense because the activity is "necessary" or "useful."

It is generally recognized that, in addition to the need to obtain food or the need for medical experimentation, there are certain other situations in which the infliction of discomfort may, as a practical matter, be accepted by the courts as "necessary." Thus, for example, it may be "necessary" to inflict pain to discipline an animal, or to train it. Discipline and training are proper and lawful ends. Therefore, the infliction of pain or suffering which can be categorized as either of these will usually be excused. *State v. Avery*[135] held that if the beating of young horses was for the purpose of training,

---

by carrying or causing the turtles to be carried from Cuba to New York on their backs upon the deck of the ship with their fins or flippers—which contain muscles, blood vessels, and nerves—perforated and tied together on each side by means of a rope passing through the perforations, violated the statute making it an offense to transport any living creature "in a cruel or inhuman manner." *Freel*, 136 N.Y.S. at 443. The court found that the manner in which the turtles were transported caused them some pain and suffering, that as he accepted the shipment for the purpose of carrying them to New York, he must have been deemed to be one who carried or caused to be carried animals in a cruel and inhuman manner. Thus, there was sufficient cause to believe that he was probably guilty of causing or permitting unjustifiable physical pain and suffering by the turtles. *Id.* 451-52.

128. State v. Allison, 90 N.C. 734 (1884).
129. State v. Bruner, 104 N.E. 103 (Ind. 1887).
130. Commonwealth v. Brown, 66 Pa. Super. 519 (1917).
131. State v. Browning, 50 S.E. 185 (S.C. 1905) (hiring out unfit mules).
132. Griffith v. State, 43 S.E. 251 (Ga. 1903).
133. Commonwealth v. Turner, 14 N.E. 130 (Mass. 1887).
134. Commonwealth v. Thorton, 113 Mass. 457 (1873).
135. 44 N.H. 393 (1862).

however severe it might be, it would not be considered malicious and would be no offense under the statute. However, if the beating was aggravated by the influence of any evil motive, cruel disposition, violent passions, spirit of revenge, or reckless indifference to the sufferings, the excess pain and suffering caused would be deemed malicious.[136]

Where the defense is necessity, the defendant bears the burden of proving the necessity. Defense of one's self, or of other persons, would appear to excuse at least some degree of assault upon the offending animal, and there are a multitude of statutes and cases which justify shooting or killing animals, especially dogs, which are attacking the defendant's livestock. *Hodge v. State*[137] held that a cruelty statute was not intended to deprive a man of the right to protect himself, his premises, and property against the intrusions of worthless, mischievous, or vicious animals by such means as are reasonably necessary for that purpose.[138] In addition, the object of the statute was to protect animals from cruelty and not from the incidental pain or suffering that may be casually or incidentally inflicted by the use of lawful means of protection against them.

As in Henry Bergh's New York statute, sometimes a legislature provides specific exemptions. The first annual report of the A.S.P.C.A. considered in some detail the pain and suffering of dogs and other animals in medical teaching facilities.[139] But for the most part, Bergh was unable to do much about this because of the specific exemption given such facilities in section 10 of the New York statute.[140] This kind of blanket exemption continues in a few of today's anti-cruelty statutes.[141]

Beside the term "cruelty," the courts have had to decide the meaning of many other terms. The words "overdrive," "override," or "overload," reflect a historical concern for those animals most closely associated with humans (beasts of burden) during a period when motorized transportation was unavailable. No standard was given to determine a violation.

---

136. *Avery*, 44 N.H. 393.
137. 79 Tenn. 528 (1883).
138. *Hodge*, 79 Tenn. 528.
139. REPORT 1867, *supra* note 125, at 19-22.
140. *See* Appendix: The 1867 New York Anti Cruelty Law, at § 10.
141. *See* Favre, *supra* note 115, at 139-40.

The number of possible variables, such as age, strength, and health of the animal, duration of load, degree of effort or weight of load, etc., made it impossible to be more precise in legislation. The riding, driving, or loading became cruel when more was being demanded of the animal than could reasonably be expected under all circumstances.[142]

Another group of terms the court has had to define was "torture" and "torment." Again the focus was not on the pain of the animal, but on the justification for the infliction of the pain. In *State v. Allison*,[143] the court found the defendant had unlawfully tortured or tormented a cow by beating her and twisting off her tail.[144] Sometimes the act itself suggested no possible justification. In one court, the pouring of turpentine on a goose and then burning it was found to be an unjustifiable act of torture.[145] In *Commonwealth v. Brown*,[146] the defendant applied a solution of nitric and sulfuric acid to the hoofs of two horses. This was found to be a violation of the law.[147]

The third area of activity by the courts was placing the specifics of the anti-cruelty law into the general context of criminal law. Only the problem of criminal intent will be mentioned in this short history.[148] As a broad statement, a person cannot be found guilty of a crime unless he intended to commit the crime. Thus, if a cat climbs into the motor compartment of a sitting car, without the knowledge of the owner of the car, and later the owner starts the car and maims the cat, it is not a criminal act since the individual did not understand that his actions would cause harm to the cat. The problem with this requirement in the context of animal treat-

---

142. *See* State v. Browning, 50 S.E. 185 (S.C. 1905) (defendant's mule, with defendant's knowledge and permission, was cruelly worked when it was unfit for labor). The enforcement of this part of the cruelty law was particularly important to Mr. Bergh in the City of New York. Henry Bergh himself would stand on street corners and examine the condition of horses and mules. When Bergh judged a violation, he would warn or arrest the person in charge. SYDNEY H. COLEMAN, HUMANE SOCIETY LEADERS IN AMERICA 44 (1924).

143. 90 N.C. 733 (1884).

144. *Allison*, 90 N.C. 733.

145. State v. Bruner, 104 N.E. 103 (Ind. 1887).

146. 66 Pa. Super. 519 (1917).

147. *Brown*, 66 Pa. Super. 519.

148. *See* Favre, *supra* note 115, at § 9.6.

ment is that the primary motivation for human conduct is often other than to harm an animal, even though it is foreseeable that there is a risk of harm to that animal.

In *People v. Tinsdale*,[149] a New York court pondered the effect of a defendant's intent in a cruelty prosecution and predicated their decision upon whether the intent or lack of intent was evident from the facts. *Tinsdale* involved a charge of cruelty to animals made against the driver and the conductor of a horse-drawn railroad car for overloading, overdriving, torturing, and tormenting two horses who were unable to draw a carload of passengers over portions of the route.[150] The conductor was in charge of admission of passengers to the car and the driver was in charge of driving the horses pulling the car. Both defendants were employees of the company who owned the cars and horses.[151] It is important to note that both claimed and may, in fact, have been acting under orders of their superiors and employers. Thus, their primary intent was not to inflict pain and suffering on the animals, but to fill the cars with passengers so as to make a profit. Yet, the suffering which occurred was a foreseeable by-product of their conduct. The judge charged the jury "[n]o company can compel their conductor or other employee to do an act which is against the law."[152]

Although the mental state of both men may not have been that of seeking to abuse their animal charges, the judge stated that both the conductor and the driver responsible could nevertheless be liable for the overloading of the car and driving the horses while the car was in that overloaded state. The *Tinsdale* court thus faced the issue of intent squarely. If a person intentionally does or does not do an act and the risk to an animal is foreseeable, then the individual is criminally liable when his action or inaction in fact inflicts pain or suffering on an animal.[153] The reasoning in *Tinsdale* is consistent

---

149. 10 Abb. Pr. (n.s.) 374 (N.Y. 1886).
150. *Tinsdale*, 10 Abb. Pr. (n.s.) at 374. The general statute at the time was section 1 of the New York Laws of 1867.
151. *Tinsdale*, 10 Abb. Pr. (n.s.) at 376.
152. *Id.*
153. Favre, *supra* note 115, at § 9.6.

with the majority of opinions in the country today concerning this important issue of criminal intent.[154]

Negligent or accidental infliction of suffering is usually not criminally actionable.[155] In a prosecution for cruelly overdriving a horse, there was evidence that defendants rented a horse for an afternoon drive and later informed the livery keeper that the animal was sick.[156] It was actually found to be "suffering from pulmonary congestion, which is usually caused by over-exertion . . . the horse died shortly afterward. . . ."[157] The livery keeper testified that, in his opinion, the horse had been overdriven, and defendants contended that they drove the animal "for a reasonable distance at a moderate gait, and that the animal was sick when they hired it."[158] The court held that a conviction was not warranted, for although the evidence tended to establish that the horse had been overdriven, it was not inconsistent with an accidental overdriving and in no way negated the conclusion that the horse may have overexerted itself, although the defendants were evidently careful.[159] The court said that "overdriving, alone, is not a statutory crime, [since] it must be willful as distinguished from accidental."[160]

V. A VOICE OF CONCERN

Twenty years after Bergh started his efforts in New York, Judge Arnold in far away Mississippi provided eloquent words for how the legal system now viewed animals, after a century of significant change.

> This statute is for the benefit of animals, as creatures capable of feeling and suffering, and it was intended to protect them from cruelty, without reference to their being property, or to the damages which might thereby be occasioned to their owners . . . .
>
> . . . .

---

154. *Id.*
155. The 1866 N.Y. Act had made the negligent maiming, etc., illegal. But since the word was modified with "maliciously" it was meaningless. In the 1867 Act, "negligent" does not appear.
156. State v. Roche, 37 Mo. App. 480, 481 (1889).
157. *Roche*, 37 Mo. App. at 481.
158. *Id.*
159. *Id.* at 482.
160. *Id.*

. . . [L]aws, and the enforcement or observance of laws for the protection of dumb brutes from cruelty, are, in my judgment, among the best evidences of the justice and benevolence of men. Such statutes were not intended to interfere, and do not interfere, with the necessary discipline and government of such animals, or place any unreasonable restriction on their use or the enjoyment to be derived from their possession. The common law recognized no rights in such animals, and punished no cruelty to them, except in so far as it affected the right of individuals to such property. Such statutes remedy this defect . . . . To disregard the rights and feelings of equals, is unjust and ungenerous, but to willfully or wantonly injure or oppress the weak and helpless is mean and cowardly. Human beings have at least some means of protecting themselves against the inhumanity of man,—that inhumanity which 'makes countless thousands mourn,'—but dumb brutes have none. Cruelty to them manifests a vicious and degraded nature, and it tends inevitably to cruelty to men. Animals whose lives are devoted to our use and pleasure, and which are capable, perhaps, of feeling as great physical pain or pleasure as ourselves, deserve, for these considerations alone, kindly treatment. The dominion of man over them, if not a moral trust, has a better significance than the development of malignant passions and cruel instincts. Often their beauty, gentleness and fidelity suggest the reflection that it may have been one of the purposes of their creation and subordination to enlarge the sympathies and expand the better feelings of our race. But, however this may be, human beings should be kind and just to dumb brutes; if for no other reason than to learn how to be kind and just to each other.[161]

CONCLUSION

Henry Bergh's efforts in New York established a foundation that was to define the accepted legal relationship between humans and the animals around them over the next century. Discussion in the courts today are comfortably within the framework established by the end of the nineteenth century. The actions in the legislatures today may be more protective of the interests of animals, but are not of a different kind and still reflect the philosophical attitude of Judge Arnold quoted above.[162]

---

161. Stephens v. State, 3 So. 458-59 (Miss. 1887).
162. A survey of current state cruelty laws can be found in ANIMAL WELFARE INSTITUTE, ANIMALS AND THEIR LEGAL RIGHTS 7-47 (4th ed. 1990).

This area of the law reflects extraordinary stability or stagnation depending on one's view. The legal system evolves as the needs and attitudes of its members change. Few would suggest that the powers and rights of husbands regarding their wives as property as existed in the 1880's should be used today. Or, that the rights of children within the legal system should remain unchanged for over a century. Yet, laws made for the protection of animals have remained stagnate for a hundred years.

The social stirring of the animal rights movement may change the laws as the next century approaches, but only if it is able to convince the members of this society that a new perspective is justified.[163] Until such time, the legal rights won for animals in the 1860's and 1870's remain the base for today's attitude about and concerning man's legal relationship with animals.

---

163. *See* David Favre, *Wildlife Rights: The Ever-Widening Circle*, 9 ENVT'L L. 241 (1979); TOM REGAN, ALL THAT DWELL THEREIN 148-64 (1982); JOEL FEINBERG, *Can Animals Have Rights, in* ANIMAL RIGHTS AND HUMANS OBLIGATIONS 190-96 (Tom Regan & Peter Singer eds. 1976); Joyce S. Tischler, Comment, *Rights for Nonhuman Animals: A Guardianship Model for Dogs and Cats*, 14 SAN DIEGO L. REV. 484 (1977); Roger W. Galvin, *What Rights for Animals? A Modest Proposal*, 2 PACE ENVTL. L. REV. 245 (1985); Susan L. Goodkin, *The Evolution of Animal Rights*, 18 COL. HUM. RIGHTS L. REV. 259 (1987). An argument for whales' rights in the international context can be found in Anthony D'Amato & Sudhir K. Chopra, *Whales: Their Emerging Right to Life*, 85 AM. J. INT'L L. 21 (1991).

Appendix A: The 1867 New York Anti-Cruelty Law

Section 1. *PENALTY FOR OVERDRIVING, CRUELLY TREATING ANIMALS, ETC.*

If any person shall overdrive, overload, torture, torment, deprive of necessary sustenance, or unnecessarily or cruelly beat, or needlessly mutilate or kill, or cause or procure to be overdriven, overloaded, tortured, tormented or deprived of necessary sustenance, or to be unnecessarily or cruelly beaten, or needlessly mutilated, or killed as aforesaid any living creature, every such offender shall, for every such offence, be guilty of a misdemeanor.

Section 2. *FOR KEEPING A PLACE FOR COCK FIGHTING, BULL BAITING, DOG FIGHTING, ETC.*

Any person who shall keep or use, or in any way be connected with, or interested in the management of, or shall receive money for the admission of any person to any place kept or used for the purpose of fighting or baiting any bull, bear, dog, cock, or other creature, and every person who shall encourage, aid or assist therein, or who shall permit or suffer any place to be so kept or used, shall, upon conviction thereof, be adjudged guilty of a misdemeanor.

Section 3. *FOR IMPOUNDING ANIMALS WITHOUT GIVING SUFFICIENT FOOD AND WATER*

Any person who shall impound, or cause to be impounded in any pound, any creature, shall supply to the same, during such confinement, a sufficient quantity of good and wholesome food and water, and in default thereof, shall, upon conviction, be adjudged guilty of a misdemeanor.

Section 4. *IN WHAT CASE ANY PERSON MAY FEED, ETC. IMPOUNDED ANIMAL*

In case any creature shall be at any time impounded as aforesaid, and shall continue to be without necessary food and water for more than twelve successive hours, it shall be lawful for any person, from time to time, and as often as it shall be necessary, to enter into and upon any pound in which any such creature shall be so confined, and to supply it with necessary food and water, so long as it shall remain so confined; such person shall not be liable to any action for such entry, and the reasonable cost of such food and water may be collected by him of the owner of such creature, and the said creature shall not be exempt from levy and sale upon execution issued upon judgment therefor.

Section 5. *PENALTY FOR CARRYING ANIMALS IN A CRUEL MANNER*

If any person shall carry, or cause to be carried, in or upon any vehicle or otherwise, any creature, in a cruel or inhuman manner, he shall be guilty of a misdemeanor, and whenever he shall be taken into custody and therefor by any officer, such officer may take charge of such vehicle and its contents, and deposit the same in some safe place of custody; and any necessary expenses which may be incurred for taking charge of and keeping and sustaining the same, shall be a lien thereon, to be paid before the same can lawfully be recovered. Or the said expenses or any part thereof remaining unpaid, may be recovered by the person incurring the same, of the owner of said creature, in any action therefor.

Section 6. *LICENSE FOR USING DOGS BEFORE VEHICLES*

Every person who shall hereafter use any dog or dogs, for the purpose of drawing or helping to draw any cart, carriage, truck, barrow, or other vehicle, in any city or incorporated village, for business purposes, shall be required to take out a license for that purpose, from the mayor or president thereof, respectively, and shall have the number of said license and the residence of the owner distinctly painted thereon; and for each violation of this section shall forfeit and pay a fine of one dollar for the first offence, and a fine of ten dollars for each subsequent offence.

Section 7. *PENALTY FOR ABANDONING INFIRM ANIMALS IN PUBLIC PLACE*

If any maimed, sick, infirm or disabled creature shall be abandoned to die, by any person, in any public place, such person shall be guilty of a misdemeanor, and it shall be lawful for any magistrate or captain of police in this state, to appoint suitable persons to destroy such creature if unfit for further use.

Section 8. *WHEN AGENT OF SOCIETY MAY ARREST FOR VIOLATIONS OF THIS ACT*

Any agent of the American Society for the Prevention of Cruelty to Animals, upon being designated thereto by the sheriff of any county in this state, may, within such county, make arrests and bring before any court or magistrate thereof, having jurisdiction, offenders found violating the provisions of this act, and all fines imposed and collected in any such county, under the provisions of this act, shall inure to said society, in aid of the benevolent objects for which it was incorporated.

Section 9. WHO SHALL PUBLISH THIS ACT, AND WHEN SHALL IT BE PUBLISHED.

This act shall take effect on the first day of May next. And the said American Society for the Prevention of Cruelty to Animals shall cause the same to be published once in each week for three weeks, in four daily papers published in New York City, or in default thereof shall forfeit the right to receive the penalties and fines as provided.

Section 10. PROVISO.

Nothing in this act contained shall be construed to prohibit or interfere with any properly conducted scientific experiments or investigations, which experiments shall be performed only under the authority of the faculty of some regularly incorporated medical college or university of the state of New York.

SECTION 2: INTEGRATIVE REVIEWS

The first article in this section, by Alan R. Felthous and Stephen R. Kellert, is very significant in the literature on the connection between animal cruelty and human aggression. Although it is the basic premise of this book that such a connection is real and well documented, this article confronts the fact that this association is not uniformly accepted by psychiatrists. This entry addresses concerns that must be recognized if our knowledge and understanding of the dynamics of animal cruelty are to have any useful application to the prevention of, and intervention in, violence against people and animals.

Questions about the strength or reality of this association generally fall into three categories. The first is the concern that undue importance may be given to a single symptom (such as animal abuse) in the attempt to make a diagnosis or prediction about later behavior. While animal abuse may be one of the earliest and most significant indicators of violence, it is rarely argued that this measure can, or ever should, be used in isolation. The second issue is that much of the data on the issue is "soft"—not generated through rigorously controlled studies. However, the history of psychiatry and psychology is built on a foundation of "case histories," which are, in effect, anecdotes. Science progresses by using this "natural history" to generate testable hypotheses that can be subjected to more formal evaluation. The diversity of articles in this book reflects the productive synthesis that can result from taking the issues raised by individual case studies and recasting them in a more experimental model. The third and main issue confronted by Felthous and Kellert is the existence of contradictory findings, particularly the nine studies they review that tested for an association between animal cruelty and later violence but failed to find it to a significant degree.

In addressing this last concern, Felthous and Kellert note that half of the studies failing to find this association used the methodology of chart review—that is, noting whether or not mention had been made of animal cruelty in the records of these violent individuals. Since animal cruelty was not listed as a symptom of any behavior disorder before the 1987 revision of the *Diagnostic and Statistical Manual of Mental Disorders* (the *DSM-III-R;* see the introduction to section 6), it is not surprising that attempts were rarely made to prompt for such information in preparing the charts of those individuals studied by this method. In contrast, all of the studies that do demonstrate an association used direct personal interviews, with specific protocols for asking about animal cruelty.

Another common element in studies failing to find a connection between animal cruelty and other violence was a poor definition of what constitutes cruelty. This has been a problem in studies of domestic violence as well. The authors note that the definition can become so broad that it can be applied to behavior that is essentially "normative," such as killing insects, and thus fails to distinguish between normal and disturbed populations. Likewise, the operational definition of "violence" in these studies may be too broad to reveal a connection. Animal cruelty seems most strongly associated with later recurrent, impulsive violence.

Felthous and Kellert call for methodological rigor and replication, with an emphasis on methods that directly address the involvement of individuals in clearly defined acts of cruelty and well-defined violent behavior. Their closing sentiments, echoed by most of the contributors to this volume, express the hope that an ethic of compassion and respect for animals can carry over to humans.

The second review, by Randall Lockwood and Guy R. Hodge, represents one of the earliest attempts to present a compilation of material on the connection between animal cruelty and other forms of violence to the humane and animal-care and -control communities. It was prepared specifically to address the needs of the many local humane societies and animal-control agencies that had been frustrated by unresponsiveness on the part of law-enforcement agencies and the courts to serious animal-cruelty cases. It not only discusses the association of early instances of animal abuse with serial killers and mass murderers but also reviews the literature linking animal-related offenses to child abuse, juvenile violence, domestic violence, and other antisocial behaviors. This report has subsequently been reissued by dozens of humane agencies and by the International Association of Chiefs of Police and has helped promote the passage of stronger anticruelty laws and increased law-enforcement sensitivity to the importance of animal-abuse cases.

The next contribution, by Frank R. Ascione, provides a review of the literature from the perspective of normal and pathological child development. He addresses the shortcomings of many studies by reviewing the problem of defining animal cruelty. As with child and spouse abuse, animal abuse can encompass commissions and omissions that vary in form and severity. This problem has been reflected in the evolution of the legal definition of animal cruelty (see the Favre and Tsang essay in section 1), and our society's mixed attitudes toward different types of animals continues to present problems (see Grandin's paper in section 9).

Ascione also provides original data on the incidence of self-reported cruelty within populations of incarcerated youths. In addition, it analyzes how animal cruelty fits into the constellation of symptoms of conduct disorder (see section 6 for a discussion of conduct disorder and its symptoms). Finally, it discusses the influences that might protect children from developing into violent offenders and those that put them at greater risk.

Ascione also presents an overview of anecdotal and survey research on animal cruelty in the context of family violence and the potential effects of this exposure on children's development. The report, like that of Felthous and Kellert in this section, concludes with a detailed call for additional research to help clarify the processes by which empathy and prosocial skills can flourish or be crushed,

and the importance of relationships with animals in determining how this development proceeds.

The final entry, by Michael Robin and Robert ten Bensel, provides a thorough overview of the literature on the role of pets in the development of the social lives of children. They point out the complexity of this relationship: pets may serve as source of support for victimized children, but they may also be an additional source of stress in a disturbed family and may become targets of abuse by children or their abusers. The authors also describe the often overlooked significance of pet loss to children and adolescents as a major traumatic event that can have far-reaching consequences for later development.

One of the more significant findings they report is that the disturbed youths they studied suffered more pet loss and were more likely to have had a pet killed than normal children. On the other hand, they were less likely to have someone available to help them deal with the pet's loss. Robin and ten Bensel also provide a good review of literature on childhood cruelty to animals and later violence, citing many of the papers included in this volume. They correctly point out the failure of many studies to look beyond the acts of cruelty to explore the history of these violent perpetrators' relationships with animals. Evidence from their studies and others seems to indicate that violence against animals and others may often not be due to an inability to feel empathy for others but rather to violation of the ability to care. It is significant that 86 percent of the violent offenders they surveyed had owned a special pet and that 60 percent had lost this beloved animal through death (often violent) or theft. As with the findings of Elizabeth DeViney and her coauthors (included in section 7), they note that the abuse of animals within disturbed families is usually at the hands of someone other than the child. We are offered some hope for the prospect of prevention and intervention by their observation that most of those children who were responsible for injuring animals felt badly about it.

Childhood Cruelty to Animals and Later Aggression Against People: A Review

Alan R. Felthous, M.D., and Stephen R. Kellert, Ph.D.

The existing literature on the relationship between childhood cruelty to animals and later violence against people appears to be inconsistent. The authors review the controlled studies that did not support this relationship and those that did and identify several methodological factors that may have contributed to the contradictory findings. Studies using direct interviews to examine subjects with multiple acts of violence point to an association between a pattern of childhood animal cruelty and later serious, recurrent aggression against people. Identification of such a relationship could improve understanding of impulsive violence and facilitate early intervention and prevention.

(Am J Psychiatry 1987; 144:710–717)

In 1806 Phillipe Pinel advanced the diagnostic concept of "mania without delirium," often cited as a nosological forerunner of antisocial personality disorder. Individuals with this disorder were not lacking in understanding, but they "were under the domination of instinctive and abstract fury, as if the active facilities alone sustained the injury" (1). The first of Pinel's two examples of this disorder involved a man who aggressed against people in various ways and eventually killed a person. "If a dog, a horse, or any other animal offended, he instantly put it to death" (1).

Since Pinel's observation, a number of case examples of dangerously aggressive men who had been cruel to animals during childhood have been entered in the literature. Some of the most notorious mass and multiple murderers, historically and in recent years, reportedly had behavioral patterns of excessive cruelty to animals in childhood (2–4). At least in these few but extremely violent individuals, animal cruelty was one of several symptomatic behaviors indicative of poorly controlled aggression.

Received Sept. 13, 1985; revised March 12, 1986; accepted April 22, 1986. From Forensic Services, Department of Psychiatry and Behavioral Sciences, University of Texas Medical Branch at Galveston; and the School of Forestry and Environmental Studies, Yale University, New Haven, Conn. Address reprint requests to Dr. Felthous, Department of Psychiatry and Behavioral Sciences, University of Texas Medical Branch, Galveston, TX 77550.

Copyright © 1987 American Psychiatric Association.

Nevertheless, an association between cruelty to animals and violence against people is not uniformly accepted by psychiatrists for several reasons. There is concern about attaching undue importance to any single symptom. Empirical studies that have tested this hypothetical association appear to have resulted in contradictory findings. The data supporting this association are considered "soft" and of dubious reliability. The methods of sample selection limit the generalizability of the positive findings and conclusions. Therefore, the claims for the value of animal cruelty and other behaviors in predicting violence seem to have been overstated. And, if the predictive value is meager, any real association is interesting but useless.

In the present inquiry we will review controlled studies that pertain to a possible association between animal cruelty and violence against people. We will summarize the current state of scientific knowledge on this issue. Many of the studies cited here included animal cruelty as only one item of a more widely encompassing inquiry. Our focus precludes analysis of methods and findings that do not directly relate to animal cruelty in particular.

Before reviewing studies that pertain to animal cruelty, we should address the concern about focusing too much attention on a single symptom. Certainly for purposes of diagnosis, one symptom should not be elevated to the exclusion of others that are also clinically significant. This is especially true for disorders manifested by multiple aggressive and antisocial behaviors. In terms of *DSM-III*, this criticism does not apply to animal cruelty because this behavior is not mentioned as symptomatic of any disorder.

The question addressed in this review is whether the scientific literature supports an association between a pattern of repeated, substantial cruelty to animals in childhood and later violence against people that is serious and recurrent. First, controlled studies that tested this association but did not find it to be significant will be reviewed. Second, we will examine controlled studies that did find a statistically significant association. Unfortunately, the constraints of space do not allow inclusion of a number of uncontrolled studies that pertain to this issue (5–13). This review will not include reports of single cases involving animal cruelty or studies of aggressive behaviors that are not clearly injurious or dangerous.

Reprinted from the *American Journal of Psychiatry* 144 (1987): 710–17. Copyright 1987 by the American Psychiatric Association. Reprinted by permission.

TABLE 1. Studies That Found No Clear Association Between Childhood Cruelty to Animals and Later Violence Against People

Author	Setting	Subjects Type	N	Sex	Method of Data Collection	Childhood Cruelty to Animals (%)
Macdonald (14)	VA hospital psychiatric unit	Nonaggressive patients	20	—	Interview	—
		Patients who threatened to kill	20	—	Interview	—
		Killers	20	—	Interview	—
Climent et al. (15)	Hospital emergency room	Violent patients	40	M/F	Interview	—
		Nonviolent patients	40	M/F	Interview	—
Climent et al. (16)	State prison	Prisoners	95	F	Interview	—
Sendi and Blomgren (17)	Children's psychiatric service	Homicidal adolescents	10	M	Chart review	20
		Adolescents who threatened or attempted homicide	10	M	Chart review	30
		Control patients	10	M	Chart review	30
		Nonviolent patients	40	M/F	Interview	—
Rada (18)	Prison	Rapists	20	M	Interview	35
		Nonviolent child molesters	20	M	Interview	30
Felthous and Bernard (19)	Private psychiatric hospital	Patients	133	M/F	Chart review	—
Lewis et al. (20)	Children's inpatient psychiatric service	Homicidal patients	21	M/F	Chart review	14
		Nonhomicidal patients	30	M/F	Chart review	3
Shanok et al. (21)	Children's psychiatric service	Delinquent adolescents	29	M	Chart review	0.0
		Nondelinquent adolescents	25	M	Chart review	8.3
Langevin et al. (22)	Forensic inservice	Killers	109	M/F	Chart review	8
		Nonviolent offenders	38	M/F	Chart review	0
	Community	Normal control subjects	54	M/F	Chart review	—
Prentky and Carter (23)	Prison hospital	Sex offenders	206	M	Chart review	7.8

STUDIES THAT FOUND NO CLEAR ASSOCIATION

Controlled studies that found no clear association between cruelty to animals and personal violence are summarized in table 1. In 1968 Macdonald (14) reported a controlled study that was designed to test nine variables, including cruelty to animals, thought to predict homicide. Three groups of patients in a VA hospital psychiatric unit were interviewed: 20 homicide offenders, 20 inpatients who had threatened to kill, and 20 inpatients with no history of homicide or homicidal threats. Macdonald conducted a semi-structured interview with each subject. Animal cruelty was defined as the deliberate infliction of injury or death on "animals or birds" in a sadistic manner.

None of the variables was significantly associated with any of the three groups. However, in discussing the homicide offenders, Macdonald commented, "The incidence of only one factor, cruelty to animals, exceeded the higher incidence of the various factors in the homicide-threat and matched homicide-offender groups. The higher incidence of cruelty to animals might be expected in a group which included more sadistic offenders" (14, p. 62).

In a well-controlled study of 40 violent and 40 nonviolent patients in a hospital emergency room, Climent et al. (15) found no discernible difference in childhood cruelty to animals. The violent subjects had come to the emergency room with a chief complaint of violence. Their acts were typically repetitive. A trained research assistant, who was blind to the objectives and hypotheses of the investigation, obtained data by administering a questionnaire. Fourteen of the items dealt with "neurotic childhood traits." Cruelty to

animals was one of several items for which no difference was found between the two groups. Stubbornness, temper tantrums, and emotional deprivation were associated with the violent sample.

Climent et al. (16) reported in 1973 a multidisciplinary study of 95 female prisoners. The authors did not define violence, and the nature of aggression studied can be inferred only from the five variables used to distinguish violent from nonviolent inmates: 1) a particular MMPI profile, 2) reports and ratings by correctional officers, 3) commission of a violent crime, determined by prison administrators who reviewed the inmates' criminal histories, 4) length of current sentence beyond the mean sentence of 5.2 years, and 5) an elevated score on a self-evaluation questionnaire about various violent behaviors.

The data were gathered by several methods, but it appears that the historical items were tested by means of a 189-item standardized questionnaire. An item that was associated with all five measures of violence was considered to be associated with violence.

Childhood cruelty to animals was one of several items that Climent et al. identified as reaching "near-significance" in association with violence. From this study of incarcerated women, it cannot be concluded whether or not cruelty to animals is associated with recurrent, diffuse physical aggression directed against people.

Sendi and Blomgren (17) reported a comparative study of 10 adolescent boys who had committed homicide, 10 who had attempted or threatened homicide, and 10 psychiatric control subjects. The subjects in all three groups had been admitted to a child psychiatric inpatient service. An evaluative form was prepared for systematic data collection. The case histories were reviewed, and the boys' behavior was observed for 1 week by two independent raters.

The triadic behaviors of persistent enuresis, fire setting, and animal cruelty were evenly distributed among the three groups. None of the patients had the complete triad. Most of the adolescent murderers had a diagnosis of schizophrenia, whereas most who threatened or attempted homicide had a diagnosis of organic brain syndrome. Exposure to parental brutality and domestic violence was associated with the homicide group.

Rada (18) briefly reported the results of a comparative retrospective study of 20 rapists and 20 nonviolent child molesters. Evidently, the subjects in both groups were interviewed directly. Childhood enuresis was reported by 45% of the rapists, cruelty to animals by 35%, and fire setting by 30%. The comparable figures for the child molesters were 45%, 30%, and 15%, respectively. Ten percent of the rapists had a positive triad, as did 5% of the child molesters. Rada concluded that the predictive value of the triadic behaviors was undetermined.

In 1979 Bernard and one of us (A.R.F.) (19) reported a retrospective study of 133 male and female patients in a private psychiatric hospital. Charts of male and female patients between 15 and 30 years of age were selected in order of hospital discharge. Information was collected by means of a data retrieval outline and chart review. Most patients with a single triadic behavior lacked a history of interpersonal violence. Those with two or three triadic behaviors also had a recorded history of at least two of the following behaviors: homicidal threats, carrying a deadly weapon, and physical assaults. The numbers were too small for statistical analysis. One useful result of this study was its demonstration that chart review is a weak means of systematically obtaining comprehensive and reliable historical data.

In 1983 Lewis et al. (20) reported a study of 55 children, 3 to 12 years of age, who were admitted to a psychiatric inpatient service. Only one episode of "homicidal behavior" was required to classify the child as homicidal. The behavior was assessed by four independent raters, each of whom determined whether the act would have resulted in death or serious injury had it been performed by an adult. Threatening with a lethal weapon was considered equivalent to a homicidal act. For the purposes of the study, 21 children were classified as homicidally aggressive, and 30 were considered not homicidally aggressive. The data were obtained from the patients' hospital records. Lewis et al. found, "The proportions of homicidally aggressive and nonhomicidal children with histories of cruelty to animals (14% and 3%) . . . [were] not significantly different" (20).

They conceded, "Data are not uniform or complete because they are not collected primarily for research purposes. On the other hand, data obtained from retrospective chart reviews of symptoms and behaviors are unbiased by the possible prejudices of the investi-

gators." Since the aggressive sample was selected on the basis of a single episode of homicidal behavior, the study did not discriminate recurrently aggressive children.

Shanok et al. (21) reported a study of 29 delinquent and 25 nondelinquent adolescent boys admitted to an inpatient psychiatric service. Data were gathered from hospital and probation department records. A symptom was considered to be present if a clinician had noted its occurrence and given an example in the chart. Significantly more delinquent than nondelinquent boys had acted violently in the past, and significantly more delinquent boys had been hospitalized before. But the triadic elements did not distinguish the two groups. Cruelty to animals was reported in the charts of only two nondelinquent boys; it was not recorded in any of the delinquent boys' charts.

In 1983 Langevin et al. (22) reported a study of 109 killers and 38 nonviolent offenders in a forensic in-service and 54 normal control subjects. The records of 50% of the offenders included a standardized Parent-Child Relations Questionnaire. Data were obtained from each chart by two raters and were checked for interrater reliability. The killers had disturbed parent-child interactions, but they did not differ from the nonviolent offenders in this regard. Compared to the killers, more of the nonviolent offenders ran away from home, more were adopted, but fewer stole in childhood. The triadic behaviors were not significantly associated with any of the three groups, but the only subjects with either two (N=6) or three (N=1) of the triadic behaviors belonged to the killer sample. Cruelty to animals was noted more often in the killers than in the nonviolent offenders (8% versus 0%).

As Langevin et al. pointed out, cruelty to animals and other childhood behaviors will not be registered if an initial evaluator, unconnected with the study, failed to inquire about this behavior or to record it in the patient's chart. For this reason, historical information gleaned from charts can be expected to yield lower frequencies than direct interviews with subjects. In comparing Langevin et al.'s results with those of other studies, one should also note that the index sample consisted of patients charged with a homicidal offense. Aggressive individuals were not defined as those with long-standing patterns of diffuse, impulsive personal violence.

Prentky and Carter (23) reported in 1984 a study of 206 male sexual offenders who were incarcerated for evaluation and treatment, having been adjudged to be "sexually dangerous." Data were obtained by systematic review of each inmate's chart. The charts were randomly assigned to three research assistants to review. The variables tested for association with the triadic behaviors fell into four groupings: family, childhood, juvenile, and criminal. The variables that most closely correspond to recurrent personal violence appear to be "total number of adult and juvenile serious sexual . . . crimes" and "degree of violence of the most violent offense."

TABLE 2. Controlled Studies That Found a Significant Association Between Childhood Cruelty to Animals and Later Violence Against People

| Author | Setting | Subjects | | | Method of Data Collection | Childhood Cruelty to Animals (%) | Significance |
		Type	N	Sex			
Hellman and Blackman (24)	Prison hospital	Violent prisoners	31	M	Interview	52	$\chi^2=16.63$, p<.001
		Nonviolent prisoners	53	M	Interview	17	
Felthous and Yudowitz (25)	State prison	Violent prisoners	11	F	Interview	36	p<.02 (chi-square analysis)
		Nonviolent prisoners	13	F	Interview	0	
Felthous (26)	Inpatient psychiatric service of military hospital	Violent patients	74	M	Interview	18	p<.025 (chi-square analysis)
		Nonviolent patients	75	M	Interview	5	
Kellert and Felthous (28, 29)	Federal prisons	Violent prisoners	32	M	Interview	25	$\chi^2=30.56$, df=9, p<.005
		Prisoners of intermediate violence	18	M	Interview	0	
		Nonviolent prisoners	52	M	Interview	6	
	Community	Nonprisoners	50	M	Interview	0	

To the extent that the variables were tested for an association with measures of aggression, the study was controlled, but all the subjects were adjudged to be "sexually dangerous"; no "sexually nondangerous" control subjects were studied for comparison.

Although cruelty to animals and arson were not defined, the study apparently identified a respectable number of subjects with a partial or complete triad (N=81). Compared with the subjects without any triadic elements (N=103), more of the triadic subjects came from abusive family backgrounds. In comparison with the subjects who had not been physically abused, over twice as many subjects who were physically abused in childhood also had histories of triadic behaviors. Compared with the subjects who had not been sexually abused, over four times as many subjects who had been sexually abused in childhood had triadic behaviors. Prentky and Carter concluded that triadic behaviors represent "primarily a maladaptive response to turmoil and abuse in the home prior to and during adolescence" (23). The study did not find a relationship between adult crime and the complete triad (N=4), a dyad (N=14), or a monad (N=63). Sixteen of the subjects (7.8%) had been cruel to animals.

Because the data were obtained from chart reviews, it is not clear that all subjects had been asked directly about cruelty to animals. And since the variables relating to aggression were convictions of violent crimes, the question of whether animal cruelty and other triadic behaviors are associated with recurrent personal violent acts, which do not invariably result in conviction, remained unanswered.

STUDIES THAT FOUND AN ASSOCIATION

Controlled studies that found an association between cruelty to animals and personal violence are summarized in table 2. The most frequently cited study and the first to lend statistical support to the impression that childhood triadic behaviors are associated with later aggression against people was reported by Hellman and Blackman in 1966 (24). The study involved interviews of 31 male prisoners charged with violent crimes and 53 male prisoners charged with nonaggressive crimes. Three-fourths of the aggressive men gave histories of triadic elements, whereas only 15 of the 53 nonviolent men had these childhood behaviors. Two-thirds of those revealing a positive triad belonged to the aggressive group. Animal cruelty was reported by 16 (52%) of the 31 aggressive prisoners and by nine (17%) of the 53 nonaggressive prisoners ($\chi^2=16.63$, p<.001).

The subjects were selected and assigned to the violent or nonviolent sample on the basis of a single charge; thus, this study did not differentiate recurrent from isolated aggressive acts. However, 75% of the violent subjects had a background of rapes, burglaries, and assaults before the index offense, so most may have been recurrently and diffusely aggressive, even though they were not selected on the basis of multiple acts of aggression. One must wonder whether the association would have been more specific had the investigators discriminated recurrent violence.

Hellman and Blackman noted that a social history was not always effective in obtaining a history of cruelty to animals. As in the case of fire setting, the relatives were not always aware of this behavior. Our experience also suggests that confirmation by relatives is often impossible.

In 1977 Yudowitz and one of us (A.R.F.) (25) reported a two-part study of female offenders that was designed to test variables thought to be associated with violence against people. One portion of the study compared 31 female offenders with 19 male offenders to determine whether historical items distinguished the women from the men. Data were obtained by administering a questionnaire and then an interview. The male sample had a higher prevalence of killing animals, but torturing animals, like enuresis and fire setting, was of nearly equal prevalence in the two samples. The numerical data did not differentiate animal killings that were deviant or gratuitous from socially acceptable killings.

In the second part of this study, assaultive and nonassaultive women were compared. An assaultive woman was defined as one convicted of a violent offense against a person (N=11), whereas a nonassaultive woman had no record of charges or convictions of a violent offense (N=13). Cruelty to animals was the only childhood behavior that differentiated the two groups with statistical significance (chi-square analysis, p<.02).

It should be noted that a conviction of a violent offense does not establish a pattern of recurrent aggression, and lack of a charge of a violent offense does not rule out a pattern of interpersonal violence.

One of us (A.R.F.) (26) reported in 1980 a study of 429 patients who were admitted to a Navy hospital, 346 men and 83 women. The subjects were not selected on the basis of aggressive behaviors or any other symptoms; they were patients successively admitted to the psychiatric service who were available and willing to participate. From the 346 men interviewed, 74 were identified as aggressive on the basis of 1) a history of assault serious enough to require the victim to obtain medical treatment or dental restoration or 2) either threatening serious harm against others or carrying a knife or gun for potential use against others. Most who manifested several types of aggressive behaviors also had histories of recurrent assaults. The nonaggressive male subjects (N=75) lacked a history of any of these behaviors since the age of 15. Historical variables thought to be associated with violence were tested via an interview schedule.

Killing dogs or cats and animal cruelty were significantly associated with the aggressive group (chi-square analysis, p<.025), but other childhood behaviors showed a stronger correlation: violent outbursts, fights, fights resulting in injury, school suspensions, school truancy, and frequent temper tantrums (in all cases, p<.005).

The latter behaviors correlated more strongly because they were reported by more of the aggressive subjects. However, these behaviors were not uncommonly reported by the nonaggressive subjects as well. The number of subjects who were pugnacious as young children but nonaggressive after 15 years of age was over half the number who were pugnacious as children and dangerously aggressive later on. In contrast, although childhood animal cruelty was reported by only 18% of the aggressive sample, the number of subjects with this behavior was several times higher among the aggressive subjects (N=13) than among the nonaggressive subjects (N=4).

The aggressive sample was also compared with a nonpsychiatric sample of men admitted to another service of the same hospital (N=26). The symptomatic items for which statistical significance was upheld in both comparisons included fights with or without injury, school truancy, school suspensions, frequent headaches, and killing dogs or cats (chi-square analysis, p<.05 in all cases).

From the 346 male psychiatric inpatients included in that study, those whose history of cruelty to animals consisted of repeatedly torturing and injuring dogs or cats (N=18), regardless of level of aggression, were singled out (27). This animal cruelty group was clearly skewed toward a higher level of aggression against people. Specifically, nine animal cruelty subjects belonged to the most aggressive level, whereas only one belong to the least aggressive level and the other eight were disturbed over intermediate levels of aggression. A control group was defined as subjects with the highest level of aggression toward people who denied a history of cruelty to animals in childhood (N=53).

The historical items reported by a majority of both samples included childhood fighting, temper tantrums, brutal punishments by a father figure, brutal punishments by a mother figure, violent outbursts, and school truancy. Setting uncontrolled fires was significantly associated with the animal cruelty group. Poor school work, setting destructive fires, and bed-wetting beyond 5 years of age showed a trend toward significance (chi-square analysis, p<.10), suggesting the possibility that the triadic behaviors are linked. Separation from a father figure longer than 6 months and presence of an alcoholic father figure also discriminated the animal cruelty group.

In summary, both the animal cruelty group and the noncruelty assaultive group gave histories of impulsive and aggressive behaviors in childhood. Parental brutality was commonly reported in both groups. In contrast to the noncruelty subjects, the men with histories of animal cruelty tended to have absent or emotionally unavailable father figures. It was hypothesized that the combination of parental brutality and lack of a stable father figure may affect a boy's psychological development in a manner that is qualitatively different from the effect of either brutality or deprivation alone.

We believe that the most comprehensive retrospective study of cruelty to animals to date was one conducted by us (28, 29). Using previously reported studies for guidance, we began our study with several assumptions. First, repeated acts of serious cruelty to socially valued animals (e.g., dogs) are more apt to be associated with violence toward people than are isolated acts of cruelty, minor abuses, and victimization of less socially valuable species (e.g., rats). Second, if animal cruelty is associated with aggression against people, it is most likely associated with serious, recurrent personal violence. A single violent offense or act would not identify this core population with continuous aggression. Third, subjects must be interviewed directly because prison records and other documents do not contain systematically gathered and adequately detailed historical data. Fourth, if a positive history of cruelty to animals exists, it will most likely be elicited by inquiry into a number of areas wherein animal involvement is possible. One or two questions on cruelty to animals do not sufficiently tap the history of an individual's involvements with animals.

Looking for samples that would include a sizable

number of recurrently aggressive subjects, we turned to U.S. penitentiaries in Connecticut and Kansas. Prison counselors were asked to rate their assigned prisoners on a scale of aggressiveness from 1 to 10. The aggressive behaviors rated on this scale included threatening speech, preparatory behaviors, and violent acts. High scores reflected the combination of frequent, severe, and multiform aggressive behaviors and, therefore, violence that was both recurrent and impulsive. Only those subjects with extremely high or low scores were asked to participate in this study. The ratings were never shared with the subjects and were communicated to the interviewers only after the interviews were completed. In addition to these objective measurements, the most violent subjects themselves confirmed that they had been recurrently and impulsively aggressive toward others. In addition to the prisoners, randomly selected young men in New Haven and Topeka were interviewed as noninstitutional control subjects. Of the 152 men who participated in this study, 32 were aggressive criminals, 18 were moderately aggressive criminals, 52 were nonaggressive criminals, and 50 were noncriminals.

A standard interview schedule with over 440 closed- and open-ended questions was administered to each subject. The interview items pertained to antisocial behaviors, environmental background, and various aspects of animal involvements, such as owning family pets, raising livestock, training animals, trapping and hunting, and attending dog, cock, or bull fights. The subjects were asked about 16 specific types of animal cruelty. A closed-ended survey on attitudes toward animals was administered. For each subject who consented, a parent or family member who knew him in childhood was contacted and interviewed.

Rigorous statistical analysis showed a significant association between acts of cruelty to animals in childhood and serious, recurrent aggression against people as an adult ($\chi^2=30.56$, df=9, p<.005) (28). From the responses to the closed-ended questions it was found that 25% of the aggressive criminals (N=8) had abused animals five or more times in childhood. In contrast, the figure for the nonaggressive criminals was 5.8% (N=3) and for noncriminals it was 0%.

In the second part of the study, the investigators identified the subjects in all four groups who had a pattern of substantial animal abuse in childhood, specifically, "a pattern of deliberately, repeatedly, and unnecessarily hurting vertebrate animals in a manner likely to cause serious injury" (29). Of the 20 prisoners who gave this history, 16 belonged to the most aggressive group, whereas only four fell into the nonaggressive category. Three of the 50 nonprisoners had shown a pattern of animal cruelty. With only a single exception, all animal cruelty subjects in the nonaggressive criminal and noncriminal groups had been more pugnacious toward people than one would expect from group assignment alone. A history of substantial animal abuse in childhood showed a statistically significant association with the recurrent, impulsive violence

of the most aggressive sample ($\chi^2=37.2$, df=3, p< .005) (29).

The extensive qualitative data on animal cruelty obtained by directly administering a comprehensive interview to each subject allowed us to suggest a tentative classification of motivation for animal cruelty (28). Other interesting findings were derived from this study, but the important point is that the most thorough retrospective study of animal cruelty to date found a firm relationship between cruelty to animals during childhood and later recurrent violence against people regardless of whether the control group comprised nonaggressive prisoners or randomly selected nonprisoners.

DISCUSSION

At first glance, one might review the discrepant results of the various studies and conclude that a relationship between cruelty to animals in childhood and later personal violence has not yet been demonstrated. There were more controlled studies, involving more investigative teams, that failed to find an association than controlled studies that did. Upon closer examination, factors can be identified that probably contributed to the apparently contradictory findings.

The first consideration is definition of the behaviors studied. The definition of animal cruelty can be broadened to the point where it is essentially normative. For example, swatting at house flies or disciplining a pet dog with a gentle slap are presumably common. A vague definition of cruelty, or no definition, allows for inclusion of these and other behaviors that may not be particularly symptomatic of abnormal aggression. Most studies, particularly those that did not find an association, did not define the behavior.

Even more important is the definition of personal aggression. Violence against people occurs in many forms. We postulate that repeated acts of animal cruelty are associated with personal violence which is serious and recurrent. Recurrent violence may result in death, but not necessarily. A single violent act, threat, or attempt is insufficient to identify recurrent violence, and too many measures of violence may cloud the recurrent nature of aggression. With the possible exception of Climent et al.'s 1972 study (15), investigators who identified recurrent impulsive violence found an association with animal cruelty.

In attempting to understand discrepant findings, one must consider the various methods of data collection. Over half of the studies that found no association between childhood cruelty to animals and later violent or deviant behavior used the chart review method of data collection rather than direct interview of subjects (table 1). All studies that found an association between animal cruelty and personal aggression obtained data by means of interviewing the subjects directly (table 2). Investigators who relied only on written material cannot know whether every subject was systematically queried about cruelty to animals and other historical variables. Having used both methods, at both hospital and prison facilities, one of us (A.R.F.) has found that even the most comprehensive clinical records do not uniformly contain adequate historical information.

Those who favor the chart review method reason that data obtained only for clinical purposes is less apt to be prejudiced than data obtained through interviews by investigators or their research assistants. On the contrary, there is no reason to believe that recording clinicians cannot be equally biased; they may exercise considerably more discretion regarding what questions to ask and what information to record than interviewers who are bound by predesigned investigative procedures.

Another factor that can account for discrepant results is variation in the thoroughness of the interviews. An interview schedule that taps several major life areas in which animals may be involved is more apt to elicit acts of cruelty in an individual's past than a schedule with just a few questions on animal cruelty.

If a pattern of animal abuse in childhood is associated with recurrent, impulsive violence toward people that continues into childhood, is animal abuse an early sign of antisocial personality disorder? A number of fine studies on delinquency or "sociopathy" (30–33) did not systematically look for a history of animal cruelty, so variables that were untested in the classic studies of criminal behavior are not widely accepted as correlates of antisocial personality disorder or recurrent aggression. Although Bowlby's writings do not indicate that he systematically investigated cruelty, he observed, "Cruelty to animals and other children is a characteristic, though not common, feature of the affectionless psychopath" (30, pp. 79, 80).

Prediction of a single act (e.g., homicide) on the basis of a preceding act (e.g., animal abuse) would be risky indeed. However, further acts of cruelty can be reasonably expected in a child who has already demonstrated an ongoing pattern of animal cruelty. In addition, although an isolated violent act in an overcontrolled individual would be difficult to predict, one could say that someone with a pattern of repeated assaults is more likely to commit assault again than someone who has never committed assault. Different patterns of aggressive behaviors also appear to be associated in many individuals. The literature suggests an association between a pattern of cruelty to animals in childhood or adolescence and a pattern of dangerous and recurrent aggression against people at a later age.

Further research on this aspect of human aggression is certainly indicated, but replication studies must apply the minimal methodological rigor suggested here lest findings serve only to confuse rather than clarify the issue. Replication studies should adopt the direct interview method of data collection. A few questions on animal cruelty are not enough. Studies should endeavor to obtain a comprehensive history of animal involvements in childhood. Identification of violent individuals based on a single act misses the point. The nature of the violence in question is *recurrent,* dangerous aggression against people. An interesting question for future investigation is whether motivation for recurrent animal cruelty correlates with motivation for recurrent personal aggression (e.g., revenge, sadistic pleasure).

Meanwhile, clinicians, jurists, school teachers, parents, and others who work and play with children should be alert to the potentially ominous significance of this behavior in childhood and the advisability of concerned, helpful intervention. Also, on a preventive note, if aggression to animals can become generalized to involve humans, perhaps an ethic of compassion and respect for animals can also carry over to humans.

REFERENCES

1. Pinel P: A Treatise on Insanity (1806). New York, Hafner, 1962, pp 150–156
2. Macdonald JM: The Murderer and His Victim. Springfield, Ill, Charles C Thomas, 1961, pp 175–216, 247–253
3. Hollie PG: Coast sniper vowed she would do something big. New York Times, Jan 31, 1979
4. Olafson S, Lucas Toole: Two lives that read like a nightmare. Houston Post, July 1, 1984, p 22A
5. Macdonald JM: The threat to kill. Am J Psychiatry 1963; 120: 125–130
6. Lion JR, Bach-y-Rita G, Ervin FR: Violent patients in the emergency room. Am J Psychiatry 1969; 125:1706–1711
7. Bach-y-Rita G, Lion JR, Climent CE, et al: Episodic dyscontrol: a study of 130 violent patients. Am J Psychiatry 1971; 127: 1473–1478
8. Tapia F: Children who are cruel to animals. Child Psychiatry Hum Dev 1971; 2:70–77
9. Rigdon JD, Tapia F: Children who are cruel to animals—a follow-up study. J Operational Psychiatry 1971; 8:27–36
10. Wax DE, Haddox VG: Enuresis, fire setting, and animal cruelty: a useful danger signal in predicting vulnerability of adolescent males to assaultive behavior. Child Psychiatry Hum Dev 1974; 4:151–156
11. Wax DE, Haddox VG: Sexual aberrance in male adolescents manifesting a behavioral triad considered predictive of extreme violence: some clinical observations. J Forensic Sci 1974; 19: 102–108
12. Wax DE, Haddox VG: Enuresis, firesetting, and animal cruelty in male adolescent delinquents: a triad predictive of violent behavior. J Psychiatry and Law 1974; 2:45–71
13. Justice B, Justice R, Kraft IA: Early-warning signs of violence: is a triad enough? Am J Psychiatry 1974; 131:457–459
14. Macdonald JM: Homicidal Threats. Springfield, Ill, Charles C Thomas, 1968
15. Climent CE, Hyg MS, Ervin MD: Historical data in the evaluation of violent subjects. Arch Gen Psychiatry 1972; 27: 621–624
16. Climent CE, Rollins A, Ervin FR, et al: Epidemiological studies of women prisoners, I: medical and psychiatric variables related to violent behavior. Am J Psychiatry 1973; 130:985–990
17. Sendi IB, Blomgren PG: A comparative study of predictive criteria in the predisposition of homicidal adolescents. Am J Psychiatry 1975; 132:423–427
18. Rada RT: Psychological factors in rapist behavior, in Clinical Aspects of the Rapist. New York, Grune & Stratton, 1978
19. Felthous AR, Bernard H: Enuresis, firesetting, and cruelty to animals: the significance of two-thirds of this triad. J Forensic Sci 1979; 24:240–246
20. Lewis DO, Shanok SS, Grant M, et al: Homicidally aggressive young children: neuropsychiatric and experiential correlates. Am J Psychiatry 1983; 140:148–153

21. Shanok SS, Malani SC, Ninan OP, et al: A comparison of delinquent and nondelinquent psychiatric inpatients. Am J Psychiatry 1983; 140:582–585

22. Langevin R, Paitich D, Orchard B, et al: Childhood and family background of killers seen for psychiatric assessment: a controlled study. Bull Am Acad Psychiatry Law 1983; 11:331–341

23. Prentky RA, Carter DL: The predictive value of the triad for sex offenders. Behav Sci Law 1984; 2:341–354

24. Hellman DS, Blackman N: Enuresis, firesetting and cruelty to animals: a triad predictive of adult crime. Am J Psychiatry 1966; 122:1431–1435

25. Felthous AR, Yudowitz B: Approaching a comparative typology of assaultive female offenders. Psychiatry 1977; 40:270–276

26. Felthous AR: Childhood antecedents of aggressive behaviors in male psychiatric patients. Bull Am Acad Psychiatry Law 1980; 8:104–110

27. Felthous AR: Aggression against cats, dogs, and people. Child Psychiatry Hum Dev 1980; 10:169–177

28. Kellert SR, Felthous AR: Childhood cruelty toward animals among criminals and noncriminals. Hum Relations 1985; 38: 1113–1129

29. Felthous AR, Kellert SR: Violence against animals and people: is aggression against living creatures generalized? Bull Am Acad Psychiatry Law 1986; 14:55–69

30. Bowlby J: Maternal Care and Mental Health. Geneva, World Health Organization, 1952

31. Glueck S, Glueck E: Predicting Delinquency and Crime. Cambridge, Harvard University Press, 1960

32. Andry RG: Delinquency and Parental Pathology: A Study in Forensic and Clinical Psychology. London, Methuen, 1960

33. Robins LN: Deviant Children Grown Up: A Sociological and Psychiatric Study of Sociopathic Personality (1966). Huntington, NY, Robert E Krieger, 1974

THE TANGLED WEB OF ANIMAL ABUSE:

The Links between Cruelty to Animals and Human Violence

—Wide World Photos, Inc.

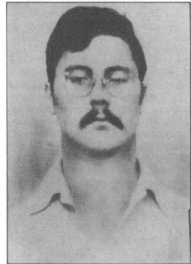

Four of the most famous violent criminals in recent years had histories of abusing animals: (top left to right) Edmund Emil Kemper III; David Berkowitz; James Oliver Huberty; and (below) Albert DeSalvo.

—The San Francisco Society for the Prevention of Cruelty to Animals

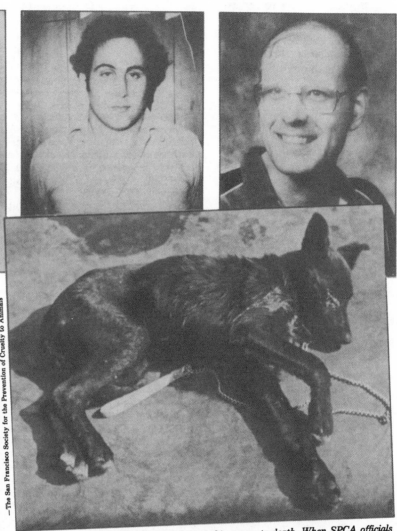

Witnesses said a San Francisco man kicked this puppy to death. When SPCA officials checked police files to see if the accused had a prior criminal record, they discovered he was also wanted on a felony charge. The man later was found guilty of a violent crime and sentenced to the state penitentiary. The link between violent behavior and animal abuse is only now coming to the attention of many in the criminal justice system.

The Humane Society of the United States
2100 L Street, NW, Washington, DC 20037

Reprinted from *The Humane Society News* (Summer 1986), 1–6, with permission of the Humane Society of the United States.

77

> "Anyone who has accustomed himself to regard the life of any living creature as worthless is in danger of arriving also at the idea of worthless human lives."
> —ALBERT SCHWEITZER

Animal abuse is not just the result of some personality flaw in the abuser, but a symptom of a deeply disturbed family.

Scientists and lawmakers are slowly beginning to acknowledge the humane movement's long-held position that society's treatment of animals is inseparable from its treatment of human beings.

by Dr. Randall Lockwood and Guy R. Hodge

In 1984, Pennsylvania SPCA officials arrested Dwayne Wright for attacking six dogs with lye in a highly publicized cruelty case. The SPCA reported that "the grisly attacks apparently were committed just to see the dogs suffer." Before Mr. Wright could stand trial for these offenses in Pennsylvania, however, law enforcement officials in New Jersey requested his extradition to face murder charges in the death of a disabled man. Mr. Wright is presently serving a twenty-year sentence for murder.

Such stories of people who exhibit violence toward both human beings and animals are disturbingly common and come as little surprise to those involved with animal welfare. The belief that one's treatment of animals is closely associated with the treatment of fellow human beings has a long history in philosophy. This idea served as the ethical foundation for the rise of the animal-welfare movement during the nineteenth century.

Despite the widespread historical recognition of the link between cruelty to animals and other forms of violent or antisocial behavior, this connection has, until recently, largely been ignored by law-enforcement agencies, the judicial system, social service agencies, and others in a position to take action. This is not surprising when we consider how long it has taken society to recognize widespread problems of child abuse and other manifestations of domestic violence.

Over the last decade, social scientists and human-service agencies have finally begun to examine cruelty to animals as a serious *human* problem. What has prompted this concern? First, there have been many dramatic cases such as that of Mr. Wright. Second, social scientists have been paying increasing attention to all forms of family violence, including abuse and neglect of children, spouses, and the elderly. Researchers studying human-animal relationships have repeatedly demonstrated the central role that pets can play in many normal and disturbed families. Increasing numbers of investigations of organized cruelty, such as dogfighting, have revealed that a multitude of other, unrelated offenses co-exist with that activity. Finally, greater attention has been drawn to animal abuse by an increasingly concerned public that has responded negatively to mild punishments handed down in animal-cruelty cases.

Scientific studies of the connections between animal abuse and human violence are still few in number, but those that exist are providing valuable insights into the roots of antisocial behavior.

Animal Cruelty and Adult Violence

Much of the early evidence that inspired interest in this issue came from anecdotal case histories of individual criminals. There is compelling circumstantial evidence linking two groups of criminals—serial and mass murderers—with acts of cruelty to animals. There is a significantly high incidence of such acts, usually prior to age twenty-five, among people who have engaged in multiple murders:

• Albert DeSalvo, the self-confessed "Boston Strangler" who killed thirteen women in 1962–63 and was sentenced to life imprisonment on unrelated charges of armed robbery, assault, and sex offenses involving four women, had, in his youth, trapped dogs and cats in orange crates and shot arrows through the boxes.

• Edmund Emil Kemper III, convicted in 1973 on eight counts of first-degree murder for killing eight women, including his mother, had revealed at his trial that he had a history of abusing cats and dogs.

• David Berkowitz, New York City's "Son of Sam" gunman who pleaded guilty to thirteen murder and attempted murder charges, had shot a neighbor's Labrador retriever. Berkowitz claimed that the dog was the spiritual force that compelled him to kill.

• Brenda Spencer fired forty shots from a rifle at arriving San Diego school children, fatally wounding two and injuring nine others. During the subsequent investigation, neighbors informed police that Ms. Spencer had repeatedly abused dogs and cats, often by setting their tails on fire.

• Carroll Edward Cole, one of the most prolific killers in modern history, was executed in December of 1985 for five of the thirty-five murders of which he was accused. Mr. Cole had said that his first act of violence

Reporting Cruelty

As a rule, failure to provide adequate food, water, and shelter or the use of physical force sufficient to leave a mark or otherwise cause injury constitutes cruelty to animals according to most state laws.

If you believe an animal is being mistreated, promptly telephone your local animal-welfare agency. If you cannot obtain a listing for a local humane society, call the local police for assistance. If there is no humane society in the area, then the police should investigate your complaint. Provide the dispatcher with all the details, including:

• A description of the incident and type of abuse

• The date and time of the incident

• A description of the animal(s)

• The exact address at which the animal can be found

• The name of the animal's owner, if any

• A description of the abuser (age, height, weight) and name, if known

• Any other relevant details such as license plate numbers that may aid in apprehending the abuser

• Your name, address, and telephone number. Also inform the dispatcher if you were an eyewitness to the incident. If your information is to be of value to law-enforcement and animal-welfare agencies, you must be willing to testify against animal abusers.

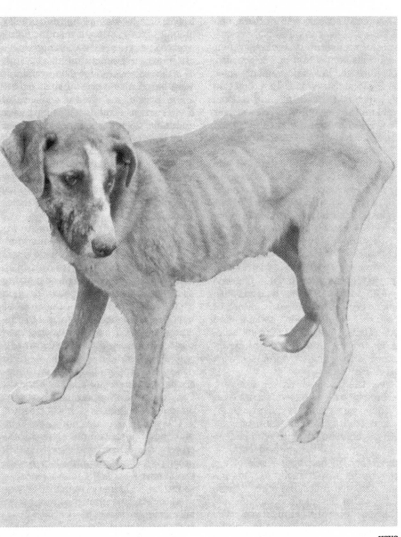

—HSUS

as a child was to strangle a puppy.

• In 1984, James Huberty was shot by police after killing twenty-one children and adults at a McDonalds restaurant in San Ysidro, California. As a teenager, Mr. Huberty had been accused of having shot his neighbor's dog with an airgun.

Although most animal abusers will *not* commit sensational murders, serial killers almost invariably have histories of animal abuse earlier in their lives. This connection has serious implications for law enforcement, since the Federal Bureau of Investigation has indicated that brutal and irrational serial killings account for one-quarter of all unsolved murders in the United States each year.

Single case histories do not provide much insight into the origins of animal abuse and its connections to other forms of violence. For this reason, a number of scientists have looked at larger populations of criminals to explore this association. In 1966, Drs. D.S. Hellman and Nathan Blackman published one of the first formal studies. Their analysis of life histories of eighty-four prison inmates showed that 75 percent of those charged with violent crimes had an early record of cruelty to animals, fire-setting, and bed-wetting. Several subsequent studies looked for this "triad" of symptoms in other violent criminals, with mixed results.

Over the last few years, a different picture has emerged. Psychiatrist Alan Felthous surveyed several groups of violent adults. In one group of eighteen psychiatric patients who had repeatedly tortured dogs and cats, he found that all had high levels of aggression to people, including one patient who had murdered a boy. These abusers also shared a common history of brutal parental punishment. Dr. Felthous and others have thus identified a slightly different triad consisting

of physical abuse by parents, cruelty to animals, and violence toward people. Almost all serious animal abusers are males, but Dr. Felthous has found similar patterns in the lives of assaultive women as well.

One of the most detailed surveys of adult criminals has recently been done by Dr. Felthous and Dr. Stephen Kellert. They looked at animal cruelty among three groups of men including aggressive criminals, nonaggressive criminals, and noncriminals. Ratings of aggressiveness for the criminals were based on reports of their *behavior* in prison, not on the violence of their crimes. Among the aggressive criminals, 25 percent reported five or more childhood acts of cruelty toward animals, compared to 6 percent of the nonaggressive criminals and none in the sample of noncriminals. Aggressive criminals were also more likely to report fear or dislike of particular animals.

This study is one of the first to explore the specific motives behind animal cruelty in these violent men. Some resorted to cruelty to control an animal's behavior, for example, using beatings and electric prods to gain compliance from dogs. Many of the men used violence as a form of retaliation. One burned a cat that had scratched him, and another drowned a dog that barked too much. A third motivation was prejudice. Many abusers harbor hatred for specific animals. Cats were victims because they were often seen as "sneaky" and "creepy."

This study identified additional complex motives for animal abuse. Some cruelty came from a desire to shock other people or to impress them with the abuser's capacity for violence. In some cases, cruelty to animals was used to retaliate against others, especially neighbors.

Animal cruelty has been correlated with other forms of adult wrongdoing.

A recent study by Dr. Michael Bessey of the University of Manitoba concluded that "violators of wildlife laws may be involved in multitudinous illegal activities." He identified three clusters of offenses that seemed to go together. People who engaged in "unethical" acts such as aerial hunting were also likely to hunt endangered species, injure wildlife with snowmobiles, or illegally hunt game at night. Those who were guilty of "dangerous" acts typically violated laws related to firearm handling and public intoxication. A third group of violators typically broke laws related to property and had histories of poaching and trespassing.

Organized abuse of animals also has its links to other crimes. HSUS investigator Bob Baker, who has extensive experience with dogfighting, says, "Dogfights are the scene of all kinds of crimes, including gambling, drug dealing, and possession of illegal weapons." He adds, "One of the most disturbing things is the number of children in attendance at these fights —from infants to teenagers. These children are exposed to all the brutality and illegal acts that go along with this sport!"

Animal Cruelty and Juvenile Violence

Most of the research on animal abuse and adult crime has indicated that the first instances of cruelty to animals take place early in the abusers' lives. As anthropologist Margaret Mead noted, "One of the most dangerous things that can happen to a child is to kill or torture an animal and get away with it." Nearly all young children go through a stage of "innocent" cruelty during which they may harm insects or other small animals in the process of exploring the world and discovering their abilities. Most children, however, with proper guidance from parents and teachers, can become sensitive to the fact that animals can experience pain and suffering and thus try to avoid causing such pain. Some, however, seem to become locked into a pattern of cruelty that can last a lifetime.

In 1971, Dr. Fernando Tapia reviewed the cases of eighteen boys who were under treatment because of incidents of severe cruelty to animals. All showed other problems of violence including bullying, theft, and arson. Most had histories of parental neglect, brutality, and rejection. Seven years later, Dr. Tapia was able to follow up on thirteen of these cases, now entering young adulthood. Eight of the thirteen were *still* involved in animal cruelty. In general, animal abuse ended only in the case of the boys who had been removed from abusive parents and placed in foster homes.

What starts young boys on the road to animal cruelty and later violence against people? Some have suggested that these children lack the capacity to love, to form close ties to either people or animals, but recent research suggests that it is not that simple. A University of Minnesota study by Dr. Michael Robin and others looked at attitudes towards animals in 507 delinquent and nondelinquent adolescents. Nearly all of these children (91 percent) reported having had a "special pet" at some time in their lives. The delinquent children were three times more likely to report that they sought out their pet during times of trouble and discussed their problems with it. A key difference between the delinquent and nondelinquent groups was that 34 percent of the delinquent children had lost their special pet through intentional or accidental killing. In many cases, an abusive father had disposed of this loved animal in some violent way, resulting in deep resentment on the part of the child.

It may be that some juveniles begin to abuse animals to convince themselves that they don't care about the things they often seem to lose. Some are convinced of their "badness" by parents and behave in the way that they think is expected of them. Some are imitating the family violence that seems to be a "normal" way of life for them. Others feel helpless and use animals as victims to demonstrate their power and authority or as scapegoats for the anger they feel against parents or society as a whole. Finally, some of these young abusers simply seem to have never learned to value the lives of others.

Animal Abuse and Family Problems

The research we have described strongly suggests that animal abuse is not just the result of some personality flaw in the abuser, but a symptom of a deeply disturbed family. As Boris Levinson has observed, "Pets mirror the tensions of their adopted families." Research specifically looking at family dynamics supports this idea.

In 1980, James Hutton reviewed RSPCA cruelty reports for one community in England. Of twenty-three families with a history of animal abuse, 83 percent had been identified by human social service agencies as having children at risk of abuse or neglect. In 1983, Deviney, Dickert, and Lockwood reported on the care of pets within fifty-seven families being treated by New Jersey's Division of Youth and Family Services because of the incidents of child abuse. At least one person had abused pets in 88 percent of the families in which children had been physically abused! In about two-thirds of these cases, it was the abusive *parent* who had killed or injured a pet. Children were the abusers in the remaining third. These and other studies confirm that cruelty to animals can be one of many signs of a family in need of professional help.

Animal Abuse and Mental Illness

Although it would seem to be clear that many animal abusers are in need of help, the psychiatric community has been very slow to recognize this. Surprisingly, the *Diagnostic and Statistical Manual of Mental Disorders*, the "handbook" for many professionals in the American Psychiatric Association, makes *no* mention of cruelty to animals as a sign of mental illness. This troubles many concerned psychiatrists, including Dr. Peter Field of the Psychologists for the Ethical Treatment of Animals. That organization recommends that "children who abuse animals be referred for appropriate treatment inasmuch as this is not a benign stage of growing up, but rather a sign of emotional illness."

Other psychiatrists have found additional links between animal abuse and mental disorders. Dr. Eugene Bliss, a University of Utah psychiatrist and expert on multiple personalities, has described the strange case of "Andrea." This woman had twenty-eight distinct personalities, two of which had killed cats. Like many patients with this disorder, her personality had begun to split when she was a victim of physical and psychological abuse. On at least one occasion, her father had punished her by forcing her to watch him throw kittens in a roaring furnace. Dr. Frank Putnam of the National Institutes of Mental Health has noted that witnessing such acts of cruelty can be as traumatic as being a victim of physical abuse.

Animal abuse rarely involves a single act of cruelty against one victim. It is part of a complex net of disturbed relationships that we are just beginning to understand. Within this tangled web, an abused child becomes violent to others, including animals.

It is likely that he, too, is at risk of becoming an abusive parent who, in turn, may produce another generation of violent children.

What can those of us involved in animal welfare do to help the people and animals caught in this web? First, although the connection between cruelty to animals and other human problems has been well established by careful research, many professionals seem unaware of this work. It is important to share this information with those who are in a position to see such problems, including veterinarians, law-enforcement officers, animal-control officers, humane agents, shelter workers, and child-welfare professionals. It is also helpful to get people in these professions talking to each other. Often, they discover that they have been dealing with some of the same families or individuals.

Second, as Drs. Kellert and Felthous point out, "Most judicial authorities tend to minimize the importance of animal cruelty among children." It is essential to urge appropriate psychiatric intervention in the case of adult and juvenile offenders. Ideally, such treatment must deal with the entire family, not just the abuser.

Crime is not only a symptom of other disorders, but animal abuse in and of itself is also a *crime* that often occurs alongside other crimes. Cruelty to animals is generally a misdemeanor punishable by fine and imprisonment, but such penalties are rare. The humane public can voice its concern. In recent cases in Florida, California, Virginia, and Louisiana, outspoken citizens have played a major role in getting stiff penalties for animal abusers.

In a recent case, two seventeen-year-old boys were caught as they attempted to decapitate a cat but went unpunished. The local district attorney offered sound advice to several HSUS members who complained about this mild treatment. He wrote: "It is obvious by the number of letters I have received that this case has stirred the emotions of many, many people. It would be my suggestion that you advise your local legislators of your concerns and urge them to act on strengthening our Juvenile Court System. Your position is correct and, perhaps, working together, we can effect change which would help stop such violent acts." Another way in which you can help is to be alert to the possibility of animal abuse in your community. Many abusers are able to hide their actions from law enforcement officials as well as from friends and even families. Their best protection has been the fear and silence of others. There are definite steps you can take when you see or suspect cruelty to animals (see sidebar).

Some states, recognizing the severity of the problem, are making it easier to fight cruelty. Wisconsin and Minnesota have enacted unusual statutes that ensure the investigation of cruelty complaints even in the absence of a local humane society. The laws allow a citizen who has reason to believe that an act of cruelty has occurred to apply to a circuit court for a search warrant. A judge will question the citizen and any other witnesses under oath. If the court is satisfied that there is probable cause to believe that an act of abuse has occurred, the judge may issue a warrant directing a local law enforcement officer to "proceed immediately" to the location, conduct a search, and take custody of any animals on the property. The judge also has the authority to direct that a veterinarian accompany law enforcement officers to help with the investigation or to aid the animals. If your community lacks the resources to investigate animal cruelty, similar statutes might be helpful in combating this problem.

Perhaps the most important approach to the problem of animal cruelty is *prevention*. Some acts take place because authority figures *allow* them to occur by failing to discipline childhood episodes of cruelty. Without proper intervention, children may graduate to more serious abuses including violence against people. Do not ignore even minor acts of cruelty. Correct the child and, when possible, express your concerns to his or her parents. Appropriate intervention may, in this way, stop a cycle of escalating abuse.

We also know that some abuse is motivated by fear and ignorance of animals and an inability to empathize with the needs and feelings of others. Humane educators constantly work to instill the knowledge and values that can help prevent children from starting on a destructive path. These efforts cannot undo generations of abuse and other family problems, but they can be an effective step in breaking the vicious cycle of family violence.

Scientists and lawmakers are slowly beginning to acknowledge the humane movement's long-held position that society's treatment of animals is inseparable from its treatment of human beings. This "new" realization echoes the sentiment of eighteenth-century philosopher Immanuel Kant: "He who is cruel to animals becomes hard also in his dealings with men. We can judge the heart of a man by his treatment of animals."

A bibliography on this subject is available from Dr. Randall Lockwood, The HSUS, 2100 L St., N.W., Washington, DC 20037.

Dr. Randall Lockwood is director of Higher Education Programs and Guy R. Hodge is director of Data and Information Services for The HSUS.

CHILDREN WHO ARE CRUEL TO ANIMALS: A REVIEW OF RESEARCH AND IMPLICATIONS FOR DEVELOPMENTAL PSYCHOPATHOLOGY

Frank R. Ascione

Abstract. *The relation between childhood cruelty toward animals and interpersonal aggression has long been of interest to developmental psychology, psychiatry, and related disciplines but the empirical study of this relation is relatively recent. This review highlights existing quantitative and qualitative research on childhood animal cruelty, organized according to four areas: (1) the relation between childhood cruelty to animals and concurrent and later antisocial behavior; (2) the significance of cru-elty to animals as a specific symptom in the DSM-III-R classification Conduct Disorder; (3) the implication of cruelty to animals in various forms of family and community violence, including child physical and sexual abuse and wife battering; and (4) suggestions for research in the areas of definition, prevention, and intervention.*

Department of Psychology, Utah State University, Logan, Utah 84322-2810. E-Mail Address: FRANKA @ F51.ED.USU.EDU.

Based on a presentation at the Biennial Meeting of the Society for Research in Child Development, March 25, 1993, New Orleans. Completion of this review was funded, in part, by a grant from the Humane Society of the United States, the American Society for the Prevention of Cruelty to Animals, the Massachusetts Society for the Prevention of Cruelty to Animals, the American Humane Association, and the Geraldine R. Dodge Foundation. The cooperation and interest of Dr. Bob Downing and Dr. John DeWitt as well as Youth Corrections staff were invaluable in securing data at the Utah Division of Youth Corrections. Preparation of this paper was facilitated by Karen Ranson's care and attention. Thanks are also due to Teresa Thompson, Shayne Bland, Tracy Black, Claudia Weber, and Dan Miggin for their assistance in bibliographic work. My thanks to Phil Arkow for prompting and encouragement and Hal Herzog for comments on an earlier draft. To Jean Anderson, particular appreciation for renewing monographs on loan "just one more time." To Debbie, Matt, Cathy, and Dave, thanks for patience and encouragement.

Cruelty to animals as a specific symptom in the DSM-III-R classification Conduct Disorder; (3) the implication of cruelty to animals in various forms of family and community violence, including child physical and sexual abuse and wife battering; and (4) suggestions for research in the areas of definition, prevention, and intervention.

Cruelty. The expression of hostile feelings may take the form of recurrent cruelty, as when a child hatches some scheme to hurt another innocent person, or sets fire to ant hills, or goes out of his way to kill frogs, toads, or other creatures. The subject of cruelty in children is in need of study from a developmental point of view, for "cruel" behavior may represent varying combinations of hostility, thoughtlessness, and exploratory interest at different developmental levels.

—A. T. Jersild

[Conduct disorder is] a mental disorder that may begin in the preschool years, but does not become fully apparent until later childhood or adolescence. The essential feature is a persistent pattern of behavior in which children violate social rules and the basic rights of others. Physical aggression is common. Young people with conduct disorder initiate fights and can be physically cruel to people and animals.

—National Advisory Mental Health Council

INTRODUCTION

Cruelty, which can be defined as an emotional response of indifference or taking pleasure in the suffering and pain of others or as actions that unnecessarily inflict such suffering and pain, has long been consid-

Reprinted from *Anthrozoös* 6 (4): 226–47, with kind permission of the editors.

ered a sign of psychological disturbance. Children's cruelty toward other people is a diagnostic sign included in psychiatric nosology related to antisocial and conduct disorders. Yet, only recently has cruelty to animals been added to the list of diagnostic criteria for Conduct Disorder (DSM-III-R, American Psychiatric Association 1987) in children and adolescents.

As a result, in part, of increased attention to animal cruelty, we are becoming aware that very basic information and data are lacking about the prevalence (existing cases) and incidence (new cases) of such behavior. Questions about the age of onset of cruelty toward animals, potential gender differences among perpetrators, relations to child and family interaction patterns, stability from childhood to adolescence to adulthood, and the design and evaluation of prevention and intervention programs are among the many issues that require research attention.

This article begins with an examination of definitional issues followed by a brief review of examples of the renewed focus on childhood cruelty to animals and research on its link to antisocial behavior in adolescence and adulthood. Next, the relevance of childhood cruelty to animals for the diagnosis of conduct disorder in children and adolescents will be highlighted since this disorder is one of the best examples of the continuity of psychological disturbance from childhood to adulthood. The focus will then be directed to ecological factors in families and communities that can shed light on processes that may be operative in cases of childhood animal cruelty. This focus will lead to consideration of various forms of family violence, including the physical abuse and/or neglect of children and spouse abuse, sexual abuse of children, both within the family and in alternative care settings, and the relation of these conditions to distortions

in the development of empathy. The article concludes with a discussion of prevention and intervention issues and directions for future research.

DEFINITION OF CRUELTY TO ANIMALS

The dance of bloodless categories that broad theories present to us cannot show us the particular textures of the horrors.
—P. P. Hallie

The task of defining cruelty to animals (for the sake of simplicity, "animals" will be used to refer to nonhuman animals) is, in many respects more daunting than defining cruelty to children. There are also common features of cruelty to animals and to children that may facilitate resolution of definitional issues. Categories of child maltreatment often include the following forms of abuse: physical, sexual, emotional/psychological, and neglect. It is not difficult to produce a litany of examples in which animals have experienced each of these forms of abuse. Each of these forms, however, requires further elaboration since the commissions and omissions they denote vary in form and severity. For example, physical abuse may range from teasing to torture, with gradations in this range being more subjective than objective in nature (from the perspectives of the victim, the victimizer, and potential observers).

The Compact Edition of the Oxford English Dictionary (1971, p. 614) includes the following characteristics of persons who display cruelty: "disposed to inflict suffering ... indifferent to or taking pleasure in another's pain or distress ... destitute of kindness or compassion ... merciless, pitiless, hardhearted...." This definition and a similar version in the *Random House Dictionary of the English Language* (1987, p.

438), suggest both behavioral and affective dimensions of cruelty.

Definitions that focus specifically on cruelty to animals have also been offered. Felthous and Kellert (1987) defined "substantial cruelty to animals" as a "pattern of deliberately, repeatedly, and unnecessarily hurting vertebrate animals in a manner likely to cause serious injury" (p. 1715). This definition includes limitations on the species considered and introduces a quantitative dimension (frequency of cruelty). Brown (1988) defined cruelty as "unnecessary suffering knowingly inflicted on a sentient being (animal or human).... The suffering may be a sensation of pain induced by physical means, or it may be distress resulting from acts of enforced confinement, for instance, or of maternal deprivation. Cruelty to animals has both positive and negative forms, the first referring to an act committed against an animal, the second to omission or failure to act, as in neglecting to provide adequate food, water, or shelter..." (p. 3). Both Felthous and Kellert and Brown introduce "deliberately" and "knowingly" as characteristics of cruelty, presumably to exclude accidental acts. This is not the case, however, in a definition provided by Vermeulen and Odendaal (1992): "the intentional, malicious and irresponsible, as well as the unintentional and ignorant infliction of physiological or psychological pain, suffering, deprivation, death or destruction of a companion animal, by both single or repeated incidents."

Although developing a widely accepted definition of cruelty to animals is probably as difficult as defining human interpersonal aggression, the following working definition is offered for the purpose of this review:

CRUELTY TO ANIMALS IS DEFINED AS SOCIALLY UNACCEPTABLE BEHAVIOR THAT INTENTIONALLY CAUSES UNNECESSARY PAIN, SUFFERING, OR DISTRESS TO AND/OR DEATH OF AN ANIMAL.

Excluded by this definition are socially approved practices related to the treatment or use of animals in veterinary practices and livestock production (including humane slaughter) or other animal husbandry practices. The definition also excludes activities involved in more controversial uses of animals, for example, in hunting and in laboratory research [see Arluke (1992) for descriptions of both compassionate and cruel treatment of laboratory primates].

Some elaboration of terms chosen for the definition may be helpful. "Behavior" is meant to include acts of commission (e.g., striking a dog's head with an iron bar) and acts of omission (e.g., depriving a house-bound cat of food). "Socially unacceptable" behavior may, in some cases, be general across cultures (e.g., setting a live bird on fire); however, there should be sensitivity to cultural variations in judgments of acceptability (as there is variation, for example, in the species of mammals judged acceptable for human consumption). "Intentional" denotes acts of commission or omission that are performed willfully and on purpose as distinct from acts performed accidentally or unknowingly (this admittedly complex distinction will be addressed below when the concept of culpability is examined).

"Pain, suffering, or distress" refer, most often, to the effects of noxious physical acts performed on an animal's body either directly or with some instrument or other agent (e.g., weapon, caustic solution, poison). Pain, suffering, and distress are judged from knowledge of species-characteristic response patterns. Physical pain, suffering, and distress may be distinguished from emotional or psychological pain, suffering, and distress, the latter being more subjective and difficult to define and verify. However, attention should also be paid to cruelty that may be psychological in nature (e.g., maintaining an animal separated from but in physical proximity to its natural predator).

Passive behavior and affective signs of pleasure when witnessing cruelty to animals are not directly addressed in the definition. However, a child who delights in the pain a peer may be producing by torturing an animal should be an object of concern. Also, bestiality may be considered cruel even in cases when physical harm to an animal does not occur (this is similar to the case of adult sexual activity with children where consent is presumed to be impossible).

RESEARCH CONTEXT

Links Between Childhood Cruelty to Animals and Later Antisocial, Aggressive Behavior

The relation between violence toward animals and violence toward humans, especially children, has been the subject of philosophical and theoretical attention for centuries (see Baenninger 1991; Mead 1964; Menninger 1951; Robin and ten Bensel 1985). Fictional accounts that have incorporated this presumed relation range from William Golding's 1954 *Lord of the Flies,* in which violence toward animals becomes a prelude to the stranded, young boys' interpersonal cruelty and aggression, to Andrew Vachss' 1991 novel *Sacrifice,* in which a sexually abused child, forced to observe animal mutilations, later turns his rage toward an infant victim. The scientific study of this relation, however, is relatively recent.

A variety of efforts have been made to illustrate the association between repetitive acts of severe cruelty in childhood and severe antisocial behavior in adulthood. These include press reports outlining the reported childhood cruelty to animals in the histories of a number of serial or multiple murderers (e.g., [Flynn 1988] "Torturing pets could be prelude to human murder," *San Francisco Examiner,* October 27, 1988), electronic media coverage of childhood animal cruelty (National Public Radio report, June 23, 1990), more extensive treatments in animal-welfare society periodicals (e.g., Lockwood and Hodge, 1986), and published research reports. The latter are represented by case studies and a few prospective and retrospective studies below.

There are numerous case studies of cruelty to animals by children and adolescents, cruelty that fits Fromm's (1973) category of "malignant" aggression (distinguished from defensive, instrumental, or "benign" aggression). Early examples include Krafft-Ebing's (1906) descriptions of sadistic behavior toward animals associated with various forms of bestiality and Ferenczi's (1916) analysis of "A Little Chanticleer":

> The case was that of a five-year-old boy, Árpâd by name…. Whenever fowl were offered for sale … Árpâd … gave no peace until his mother bought some. He wanted to witness their slaughter … Árpâd's curious sayings and actions … mostly display an unusual pleasure in phantasies about the cruel torturing of poultry…. His cruelty was often displayed in regard to human beings also….

More recent case studies include Bettelheim's (1955) analysis of the case of Mary (p. 157), who, at approximately five years of age, attempted to kill animals and set them on fire and who assaulted other children and Redl and Wineman's (1951) predictions of cruelty to animals (in con-

Figure 1. Boy in War Zone Stomping on Dog

Credit: Kari René Hall, *Beyond the Killing Fields,* 1992. New York: Aperture and Asia 2000 Ltd.

trast, see Levinson 1969) in the antisocial children attending their Pioneer House therapeutic setting. In actual observations of some of the boys interacting with a dog, Redl and Wineman note "The fascinating thing ... is that each child duplicates in his relationship to him some of the essential symptomatic patterns that occur in the relationships to humans...." (p. 113). These case studies provide rich descriptions of childhood cruelty to animals but do not directly examine the developmental continuity or discontinuity of such behavior.

The case histories of 18 children referred for clinical evaluation, in part, for cruelty to companion (pets) and non-companion animals were detailed by Tapia (1971). These children, aged 5 to 15 years, were reported to have engaged in varying degrees of cruelty toward family pets, livestock, farm animals, and wild animals. In a followup study of these children and adolescents (2 to 9 years later), Rigdon and Tapia (1977) reported that, of the 13 original clients who could be relocated, 62% were reported still to display abusive behavior toward animals (a more conservative 38% were reported to be engaging in clearly cruel animal treatment). Unfortunately, verification of cruelty incidents was not included in either report, nor was there any attempt to scale the severity of cruelty displayed by these children, problems common to research in this area. In addition, comparisons with clinic-referred children who were not reported to be cruel and with nonclinic children were not made. These early case studies were important in providing prospective information on childhood animal

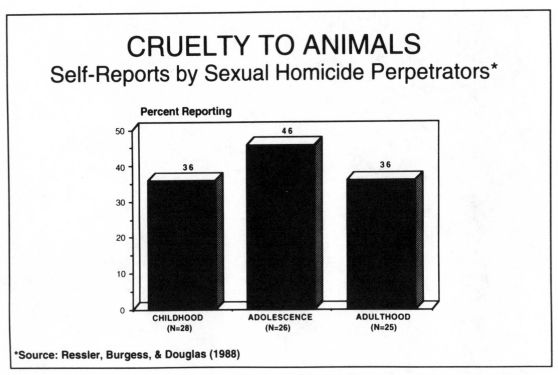

Figure 2. Sexual Homicide and Animal Cruelty Reports

cruelty and rich clinical detail about familial factors possibly related to such behavior.

Critical retrospective research has been conducted by Alan Felthous, Stephen Kellert, and their associates. Childhood histories of animal cruelty (reported percentages are in parentheses) were examined in men who were psychiatric patients (25%) (Felthous 1980), aggressive men (25% "substantial cruelty") in prison and a comparison group of nonincarcerated men (0%) (Kellert and Felthous 1985), and assaultive (36%) and nonassaultive (0%) women offenders (Felthous and Yudowitz 1977). These studies generally support the relation between contemporary patterns of chronic interpersonal aggression and childhood histories of animal cruelty. Although this and related research have been acknowledged to contain some inconsistencies and to share some methodological shortcomings (Felthous and

Kellert 1987), a case for the prognostic value of childhood animal cruelty has been made.

Retrospective research with more "select" samples of adults yield even higher rates of reported cruelty to animals. In a study of 28 convicted and incarcerated sexual homicide perpetrators (all men), Ressler, Burgess, and Douglas (1988) found that prevalence of cruelty to animals was 36% in childhood and 46% in adolescence. Tingle, Barnard, Robbins, Newman, and Hutchinson (1986) found that, in their sample of 64 men, 48% of convicted rapists and 30% of convicted child molesters admitted to cruelty to animals in their childhood or adolescence. In some cases, killing animals may follow killing humans. Hickey (1991) observed, "one offender admitted killing several puppies in order to relive the experience of killing his first child victim" (p. 11).

With the assistance of the Utah Division

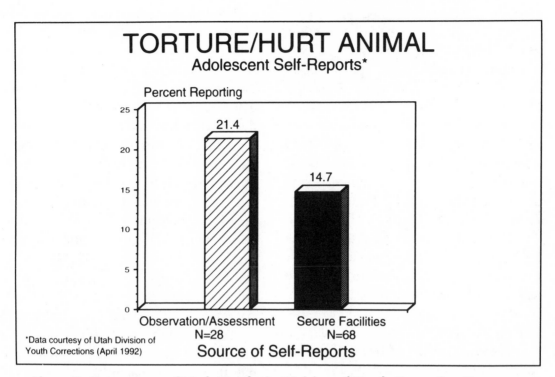

Figure 3. Percentage of Utah Youths in Division of Youth Correction Programs Reporting Abuse of Animals

of Youth Corrections, data were gathered, in the spring of 1992, on youth undergoing evaluations (Observation and Assessment) and youth currently incarcerated (Secure Facilities). Nearly all of these 96 participants were boys and their ages ranged from 14 to 18 years (65% were either 16 or 17). Twenty-one percent of the youths being evaluated and 15% of the incarcerated youth reported torturing or hurting animals on purpose within the past 12 months.

Two other studies provide examples of research with clinical samples of youth in which cruelty to animals was assessed (primarily from review of case histories—a problematic methodology since failure to find mention of cruelty to animals is an ambiguous outcome). Lewis, Shanok, Grant, and Ritvo (1983) studied fifty-one 8–12-year-olds on an inpatient ward; 21 had been judged homicidally aggressive, 30 were not. The prevalence of reported cruelty to animals for these two groups was 14% and 3%, respectively. Wochner and Klosinski (1988) selected fifty children and adolescents, from inpatient and outpatient settings, half of whom had records of cruelty to animals and half who did not. The prevalence of sadistic behavior toward people was 32% and 12% for these two groups, respectively.

Lest the reader think that cruelty to animals is confined to prison samples and patients in psychiatric care, it should be noted that the breadth of the problem includes adult tolerance of child cruelty toward and abuse of animals at livestock auctions (Grandin 1988) and anecdotal evidence that children exposed to chronic war-time violence display violent and cruel behavior toward animals (Randal and Boustany 1990).

A final, yet significant, example of renewed attention to this area is a series of professional-conference sessions, sponsored by societies devoted to humane animal treatment, on the childhood animal cruelty/later violence link. Such sessions have been included in the meetings of the Animal Protection and Child Protection Divisions of the American Humane Association (September 1990), the Delta Society (October 1990), and in a workshop sponsored by the Latham Foundation. In November 1991, a conference, jointly sponsored by the Child Protection and Animal Protection Divisions of the American Humane Association, focused specifically on violence to children and animals (Moulton, Kaufmann, and Filip 1992). Presentations have also been made at the 6th International Conference on Human–Animal Interactions (Ascione 1992, July) and a conference sponsored by the Geraldine R. Dodge Foundation (Ascione 1992, September).

The Relation Between Childhood Animal Cruelty and the Psychiatric Diagnostic Category Conduct Disorder (DSM-III-R).

> Cruelty to animals and other children is a characteristic, though not common, feature of the affectionless delinquent, and occasional outbursts of senseless cruelty are well known in some forms of mental illness.
> —J. Bowlby

Included in a description of conduct disorder in the most recent revision of the *Diagnostic and Statistical Manual of Mental Disorders* (American Psychiatric Association, 1987) is the following: "The essential feature of this disorder is a persistent pattern of conduct in which the basic rights of others and major age-appropriate societal norms or rules are violated.... Physical aggression is common. Children or adolescents with this disorder usually initiate aggression, may be physically cruel to other

people or to animals, and frequently deliberately destroy other people's property (this may include firesetting). They may engage in stealing with confrontation of the victim, as in mugging, purse snatching, extortion, or armed robbery. At later ages, the physical violence may take the form of rape, assault, or, in rare cases, homicide...The child may have no concern for the feelings, wishes, and wellbeing of others, as shown by callous behavior, and may lack appropriate feelings of guilt or remorse" (p. 53). It is important to note that the 1987 edition of DSM-III-R is the first to list specifically physical cruelty to animals among the symptoms indicative of conduct disorder. Had the current diagnostic criteria been in effect when the prospective and retrospective animal cruelty studies cited earlier were conducted, the conduct disorder diagnosis might have been applied to many of the subjects in those studies.

Because cruelty to animals is only one of several symptoms of conduct disorder (Spitzer, Davies, and Barkley 1990), the prevalence of such cruelty is difficult to estimate. Research using checklists of behavior problems in children suggests that cruelty to animals is reported more frequently by parents of children being seen at mental health clinics than by parents of a nonclinic sample (Achenbach and Edelbrock 1981; Achenbach, Howell, Quay, and Conners 1991). A recent Canadian study reports an approximate 2% prevalence rate in a census-based sample of 12–16-year-olds (less than 2% in 4–11-year-olds), using mothers' reports; however, when the children in this sample self-reported cruelty to animals, the rate was closer to 10% (Offord, Boyle, and Racine 1991). This discrepancy may be due to differences between respondents in interpretation of "cruelty to animals" and/or to the often covert nature of the cruelty. Nevertheless, a recent meta-analysis of studies of oppositional defiant and conduct disorders reveals that cruelty to animals loads very strongly on the destructive pole of a destructive–nondestructive dimension derived from a multidimensional scaling and that hurting animals is one of the earliest reported symptoms of conduct disorder (median age of onset reported by parents = 6.5 years of age) (Frick, Lahey, Loeber, Tannenbaum, Van Horn, Christ, Hart, and Hanson 1993).

Not all children diagnosed with conduct disorder will display the symptom of animal cruelty. However, certain issues addressed by research on conduct disorder and, more specifically, interpersonal aggression in children and adolescents may have relevance for our understanding of animal cruelty.

Kazdin (1990) has summarized definitional, theoretical, conceptual, and research issues pertaining to the prevention and treatment of conduct disorder. He notes that 1989 Institute of Medicine data suggest that 2–6% of American children display symptoms that fit the conduct disorder diagnosis. Data provided by Rosenstein (1990, personal communication) at the Statistical Research Branch of the National Institute of Mental Health suggest that in 1986, nearly 100,000 children under the age of 18, diagnosed with this disorder, were admitted to inpatient and outpatient mental health facilities. If even a small percentage (assume 5%) of these children and adolescents displayed animal cruelty, the problem would involve thousands of children in the United States.

Kazdin emphasizes that conduct disorder is (1) often stable over time, (2) related to the prediction of adult disorders, and (3) often present across generations within families. Although these features are not always or consistently characteristic of this disorder, other researchers have also

called attention to their significance (e.g., Loeber 1988, Widom 1989).

Recent research on conduct disorder has focused on risk and protective factors in childhood that may increase and reduce, respectively, the likelihood and severity of conduct disordered behaviors (see Garmezy 1988, Robins 1988, and Rutter 1988). Two theory-based approaches describe risk factors related to the development and escalation of aggression in children: coercive family interaction patterns and children's attributional biases.

The first approach is illustrated in the work of Gerald Patterson and colleagues (Patterson, DeBaryshe, and Ramsey 1989) which provides a research-based model of the escalation of aggression in families. Ineffective parenting styles, relying heavily on punitive or aversive control, present children with models of coercion such that family members become enmeshed in a cycle where parent and child use aversive techniques to terminate each others' behavior. This pattern is often coupled with an absence of parental behavior directed at fostering prosocial behavior. The implication for childhood animal cruelty is that children reared in such families may learn to generalize aversive control techniques to their companion animals, if present.

The second approach is exemplified in the work of Price and Dodge (1989) on peer rejection and social maladjustment in boys. These authors suggest that rejected boys who display atypical levels of aggression often show deficits in intention-cue detection. That is, in situations where peers' intentions may be ambiguous, these socially rejected boys display an attributional bias and impute hostile intentions to peer behavior that may be neutral (e.g., being accidentally bumped in a lunch line). This bias may lead such boys to respond to such situations with aggression, with subsequent retaliation by peers. Repetitions of such interactions may reinforce the rejected child's negative self-perceptions and belief in a hostile peer environment and reinforce the rejecting peers' aggressive stereotype of the child. Again, potential parallels to children who display cruelty toward animals are not difficult to conceive. If peers' intention cues are at times ambiguous to rejected children, intention cues provided by animals, both companion and noncompanion, may be even more difficult to discern. A vivid example of this possibility was included in the National Public Radio report referred to above. A young boy who brutalized, sexually assaulted, and eventually killed a stray dog reported how, when he heard the dog barking at him, he interpreted the dog's behavior as personally directed aggression, something the boy was not going to allow. There was no sensitivity to the possibility that the animal's behavior reflected being startled or frightened. Clearly, such attributional bias toward animals needs to be examined empirically.

Before leaving this topic, one additional parallel between conduct disorder research and research on childhood animal cruelty needs to be highlighted. Child and adolescent firesetting is also included in DSM-III-R diagnostic criteria for conduct disorder. [The firesetting-enuresis-cruelty to animals "triad," has received inconsistent support (see, for example, Hellman and Blackman 1966; Wax and Haddox 1974a; Wax and Haddox 1974b; in contrast, see Justice, Justice, and Kraft 1974) and its discussion, which is beyond the scope of this review.] Kolko and Kazdin (1989), in elaborating a risk model for children displaying such behavior, have developed the *Children's Firesetting Interview* to ascertain qualitative information about children's firesetting as distinct from simplistic presence-absence ratings. They note that firesetting is a relatively low frequency behavior and is often covert, characteristics it shares with childhood animal cruelty. Wooden and Berkey (1984) found that young (4–8 years old) firesetters were more likely to be cruel to animals than older (9–17 year old) firesetters.

The development of an assessment instrument, patterned after Kolko and Kazdin's, for animal cruelty would assist our definition and understanding of qualitative variations in childhood animal cruelty. Current assessment instruments (Achenbach 1988, Achenbach and Edelbrock 1981—*Child Behavior Checklist;* Kazdin and Esveldt-Dawson, 1986—*Interview for Antisocial Behavior*) are lacking in this regard. The intensity, duration, and breadth of certain antisocial behaviors may be more important than their frequency (Kazdin 1990). Information about these dimensions for childhood animal cruelty would allow us to move beyond anecdotal evidence (e.g., Magid and McKelvey 1987).

Relations to Family Violence and Violence in Alternative Child Care Settings

"We have talked with two young women each of whom told us that when her father was angry with her he killed her favorite pet." (p. 68) "Cindy remembers seeing her father hit her mother on many occasions. Bill (the father) rarely spanked Cindy. When he did, it was rather mild. But his other punishments were extraordinarily cruel. Cindy's clearest childhood memory was of her father shooting her pet cat." (p.119) These anecdotes from Gelles and Straus' (1988) book *Intimate Violence* are two of many references to the abuse, torture, and killing of companion animals that one encounters in the literatures on family violence and alternative child care sexual abuse.

A number of review articles have appeared recently on family violence (e.g., Emery 1989), characteristics of abusing and/or neglecting parents (e.g., LaRose and Wolfe 1987), and the psychological effects of abuse on children (Cicchetti 1990). In addition, there have been reports dealing with sexual abuse of children in day care (e.g., Faller 1990; Finkelhor, Williams, and Burns 1988) that include reference to the torture and killing of animals by adults as a coercive technique. In this section, I will not attempt to summarize the extensive research in these areas but rather will highlight how aspects of this research have relevance for our understanding of childhood animal cruelty. Special note will be made of potential distortions of children's empathic development that may result from their observation and direct experience of family violence.

Illustrating the relation between the violent and abusive environments in which some children are reared and the children's own violent reactions, Besharov (1990) reminds us of the case of Wayne Dresbach who, when 15 years of age, killed both of his parents (Mewshaw 1980). Wayne had been subjected to years of verbal and physical abuse at the hands of his father and had witnessed his father's beatings of his mother. Mewshaw describes an incident involving cruelty to animals by Wayne's father that no doubt included Wayne's psychological abuse:

> But one weekend morning his father scooped the kittens into a paper sack, picked up the .22, and headed out the back door. Worried, Wayne went with him.
>
> "What are you doing?" he asked as they crossed the yard, passed the stables, and set off toward a creek at the property line.

> "Going to get rid of these fucking things," Dresbach said.
>
> "I thought we were going to give them away."
>
> "I'm tired of waiting. Tired of them whining all night and stinking up the house."

At the creek Dresbach rolled the top of the bag tight, then tossed it into the shallow water. While the kittens screeched, and pawed to get out, and Wayne sobbed for him not to do it, his father took aim and emptied the rifle. At that range he couldn't miss. The slugs tore the sack to pieces, and blood poured out in trickles, then in a great rush as the bottom gave way.

Wayne wanted to bury the kittens, but Pat told him not to bother. Dogs and buzzards would take care of them.

It is also increasingly more common to find cruelty to animals (especially pets) listed in behavioral checklists used in domestic violence assessment. For example, Klingbeil and Boyd (1984, referred to in Jaffe, Wolfe, and Wilson [1990]) note that "Children in violent homes are characterized by ... frequently participating in pecking order battering (maim or kill animals, batter siblings)...." (p. 30).

In addition to experiencing the abuse of their pet animals, battered women may be forced to perform acts of bestiality by their husbands or boyfriends (Dutton 1992, Walker 1979). We do not know how often children witness these abuses. In a study of partner abuse in lesbian relationships, Renzetti (1992) reports, "At least 35 of the respondents lived with children either their own or their partners'. In almost 30% of these cases, the children also were abused by the partner. Pet abuse was frequent as well; 38% of the respondents who had pets reported that their partners had abused the animals" (p. 21). These phenomena are not limited to the admittedly violent nature of American society. In a major crosscultural analysis, Levinson

(1989) observed, "Women are more likely to be permanently injured, scarred, or even killed by their husbands in societies in which animals are treated cruelly...." (p. 45).

Hughes (1988) studied 3–12-year-olds accompanying their mothers to a shelter for abused women; 60% of the children were reported, by mothers, to have been physically abused. She notes that these child witness victims were least well adjusted (as measured by the Eyberg Child Behavior Inventory) when compared with either child witnesses who were not themselves abused or a control group of children. Jouriles, Murphy, and O'Leary (1989) reported that marital aggression (as distinct from marital discord) was associated with conduct-disordered behavior in 5–12-year-old boys whose parents were in marital therapy. One may speculate that witnessing marital aggression may be a form of observational learning through which children may learn violent problem-"solving" behaviors. If companion animals are present in such situations and are also targets of parental aggression, children may imitate parents' behavior. Evidence for this relation in nondistressed families has been provided by Zahn-Waxler, Hollenbeck, and Radke-Yarrow (1984).

Cicchetti (1990) has outlined a number of negative psychological correlates of child maltreatment including deficits in children's emotion language, problematic attachment relationships, and deficits in children's ability to decode facial expressions of emotions in others [see also, Camoras, Ribordy, Hill, Martino, Sachs, Spaccarelli, and Stefani (1990)]. A more commonly reported correlate of child maltreatment is victims' disordered and aggressive peer relations (e.g., prospective research by Dodge, Bates, and Pettit, 1990). Mueller and Silverman (1989) note that maltreated preschoolers may respond to peer distress either by ignoring or in some cases aggressing toward the child displaying the distress (e.g., Klimes-Dougan and Kistner, 1990). Although the processes involved in such atypical reactions are not clear, maltreated children may be hypersensitive to displays of distress (because of their own experiences associating distress with maltreatment) and may resort to aggression in an effort to terminate such displays. No information (beyond case study reports, e.g., Furman 1986) is available on how maltreated children might respond to animals in distress.

Although most cases of child abuse involve perpetrators who are parents or parent figures, in some cases, children suffer abuse from siblings. Wiehe (1990), in a study of 150 adult respondents to a questionnaire on sibling abuse, described how emotional abuse by siblings either took the form of or accompanied the torture or killing of the victim's pet (neither an uncommon nor only a recent phenomenon—see Burk, 1897). The immediate effects of such trauma included the inability to care for another pet and, in some cases, the victim's emotional abuse of younger siblings. Although exposure to distressing childhood experiences may be related to higher levels of empathy in adulthood (Barnett and McCoy 1989), negative effects may be more likely when the distressing experiences take the form of physical, emotional, or sexual abuse. The factors leading to these differential outcomes are, as yet, unclear.

Only one published study exists (to my knowledge) that has directly addressed the relation between child abuse and neglect and companion animal abuse and neglect. Deviney, Dickert, and Lockwood (1983) studied 53 families who met New Jersey legal criteria for child abuse or neglect and who also had companion animals in their homes. Although only one observer was present, precluding reliability assessment, observations during home interviews revealed that pets were abused or neglected in 60% of these families. As potential support for observational learning of abusive tactics, one finds that 26% of the children in these families abused or were cruel to their pets. When the sample was categorized into physically abused (40%), sexually abused (10%), and neglected (58%), an alarming finding was that in 88% of families displaying child physical abuse (in contrast to 34% in sexually abusing or neglecting families), pet abuse was also present. An unpublished study by Walker (1980) examined records of families' contacts with child protection and animal protection agencies. Appearance in the records of both agencies was found for 9% of the families studied.

Some case studies of sexual abuse of children include reports of forcing children to interact sexually with animals or warning a child to maintain silence about abuse by threatening to harm or destroy the child's pet animals (Faller 1990; Finkelhor, Williams, and Burns 1988; Kelley 1989; Hunter 1990). Although Faller (1990) notes that the killing of animals at a day care facility occurred in only 4% of the cases she directly studied, Finkelhor, Williams, and Burns (1988) reported such coercion in 14% of their cases. Faller also describes a study (in Waterman, Kelly, Oliveri, and McCord 1993) in which 80% of the child victims in the Manhattan Beach molestation case reported exposure to the killing of animals as a part of teachers' threats to maintain secrecy. The long-term effects of these experiences on the child victims are, of course, not yet known. Sexual or violent "play" with animals is mentioned as a potential sign that a child has been sexually or physically abused—one report of such inappropriate play involved a three-and-one-half-year-old child (Hewitt 1990). Adult homicide perpetrators who report being sexually abused as children report higher rates of childhood animal cruelty (58%) than perpetrators not reporting sexual abuse (15%) (Ressler, Burgess, Hartman, Douglas, and McCormack 1986; Ressler, Burgess, and Douglas 1988).

The relation between physical and sexual abuse of children and children's dysfunctional interactions with animals has received attention in the clinical literature. Sterba (1935) related the case of a severe dog phobia in a seven-and-one-half-year-old girl who had been given daily enemas for over a month. Weil (1989) has reviewed a hundred case studies involving children exposed to erogenous and erotic contact with adults and to beatings and violent yelling. Examples of destructive behavior toward objects, other children, and animals were common among the symptoms many of these children presented. Cruelty to animals and sexual behavior with animals are listed in an assessment for adult and juvenile sex offenders (Hindman, no date). Hindman (1992) also includes in her *Juvenile Culpability Assessment* (to be used in judging responsibility in youth who act out sexually) an index of "social capacity for empathy" that includes whether a young person "indicates understanding of needed concern or sensitivity for animals."

Although much of the information we have on the relation between sexual abuse of children and children's cruelty toward animals is derived from retrospective research, some existing data sets (e.g., Friedrich, Urquiza, and Beilke 1986) allow for contemporary analysis of this relation. William Friedrich (April, 1992, personal communication) provided data from a large-scale study of substantiated cases of sexual abuse in children 2–12 years of age. Most of these children had been victim-

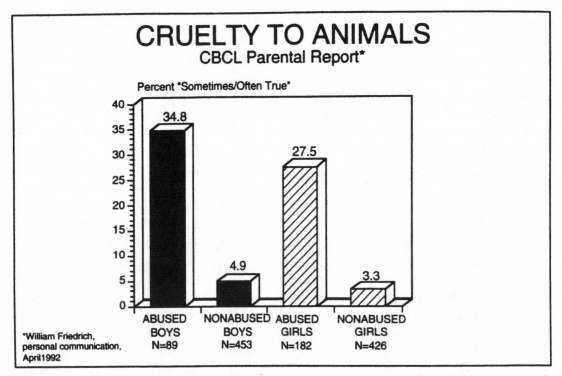

Figure 4. Relationship Between Sexual Abuse of Children and the Child's Reported Abuse of Animals

ized within twelve months of data collection that included administration of the Child Behavior Checklist (Achenbach 1988). Parental reports of cruelty to animals were 35% for abused boys and 27% for abused girls; the percentages were 5% for nonabused boys and 3% for nonabused girls, a highly significant difference based on clinical status.

Anecdotal reports of animal cruelty also surface in the literature on alternate child care where allegations of molestation are present. The reports are present in cases where there may be a single perpetrator and victim but are even more prominent in "multidimensional child sex ring" reports (or in cases reported to involve so-called "ritual" abuse) (Boat 1991; Lanning 1989a, 1989b; Uherek 1991). Determining the degree of validity of such reports remains controversial (Lanning 1991, Putnam 1991), yet it is difficult to ignore common threads describing animal cruelty. Reports include mutilation and killing of animals, threatening to destroy or actually destroying animals to frighten children into secrecy, and forcing children to engage in sexual activity with animals (Jonker and Jonker-Bakker 1991). A recent study of 37 adult clients diagnosed with dissociative disorders noted that all of the clients reported witnessing animal mutilation or killing as part of their own childhood abuse experiences (Young, Sachs, Braun, Watkins 1991). In reviewing the relation between severe abuse and the development of dissociative problems in children, Peterson (1990) notes that cruelty to animals is one of a number of conduct disorder problems listed among other symptoms of dissociation. In constructing his Child Dissociation Problem Checklist, Peterson (1991) has included the item "hurt animals" along with a variety of antisocial behaviors. On balance, it should also be noted that abuse victims may find interactions with a family pet a source of comfort (Zimrin 1986) and that learning to touch pets appropriately may be a useful adjunct to therapy (Lew 1988). It is not clear what factors would allow us to predict whether animals would be the target of affectional or disordered behavior in cases of abuse.

Cruelty and Empathy

Finally, the potential relation between empathy and childhood animal cruelty will be examined. In earlier work (Ascione 1992, Weber and Ascione 1992), I have reviewed research, with nondistressed children and adults, showing a positive relation between children's empathy (ability to understand and relate to the emotional experiences of others) toward animals and other aspects of their psychological development. In Ascione (1992), I reported that, at certain elementary grades, a year-long humane education program not only enhanced children's attitudes toward animals (Ascione 1988a, 1988b) but this change generalized to a measure of human-directed empathy. Similar research with distressed children (e.g., abused, conduct-disordered) has not yet been accomplished. Feshbach (1989), however, reviewed a small number of studies of empathy in abusing parents and abused children (without, unfortunately, consideration of animal-directed empathy). She notes that "the relationship between empathy and prosocial behavior and empathy and aggression suggests that the abusive parent should be low in empathy and that the abused child should also manifest a lack of empathy" (p. 355).

Studies show that even in nonabusing families, toddlers exposed to frequent maternal child-directed anger are less empathic when witnessing others' distress (Crockenberg 1985). Reporting on unpublished data, Feshbach (1989) notes that "Abusive parents appear more indifferent to emotional pain in others than do the control or psychiatric patients." (p. 369). Low maternal empathy has also been found to be more strongly related to physical child abuse than a measure of maternal stress (Letourneau 1981). Parental deficits in empathy warrant attention since there is consensus that empathy development in children is strongly related to parental socialization practices (Zahn-Waxler, Hollenbeck, and Radke-Yarrow 1984) and evidence that higher levels of empathy in children are associated with greater prosocial behavior (Strayer and Roberts 1989). There is a critical need for research relating both human- and animal-directed empathy in children to child abuse and childhood animal cruelty.

Freud (1905), noting that clinicians should attend to "children who are distinguished for evincing especial cruelty to animals and playmates" also observed that "The absence of the barrier of sympathy carries with it the danger that a connection found in childhood between cruelty and the erogenous impulses will not be broken later in life" (p. 594).

RESEARCH NEEDS

Companion animals are an integral part of the lives of children in the United States. Pet ownership has been found to be significantly more common in families with school-aged children and adolescents than in families without children (Albert and Bulcroft 1988). In samples from California and Connecticut, children reported pet ownership ranging from 52%, for kindergartners, to 75%, for fifth graders (Ascione, Latham, and Worthen 1985). Seventy-seven percent of a northern Utah sample of first, second, fourth, and fifth graders (Ascione 1992) reported having at least one pet at home. Higher rates of pet ownership in a sample of older children have been reported by Bryant (1990). The numbers confirm the importance of attending to the human–companion animal bond (Kidd and Kidd 1987, Levinson 1972, National Institute of Health 1988). Given the demonstrated or potential implication of childhood animal cruelty in a variety of psychological disturbances in children, adolescents, and adults, it is regrettable that we have so little information about the prevalence and incidence of seriously dysfunctional human–animal relations.

Given the infancy of research development in this area, many basic issues have yet to be addressed. For example, although "cruelty" and "maltreatment" may be used to describe behavior toward animals, operational definitions of these terms have yet to be developed or accepted (Arkow, Walker, Ascione, and Boatfield 1990). Clearly, these terms may refer to a spectrum of behavior that will vary in severity, intensity, and generality of contexts where it is displayed. There may even be differences in judgments of cruelty severity based on the species of animal(s) involved. Adult and child-adolescent differences in definitions may also make comparisons of parent reports and self-reports by children problematic.

An operational definition should include qualitative dimensions of cruelty to animals (e.g., forms of physical cruelty [sexual and nonsexual], whether it was performed overtly or covertly, whether it was performed alone or with the help of other individuals) with a measure of severity (perhaps based on degree of pain/distress as well as physical injury inflicted). Once a definition has been developed, other characteristics that should be ad-

dressed would include estimates of the onset or first occurrence of cruelty, listing of the types of animals (e.g., farm, companion, wild/stray) toward which the behavior was directed, describing opportunities to have contact with animals (including whether the individual currently has or has had companion animals), and some measure of positive behaviors toward animals (attending to patterns of behavior that include cruelty and kindness may be important).

> Lennie sat in the hay and looked at a little dead puppy that lay in front of him.... And Lennie said softly to the puppy, "Why do you got to get killed? You ain't so little as mice. I didn't bounce you hard."
>
> —John Steinbeck,
> *Of Mice and Men*, p. 85

Combinations of kindness and putative cruelty raise the issue of judging responsibility or culpability for acts of cruelty. (Lennie Small's desire to caress is overwhelmed by his inability to control the intensity of his touches, with tragic consequences.) One approach that could serve as a model has been used to judge culpability in cases of juvenile sex offending (Hindman 1992). The method considers a youth's cognitive and social skill levels as well as the youth's own history of abuse to assess level of responsibility. This general approach would be helpful in distinguishing cruelty derived from developmental immaturity from cruelty that may be malicious.

Process-oriented research that is sensitive to developmental issues is also needed. Childhood animal cruelty has been discussed in the context of observational learning, [children may learn both the roles of victim and victimizer (see Wertsch 1991, pp. 234–6)], displacement of aggression (Bandura and Walters 1959,

p. 91), as an outcome of psychological trauma (Green 1985, Terr 1990) [one report notes higher rates of parent-reported animal cruelty for children who lived near the Three Mile Island accident (Davidson and Baum 1990)], and in relation to distortions in empathic development in children (Crockenberg 1985, Feshbach 1989). Basic developmental research in a number of these areas could inform studies on the ontogeny of animal maltreatment in children. Such research could also help identify factors that place children at risk for or protect them from developing cruelty toward animals.

Prevention and intervention issues will no doubt be related to our understanding of the processes of different forms of animal cruelty. Primary prevention may focus on educational programs (Ascione 1992) that provide children with clear guidelines for acceptable behavior with animals (Zahn-Waxler, Hollenbeck, and Radke-Yarrow 1984). Parents and other significant adults may also need to be informed that certain forms and/or patterns of cruelty should be of concern and not summarily dismissed as typical childhood exploration. Intervention for children who already display cruelty toward animals will need to consider ecological factors that may be related to such behavior, including family violence (Dodge, Bates, and Pettit 1990; Emery 1989; Jouriles, Murphy, and O'Leary 1989; Widom 1989, 1991), dysfunctional peer relations (Cicchetti 1990; Dodge, Bates, and Pettit 1990; Klimes-Dougan and Kistner 1990; Mueller and Silverman 1989), and the specific modeling of animal cruelty, live and in various forms of media.

FINAL COMMENTS

In Ramon's classroom ... at least four of the

children face significant problems or are evidencing developmental harm: four-year-old Jamilla, who killed her brother's pet bird, plucking out its feathers one by one and stomping on it because it "made too much noise...."

—Garbarino, Dubrow, Kostelny, and Pardo, p. 163

We are in the final years of a century of great promise and yet we are still struggling to understand and prevent violence (Reiss and Roth 1993). Violent environments, such as the one that envelops Jamilla, can foster cruelty or caring. The dangerous environments children endure can lead them to seek out animals for affection or to train animals to be weapons (Kotlowitz 1991, pp. 6, 43, 78). A better understanding of how cruelty to animals is related to the more general domain of interpersonal violence may facilitate prevention and intervention efforts. Parents know that cruelty to animals may be serious (Weisz and Weiss 1991); children seem to know as well (Triplett 1903).

REFERENCES

Achenbach, T. M. 1988. *Child Behavior Checklist* (for ages 2–3, for ages 4–16). Burlington, VT: Center for Children, Youth, and Families.

Achenbach, T. M., and C. S. Edelbrock. 1981. Behavioral problems and competencies reported by parents of normal and disturbed children aged four through sixteen. *Monographs of the Society for Research in Child Development* 46 (1, Serial No. 188).

Achenbach, T. M., C. T. Howell, H. C. Quay, and C. K. Conners. 1991. National survey of problems and competencies among four to sixteen-year-olds. *Monographs of the Society for Research in Child Development* 56, Serial No. 225.

Albert, A., and K. Bulcroft. 1988. Pets, families, and the life course. *Journal of Marriage and the Family* 50, 543–52.

American Psychiatric Association 1987. *Diagnostic and Statistical Manual of Mental Disorders* (3rd ed. rev.). Washington, DC: Author.

Arkow, P., J. R. Walker, F. R. Ascione, and M. P.

Boatfield. 1990, April. *The links between animal abuse and child abuse*. Panel presentation at the Delta Society Ninth Annual Conference, Houston, TX.

Arluke, A. 1992, July. *The ethical cultures of animal labs.* Paper presented at the Sixth International Conference on Human–Animal Interactions, Montreal, Canada.

Ascione, F. R. 1988a. *Primary Attitude Scale.* Assessment of kindergarten through second graders' attitudes toward the treatment of animals. Logan, UT: Wasatch Institute for Research and Evaluation.

————. 1988b. *Intermediate Attitude Scale.* Assessment of third through sixth graders' attitudes toward the treatment of animals. Logan, UT: Wasatch Institute for Research Evaluation.

————. 1992. Enhancing children's attitudes about the humane treatment of animals: Generalization to human-directed empathy. *Anthrozoös,* 5:176–91.

————. 1992, July. Cruelty to animals in childhood and adolescence: An overview of research. Presentation at the "Risks for Animals Workshop," R. Arkow, C. Moulton, F. Ascione, J. Filip, and M. Kaufmann, *Cruelty to animals and child abuse: Connections and creative community strategies,* Sixth International Conference on Human–Animal Interactions, Montreal, Canada.

————. 1992, September. *Cruelty to animals in childhood and adolescence.* Presentation at the American Humane Association Conference, "Protecting children and animals: Agenda for a nonviolent future," Herndon, VA.

Ascione, F. R., G. I. Latham, and B. R. Worthen. 1985. Final report, Year 2: An experimental study. *Evaluation of the Humane Education Curriculum Guides.* Report to the National Association for the Advancement of Humane Education.

Baenninger, R. 1991. Violence toward other species. In *Targets of violence and aggression,* ed. R. Baenninger, pp. 5–43. New York: North-Holland.

Bandura, A., and R. H. Walters. 1959. *Adolescent aggression.* New York: Ronald Press.

Barnett, M. A., and S. J. McCoy. 1989. The relation of the distressful childhood experiences and empathy in college undergraduates. *Journal of Genetic Psychology* 15:417–26.

Besharov, D. J. 1990. *Recognizing child abuse.* New York: The Free Press.

Bettelheim, B. 1955. *Truants from life.* New York: The Free Press.

Boat, B. W. 1991. Caregivers as surrogate therapists in treatment of a ritualistically abused child. In *Casebook of sexual abuse treatment,* ed. W. N. Friedrich, pp. 1–26. New York: W. W. Norton.

Bowlby, J. 1953. *Child care and the growth of love.* Baltimore: Pelican Books.

Brown, L. 1988. *Cruelty to animals: The moral debt.* London: Macmillan.

Bryant, B. K. 1990. The richness of the child–pet relationship: A consideration of both benefits and costs of pets to children. *Anthrozoös* 3:253–61.

Burk, F. L. 1897. Teasing and bullying. *Pedagogical Seminary* 4:336–71.

Camoras, L. A., S. Ribordy, J. Hill, S. Martino, V. Sachs, S. Spaccarelli, and R. Stefani. 1990. Maternal facial behavior and the recognition and production of emotion expression by maltreated and nonmaltreated children. *Developmental Psychology* 26:304–12.

Cicchetti, D. 1990. The organization and coherence of socioemotional, cognitive, and representational development: Illustrations through a developmental psychopathology perspective on Down syndrome and child maltreatment. In *Socioemotional development,* ed. R. A. Thompson (Nebraska Symposium on Motivation, 1988), pp. 259–366. Lincoln: University of Nebraska Press.

The Compact Edition of the Oxford English Dictionary. 1971. New York: Oxford University Press.

Crockenberg, S. 1985. Toddlers' reactions to maternal anger. *Merrill-Palmer Quarterly* 31:361–73.

Davidson, L. M., and A. Baum. 1990. Posttraumatic stress in children following natural and human-made trauma. In *Handbook of developmental psychopathology,* ed. M. Lewis and S. M. Miller, pp. 251–59. New York: Plenum Press.

Deviney, E., J. Dickert, and R. Lockwood. 1983. The care of pets within child abusing families. *International Journal for the Study of Animal Problems* 4:321–9.

Dodge, K. A., J. E. Bates, and G. S. Pettit. 1990. Mechanisms in the cycle of violence. *Science* 250:1678–83.

Dutton, M. A. 1992. *Empowering and healing the battered woman.* New York: Springer.

Emery, R. E. 1989. Family violence. *American Psychologist* 44:321–8.

Faller, K. C. 1990. *Understanding child sexual maltreatment.* Newbury Park, CA: Sage Publications.

Felthous, A. R. 1980. Aggression against cats, dogs and people. *Child Psychiatry and Human Development* 10:169–77.

Felthous, A. R., and S. R. Kellert. 1987. Childhood cruelty to animals and later aggressive against people: A review. *American Journal of Psychiatry* 144:710–17.

Felthous, A. R., and B. Yudowitz. 1977. Approaching a comparative typology of assaultive female offenders. *Psychiatry* 40:270–6.

Ferenczi, S. 1916. *Sex in psycho-analysis* (pp. 240–252). Boston: Richard G. Badger, the Gorham Press.

Feshbach, N. D. 1989. The construct of empathy and the phenomenon of physical maltreatment of children. In *Child maltreatment*, ed. D. Cicchetti and V. Carlson, pp. 349–73. New York: Cambridge University Press.

Finkelhor, D., L. M. Williams, and N. Burns. 1988. *Nursery crimes: Sexual abuse in day care*. Newbury Park, CA: Sage Publications.

Flynn, J. 1988, October 27. Torturing of pets could be prelude to human murder. *San Francisco Examiner*.

Freud, S. 1905. Three contributions to the theory of sex. In *The basic writings of Sigmund Freud*, ed. A. A. Brill (1938). New York: Random House.

Frick, P. J., B. B. Lahey, R. Loeber, L. Tannenbaum, Y. Van Horn, M. A. G. Christ, E. A. Hart, and K. Hanson. 1993. Oppositional defiant disorder and conduct disorder: A meta-analytic review of factors analyses and cross-validation in a clinic sample. *Clinical Psychology Review*, in press.

Friedrich, W. N., A. J. Urquiza, and R. L. Beilke. 1986. Behavior problems in sexually abused young children. *Journal of Pediatric Psychology* 11:47–57.

Fromm, E. 1973. *The anatomy of human destructiveness*. New York: Henry Holt.

Furman, E. 1986. Aggressively abused children. *Journal of Child Psychotherapy* 12:47–59.

Garbarino, J., N. Dubrow, K. Kostelny, and C. Pardo. 1992. *Children in danger: Coping with the consequences of community violence*. San Francisco: Jossey-Bass.

Garmezy, N. 1988. Stressors of childhood. In *Stress, coping, and development in children*, ed. N. Garmezy and M. Rutter, pp. 43–8. Baltimore: Johns Hopkins University Press.

Gelles, R. J., and M. A. Straus. 1988. *Intimate violence*. New York: Simon and Schuster.

Golding, W. 1959. *Lord of the flies*. New York: Capricorn Books.

Grandin, T. 1988. Behavior of slaughter plant and auction employees toward animals. *Anthrozoös* 1:205–13.

Green, A. H. 1985. Children traumatized by physical abuse. In *Post-traumatic stress disorder in children*, ed. S. Eth and R. S. Pynoos, pp. 135–54. Washington, DC: American Psychiatric Press.

Hallie, P. P. 1982. *Cruelty*. Middletown, CT: Wesleyan University Press.

Hellman, D. S., and N. Blackman. 1966. Enuresis, firesetting and cruelty to animals: A triad predictive of adult crime. *American Journal of Psychiatry* 122:1431–5.

Hewitt, S. 1990. The treatment of sexually abused preschool boys. In *The sexually abused male: Application of treatment strategies*, ed. M. Hunter, Vol. 2, pp. 225–48. Lexington, MA: Lexington Books.

Hickey, E. W. 1991. *Serial murderers and their victims*. Belmont, CA: Wadsworth.

Hindman, J. L. No date. *Adult and Juvenile Data Collection Form*. Ontario, OR: Alexandria Associates.

———. 1992. *Juvenile Culpability Assessment, 2nd revision*. Ontario, OR: Alexandria Associates.

Hughes, H. M. 1988. Psychological and behavioral correlates of family violence in child witnesses and victims. *American Journal of Orthopsychiatry* 58:77–90.

Hunter, M. 1990. *Abused boys: The neglected victims of sexual abuse*. New York: Fawcett Columbine.

Jaffe, P. G., D. A. Wolfe, and S. K. Wilson. 1990. *Children of battered women*. Newbury Park, CA: Sage Publications.

Jersild, A. T. 1954. Emotional development. In *Manual of child psychology*, 2nd ed., ed. L. Carmichael, pp. 833–917. New York: Wiley.

Jonker, F., and P. Jonker-Bakker. 1991. Experiences with ritualist child sexual abuse: A case study from The Netherlands. *Child Abuse and Neglect* 15:191–6.

Jouriles, E. N., C. M. Murphy, and K. D. O'Leary. 1989. Interspousal aggression, marital discord, and child problems. *Journal of Consulting and Clinical Psychology* 57:453–5.

Justice, B., R. Justice, and I. A. Kraft. 1974. Early-warning signs of violence: Is a triad enough? *American Journal of Psychiatry* 131:457–9.

Kazdin, A. E. 1990, June. *Prevention of conduct disorder*. Paper prepared for the National Conference on Prevention Research, National Institute of Mental Health, Bethesda, MD.

Kazdin, A. E., and K. Esveldt-Dawson. 1986. The interview for antisocial behavior: Psychometric characteristics and concurrent validity with child psychiatric inpatients. *Journal of Psychopathology and Behavioral Assessment* 8:289–303.

Kellert, S. R., and A. R. Felthous. 1985. Childhood cruelty toward animals among criminals and noncriminals. *Human Relations* 38:1113–29.

Kelley, S. J. 1989. Stress responses of children to sexual abuse and ritualistic abuse in day care centers. *Journal of Interpersonal Violence* 4:502–13.

Kidd, A. H., and R. M. Kidd. 1987. Seeking a theory

of the human/companion animal bond. *Anthrozoös* 1:140–5.

Klimes-Dougan, B., and J. Kistner. 1990. Physically abused preschoolers' responses to peers' distress. *Developmental Psychology* 26:599–602.

Klingbeil, K. S., and V. D. Boyd. 1984. Emergency room intervention: Detection, assessment, and treatment. In *Battered women and their families,* ed. A. R. Roberts, pp. 5–32. New York: Springer.

Kolko, D. J., and A. E. Kazdin. 1989. The Children's Firesetting Interview with psychiatrically referred and nonreferred children. *Journal of Abnormal Child Psychology* 17:609–24.

Kotlowitz, A. 1991. *There are no children here.* New York: Doubleday.

Krafft-Ebing, R. V. 1906. *Psychopathia sexualis,* rev. ed., 1934. Brooklyn, NY: Physicians and Surgeons Book Company.

Lanning, K. V. 1989a. *Satanic, occult, ritualistic crime: A law enforcement perspective.* Quantico, VA: National Center for the Analysis of Violent Crime, FBI Academy, October.

———. 1989b. *Child sex rings: A behavioral analysis.* Arlington, VA: National Center for Missing and Exploited Children, December.

———. 1991. Ritual abuse: A law enforcement view or perspective. *Child Abuse and Neglect* 15:171–3.

LaRose, L., and D. A. Wolfe. 1987. Psychological characteristics of parents who abuse or neglect their children. In *Advances in clinical child psychology,* ed. B. B. Lahey and A. E. Kazdin (Vol. 10), pp. 55–97. New York: Plenum Press.

Letourneau, C. 1981. Empathy and stress: How they affect parental aggression. *Social Work* 26:383–9.

Levinson, D. 1989. *Family violence in cross-cultural perspective.* Newbury Park, CA: Sage Publications.

Lew, M. 1988. *Victims no longer.* New York: Harper and Row.

Lewis, D. O., S. S. Shanok, M. Grant, and E. Ritvo. 1983. Homicidally aggressive young children: Neuropsychiatric and experiential correlates. *American Journal of Psychiatry* 140:148–53.

Lockwood, R., and G. R. Hodge. 1986, Summer. The tangled web of animal abuse: The links between cruelty to animals and human violence. *The Humane Society News.*

Loeber, R. 1988. Natural histories of conduct problems, delinquency, and associated substance abuse. In *Advances in clinical child psychology,* ed. B. B. Lahey and A. E. Kazdin (Vol. 11), pp. 73–124. New York: Plenum Press.

Magid, K., and C. A. McKelvey. 1987. *High risk:*

Children without a conscience. New York: Bantam Books.

Mead, M. 1964. Cultural factors in the cause and prevention of pathological homicide. *Bulletin of the Menninger Clinic* 28:11–22.

Menninger, K. A. 1951. Totemic aspects of contemporary attitudes toward animals. In *Psychoanalysis and culture,* ed. G. B. Wilbur and W. Muernsterberger, pp. 42–74. New York: International Universities Press, Inc.

Mewshaw, M. 1980. *Life for death.* Garden City, NY: Doubleday.

Miller, A. 1990. *For your own good.* New York: Noonday Press.

Mueller, E., and N. Silverman. 1989. Peer relations in maltreated children. In *Child maltreatment,* ed. D. Cicchetti and V. Carlson, pp. 529–78). New York: Cambridge University Press.

National Advisory Mental Health Council 1990. *National Plan for Research on Child and Adolescent Mental Disorders.* A report requested by the U.S. Congress, DHHS Publication No. (ADM)90-1683. Rockville, MD: National Institute of Mental Health.

National Institute of Health 1988. *Health benefits of pets.* Summary of Working Group, NIH Technology Assessment Workshop. (Publication 1988-216-107). Bethesda, MD: U.S. Government Printing Office.

Offord, D. R., M. H. Boyle, and Y. A. Racine. 1991. The epidemiology of antisocial behavior in childhood and adolescence. In *The development and treatment of childhood aggression,* ed. D. J. Pepler and K. H. Rubin. Hillsdale, NJ: Lawrence Erlbaum Associates.

Patterson, G. R., B. D. DeBaryshe, and E. Ramsey. 1989. A developmental perspective on antisocial behavior. *American Psychologist* 44:329–35.

Peterson, G. 1990. Diagnosis of child multiple personality disorder. *Dissociation* 3:3–9.

———. 1991. Children coping with trauma: Diagnosis of "Dissociation Identity Disorder." *Dissociation* 4:152–64.

Price, J. M., and K. A. Dodge. 1989. Peers' contributions to children's social maladjustment. In *Peer relationships in child development,* ed. T. J. Berndt and G. W. Ladd, pp. 341–70. New York: Wiley.

Putnam, F. W. 1991. The satanic ritual abuse controversy. *Child Abuse and Neglect* 15:175–9.

Randal, J., and N. Boustany. 1990. Children of war in Lebanon. In *Betrayal: A report on violence toward children in today's world,* ed. C. Moorehead, pp. 59–82. New York: Doubleday.

Random House Dictionary of the English Language. 1987. New York: Random House.

Redl, F., and D. Wineman. 1951. *Children who hate.* New York: The Free Press.

Reiss, Jr., A. J., and J. A. Roth, Eds. 1993. *Understanding and preventing violence.* Washington, DC: National Academy Press.

Renzetti, C. M. 1992. *Violent betrayal: Partner abuse in lesbian relationships.* Newbury Park, CA: Sage Publications.

Ressler, R. K., A. W. Burgess, and J. E. Douglas. 1988. *Sexual Homicide: Patterns and motives.* Lexington, MA: Lexington Books.

Ressler, R. K., A. W. Burgess, C. R. Hartman, J. E. Douglas, and A. McCormack. 1986. Murderers who rape and mutilate. *Journal of Interpersonal Violence* 1:273–87.

Rigdon, J. D., and F. Tapia. 1977. Children who are cruel to animals-A follow-up study. *Journal of Operational Psychology* 8:27–36.

Robin, M., and R. ten Bensel. 1985. Pets and the socialization of children. In *Pets and the family,* ed. M. B. Sussman, pp. 63–78. New York: Haworth Press.

Robins, L. N. 1988. Some methodological problems and research directions in the study of the effects of stress on children. In *Stress, coping, and development in children,* ed. N. Garmezy and M. Rutter, pp. 335–46. Baltimore: Johns Hopkins University Press.

Rutter, M. 1989. Pathways from childhood to adult life. *Journal of Child Psychology and Psychiatry* 30:23–51.

Spitzer, R. L., M. Davies, and R. A. Barkley. 1990. The *DSM-III-R* field trial of disruptive behavior disorders. *Journal of the American Academy of Child and Adolescent Psychiatry* 29:690–7.

Steinbeck, J. 1938. *Of mice and men.* New York: Viking Press.

Sterba, E. 1935. Excerpt from the analysis of a dog phobia. *Psychoanalytic Quarterly* 4:135–60.

Strayer, J., and W. Roberts. 1989. Children's empathy and roletaking: Child and parental factors, and relations to prosocial behavior. *Journal of Applied Developmental Psychology* 10:227–39.

Tapia, F. 1971. Children who are cruel to animals. *Child Psychiatry and Human Development* 2:70–7.

Terr, L. 1990. *Too scared to cry.* New York: Harper and Row.

Tingle, D., G. W. Barnard, L. Robbins, G. Newman, and D. Hutchinson. 1986. Childhood and adolescent characteristics of pedophiles and rapists. *International Journal of Law and Psychiatry* 9:103–16.

Triplett, N. 1903. A study of the faults of children. *Pedagogical Seminary* 10:200–38.

Uherek, A. M. 1991. Treatment of a ritually abused preschooler. In *Casebook of sexual abuse treatment,* ed. W. N. Friedrich, pp. 71–92. New York: W. W. Norton.

Vachss, A. 1991. *Sacrifice.* New York: Alfred A. Knopf.

Vermeulen, H., and J. S. J. Odendaal. 1992, July. *A typology of companion animal cruelty.* Paper presented at the Sixth International Conference on Human–Animal Interactions, Montreal, Canada.

Walker, J. R. 1980. *A study on the relationship of child abuse and pet abuse.* Unpublished professional project. University of Pennsylvania School of Social Work, Philadelphia.

Walker, L. E. 1979. *The battered woman.* New York: Harper and Row.

Waterman, J., R. J. Kelly, M. K. Oliveri, and J. Mc-Cord. 1993. *Behind the playground walls: Sexual abuse in preschools.* New York: Guilford Press.

Wax, D. E., and V. G. Haddox. 1974a. Enuresis, firesetting, and animal cruelty: A useful danger signal in predicting vulnerability of adolescent males to assaultive behavior. *Child Psychiatry and Human Development* 4:151–7.

———. 1974b. Sexual aberrance in male adolescents manifesting a behavioral triad considered predictive of extreme violence: Some clinical observations. *Journal of Forensic Sciences* 4:102–8.

Weber, C., and F. R. Ascione. 1992, July. *Humane attitudes and human empathy: Relations in adulthood.* Paper presented at the Sixth International Conference on Human–Animal Interactions, Montreal, Canada.

Weil, J. L. 1989. *Instinctual stimulation of children: From common practice to child abuse (Vol. I: Clinical findings).* Madison, CT: International Universities Press.

Weisz, J. R., and B. Weiss. 1991. Studying the "referability" of child clinical problems. *Journal of Consulting and Clinical Psychology* 59:266–73.

Wertsch, M. E. 1991. *Military brats: Legacies of childhood inside the fortress.* New York: Harmony Books.

Widom, C. S. 1989. Does violence beget violence? A critical examination of the literature. *Psychological Bulletin* 106:3–28.

———. 1991. *Long-term consequences of early childhood victimization.* Paper presented at the annual meeting of the American Association for the Advancement of Science, Washington, DC, February 16.

Wiehe, V. R. 1990. *Sibling abuse.* Lexington, MA: Lexington Books.

Wochner, M., and G. Klosinski. 1988. Kinder-und jugendpsychiatrisch auffällige Tierquäler. (Children and adolescents with psychiatric problems who mistreat animals.) *Schweizer "Archiv für Neurologie und Psychiatrie"* 139:59–67.

Wooden, W. S., and M. L. Berkey. 1984. *Children and arson: America's middle class nightmare.* New York: Plenum Press.

Young, W. C., R. G. Sachs, B. G. Braun, and R. T. Watkins. 1991. Patients reporting ritual abuse in childhood. A clinical syndrome report of 37 cases. *Child Abuse and Neglect* 15:181–9.

Zahn-Waxler, C., B. Hollenbeck, and M. R. Radke-Yarrow. 1984. The origins of empathy and altruism. In *Advances in animal welfare,* ed. M. W. Fox and L. D. Mickley, pp. 21–41. Norwell, MA: Kluwer Academic.

Zimrin, H. 1986. A profile of survival. *Child Abuse and Neglect* 10:339–49.

Pets and the Socialization of Children

Michael Robin
Robert ten Bensel

ABSTRACT. Despite the widespread ownership of pet animals in American families, there is very little analysis of the role of pets in child development. This paper will examine the influence of pet animals on child development; the impact of pet loss and bereavement on children; the problem of child cruelty to animals and its relationship to child abuse; and the role of pets in both normal and disturbed families. The authors will also review their own research study of adult prisoners and juveniles in institutions in regard to their experiences with pet animals.

INTRODUCTION

Given the large numbers of children who have had pets, it is striking how little attention has been paid to the role pets play in the emotional and developmental lives of children. In addition to the mythological, symbolic and utilitarian aspects of the animal/human relationship, recent research has focused on the developmental aspects of this relationship. While there is a literature on the role of animals in myths, fairytales, dreams and nightmares, very little has been written on companion animals and children. This paper will focus on what is known about the normal developmental interactions between animals and children and the implications of this knowledge to the everyday lives of children. In addition to a review of the literature on companion animals and children, we will also report on our surveys of juveniles and adults in correctional institutions and their experiences with pet animals (Robin, ten Bensel, Quigley and Anderson, 1983, 1984; ten Bensel, Ward, Kruttschnitt, Quigley and Anderson, 1984).

Michael Robin and Robert ten Bensel are at the University of Minnesota, School of Public Health, Program in Maternal and Child Health, Box 197, Mayo Memorial Building, 420 Delaware Street Southeast, Minneapolis, Minnesota 55455.

Reprinted from *Pets and the Family,* edited by M. Sussman (Binghamton, N.Y.: Haworth Press, 1985), 63–78.
Reprinted with permission.

COMPANION ANIMALS AND CHILDREN

Companion animals are a vital part of the healthy emotional development of children. As children develop, animals play different roles for the child at each stage of development. The period of childhood encompasses a number of developmental tasks—the acquisition of basic trust and self-esteem, a sense of responsibility and competence, feelings of empathy toward others and the achievement of autonomy—that can be facilitated for the child by a companion animal. The constancy of animal companionship can help children move along the developmental continuum and may even have an inhibiting effect toward mental disturbances (Levinson, 1970).

In what ways can a pet meet the mental health needs of a child? In the first instance, a pet is an active and energetic playmate, which facilitates the release of a child's pent-up energy and tension (Feldman, 1977). In general, a child who is physically active is less likely to be tense than one who is not. The security of the companion animal may encourage exploratory behavior, particularly for fearful children in unfamiliar situations. It may also serve as a bridge or facilitator towards relationships with other children. And for those living in situations without other children, a pet may be a substitute for human companionship. As one child said, "Pets are important especially for kids without brothers and sisters. They can get close to this animal and they both can grow up to love one another" (Robin, ten Bensel, Quigley and Anderson, 1983).

Caring responsibly for a pet will help a child experience the pleasures of responsible pet ownership. Levinson (1972) suggests that responsibility for pet care should be introduced gradually and that parents should recognize there will be periods when even for a conscientious child the care of a pet will be too much. Adolescents living in normal family environments more often shared the responsibility of pet care with other family members which became a source of mutual enjoyment (Robin, ten Bensel, Quigley and Anderson, 1983). The successful care of a valued pet will promote a sense of importance and being needed. By observing the pet's biological functions, children will learn about sexuality and elimination (Levinson, 1972; Schowalter, 1983).

In laboratory experiments, it was found that people of all ages, including children, use animals to feel safe and create a sense of intimacy. As Beck and Katcher (1983) have noted, pairing an animal with a strange human being apparently acts to make that person, or the situation surrounding that person, less threatening. For example, in an experiment where children were brought into a room with an interviewer alone or with with an interviewer with a dog, the children were found to be more relaxed as measured by blood pressure rates when entering a room with the interviewer and an animal (Beck and Katcher, 1983). In another study in England, Messant (1983) found people in public parks were considered more approachable for conversation when accompanied by a pet. In general, the presence of companion animals seems to have a relaxing and calming effect on people. When people talk to other people there is a tendency for blood pressure to rise; however, when people talk to or observe animals there is a tendency for blood pressure to lower.

Pets as Transitional Objects

It is widely accepted that the key factor in the relationship between children and companion animals is the unconditional love and acceptance of the animal for the child, who accepts the child ''as is'' and does not offer feedback or criticism (Levinson, 1969, 1972; Beck and Katcher, 1983). As Siegel (1962) has written, ''The animal does not judge but offers a feeling of intense loyalty. . . . It is not frightening or demanding, nor does it expose its master to the ugly strain of constant criticism. It provides its owner with the chance to feel important.'' The simple, uncomplicated affection of an animal for his master was also noted by Freud in a letter to Marie Boneparte, ''It really explains why we can love an animal like Topsy (or Jo-Fi) with such an extraordinary intensity: affection without ambivalence . . . that feelings of an intimate affinity, of an undisputed solidary. Often when stroking Jo-Fi, I have caught myself humming a melody which, unmusical as I am, I can't help recognizing as the aria from Don Giovanni: A bond of friendship units us both'' (Freud, 1976).

Pets as Parents

Beck and Katcher (1983) have suggested that as children get older, the pet acquires many of the characteristics of the ideal mother. The pet is unconditional, devoted, attentive, loyal and non-verbal—all elements of the primary symbiotic relationship with the mother. From a developmental point of view, a major task of childhood is the movement away from the primary symbiotic relationship with the mother and the establishment of a separate and distinct identity (Erickson, 1980). This process of separation and individuation creates feelings of ''separation anxiety'' that occur throughout the life process, particularly at stressful times of loss or during new experiences (Perin, 1983). ''One could regard the entire life cycle as constituting a more or less successful process of distancing from and introjection of the lost symbiotic mother, an eternal longing for the actual or fantasied ideal state of self'' (Mahler, 1972).

Pets function, particularly for adolescents, as transitional objects, much like the blanket or teddy bear does for infants. As transitional objects, pets help children feel safe without the presence of parents. Pets are more socially acceptable as transitional objects for older children than are inanimate objects. Adolescence brings with it a changing relationship to pets, in large part due to this emergence of pets as transitional objects. At this period pets can be a confidant, an object of love, a protector, a social facilitator or a status symbol (Fogle, 1983). Moreover, the bond between children and pets is enhanced by its animate quality. The crucial attachment behaviors of proximity and caring between children and pets forms an alive reciprocating alliance (Bowlby, 1969). The relationship is simpler and less conflicted than are human relationships.

Like other transitional objects, most of the shared behaviors between animals and children are tactile and/or kinetic rather than verbal. Levinson (1969) has stated that pets may satisfy the child's need for physical contact and touch without the fear of entanglements that accompany contact with human beings. Children have a great need for empathetic listening and association with others. It is the non-interventiveness and empathy that makes animals such good companions. Pets are often perceived by children as attentive and empathetic listeners. As one child wrote, ''My dog is very special to me. We have had it for seven years now. When I was little I used to go to her and pet her when I was depressed and crying. She seemed to understand. You could tell by the look in her eyes'' (Robin, ten Bensel, Quigley and Anderson, 1983).

Pets as Children

Along with the parental role, pets simultaneously or alternately function as children for the pet owner (Beck and Katcher, 1983). This idea was expressed by the prophet Nathan during antiquity (2

Sam. 12:3): "The poor man had nothing save one little ewe lamb, which he bought and nourished up; and it grew up together with him, and with his children; it did eat of his own morsel, and drank of his own cup, and lay in his bosom, and was to him as a daughter." Midgley (1984) notes in her discussion of this passage that the lamb was not a substitute for the poor man's children as he had children. His love for the lamb was nonetheless the kind of love suited to a child. The lamb was a live creature needing love, and was able to respond to parental cherishing. The helplessness of the animal drew out from the man nurturing and humane caring.

Fogle (1983) notes that studies in New York State show that pets can elicit maternal behaviors in children as young as three years old. In fact, according to Beck and Katcher (1983), much of the usual activity of children and pet animals resembles a parent/child relationship with the animal representing the child as an infant. Children unconsciously view their pets as an extension of themselves and treat their pets as they want to be treated themselves. This process is what Desmond Morris has called "infantile parentalism," suggesting this is one way children cope with the loss of their childhood (Morris, 1967). Schowalter (1983), for example, discussed the case of a five-year-old insecure boy referred for psychiatric care due to his habit of petting his goldfish. For this boy, petting the fish helped him feel both caring and cared for. Gradually he was able to transfer his affection toward a dog. With increased parental nurturance, he became more confident and outgoing.

Sherick (1981) also presented a case of a nine-year-old girl whose pets became symbolic substitutes for her ideal self. The sick pets that she cared for and nursed back to health represented the cared-for, protected and loved child that she longed to be. The girl's mother was a vain woman concerned with appearances who turned most of her maternal instincts toward the family pet rather than her daughter. The girl's behavior toward her pet was an unconscious effort to model "good enough" mothering to her mother. Searles (1960) points out that many children grow up with parents unable to nurture them, because of their own disturbance, but who can show affection to an animal. The child then grows up thinking if only he or she were an animal then they might receive parental love. Kupferman (1977) presented a case of a seven-year-old boy whose ego development was so faulty that he took on the identity of a cat and meowed to his psychiatrist.

Pets and Families

The role of a pet in a family will be dependent upon the family's structure, its emotional undercurrents, the emotional and physical strengths and weaknesses of each of its members, and the family's social climate (Levinson, 1969). When a pet is acquired by a family a variety of changes frequently occurs in family relationships and dynamics. Cain (1983) found in her study of pets in family systems that families reported both positive and negative changes after acquiring a pet. Some families reported increased closeness expressed around the care of a pet, more time spent together playing with a pet, more happiness of family members, and less arguing. However, other families reported more arguing and problems over the rules and care of the pet and less time spent with other family members; for example, children spent less time with their parents and husbands spent less time with their wives (Cain, 1983).

Pets become, according to the theory of Murray Bowen, part of the "undifferentiated ego mass" of the family and form part of the emotional structure of that family (Bowen, 1965). Many people indeed consider their pet as a member of the family. In Cain's survey of 60 families, 87 percent considered their pet as a member of the family (Cain, 1983). Ruby has also noted that most families include their pets in their family photographs (Ruby, 1983). Family members not only interact with their pets in their own characteristic manner, but they also interact with each other in relationship to the pet. In some families, pets become the major focus of attention and assume a position even more important than human family members (Levinson, 1969).

As Levinson has cautioned, pets may be involved in family pathology (Levinson, 1969). For example, one young woman committed suicide after being ordered by her parents to kill her pet dog for punishment for spending the night with a man. The woman used the same gun on herself that she used to kill her dog (Levinson, 1969). In another case, Rynearson (1978) discussed a severely disturbed adult woman who as a child had a profound fear of her parents and siblings. She turned to her cat as a confidant with whom she shared her troubles. One day her younger sister was scratched by the cat and the woman watched her enraged mother kill the cat with a shovel and then her mother turned to her and said, "Never forget that you are the one who really killed her, because you weren't watching her closely—it's all your fault."

Children can involve their animals psychodynamically in their use of such defense mechanisms as displacement, projection, splitting and identification (Schowalter, 1983). There are times when a child living in a disturbed family will become overly attached to a pet to the detriment of human relationships. Such children have a basic distrust of people which becomes overgeneralized. This basic distrust of human attachments contributes to the intense displacement of attachment to a pet who is consistently receptive as a source of love and caring. In anxiously attaching to the animal, a child can gratify part of the self without risking interpersonal involvement. Disturbed children with limited ego strength will turn to their pets for warmth and caring to meet their regressed, insatiable need for closeness and love (Rynearson, 1978; Levinson, 1972).

In a study of 269 disturbed children institutionalized for delinquency problems, 47 percent said pets were important for children growing up because they provided someone for them to love. For the control group of students in regular public schools, a pet was important to them because it taught responsibility. For many abused and disturbed children, a pet becomes their sole love object and a substitute for family love. As one boy said of his pet, "My kitty was the joy of my life. It never hurt me or made me upset like my parents. She always came to me when she wanted affection." Another boy wrote, "My favorite pet was my dog Bell. I loved her very much. I took care of her all the time and never mistreated her. Sometimes she was the only person I could talk to." Overall, abused and disturbed children in this study were more likely to talk to their pets about their problems. Pets became their sole source of solace at times of stress, loneliness or boredom (Robin, ten Bensel, Quigley and Anderson, 1983).

PET LOSS

For many children, the loss or death of a companion animal is the first experience with death and bereavement. In fact, it is often stated that one of the most important aspects of pet ownership for children is that it provides the child with experiences of dealing with the reality of illness and death which will prepare them for these experiences later in life (Fox, 1983). By fully experiencing the grief of losing a pet, the child learns that death is a natural part of the life process, is painful, but is tolerable and does not last forever. A child can learn that death is permanent and that dead animals will not come back to haunt them. The children can also be taught that guilt feelings following the death of a loved object are common and can be overcome (Levinson, 1972).

There is a tendency, however, to minimize a child's grief over a lost pet. In the vast literature on children and bereavement there are few references to bereavement from pet loss (Nieburg, 1982). The death of a pet has been considered an "emotional dress rehearsal" and preparation for greater losses yet to come (Levinson, 1967). However, there are strong indicators that the loss of a pet is more than a "rehearsal," and it is a profound experience in itself for many children.

In a study of 507 adolescents in Minnesota, over one-half had lost their "special pet" and only two youths reported feeling indifferent to the loss (Robin, ten Bensel, Quigley and Anderson, 1983). Most of the youths whose pets had died had deep feelings of regret and sadness such as those who wrote, "My sorrows are very deep for my special pet, but I know she is in some place where she is treated very well. And I know she is thinking of me because I always think of her." And, "I was sad that he had to be put to sleep but I was glad that he didn't die painfully."

Stewart (1983) also surveyed 135 schoolchildren in central Scotland on their experiences and feelings toward pet loss. She asked the children to write about their pets and how they felt if their pet had died. She found that 44 percent had pets that died and two-thirds of these children expressed profound grief at their loss, such as the child who said, "I didn't believe it, I didn't know where I was." In most cases, the children got over the loss, usually with parental support. But in all the bereavements that seemed unresolved the parents were unwilling to have another animal.

How a child reacts to the loss of a pet depends largely on his or her age and emotional development, the length of time the child had the pet, the quality of the relationship, the circumstances surrounding the loss of the pet, and the quality of support available to the child. Pre-school children are less likely to become deeply attached to their pets, and are less likely to view the pet loss as irrevocable. According to Nieburg and Fischer (1982), children under five years usually experience the pet loss as a temporary absence, and from five years to nine years or so, pet loss is not seen as inevitable and is believed possible to avoid. Stewart (1983) found that school-aged children often expressed profound grief for a short time, and then seemed to quickly adapt to normal, especially if a new animal was introduced. Most young children miss their deceased animals, but more as a playmate than as an object that satisfies basic emotional needs.

It is usually adolescents who have the most profound experiences with pet loss. From early adolescence on, children begin to develop an adult perception that death is final, permament and inevitable (Nieburg and Fischer, 1982). Adolescents tend to take longer to get over their grief, in part because their relationships with pets tends to be more intense at this age (Stewart, 1983; Nieburg and Fisher, 1982). How a young adolescent will react to pet loss will depend on the circumstances surrounding the death of a pet. A pet may be lost in a variety of ways such as old age or illness, being run over, theft, given away or traumatic death. Unfortunately, there are very few empirically based epidemiological studies on the nature of pet loss. In Minnesota it was found that abused and disturbed youths suffered more pet loss, had their pets for shorter times, and were most likely to have had their pet killed accidentally or purposely more than any other factor (Robin, ten Bensel, Quigley and Anderson, 1983, 1984). Most of those children whose pets were traumatically killed were saddened by the loss of their pet, and, in a few cases, were angry and revengeful toward the person who killed their pet. For example, one child wrote, "He was 11 years old and my mother had my little brother and Duke started being grouchy and nipping at people. So my brother-in-law shot him. It really hurt bad, like one of my brothers died. It was really hard to accept" (Robin, ten Bensel, Quigley and Anderson, 1983). Another child wrote, "My sister was taking it for a walk and this man drove over it, then backed over it and then drove over it again. I was hurt very bad. I hated that man. I cried for two days straight" (Robin, ten Bensel, Quigley and Anderson, 1983). Not only did abused and disturbed youths experience more traumatic pet loss than did the controls, they were also less likely to have someone to talk to about their grief. Only 56 percent of those youths whose pets died traumatic deaths had someone to talk to about their grief, as compared to 79 percent of the control group who had support after traumatic pet loss.

Most mental health practitioners indicate that the forms of bereavement from pet loss are similar to those of human loss (Levinson, 1967). Some children might be surprised and embarrassed by the intensity of their grief and feel the need to conceal their grief from the outside world. Parents should be sensitive to the child's grief and not minimize or ridicule its impact. Some young children tend to view the death of a pet as punishment from their misdeeds. If so, children should be assured that they were not to blame for their pet's death. Given that our society has no public rituals for the death of pets, families may enact funerals to acknowledge the importance of the pet to the family (Levinson, 1967; Nieburg and Fischer, 1982). Children should also be offered a replacement pet; however, there is disagreement if the replacement should be deferred for a time (Levinson, 1981; Nieburg and Fischer, 1982) or take place immediately (Stewart, 1983).

CHILDHOOD CRUELTY TO ANIMALS

Interest in childhood cruelty to animals grew out of the notion that cruelty to animals has a disabling effect on human character and leads to cruelty among people (ten Bensel, 1984). This idea was articulated by Saint Thomas Aquinas (1225–1274) who said: "Holy scriptures seem to forbid us to be cruel to brute animals . . . that is either . . . through being cruel to animals one becomes cruel to human beings or because injury to an animal leads to the temporal hurt of man" (Thomas, 1983). Likewise the philosopher Montaigne (1533–1592) wrote that "men of bloodthirsty nature where animals are concerned display a natural propensity toward cruelty" (Montaigne, 1953).

Until the seventeenth and eighteenth centuries, there was relatively little awareness that animals suffered and needed protection because of this suffering. This new sensibility was linked to the growth of towns and industry which left animals increasingly marginal to the production process. Gradually society allowed animals to enter the house as pets, which created the foundation for the view that some animals at least were worthy of moral consideration (Thomas, 1983). The English artist, William Hogarth (1697–1764) was the first artist to both condemn animal cruelty and theorize on its human consequences. His *Four Stages of Cruelty* (1751) was produced as a means of focusing attention on the high incidence of crime and violence in his day. The four drawings trace the evolution of cruelty to animals as a child, to the beating of a disabled horse as a young man, to the killing of a woman, and finally to the death of the protagonist himself. As Hogarth declared in 1738, "I am a professional enemy to persecution of all kinds, whether against man or beast" (Lindsay, 1979).

The link between animal abuse and human violence has been made more recently by Margaret Mead (1964) when she suggested that childhood cruelty to animals may be a precursor to anti-social violence as an adult. Hellman and Blackman (1966) postulated that childhood cruelty to animals, when combined with enuresis and fire-setting, were indeed effective predictors of later violent and criminal behaviors in adulthood. They found that of 31 prisoners charged with aggressive crimes against people, three-fourths (N = 23) had a history of all or part of the triad. The authors argued that the aggressive behaviors of their subjects were a hostile reaction to parental abuse or neglect. Tapia (1971) found additional links between animal abuse, child abuse, and anti-social behavior. Of 18 young boys who were identified with histories of cruelty to animals, one-third had also set fires, and parental abuse was the most common etiological factor. Felthous (1980), in another study, found that Hellman and Blackman's behavioral triad did have predictive value for later criminal behavior. He found extreme physical brutality from parents common, but he felt that parental deprivation rather than parental aggressiveness may be more specifically related to animal cruelty.

Kellert and Felthous (1983) also found in their study of 152 criminals and non-criminals in Kansas and Connecticut an inordinately high frequency of childhood animal cruelties among the most violent criminals. They reported that 25 percent of the most aggressive criminals had five or more specific incidents of cruelty to animals, compared to less than six percent of moderate and non-aggressive criminals, and no occurrence among non-criminals. Moreover, the family backgrounds of the aggressive criminals were especially violent. Three-fourths of all aggressive criminals reported excessive and repeated abuse as children, compared to only 31 percent for non-aggressive criminals and 10 percent among non-criminals. Interestingly, 75 percent of non-criminals who experienced parental abuse also reported incidents of animal cruelty.

These studies identified extreme parental cruelty as the most common background element among those who abuse animals. As Erich Fromm has noted in his study, *The Anatomy of Human Destructiveness* (1973), persons who are sadistic tend themselves to be victims of terroristic punishment. By this is meant punishment that is not limited in intensity, is not related to any specific misbehavior, is arbitrary and is fed by the punisher's own sadism. Thus, the sadistic animal abuser was, himself, a victim of extreme physical abuse.

While most children are usually sensitive to the misuse of pets, for some abused or disturbed children, pets represent someone they can gain some power and control over. As Schowalter (1983) has said, "No matter how put upon or demeaned one feels, it is still often possible to kick the dog." Cruelty to animals thus represents a displacement of aggression from humans to animals. Rollo May (1972) suggests that when a child is not loved adequately by a mother or father, there develops a "penchant for revenge on the world, a need to destroy the world for others inasmuch as it was not good for him." Severely abused children, lacking in the ability to empathize with the sufferings of animals, take out their frustrations and hostility on animals with little sense of remorse. Their abuse of animals is an effort to compensate for feelings of powerlessness and inferiority.

A weakness of the previous studies of childhood cruelty to animals is that they did not consider the patterns of pet ownership among their subjects. These studies did not distinguish if the abused animal was the child's own animal or if the child had ever had a companion animal and what the nature of that relationship might have been. Other than a passing comment by Brittain (1970) in his study of the sadistic murderer, little mention has been made of the child and his relationship to animals prior to the incident of cruelty. Brittain wrote, "There is sometimes a history of extreme cruelty to animals. Paradoxically they can also be very fond of animals. Such cruelty is particularly significant when it relates to cats, dogs, birds and farm animals, though it can also be directed toward lower forms of animal life, and the only animal which seems to be safe is the one belonging to the sadist himself." It is with these ideas in mind that we studied adult prison populations along with abused adolescents institutionalized for delinquency and emotional disturbances to determine their patterns of pet ownership and their feelings toward their pets.

In our study of 81 violent offenders imprisoned in Minnesota, 86 percent had had a pet sometime in their life that they considered special to them. Overall, 95 percent of the respondents valued pets for companionship, love, affection, protection and pleasure. Violent offenders were more likely to have a dog in their home while growing up. The control group had more animals as pets other than dogs or cats, but the offender group had more "atypical" pets such as a baby tiger, cougar, and wolf pup. When we asked what has happened to the special pet, over 60 percent of both groups lost their pets through death or theft; however, there were more pets that died of gunshots in the inmate group. In addition, the offender group tended to be more angry at the death of the pet. Strikingly, among the violent offenders, 80 percent wanted a dog or cat *now* as compared to 39 percent of the control group. This suggests something about the deprivation of the prison environment as well as the possibility of therapeutic intervention with pets among prison populations. Like the Kellert and Felthous study (1983), this study also found that most violent offenders had histories of extreme abuse as children (ten Bensel, Ward, Kruttschnitt, Quigley and Anderson, 1984).

We also surveyed 206 teenagers between the ages of 13 and 18 living in two separate juvenile institutions and 32 youth living in an adolescent psychiatric ward in regard to their experiences with pets. We compared them to a control group of 269 youths from two urban public high schools. Of the 238 abused institutionalized youths we surveyed, 91 percent (N = 218) said that they had had a special pet and of these youths 99 percent said they either loved or liked their pet very much. Among our comparison group 90 percent (N = 242) had had a special pet and 97 percent said they either loved or liked their pet very much. This suggests that companion animals do indeed have a prominent place in the emotional lives of abused as well as non-abused children. It is also a corrective to those who suggest that pet ownership in itself will prevent emotional or behavioral disturbances in children. Merely having a special pet played no part in whether or not a child was eventually institutionalized (Robin, ten Bensel, Quigley and Anderson, 1983, 1984).

In considering the issue of abuse of animals, the authors found that the pets of the institutionalized group suffered more abuse; however, the abuser was usually someone other than the child. In a few instances, youths had to intervene against their parents to protect their pets. As one youth wrote, 'He jumped on the bed and my mom beat him and I started yelling at her because she was hurting my dog.'' Another child wrote, ''My dad and sister would hit and kick my cat sometimes because he would get mad when they teased him. I got mad and told them not to hurt him because he's helpless'' (Robin, ten Bensel, Quigley and Anderson, 1983, 1984).

Of those youths who indicated that they mistreated their pets, sadness and remorse were the most common responses. For example, one child said, ''I remember once I was punished for letting the dog out and so I hit him for that. I felt real bad after that and comforted it a lot.'' All of those who mistreated their pets, except for one youth, indicated that they loved or liked their pets very much and felt bad about hurting their pets. Only one youth said he did not care that he hurt his pet. There was no self-reported evidence of sadism toward pets.

There were several instances of pets being harmed or killed as punishment to a child. According to Summit (1983), threatening to harm a child's pet is a common technique of child abusers to keep the child quiet about the abuse. In a recent child sexual abuse case discovered in a Los Angeles day care center, the adults involved allegedly silenced the children by butchering small animals in front of the children and threatening to do the same to their parents if they revealed the abuse. Mental health practitioners should routinely ask young people if anyone has ever hurt or threatened to hurt their animal.

Lenore Walker (1983) has suggested in her study on domestic violence that the best predictor of future violence was a history of past violent behavior. In her definition she included witnessing violent acts toward pets in the childhood home. At this point, without further studies, it is unclear what role, if any, violence toward pets plays in the emotional and behavioral disturbances of adolescents. Nonetheless, the abused institutionalized population experienced more violent pet loss than did the comparison group. They showed no evidence of callousness toward the sufferings of their pets and seemed to be troubled by the mistreatment of their pets.

CONCLUSION

Pets clearly play an important role in the lives of children. The relationship is characterized by deep feelings of love and care. It is enhanced by children's empathy toward the feelings of animals and their intuitive sense of having a common status with animals. As Freud (1953) wrote, ''Children show no trace of arrogance which urges adult civilized men to draw a hard-and-fast line between their own nature and that of all other animals. Children have no scruples over allowing animals to rank as their full equals. Uninhibited as they are in the avowal of their bodily needs, they no doubt feel themselves more akin to animals than to their elders, who may well be a puzzle to them.''

REFERENCES

Anderson, R.K., Hart, B., and Hart, L. The pet connection: Its influence on our health and quality of life. Minneapolis: CENSHARE, 1984.

Beck, A., and Katcher, A.H. Between pets and people: The importance of animal companionship. New York: G.P. Putnam's Sons, 1983.

Bowen, M. Family psychotherapy with a schizophrenic in the hospital and in private practice. In I. Borzormenyi-Nagy and J.L. Framo (Eds.), *Intensive family therapy*. New York: Harper and Row, 1965.

Bowlby, J. Attachment and loss. In *Attachment*, Vol. I. London: Hogarth Press, 1969.

Brittain, R.P. The sadistic murderer. In *Medicine, Science and the Law*, 1970, 10:198–207.

Cain, A. A study of pets in the family system. In A. Katcher and A. Beck (Eds.), *New perspectives on our lives with companion animals*. Philadelphia: University of Pennsylvania Press, 1983.

Erickson, E. *Identity and the life cycle*. New York: W.W. Norton, 1980.

Feldmann, B.M. Why people own pets. In *Animal Regulation Studies*, 1977, 1:87–94.

Felthous, A. Aggression against cats, dogs and people. In *Child Psychiatry and Human Development*, 1980, 10:169–177.

Fogle, B. (Ed.) *Interrelations between people and pets*. Springfield, Illinois: Charles C. Thomas, 1981.

Fogle, B. *Pets and their people*. New York: The Viking Press, 1983.

Fox, M. Relationships between the human and non-human animals. In B. Fogle (Ed.), *Interrelationships between people and pets*. Springfield, Illinois: Charles C. Thomas, 1981.

Freud, S. Letter to M. Boneparte. In I. Simitis-Grubrich (Ed.), *Sigmund Freud*. New York: Harcourt Brace Jovanovich, 1976.

Freud, S. *Totem and taboo*. Standard edition. London: Hogarth Press and the Institute of Psychoanalysts, 1953, 1–161.

Fromm, E. *The anatomy of human destructiveness*. New York: Holt, Rinehart and Winston, 1973.

Hellman, D., and Blackman, N. Enuresis, firesetting and cruelty to animals: A triad predictive of adult crime. In *American Journal of Psychiatry*, 1966, 122:1431–1435.

Katcher, A.H. Interactions between people and their pets: Form and function. In B. Fogle (Ed.), *Interrelations between people and pets*. Springfield, Illinois: Charles C. Thomas, 1981.

Katcher, A.H., and Beck, A. (Eds.) *New perspectives on our lives with companion animals*. Philadelphia: University of Pennsylvania Press, 1983.

Kellert, S., and Felthous, A. Childhood cruelty toward animals among criminals and non-criminals. Manuscript submitted for publication, 1983.

Kupferman, K. A latency boy's identity as a cat. In *Psychoanalytic Study of the Child*, 1977, 32:193–215.

Levinson, B. *Pet-oriented child psychotherapy*. Springfield, Illinois: Charles C. Thomas, 1969.

Levinson, B. The pet and the child's bereavement. In *Mental Hygiene*, 1967, 51:197–200.

Levinson, B. Pets, child development, and mental illness. In *Journal of the American Veterinary Medical Association*, 1970, 157:1759–1766.

Levinson, B. *Pets and human development*. Springfield, Illinois: Charles C. Thomas, 1972.

Levinson, B. Pets and personality development. In *Psychological Reports*, 1978, 42:1031–1038.

Lindsay, J. *Hogarth: His art and his world*. New York: Taplinger Publishing Co., 1979.

Mahler, M.S. On the first three subphases of the separation-individuation process. In *International Journal of Psycho-Analysis*, 1972, 53:333–338.

May, R. *Power and innocence*. New York: W.W. Norton and Co., 1972.

Mead, M. Cultural factors in the cause of pathological homicide. In *Bulletin of Menninger Clinic*, 1964, 28:11–22.

Midgley, M. *Animals and why they matter*. Athens: University of Georgia Press, 1984.

Montaigne, M. de. *The essays of Montaigne*. New York: Oxford University Press, 1953.

Morris, D. *The naked ape*. New York: McGraw-Hill, 1967.

Nieburg, H.A., and Fischer, A. *Pet loss: A thoughtful guide for adults and children*. New York: Harper and Row, 1982.

Perin, C. Dogs as symbols in human development. In B. Fogle (Ed.), *Interrelations between people and pets*. Springfield, Illinois: Charles C. Thomas, 1981.

Robin, M., ten Bensel, R.W., Quigley, J., and Anderson, R.K. Childhood pets and the psychosocial development of adolescents. In A. Katcher and A. Beck (Eds.), *New perspectives on our lives with companion animals*. Philadelphia: University of Pennsylvania Press, 1983.

Robin, M., ten Bensel, R.W., Quigley, J., and Anderson, R.K. Abused children and their pet animals. In R.K. Anderson, B. Hart, and L. Hart (Eds.), *The pet connection: Its influence on our health and the quality of life*. Minneapolis: CENSHARE, 1984.

Ruby, J. Images of the family: The symbolic implications of animal photography. In A. Katcher and A. Beck (Eds.), *New perspectives on our lives with companion animals*. Philadelphia: University of Pennsylvania Press, 1983.

Rynearson, E.K. Humans and pets and attachment. In *British Journal of Psychiatry*, 1978, 133:550–555.

Schowalter, J.E. The use and abuse of pets. In *Journal of the American Academy Child Psychiatry*, 1983, 22:68–72.

Searles, H.F. *The nonhuman environment*. New York: International University Press, 1960.

Sherick, I. The significance of pets for children. In *Psychoanalytic Study of the Child*, 1981, 36:193–215.

Siegel, A. Reaching severely withdrawn through pet therapy. In *American Journal of Psychiatry*, 1962, 118:1045–1046.

Stewart, M. Loss of a pet—loss of a person: A comparative study of bereavement. In A. Katcher and A. Beck (Eds.), *New perspectives on our lives with companion animals*. Philadelphia: University of Pennsylvania Press, 1983.

Summit, R. The child sexual abuse accommodation syndrome. In *Child Abuse and Neglect*, 1983, 7:181.

Tapia, F. Children who are cruel to animals. In *Child Psychiatry and Human Development*, 1971, 2:70–77.

ten Bensel, R.W. Historical perspectives on human values for animals and vulnerable people. In R.K. Anderson, B. Hart, and L. Hart (Eds.), *The pet connection: Its influence on our health and quality of life*. Minneapolis: CENSHARE, 1984.

ten Bensel, R.W., Ward, D.A., Kruttschnitt, C., Quigley, J., and Anderson, R.K. Attitudes of violent criminals towards animals. In R.K. Anderson, B. Hart, and L. Hart (Eds.), *The pet connection: Its influence on our health and quality of life*. Minneapolis: CENSHARE, 1984.

Thomas, K. *Man and the natural world*. New York: Pantheon Books, 1983.

Walker, L. The battered women syndrome story. In D. Finkelhor (Ed.), *The dark side of families*. Beverly Hills: Sage Productions, 1983.

Section 3: Case Studies, Case Control, and Prospective Research

In the last section we referred to a number of reviews of research that refer to the variety of methodologies used to examine the phenomenon of cruelty toward animals. Here we highlight examples of three methodological strategies that have facilitated scientific understanding in a number of disciplines, especially those with a developmental emphasis. These strategies are the case study, case-control research, and prospective research.

Case studies typically involve the description of one individual and are most often related to relatively rare phenomena and to the preliminary investigation into a new research area. Ferenczi's paper in section 1 is an early example of such a study. Although case studies do not promise either representative or generalizable results, they do paint a richly detailed portrait of the individual's history and current behavior and their context. Such detail is obviously not feasible in studies of large groups of individuals.

The first article, by Alan R. Felthous, describes case studies of three adult men whose psychoses involved bizarre perceptions of pet animals. In two cases, the men were alleged to have killed their wives. In the third case, alleged violence involved a neighbor. Although Felthous includes recent examples of the individuals' cruelty toward animals, he does not provide information about their childhood relations with animals. The value of these case studies, as noted by Felthous, is that "In each case, information about psychotic perceptions of pet animals was helpful in reconstructing the defendant's state of mind at the time of the alleged attack."

If there is a "classic" case study in the area of childhood cruelty to animals, it would be Fernando Tapia's 1971 paper. Case *studies* is more accurate, since Tapia includes information on eighteen children and adolescents who had been referred to a psychiatric clinic and for whom cruelty

to animals had been the "chief complaint or one of the complaints." In some cases, Tapia describes the cruelty performed in general terms, so that it is difficult for the reader to gauge the severity and frequency of the behavior (examples of such general terms are "constant mistreatment of family pets," "cruel and sadistic"). However, in most of these cases (which involved five-year-old to eighteen-year-old boys), Tapia provides vivid descriptions of the animals' victimization, leaving no confusion about which cases represented teasing of animals and which exemplified torture and killing.

Tapia also provides information about other symptoms or problem behaviors listed in the boys' clinical files. This information is conveniently organized into a table that allows the reader to see that cruelty to animals rarely appears as an isolated indicator of psychological problems. (Tapia's essay also anticipates later research by identifying a number of symptoms that were eventually associated with conduct disorder in *DSM-III-R* and *DSM-IV;* see section 6.) The brief narratives also show that cruelty to animals was associated with the child's actual or threatened violence toward other human beings (such as classmates, siblings, and parents) in 89 percent of the cases and that the "common though not essential" features of these children's histories included child abuse (physical and sexual), domestic violence, and juvenile sex offending.

One of the shortcomings of Tapia's study is the lack of detail about the process used to select his case studies. Since we do not know how many files were examined to yield the eighteen cases, it is impossible to estimate the prevalence of cruelty in this clinical sample. Nor can we determine how often cruelty to animals would have been present if cases had been initially screened for fighting and aggression (instead of for animal maltreatment). Nevertheless, Tapia's study is a landmark that illustrates the potential severity of cruelty to animals and its relation to interpersonal violence.[1]

The final study in this section is a rare example of a prospective study of cruelty to animals, in which John D. Rigdon and Tapia followed up on the sample of boys described in Tapia's previous essay. Using an enhanced multisource method of assessment, Rigdon and Tapia contacted the children, their parents/guardians, employers, teachers, and, if applicable, the children's current therapists and acquired information on thirteen of the original sample of eighteen boys (the period of follow-up ranged from two to nine years). The authors evaluated whether the youths were considered to have improved, using a five-point scale ranging from "much improved" to "much worse" (eleven of the thirteen were reported to be "doing better"). Despite general improvements, Rigdon and Tapia reported, eight of the boys (61.5 percent) continued to display cruelty to animals at follow-up. But again, no standard definition of cruelty was provided, nor was there a rating of the severity of cruelty. If one examines the case descriptions and uses a definition of "severe" cruelty as physically damaging, torturing, or killing animals, only four (31 percent) displayed severe cruelty. Nevertheless, cruelty in whatever degree persisted in a substantial number of cases, despite ongoing interventions. Some children clearly do not "grow out" of this problem.

---

1.   Some of the shortcomings of the case-study approach are avoided in a German case-control research project reported by V. M. Wochner and G. Klosinski. They reviewed clinical files for 1,502 inpatient and outpatient children and adolescents admitted to a psychiatric clinic for aggressive behavior. They selected twenty-five cases where there were also reports of cruelty to animals, and these cases were matched for age, gender, and nationality to twenty-five youths for whom there were no reports of animal cruelty. They found that "sadism" toward people was more common in the "cruel" group (32 percent) than in the "aggression-only" group (12 percent). Unfortunately, they did not define the criteria they used to assess sadism. This generalization of violence to people and animals is of interest because the authors also report that 24 percent of the "cruel-to-animals" group reported their love of pets (V. M. Wochner and G. Klosinki, "Kinder- und jugendpsychiatrisch auffällige Tierquäler," *Schweizer Archiv für Neurologie und Psychiatrie* 139[3] [1988]: 59–67).

Psychotic Perceptions of Pet Animals in Defendants Accused of Violent Crimes

Alan R. Felthous, M.D.

ABSTRACT

Some defendants charged with aggressive crimes against people have a history of psychotic perceptions and delusions involving their pet animals. Careful history of this phenomenon can contribute towards better understanding of a defendant's state of mind at the time of the alleged offense. Three case examples are presented and discussed.

INTRODUCTION

"The corpse, already greatly decayed and clotted with gore, stood erect before the eyes of the spectators. Upon its head, with extended mouth and solitary eye of fire, sat the hideous beast whose craft had seduced me into murder . . ." (Poe, 1951).

This statement climaxed the well known account of an alcoholic who first maimed, then killed his beloved pet cat. Psychotic experiences preceded and followed his foiled attempt to kill his second pet cat and the actual killing of his wife. This eerie, riveting tale should be recognized as "The Black Cat" by Edgar Allen Poe. Fiction such as this and anecdotes by clinicians of pet animal killing followed by psychotic homicide caused the author to be alert to the possibility that some psychotic individuals who aggress violently against a person may have a history of psychotic perceptions of animals that can relate to the aggressive crime.

A literature search failed to reveal any articles on the phenomenon of psychotic perceptions involving pet animals followed by a violent act against a person. A number of reports suggest an association between repetitive cruelties to animals in childhood and serious assaults against people at a later age (Mead, 1964; Felthous & Yudowitz, 1977; Felthous, 1980; Felthous, 1981). Case studies demonstrate that some individuals who have been cruel to animals have

Alan R. Felthous, M.D., is Associate Professor of Psychiatry and Chief of Forensic Services in the Department of Psychiatry and Behavioral Sciences at the University of Texas Medical Branch. *Correspondence and reprint requests should be addressed to: Alan R. Felthous, M.D. Department of Psychiatry and Behavioral Sciences, University of Texas Medical Branch, Galveston, TX 77550.*

Reprinted from *Behavioral Sciences and the Law* 2 (1984): 331–39. Reproduced by permission of John Wiley & Sons Limited.

poor control over aggressive impulses in general (Wax & Haddox, 1974; Felthous, 1982). Some sadistic sex murderers and sadistic rapists reportedly have histories of animal cruelties that compared with their later cruelties against people (MacDonald, 1961; Groth & Birnbaum, 1979). However, most individuals who have aggressed against both animals and people are not psychotic, and they do not have psychotic perceptions of animals or people.

The literature on hallucinations or delusions having animal content does not pertain to psychotic perceptions of pet animals. Animal content in organic psychoses, such as with alcohol withdrawal, involves negatively regarded creatures such as insects and reptiles, not pet animals (Deiker & Chambers, 1978). Lycanthropy, also termed therianthropy (Eister, 1953), may bear some relationship to the phenomenon presented here. Lycanthropy is a rare paranoid phenomenon in which the patient believes he or she is a wild animal (Polatin, 1975; Rosenstock & Vincent, 1977). The lycanthrope may feel him/herself harmed by the "evil eye" (Rosenstock & Vincent, 1977). Lycanthropy can be associated with bizarre sexual and aggressive behaviors (Polatin, 1975; Rosenstock & Vincent, 1977). In contrast to the phenomenon described here, however, lycanthropy does not involve psychotic perceptions of the patient's pet.

The mass-murderer Wagner (1874–1938) reportedly slew his wife and four children with a knife, shot and killed nine more people and several cows, and set several houses and barns on fire (Berger, 1939; MacDonald, 1961). It is not clear whether his mental disorder, diagnosed as "paranoia," involved psychotic perceptions of cows. David Berkowitz ("Son of Sam"), who was convicted of murdering courting couples in New York City, said he acted on command hallucinations from demon dogs, but he later stated that his demon story was a hoax (Abrahamsen, 1979).

Dr. Karl Menninger presented and discussed a case example of a 32-year-old married farmer who experienced psychotic perceptions of his stallion (Menninger, 1951). Although this man did not aggress against a person, features of the psychotic symptoms centering on his horse correspond to aspects of the first two cases presented here. He was proud of this stallion that he used for breeding purposes. The horse grew old and less able, however, so he sold it. He soon purchased another stallion, but only after some difficulties attending the transaction.

> From this point on, the symptoms of the present illness developed rapidly. He became convinced that something was wrong with the horse. The horse was not acting right. It did not "look" right. Something about the veins in the horse's forehead and *some tinge in the whites about the horse's eyes seemed not to be quite right* (emphasis added). (Menninger, 1951)

Delusions concerning this stallion crystallized and expanded. He believed his horse was afflicted with syphilis and that it had transmitted the disease to breeding mares. These mares, he feared, would infect their owners. He concluded that he had contracted syphilis from his stallion and that he had afflicted his wife and children. Fortunately, this man sought medical help and hospital treatment was successful in overcoming his psychosis.

An examining psychiatrist may gather abundant evidence that suggests that a defendant was psychotic when he or she was thought to have committed an aggressive crime and yet be able to provide only minimal understanding of how psychotic processes might have contributed to the violent act. Diagnostic interviews of psychotic defendants who were accused of seriously aggressive crimes revealed that several had, according to history, experienced psychotic perceptions of one or more of their pet animals. In each case, information about psychotic perceptions of pet animals was helpful in reconstructing the defendant's state of mind at the time of the alleged attack.

CASE HISTORIES

Case One

A 52-year-old widower, Mr. A, was referred for a psychiatric evaluation to help in the determination of whether he was competent to stand trial and whether he had mental illness which met criteria for the insanity defense. Reconstruction of his state of mind was hampered by his failure to remember events at the moment of the alleged homicide. Since he demonstrated ongoing signs of emotional instability and paranoid delusions, it would have been imprudent to attempt barbiturate or hypnotic interview.

Several weeks before the alleged killing, Mr. A's cat appeared to be pregnant, so he made a nesting box for it. He said his wife disliked his cat because of its grey color. One day Mr. A dropped a jar of molasses, thereby spilling the contents. He lamented to himself that he no longer had control over picking up and holding objects. Upon seeing the cat's strange green eyes, he concluded that voodoo was being perpetrated against him through the cat as a medium, and the cat was therefore responsible for his loss of control. It occurred to him that Cleopatra and the ancient Egyptians were surrounded by cats. He associated cats with the ancient past and evil spirits. He decided to shoot the cat in order to "break the spell" against him. However, killing his cat failed to dispel his sense of being fragmented and persecuted.

From the time he shot his cat until his wife was mortally shot several days later, Mr. A's psychosis worsened; his thinking became more disorganized and lacking in reality adherence. Time seemed to have stopped. He perceived a striking deterioration in his wife's appearance. "She looked so grey (her criticism of the cat), like a craven image . . . she looked sick." He wondered why she always left the front door unlocked at night and why she sat alone and talked to herself throughout the night. He surmised that she was emotionally disturbed and that they were somehow driving each other crazy. But he also believed that she was in a conspiracy with his unnamed enemies to ensorcel him.

On the eve of his wife's death, Mr. A observed her lying on the sofa and noted that she resembled Marie Antoinette. He believed that Mrs. A was a historically displaced, hooded executioner who once operated guillotines in France. He envisioned her wearing a black hood. It seemed to him that cockroaches were drawn to corpses under his house. His wife, he thought, was colluding with his enemies by burning candles late at night in order to do something with the corpses. He then retired to his room. He denied recollection of having seen her or of hearing a gun discharge later that night.

Mr. A suffered from schizophrenia, paranoid subtype. The bulk of the evidence for this diagnosis is omitted from this report. As is generally true for retrospective mental status examinations, contributory data was largely historical and subjective. Unfortunately, there were no close acquaintances to provide collateral information.

Mr. A externalized the cause of his frightening decompensation onto his grey, mysterious, and pregnant cat, and onto his perceivedly grey, mysterious, and afflicted wife. He believed both were instrumental in directing harmful witchcraft against him. He believed both had connections with evil and powerful forces in history. In Cameron's terminology (Cameron, 1943; Cameron, 1959a; Cameron, 1959b; Cameron, 1963), both were agents of an inimical, collusive pseudocommunity. Mr. A had hoped that by killing his cat he would short-circuit his persecution; however, his psychotic perceptions and delusions persisted. Psychotic symptoms involving his pet cat were essentially the same as those involving his wife.

Case Two

The patient, Mr. B, was a 48-year-old unemployed man who had been dependent on alcohol for many years. His attorney requested a psychiatric evaluation in order to help determine whether Mr. B. was competent to stand trial and to help assess his state of mind at the time his wife was allegedly shot and killed. The fact that his pet Doberman pinscher died inexplicably on the day of his wife's death led to further inquiry which advanced retrospective understanding of his state of mind.

For years Mr. B believed that his wife was having sexual affairs with other men while he slept at night. He cited numerous signs to support this belief, and he took special measures to prevent her from engaging in such activities. For example, after placing padlocks on all outside doors, he locked them every evening to prevent her from leaving the house for coital rendezvous. Despite these precautions, he was certain that she was able to continue to satisfy her desires by climbing out of windows. He never actually witnessed her in adulterous involvement, and she never admitted infidelity. Intermittently over the years, Mr. B also believed his wife wanted to get rid of him either by killing him or by sending him to a nursing home.

Some time ago one of his sons gave Mr. B a Doberman pinscher to serve both as a pet and a watchdog. At first he liked this dog and valued it for protection. Over time, however, he developed some peculiar beliefs about his dog. He believed the dog was previously owned by a single woman who had trained it to perform sexual acts with her. He believed that his dog had lustful desires for his wife and for his daughter. Whenever one of them was in the back yard with his dog, according to Mr. B, the animal would follow her around, lick her legs, and try to mate with her. In order to discourage his dog's assumed sexual inclinations toward family members, he would strike it in the presence of his wife and children. Mr. B said his dog hated and feared him and was becoming dangerous. Because his dog appeared strange and vicious, he asked his wife and son to get rid of it, before it killed someone.

Shortly after awakening early on the morning of his wife's death, he perceived something to be the matter with his dog. He thought it had a mental illness or an infection of the brain. His dog seemed to stare at him with eyes that appeared eerie, colorless, blurred, and cross-eyed. Upon arising from his chair after having had a studied look at his dog, Mr. B no longer felt like the same person. That morning his dog salivated profusely, refused to eat, and drank copious amounts of water. Mr. B believed his dog was becoming psychotic. His perception that his dog wore a purple collar that morning confirmed his impression that the dog was afflicted with a brain infection. But he also believed his dog had been transformed into a dangerous black ghost. Even though he was inside the house his dog was outside, and the doors were shut, he felt impelled to retreat further into the interior of his house. He told his wife and son of his fears and advised his son to secure the pet in the garage, but his son did not share his father's concerns.

Diagnostic information was obtained through interviews with Mr. B and his family members, hospital reports, psychological testing, and laboratory and procedural studies that included CT scan and electroencephalography. Diagnoses included alcohol abuse and dependance, paranoia or delusional jealousy associated with alcohol dependence, severe dementia associated with alcohol dependence, and atypical psychosis following his wife's death and his confinement.

Mr. B's long-standing delusional system involved a pseudocommunity of many men who, he believed, were having ongoing sexual relations with his wife. He thought some of these men were extremely dangerous. Presenting both the threats of sexual congress with his wife and direct harm to himself, Mr. B's pet Doberman was a principle member of his delusional pseudocommunity. On the day his wife was shot, Mr. B's psychotic perceptions of his pet became more fragmentary, and his ego boundaries collapsed. He projected fear, hatred, and psychosis onto the animal. Psychotic perceptions of his dog helped to substantiate his further psychotic decompensation on that day.

Case Three

Mr. C was a 39-year-old married but separated man who had been unemployed for many years. His attorney referred him for a psychiatric evaluation to help determine whether he was competent to stand trial and to help assess his mental state at the time of alleged aggravated assault and aggravated battery—offenses involving exchange of gunfire with a neighbor, Mr. D.

Mr. C appeared in outpatient interviews dressed in Indian attire and identified himself by various Indian names. He claimed that he was born to wealthy American Indians who did not want him to remain alive because he was in line to inherit much valuable land, and that he was adopted by his present parents. His mother denied these claims and asserted that he was her biological son. He believed his dogs were his children, and he referred to them by Indian names. For years he believed that members of the Black Mafia kept him under close surveillance because they had intentions of eventually either abducting or killing him so they could gain possession of his inheritable wealth. He believed they wanted to abduct or kill his pets so that he would be provoked to action, which would then provide them with an excuse to dispose of him.

Two years earlier, Mr. D, a neighbor whom Mr. C believed to be an agent of the Black Mafia, attempted to visit the defendant's sister, but Mr. C's German shepherd did not permit the man entry into the yard. Mr. D telephoned Mr. C and theatened to kill his dog, just as Mr. C had once killed a farmer's dog. When asked about the latter, Mr. C said he once went to a farm to examine some livestock. The farmer opened a door and released his large Labrador retriever. Mr. C said the dog attacked him without barking. As the dog lunged at him, he threw his Indian blanket over the dog and mortally stabbed it.

Later in the same year, Mr. C went on a trip. Upon returning he discovered that his sister's house, where he had been staying, had burned down and four of his five dogs were missing. He assumed that his enemies deliberately torched the house, and they either took the dogs or the animals were killed in the fire. He considered this to be another attempt to provoke him by abducting or killing his dogs. Not long after, he said, his enemies bludgeoned to death his fifth dog.

The patient again moved in with his sister, this time along with his seven dogs and two raccoons. The raccoons were kept in his bedroom behind shut door in order to protect them from two large dogs that had free run of the other rooms. According to Mr. C, his principle provoker made several attempts to harm his beloved pets. Mr. C said his sister and Mr. D together broke into her house by kicking open the back door, which had been locked. Then Mr. D kicked open the door to the bedroom in order to allow the hunting dogs to enter and kill his raccoons. None of the animals were harmed, but Mr. C was convinced the Black Mafia was again trying to provoke him to react, so as to give the Mafia a pretext to abduct or kill him. On another occasion, Mr. D set free one of his dogs that was tethered in the yard. Mr. D explained to him that he tried to disentangle the dog, but Mr. C insisted that the animal had been released onto a busy intersection so that it would be killed and he would be provoked.

He believed that agents of the Black Mafia were feeding arsenic to his outdoor dogs. One appeared to behave differently, as if affected by poison. He believed agents infested all of his dogs with heartworms by implanting worms in the dog food. He also believed agents were slipping worms in his food. He said he actually saw worms in his food, and that he had worms in his heart.

On the evening of the alleged exchange of gunfire, Mr. D came to visit the patient's sister, but Mr. C thought the man was sent by the Black Mafia to kill him. Not wanting to give his tormentor an opportunity to approach him, Mr. C went outside. While sitting on the tailgate of his truck, he wondered how he could protect his dogs from this man. Mr. D came out of the house, complained that the German shepherd that was tied to the front porch was barking at him, and threatened to kill the animal. Mr. C said his shepherd sensed impending danger. She looked in a northwesterly direction and talked to herself. She seemed to know what was about to happen. Mr. C told Mr. D to leave. He did, but returned with a rake, and Mr. C assumed he intended to kill his dogs with it. An argument and fight ensued. Mr. D left again and this time returned with a pistol. Mr. C thought his adversary was about to carry out the Black Mafia's design of killing him. He quickly armed himself, and the gunfire was exchanged which led to criminal charges.

While he was in jail, Mr. C believed Mafia agents poisoned one of his raccoons and attempted to kill his dogs. After he was released on bond, he continued to believe Mafia agents were trying to kill or abduct his pets in order to provoke him, and he insisted agents infected two of his dogs with distemper and killed his mother's cat.

The diagnosis of schizophrenia, paranoid subtype, was supported by Mr. C's symptoms of bizarre, grandiose, persecutory, and somatic delusions, ideas of reference, flat affect broken by inappropriate laughter, illogical thinking, and auditory hallucinations. This was a chronic disorder which had existed for many years. Information supportive of these conclusions was obtained from interviews with Mr. C, interviews with his mother, and numerous summaries of prior psychiatric hospitalizations.

It is notable that Mr. C surrounded himself with so many dogs of breeds known for hunting or protection and that he also carried three hunting knives on his person. Dogs and knives provided a fragile sense of protection for this frightened man.

If the Black Mafia had been a persecuting pseudocommunity in Mr. C's delusional system, his pet dogs and raccoons belonged to a positive pseudocommunity (Weinstein & Lyerly, 1969; Rothstein, 1975) of which he was the central member. Delusions of persecution against his pet animals paralleled delusions of persecution against him. His pets were believed to be special Indians with special powers like him. Agents of the Black Mafia intended to abduct his pets, he felt, as they intended to abduct him. Agents tried to kill his pets, as they tried to kill him. Agents tried to poison his pets, as they tried to poison him. Although some real threats may have stressed the patient, because of his paranoid delusions and loss of ego boundaries, his need to protect his pets and his need to protect himself were essentially one and the same.

SUMMARY AND CONCLUSIONS

Three cases are presented wherein men who were accused of violent crimes offered a history of psychotic perceptions involving one or more pet animals. All three were middle-aged men who suffered from profound and chronic psychosis involving paranoid delusions. In each case the psychotic disturbance had lasted for years but exacerbated with increasing psychotic perceptions of the defendant's pet animal(s) shortly before the alleged violent offense against a person. The impression is that all were socially isolated, and none had enjoyed a reciprocal relationship of intimacy.

The first two men became frightened of their pets and felt psychologially afflicted by their pets' strange-looking eyes. (This might be compared with the "evil eye" symptom that has been described in some patients exhibiting lycanthropy.) Shortly after, they allegedly killed their wives to whom they had been ambivalently bonded for years. Like their pets, their wives were perceived as maliciously causing them to become psychotic. Both their pets and their wives were identified as principle agents of a larger, hostile pseudocommunity bent on destroying them. Although the animal deaths were not investigated, the possibility exists that each defendant took measures to destroy his persecuting pet first and then his persecuting wife, before either pet or wife could destroy him by causing further psychotic decompensation.

The third man also experienced loss of ego boundaries in his relationships with pets which belonged to a pseudocommunity. But his pets were regarded as extensions of himself and belonged to a positive pseudocommunity. While his pets served to protect him from a hostile pseudocommunity, like him, they were vulnerable to destruction. It is conceivable, though not known, that the attacking black Labrador was perceived as an agent of his negative pseudocommunity, the Black Mafia.

One should not conclude from these reports that psychotic aggression against animals is necessarily a harbinger of psychotic violence against people. There are no data either on the frequency of this association or on the frequency of psychotic aggression against animals that is not followed by violence directed against people. However, psychotic aggression against animals per se suggests serious disturbance with poor control of aggressive impulses.

In a given individual, psychotic perceptions involving pet animals can parallel such symptoms focused on people. The examining psychiatrist must, however, remain alert to the possibilities of malingered symptoms in an unreliable defendant and of delusional reconstruction in someone with ongoing psychosis. Although psychotic delusions involving pets do not by themselves fully explain or even confirm aggressive behavior, a careful history of such phenomena, together with other historical and examinational data, can contribute towards a more complete and consistent reconstruction of the mental state of some defendants. Apart from psycho-legal issues, a striking change in a patient's relationship with his or her pet animal should be fully explored as it may provide valuable information about the evolution of the illness.

REFERENCES

Abrahamsen, D. (1979, July 2) When is a killer sane? *Chicago Tribune*: Tempo 1 and 7.

Berger, H. (1939). Illness and the death of a paranoiac mass murderer. *Journal of Criminal Psychopathology, 1*(1), 68–69. Abstract translated from R. Gaupp (1938) *Zeitschrift für die gesamte Neurologie and Psychiatrie, 163,* 48.

Cameron, N. (1943). The development of paranoid thinking. *Psychological Review, 50*(2), 219–233.

Cameron, N. (1959a). The paranoid pseudo-community revisited. *The American Journal of Sociology, 65*(1), 52–58.

Cameron, N. (1959b). Paranoid conditions and paranoia. In S. Arieti (Ed.), *American Handbook of Psychiatry* (pp. 508–539). New York: Basic Books, Inc., Publishers.

Cameron, N. (1963). *Personality development and psychopathology*. Boston: Houghton MIfflin Company, pp. 470–515.

Deiker, T., & Chambers, H.E. (1978). Structure and content of hallucinations in alcohol withdrawal and functional psychosis. *Journal of Studies on Alcohol, 39*(11), 1831–1840.

Eister, R. (1953). Therianthropy. In E. Podulsky (Ed.), *Encyclopedia of aberrations: A psychiatric handbook.* New York: Philosophical Library, pp. 523–527.

Felthous, A.R. (1980). Aggression against cats, dogs and people. *Child Psychiatry and Human Development, 10*(3), 169–177.

Felthous, A.R. (1981). Childhood cruelty to cats, dogs and other animals. *The Bulletin of the American Academy of Psychiatry and the Law, 9*(1), 48–53.

Felthous, A.R. (1982). The urge to kill: A case study of aggressive drives in an adolescent boy. *McLean Hospital Journal, 7*(1), 49–60.

Felthous, A.R., & Yudowitz, B. (1977). Approaching a comparative typology of assaultive female offenders. *Psychiatry, 40*(3), 270–276.

Groth, A.N., & Birnbaum, H.J. (1979). *Men who rape: The psychology of the offender.* New York: Plenum Press, pp. 44–57.

MacDonald, J.M. (1961). *The murderer and his victim.* Springfield, Ill.: Charles C. Thomas, 186–188.

Mead, M. (1964). Cultural factors in the cause of pathological homicide. *Bulletin of the Menninger Clinic, 28*(1), 11–22.

Menninger, K. (1951). Totemic aspects of contemporary attitudes toward animals. In G. B. Wilber and W. Muensterberger (Eds.), *Psychoanalysis and culture: Essays in honor of Géza Róheim* (pp. 42–74). New York: International Universities Press.

Poe, E.A. (1951). The black cat: In *Great tales and poems of Edgar Allan Poe,* (pp. 26–36). New York: Washington Square Press.

Polatin, P. (1975). Psychotic disorders: Paranoid states. In A.F. Freedman, H.I. Kaplan, and B.J. Sadock (Eds.), *Comprehensive textbook of psychiatry,* 2nd ed., Vol. 2, (p. 995). Baltimore: Williams and Williams Co.

Rosenstock, H.A., & Vincent, K.R. (1977). A case of lycanthropy. *The American Journal of Psychiatry, 134*(10), 1147–1149.

Rothstein, D.A. (1975). On presidential assassination: The academia and the pseudocommunity. In S.C. Feinstein & P.L. Giovacchini (Eds.), *Adolescent Psychiatry, Vol. IV* (pp. 264–298). New York: Jason Aronson, Inc.

Wax, D.E., & Haddox, V.G. (1974). Sexual aberance in male adolescents manifesting a behavioral triad considered predictive of extreme violence. *Journal of Forensic Sciences, 4*(1), 102–108.

Wax, D.E., & Haddox, V.G. (1974). Enuresis, firesetting and animal cruelty: A useful danger signal in predicting vulnerability of adolescent males to assaultive behavior. *Child Psychiatry and Human Development, 4*(3), 151–156.

Wax, D.E., & Haddox, V.G. (1974). Enuresis, firesetting and animal cruelty in male adolescent delinquents: A triad predictive of violent behavior. *The Journal of Psychiatry and Law, 2*(1), 45–72.

Weinstein, E.A., & Lyerly, O.G. (1969). Symbolic aspects of presidential assassination. *Psychiatry, 32*(1), 1–11.

CHILDREN WHO ARE CRUEL TO ANIMALS

Fernando Tapia, M.D., University of Missouri School of Medicine, Columbia, Missouri

A review of the literature reveals that no systematic study is available on the subject of children who are cruel to animals. Although it is frequently mentioned in texts and often appears in case histories, a good analysis of a series of cases apparently has not been made. The study done by Hellman and Blackman [1] in which they concerned themselves with a triad of symptoms— enuresis, fire setting, and cruelty to animals—as being predictive of adult crime heightens one possible reason for interest in this symptom. In their series of 84 prisoners, 75 percent of the 31 prisoners charged with aggressive crimes had the symptom triad whereas only 15 of the 53 (28 percent) involved in nonaggressive crimes had the triad or even part of the triad.

Margaret Mead [2], in an article on cultural factors in the cause of pathological homicide, stated that the torturing or killing of "good animals" by the child might be a precursor of violent acts as an adult.

In an example of comments commonly given in textbooks one is able to note from A. H. Chapman [3: p. 143] such a statement:

> CRUELTY: A severe acting out problem occasionally may take the form of vicious physical cruelty to siblings, to other children and friends. I have seen a few chaotically hostile boys who in their late childhood and early adolescence tortured stray dogs and cats by tying them and inflicting painful wounds on them. Such cruelty to animals usually indicates severe personality problems and it may be coupled with mental retardation. These children have been subjected to gross parental neglect, brutality, or hostility. They have a cold indifference or even a delight in inflicting suffering and often they are borderline psychotic. They require careful prolonged psychiatric evaluation and management.

An overall look at the cases noted and discussed throughout the available literature reveals that these children usually have other symptoms besides the matter of cruelty to animals. Among the concomitant symptoms most often mentioned are: (*a*) aggressiveness to younger siblings and smaller peers; (*b*) fire setting; (*c*) interest in sex; (*d*) hoarding; (*e*) enuresis; (*f*) problems with learning; (*g*) bullemia; and (*h*) imperviousness to pain.

Reprinted from *Child Psychiatry and Human Development* 2 (1971): 70–77, with kind permission of Plenum Publishing Corporation.

Whether these other symptoms have a correlation or significance is not really known. It would seem, however, that seldom is the symptom of cruelty to animals an isolated problem in the child. Nurcombe [4] in an article about children who set fires noted that these incidents were often seen in conjunction with children who were cruel. Examples included a 7-year-old fire setter who was "sadistic to younger children" and a 3½-year-old boy who was destructive, cruel, and sadistic with his younger sibling, whose fingers he jammed into the door hinge, whose hair he lit, and whose finger he amputated with a razor blade. This 3½-year-old youngster also had tantrums, night terrors, encopresis, and trichotillomania and was a head banger. Incidentally, Nurcombe felt that brain damage and severe deprivation, both emotional and material, were the etiological causes.

The literature mentions other causes that are reputedly common—for instance, exposure to aggressive models such as parents who vent their hostility on the child or on each other. Thus, the child imitates the cruelty done to himself or to others. The children described by Bender and Schilder [5] who had somewhat similar aggressive characteristics were generally believed to be suffering a specific disorder akin to adult obsessive-compulsions, but in children it was considered an impulsion. Kaufman [6] discussed children involved in crimes of violence who were diagnosed as schizophrenic. As one browses through the literature further, it is noted that the patient is invariably male. One is also struck by the frequency with which the child is a preadolescent or rather young.

CASE HISTORIES

The analysis of the following 18 cases should help us view the problem of cruelty to animals from the standpoint of etiology, possible concomitant symptoms that may spell a syndrome, as well as other characteristics of this condition. These cases were selected from the clinic files of the Child Psychiatry Section of the University of Missouri School of Medicine. They represent those cases where cruelty to animals was the chief complaint or one of the complaints. Cases in which cruelty to an animal was an incidental rather than a common or persistent act were eliminated. A brief account of each case is given below.

Case 1: R.H., age 12, was referred to us because of "mad fits," threatening to shoot his mother and the livestock. He killed small animals which he took to school to frighten the children. He also suffered from enuresis and had regular grand mal seizures. The family history included a father who was considered an ambulatory paranoid schizophrenic with a severe temper. The patient's electroencephalogram was "abnormal and paroxysmal." Full-scale IQ was 82, verbal 76, and performance 92. Diagnosis: Chronic Brain Syndrome associated with brain trauma, Incipient Childhood Schizophrenia.

Case 2: R.S., age 10, was referred because he was uncontrollable at school, belligerent with children, and aggressive with his younger sibling. He was known to be cruel and sadistic with animals including his dogs, cats, and pony. This youngster was short-tempered, defiant, and a "notorious liar." His natural father was an abusive, assaultive alcoholic, and, at the time, the youngster was obviously being rejected by his stepfather. It was noted that when his stepfather was away from the home the boy's behavior improved considerably. No electroencephalogram was done. Full-scale IQ was 90, verbal 93, and performance 91. Diagnosis: Adjustment Reaction of Childhood, Conduct Disturbance.

Case 3: R.B., age 10, was difficult to control and in complete defiance of authority. He was aggressive, overactive, and destructive. Besides being cruel to any animal he could catch, he was known to set fires, to have mistreated a baby, and to delight in tormenting and hurting other people. In the home situation, the mother was reputedly a behavior problem herself. The father, when drunk, was brutal to the wife and the son; this was frequent since he was an alcoholic. The father continually threatened to shoot the wife, and at one time they had been divorced but remarried. An electroencephalogram was not done. Full-scale IQ was 96, verbal 101, and performance 90. Diagnosis: Adjustment Reaction of Childhood, Conduct Disturbance.

Case 4: M.E., age 9, was cruel and obsessed with violence. He was constantly fighting and would use a knife, rock, wrench, or anything at hand. Oftentimes he would provoke and threaten to kill children who hadn't even provoked him. At one time he attempted to smother and later to choke his pet dog. He killed two pets at the age of 4½. He once dismembered a frog, then laid it on the sidewalk and ran over it with his bicycle. He was reputedly very destructive and was a known liar. Other symptoms noted in his case were hyperactivity, enuresis, night terrors, and tics. This youngster was dramatically helped by Ritalin medication. The home situation was marked by the fact that the mother was a difficult, contentious person who was concluding her third marriage. The father was a known bank robber and constantly had illegal sources of income. At one time the father was jailed for shooting someone. The electroencephalogram was read as "mildly abnormal, showing diffuse slowing and disorganization for the age." IQ was 120. Diagnosis: Unsocialized Aggressive Reaction of Childhood.

Case 5: C.S., age eight, was accused of pinching, slapping, and kicking pet animals until they snapped or scratched back. He set two fires and was known to be very aggressive in his peer group. The mother reputedly provided a "messy home situation for the boy." She admitted being on "booze and bennies" for several years prior to and during her pregnancy. The true natural father was unknown, but the stated natural father rejected the boy on discovering that he was probably not the natural father. An electroencephalogram was not done. Despite a Peabody IQ of 128, the boy was a poor reader. Diagnosis: Adjustment Reaction of Childhood.

Case 6: C.G., age 10, was referred for fighting, lying, stealing, destructiveness, and violence. He was frequently cruel to animals and once stabbed a cat and nearly killed it by dismembering it. He was a bedwetter until age 9. The family situation was composed of an alcoholic father who once attempted suicide. The father was hostile and abusive with the family and indiscreetly tried incest with his 18-year-old daughter. The mother was passive, fearful of her husband, and suffered from migraine. The electroencephalogram was normal. Full-scale IQ was 70, verbal 62, and performance 85. Diagnosis: Nonpsychotic Organic Brain Dysfunction.

Case 7: D.A., age 15, was referred because of stealing, fighting, and cruelty to animals—both pets and livestock. Other symptoms were enuresis, "picking his own skin with a knife," excessive interest in sex, indiscreet masturbation, sexually molesting his siblings, and making sexual overtures at his grandmother. The boy was a known ferocious and voluminous eater. The home was generally a deprived one. The patient's natural father, an ex-convict, was divorced, and his stepfather (since age 7) was an alcoholic. The mother was of "questionable character and irresponsible." An electroencephalogram was normal. Full-scale IQ was 86, verbal 74, and performance 90. Diagnosis: Adjustment Reaction of Adolescence.

Case 8: D.R., age 10, was distinctly cruel to animals, having tortured turtles and killed a puppy by kicking it. He stole, lied, and set fires. He was aggressive toward his siblings: he once broke his sister's arm and tried to drown his brother; another time he was found choking his brother. In school he cut a girl with a piece of metal. The boy suffered many nightmares. The natural mother was emotionally disturbed with repeated institution-alizations. The natural father was an alcoholic and a bully, and the stepfather rejected the boy. An electroencephalogram was paroxysmal and suggestive of seizure disorders. Full-scale IQ was 99, verbal 91, and performance 107. Diagnosis: Adjustment Reaction of Childhood.

Case 9: J.C., age 12, was referred because of cruelty to animals, hyperactivity, poor peer relations (teasing and fighting), and abusiveness to younger children. He was also destructive, had an explosive temper, was expelled from two schools, and had learning difficulties. This child was born prematurely, suffered polio at age 2, and during his first 5 years of life had convulsions whenever he had high fevers. The home situation was fairly average, stable, and normal. The electroencephalogram was abnormal with "right temporal asynchrony, consistent with old focal lesion." Full-scale IQ was 106, verbal 99, and performance 113. Diagnosis: Organic Brain Syndrome of Unknown Etiology.

Case 10: J.R., age seven, was referred for constant mistreatment of family pets, bad temper, loud and foul mouth, aggressiveness, and being extremely demanding. He was born prematurely and had a cleft palate and a supernumerary finger. The home situation was an adoptive one from the age of three months. The home was apparently adequate although the parents represented an overindulgent couple. The electroencephalogram had paroxysmal discharges with no focus. Full-scale IQ was 72, verbal 71, and performance 79. Diagnosis: Organic Brain Syndrome with other physical conditions.

Case 11: I.B., age 10, was referred because of profanity and being verbally abusive. He was cruel to animals, having crushed the heads of mice with a hammer and fed live birds to his cats. He once ripped an entire collection of tropical fish apart and in temper tantrums at school attacked teachers and classmates. The boy was born prematurely. The home situation was composed of a very aggressive and tempestuous mother and a mild, dominated father. The electroencephalogram was "Diffusely abnormal. Temporal lobe, transient paroxysmal slowing." Full-scale IQ was 87, verbal 82, and performance 94. Diagnosis: Organic Brain Syndrome with Severe Maladjustment of Childhood (Pre-Schizophrenia).

Case 12: J.L., age seven, was referred for beating the family dog continuously and for threatening to burn the house. He actually went as far as stashing a can of gasoline. He once tried to stick a three-year-old girl in the rectum with a stick. He was encopretic and a bed rocker. The father was an alcoholic. The mother, who was seen in the Child Guidance Clinic during her childhood, seemed relatively well adjusted. The maternal grandmother was called a "pathologic liar." The electroencephalogram was abnormal—"paroxysmal record consistent with a systematic mixed psychomotor and petit mal seizure disorder." The boy had positive soft neurological signs. Full-scale IQ was 110, verbal 116, and performance 101. Diagnosis: Organic Brain Syndrome of Unknown Etiology.

Case 13: J.P., age 12, was referred because of sadistic treatment of animals. He killed his foster mother's prize bantams and pedigreed Siamese cat. He killed chickens and barnyard rabbits and squeezed little chicks. He actually killed pets that were close to him. He continually threatened to kill the foster mother and others. This child seemed to have an obsession with killing. The natural mother was an unstable, tempestuous person who abandoned the patient at the welfare office and later was arrested for forgery. The father, who had received a dishonorable discharge from the service, was an ex-convict and known brawler. The electroencephalogram was borderline with minimal abnormality. Full-scale IQ was 83, verbal 82, and performance 86. Diagnosis: Passive-Aggressive, Aggressive Personality.

Case 14: M.R., age five, generally destroyed pets and other available animals. He was known for excessive masturbation, destructiveness, and for so much fighting that he had no playmates. He came from a rather hectic home. The mother was reputedly a very promiscuous woman who sexually stimulated the patient. The father, who was unstable and immature, eventually shot the mother dead. The electroencephalogram was mildly abnormal—paroxysmal consistent with seizure disorder or other paroxysmal disorders. Full-scale IQ was 88, verbal 97, and performance 79. Diagnosis: Adjustment Reaction of Childhood.

Case 15: J.G., age 14, was referred because of sadistic treatment of animals. He once slowly choked a cat to death and another time stuck an ice pick through a dog's head from ear to ear. He was also well known for lying and stealing, restlessness, and destructiveness, and for having a seriously difficult temper. The boy had grand mal seizures early in life, but they stopped at age 2½. He received a serious head trauma at age 6. The home would be considered average to good, although the father was said to have a short temper. The electroencephalogram was "borderline for seizure disorders while resting with hyper-ventilation, paroxysmal from left interior and left temporal leads. This is a seizure disorder of focal origin." Full-scale IQ was 120, verbal 119, and performance 117. Diagnosis: Organic Brain Syndrome, Seizure Disorders, Idiopathic.

Case 16: G.F., age eight, was referred because he was constantly trying to smother his baby brother and because he burned his sister's arm on purpose. He was constantly killing the chickens in the barnyard. He was a fire setter and was always fighting with younger children and stealing. He was very interested in sex and masturbated freely. One outstanding note is that he was reputedly "insensitive to pain." The home situation was marked by a promiscuous mother who was careless regarding the primal scene. The father, who was in prison at the time, was an alcoholic and also a cruel person who once tried to run over his own children. This home could be called a chaotic one in an understatement. The electroencephalogram was "Abnormal and markedly paroxysmal, consistent with mixed type of seizure disorder—petit mal predominant." Full-scale IQ was 86, verbal 84, and performance 106. Diagnosis: Adjustment Reaction of Childhood, Conduct Disturbance.

Case 17: D.C., age five, was referred for cruelty to animals, fire setting, and excessive curiosity about sex. He was hyperactive. The natural father abused the boy and was known to have a severe temper. The mother suffered a nervous breakdown during pregnancy, and the stepfather who was rearing the boy was an alcoholic. An electroencephalogram was not done. Neurological examination showed grossly poor motor and visual motor performance. Developmental IQ was 51. Diagnosis: Organic Brain Syndrome, Moderate Mental Retardation.

Case 18: K.H., age eight, was cruel to the family's pets, killed a kitten by drowning, and smothered a dog in a jar. He was hyperactive and aggressive. He was considered to have a peculiar facial appearance—wide-set eyes and broad bridge of the nose. He had hypotonic musculature and a hyperextensibility of the joints. He came from a generally adequate home with several siblings who were all well adjusted. The electroencephalogram was indefinite with mild mixed slow and fast record. Full-scale IQ was 68, verbal 72, and performance 69. Diagnosis: Mental Retardation, Adjustment Reaction of Childhood.

DISCUSSION

The careful reader will note that the diagnostic categories may be inconsistent and that some children were diagnosed as Organic Brain Syndrome when no apparent reason was given. At the same time some children were called Adjustment Reaction of Childhood in spite of, say, a rather abnormal electroencephalogram. However, this study spans 11 years of intake and two diagnostic manuals. At the same time there has been no attempt to alter the diagnoses given, presumably after careful consideration, at the time of initial evaluation.

The criteria used for diagnosing an Organic Brain Syndrome have been detailed in a previous article on the medication of brain-damaged children [7]. The diagnosis was based on clinical judgment that took into consideration the following six areas of investigation:

1. Clinical picture—hyperactivity, short attention span, irritability, temper, destructiveness, and the like.

2. Medical history—birth trauma, physical illness, head injury, and so forth.

3. Psychological tests.

4. Neurological examination with special attention paid to "soft" neurologic signs.

5. Electroencephalogram.

6. Lack of environmental and interpersonal determinants.

This series of cases reveals certain obvious characteristics. It confirms the high male prevalence and the relative youthfulness of the group—average age was 9½. The age span was 5 to 15 with half the cases being between 8 and 10.

The etiological background of gross parental neglect, brutality, rejection, and hostility seems very common although not an essential. Four of the cases—9, 10, 15, and 18—had what seemed to be a rather average, sedate type of home. In three of the cases the contribution of brain damage seems to stand out as being significant. In cases 9, 10, and 15, an organically based etiological factor was the only evident contribution to the pathology. In cases 1, 6, and 11, biologic and environmental factors were both contributors. The remaining 11 cases appear environmentally determined. Thus the type of home and its parental models seem to have contributed greatly to these children's aggressiveness.

A large number of these children came from rural Missouri which is the area served by the clinic facilities from which the cases were selected. However, a larger than the usual clinic case proportion came from very small towns and completely rural areas. One possible explanation, of course, is that this type of youngster would invariably be brought in for an evaluation whereas children who are equally disturbed but not so problematic might not be brought to us from these more rural and less sophisticated areas. Availability of animals and normal agrarian concern for animals would further enhance the rural proportion of referrals.

A study of the IQ test results might indicate some interesting characteristics. Generally the Wechsler Intelligence Scale for Children (WISC) was administered. This test renders a verbal and a performance scale as well as the full-scale IQ. In 15 of the cases we obtained a WISC. However, other tests, mainly the Peabody, were given with the following overall results: (*a*) the average IQ was 91; and (*b*)

Table 1: Reported presence of other symptoms in children who were cruel to animals

Symptom										Case number									Total
	1	2	3	4	5	6	7	8	9	10	11	12	13	14	15	16	17	18	
Cruelty to animals	x	x	x	x	x	x	x	x	x	x	x	x	x	x	x	x	x	x	18
Bullying and fighting	x	x		x	x	x	x	x	x					x		x			10
Temper	x	x	x	x		x		x	x	x					x				9
Lying and/or stealing		x				x	x	x							x	x			6
Destructiveness			x	x		x			x					x	x				6
Hyperactivity				x					x						x		x	x	5
Excessive interest in sex									x					x		x	x		4
Night terrors				x				x											2
Enuresis	x			x			x												3
Fire setting			x		x			x								x	x		5
Sadism			x										x						2
Encopresis												x							1

in those tests where verbal and performance scales could be compared, an average of 6.6 points higher in the performance test was noted.

This discrepancy might reflect the cultural background of these boys. However, higher performance scores are often found in delinquent adolescents and in this case might reflect their action orientation in preference to a verbal and intellectual approach to problems and frustrations. This study, however, certainly does not limit cruelty to animals to borderline or retarded children.

The overall picture must be viewed as one of aggression with poor control of impulses. The aggressiveness was exhibited in many ways including fire setting (5 cases), bullying and fighting (10 cases), temper (9 cases), lying and/or stealing (6 cases), destructiveness (6 cases), sadism (2 cases), and excessive interest in sex (4 cases). Other types of symptoms were less frequent—enuresis (3 cases), encopresis (1 case), and night terrors (2 cases). (See table 1.)

CONCLUSIONS

Eighteen cases of children who raised concern because of their cruelty to animals were reviewed. The results revealed that they were all boys, usually young (average age 9½), and of normal intelligence, and that they showed many other aggressive symptoms, such as destructiveness, bullying, fighting, stealing, and fire setting. Etiologic factors ranged from strictly biologic factors (Organic Brain Syndrome) to strictly environmental factors or to a combination of psycho-bio-social factors. The chaotic home with aggressive parental models was the most common factor.

Dr. Tapia is Professor of Psychiatry (Child Psychiatry), Department of Psychiatry, University of Missouri-Columbia, 803 Stadium Road, Columbia, Missouri 65201.

REFERENCES

1. Hellman DS, Blackman N: Enuresis, firesetting, and cruelty to animals: A triad production of adult crime. *Amer J Psychiat* **122**:1431-35, 1966.
2. Mead M: Cultural factors in the cause of pathological homicide. *Bull Menninger Clin* **28**:11-22, 1964.
3. Chapman AH: *Management of Emotional Problems of Children and Adolescents.* Philadelphia, Lippincott, 1965.
4. Nurcombe B: Children who set fires. *Med J Australia* **1**:579-84, 1964.
5. Bender L, Schilder P: Impulsions: A specific disorder of the behavior of children. *Arch Neurol Psychiat* **44**:990-1008, 1940.
6. Kaufman I: Crimes of violence and delinquency in schizophrenic children. *J Amer Acad Child Psychiat* **1**:269, 1962.
7. Tapia F: Medication of "brain damaged" children. *Dis Nerv Syst* **26**:490-95, 1965.

Children Who Are Cruel to Animals — A Follow-Up Study

JOHN D. RIGDON, M.D. AND FERNANDO TAPIA, M.D.

This paper reports the current status of eighteen children who, from two to nine years earlier, had been admitted to a child psychiatry clinic and in whose cases an important feature was cruelty to animals. An earlier paper (Tapia, 1971) provided brief descriptions of the case of each child which seemed to support the conclusion that cruelty to animals occurs in conjunction with other hostile behavior and that a chaotic home, together with aggressive parent models, was a common etiologic factor.

The purpose of the follow-up study was to assess the degree of improvement, if any, in the child's behavior and to derive suggestions regarding the correlates of differential outcomes. Levy (1969) contended that low I.Q. had a "grim prognostic significance". Nurcombe (1964) attributed causal significance, in cases of another type of hostile behavior (fire setting), to brain damage combined with severe deprivation. Chapman (1965) stated that prolonged psychiatric management was indicated for children who are cruel to animals. In addition to assessing the prognostic significance of variables that investigators believed to be important, we were interested in whether the outcomes suggested the relative effectiveness of various treatment approaches and whether the course and outcome might be related to the social situation. In other words, we wanted to know if the follow-up study would suggest what one could say about prognosis when cruelty to animals was a significant feature of the problem.

Data for the study were obtained by interviews with: (1) the child in his present home; (2) the guardian; (3) the natural parents, if not also the guardians; (4) the employers and/or teachers; (5) the present therapist, if any. The interview dealt with the course of each presenting symptom and the appearance of additional symptoms. Data were also obtained on educational progress, family adjustment, job performance, peer group relations, current treatment, and contacts with police, judicial or correctional authorities. The parents were asked to rate the child's progress from first admission to the present, assigning a rating of one if much improvement had occurred; two, some improvement; three, no change; four, worse; five, much worse.

Five of the original eighteen children could not be located and the adoptive parents would not permit one child to be interviewed. In one case, (number 15), the interview with the parents and child was conducted by telephone. In another case, (number 12), the child was not interviewed because he was out of state, but parents, teachers and the therapist were seen.

The following case histories present a comparison of each patient on first admission and on follow-up. The admission note is quoted from the original article.

Dr. Rigdon is in private practice in Kennett, Missouri. Reprint requests should be sent to Dr. Tapia, Professor of Psychiatry, University of Oklahoma School of Medicine, 800 N. E. 13th Street, Oklahoma City, Oklahoma 73190

Reprinted from the *Journal of Operational Psychiatry* 8, no. 1 (1977): 27–36.

Case Histories

Admission

Case 1: R.H., age 12, was referred because of "mad fits", threatening to shoot his mother and the livestock. He killed small animals which he took to school to frighten the children. He also suffered from enuresis and had regular grand mal seizures. The family history included a father who was considered an ambulatory paranoid schizophrenic with a severe temper. The patient's electroencephalogram was "abnormal and paroxysmal". Full Scale I.Q. was 82, Verbal 76 and Performance 92. Diagnosis: Chronic Brain Syndrome associated with brain trauma, Incipient Childhood Schizophrenia.

Follow-Up

The patient, now age 18, has been in and out of a state mental hospital. He is still cruel to animals and enjoys kicking the family's pet dog and cat. He is impulsively aggressive toward his younger brother and tends to bully him around. Within the past year he has cut up some of his brother's shirts and other personal belongings "because he is so jealous of him". He says that this brother is his mother's favorite. The patient is destructive with belongings of others but takes good care of his own things. He steals from and lies to his family and friends. He has a severe temper, becoming violent when anyone crosses him. He still suffers from enuresis but has had no grand mal seizures for several years and is presently on no medication.

His formal education terminated upon completion of the 5th grade. The only job he has held was a construction job that lasted only three months about one year ago. He spends his days and nights at the local pool hall and so far has stayed out of trouble with the authorities. His mother gives him a rating of 4 (worse). The patient's father and mother are divorced and he lives with his mother.

Admission

Case 2: R.S., age 10, was referred because he was uncontrollable at school, belligerent with children and aggressive with his younger siblings. He was known to be cruel and sadistic with animals including his dogs, cats and pony.

This youngster was short-tempered, defiant and a "notorious liar". His natural father was an abusive, assaultive alcoholic and, at the time, the youngster was obviously being rejected by his step-father. It was noted that when his step-father was away from the home, the boy's behavior improved considerably. No electroencephalogram was done. Full Scale I.Q. was 90, Verbal 93 and Performance 91. Diagnosis: Adjustment Reaction of Childhood, Conduct Disturbance.

Follow-Up

This patient, now age 12, has done well since his natural mother and step-father were divorced. Interestingly, he lives with his step-father who remarried and whose second wife was recently killed in an automobile accident. The patient misses his step-mother very much but is adjusting well to the situation. He has not been cruel to animals recently and does not lie or steal. He gets along well with his teachers and peers at school and is making average grades. He sometimes bullies other children but will not fight them. His step-father stated that "since his real mother left the home he has been a much improved child". He rated him as 1 (much improved).

Case 3 could not be located for follow-up interview.

Admission

Case 4: M.E., age 9, was cruel and obsessed with violence. He was constantly fighting and would use a knife, rock, wrench or anything at hand. Oftentimes he would provoke and threaten to kill children who hadn't even provoked him. At one time he attempted to smother and later to choke his pet dog. He killed two pets at the age of 4½. He once dismembered a frog, then laid it on the sidewalk and ran over it with his bicycle. He was reputedly very destructive and was a known liar. Other symptoms noted in his case were hyperactivity, enuresis, night terrors and tics. This youngster was dramatically helped by Ritalin medication. The home situation was marked by the fact that the mother was a difficult, contentious person who was concluding her third marriage. The father was a known bank robber and constantly had illegal sources of income. At one time the father was jailed for shooting someone. The electroencephalogram was read as "mildly abnormal, showing diffuse slowing and disorganization for the age". I.Q. was 120. Diagnosis: Unsocialized Aggressive Reaction to Childhood.

Follow-Up

This patient, now age 12, continues to be hyperactive and is moderately controlled on 80 mg. Ritalin daily. He is cruel to animals but in a teasing rather than a physical way. He chases them and pulls their ears. This child has not been enuretic for one year and his night terrors have decreased to approximately one per month. He continually fights with his 15-year-old sister and with his peers at school. As a result of this he has no close friends. He gets angry once or twice a day and has several temper tantrums each week. He is impatient with everybody and everything (including animals). The patient is not so destructive as he formerly was but still manages to keep his mother busy keeping the house in order. His mother states that he is "mad" over money and wants excessive amounts all the time. He has stolen money from both his mother and his grandmother. He does not lie as much as he did when he was younger. His mother feels that his interest in the opposite sex is excessive for his age. He has been "in love" with several girls during the last two years.

He will be in the 7th grade and does well in school. His mother rated him as 2 (improved). She stated that he used to cry over minor things and was depressed. He no longer does this and is much happier now. He has no more tics.

He does not respond well to corporal punishment but it is believed that he will benefit from a structured environment. He is leaving his present home with his mother and will be admitted to Boys Town in Missouri.

Case 5 could not be located for follow-up interview.

Admission

Case 6: C.G., age 10, was referred for fighting, lying, stealing, destructiveness and violence. He was frequently cruel to animals and once stabbed a cat and nearly killed it by dismembering it. He was a bedwetter until age 9. The family situation included an alcoholic

father who once attempted suicide. The father was hostile and abusive with the family and indiscreetly tried incest with his 18-year-old daughter. The mother was passive, fearful of her husband and suffered from migraine. The electroencephalogram was normal. Full Scale I.Q. was 70, Verbal 62 and Performance 85. Diagnosis: Nonpsychotic Organic Brain Dysfunction.

Follow-Up

The patient, now age 15, is in a state institution for the educable, mentally retarded. He continues to be hyperactive, lies, steals and has temper tantrums. He is very cruel to animals and kills frogs with scissors. He is enuretic. He still likes to fight and gets into fights with peers often. The hyperactivity and temper are controlled with medication and a structured environment. His father, having been committed by his mother, is now in a state mental hospital. She rated the patient as 1 (much improved). The patient visits home several times a year and does very well. The mother seems to be handling a difficult home situation very well; she has to work to maintain the home and care for five other children.

Admission

Case 7: D.A., age 15, was referred because of stealing, fighting and cruelty to animals — both pets and livestock. Other symptoms were enuresis, "picking his own skin with a knife", excessive interest in sex, indiscreet masturbation, sexually molesting his siblings and making sexual overtures toward his grandmother. The boy was a ferocious and voluminous eater. The home was generally a deprived one. The patient's natural father, an ex-convict, was divorced and the child's step-father (since age 7) was an alcoholic. The mother was of "questionable character and irresponsible". An electroencephalogram was normal. Full Scale I.Q. was 86, Verbal 74 and Performance 90. Diagnosis: Adjustment Reaction of Adolescence.

Follow-Up

The patient, now age 19, has been married for three years and has a two year old son. He is unemployed and his wife works to support the family. He says he cannot work because he has a hernia. He is consistently getting into fights and seems to enjoy it. He has a temper which causes many of the fights. He has an excessive interest in sex and has several girlfriends. Until recently he was living with another woman. He lies to his wife about his affairs but she doesn't believe him. He steals small things like candy bars from the stores but has never been caught. The patient is no longer cruel to animals and gets along well with them. He ceased enuresis at age 18. He is rated as 2 (improved).

Admission

Case 8: D.R., age 10, was distinctly cruel to animals, having tortured turtles and killed a puppy by kicking it. He stole, lied and set fires. He was aggressive toward his siblings. He once broke his sister's arm and tried to drown his brother; another time he was found choking his brother. In school he cut a girl with a piece of metal. The boy suffered many nightmares. The natural mother was emotionally disturbed with repeated institutionalizations. The natural father was an alcoholic and a bully and the step-father rejected the boy. An electroencephalogram was paroxysmal and suggestive of seizure disorders. Full Scale I.Q. was 99, Verbal 91 and Performance 107. Diagnosis: Adjustment Reaction of Childhood.

Follow-Up

This young man, now age 13, is very destructive of the belongings of others and even his own prized possessions. Within the past year he has destroyed a tape recorder, a walkie-talkie, a transistor radio, a watch and a rod and reel. These were Christmas and birthday gifts which lasted for a maximum of 10 days. He is not so cruel to animals as he once was but does still tease dogs. The patient bullies younger children and siblings and likes to pick fights with them. He is easily provoked and pouts when he doesn't get his way. However, he no longer has temper tantrums. He seems nervous and "fidgets around all the time" but is not hyperactive. Recently he has shown an excessive interest in sex and at the age of 12 molested his 6-year-old brother. He no longer has night terrors nor does he set fires.

This patient is now a ward of the court and has been placed in a group home. However, since in the group home he has been in trouble for stealing a B-B gun from a local store. His step-father rates him as 2 (improved) and his step-mother rates him as 1 (much improved). The step-father continues to reject him but the step-mother is much more accepting. Both report that the patient has made great improvement since being placed in the group home.

Cases 9 and 10 could not be located for follow-up interview.

Admission

Case 11: I.B., age 10, was referred because of profanity and being verbally abusive. He was cruel to animals, having crushed the heads of mice with a hammer and fed live birds to his cats. He once ripped an entire collection of tropical fish apart and in temper tantrums at school attacked teachers and classmates. The boy had been born prematurely. The home situation was composed of a very aggressive and tempestuous mother and a mild, dominated father. The electroencephalogram was "diffusely abnormal. Temporal lobe, transient paroxysmal slowing." Full Scale I.Q. was 98, Verbal 82 and Performance 94. Diagnosis: Organic Brain Syndrome with Severe Maladjustment of Childhood (Pre-Schizophrenia).

Follow-Up

This teenager, now age 16, is still hyperactive (on no medication) and hasn't been in school since the 3rd grade. He was expelled at that time and was not allowed to return. He has a temper, gets violently angry at his mother and uses profanity. After a temper tantrum he may pout for hours or days. He is not cruel to animals and hasn't been for many years. He loves the family's cat. He enjoys swimming, fishing, camping and doing odd jobs around town. This patient can neither read nor write but still has friends his own age who seem to accept him. He show no anti-social behavior.

The mother is a very dominant and verbose woman who does not admit that the child has any problems. She blames all problems on others and is unwilling to accept any responsibility for them. The father is quiet and says very little. They rated the patient as 1 (much improved).

Admission

Case 12: J.L., age 7, was referred for beating the family dog repeatedly and for threatening to burn the house. He actually went as far as stashing a can of gasoline for this purpose. He once tried to place a stick in the rectum of a three-year-old girl. He was encopretic and a bed rocker. The father was an alcoholic. The mother, who had been seen in a Child Guidance Clinic during her childhood, seemed relatively well adjusted. The maternal grandmother was called a "pathologic liar". The electroencephalogram was abnormal — "paroxysmal record consistent with a systematic mixed psychomotor and petit mal seizure disorder". The boy had positive soft neurological signs. Full Scale I.Q. was 110, Verbal 116 and Performance 101. Diagnosis: Organic Brain Syndrome of Unknown Etiology.

Follow-Up

This patient, now age 13, is michievous and seems to always be getting into trouble. At the age of 12, he sprayed "Lysol" in the maid's eyes and threw a sharp letter opener at his 8-year-old sister. He also killed a number of fish in a neighbor's aquarium with a rubber band. At age 10, he killed some guinea pigs by puncturing them with an ice pick. Even though he is cruel to many animals he does not mistreat his own dog and rabbit. When he hurts animals he never expresses guilt about it and usually lies about doing it. This teenager is popular at school and was elected class president for one year. He has a violent temper and when provoked throws furniture and uses profanity in fits of rage. He fights and bullies only his 8-year-old, hyperkinetic sister. Within the past year he has stolen cigarettes, money and liquor from his parents. This patient has not set any fires since a small child and no longer soils his pants.

Both father and mother are college graduates but are unable to cope with either their son's problems or their own. Both are receiving family counselling. Their therapist believes the patient is partly reacting to inconsistencies in parental child-rearing practices. The parents rate him as 2 (improved).

Admission

Case 13: J.P., age 12, was referred because of sadistic treatment of animals. He killed his foster mother's prize bantams and pedigreed Siamese cat. He killed chickens and barnyard rabbits and squeezed little chicks. He actually killed pets that were close to him. He continually threatened to kill the foster mother and others. This child seemed to have an obsession with killing. The natural mother was an unstable, tempestuous person who abandoned the patient at the welfare office and later was arrested for forgery. The father, who had received a dishonorable discharge from the service, was an ex-convict and known brawler. The electroencephalogram was borderline with minimal abnormality. Full Scale I.Q. was 83, Verbal 82 and Performance 86. Diagnosis: Passive-Aggressive, Aggressive Personality.

Follow-Up

This teenager, now age 19, completed the 8th grade in school. At the age of 16 he left his foster home and has been working as a farm laborer. He is still cruel to animals and seems to have very little patience with them. He has been known to kick and "take a board" to cattle when they didn't follow his orders. However, he is a likeable kind of guy who is described as being a lot of fun. His foster parents state that he lies all the time and "you can't believe a thing he says." He does not have an excessive temper and never gets into fights. He gets along well with his peers and with his foster parents, brothers and sisters. He seems to be well adjusted to his farm job and likes it. His employer feels he does well as long as he stays away from the animals. His foster parents rate him as 2 (improved).

Case 14 could not be located for follow-up interview.

Admission

Case 15: J.G., age 14, was referred because of sadistic treatment of animals. He once slowly choked a cat to death and another time stuck an ice pick through a dog's head from ear to ear. He was also well known for lying and stealing, restlessness and destructiveness and having a seriously difficult temper. The boy had grand mal seizures early in life, but they stopped at age 2½. He received a serious head trauma at age 6. The home would be considered average to good, although the father was said to have a short temper. The electroencephalogram was "borderline for seizure disorders while resting with hyperventilation, paroxysmal from left interior and left temporal leads. This is a seizure disorder of focal origin." Full Scale I.Q. was 120, Verbal 119 and Performance 117. Diagnosis: Organic Brain Syndrome, Seizure disorders, Idiopathic.

Follow-Up

This patient, now age 23, spent some time at age 16 in a state training school for riding in a stolen car. After a few months he got out and worked as a carpenter for three years. He then spent four months in a county jail for stealing drugs from a pharmaceutical supplier. For the past two years he has been unemployed and his only supply of money is from "pushing" drugs. He uses marijuana, amphetamines, barbiturates and alcohol regularly. He is not a "pusher" or user of heroin. At the time of the follow-up study, this patient had just been discharged from the Federal Hospital for Drug Addicts in Lexington, Kentucky. He had entered on his own because "he was mixed up in the head" and was discharged two weeks later. His parents rate him as 4 (worse) and state that his main problems are drugs, a hot temper and the wrong kind of friends. He has not shown any cruelty to animals.

Admission

Case 16: G.F., age eight, was referred because of his repeated attempts to smother his baby brother and because he burned his sister's arm on purpose. He frequently killed chickens in the barnyard. He was very interested in sex

and masturbated freely. One outstanding note is that he was reputedly "insensitive to pain". The home situation was marked by a promiscuous mother who was careless regarding the primal scene. The father, who was in prison at the time, was an alcoholic and also a cruel person who once tried to run over his own children. That this home could be called a chaotic one is an understatement. The electroencephalogram was "abnormal and markedly paroxysmal, consistent with mixed type of seizure disorder — petit mal predominant." Full Scale I.Q. was 86, Verbal 84 and Performance 106. Diagnosis: Adjustment Reaction of Childhood, Conduct Disturbance.

Follow-Up

For the past 9 years, this patient, now age 17, has been living with loving and concerned foster parents who recently adopted him. He gets along very well with his adoptive parents and his peers. He is honest and doesn't lie or steal. He had had no enuresis since age 9. He does have a temper and gets mad over little things but does not throw temper tantrums any more. He is still cruel to animals and gets angry when they don't do what he wants them to do. At the age of 16 he ran his favorite horse into an iron post because it did not turn when he commanded. This almost cost the animal his leg. This impatience seems to be his only problem. He has set no more fires and does not have any excessive interest in sex. He is adjusting very well at home and at school. Both parents are very proud of him and rate him as 1 (much improved).

Admission

Case 17: D.C., age five, was referred for cruelty to animals, fire setting and excessive curiosity with sex. He was hyperactive. The natural father abused the boy and was known to have a severe temper. The mother suffered a nervous breakdown during pregnancy and the step-father who was rearing the boy was an alcoholic. An electroencephalogram was not done. Neurological examination showed grossly poor motor and visual motor performance. Developmental I.Q. was 51. Diagnosis:

Organic Brain Syndrome, Moderate Mental Retardation.

Follow-Up

This hyperkinetic child, now 7, has been in a good foster home for two years. He is maintained on 15 mg. Ritalin which greatly increases his attention span and "slows him down". Since being in the foster home he has shown no firesetting, cruelty to animals (loves dogs) or abnormal interest in sex. He is not deliberately destructive and is always sorry when he does something wrong. This patient gets along well with others at home and school but is somewhat stigmatized due to a speech defect. He has been seeing a speech pathologist for two years. The other siblings in the family (boy 12 and girls 10) are very accepting of the patient and try to help him. He has much difficulty in school and can't read or write. He needs special education but his school doesn't have it. His foster mother feels that his main problem is hyperactivity and a short attention span. She rates him as 1 (much improved). He is quieter, listens, takes part wholeheartedly in family projects and tries to be part of the family.

Admission

Case 18: K.H., age eight, was cruel to the family's pets, killed a kitten by drowning and smothered a dog in a jar. He was hyperactive and aggressive. He was considered to have a peculiar facial appearance — wide set eyes and broad bridge of the nose. He had hypotonic musculature and a hyperextensibility of the joints. He came from a generally adequate home with several siblings who were all well adjusted. The electroencephalogram was indefinite with mild mixed slow and fast record. Full Scale I.Q. was 63, Verbal 72 and Performance 69. Diagnosis: Mental Retardation, Adjustment Reaction of Childhood.

Follow-Up

This hyperkinetic child, now age 10, is maintained on 5-10 mg. Ritalin each day. This seems to slow him down significantly and increase his attention span. He does not have temper tantrums but does get impatient sometimes and loses his temper. He is not so cruel

with animals as he once was but is still very impatient with them. He is also very impatient with his baby sister when she doesn't do as he wishes. He gets along well with his peers but is having significant educational difficulty at school. He attends a country school with no adequate provisions for special education. He is more destructive than most children his age and enjoys breaking glass bottles with a hammer every chance he gets. He is no longer enuretic. His mother rates him as 2 (improved).

Discussion

Of the 13 cases, all of whom were originally cruel to animals, 8 were still cruel to animals at follow-up (cases 1, 4, 6, 8, 12, 13, 16, 18). (See Table 1). Among those cases in which the children were no longer cruel to animals, several interviewees no longer remembered their original complaint or considered it exaggerated (cases 2, 7, 17). The parents of cases 11 and 15 remembered the original complaint of "cruelty to animals" and stated that it was minimal, considering the child's overall behavior problems. Because this study did not qualify the severity of the cruelty to animals, it is not possible to say whether or not the severity of the cruelty to animals is significant, although the slant of the reports indicate as much.

An interesting but not surprising relationship can be seen between I.Q. and educational achievement. Those who are presently in school and doing well (2, 4, 6, 12, 16) have I.Q.'s of 90, 120, 99, 110 and 86 respectively. Those children who were school dropouts (1, 7, 11, 13, 15) have I.Q.'s of 82, 86, 87, 83 and 120 respectively. Case number 15 with an I.Q. of 120 seems to have diverted his intelligence into the marketing of drugs.

Backgrounds of 11 of the 13 cases showed family discord. Seven of these have parents who are divorced (1, 2, 4, 8, 13, 17). Case number 2 indicated that his condition improved greatly after the divorce. Four additional cases (6, 11, 12, 16) showed extreme family instability. In case number 6 the father is an alcoholic schizophrenic who is a patient in a mental hospital. The mother in case number 11 is a very aggres-

Table I

Follow-Up Study of Children Who Were Cruel to Animals

Reported presence of symptoms on first admission (A) and on follow-up (B)

Case Numbers

Symptom	1 A	1 B	2 A	2 B	4 A	4 B	6 A	6 B	7 A	7 B	8 A	8 B	11 A	11 B	12 A	12 B	13 A	13 B	15 A	15 B	16 A	16 B	17 A	17 B	18 A	18 B	TOTAL A	TOTAL B
Cruelty to Animals	X	X	X		X	X	X	X	X		X	X	X		X	X	X	X	X		X	X	X		X	X	13	8
Bullying and Fighting	X	X	X		X	X	X	X	X	X	X	X									X						7	5
Temper	X	X	X	X	X	X						X	X	X		X			X	X	X	X					6	8
Lying and Stealing	X	X	X		X	X	X	X	X	X	X	X			X			X	X	X		X					8	8
Destructiveness	X				X	X	X	X				X						X								X	3	5
Hyperactivity					X	X	X	X					X	X					X	X			X	X	X	X	6	6
Excessive Interest In Sex						X			X	X		X									X	X					2	4
Night Terrors			X	X							X																2	1
Enuresis	X	X			X		X																				3	1
Fire Setting											X										X		X				3	0
Sadism																	X	X									1	1
Encopresis																	X										1	0

sive and tempestuous woman who dominates a quiet, passive father. The parents of case number 12 are being seen together in therapy for their own personal as well as marital problems. In case number 16 the natural mother has marital problems. In case number 16 the natural mother was reputedly promiscuous and the father an alcoholic with a prison record. Following this child's placement in a foster home, he has made obvious progress. The chaotic background of most of these children is evident; there is a history of mental illness in nine cases and a history of alcoholism in seven of the cases. In four of the homes the father has a prison record. Only two natural homes (cases 15 and 18) are described as good and adequate.

The individual parental ratings indicate that the rating of 3 (same) and 5 (much worse) were never used by any parent or guardian. Only in two cases (1 and 15) was the rating of 4 (worse) used. (See Table II) In both of these cases the original diagnosis was Organic Brain Syndrome and in neither case is the individual presently receiving any medication or treatment. One case (4) overtly refuses therapy and case 15 never sought therapy after the original diagnostic work-up. All the other original diagnostic categories were rated by the parents as 1 or 2, much improved or improved.

The extent and type of treatment varied greatly with the individuals. But in most cases a *change in home environment seemed to be the most effective form of therapy.* Patient 16 showed astounding progress when placed in a good foster home. He did not require any medication nor further inpatient or outpatient treatment. Case number 17 also showed much improvement when placed in a foster home. He is also maintained on 15 mg. Ritalin daily for his hyperactivity. The medication seems to be effective and he is being followed medically. Furthermore, two patients (cases 4 and 8)

Table II
Follow-Up Study of Children Who Were Cruel to Animals
Relationship between Original Diagnosis and
Parental Rating on Follow-Up

Diagnosis	No. of cases out of 13 with Diagnosis of:	Case numbers rated (1, 2) improved	Case numbers rated (3) same	Case numbers rated (4) worse
Organic Brain Syndrome	5	11, 12, 17	0	1, 15
Non-Psychotic O.B.S.	1	6	0	0
Childhood Schizophrenia	1	0	0	1
Adjustment Reaction of Childhood	4	2, 6, 16, 18	0	0
Unsocialized Aggressive Reaction of Childhood	1	4	0	0
Adjustment Reaction of Adolescence	1	7	0	0
Conduct Disturbance	2	2, 16	0	0
Pre-Schizophrenia	1	11	0	0
Passive-Aggressive Personality	1	13	0	0
Seizure Disorder	1	0	0	15
Mental Retardation	1	18	0	0

Key to Rating   3 = same
1 = much improved   4 = worse
2 = improved   5 = much worse

responded well to the structured environment of a group home. Patient number 4 is also maintained on 80 mg. Ritalin daily which is apparently necessary to control his hyperactivity. Case number 6 is responding well in a home for the mentally retarded and his hyperactivity is also controlled with medication. In case number 1, whose mother rated him as 4 (worse), the patient has been in and out of state mental hospitals the past six years. He has been on both major and minor tranquilizers and on seizure medications but is presently taking no medication and receiving no therapy or counselling. At the present time he refuses any medication or therapy and is unable to hold a job. He spends his days loitering around the local pool hall. The only other patient (case 15) whose parents rated him as 4 never received any form of therapy. He was seen initially for diagnostic evaluation but the parents moved out of state and he did not return for any therapy. This boy has been repeatedly in trouble with the law and has been involved in drugs. Case number 18's hyperactivity is controlled with 5-10 mg. Ritalin daily and is being followed at the Rolla Regional Diagnostic Clinic. In the case of patient number 12, the whole family is receiving family therapy and the child is also receiving individual psychotherapy on an outpatient basis. None of the other cases studied (2, 7, 11, 13) received any type of therapy after discharge from the inpatient service.

Table III
Follow-Up Study of Children Who Were Cruel to Animals
Parental rating, years since admission, and age at time of follow-up

Case Numbers	Age at Time of Follow-Up	Age at Admission	Years Since First Admission	Present Parental Rating
1	18	12	6	4
2	12	9	3	1
4	12	9	3	2
6	15	10	5	1
7	19	15	4	2
8	13	10	3	1
11	16	10	6	1
12	13	7	6	2
13	19	12	7	2
15	23	14	9	4
16	17	8	9	1
17	7	5	2	1
18	10	8	2	2

Key to Parental Ratings
1 = much improved
2 = improved
3 = same
4 = worse
5 = much worse

Time alone does not seem to improve the condition. Cases 2, 4, 7, 8, 17 and 18, averaging 2.8 years from admission to rating of outcome had an average rating of 1.5 while cases 1, 6, 11, 12, 13, 15 and 16, averaging 6.8 years from admission to rating of outcome had an average rating of 2.1. The first set of 6 cases had 4 or less years of follow-up time while the second set of 7 cases had 5 or more years of follow-up time.

Conclusions

Thirteen cases out of an original study of eighteen children who were cruel to animals were reviewed on the follow-up. Eight of these 13 children were still cruel to animals from 2 to 9 years after the initial evaluation. Most of these children are the products of a chaotic home situation with aggressive parents who administered harsh corporal punishment. Parental ratings indicated that only two cases were rated as worse and both cases were originally diagnosed

as Organic Brain Syndrome. Time alone did not seem to improve the condition. Low I.Q. did not carry the "grim prognostic significance" that had been noted by Levy (5) in his follow-up study of children treated at Menninger. The most effective form of therapy seemed to be removal from or a significant change in the chaotic home situation.

References

1. Tapia F: Children who are cruel to animals. Child Psychiatry and Human Development, 2(2): 70-77, 1971.
2. Nurcombe B: Children who set fires. Medical Journal of Australia. 1:579-84, 1964.
3. Chapman AH: Management of Emotional Problems of Children and Adolescents. Philadelphia: Lippincott, 1965.
4. Levy EL: Long-Term Follow-Up of Former Inpatients at the Children's Hospital of the Menninger Clinic. Amer J Psychiatry 125: 1633-1639, 1969.

SECTION 4: PSYCHIATRIC AND BIOMEDICAL STUDIES

The papers in this section represent research that ties the issues of cruelty to animals to the psychiatric and biomedical literature on interpersonal violence. The first two papers are by Alan R. Felthous, a pioneer in research on the links between animal maltreatment and human aggression, and focus on a large sample of psychiatric inpatients. The patients, all men, were interviewed about a variety of background family variables as well as their experiences with animal abuse. In the first study, these patients were categorized into aggressive and nonaggressive groups and compared with nonpsychiatric inpatients with urological problems. One of the positive features of this study is its focus on fairly severe forms of animal maltreatment (such as "purposeless slaying" of cats and dogs and injuring and torturing animals) and its inclusion of a nonpsychiatric comparison group. In addition to finding higher rates of killing animals (23 percent) and animal cruelty (18 percent) in the aggressive group, Felthous discovered higher rates of childhood parental brutality for these men. In fact, nearly a third of the aggressive group had experienced blows to the head that resulted in a loss of consciousness. This latter finding is in line with research on violent juveniles, for whom head injuries are common; their violence may be related to varying levels of brain trauma. Severe corporal punishment and paternal alcoholism were also more common in the aggressive group.

In a follow-up study of the aggressive group, Felthous rated the men's histories of violent and aggressive behavior toward people and related these ratings to histories of cruelty to animals. For aggressive men who admitted to hurting animals, the level of interpersonal aggression was clearly associated with a higher frequency of cruelty to cats and dogs. The men who admitted to animal cruelty also had higher rates of setting fires (50 percent) than those who said they had not been cruel (26 percent), but there were no differences in histories of enuresis (bed-wetting) (see section 6 for a discussion of this cluster of symptoms). The entire sample reported high rates of parental brutality, ranging from 60 to 82 percent, by both mothers and fathers.

These studies underscore the association of significant interpersonal violence with histories of animal maltreatment and the role that parental physical abuse may play in the development of both forms of aggression. Felthous ends this paper with a call for research on assaultive females, a group that has received less study.

As in many areas of psychiatry and psychology, questions have been raised here about the roles of nature and nurture, biology and experience, in accounting for individual and group differences in aggression. The papers by Markus J. P. Kruesi and by Graham A. Rogeness and his colleagues suggest that violent behavior, including cruelty to animals, may be associated with neurobiological factors. Kruesi reported on an adolescent girl with a history of animal abuse and a low level of a neurochemical related to aggression, serotonin. In a more extensive study, Rogeness and his colleagues examined children hospitalized in a psychiatric facility for a variety of disorders. They found that levels of a dopamine-related neurochemical were significantly lower for children who had been cruel to animals than for those who had not. The children with lower levels of the neurochemical also had more frequent histories of abuse and neglect.

As noted in the Rogeness essay, regardless of whether these neurobiological factors are the causes and/or consequences of violent behavioral dispositions, information about neurochemical differences could serve to identify individuals with a propensity toward violence to people and to animals. It is clear that we will need to attend to brain-behavior relations as we seek a better understanding of the phenomenon of cruelty to animals, both from the perspectives of identification, diagnosis, and prevention as well as from the perspective of intervention (such as pharmacological therapy as an adjunct to psychological intervention).

Childhood Antecedents of Aggressive Behaviors In Male Psychiatric Patients†

ALAN R. FELTHOUS, M.D.*

Most studies which have investigated the relationship between childhood variables and aggressive behaviors at a later age, selected subjects who were already identified as murderous, violent or aggressive.[1-15] This is a useful and needed method of sample selection which has the advantage of few false positives in the aggressive sample. The disadvantage is that persons whose aggressive deeds went unnoticed are excluded from such samples. Studies which define a nonaggressive control group by absence of charges, convictions, or complaints of violent behaviors run the risk of containing subjects in the control group whose aggressive behaviors were simply not reported.

The present study tried to avoid these methodologic drawbacks by obtaining a careful history of aggressive behaviors before assignment to aggressive and nonaggressive samples. A weakness of this approach is that it is only as reliable as the subjects, but when history is obtained by clinical interview, the investigator can obtain an impression about the subject's reliability.

If comparison of aggressive and nonaggressive samples shows that certain childhood variables correlate with aggressive behaviors at a later age, it should be of interest to determine which of these factors are significant when the aggressive sample is compared with a nonpsychiatric sample. Childhood factors which are significantly associated with the aggressive psychiatric sample in both comparisons may be helpful in understanding the pathogenesis of aggressiveness in psychiatric patients.

Materials and Methods

Subjects consisted of successive admissions over an 11 month period to the Inpatient Psychiatric Service of Naval Regional Medical Center, Oakland, California. From a total of 823 admissions, 429 subjects were interviewed: 346 males and 83 females. The most common reasons for noninclusion were: (1) early discharge; (2) subject confusion or unreliability; and (3) subject refusal. Subjects were not prescreened on the

†This paper was presented at the Annual AAPL Meeting in Baltimore, Maryland, October, 1979.
From the Psychiatry Service, Naval Regional Medical Center, Oakland, California 94627.
This study was supported by funds provided by the Bureau of Medicine and Surgery, Navy Department, for CIP 7-48-932.
The opinions or assertions contained herein are those of the author and are not to be construed as official or as reflecting the views of the Navy Department or the Naval Service at large.
*Dr. Felthous is formerly of the Naval Regional Medical Center, Oakland, and is now Associate Psychiatrist, The Menninger Foundation, Topeka, Kansas 66601.

basis of diagnosis or presence or absence of known violent behavior. The most common diagnoses by admitting physicians were alcoholism, character disorder, situational adjustment reaction, depression, and schizophrenia. Twenty-six nonpsychiatric male subjects on the urology inpatient service were also studied for comparison with the Aggressive Psychiatric Sample. Fortuitously, none of these patients was hospitalized for enuresis or trauma. Informed consent was obtained from all subjects.

All subjects participated in a two-phase evaluation consisting of a clinical interview and questionnaire. The purpose of the interview was to obtain the subject's history of aggressive behaviors. Subjects were asked about past assaults, murders, threats of violence, and use of deadly weapons.

The Aggressive Psychiatric Sample (n=74) consisted of those subjects who gave a history of (1) assaultively injuring someone seriously enough to require medical treatment or dental restoration plus either (2) threatening serious harm against others or (3) carrying a knife or firearm for potential use against others (except for legitimate job requirements). As criteria for the Aggressive Psychiatric Sample, these items needed to be present since 15 years of age in order to exclude the less dangerous threats and assaults of children. Psychiatric subjects who denied a history of any aggressive behavior since 15 years were assigned to the Nonaggressive Psychiatric Sample (n=75). Subjects who gave histories of some aggressive behaviors but did not meet the criteria of the Aggressive Psychiatric Sample, were of intermediate levels of aggression and therefore excluded from this comparative study.

Items on the questionnaire asked about demographic information and childhood factors which were thought to relate to aggressive behaviors at a later age. Questions about childhood variables were multiple choice. Some items should be clarified: Killing dogs or cats denoted purposeless slaying; whereas cruelty referred to injuring and torturing these animals. Destructive firesetting referred to deliberate incineration of useful property or natural resources regardless whether a fire department was summoned. Uncontrolled fires eventuated in suppression by a fire department. Frequent temper tantrums referred to outbursts which occurred often. Violent outbursts, though not necessarily often, involved either assaults on people or destruction of property. Beatings more severe than bottom spankings with an open hand were termed corporal punishments. Meanings of other terms which appear in the tables and text should be evident.

Results

There were no significant demographic differences between the Aggressive Psychiatric Sample and the Nonaggressive Pychiatric Sample. Most were single, white, active duty enlisted men. Educational attainment varied from incompletion of elementary school to graduate degrees, and crested at the level of high school graduation. The 26 male subjects from the Urology Inpatient Service ranged in age from 19 to 65, and, similar to the psychiatric patients, peaked in the 20-24 group. Unlike their psychiatric counterparts, most of the nonpsychiatric subjects were married. In comparison with both Psychiatric Samples, the Nonpsychiatric Sample had more subjects who were over 40 years and more with some college education.

Aggressive and Nonaggressive Psychiatric Patients

Historical items for which deviant responses were at least 5% greater in the Aggressive Psychiatric Sample (APS) than in the Nonaggressive Psychiatric Sample were tabulated. Symptomatic items were ranked in ascending order of the differential percentages in Table 1, environmental items in Table 2. The chi square test showed that most of the early symptomatic items tabulated were significantly associated with aggressive behaviors at a later age; violent outbursts, fights with injury to others, school suspensions, school truancy, frequent headaches, frequent temper tantrums, fights with or without injury to others, setting uncontrolled fire(s), animal cruelty, killing dogs or cats, and enuresis beyond nine years of age.

Environmental items in childhood which were significantly associated with later assaultive behaviors included corporal punishments by mother, head blows by father, alcoholic father, head injury with loss of consciousness, head blows by mother, and corporal punishments by father.

Aggressive Psychiatric Patients and Nonpsychiatric Patients

Symptomatic items for which deviant responses were at least 10% greater in the Aggressive Psychiatric Sample than in the Nonpsychiatric Sample were tabulated (Table 3). Comparison by application of the chi square test showed the APS had a significantly higher incidence of school suspensions, fights with injury to others, school truancy, frequent temper tantrums, violent outbursts, poor peer relationships, frequent headaches, killing dogs or cats, fights with or without injury, and destructive firesetting. Setting uncontrolled fire(s), animal cruelty, and turning in false fire alarms showed a trend toward association with aggressive behaviors (p < 0.10). Poor school work was not significant.

Environmental items which were significantly associated with the Aggressive Psychiatric Sample include unjust punishments by mother, alcoholic father, unjust punishments by father, head blows by father and head injury with loss of consciousness. Aggressive subjects revealed a trend toward a higher incidence of injurious punishments by father (p < 0.10). Corporal punishments (regardless whether injury was inflicted) did not show a significant association.

Discussion

A number of items were significantly associated with the Aggressive Psychiatric Sample in comparison with both the Nonaggressive Psychiatric Sample and the Nonpsychiatric Sample. Symptomatic items which were significant in both statistical comparisons were violent outbursts, fights with injury, fights with or without injury, school suspensions, school truancy, frequent temper tantrums, killing dogs or cats, and frequent headaches. Four symptomatic items — fights with injury, frequent headaches, killing dogs or cats, and school suspensions — may be especially useful in assessing aggressive disorders. None of these items was reported by more than 20 percent of control subjects in either comparison. For each of these items, the percentage of APS subjects who gave a positive history was over two and one-half times that of both control samples.

Even though these items were significantly associated with APS in both comparisons, most were also reported by nonaggressive psychiatric subjects and nonpsychiatric subjects, so they should not be considered as

TABLE 1
SYMPTOMATIC ITEMS OF HIGHER INCIDENCE IN THE AGGRESSIVE PSYCHIATRIC SAMPLE THAN IN THE NONAGGRESSIVE PSYCHIATRIC SAMPLE*

| | Percent of Deviant Responses | | | |
Item	Aggressive Psychiatric Sample (N=74)	Nonaggressive Psychiatric Sample (N=75)	Differential Percentage	p
1. Violent outbursts	63%	21%	42%	0.0005
2. Fights with injury	52%	19%	33%	0.0005
3. School suspensions	43%	12%	31%	0.0005
4. School truancy	68%	39%	29%	0.0005
5. Frequent temper tantrums	82%	56%	26%	0.0005
6. Fights	93%	68%	25%	0.0005
7. Frequent headaches	27%	10%	17%	0.01
8. Uncontrolled fires	26%	10%	16%	0.01
9. Killed dogs or cats	23%	10%	13%	0.025
10. Animal cruelty	18%	5%	13%	0.025
11. Enuresis after 9 years	11%	3%	8%	0.01
12. Destructive fires	16%	10%	6%	n.s.
13. False fire alarms	12%	6%	6%	n.s.

*Items for which deviant responses were at least 5% greater in the Aggressive Psychiatric Sample are tabulated.

TABLE 2
ENVIRONMENTAL ITEMS OF HIGHER INCIDENCE IN THE AGGRESIVE PSYCHIATRIC SAMPLE THAN IN THE NONAGGRESSIVE PSYCHIATRIC SAMPLE*

| | Percentage of Deviant Responses | | | |
Item	Aggressive Psychiatric Sample (N=74)	Nonaggressive Psychiatric Sample (N=75)	Differential Percentage	p
1. Corporal punishment by mother	68%	37%	31%	0.0005
2. Head blows by father	31%	4%	27%	0.0005
3. Alcoholic father	42%	19%	23%	0.0005
4. Corporal punishment by father	76%	55%	21%	0.01
5. Head injury with loss of consciousness	32%	12%	20%	0.0005
6. Head blows by mother	26%	7%	19%	0.0005
7. Injurious punishments by father	12%	5%	7%	n.s.

*Items for which deviant responses were at least 5% greater in the Aggressive Psychiatric Sample are tabulated.

TABLE 3
SYMPTOMATIC ITEMS OF HIGHER INCIDENCE IN THE
AGGRESSIVE PSYCHIATRIC SAMPLE THAN IN THE NONPSYCHIATRIC SAMPLE*

Percentage of Deviant Responses

Item	Aggressive Psychiatric Sample (N=74)	Nonpsychiatric Sample (N=26)	Differential Percentage	p
1. School suspensions	43%	4%	39%	0.0005
2. Fights with injury	52%	15%	37%	0.0005
3. School truancy	68%	42%	26%	0.025
4. Frequent temper tantrums	82%	58%	24%	0.025
5. Violent outbursts	63%	39%	24%	0.050
6. Poor peer relationships	30%	8%	22%	0.025
7. Frequent headaches	27%	8%	19%	0.050
8. Killed dogs or cats	23%	4%	19%	0.050
9. Uncontrolled fire(s)	26%	8%	18%	0.100
10. Destructive firesetting	16%	0%	16%	0.05
11. Fights	93%	77%	15%	0.0005
12. Animal cruelty	18%	4%	14%	0.100
13. False fire alarms	12%	0%	12%	0.100
14. Poor school work	15%	4%	11%	n.s.

*Items for which responses were at least 10% greater in the Aggressive Psychiatric Sample are tabulated.

TABLE 4
ENVIRONMENTAL ITEMS OF HIGHER INCIDENCE IN THE
AGGRESSIVE PSYCHIATRIC SAMPLE THAN IN THE NONPSYCHIATRIC SAMPLE*

Percentage of Deviant Responses

Item	Aggressive Psychiatric Sample (N=74)	Nonpsychiatric Sample (N=26)	Differential Percentage	p
1. Unjust maternal punishments	40%	13%	27%	0.025
2. Alcoholic father	42%	15%	27%	0.025
3. Unjust paternal punishments	46%	20%	26%	0.025
4. Head blows by father	31%	8%	23%	0.025
5. Head injury with loss of consciousness	32%	12%	20%	0.050
6. Corporal punishments by father	76%	60%	16%	n.s.
7. Injurious punishments by father	12%	0%	12%	0.100

*Items for which deviant responses were at least 10% greater in the Aggressive Psychiatric Samples are tabulated.

pathognomonic correlates of aggression. One would expect, however, that a combination of several of these symptoms in a child indicates a burgeoning difficulty in controlling aggressive impulses which could worsen in his adolescent and adult years.

It should not be assumed if items were not significantly associated with APS in both comparisons, they are of no value in assessing disorders of aggression. There is evidence, for example, that the presence of two-thirds of the childhood triad of animal cruelty, destructive firesetting, and persistent enuresis is associated with an assaultive disposition at a later age.[15] Also, an item such as enuresis, which is not significant by itself, may be diagnostically useful when attended by other signs of an aggressive disorder.

Only three environmental items were significantly associated with APS in both comparisons: alcoholic father, head blows by father, and head injury with loss of consciousness. None of these items was reported by more than 20 percent of either control group. All of these items showed at least a two-fold increase in the APS in both comparisons. Head blows by father, reported by only 4% of the nonaggressive psychiatric sample, demonstrated a near eight-fold increase in the APS.

Parental brutality, an etiologic factor in many cases of homicide,[1,2,10,16] and child abuse[17] may also predispose a child toward impulsive, assaultive behaviors in general at a later age. A more specific inference from this study is that the psychological impact (and possibly neurological trauma) from a father's blow to his son's head may predispose him to strike others.

Since psychiatric diagnoses were not investigated in this study, it is not known how much the association of childhood factors with aggressive behaviors varies with the psychopathological setting. Does a history of killing dogs or cats, for example, show a higher correlation with aggressive behavior in an Antisocial Personality Disorder compared with that attending Chronic Paranoid Schizophrenia? Studies of aggressive behaviors subtyped according to psychiatric diagnosis should further our understanding of this complex subject. Nonetheless, a relationship between the following three items will likely prevail regardless of individual psychopathology: (1) How the individual's parents dealt with their aggression, and his, during his formative years, (2) how he handled his aggression as a child, and (3) how he controlled and directed his aggression in adolescence and adulthood.

Acknowledgements

Appreciation is extended to Captain G. A. Conkey, MC, USN, Ret., former Chief of Psychiatry, NRMC, Oakland, California, and to Captain G. A. LeBlanc, MC, USN, Ret., former Chief of Urology Service for their suggestions.

Lolafaye Coyne, Ph.D., Staff Psychologist, The Menninger Foundation, Topeka, Kansas, provided help with statistical methods.

References

1. Duncan GM, Frazier SH, Litwin EM, *et al.*: Etiological factors in first degree murder. JAMA 168:1755-1758, 1958
2. Satten J, Menninger K, Rosen I, *et al.*: Murder without apparent motive: A study in personality disorganization. Am J Psychiatry 117:48-53, 1960
3. MacDonald JM: The threat to kill. Am J Psychiatry 120:125-130, 1963
4. Hellman DS and Blackman N: Enuresis, firesetting and cruelty to animals: A triad predictive of adult crime. Am J Psychiatry 122:1431-1435, 1966
5. Climent CE and Ervin FR: Historical data in the evaluation of violent subjects: A hypothesis generating study. Arch Gen Psychiatry 27:621-624, 1972
6. Climent CE, Rollins A, Ervin FR, *et al.*: Epidemiological studies of woman prisoners, I: Medical and psychiatric variables related to violent behavior. Am J Psychiatry 130:985-990, 1973
7. Justice B, Justice R, and Kraft IA: Early warning signs of violence: Is a triad enough? Am J Psychiatry 131:457-459, 1974
8. Wax DE and Haddox VG: Sexual aberrance in male adolescents manifesting a behavioral triad considered predictive of extreme violence. J Forensic Science 19:102-108, 1974

9. Wax DE and Haddox VG: Enuresis, firesetting, and animal cruelty: A useful danger signal in predicting vulnerability of adolescent males to assaultive behavior. Child Psychiatry Hum Dev 4:151-156, 1974

10. Frazier SH: Murder — single and multiple. Frazier SH (ed): Aggression: Research Publications, Association for Research in Nervous and Mental Disease, Vol. 52. Baltimore, The Williams and Wilkins Company, 1974, p. 304-312

11. Felthous AR and Yudowitz B: Approaching a comparative typology of assaultive female offenders. Psychiatry 40:270-276, 1977

12. Toch H: Violent Men. Chicago, Aldine Publishing Co. 1969

13. Yarvis RM: Psychiatric pathology and social deviance in 25 incarcerated offenders. Arch Gen Psychiatry 26:79-84, 1972

14. Bach-Y-Rita G and Veno A: Habitual violence: A profile of 62 men. Am J Psychiat 131:1015-1017, 1974

15. Felthous AR and Bernard H: Enuresis, firesetting and cruelty to animals: The significance of two-thirds of this triad. J Forensic Science 24:240-246, 1979

16. Miller D and Looney J: The prediction of adolescent homicide: Episodic dyscontrol and dehumanization. Am J Psychoanal 34:187-198, 1975

17. Silver LB, Dublin CC, and Lourie RS: Does violence breed violence? Contributions from a study of the child abuse syndrome. Am J Psychiat 126:404-407, 1969

Aggression Against Cats, Dogs and People

Alan R. Felthous, M.D.
Naval Regional Medical Center, Oakland, California 94627

ABSTRACT: In order to investigate the nature of animal cruelty in childhood two groups of male psychiatric patients were compared: an Animal Cruelty Group and an Assaultive Group. Most in both groups showed other signs of aggression dyscontrol in childhood. Most in both groups were subjected to parental brutality. Emotional or physical unavailability of a father figure may be a common etiologic factor in childhood cruelty to animals. This may compare with the absense of a father figure noted by several investigators in boys who set fires.

Animal cruelty is one of several signs of aggression dyscontrol in childhood [1-8]. Little has been written about animal cruelty per se [9], so knowledge about this behavior is scant. Margaret Mead was apparently the first to suggest that if children torture small animals, this may be an ominous sign of impulsive character development with potential for harming others [8]. There is empirical evidence that in combination with persistent enuresis and firesetting, animal cruelty is part of a behavioral triad in childhood which may be associated with dangerous agression against others at a later age [2-5, 7]. Is cruelty itself associated with assaultive behaviors? Are there significant differences or commonalities between males who in childhood have been cruel to animals and danger-ously assaultive males who deny a history of animal cruelty.

Tapia reported a study of 18 children who were referred for psychiatric treatment in part because they had been cruel to animals [9]. All 18 were males as is the case in the present study. Though females have been reported who had a history of animal cruelty during childhood [6,7,10] most subjects with this history are male [9].

Alan R. Felthous, M.D., is now a staff psychiatrist at the C.F. Menninger Memorial Hospital, Topeka, Kansas.

This study was supported by funds provided by the Bureau of Medicine and Surgery, Navy Department, for CIP 7-48-932. The opinions or assertions contained herein are those of the author and are not to be construed as official or as reflecting the views of the Navy Department or the Naval Service at large.

Reprinted from *Child Psychiatry and Human Development* 10 (1980): 169–77, with kind permission of Plenum Publishing Corporation.

Subject's of Tapia's study showed other aggressive behaviors including destructiveness, bullying, fighting, stealing, firesetting and temper outbursts. He observed associated organic factors in some subjects, environmental factors in some, and a combination of both organic and environmental factors in others. The most common factor was a chaotic home with aggressive parental models. In brief case vignettes, five fathers were described as alcoholic and eight were either physically abusive or given to severe temper outbursts. Since there was no control group in this study, it is hard to draw conclusions specific to animal cruelty. Tapia's findings might apply to children with disorders of aggression in general rather than just those who are cruel to animals.

The present study compared two groups of male psychiatric patients: an Animal Cruelty Group and an Assaultive Group. One purpose of this study was to determine what symptomatic and environmental factors in childhood these two groups have in common. A second objective was to find which factors tend to set these two groups apart. Such information could invite useful hypotheses on the etiology of animal cruelty in childhood and of aggressive behaviors in general.

Method

In a study of 346 male patients admitted to an inpatient psychiatric service (11), each subject was rated according to his level of aggressiveness against people. Data for these determinations were obtained by structured clinical interviews in which subjects were asked about prior aggressive behaviors. The most aggressive level, level 5, these behaviors needed to be present after 15 years of age. Nonagressive enough to require medical or dental treatment and either (b) threatening serious bodily harm or (c) carrying a knife or firearm for use as a weapon. As criterea for level 5, these behaviors needed to be present after 15 years of age. nonaggressive subjects of level 1 gave no history of any of these behaviors. Levels 2, 3 and 4 represent intermediate degrees of aggressiveness.

In the present study, the Assaultive Group (N=53) consisted of all level 5 subjects who denied repetetive cruelty in childhood. Animal Cruelty Group subjects (N=18) gave an history of repeatedly torturing and injuring dogs and cats. Level of aggressiveness was not a factor in assigning subjects to the Animal Cruelty Group.

Subjects in both groups completed a multiple choice questionnarie designed to test childhood variables which were thought to be related to aggressive behaviors at a later age. Whenever a subject responded affirmatively to a question about animal torture or killing, he was asked in interview for more detailed information about these behaviors.

Results

The Animal Cruelty Group was skewed towards higher levels of aggressiveness against people (Table 1). Only one animal cruelty subject gave no history of aggressive behaviors against others after 15. One animal cruelty subject killed another boy in a fight, but since he was only 13 at the time and he successfully vowed never to fight again, his level of aggressiveness was rated low (level 2).

All but one of the 18 animal cruelty subjects tortured cats. The only subject who tortured dogs but not cats showed level 5 aggressiveness against people. All six of the subjects who tortured both cats and dogs belonged to the more aggressive levels, 4 and 5.

Four subjects said they tortured cats by hanging them by the neck until they died. These four belonged to level 5 aggressiveness. Six of the eight who set cats or dogs on fire or injected lit firecrackers per rectum, also gave histories of setting fires which required suppression by a fire department. Other sadistic methods of injury included limb amputation, decapitation, choking, brutal beatings, fracturing bones and scalding with hot water. Three subjects found amusement in tying two cats or dogs by their tails to a clothesline and watching them tear each other apart.

A number of historical items were reported with high incidence in both the Animal Cruelty Group and the Assaultive Group (Table 2). Over 60 percent of subjects in each group gave deviant (positive) responses to items on brutal punishments by father, brutal punishments by mother, temper tantrums, destructive or assaultive outbursts, childhood fights and school truancy.

Table 1

Repetitive Cruelty to Cats or Dogs:
Level of Aggressiveness Against People

Animal Tortured	1	2	3	4	5
Cats only	1	3	2	1	5
Dogs only	0	0	0	0	1
Cats and Dogs	0	0	0	2	3
Cats or Dogs	1	3	2	3	9

Table 2

Historical Items for which more than 60% of Subjects in
Each Group gave Deviant Responses are Tabulated

Percentage of Deviant Responses

	Animal Cruelty Group (N=18)	Assaultive Group (N=53)	Differential Percentage
1. Childhood fighting	83.33	95.75	-12.42
2. Temper Tantrums	83.33	82.44	+0.89
3. Brutal punishments by father	82.35	75.00	+7.35
4. Brutal punishments by mother	72.22	60.27	+11.95
5. Violent outbursts	70.59	63.89	+6.70
6. School truancy	66.67	67.57	-0.90

Childhood factors for which the percentage of deviant responses in the Animal Cruelty Group was at least 12 percent greater than that for the Assaultive Group are presented in Table 3. Items which correlated significantly (chi square test) with the Animal Cruelty Group in comparison with the Assaultive Group were prolonged separation from father figure, alcoholic father figure, and setting uncontrolled fires. Enuresis beyond five years of age, setting destructive fires and poor school work showed a trend towards significance ($p < 0.10$).

Of the items reported by a larger percentage of Assaultive Group in comparison with the Animal Cruelty Group, the differential percentage was greater than 12 percent for two items: unjust punishments by a mother figure and head blows by a father figure.

Discussion

As one might expect, most subjects of the Animal Cruelty Group gave histories compatible with higher levels of aggressiveness against people. There appears to be considerable overlap in populations of male psychiatric patients who have been cruel to animals and those who have assaulted and injured people. Most subjects in both groups showed early signs of impaired modulation of aggression (temper tantrums, destructive

Table 3

Historical Factors for which the percentage of Subjects in the
Animal Cruelty Group who gave Deviant Responses was at least
12% greater than that for the Assaultive Group are Tabulated

Percentage of Deviant Responses

	Animal Cruelty Group (N=18)	Assaultive Group (N=53)	Differential Percentage	x^2 df=1	p
1. Alcoholic father	66.67%	38.89%	27.78%	4.9192	0.050
2. Set uncontrolled fires	50.00	25.68	24.32	4.0766	0.050
3. Enuresis beyond age five	38.89	17.81	21.08	2.9576	0.100
4. Separated from father	38.89	19.18	19.18	6.6143	0.025
5. Set destructive fires	33.33	16.22	17.11	3.6386	0.100
6. Poor school work	27.78	14.86	12.92	2.7795	0.100

or assaultive outbursts and childhood fights). Most in both groups were subjected to brutal punishments by a mother or father figure. It seems that parental brutality may predispose a boy to assault other people, torture pet animals, or both.

Cruelty to Animals and Firesetting

There is evidence for population overlap in boys who set fires and those who are cruel to animals. Tapia found that five of the 18 boys in his study who had been cruel to animals had also set fires and another boy had obtained gasoline for the purpose of burning a house [9]. In other words, nearly one third of the boys in his study who had tortured animals also set fires. In the present study one half of the animal cruelty subjects had set fires and setting uncontrolled fires was significantly associated with the Animal Cruelty Group in comparison with the Assaultive Group.

A number of authors suggest a relationship between sadistic drives or fantasies and childhood firesetting [12-17]. Nurcombe [17] studied 21 boys who had set fires, and of these nine also showed sadistic behaviors towards younger siblings.

Several investigators suggest a relationship between absense of a father figure and firesetting in young boys. In the above mentioned study by Nurcombe, fathers of six of the 21 young firesetters were frequently or permanently separated from the family. Kaufman et al. [18] who studied 30 boys who had set fires, hypothesized that a boy may set fires in order to reunite with both of his parents, but his firesetting is more likely an attempt to bring back his departed father.

Macht and Mack presented case histories of four adolescent boys who had set fires [19]. They suggested that firesetting has multiple determinants. But they observed that each boy started fires only when his father was absent and each boy's father had some involvement with fires. The authors thought that the act of firesetting was intended to recapture a lost relationship with a father figure and to achieve distance from an overpowering mother figure at a time in the boy's development when Oedipal conflicts are resurgent.

Vandersall and Wiener studied 20 children (19 boys and one girl) who had set fires [20]. Absence of a father occurred to some extent "in all the families"."The consistency with which fathers were either completely absent or affectively unavailable was striking". Ten children were completely separated from their fathers for many years.

Deprivation by and separation from father figures, factors thought to be associated with firesetting, are apparently common findings in boys who are cruel to animals. Although Tapia did not distinguish these as separate items, terms in his 18 case vignettes suggest that deprivation by father figures ("alcoholic", "rejected the boy") and separation from father figures ("father was in prison,", "divorced") were common patterns. In the present study "alcoholic father" and "separation from father" showed a significantly higher association with the Animal Cruelty Group in comparison with the Assaultive Group. Actual or emotional unavailability of father figures may then predispose a boy to set fires or injure pet animals.

Projections onto Fire, Cats and Dogs

Piaget [21] theorized,"...a child frightened by the sight of fire, endows the fire with malicious designs..." This is not simply a fear of the essential destructive potential of fire but rather, "a reciprocal sentiment of maliciousness which is projected."

Cats and dogs can likewise be feared or hated by children because of reciprocal hostility or destructiveness which the child projects onto the animal. Cats, more so than dogs, seem to educe a child's sadistic projections and cruel behaviors. The numer of subjects in this study who had tortured cats was nearly triple the number who had tortured dogs. Most who had tortured cats admitted an intense dislike of this animal in particular, but none disclosed any insight into his animosity.

The history of western civilization is rich with examples of cultural persecutions of cats [22,23]. Ailurophobia and cat persecution were especially rampant in mediaeval Europe where people believed these animals were witches' familiars and vessels of the Devil. Even today cat killing is regarded by many as an acceptible if not respectible activity. Although wild canids such as wolves and foxes have been villianized and systematically decimated [24-26], the domestic dog has evidently not been persecuted to the same extent as cats [22,23,27]. This is not to deny that some notable cults and delinquent groups have tortured or killed dogs. Members of the Manson Family reportedly tortured and killed dogs and drank the animals' blood [28]. Such practices however, are apparently limited compared to historic and contemporary persecutions of cats.

Etiology

Physical abuse from a parent can increase a boy's titer of aggression, stimulating sadistic and masochistic fantasies and impulses. A physcially abusive parent becomes an aggressive object for identification and a model for learning aggressive behaviors. The child who is treated like an enemy of the parent is apt to regard himself as evil and to project maliciousness onto others.

Alcoholic father figures and prolonged separations from father figures are significantly associated with childhood cruelty to animals. The presence of an emotionally available, stable father figure provides a boy with an effective model for learning suitable methods of dealing with anger and an object for development of an age/sex appropriate identity. Without a secure identity and ego functions which can handle strong aggressive drives, the boy who has been subjected to parental brutality is especially prone to aggression dyscontrol of a diffuse nature.

Conclusions

Animal cruelty in childhood is often associate with other signs of poor control over aggressive impulses. The present study compared a group of male psychiatric patients who gave a history of animal cruelty with a group of patients who had been dangerously assaultive but denied animal cruelty. Both groups had a high incidence of aggressive behaviors in childhood. In both groups, early aggressiveness may have been due in large part to parental brutality.

Although parental brutality increases a boy's aggressiveness and can therefore be etiologic for both animal cruelty and assaultive behaviors, paternal deprivation may be more specifically related to animal cruelty. Paternal deprivation may be etiologic both in boys who are cruel to animals and in those who set fires. This would underscore the importance of a stable father figure in a boy's developing capacity to control and channel aggressive impulses. Psychodynamic case reports of boys who have been cruel to animals would help to validate, invalidate or elaborate upon this hypothesis. It would also be worth investigating whether girls who are cruel to animals were emotionally deprived by father or mother figures.

References

1. MacDonald JM: The threat to kill. *Am J Psychiatry 120:* 125-130, 1963.
2. Hellman DS, Blackman N: Enuresis, firesetting and cruelty to animals: A triad predictive of adult crime. *Am J Psychiatry 122:* 1431-1435, 1966.
3. Wax DE, Haddox VG: Sexual aberrance in male adolescents manifesting a behavioral triad considered predictive of extreme violence. *J Forens Scienc 19:* 102-108, 1974.
4. Wax DE, Haddox VG: Enuresis, firesetting and animal cruelty: A useful danger signal in predicting vulnerability of adolescent males to assaultive behavior. *Child Psychiatry Hum Dev 4:* 151-156, 1974.
5. Wax DE, Haddox VG: Enuresis, firesetting and animal cruelty in male adolescent delinquents: a triad predictive of violent behavior. *J Psychiatry Law 2:* 45-71, 1974.

6. Felthous AR, Yudowitz B: Approaching a comparative typology of assaultive female offenders. *Psychiatry 40:* 270-276, 1977.

7. Felthous AR, Bernard H: Enuresis, firesetting and cruelty to animals: the significance of two thirds of this triad. *J Forens Scienc 24:* 240-246, 1979.

8. Mead M: Cultural factors in the cause of pathological homicide. *Bull Menninger Clinic 28:* 11-22, 1964.

9. Tapia F: Children who are cruel to animals. *Child Psychiatry Hum Dev 2:* 70-71, 1971.

10. MacDonald M: *The Murderer and His Victim.* Springfield, Illinois: Charles C. Thomas, 1961, p. 262.

11. Felthous AR: Childhoods antecedents of aggressive behaviors in male psychiatric patients (unpublished manuscript).

12. Stekel W. *Peculiarities of Behavior.* New York: Boni and Liveright, 1924, 124-181.

13. Klein M: *Psychoanalysis of Children.* London: Hogarth Press, 1932, pp. 186-187, 240-241.

14. Yarnell H: Firesetting in children. *Am J Orthopsychiatry 10:* 272-286, 1940.

15. Fenichel O: *The Psychoanalytic Theory of Neurosis.* New York: W.W. Norton, 1945, 371-372.

16. Grinstein A: Stages in the development of control of fire. *Int J Psychoanal 33:* 416-420, 1952.

17. Nurcombe B: Children who set fires. *Med J Austral 1:* 579-584, 1964.

18. Kaufman I, Heims LW, Reiser DE: A re-evaluation of the psychodynamics of firesetting. *Am J Orthopsychiatry 22:* 63-72, 1961.

19. Macht LB, Mack JM: The firesetter syndrome. *Psychiatry 31:* 277-288, 1968.

20. Vandersall JA, Wiener JM: Children who set fires. *Arch Gen Psychiatry 22:* 63-71, 1970.

21. Piaget J: *The Child's Conception of the World* (Translated by Joan and Andrew Tomlinson), Totowa, New Jersey: Littlefield, Adams and Co. 1969, p. 35.

22. Dale-green P: *Cult of the Cat.* Boston: The Riverside Press, 1963, pp. 120-130, 137-177.

23. Oldfield M: *The Cat in the Mysteries of Magic and Religion.* New York, Castle Books, 1956.

24. Allen TB: *Vanishing Wildlife of North America.* Washington DC: National Geographic Society, 1974.

25. Lopez BH: *Of Wolves and Men,* New York, Charles Scribner's Sons, 1978.

26. Rue LL: *The World of the Red Fox.* New York: J.B. Lippincott Company, 1969.

27. Dale-Green P: *Lore of the Dog.* Boston: Houghton Mifflin Company, 1966.

28. Sanders E: *The Family.* New York, Avon Books, 1971.

Letter

Cruelty to Animals and CSF 5HIAA

To the Editors:

Serotonergic systems are implicated in aggressive behavior modulation in all mammalian species studied (Albert et al., 1984). Across a number of adult studies, both self- (Åsberg et al., 1986) and other-directed (Brown et al., 1982; Virkkunen et al., 1987) forms of human aggression have been associated with low cerebrospinal fluid (CSF) concentrations of the serotonin metabolite 5-hydroxyindoleacetic acid (5HIAA). Because cruelty to animals is a predictive risk factor for later aggression toward humans (Felthous et al., 1986) and there are few predictive data in children from CSF measures, I report prospective followup of a child with low CSF 5HIAA, who had been cruel to animals.

The Case

A 12-year-old white girl of normal intelligence with conduct disorder has been described in detail earlier because of her carbohydrate craving (Kruesi et al., 1985). She was 155 cm tall, and menarche had just begun. In response to the Diagnostic Interview for Children and Adolescents (DICA) (Herjanic et al., 1982) question, "Have you ever injured or killed a small animal such as a cat or a squirrel just for fun?", the patient answered no. However, she then described having found a baby bird and throwing it in the air repeatedly to watch it attempt to fly, until it died. Parents noted that the child had mistreated her pet hamsters by attempting to cram them into confined spaces (e.g., the interior of toys). Ratings by the child's adoptive mother on the Child Behavior Checklist (Achenbach et al., 1983) were above the 99.9 percentile on the aggressive and cruel subscales. She had no history of suicide gestures or attempts.

CSF was obtained for measurement of concentrations of monoamine metabolites via L4-L5 lumbar puncture. Results in picomoles/ml were as follows: 5HIAA, 50.3; homovanillic acid (HVA), 165.7; and 3-methoxy-4-hydroxyphenylglycol (MHPG), 41.6. The midpoint of the aliquot assayed was 2.5 ml. As noted in the discussion below, this is low for 5HIAA but not for HVA concentration.

On followup 4 years later, the child was being held in a detention center after being arrested for passing bad checks at age 15. Her conduct disorder symptoms had continued and increased in variety. She had a confirmed history of superficially lacerating her wrists, a behavior she had not engaged in when originally seen. She stated she had made other suicidal gestures as well.

Discussion

This adopted female reared in a middle class household, who had a low CSF concentration of 5HIAA and a history of physically cruel behavior toward animals by age 12, has subsequently gone on to self-laceration.

Her 5HIAA is low when compared with 18 other pubertal or older children studied in the same facility (Kruesi et al., 1988). Mean levels for 16 children for the 2.6 ml aliquot were HIAA 82.7 (SD 27.1), HVA 194.6 (SD 72.2), and MHPG 50.6 (SD 12.4). Seven of eight patients who had 5HIAA concentrations close to this subject's were a minimum of 10 cm taller and a minimum of 2 years older. Concentrations of 5HIAA decrease with age in children and adolescents (Riddle et al., 1986; Kruesi et al., 1988). Thus, this patient's 5HIAA concentration would be expected to be higher. The lone child younger and shorter than this case with lower 5HIAA concentra-

Reprinted from *Psychiatry Research* 28 (1989): 115–16, with kind permission from Elsevier Science Ireland Ltd., Bay 15K. Shannon Industrial Estate, Co. Clare, Ireland.

tion had killed his family pet. All seven patients with 5HIAA concentrations close to this patient's values had lower HVA concentrations. This also suggests that the case described above has low 5HIAA, because CSF 5HIAA and HVA concentrations are highly correlated (Riddle et al., 1986).

The present case study suggests that relationships between cruelty to animals and low 5HIAA concentrations warrant further investigation and prospective followup.

References

Achenbach, T., and Edelbrock, C. *Manual for the Child Behavior Checklist and Revised Child Behavior Profile.* Burlington: University of Vermont, 1983.

Albert, D.J., and Walsh, M.L. Neural systems and the inhibitory modulation of agonistic behavior: A comparison of mammalian species. *Neuroscience and Biobehavioral Reviews,* 8:5-24, 1984.

Åsberg, M.; Nordstrom, P.; and Träskman-Bendz, L. CSF studies in suicide: An overview. *Annals of the New York Academy of Sciences,* 487:243-255, 1986.

Brown, G.L.; Ebert, M.H.; Goyer, P.F.; Jimerson, D.C.; Klein, W.J.; Bunney, W.E., Jr.; and Goodwin, F.K. Aggression, suicide and serotonin: Relationships to CSF amine metabolites. *American Journal of Psychiatry,* 139:741-746, 1982.

Felthous, A.R., and Kellert, S.R. Violence against animals and people: Is aggression against living creatures generalized? *Bulletin of the American Academy of Psychiatry and the Law,* 14:55-69, 1986.

Herjanic, B., and Campbell, W. Differentiating psychiatrically disturbed children on the basis of a structured interview. *Journal of Abnormal Child Psychology,* 10:173-189, 1982.

Kruesi, M.J.P.; Linnoila, M.; Rapoport, J.L.; Brown, G.L.; and Petersen, R. Carbohydrate craving, conduct disorder, and low 5-HIAA. *Psychiatry Research,* 16:83-86, 1985.

Kruesi, M.J.P.; Swedo, S.E.; Hamburger, S.D.; Potter, W.Z.; and Rapoport, J.L. Concentration gradient of CSF monoamine metabolites in children and adolescents. *Biological Psychiatry,* 24:507-514, 1988.

Riddle, M.A.; Anderson, G.M.; McIntosh, S.; Harcherik, D.F.; Shaywitz, B.A.; and Cohen, D.J. Cerebrospinal fluid monoamine precursor and metabolite levels in children treated for leukemia: Age and sex effects and individual variability. *Biological Psychiatry,* 21:69-83, 1986.

Virkkunen, M.; Nuutila, A.; Goodwin, F.K.; and Linnoila, M. Cerebrospinal fluid monoamine metabolite levels in male arsonists. *Archives of General Psychiatry,* 44:241-247, 1987.

Markus J.P. Kruesi, M.D.
Child Psychiatry Branch
National Institute of Mental Health
Bldg. 10, Rm. 6N240
9000 Rockville Pike
Bethesda, MD 20892, USA

Received May 9, 1988; revised August 24, 1988.

Clinical Characteristics of Emotionally Disturbed Boys with Very Low Activities of Dopamine-β-hydroxylase

GRAHAM A. ROGENESS, M.D. JOSE M. HERNANDEZ, M.D., CARLOS A. MACEDO, M.D., ELIZABETH L. MITCHELL, M.D., SUCHAKORN A. AMRUNG, M.D., AND WILLIAM R. HARRIS, M.D.

Twenty boys with very low levels of plasma dopamine-β-hydroxylase (DβH) are compared to 20 boys with plasma DβH greater than 15 μM/min/L. All 40 had been hospitalized in a children's psychiatric hospital. We report an association between zero DβH and a cluster of symptoms, and the diagnoses of conduct disorder, undersocialized, and borderline personality disorder. The association between zero DβH and the group of symptoms is strong enough to suggest a direct relationship between the clinical picture and very low activities of DβH. The triad of firesetting, enuresis, and cruelty to animals frequently appears to be associated with zero DβH. Interestingly, there were significantly more cases of neglect or abuse in the zero DβH group.

Journal of the American Academy of Child Psychiatry, 23, 1:203–208, 1984.

Dopamine-β-hydroxylase (DβH) is an enzyme involved in the conversion of dopamine to norepinephrine. Its activity in plasma is genetically determined and is constant over time from about age 6 (Ciaranello and Boehme, 1981; Weinshilboum et al., 1973). It is unclear as to whether or not its activity in plasma relates to noradrenergic activity, either peripherally or centrally (Rush and Geffen, 1980). A deficiency of DβH would be relevant to the dopamine hypothesis of schizophrenia or the norepinephrine hypothesis of depression since deficient DβH could theoretically result in either excess dopamine or deficient norepinephrine being produced. Clinical studies to test these possibilities have been inconsistent. Studies in adult psychiatric disorders show significantly lower DβH activities in schizophrenics (Book et al., 1978; Fujita et al., 1978) or no differences (DeLisi et al., 1981; Dunner et al., 1973; Meltzer et al., 1976; Ross et al., 1981). DβH activities in major depressive disorders and bipolar disorders have been found to be higher, lower, and not different than comparison populations (Leckman, 1977; Markianos et al., 1976; Meltzer et al., 1976; Strandman et al., 1978; Wetterberg et al., 1972). Several studies in children's psychiatric disorders have shown either lower or no difference in DβH activities in autistic children (Lake et al., 1977, Young et al., 1980), elevated DβH activities in functional psychosis (Belmaker et al., 1978), and either no difference or elevated activities in children with attention deficit disorder (Mikkelsen et al., 1981; Rapoport et al., 1974).

The inconsistencies shown in these studies can be due in part to the marked interindividual variation in DβH activities as well as a lack of homogeneity in the diagnostic groups. Two studies correlating DβH activities with MMPI scores were consistent with each other. Winter et al. (1978) studied a non-patient population and Major et al. (1980) studied patients in an alcoholic treatment program. They both showed that elevated scores on the psychopathic deviant and schizophrenia scales were negatively correlated with DβH activities. In the study by Major et al., 10 of 11 patients with a diagnosis of personality disorder were in the low DβH group.

If DβH activities relate to personality factors as suggested by the studies of Winter et al. (1978) and Major et al. (1980), the chances of finding consistent differences in DβH activities in the major psychiatric disorders may not be great since it is possible to have a range of personality traits in both the major diagnostic groups and the comparison groups. In addition, a tendency toward psychotic decompensation and DβH activities could occur and not correlate directly with the major psychiatric disorders. Major et al. (1979) found that alcoholics who had psychotic reactions when treated with disulfiram had significantly lower cerebrospinal fluid DβH.

In a recent study we reported that children with

Dr. Rogeness is Clinical Associate Professor and Dr. Hernandez, Dr. Macedo, Dr. Mitchell, Dr. Amrung, and Dr. Harris are Clinical Assistant Professors of Psychiatry in the Division of Child and Adolescent Psychiatry at The University of Texas Health Science Center at San Antonio and Child Psychiatrists at San Antonio Children's Center.

Reprints may be requested from Dr. Rogeness, The University of Texas Health Science Center at San Antonio, Department of Psychiatry, 7703 Floyd Curl Drive, San Antonio, TX 78284.

This work was supported by grants from the Meadows Foundation, Ewing Halsell Foundation, the Mary Yates Fund, and an Institutional Grant from The University of Texas Health Science Center at San Antonio, Texas.

The authors thank Ms. Natalee Shelton and Ms. Rosa De Luna for their technical assistance.

conduct disorder, undersocialized (CDU), had significantly lower plasma DβH activities than children with conduct disorder, socialized, and a comparison group (Rogeness et al., 1982). Children with CDU are at risk for significant psychopathology, especially personality disorders, as adults (Robins, 1966) so this finding is consistent with the MMPI-DβH correlations found by Winter et al. (1978) and Major et al. (1980). There were 18 children diagnosed with CDU in our study (Rogeness et al., 1982), 6 of whom had very low levels of plasma DβH, activities less than 2 μM/min/L plasma. Weinshilboum et al. (1973) reported that about 5% of a normal population have very low plasma DβH activities. Young et al. (1980) found 6.5% of their normal population to have this low level. We observed that children with this very low level of DβH in our inpatient population had symptoms in common and were some of our more difficult and more aggressive patients.

In order to determine if DβH activities relate to a specific pattern of psychopathology, we devised a study comparing 20 emotionally disturbed boys with DβH values less than or equal to 2 μM/min/L plasma with 20 emotionally disturbed boys with DβH values greater than 15 μM/min/L. Most of the boys in the low DβH group had measured values of zero, and in this paper we will refer to this group as the zero DβH group. The children in this study had all had psychiatric disorders severe enough to cause their hospitalization in a children's psychiatric hospital. The strategy of comparing those with a possible enzyme disorder to those without a disorder is a method discussed by Buchsbaum and Rieder (1979). This strategy may show results that are obscured when two diagnostic groups are compared because a diagnostic group may not be homogeneous.

In comparing the zero DβH group with the comparison group we are attempting to show that there is a cluster of symptoms associated with zero DβH and that this group of patients is more disturbed and more aggressive than the comparison group. The clustering of diagnostic groups and symptoms with zero DβH shown in this paper suggests a direct relationship between zero DβH and the clinical picture. An additional surprising finding was an association with zero DβH and abuse and neglect in this hospitalized population.

Method

Subjects

Subjects were selected from children hospitalized at a private, not for profit, children's psychiatric hospital. The hospital serves children 16 and below and is the only psychiatric hospital in the area serving children 12 and under. Public as well as private funds are available to hospitalize children 12 and under and the majority of the children served by our hospital are 12 and under. Participants were those on whom written informed consent was obtained after the experimental procedures were fully explained.

All boys who had a DβH value less than or equal to 2 μM/min/L were the study group. There were 22 boys who met this criterion. This was about 10% of the boys on whom we measured DβH. Two were excluded because of their age—5 years—and mild mental retardation. They did, however, fit into the general pattern described in this paper. One of the two had a history of firesetting and threatening behavior toward a parent and the other had been excluded from nursery school for choking peers.

Each boy in the zero group was matched with a boy who was admitted nearest to him in time who met the criteria of having a DβH activity greater than 15 μM/min/L, had a similar IQ, and was within 1 year of age. This resulted in 2 groups of 20 matched for age and IQ. The range in age of the 2 groups was from 6 to 16 years with a mean age of 11.4 for the zero group and 11.2 for the comparison group. Fifteen in each group were 12 or younger. The mean full scale IQ for the zero group was 95 and 94 for the comparison group. Racially, the zero group contained 12 Anglo, 1 Anglo-Asian, 5 Mexican-American, and 2 black patients. The comparison group contained 14 Anglo, 5 Mexican-American, and 1 black patient. The varied makeup of these two groups reflects the racial mix of our hospitalized population and the geographic area from which we draw.

Dopamine-β-Hydroxylase Measurement

Blood for DβH was drawn into tubes containing sodium heparin (143 IU) as the anticoagulant before breakfast between 7:30 and 8:30 a.m. at the same time that the admission blood work was obtained. This was within 1 to 4 days after admission. The blood was placed on ice immediately after it had been drawn and the plasma was prepared and frozen within 2 hours of being drawn. Plasma DβH was measured photometrically by the method described by Nagatsu and Udenfriend (1972). An internal standard was run each time one of the above assays was conducted to ensure consistency of the method over time. The measurement of DβH was stable over time on a given individual. Twenty subjects who had a repeat DβH analysis weeks to as long as a year later showed a high correlation between the first and second measurement of r = 0.97. Seven in the zero group had 2 or more DβH determinations for a total of 19 separate determinations. Some were more than a year apart. The repeat determinations were all 2 μM/min/L or less whether or not the subject was on medication on one occasion and off on another.

Five in the zero group were on medication at the time the blood was drawn: imipramine, haloperidol, thioridazine, methylphenidate and chlorpromazine, thioridazine and phenytoin; and three in the comparison group; two on thioridazine and one on trifluoperazine. The rest were drug free for at least 2 weeks. The eight on medication are being included in the data analysis since medication effects reported in the literature and observed by us would have no significant effects on the two groups. Fujita et al. (1978) reported no significant effects of neuroleptics on plasma DβH activities but DeLisi et al. (1981) found a 27% decrease in activity in those of neuroleptics. Rapoport et al. (1974) found that methylphenidate and imipramine increased DβH activities. If neuroleptics lowered DβH activities by 50%, the one child in the zero group who was on medication and had a value of 2 μM/min/L would have had a value of at most 4 without medication. The other 4 on medication had values of zero. If medication lowered the DβH values in the comparison group it would make no difference since the criterion for being in this group is having a DβH value greater than 15 μM/min/L.

Clinical Data

The patients were diagnosed according to DSM-III criteria by the authors. The diagnosis was determined from a history provided by the child, his family, referral sources and school, direct evaluation of the child, and observation of the child in the hospital. The diagnoses used in this study were assigned after the 2-week evaluation process had been completed. Often more than one diagnosis was given to a child. In addition to the diagnosis, the psychiatrist rated the child's relationship capacity by the DSM-III criteria used to differentiate the socialized from the undersocialized conduct disorder.

A data form was prepared for use in abstracting data from the chart. The purpose of the data form was to obtain additional data, separate from the psychiatrist's diagnoses, that might show clustering of symptoms in the zero group and reveal data consistent with the psychiatric diagnoses. The data recorded included items related to aggressiveness and psychiatric functioning, family data, number of hospitalizations, number of days spent in a psychiatric hospital, and medication on discharge. It was our impression that the zero DβH child was more aggressive and more difficult to treat. The medication on discharge, and length and number of hospitalizations were used as one way of determining severity and chronicity of the disorder.

The technician running the DβH assay was blind to the clinical data. The psychiatrists and clinicians recording the clinical data and treating the patients were blind to the biochemical data. A research assistant was hired to abstract the data from the chart using the data form. This was done after the child had been discharged from the hospital. The research assistant was blind to which group the child was in. The data on all 40 subjects were abstracted by the same individual.

Results

Diagnoses

Table 1 shows the diagnoses in the two groups. Fourteen of 20 in the zero DβH group had axis I diagnoses of CDU and 4 had a diagnoses of schizophrenia. Three of the 4 with a schizophrenic diagnosis were similar to the conduct disorder group and met DSM-III criteria for CDU had they not been schizophrenic. Two of the 3 had firesetting behavior and all 3 had a history of cruelty to animals. The individual with schizophrenia who did not have the pattern had the onset of schizophrenic symptoms at age 15. The 14 with CDU and the 3 with schizophrenia and CDU symptoms all had the onset of significant behavioral symptoms before age 6. Therefore 17 of 20 children with zero DβH were similar in that they met the symptom criteria of CDU and had the onset of problems before age 6. The comparison group, in contrast, did not have a similar clustering of diagnostic groups, except for 7 with a diagnosis of conduct disorder, socialized. Seven in the zero group and 5 in the com-

TABLE 1

Diagnoses for Groups

Primary Diagnoses	Dopamine-β-hydroxylase	
	≤2 μM/ min/L (N = 20)	>15 μM/ min/L (N = 20)
Axis I		
Schizophrenia	4	3
Conduct Disorder, undersocialized	14[a]	1
Conduct Disorder, socialized		7[a]
Major Depression	1	1
Dysthymic Disorder	1	1
Atypical Psychosis		1
Overanxious Disorder		2
Intermittent Explosive Disorder		1
Atypical Dissociative Disorder		1
Axis II		
Borderline Personality Disorder	8[a]	1
Narcissistic Personality Disorder		1
Paranoid Personality Disorder	1	
Schizotypal Personality Disorder	1	

[a] Groups significantly different *p* < 0.05 or better. Chi square test of significance.

parison group had the secondary axis I diagnosis of attention deficit disorder.

More severe psychopathology in the zero group is indicated by the axis II diagnoses. In the zero group, 10 were given personality disorder diagnoses compared to 2 in the comparison group. In those not diagnosed as schizophrenic, 6 in the zero group and 1 in the comparison group had reports in the chart of psychotic episodes (Table 2). The presence of psychotic episodes and the severe impulse control problems (Table 2) are consistent with the borderline personality diagnoses.

In summary, the zero group differed from the comparison group in two ways: (1) 85% of the zero group had a symptom pattern consistent with CDU, and (2) of the 16 in the zero group who did not have a diagnoses of schizophrenia, 10 had a diagnosis of personality disorder compared to 2 of 17 in the comparison group. The personality diagnoses in the zero group reflected the more pervasive psychopathology and more impaired reality testing in the zero group.

Data Extracted from the Charts

Table 2 shows the presence of certain symptoms in the two groups to determine if the clinical record showed a qualitative difference in symptom picture between them. The severity of the symptoms was not rated. For example, 6 of the 8 children with firesetting in the zero group had set fires causing damage, compared to 1 of 3 in the comparison group. The other

two episodes in the comparison group involved single episodes of setting a fire outside that did no damage, i.e. setting a fire inside a garbage can.

Aggression toward peers was high in both groups, reflecting that severe conduct problems are what usually cause admission of a child to a psychiatric facility. The zero group showed more firesetting behavior, cruelty to animals, and dangerous aggressive behavior. If one looks at the number of children in each group with at least two of the following severe aggressive behaviors, the differences between the two groups becomes more evident. Twelve of the zero group compared to 4 of the comparison group evidenced at least two of the following kinds of behavior: homicidal ideation or threats, threatening others with a knife or gun, threatening behavior toward a parent, cruelty toward animals, and firesetting behavior. At least 2 children were placed on assaultive precautions while an inpatient.

Seventy-five percent of the zero group were rated as having moderate to severe impulse control problems on psychological evaluation. In the zero group 90% showed an impaired ability to relate to others.

We hypothesized that the zero group might have more severe psychopathology as a result of more family psychopathology (Table 3). There was no apparent difference in family psychopathology between the two groups. Interestingly, 11 in the zero group had a history of neglect or abuse, compared to 3 in the comparison group.

Table 4 shows that the zero group had more psychiatric hospitalizations and had spent more days in the hospital, consistent with more severe psychopathology in the zero group.

Nineteen of 20 in the zero DβH group were discharged on medication, compared to 8 of 20 in the comparison group. The one in the zero group who was

TABLE 2
Psychopathology[a]

Clinical Data	Dopamine-β-hydroxylase	
	$\leq 2\ \mu M/$ min/L $(N = 20)$	$>15\ \mu M/$ min/L $(N = 20)$
Homicidal ideation threats	8	5
Threatening others with a knife or gun	6	2
Threatening behavior toward a parent	7	4
Cruel toward animals	5[b]	0
Firesetting behavior	8	3
Placed on assaultive precautions	8	5
Has 2 or more of the above items	12[b]	4
Physically cruel toward others	18	16
Verbally abusive toward others	11	9
History of enuresis	8	6
Psychotic episodes in those not diagnosed schizophrenic	6[b]	1
Psychologicals show		
1. Moderate impulse control problems	7	7
2. Severe impulse control problems	8	2
Failure to establish a normal degree of relatedness to others (psychiatrist's assessment)	18[b]	3

[a] Data abstracted from the clinical record following discharge.

[b] Groups significantly different, $p < 0.05$ or better. Chi square test of significance.

TABLE 3
Family Data[a]

Data	Dopamine-β-hydroxylase	
	$\leq \mu M/min/$ L $(N = 20)$	$>15\ \mu M/$ min/L Non-zero $(N = 20)$
Adopted	3	1
No reported family mental illness (nuclear or extended family)	5	5
Mother or father with mental illness	13	14
Father and mother with mental illness	5	4
Family situation is moderately to severely disruptive	14	14
History of neglect or abuse	11[b]	3

[a] Data abstracted from the clinical record following discharge.

[b] Groups significantly different $\chi^2_{(1)} = 7.03$, $p < 0.01$.

TABLE 4
Hospitalization and Discharge Data[a]

	Dopamine-β-hydroxylase	
	≤2 μM/min/L Zero (N = 20)	>15 μM/min/L (N = 20)
Hospitalization		
Total number of hospitalizations	41[b]	27
Mean days in the hospital	198	100
Median days in the hospital	96	58
Psychotropic Medications on Discharge		
Discharged on medication	19[b]	8
Neuroleptic alone	7	6
Methylphenidate	2	0
Neuroleptic plus methylphenidate	5[b]	0
Imipramine	5	2

[a] Data abstracted from the clinical chart following discharge.
[b] Groups significantly different, $p < 0.05$ or better. Chi square test of significance.

not on medication had signed out against medical advice after 2 weeks in the hospital. A review of 100 consecutive discharges from our hospital showed that 47 out of 100 were discharged on medication. This figure is similar to the percent in the comparison group. Ninety-five percent were discharged on medication, and a pattern appeared to be developing in the type of medication that was used. There was no difference between the use of neuroleptics alone in each group. However, 7 in the zero group were on methylphenidate, alone or in combination with a neuroleptic, and 5 were on imipramine.

Discussion

The results show that the zero DβH group has more severe psychopathology than the comparison group, and that the patients in the zero group have a clinical picture that is similar enough to suggest a direct relationship between zero DβH and the symptom picture. The symptom picture has many components of the attention deficit disorder syndrome, and if one viewed it as a subgroup of attention deficit disorder, it would fall into the poorer prognosis, aggressive subgroup defined by Langhorne and Loney (1979). However, this would not account for the presence of the borderline psychotic functioning in this group. The children with zero DβH sound similar to the clinical description of a latency age group of firesetters described by Kaufman and Heims (1961) and to the clinical descriptions of children with the triad of enuresis, firesetting, and cruelty to animals (Felthous and Bernard, 1979; Hellman and Blackman 1966; Wax and Haddox 1974). It is possible that many of the children described in these studies would fall into the zero DβH group.

The increase in child abuse in the zero group is interesting. There are several possibilities for this relationship. The most probable is that the child has a very difficult temperament from an early age. For example, one parent who had not abused her child had called protective services for help because she was afraid she would lose control and abuse her child. When such a child is in a family with limited coping skills, his abuse risk goes way up. The abuse reinforces the difficult behavior and a vicious cycle is started. Another less likely possibility is that the abuse affects the noradrenergic system in some developing infants and children and the normal increase in plasma DβH activity that occurs during the first 6 years of life does not occur.

The meaning of very low levels of plasma DβH as it exists in the zero DβH group is unclear. In addition to those with the zero DβH described in this paper, a small percentage of normal individuals have zero DβH. Since plasma DβH activities are genetically determined, an association with zero DβH and a specific group of symptoms may be associated with the genetics of zero DβH and not the biochemistry of DβH. An association between zero plasma DβH and a relative deficiency of brain DβH seems to be the more interesting possibility.

If the symptoms are related to a deficiency of central nervous system DβH, several possibilities exist. The normal group with zero DβH may have adequate compensatory mechanisms, zero DβH may be associated with a CNS deficiency in the patient group but not in the normal group, a second neurophysiologic disorder such as that causing attention deficit disorder must also be present in order for the symptoms to become manifest, or the symptoms only occur in vulnerable individuals when they are subjected to a traumatic environment in their early years of life.

Significantly more of the boys in the zero DβH group were treated with psychotropic medications than those in the comparison group. This is consistent with the zero group being less responsive to the environmental change and structure that exists in an inpatient service and is consistent with the zero group having a neurophysiologic basis to their disorder. The increased use of methylphenidate and imipramine in this group is interesting, especially the combination of methylphenidate and a phenothiazine. In several of the patients, this combination was arrived at after a variety of medications, including lithium, had been tried and had proven unsuccessful. Methylphenidate alone and a neuroleptic alone had also been unsuccessful. Three patients who could not be maintained outside the hospital for extended periods of time were able to function outside the hospital on a combination of methylphenidate and chlorpromazine. In retrospect, several of the children who were discharged on methylphenidate alone or a neuroleptic alone may have done better on the combination, but it was not considered at the time. Methylphenidate has both dopaminergic and noradrenergic stimulating effects and chlorpromazine has both dopaminergic and noradrenergic blocking effects. It is possible that the combination somehow acts to decrease an imbalance caused by a DβH deficiency and thereby helps the child improve his functioning. Imipramine may also act in a similar manner through its dopaminergic, noradrenergic and serotoninergic effects. The proven efficacy of these medications in the zero DβH group needs to be determined in future studies.

The implications of a specific group of symptoms associated with zero DβH are many. It may help us diagnose a subgroup of conduct disorders, understand the biochemistry of certain behavioral disorders of children, and develop earlier and more effective interventions. Further studies will clarify these issues.

References

BELMAKER, R. H., HATTAB, J. & EBSTEIN, R. P. (1978), Plasma dopamine-β-hydroxylase in childhood psychosis. *J. Aut. Child. Schizo.*, 8:293–298.

BOOK, J. A., WETTERBERG, L. & MODRYENSKI, K. (1978), Schizophrenia in a North Swedish geographical isolate, 1900–1977. Epidemiology, genetics and biochemistry. *Clin. Genet.*, 14:373–394.

BUCHSBAUM, M. S. & RIEDER, R. O. (1979), Biologic heterogeneity and psychiatric research. *Arch. Gen. Psychiat.*, 36:1163–1169.

CIARANELLO, R. D. & BOEHME, R. E. (1981), Biochemical genetics of neurotransmitter enzymes and receptors: relationships to schizophrenia and other major psychiatric disorders. *Clin. Genet.*, 19:358–372.

DELISI, L. E., PHELPS, B. H., WISE, C. D., APOSTOLES, P. S., BIGELOW, L. & WYATT, R. J. (1981), An effect of neuroleptic medication on plasma dopamine-β-hydroxylase activity. *Biol. Psychiat.*, 16:873–878.

DUNNER, D. L., COHN, C. K., WEINSHILBOUM, R. M. & WYATT, R. J. (1973), The activity of dopamine-β-hydroxylase and methionine-activating enzyme in blood of schizophrenic patients. *Biol. Psychiat.*, 6:215–220.

FELTHOUS, A. R. & BERNARD, H. (1979), Enuresis, firesetting, and cruelty to animals: the significance of two-thirds of the triad. *J. Forensic Sci.*, 24:240–246.

FUJITA, K., ITO, T., MARUTA, K., TERADAIRE, R., BEPPU, H., NAKAGAMI, Y. & KATO, Y. (1978), Serum DβH in schizophrenic patients. *J. Neurochem.*, 30:1569–1572.

HELLMAN, D. S. & BLACKMAN, H. (1966), Enuresis, firesetting and cruelty to animals. *Amer. J. Psychiat.*, 122:1431–1435.

KAUFMAN, I. & HEIMS, L. W. (1961), A re-evaluation of the psychodynamics of firesetting. *Amer. J. Orthopsychiat.*, 31:123–136.

LAKE, C. R., ZIEGLER, M. G. & MURPHY, D. L. (1977), Increased norepinephrine levels and decreased dopamine-β-hydroxylase activity in primary autism. *Arch. Gen. Psychiat.*, 34:553–556.

LANGHORNE, J. E. JR. & LONEY, J. (1979), A four-fold model for subgrouping the hyperkinetic/MBD syndrome. *Child Psychiat. Hum. Develpm.*, 9:153–159.

LECKMAN, J. F., GERSHON, E. S., NICHOLS, A. S. & MURPHY, D. S. (1977), Reduced MAO activity in first-degree relatives of individuals with bipolar affective disorders. *Arch. Gen. Psychiat.* 34:601–606.

MAJOR, L. F., LERNER, P., BALLENGER, J. C., BROWN, G. L., GOODWIN, F. K. & LOVENBERG, W. (1979), DβH in the CSF: relationship to disulfiram-induced psychosis. *Biol. Psychiat.*, 14:337–344.

—— ——, GOODWIN, F. K., BALLENGER, J. C., BROWN, G. L. & LOVENBERG, W. (1980), DβH in CSF: relationship to personality measures. *Arch. Gen. Psychiat.*, 37:308–310.

MARKIANOS, E. S., NYSTREM, I., REICHEL, H. & MATUSSEK, H. (1976), Serum dopamine-β-hydroxylase in psychiatric patients and normals: Effect of *d*-amphetamine and haloperidol. *Psychopharmacology*, 50:259–267.

MELTZER, H. Y., CHO, H. W. & CARROLL, P. J., RUSSO, P. (1976), DβH activity in the affective psychosis and schizophrenic. *Arch. Gen. Psychiat.*, 33:585–591.

MIKKELSEN, E., LAKE, C. R., BROWN, G. L., ZIEGLER, M. G. & EBERT, M. H. (1981), The hyperactive child syndrome: peripheral sympathetic nervous system function and the effect of amphetamine. *Psychiat. Res.*, 4:157–169.

NAGATSU, T. & UDENFRIEND, S. (1972), Photometric assay of dopamine-β-hydroxylase activity in human blood. *Clinical Chemistry*, 18:980–983.

RAPOPORT, J., QUINN, P. & LAMPRECHT, F. (1974), Minor physical anomalies and plasma dopamine-beta-hydroxylase activity in hyperactive boys. *Amer. J. Psychiat.*, 131:386–390.

ROBINS, L. N. (1966), *Deviant Children Grown Up*. Baltimore: Williams & Wilkins.

ROGENESS, G. A., HERNANDEZ, J. M., MACEDO, C. A., MITCHELL, E. L. (1982), Biochemical differences in children with conduct disorder socialized and undersocialized. *Amer. J. Psychiat.*, 139:307–311.

ROSS, S. B., BOOK, J. A. & WETTERBERG, L. (1981), Plasma dopamine-β-hydroxylase activity in a North Swedish isolate with a high frequency of schizophrenia. *Clin. Genet.*, 19:415–426.

RUSH, R. A. & GEFFEN, L. B. (1980), Dopamine-β-hydroxylase in health and disease. *CRC Crit. Rev. Clin. Lab. Sci.*, 12:241–277.

STRANDMAN, E., WETTERBERG, L., PERRIS, C. & ROSS, S. B. (1978), Serum dopamine-β-hydroxylase in affective disorders. *Neuropsychobiology*, 4:248–255.

WAX, D. E. & HADDOX, V. G. (1974), Enuresis, firesetting, and animal cruelty: A useful signal in predicting vulnerability of adolescent males to assaultive behavior. *Child Psychiat. Hum. Develpm.*, 4:151–156.

WEINSHILBOUM, R. M., RAYMOND, F. A., ELVEBACK, L. R. & WEIDMAN, W. H. (1973), Serum DβH activity: sibling-sibling correlation. *Science*, 181:943–945.

WETTERBERG, L., ABERG, H., ROSS, S. B. & FRODEN, O. (1972), Plasma-β-hydroxylase activity in hypertension and various neuropsychiatric disorders. *Scand. J. Clin. Lab. Invest.*, 30:283–289.

WINTER, H., HERCHEL, M., PROPPING, P., FRIEDL, W. & VOGEL, F. (1978), A twin study on three enzymes (DβH, COMT, MAO) of catecholamine metabolism-correlations with MMPI. *Psychopharmacology*, 57:63–69.

YOUNG, J. G., KYPRIE, R. M., ROSS, N. T. & COHEN, D. J. (1980), Serum DβH activity: clinical applications in child psychiatry. *J. Aut. Develpm. Dis.*, 10:1–14.

SECTION 5: CRIMINOLOGY

One of the most important forces driving the current interest in the connections between cruelty to animals and violence against people is the proliferation of criminological reports noting this association in studies of offender populations. This section presents several different views of the criminological approach to understanding the significance of animal cruelty in the development of violent antisocial or criminal behavior. All of the research in this section is retrospective—that is, it deals with interviews or other studies of criminals after they have already been identified as violent offenders. Because animal cruelty is still largely treated as a minor crime, and because it frequently involves juvenile offenders, whose records are usually sealed, it has been very difficult to identify offenders and follow them in a prospective way to determine how, why, and how often these offenses escalate to violence against people, or to identify the forces that prevent that from happening.

The research described in this section raises many practical and theoretical questions about the origins and dynamics of violence and offers the promise of tools for helping to identify individuals at a high risk of engaging in violent antisocial behaviors. In many ways an analysis of early animal abuse allows us to avoid the pitfalls of the traditional "nature-nurture controversy" in asking questions about who is likely to become a violent offender. Looking at a person's early treatment of animals can give us an objective and easily observed measure of what that person is temperamentally capable of doing (nature) and the behavior that his or her environment has allowed or encouraged (nurture).

The first selection, by Robert K. Ressler and his colleagues, is one of the earliest major retrospective studies of violent criminals conducted by the FBI's behavioral science unit. The main theoretical question in this study is similar to that raised by Mead in section 1: "What leads sadistic fantasies to be acted out?" Data on animal abuse is bur-

ied in the wealth of information in this report, but it is highly significant. Animal cruelty appears as one of the major differences in the childhood histories of sexually abused and nonabused killers. This confirms the importance of animal abuse as an indicator of past or ongoing sexual abuse.

In addition, the authors report that sexually abused murderers are five times more likely to report having sexual contact with animals than nonabused murderers. Animal cruelty, like rape and sexual homicide, is often motivated by a need for power and control gained at the expense of a relatively vulnerable victim. The evidence of this report suggests that perpetrators of sexual homicide, particularly those with a history of sexual abuse, will often kill their victims prior to sexual activity to achieve control of the victim. Early experience with gaining such control over others through animal cruelty seems to be a common element in the development of this pattern.

The next selection, by Stephen R. Kellert and Alan R. Felthous, is one of the most significant of the retrospective studies of criminals other than serial killers and perpetrators of sexual homicide. This study is particularly valuable for its attempt to compare controlled groups instead of relying on anecdotal or biographical material. It is also important to note that the distinction between violent and nonviolent criminals is based on the current behavior within the prison system rather than on the crimes for which these men were imprisoned.

The most significant finding is that 60 percent of the criminal subjects report at least one act of animal abuse in childhood. Within the population of aggressive criminals, 25 percent report five or more such acts, compared with only 6 percent of the nonaggressive criminals and none of the noncriminal controls. The authors' attempt to elucidate the most common reasons given for engaging in animal cruelty is a key step in unraveling the dynamics of abuse. Echoing the preceding essay, this study shows that the families of the aggressive and animal-abusing criminals were more likely to be characterized by repeated child abuse as well as by higher levels of parental alcohol and drug abuse. The authors caution other researchers that many family members contacted to cross-validate these reports were more defensive about the inmates' early behaviors than the prisoners themselves. Kellert and Felthous conclude that most of the errors in such studies are likely to be in the direction of underreporting early problems, including animal abuse.

The article by David Tingle and his colleagues, like the Ressler essay, addresses the animal-cruelty connection only tangentially, but it is significant in that it looks at a variety of measures that try to identify the dynamics of families that produce individuals with serious social adjustment problems—in this case rapists and child molesters. These individuals often come from homes with physical and sexual abuse, a conclusion that other studies in this volume concur with. Their antisocial behavior often appears early, particularly among rapists, with one-third having been expelled from elementary school and nearly half involved in cruelty to animals. Among child-molesters, who are generally less violent, 28 percent had an early history of animal cruelty. Both groups suffered from an early failure to form adequate peer relations, with 75 percent of child molesters and 86 percent of rapists having few or no friends as children.

Yet another essay by Felthous and Kellert, entitled "Psychosocial Aspects of Selecting Animal Species for Physical Abuse," builds on the data used in their earlier paper and focuses on the reasons perpetrators give for abusing certain animals. This is one of the first attempts at what has become known as "profiling," going beyond a simple victimology to understand the mechanisms of cruelty. Such an understanding is important if we are to better comprehend how animal abuse may come to be directed toward people. This analysis focuses on social attitudes toward animals, extrapolating

from Kellert's earlier works on public attitudes toward animals. While this is a good start, it unfortunately provides little insight into some of the more direct factors that might influence the selection of animals for abuse, including modeling of parental behaviors, familial or peer acceptance or encouragement of such acts, and past experiences with the species in question. Nor does it provide much insight into the origins, age of onset, and societal response to the animal cruelty that was performed.

The article by Faith H. Liebman is an example of the more traditional, biographical analysis of violent criminals from a predominantly psychoanalytic perspective. She attempts to determine the common emotional and environmental backgrounds of four serial killers in order to identify early signs that might enable detection and treatment. Several of the classic patterns that characterize serial killers are mentioned, including violent parenting, rejection by parents and/or sex partners, early contact with the mental health and criminal justice systems, lack of friends or family as a source of social support, and aberrant sexuality. Unfortunately, the author seems to overlook the potential significance of animal cruelty as an early indicator of problems of power and control and of aberrant sexuality. Although such a connection has been reported in the cases of Bundy, DeSalvo, and Kemper, she notes it only in Kemper's case, while failing to mention that one of Kemper's final victims was his mother, which would seem to be of overwhelming significance from a psychoanalytic perspective.

The final contribution in this section, by Randall Lockwood and Ann Church, shows how the awareness of the connection between animal cruelty and violent crime is used today within the FBI to measure dangerousness and profile suspects. This article also suggests the benefits that could result from establishing better collaboration between law-enforcement agencies and animal-care and -control organizations.

In comparing sexual murderers with a history of sex abuse (n = 12) with murderers without such a history (n = 16), findings that approach a level of significance between early sexual abuse and sexual deviations include zoophilia (.06) and sexual sadism (.07) with the ultimate expression of the murderer's perversion being the mutilation of the victim. Murderers with sexual abuse histories report fantasizing about rape earlier than murderers without sexual abuse histories (.05) and report aversion to peer sex in adolescence and adulthood (.05). Significant differences in behavioral indicators comparing across developmental levels of childhood include cruelty to animals (.05), and differences approaching significance include isolation (.09), convulsions (.09), cruelty to children (.09) and assaultive to adults (.09). Significant differences in adolescence between murderers with child sexual abuse history versus nonhistory include running away (.01), sleep problems (.05), daydreams (.05), rebellious (.05), assaultive to adults (.05), and indicators approaching significance include temper tantrums (.09) and self-mutilation (.09).

Murderers Who Rape and Mutilate

ROBERT K. RESSLER
FBI Academy

ANN W. BURGESS
University of Pennsylvania

CAROL R. HARTMAN
Boston College

JOHN E. DOUGLAS
FBI Academy

ARLENE McCORMACK
University of Lowell

The origins and significance of sexualized acts in the commission of a sexual crime have been implicit themes in the professional literature. Deviant sexual behaviors of offenders have been reported in terms of sexual dysfunction (Groth & Burgess, 1977), sexual

Authors' Note: Preparation of this article was supported by Department of Justice grants: Office of Juvenile Justice and Delinquency Prevention (#84-JN-AX-K010) and

180   *Robert K. Ressler et al.*

arousal (Abel, 1982), sadistic fantasies (Brittain, 1970; MacCulloch, Snowden, Wood, & Mills, 1983), and childhood sexual abuse (Groth, 1979; Seghorn, Boucher, & Prentky, in press).

In a report of a British study of 16 male patients diagnosed with psychopathic disorders and hospitalized in a psychiatric facility, the crucial link between sadistic fantasy and behavior is discussed (MacCulloch et al., 1983). The authors raise the following question: If sadistic fantasy has a role in the genesis and maintenance of sadistic behavior, what factors lead some individuals to act out their fantasies? Although they state that they believe any answer would include multiple factors, the authors speculate that factors observed in their subpopulation of 13 sadistic fantasizers include childhood abuse (being tied up and anal assault) and/or adolescent sexual experiences (MacCulloch et al., 1983).

The linking of childhood sexual abuse to subsequent problems and behavior is not a new idea. Freud in 1895 believed that hysterical symptoms of his female patients could be traced to an early traumatic experience and that the trauma was always related to the patient's sexual life. The trauma manifested itself when revived later, usually after puberty, as a memory. However, Freud later reversed his belief in 1905 and said that the sexual seductions his patients reported were not all reports of real events, but fantasies created by the individual (Masson, 1984). This reversal created a major shift in the priorities of psychological investigation. The external, realistic trauma was replaced in importance by infantile sexual wishes and fantasies.

In the past decade clinicians (Herman, 1981) and feminists (Rush, 1980) have challenged this perspective and are now proposing that sexual abuse in childhood may have a common base in a wide range of social problems. The propositions are based on observations of the prevalence of early child sexual abuse found in populations of runaways (Janus, Scanlon, & Price, 1984), juvenile delinquents (Garbarino & Plantz, 1984), prostitutes (James & Meyerding, 1977; Silbert & Pines, 1981), psychiatric patients (Carmen, Rieker, & Mills, 1984), substance abusers (Densen-Gerber, 1975), and sex offenders (Groth, 1979; Seghorn et al., in press).

Although these studies have looked at various populations, none has examined sexual murderers. In an attempt to address the question

National Institute of Justice (#82-CX-0065). We wish to acknowledge gratefully Marieanne L. Clark for contributions to earlier drafts of this article.

raised by MacCulloch and colleagues about acting out sadistic fantasies, this article discusses results of an assessment of the relationship between sexual abuse in childhood or adolescence and sexual interests, activities, and deviations in convicted sexually oriented killers.

METHOD

Apprehension of a crime suspect is the job of law enforcement. In many crimes, this task is fairly straightforward when a motive (e.g., robbery, revenge) has been identified. However, in many crimes the motive is not readily apparent. FBI agents became involved in assisting local law enforcement agencies in their profiling of unsolved homicide cases in the early 1970s. These crimes, often referred to as "motiveless," were analyzed by the agents to include a sexual component. The agents, sensitive to crime scene information, began their own efforts at classifying characteristics of the murderer by virtue of evidence found at the crime scene. From this evidence they devised a new typology that characterized crime scene patterns as being organized or disorganized. This typology inferred a motivational framework that included expectations, planning, and justification for the criminal action as well as "hunches" regarding postcrime behaviors. As a result, particular emphasis was placed on the thinking patterns dominating the murderer's actions indicating differences in acts committed against the victim and suggesting subcategories of motivational constructs.

The selection of subjects and methodology used to develop the organized/disorganized typology are reported elsewhere (Ressler et al., 1985). Briefly, FBI special agents collected data in various U.S. prisons between 1979 and 1983. The data set for each murderer consisted of the best available data from two types of sources: official records and interviews with the offenders.

To qualify for the study, a murder had to be classified through crime scene observations and evidence as a sexual homicide. These observations included the following: victim attire or lack of attire; exposure of sexual parts of the victim's body; sexual positioning of victim's body; insertion of foreign objects into victim's body cavities; or evidence of sexual intercourse. Primary analysis was conducted on information about the crime scenes of 36 sexually oriented murderers.

Identifying murderers who had earlier been sexually abused was accomplished by using interview or official record information about whether the subject had been sexually abused as a child, adolescent, or adult. Information about symptoms and criminal behaviors was obtained in a similar manner. A "yes" response required confirmation through offender disclosure and background record; an answer recorded as "suspected" was based on the offender's recollection. For this aspect of the research, both answers were coded as "yes." We acknowledge the limitations of this variable, which could be either underreported due to memory loss over the years or incorrect because of offender error in memory reconstruction. In addition, the increased public attention to sexual victimization may have influenced offenders to give a positive response. It is important to keep in mind that all subjects in this study were convicted of sexually oriented murder. This report is based on our analysis of convicted, incarcerated, sexual murderers for whom there were data available on early sexual abuse in their life histories; on their sexual/aggressive interests, fantasies, and practices; and on their criminal behaviors. At the time of data collection, these men represented a group of sexually oriented murderers who were available for research purposes (that is, whose appeal process was complete), and who were also able to participate in the in-depth interview conducted by the agents. Murderers were excluded from the sample if they were acutely mentally disordered and unable to respond to interview questions (N = 2). They were selected for a project to investigate law enforcement profiling techniques (Ressler et al., 1985); in addition, they do not represent a random sample.

FINDINGS

When questioned about prior sexual abuse, 12, or 43%, of those murderers responding (28) indicated such abuse in childhood (age 1-12); 9, or 32%, were abused in adolescence (age 13-18); and 10, or 37%, as adults (over age 18).

Symptoms and behavior indicators. The comparison of sexual abuse in childhood and adolescence by symptoms and behaviors present in childhood, adolescence, and adulthood for murderers who had and who had not been sexually abused is presented in Table 1. For the overwhelming majority of symptoms and behavioral indicators, the higher incidence is in the direction of those offenders who were sexually abused. Those sexually abused in childhood are significantly more likely than nonabused offenders to report the following symptoms in childhood: cruelty to animals, isolation, convulsions, cruelty to children, and assaultive to adults. In addition, those men sexually abused in childhood are more likely to report experiencing the following symptoms in adolescence: sleep problems, isolation, running away, self-mutilation, temper tantrums, rebelliousness, and assaultive to adults. In adulthood, differences are noted in the areas of poor body image, sleep problems, isolation, self-mutilation, and temper tantrums.

Those sexually abused in adolescence are more likely than nonabused offenders to report the following symptoms in adolescence: running away, fire setting, and cruelty to animals. In adulthood, differences for those sexually abused as an adolescent include the behavioral indicators of nightmares, daydreams, rebelliousness, and cruelty to children. (See Table 2.)

Sexual issues. Our analysis of the total murderer sample found that over 50% of the murderers report concern with various sexual issues. These include sexual conflicts (69%), sexual incompetencies (69%), sexual inhibitions (61%), sexual ignorance (59%), and sexual dysfunction (56%).

Regarding sexual activities, over 50% of all murderers report interests in pornography (81%), fetishism (stealing, wearing, or masturbating with women's undergarments; attraction to specific body parts, articles, or inanimate objects) (72%), and voyeurism (71%). A total of 39% report interests in bondage sex (S&M), and 25% indicate involvement in indecent exposure. Less than one-fourth disclose interest in sexual contact with animals (23%), obscene telephone calls (22%), rubbing against others (18%), cross-dressing (17%), prostitution (11%), and coprophilia (7%).

An analysis of the relationship between prior sexual abuse in childhood or adolescence and sexual issues shows that the sexually abused offenders are more likely to report sexual conflicts (92% versus 40%; $p = .01$), sexual dysfunction (69% versus 50%), and sexual incompetence (77% versus 60%). There is little or no difference in sexual ignorance between the two groups.

An analysis of the relationship between sexual abuse in childhood and adolescence and participation in certain sexual activities indi-

TABLE 1
Symptoms and Behaviors for Sexually and Nonsexually Abused Murderers
(in percentages)

Symptoms and Behaviors	Sexually Abused as a Child						Sexually Abused as an Adolescent			
	Symptoms as a Child		*Symptoms as an Adolescent*		*Symptoms as an Adult*		*Symptoms as an Adolescent*		*Symptoms as an Adult*	
	Sexually Abused	*Not Sexually Abused*	*Sexually Abused*	*Not Sexually Abused*	*Sexually Abused*	*Not Sexually Abused*	*Sexually Abused*	*Not Sexually Abused*	*Sexually Abused*	*Not Sexually Abused*
Enuresis	78	55	67	50	22	10	60	57	20	14
Poor body image	58	42	75	46	75	42*	56	63	56	60
Nightmares	78	50	78	55	67	45	80	60	100	40***
Eating problems	36	17	50	18	50	25	50	27	50	31
Sleep problems	60	27	70	27**	70	27**	67	40	67	40
Headaches	40	20	50	20	60	30	50	29	50	43
Accident prone	33	31	33	36	22	36	33	36	17	36
Convulsions	36	8*	30	15	28	8	14	25	14	13
Isolation	91	57*	100	62**	91	62*	88	75	75	75
Daydreams	91	71	91	71	91	71	100	71*	100	71*
Running away	36	36	73	23***	18	8	50	44		
Phobias	40	31	50	33	60	38	43	40	43	50
Chronic lying	73	64	73	71	64	64	88	65	75	59
Stealing	70	43	90	71	56	50	86	76	50	53
Destroying property	60	54	64	54	30	27	63	56	14	36
Self-mutilation	27	15	40	8*	54	17**	33	19	43	31
Temper tantrums	64	46	73	38*	70	31*	75	44	57	44
Rebellious	80	57	100	69**	90	62	100	75	100	63**
Cruelty to children	73	38*	67	62	50	25	75	59	63	25*
Fire setting	60	46	64	38	36	15	75	38*	38	19
Cruelty to animals	58	15**	58	31	40	29	67	31*	43	29
Assaultive to adults	50	17*	100	69**	90	79	100	75	100	76
Destructive to possessions	44	15	50	25	50	25	43	33	29	40
Compulsive masturbation	82	80	82	80	82	73	88	78	88	72

*p ≤ .09; **p ≤ .05; ***p ≤ .01.

TABLE 2
Behaviors with Significant Differences Between
Sexually Abused and Non-Sexually Abused Murderers

Sexually Abused as a Child			*Sexually Abused as an Adolescent*	
Symptoms as a Child	*Symptoms as an Adolescent*	*Symptoms as an Adult*	*Symptoms as an Adolescent*	*Symptoms as an Adult*
Convulsions	Sleep problems	Poor body image	Running away	Nightmares
Isolation	Isolation	Isolation	Fire setting	Daydreams
Cruelty to children	Running away	Sleep problems	Cruelty to animals	Rebellious
Cruelty to animals	Self-mutilation	Self-mutilation		Cruelty to children
Assaultive to adults	Temper tantrums	Temper tantrums		
	Rebellious			
	Assaultive to adults			

cates that the sexually abused murderers are more likely to engage in sexual contact with animals (40% versus 8%; p ≤ .06), bondage sex (55% versus 23%), fetishism (83% versus 57%), obscene phone calls (36% versus 15%), indecent exposure (36% versus 21%), pornography (92% versus 79%), frottage (27% versus 15%), and cross-dressing (18% versus 7%). There is little difference or no difference noted in the area of voyeurism. Prostitution and coprophilia were dropped from this analysis due to an inadequate number of responses.

Rape fantasies. For 19 of the 36 murderers who responded to a question about at what age they began to fantasize about rape, the ages range from 5 to 25 years old. The results of a test of mean age differences shows that sexually abused murderers (11) began to fantasize at an earlier age than did those not abused (8), or ages 11.6 years versus 15.3 years (t = 1.99, p = 0.05).

First consensual sex. For 19 murderers, the age of first significant, consensual sexual experience ranged from 11 to 35 years of age. The results of a test of mean age difference shows that sexually abused killers report an earlier age for this activity than do murderers not sexually abused (14.7 years versus 16.2 years). However, this difference was not statistically significant (t = 1.12, p = 0.14).

Aversion to sexual activity. It was clear to the interviewers that some of the murderers could not answer the question of age of consensual sex because they had never had such an experience. Thus in reply to the question about whether they experienced a marked aversion or inhibition to sexual activity with peers, the affirmative response of 26 offenders is not surprising.

Of these 26, 11 were sexually abused as children and 15 were not (see Table 3). Results indicate that there is no difference in aversion to sexual activity in childhood for sexually versus nonsexually abused murderers (9% versus 7%). Murderers who were sexually abused in childhood are more likely than their nonabused counterparts to report aversion to sex in adolescence (73% versus 27%) and in adulthood (73% versus 33%; p = 0.05).

Mutilation of murder victim. The results of assessing the relationship between sexual abuse in childhood and the mutilation of murder victims after death show a positive relationship (see Table 4). Mutilation is defined as the deliberate cutting, usually after death, of the sexual areas of the body (breasts, genitals, abdomen). Sexually abused murderers are more likely to mutilate victims than are those offenders not sexually abused (67% versus 44%). We also see a positive relationship between adolescent sexual victimization and the mutilation of the murder victim (78% versus 42%; p = .07).

DISCUSSION

Sexual Interests and Behaviors

In our examination of sexual interests and behaviors we find some association in our population between early sexual abuse and the development of sexual deviations or psychosexual disorders (DSM III, 1980). As described by the DSM III (1980), the essential feature of psychosexual disorders is that unusual or bizarre imagery or acts are necessary for sexual excitement. Additionally, the acts tend to be involuntarily repetitive and the imagery necessary for sexual arousal must be included in masturbatory fantasies. In the murderer sample, those sexually abused offenders were more likely to have the paraphilia of zoophilia and to begin to experience rape fantasies earlier than the nonabused group. The complexity and bizarreness of the offender's fantasy life needed to obtain and sustain emotional arousal suggest that the ultimate expression of his perversion is in the mutilation of the victim.

There are many significant differences of behavioral indicators comparing across developmental levels of childhood, adolescence,

TABLE 3
Inhibition or Aversion to Sexual Activity of Sexually Abused and Nonabused Murderers
(in percentages)

Aversion to Sexual Activity	Sexual Abuse			
	As a Child		As an Adolescent	
	Yes (11)	No (15)	Yes (8)	No (18)
In childhood	9	7		
In adolescence	73	27	63	39
In adulthood	73	33	63	44

NOTE: n = numbers in parentheses.
*p < 0.05

TABLE 4
Mutilation of Murder Victims and Sexual Victimization of Offender

Victimization	Mutilation of Victims		
	Yes %	No %	N
In childhood			
Yes	67	33	12
No	44	56	16
In adolescence			
Yes	78	22	9
No	42	58	19

*p = 0.07.

and adulthood for abused and nonabused murderers. We note the consistently reported behavior of isolation as an outcome of childhood sexual abuse with varied symptom clusters of sleep problems, nightmares, daydreams, poor body image, and convulsions; behaviors of self-mutilation, running away, temper tantrums, rebelliousness, fire setting, actions of cruelty to children and animals, and assault of adults. Some of the symptoms suggest internalized undisclosed sexual abuse (i.e., sleep problems, running away, self-mutilation, and poor body image) whereas other symptoms suggest externalized aggression.

Although it would not be expected to see differences between murderers who were sexually molested in childhood reporting a greater peer sex aversion than the nonmolested as a child, those molested in childhood do have more aversion of peer sex in adolescence and those molested in adolescence also have a high report rate of aversion at this time. This finding suggests that there is a complex interaction between basic developmental issues of sexuality that interact with molestation at different times in the development of the child and are linked with avoidance of peer experiences in adolescence. It is speculated that this aversion not only jeopardizes the development of constructive and normative sexual and interpersonal experiences but also increases social isolation and fosters a reliance on fantasy for impulse development and discharge.

Hypersexuality or the sexualization of relationships is an important indicator of sexually abused children, and children can be expressive both verbally and behaviorally about sex. Often when this sexuality is expressed aggressively toward others, it reflects directly on the aggressive and exploitive nature of the initial abuse (Burgess et al., 1984). Sex, rather than linking these men (abused and nonabused) with their peers, somehow impedes the connection. One speculation is that the adult role of the abuser in the original childhood victimization is maintained in the repeated fantasy and thus the preferred sexual relationship is a child/adult pairing. In addition, relationships with younger children, peers, and adults are marked by aggression.

Murder Behavior

One finding of our analysis of crime scene evidence approached a level of significance with sexual abuse. There was a striking difference in the style of sexual assaults on victims between sexually abused offenders and those offenders who did not report abuse: Those who were sexually abused in childhood tended to mutilate the body after killing, as contrasted with murderers who raped and then killed ($p = 0.07$). We speculate that undisclosed and unresolved early sexual abuse may be a contributing factor in the stimulation of bizarre, sexual, sadistic behavior characterized in a subclassification of mutilators.

Although we do not have systematic data collected on the intentions of the mutilations, some murderers volunteered information. One murderer said the mutilation was a way of disposing of the body, implying he had a pragmatic reason for the mutilation. However, the autopsy report revealed that in addition to cutting up the body, he also pulled out the victim's fingernails after death, something he claimed not to remember. This man went to prison for the first killing. When he was released he knew he would kill again. He revealed that he sought the high level of emotional arousal not in the killing, but in the successful dismemberment of his victims and the disposal of the parts without detection—an act that took thought and planning.

MacCulloch and colleagues (1983) observed in their sample of sex offenders with sadistic fantasies that from an early age, the men had difficulties in both social and sexual relationships. They suggest that this failure in social/sexual approach might be partly responsible for the development of a feeling of inadequacy and lack of assertiveness. This inability to control events in the real world moves the man into a fantasy world where he can control his inner world. This fantasy of control and dominance is bound to be repeated because of the relief it provides from a pervasive sense of failure. MacCulloch and colleagues (1983) suggest that when sexual arousal is involved in the sadistic fantasy, the further shaping and content of the fantasy may be viewed on a classical conditioning model; the strong tendency to progression of sadistic fantasies may then be understood in terms of habituation.

Eysenck (1968) argues the acting out of elements of the deviant fantasies is a relatively short step in those whose personalities predispose to repeated thinking or incubation. In these cases the fantasies would theoretically at least form part of a conditional stimulus class and possibly become a necessary condition for sexual arousal. Thus a conditioning model, writes MacCulloch and colleagues (1983), may explain not only the strength and permanence of sadistic fantasies in these abnormal personalities but their progression to nonsexual and sexual crimes. This model provides an explanation for what Reinhardt (1957) called the "forward thrust of sexual fantasies in sadistic murderers." Our last example of a mutilator murderer underscores the reality-orienting fantasy of successful disposal of the body as the cognitive set, driving repeated murders.

Although all murders in our study contained a sexual element, it was apparent that motives differed. Some victims were raped and then murdered; others were murdered and then sexually mutilated. Rapists who murder, according to Rada (1978), rarely report any sexual satisfaction from the murder nor perform sexual acts postmortem. In contrast, the sadistic murderer (Brittain, 1970), sometimes called *lust-murderer* (Hazelwood & Douglas, 1980), kills prior to or simultaneously in carrying out a ritualized sadistic fantasy.

Evidence from this study suggests that the murderer with a sexual abuse history will first kill the victim to achieve control before he makes any sexual expression. The murderer may not necessarily have any orgastic experiences with the body, but rather may masturbate on or beside the body. The release of tension may also occur through substitute action such as mutilation of the body, or perhaps using, as noted with Brittain's study (1970), a phallus substitute.

Consistent with our study are others (Brittain, 1970; MacCulloch et al., 1983) that underscore a feeling of relief and pseudonormal behavior following the murder. Many of the murderers recount going home and sleeping deeply after a murder. After several days, they would reflect on the murder in great detail.

IMPLICATIONS

The analysis of data specific to the variables of childhood sexual abuse and subsequent symptoms and criminal behaviors suggests that several variables (e.g., daydreams, isolation, cruelty to children and animals) play an important part in the subgroups (i.e., rape-murder and murder-mutilate) of sexual murderers. There is every indication that the motivation for murder is a complex developmental process that is based on needs for sexual dominance at the destructive expense of the victim. It appears from this exploratory study of convicted killers that there is an important difference in the symptom constellation among those with a history of sexual abuse and those without such a history. Although it is not clear whether there is a difference in psychological motivation for sexual murder, what is apparent is an early onset of specific behaviors that are noted in the subgroup of murderers who mutilate.

The association of the specific impact of sexual molestation in the lives of these offenders and subsequent mutilation of their victims requires further investigation. To speculate on a possible link between the adolescents who were sexually abused and those who mutilate the body suggests a premeditated pattern where acts of self-mutilation are then transferred and carried out on others.

Our exploratory study raises far more questions than it answers. Current understanding of disclosed childhood sexual abuse has focused on the initial treatment (Burgess et al., 1978; Conte, 1984; Sgroi, 1982), legal process (Buckley, 1981), sequelae (Browne & Finkelhor,

1984), and prevention efforts (Conte, 1984; Swift, 1977). Yet our understanding of undisclosed childhood sexual abuse and its long-term effects is limited in regard to gender differences and behavioral outcomes. It becomes even more imperative, given our findings on behavioral differences, that we not only learn how to detect cases of child sexual abuse early but also delve further into behavioral outcomes particularly in noncriminal abused adults.

For the men who repeat sexual murder, their internal processing and cognitive operations appear to sustain and perpetuate fantasies of sexually violent actions. As a result, clinicians are urged to take careful note of patients reporting sadistic as well as criminal fantasies and record a systematic history on the content, duration, progression, and affect triggered by the fantasy. For law enforcement, murder that appears to be motiveless—that is, the victim is a stranger and there is no profit to be gained from the death of the victim—suggests that the victim and offense must be seen as having symbolic meaning to the offender reflecting violent sadistic fantasies.

REFERENCES

Beck, A. T. (1976). *Cognitive therapy and the emotional disorders.* New York: International University Press.

Brittain, R. P. (1970). The sadistic murderer. *Medical Science and the Law, 10,* 198-207.

Browne, A., & Finkelhor, D. (1984). *The impact of child sexual abuse: A review of the research.* (Unpublished manuscript)

Buckley, J. (1981). *Child sexual abuse and the law.* Washington, DC: National Legal Resource Center for Child Advocacy and Protection, American Bar Association.

Burgess, A. W., Hartman, C. R., McCausland, M. P., & Powers, P. (1984). Response patterns in children and adolescents exploited through sex rings and pornography. *American Journal of Psychiatry, 141* (5), 656-662.

Burgess, A. W., Hartman, C. R., Ressler, R. K., Douglas, J. E., & McCormack, A. (1986). Sexual homicide: A motivational model. *Journal of Interpersonal Violence, 1* (3).

Carmen, E. H., Rieker, P. P., & Mills, T. (1984). Victims of violence and psychiatric illness. *American Journal of Psychiatry, 141* (3), 378-383.

Conte, J. R. (1984). Progress in treating the sexual abuse in children. *Social Work,* 258-263.

Densen-Gerber, J., & Benward, J. (1976). *Incest as a causative factor in antisocial behavior.* New York: Odyssey Institute.

Eysenck, H. J. (1968). A theory of the incubation of anxiety/fear response. *Behaviour Research and Therapy, 6,* 309-321.

Freud, S. (1895). *Totem and taboo.* New York: New Republic Edition.

Garbarino, J., & Plantz, M. C. (1984). *Child maltreatment and juvenile delinquency: What are the links?* Pennsylvania State University, unpublished manuscript.

Groth, A. N. (1979). Sexual trauma is the life histories of rapists and child molesters. *Victimology, 4* (1), 10-16.

Groth, A. N., & Burgess, A. W. (1977). Sexual dysfunction during rape. *New England Journal of Medicine, 14,* 764-766.

Hazelwood, R. R., & Douglas, J. E. (1980). The lust-murderer. *FBI Law Enforcement Bulletin, 49* (4), 1-5.

Herman, J. (1982). *Father-daughter incest.* Cambridge, MA: Harvard University Press.

James, J., & Meyerding (1977). Early sexual experience and prostitution. *American Journal of Psychiatry, 134* (12), 1381-1385.

Janus, M. D., Scanlon, B., & Price, V. (1984). Youth prostitution. In *Child pornography and sex rings.* Lexington, MA: Lexington Books.

MacCulloch, M. J., Snowden, P. R., Wood, P.J.W., & Mills, H. E. (1983). Sadistic fantasy, sadistic behaviour and offending. *British Journal of Psychiatry, 143,* 20-29.

Masson, J. M. (1984). *The assault on truth: Freud's suppression of the seduction theory.* New York: Farrar, Straus, and Giroux.

Rada, R. T. (1978). Psychological factors in rapist behavior. In *Clinical aspects of the rapist* (pp. 51-52). New York: Grune & Stratton.

Reinhardt, J. M. (1957). Sex perversions and sex crimes: A psychocultural examination of the causes, nature and criminal manifestations of sex perversions. *Police science series.* Springfield, IL: Charles C Thomas.

Ressler, R. K. (1985, August). Violent crimes. *FBI Law Enforcement Bulletin.*

Ressler, R. K., Burgess, A. W., Douglas, J. E., Hartman, C. R., & D'Agostino, R. B. (in press). *Sexual killers and their victims: Identifying patterns through crime scene analysis.*

Revitch, E. (1965). Sex murder and the potential sex murderer. *Diseases of the Nervous System, 26,* 640-648.

Rush, F. (1980). *The best kept secret.* Englewood Cliffs, NJ: Prentice-Hall.

Saminow, S. (1984). *Inside the criminal mind.* New York: New York Times Book Co.

Seghorn, T. K., Boucher, R. J., & Prentky, R. A. (in press). *Childhood sexual abuse in the lives of sexually aggressive offenders.*

Sgroi, S. M. (1982). *Handbook of clinical intervention in child sexual abuse.* Lexington, MA: Lexington Books.

Silbert, M. H., & Pines, A. M. (1981). Sexual child abuse as an antecedent to prostitution. *Child Abuse and Neglect, 5,* 407-411.

Swift, C. (1977). Sexual victimization of children: An urban mental health center survey. *Victimology, 2* (2), 322-326.

Robert K. Ressler, M.S., is Supervisory Special Agent, Federal Bureau of Investigation, and Program Manager, Violent Criminal Apprehension Programs, National Center for the Analysis of Violent Crime, FBI Academy, Quantico, VA.

Ann W. Burgess, R.N., D.N.Sc., is van Ameringen Professor of Psychiatric Mental Health Nursing, University of Pennsylvania, Philadelphia, and Associate Director of Nursing Research, Boston City Hospital, Boston.

Carol R. Hartman, R.N., D.N.Sc., is Associate Professor and Coordinator of Graduate Programs in Psychiatric Mental Health Nursing, Boston College, Chestnut Hill, MA.

John E. Douglas, M.S., is Supervisory Special Agent, Federal Bureau of Investigation, and Program Manager, Criminal Profiling and Crime Scene Assessment Program, FBI Academy, Quantico, VA.

Arlene McCormack is Assistant Professor of Sociology, University of Lowell, Lowell, MA.

Childhood Cruelty toward Animals among Criminals and Noncriminals[1]

Stephen R. Kellert[2]
Yale University

Alan R. Felthous
The University of Texas Medical Branch at Galveston

This paper examines the relationship between childhood cruelty toward animals and aggressive behavior among criminals and noncriminals in adulthood.

Data were derived from personal interviews with 152 criminals and noncriminals in Kansas and Connecticut. A standardized, closed, and open-ended interview, requiring approximately 1–2 hours to complete, was administered to all subjects. Aggressiveness was defined by behavioral criteria rather than by reason for incarceration.

Childhood cruelty toward animals occurred to a significantly greater degree among aggressive criminals than among nonaggressive criminals or noncriminals. Additionally, the occurrence of more than 40 cases of extreme animal crielty facilitated the development of a preliminary classification of nine distinct motivations for animal cruelty. Finally, family violence, particularly paternal abuse and alcoholism, were significantly more common among aggressive criminals with a history of childhood cruelty toward animals.

[1]This study was initiated and sponsored by the World Society for the Protection of Animals and funded by the G. R. Dodge Foundation. Many thanks to John and Joyce Walsh and to Scott McVay for making this research possible and for their considerable help, encouragement, and support. The findings in this paper indicate the views and data analysis of the authors, and do not reflect the views of the U.S. Federal Prison System.

[2]Requests for reprints should be sent to Stephen R. Kellert, School of Forestry and Environmental Studies, Yale University, New Haven, Connecticut 06511.

INTRODUCTION

Perhaps the greatest distortion of the human/animal relationship is a deliberate act of cruelty toward animals. While the perception of animal cruelty is somewhat dependent on subjective judgment, it will be defined here as the willful infliction of harm, injury, and intended pain on a nonhuman animal.

The serious social and legislative response to animal cruelty first became apparent in North America and Europe at the beginning of the eighteenth and, more decidedly, nineteenth centuries (Carson, 1972). Despite references to kindly treatment of animals in the Bible, among the ancient Greeks, and in some early ecclesiastical writings, little concern existed among the general populace toward this issue prior to the modern era (Thomas, 1983).

Concern for the possible pain and suffering experienced by animals became important only after the development of the companion, pet animal as a social phenomenon beginning in the sixteenth and seventeenth centuries. What distinguished the pet, as a kind of "humanized" animal, were three characteristics: it was allowed in the house, it was given a personal name, and it was never eaten (Levi-Strauss, 1966). The development of the companion pet phenomenon had profound implications on the perception and concern for cruelty toward animals. As Thomas remarked: "It encouraged [people] to form optimistic conclusions about animal intelligence;... it stimulated the notion that animals could have character and individual personality; and [most of all] it created the psychological foundation for the view that some animals at least were entitled to moral consideration" (Thomas, 1983). An additional force promoting a concern for animal cruelty was the emergence of a sympathy for the downtrodden and exploited, associated with the social ills of rapid urbanization and industrialization during the eighteenth and nineteenth centuries (Carson, 1972). Of particular concern were domestic beasts of burden, children, and women who were frequent victims of the depersonalization, anonymity, and crowding of the new industrial urban centers.

A dominant factor in the rising concern for animal cruelty was the presumption that abusive treatment of animals would tend to brutalize the human perpetrator and increase the likelihood of similar conduct toward human beings. Perhaps the most famous depiction of this view was Hogarth's (1750–1751) *Four Stages of Cruelty* which described "the progression of...torturing animals as a child, beating a disabled horse as a young man and, finally, killing a woman" (ten Bensel, 1983).

A concern for cruelty toward animals is currently a major interest of animal welfare and humane groups, and among people possessing a strong affection and empathetic compassion for animals (Kellert, 1979, 1983a). The popular association of animal cruelty and violent behavior against people is made and, in American journalism, sporadic reference is noted of this possible connection. The "Son of Sam" murderer in New York City, for example, was depicted by the press (Washington Star, 1977) as hating dogs and having killed a number of neighborhood animals. A mass murderer in California was described (Los Angeles Times, 1973) as having a history of cruelties toward cats and dogs. Another newspaper article (Washington Post, 1979) reported a mass killer as having immersed cats in containers of battery acid as a child. Albert DeSalvo, the notorious Boston strangler, trapped dogs and cats, placed them in orange crates, and shot arrows through the boxes (Fucini, 1978). A young man who recently admitted to "killing for fun" was described (Lowell Sun, 1982) as having put ammonia in fish tanks to watch the turtles turn white and torturing animals as a youth.

Scientific documentation of an association between animal cruelty and antisocial and violent conduct, however, has been lacking. Until credible and repeated scientific documentation occurs, most societal decision-makers will regard animal cruelty as a relatively minor issue. At present, most judicial authorities minimize the importance of animal cruelty among children if unaccompanied by violent or aggressive conduct toward human beings.

This paper will explore the subject of animal cruelty by reviewing the results of a study of 152 aggressive and nonaggressive criminals and noncriminals in Kansas and Connecticut. This research focused on the possible association of childhood cruelty toward animals and aggressive behavior toward humans among criminals in adolescence and adulthood. Additionally, a preliminary classification of motivations for cruelty toward animals was developed. Finally, the possible relationship of family violence, childhood animal cruelty, and aggressiveness toward humans was explored.

As indicated, the existing scientific literature on this subject has been relatively limited. Some empirical evidence exists suggesting a possible association of cruelty toward animals, persistent enuresis, and firesetting in childhood with dangerous, aggressive conduct against people at a later age (Hellman & Blackman, 1966; Wax & Haddox, 1974; Felthous & Bernard, 1979). On the other hand, others have not confirmed this relationship or have emphasized the presence of cruelty alone (Climent & Ervin, 1972; Bachy-Rita, et al., 1971; Felthous, 1980, 1981; Frazier, 1972; Glueck & Glueck, 1968; Justice, Justice & Kraft, 1974; Lewis, Shanok, Grant, & Ritvo, 1983; MacDonald, 1961; Mead, 1964; Rigdon & Tapia, 1977; Robin, ten Bensel, Quigley, & Anderson, 1981; Shanok, Malani, Ninan, Guggenheim, Weinstein, & Lewis, 1983; Tapia, Jekel, & Dumke, 1960; Tapia, 1971; ten Bensel, Ward, Kruttschnitt, Quigley, & Anderson, 1983). A recedntly published study by Langevin, Paitich, Orchard, Handy, and Russon (1983) found no difference in the amount of animal cruelty among killers, nonviolent offenders, and normal controls. This study, however, did not distinguish homicide from chronic aggressiveness, and employed only a very limited number of indicators of animal cruelty. The results of most studies suggest other childhood patterns of aggressive conduct are more strongly related to adult assaultiveness and violence (Alfaro, 1978; Amsterdam, Brill, Bell, & Edwards, 1977; Azrim & Holz, 1966; Button, 1973; Duncan, Frazier, & Litin, 1958; Easson, 1958; Gelles, 1974; Hunner & Walker, 1981; Langner & Gersten, 1976; Lowen, 1979; Owens & Strauss, 1975; Welsh, 1978). The research literature, thus, appears to suggest that childhood cruelty toward animals may operate as one component of a behavioral spectrum associated with violence and criminality in adolescence and adulthood.

Despite this indication of a possible association between animal cruelty and assaultiveness toward humans, the scientific literature on this subject may be regarded as sparse and inconsistent (Monahan, 1981). Additionally, most reported studies have involved small samples, only indirectly considered the phenomenon of animal cruelty, and have been characterized by various methodological deficiencies. Additionally, none of the investigations attempted to delineate a range of motivations for cruelty toward animals.

METHODOLOGY

This study explored the phenomenon of animal cruelty among three groups of males: aggressive criminals, nonaggressive criminals, and noncriminals. Criminal populations were selected from the Federal penitentiaries in Leavenworth, Kansas, and Danbury, Connecticut. A Memorandum of Understanding was signed with the U.S. Department of Justice, Federal Prison System, to permit this research and to assure the rights and privacy of prison inmates. All consenting prisoners signed an informed consent form which detailed the purposes and methodology of the study and provided assurances of confidentiality. The Federal penitentiaries at Leavenworth and Danbury incarcerate somewhat different populations of offenders. Leavenworth generally includes persons guilty of more severe, and often violent crimes than at Danbury and, relatedly, Leavenworth has a higher maximum security rating. Despite these differences, inmates from the two prisons were remarkably similar, nearly two-thirds were in their 30's, over two-thirds were of urban background, and all inmates were male. A slight tendency existed for Leavenworth inmates to be more aggressive and violent than inmates at Danbury.

In order to obtain an adequate number of aggressive criminal subjects, prison counselors were asked to rate the inmates on a scale of 1–10 for aggressiveness. These ratings were based on observations of the inmates subsequent to arriving at the facility and not on the prisoner's history prior to incarceration or on the reason for imprisonment. Ratings were, thus, based on observed behavior. This distinction is important as persons can be incarcerated for violent crimes but not be particularly aggressive individuals. A primary objective was to identify subjects characterized by chronic, recurrent, aggressive behavior. Criteria for defining aggressiveness included: aggressive speech, e.g., threats of serious bodily harm, aggressive preparatory behaviors, e.g., arming oneself for potential use against others, and aggressive actions, e.g., inflicting injury requiring medical attention. Additionally, aggressive actions of this severity were to be repetitive (at least three times) over a 1-year span. The 1–10 rating scale allowed for the identification of individuals at the extreme ends of the continuum. Interviewers were not informed of ratings until after the interviews. Inmates were never informed of this rating system or their particular designation. The final rating of aggressiveness, for purposes of analyzing the study's data, was based largely on an assessment of information provided by the inmates regarding past fighting, assaultiveness, violence, and aggressive behavior, rather than just on the judgments of counselors. Thus, two ratings of aggressiveness were used which, it should be noted, were highly correlated with one another ($R = .76$).

Noncriminals were chosen at random and resided in urban, small town, and suburban areas in proximity to New Haven, Connecticut, and Topeka, Kansas. Noncriminals were personally interviewed in their homes, and included only adult males to assure comparability with the criminal sample. The total sample of 152 persons included 63 Leavenworth and 89 Danbury penitentiary inmates, and 15 Kansas and 36 Connecticut non-inmates.

Each subject was interviewed for approximately 1–2 hours, using a standardized interview schedule which included over 440 closed and open-ended questions. The interview schedule covered the subject's demographic characteristics, childhood family relationships, childhood behavior patterns, relationships to animals in childhood, adult behavior patterns, and a closed-ended survey on attitudes toward animals and human aggression. This data was coded, keypunched, and computer analyzed. In addition, a qualitative analysis focused on situations of animal cruelty and family violence among the subjects.

The interview schedule was pre-tested and revised on three occasions. Four interviewers collected the data including the two principal investigators, one field assistant in Kansas and one field assistant in Connecticut. The Kansas field assistant had previously worked with the research staff of the Menninger Clinic. The Connecticut field assistant is a practicing family and marital therapist with over 10 years experience, including alcohol and substance abuse counseling in Vietnam.

Any retrospective study of an adult's childhood is fraught with methodological problems associated with the reliability and validity of recall information. This problem is compounded when collecting information from a population of prison inmates who are influenced by the institutional and bureaucratic context of their incarceration, and a tendency to view the "outside" world in sociopathic and paranoid terms (Edelman & Felthous, 1976). The interview schedule was, therefore, designed to include several measures of violent and aggressive behavior, and constructed to minimize tendencies toward providing socially desirable information.

One method sometimes employed to strengthen the validity of historical data is a review of criminal records for cross-validation purposes. This procedure was not attempted for several reasons. It would have required an additional element of informed consent which may have deterred subjects from participating in the project. Additionally, prison records typically do not contain much early childhood information. Prison records are also often very inconsistent among inmates and sometimes misleading.

Another method of cross-validation is contacting a significant and important figure in the subject's childhood. This procedure was attempted and largely involved parents and siblings of the inmates. Several difficulties arose, however, with this method. A number of subjects would not consent to having a significant other contacted, others gave their consent but the significant other could not be reached, and many of those contacted seemed even more defensive about the inmates' behaviors than the prisoners themselves.

The historical information was, therefore, open to a number of possible sources of unreliability including (1) inaccurate information because the meaning of a question was misunderstood, (2) inaccurate recollection, (3) the subject wanting to project an aggressive image and, thus, exaggerating a history of aggressive behaviors, and (4) the subject not wanting to convey an aggressive image and withholding or distorting information. The last distortion appeared to occur most often. At least one-half of the inmates contacted refused to participate in the study. Professional criminals, for example, who were members of organized crime syndicates categorically refused to be interviewed. Many subjects tended towards taciturnity, and the more garrulous often justified their actions and stressed how unfair the world had been to them. A few openly questioned, even after full informed consent, whether the interviewer was an agent of the Federal Bureau of Investigation. Subjects often used and interpreted terminology to minimize their aggressions. Most errors, therefore, appeared to move in the direction of *underreporting,* especially among the criminal population. This underreporting tendency should have reduced observed differences between the sample groups and, thus, the identification of major differences can be regarded as a likely understatement of the actual variations in animal cruelty and violence among the study populations.

CRUELTY TOWARD ANIMALS RESULTS

The range of acts involving undue harm and violence to animals during childhood[3] covered a wide diversity of behaviors with varying degrees of severity and cultural meaning. Presumably, cruel acts included deliberately inflicting pain and torturing a pet animal, similar acts toward wildlife and livestock, prolonged slaughter of a domestic animal, skinning a trapped animal alive, stoning or beating an animal, exploding an animal, wounding an animal on purpose, entering a dog in a dog fight, throwing an animal off a high place, pulling the wings off animals, tying two animals tails together, electrocuting an animal, burning an animal, blinding an animal, cutting off parts of an animal, deliberately starving an animal, hanging an animal, breaking an animal's bones, and pouring chemical irritants on an animal. A number of other behaviors were considered possible indicators of animal cruelty, although the social acceptability of these acts could be linked to particular value standards. These acts included participating in a cock fight, harsh physical punishment during the training of an animal, and sexual play with an animal. Particular childhood phobic fears, extreme hatred, and attendant tendencies toward harming animals who were the objects of these prejudices were also treated as possibly cruel behaviors toward animals, e.g., obsessive fear of snakes and the tendency to kill any snake.

The 152 subjects reported 373 acts involving some degree of undue harm, violence, or cruelty toward animals as measured by the various indicators. The majority of subjects, 60%, reported at least one or more childhood cruelties toward animals. Some 41% reported 1–2 cruelties, 11.2% admitted 3–4 cruel acts toward animals, and nearly 8% indicated at least five or more animal cruelties during childhood (Table II). Most specific acts occurred infrequently and often involved what many regard as relatively minor cruelties toward animals. Tearing the wings off bugs, for example, occurred among approximately one-third of the subjects, an act often not regarded as indicative of cruelty given prevailing beliefs about the sentient capacities of invertebrates (Kellert, 1983a, b).

Table I also indicates the frequency of childhood cruelties toward animals among aggressive criminals, moderately aggressive criminals (only examined separately at Leavenworth prison), nonaggressive criminals, and noncriminals in Kansas and Connecticut. Differences were highly significant with the greatest variance attributable to the inordinately high frequency of childhood animal cruelties among aggressive criminals. Twenty-five percent

[3]In this research, childhood was defined as prior to age 18.

Table I. Frequency of Childhood Animal Cruelties among Criminals and Noncriminals in Kansas and Connecticut

	Number of animal cruelties				
	0	1–2	3–4	5+	N
Aggressive criminals					
N	10	9	5	8	32
Percent	31.2	28.1	15.6	25	
χ^2	.63	1.26	.56	11.83	
Moderately aggressive criminals[a]					
N	10	5	2	1	18
Percent	55.6	27.7	11.1	5.6	
χ^2	1.07	.75	.00	.12	
Nonaggressive criminals					
N	27	20	2	3	52
Percent	51.9	38.5	3.8	5.8	
χ^2	1.8	.07	2.5	.30	
Noncriminals					
N	14	28	8	0	50
Percent	28	56	16	0	
χ^2	1.84	2.84	1.04	3.95	
Totals					
N	61	62	17	12	152
%	40.1	40.8	11.2	7.9	
$\chi^2 = 30.56$, $df = 9$, $p = < .005$					

[a]This category includes inmates at Leavenworth prison only.

of aggressive criminals reported five or more childhood cruelties toward animals, compared to less than 6% of moderate and nonaggressive criminals, and no occurrence among noncriminals.

A related scale was developed to measure childhood aggressiveness toward animals. Scale scores for each subject were an overall mean based on the summation of 1–5 severity ratings for each of the various animal cruelty behaviors, in addition to similar ratings for other aggressive acts toward animals including trying to wound an animal during hunting, hurting an animal during its training, various gratuitous injuries to animals, etc. Very significant differences occurred on the childhood animal aggression scale with aggressive criminals in both Kansas and Connecticut obtaining far higher scores (Table II). Additionally, the scale scores of moderate and nonaggressive criminals and noncriminals were insignificant, further suggesting the *fundamental* importance of aggressiveness rather than criminality in the occurrence of childhood cruelty toward animals.

Space limitations do not permit more than a cursory review of specific acts of childhood animal cruelty. Table III, for example, indicates the significantly greater frequency of childhood stoning of animals among aggressive criminals.

Table II. Mean Scores, Analysis of Variance, and Duncan's Multiple Range Test — Kansas and Connecticut Criminals and Noncriminals by Childhood Animal Aggression Scale

	Mean	N	Duncan grouping[b]
Kansas[a]			
Aggressive criminals	6.8	17	A
Moderately aggressive criminals	3.0	18	B
Nonaggressive criminals	2.1	15	B
Noncriminals	1.9	13	B
$F = 3.08$, $df = 3$, $PR > F = .034$			
Connecticut[c]			
Aggressive criminals	5.0	15	A
Nonaggressive criminals	1.8	35	B
Noncriminals	1.9	39	B
$F = 7.45$, $df = 2$, $PR > F = .001$			

[a]Inmates at the federal penitentiary at Leavenworth, Kansas.
[b]Means with the same letter are not significantly different.
[c]Inmates at the federal penitentiary at Danbury, Connecticut.

THE MOTIVATION FOR ANIMAL CRUELTY

Some descriptions of specific childhood cruelties toward animals will be reviewed. This description is not intended to shock nor be comprehensive, but to provide a more vivid indication of the behaviors encountered.

One subject reported snapping the necks of animals, shooting birds, and exploding a cat in a microwave oven as a youth. When asked to describe

Table III. Stone an Animal during Childhood among Criminals and Noncriminals in Kansas and Connecticut

	No	Yes
Aggressive criminals		
N	(21)	(10)
Percent	67.7	32.3
x^2	1.6	13.2
Moderately aggressive criminals		
N	(14)	(3)
Percent	82.4	17.6
x^2	.09	.73
Nonaggressive criminals		
N	(48)	(2)
Percent	96.0	4.0
x^2	.26	2.2
Noncriminals		
N	(49)	(1)
Percent	98.0	2.0
x^2	.44	3.59
Totals		
N	132	16
Percent	89.2	10.8
$x^2 = 22.06$, $df = 3$, $p = < .005$		

his feelings about these behaviors, he remarked it was done "for kicks, for fun, [that he] felt nothing." He also reported a prolonged history of child-hood fighting, property destruction, and firesetting.

Another subject described repeated childhood instances of deliberate-ly inflicting pain, torturing, and killing family pets. He also reported throw-ing animals off high buildings, starving dogs, and extreme fear of birds and snakes. He related these behaviors to a hatred and fear of his father, and indicated they were "a means for venting [his] anger, striking out, getting revenge, getting even."

Another subject explained that cruelty and aggression toward animals were a way of demonstrating his violence to others. He trained dogs to fight by the painful practice of feeding the animal gun powder to "toughen it up." He also reported illegally poaching an endangered species (the Florida Pan-ther, *Felis concolor*), and indiscriminately killed animals to increase his ag-gressiveness.

One subject reported various cruelties toward animals as an aspect of a violent family life characterized by frequent fighting, many arrests, sexual deviance, and excessive drug and alcohol use. Animal cruelties were described as a form of family excitement and pleasure. This subject reported putting cats in bags and throwing them in front of cars, placing rat poison in fish bowls, electrocuting rodents, tying cats' tails together, and beating and drowning pets. He repeatedly described these acts as being done "for fun and excitement."

Another subject reported various childhood animal cruelties including throwing a cat in an incinerator, beating and stoning dogs, and throwing animals off high places. Killing was a prominent theme, with shooting, trap-ping, and exploding animals occurring primarily for the pleasure derived from killing animals. This subject also reported pulling wings off birds, and an interest in doing combat with animals.

Analogous cases of excessive cruelty toward animals occurred among more than 40 of the 152 subjects. Based on a careful review of these cases, a preliminary classification of motivations for cruel and extremely aggres-sive behavior toward animals was developed. This classification scheme is tentatively offered, and will require further testing and refinement. It represents, nevertheless, a first attempt in the scientific literature to develop a classification of motives for cruelty toward animals. It should be noted, however, that the motivation to mistreat an animal is typically multidimen-sional, and most subjects who evidenced cruelty toward animals exhibited a variety of the described motivations. The following motives for cruelty toward animals were encountered:

1. *To Control an Animal.* Excessive and cruel physical punishment was at times employed to control or shape an animal's behavior or to eliminate presumably undesirable characteristics of an animal. One subject kicked his dog in the testicles when it bothered him at the dinner table, another repeat-

edly rubbed his dog's anus in turpentine to dissuade it from entering the chicken-coop, another subject used electric prods and beatings to gain compliance. These behaviors were typically excessive rather than simply intended to produce a well-behaved animal.

2. *To Retaliate against an Animal.* Some subjects inflicted extreme punishment or revenge for a presumed wrong on the part of an animal. For example, one subject shot and killed a dog which tried to mate with his dog, another burned a cat that scratched him, a third drowned a neighbor's dog for barking too much. While some provocation was evident, the delight taken in the retaliatory punishment and the intensity of the vengeful behavior identified this conduct as a type of animal cruelty.

3. *To Satisfy a Prejudice against a Species or Breed.* People will at times designate groups of animals as either good or bad, with these beliefs often associated with cultural values such as the prejudice in our society against rats or snakes. Cruelty associated with this type of bias typically involves more than simple normative prejudice, usually being manifest in violent or sadistic conduct against an animal rationalized by a particular prejudice.

For example, cat hatred was particularly common. One subject admitted to a variety of cruelties against cats because he did not like them, another exploded his girlfriend's cat in a microwave oven, a third alluded to running a cat over with a lawn mower. These and other subjects often described cats as "sneaky," "creepy," "treacherous," and one related his violent prejudice against cats to violent feelings he possessed toward people of another race. In contrast, no subject reported any categorical hatred of dogs, although a number admitted to extreme fear of dogs, and some used dogs as a device for expressing violence against other people and animals. Extreme prejudice was also evidenced toward snakes, certain rodents and insects, and a number of subjects indiscriminately shot, burned, or mutilated these creatures.

4. *To Express Aggression through an Animal.* Cruelty toward animals was sometimes used to express violent, aggressive behaviors toward other people or animals. For example, cruelty occasionally occurred as a device for instilling violent tendencies in an animal, or for attacking other animals or people. One subject inflicted extreme pain on his animal to make it "mean"; another fed his dog gunpowder so it would be "tough"; still another used his dog to attack and kill other animals without provocation.

5. *To Enhance One's Own Aggressiveness.* Some subjects reported killing and abusing animals as a way of improving their own aggressive skills, or to impress others with their capacity for violence. One subject gratuitously shot and maimed animals as a form of target practice; while another reported killing animals in an outrageous fashion to impress his fellow motorcycle gang members.

6. *To Shock People for Amusement.* Cruelty toward animals sometimes occurred as a means of generating amusement. One inmate stuffed cats in a pillowcase for a "joke," soaked them with lighter fluid, set them afire, and

turned them loose in a bar, another reported putting pigeons in milk crates and releasing them in a restaurant, still another subject cut the legs off and exploded frogs to entertain himself and his friends.

7. *To Retaliate against Another Person.* Cruelty toward animals sometimes occurred as a method for striking back and exacting revenge against other people. In such cases, this behavior often involved another person's animals, typically a pet. One subject retaliated against a neighbor by placing her cats in a gunny sack and beating them with a club, another castrated a raccoon and hung its testes on the door of a woman's house whom he disliked.

8. *Displacement of Hostility from a Person to an Animal.* A related motivation was the displacement of frustrated aggression from another person to an animal. This displaced aggression typically involved authority figures whom the subject hated or feared but was afraid to aggress against. It is often easier in childhood to be violent toward an animal than against a parent, sibling, or adult.

Many aggressive subjects were raised in violent and chaotic families and were physically abused, and cruelty toward animals often served as a displaced expression of this violence. One subject reported being cruel toward animals as a means of getting "even for my hurt," caused by parental and peer rejection. Another described beating animals as revenge for the beatings he had suffered.

9. *Nonspecific Sadism.* A final motivation was the desire to inflict injury, suffering, or death on an animal in the absence of any particular provocation or especially hostile feelings toward an animal. The primary goal was the pleasure derived from causing injury and suffering. Sadistic gratification was sometimes associated with the desire to exercise total power and control over an animal, and may have served to compensate for a person's feelings of weakness or vulnerability.

One subject reported pulling wings off sparrows and splitting open the bellies of amphibians to watch them die slowly, another reported electrocuting animals and tying the tails of cats together for "fun and excitement," another reported cutting and stabbing fish for "kicks." The act of killing was often associated in these cases with satisfying a pleasurable impulse, and extinguishing a life became a primary objective unrelated to any particular fear or hatred of an animal. One subject reported slaughtering livestock and trapping animals for the primary purpose of killing, to be "vicious" as he remarked, another reported snapping the necks of animals "for kicks, for fun, [and] feeling nothing." Still another indicated a fascination with the boundary between life and death, and an obsession with the tendency of chickens not to die immediately after decapitation and the possibility of a similar human capacity at the instant of being guillotined. This subject also reported experimenting with novel ways of killing animals.

Table IV. Mean Scores, Analysis of Variance, and Duncan's Multiple Range Test — Kansas and Connecticut Prisoners and Nonprisoners by Childhood Aggression Toward People Scale

	Mean	N	Duncan grouping[b]
Kansas[a]			
Aggressive criminals	13.5	16	A
Moderately aggressive criminals	8.2	18	B
Nonaggressive criminals	6.0	15	B
Noncriminals	5.2	13	B
$F = 10.98$, $df = 3$, $PR > F = .0001$			
Connecticut[c]			
Aggressive criminals	10.4	15	A
Nonaggressive criminals	3.4	39	B
Noncriminals	1.8	35	B
$F = 43.89$, $df = 2$, $PR > F = .0001$			

[a]Inmates at the federal penitentiary at Leavenworth, Kansas.
[b]Means with the same letter are not significantly different.
[c]Inmates at the federal penitentiary at Danbury, Connecticut.

FAMILY DYNAMICS

The family background of many subjects were so striking that some preliminary results can be presented regarding the role of childhood family experiences in the occurrence of cruelty toward animals. Far more data will be necessary, however, before confident conclusions can be offered.

The family and childhood experiences of many aggressive criminals were especially violent. For example, aggressive criminals obtained very significantly higher scores on a childhood aggressiveness toward people scale than did either nonaggressive criminals or noncriminals (Table IV). Additionally, the mean scores of nonaggressive criminals and noncriminals were insignificantly different on this scale.[4] Table V also indicates a greater tendency among aggressive criminals to inflict violence against people as a child.

Domestic violence in the families of aggressive criminals who were cruel to animals assumed many forms, although extreme paternal violence and alcoholism were especially common. Additionally, nonaggressive criminals and noncriminals who reported instances of animal cruelty often indicated being physically abused as a child, frequent fights with fathers, and parental alcoholism.

The extent of domestic violence in the families of aggressive criminals is dramatically indicated by the findings of Table VI and VII. Three-quarters of all aggressive criminal subjects reported excessive and repeated child abuse, compared to 31% of nonaggressive criminals, and only 10% among non-

---

[4]This scale was based on such indicators as fighting in school, physically hurting another person as a child, setting fires as a child, and a number of other factors.

Table V. Physical Fights as Child among Criminals and Noncriminals in Kansas and Connecticut

	No	Rarely	Sometimes	Often
Aggressive criminals				
N	0	3	9	19
Percent	0	10.0	29.0	61.1
χ^2	7.4	3.5	0.0	26.76
Moderately aggressive criminals				
N	1	7	6	4
Percent	5.6	38.9	33.3	22.2
χ^2	2.5	0.9	0.1	0.1
Nonaggressive criminals				
N	14	16	17	5
Percent	26.9	30.8	32.7	9.6
χ^2	0.2	0.3	0.2	2.8
Noncriminals				
N	21	15	12	2
Percent	42.0	30.0	24.0	4.0
χ^2	6.9	0.2	0.5	6.3
Totals				
N	36	41	34	30
Percent	25.5	29.1	24.1	21.3

$\chi^2 = 58.53$, $df = 9$, $p = < .005$

Table VI. Domestic Violence vs. Stable Family Relationships among Criminals and Noncriminals in Kansas and Connecticut[a]

	Domestic violence	Stable family	Neither domestic violence nor stable family
Aggressive criminals			
N	37	9	3
Percent	75.5	18.4	6
χ^2	14.9	11.2	0.0
Nonaggressive criminals			
N	16	31	5
Percent	30.7	59.6	9.6
χ^2	1.2	0.4	0.9
Noncriminals			
N	4	35	1
Percent	10	87.5	2.5
χ^2	9.2	8.9	0.9
Totals			
N	51	75	9
Percent	40.4	53.2	6.4

$\chi^2 = 47.6$, $df = 2$, $p = < .0001$

[a]Eleven cases were omitted due to inadequate information.

Table VII. Domestic Violence and Parental Alcoholism/Drug Abuse Among Criminals and Noncriminals in Kansas and Connecticut

	Domestic violence and parental alcohol/drug abuse	Non-occurrence
Aggressive and moderately aggressive criminals		
N	(24)	(25)
Percent	49	51
x^2	13.72	4.19
Nonaggressive criminals		
N	(6)	(46)
Percent	11.5	88.5
x^2	3.13	.96
Noncriminals		
N	(3)	(37)
Percent	7.5	92.5
x^2	4.32	1.32
Totals		
N	33	108
Percent	23.4	76.6
$x^2 = 27.64$, $df = 2$, $p = < .0001$		

criminals. Additionally, nearly one-third of nonaggressive criminals with a history of substantial family violence were rated as borderline aggressive subjects, and 75% of all noncriminals who experienced parental abuse also reported incidents of animal cruelty.

Parental alcoholism, especially among fathers, occurred to a far greater degree among aggressive subjects. Seventy-three percent of violent criminals reported alcoholism and/or drug abuse by their parents or guardians, compared to less than 20% among nonaggressive criminals and 10% of noncriminals. Not surprisingly, a strong association of substance abuse and severe family violence was observed. Nearly one-half of aggressive criminal subjects, compared to 12% of nonaggressive criminals and 7% of noncriminals, reported alcoholism and substantial family violence during childhood.

CONCLUSION

This paper has reviewed a number of results from a study of childhood cruelty toward animals, motivations for animal cruelty, and family violence. The strength of these findings suggests that aggression among adult criminals may be strongly correlated with a history of family abuse and childhood cruelty toward animals. The identification of nine motivations for animal cruelty indicates the complex multidimensional character of this behavior.

This data should alert researchers, clinicians, and societal leaders to the importance of childhood animal cruelty as a potential indicator of disturbed family relationships and future antisocial and aggressive behavior. The evolution of a more gentle and benign relationship in human society might be enhanced by our promotion of a more positive and nurturing ethic between children and animals.

REFERENCES

ALFARO, J. D. Summary report on the relationship between child abuse and neglect and later socially deviant behavior. New York: Select Committee on Child Abuse, 1978.

AMSTERDAM, B., BRILL, M., BELL, N., EDWARDS, D. Coping with abuse: Adolescents' views. *Victimology,* 1977, *4*(2), 278-284.

AZRIM, N. H., & HOLZ, W. C. Punishment (Chap. 9). In W. K. Honig (Ed.), *Operant behavior: Areas of research and application.* New York: Appleton-Crofts, 1966.

BACH-y-RITA, G., et al. Episodic dyscontrol: A study of 130 violent patients. *American Journal of Psychiatry,* 1971, *127,* 1473-1478.

BUTTON, A. Some antecedents of felonious and delinquent behavior. *Journal of Clinical Child Psychology,* 1973, *2*(3), 34-37.

CARSON, G. *Men, beasts and gods.* New York: Charles Scribner's Sons, 1972.

CLIMENT, C. E., & ERVIN, F. R. Historical data in the evaluation of violent subjects. *Archives of General Psychiatry,* 1972, *27,* 621-624.

DUNCAN, G., FRAZIER, S. H. & LITIN, E. M. Etiological factors in first degree murder. *Journal of the American Medical Association,* 1958, *168*(13).

EASSON, D. In silver, doublin, and lourie. *Journal of the American Medical Association,* 1958, *158*(13).

EDELMAN, S. E., & FELTHOUS, A. R. Some methodological problems in studying violent offenders. *Bulletin American Academy of Psychiatric Law,* 1976, *4*(1), 67-72.

FELTHOUS, A. R. Aggression against cats, dogs and people. *Child Psychiatry and Human Development,* 1980, *10*(3), 169-177.

FELTHOUS, A. R. Childhood cruelty to cats, dogs and other animals. *Bulletin American Academy Psychiatric Law,* 1981, *8*(2), 48-53.

FELTHOUS, A. R., & BERNARD, H. Firesetting and cruelty to animals: The significance of two thirds of this triad. *Forensic Sciences,* 1979, *29*(1), 240-246.

FRAZIER, S. H. Murder—single and multiple. *Aggression, Research, Public Assessment Research Nervous and Mental Disturbance,* 1972, *52, 304-310.*

FUCINI, S. The abuser, first a dog, then a child? *American Humane,* May 1978.

GELLES, R. J. *The violent home: A study of physical aggression between husbands and wives.* California: Sage, 1974.

GLUECK, S., & GLUECK, E. T. *Delinquents and nondelinquents in perspective.* Massachusetts: Harvard University Press, 1968.

HELLMAN, D. S., & BLACKMAN, N. Enuresis, firesetting and cruelty to animals: A triad predictive of adult crime. *American Journal of Psychiatry,* 1966, *122,* 1431-1435.

HUNNER, R. J., & WALKER, H. E. (Eds.). *Exploring the relationship between child abuse and delinquency.* New Jersey: Allanheld, Osmun and Co., 1981.

JUSTICE, B., JUSTICE, R., & KRAFT, I. A. Early-warning signs of violence: Is a triad enough? *American Journal of Psychiatry,* 1974, *131*(4), 457-459.

KELLERT, S. American attitudes toward and knowledge of animals: An update. *International Journal for the Study of Animal Problems 1,* 1979, *2,* 87-119.

KELLERT, S. Affective, cognitive and evaluative perceptions of animals. In I. Altman & J. F. Wohlwill (Eds.), *Behavior and the natural environment.* New York: Plenum Press, 1983. (a)

KELLERT, S. Societal and perceptual factors in species preservation. In B. G. Norton & H. Shue (Eds.), *Preservation of species.* New Jersey: Princeton University Press, 1983. (b)

LANGEVIN, P. PAITICH, D., ORCHARD, B., HANDY, L., & RUSSON, A. Childhood and family background of killers seen for psychiatric assessment: A controlled study. *Bulletin of American Psychiatric Law,* 1983, *11,* 331-341.

LANGNER, S., & GERSTEN, J. D. Family research project. *Science News,* 1976, *109,* 20.

LEVI-STRAUSS, C. *The savage mind.* Illinois: University of Chicago Press, 1966.

LEWIS, D. O., SHANOK, S. S., GRANT, M. & RITVO, E. Homicidally aggressive young children: Neuropsychiatric and experiential correlates. *American Journal of Psychiatry,* 1983, *140*(2), 148-153.

LOS ANGELES TIMES. There are 2 people inside of him. November 4, 1973.

LOWELL SUN. Man who says he killed for "fun" sentenced to 150 years in prison, 1982.

LOWEN, J. Child abuse: A contributing factor to delinquency. Washington: University of Washington, Center for Law and Justice, 1979, pp. JD-45.

MacDONALD, J. M. *The murderer and his victim.* Illinois: Charles C Thomas, 1961.

MEAD, M. Cultural factors in the cause of pathological homicide. *Bulletin Menninger Clinic,* 1964, *28,* 11-22.

MONAHAN, J. *The clinical prediction of violent behavior.* Maryland: National Institute of Mental Health, 1981.

OWENS, D. J., & STRAUSS, M. A. Childhood violence and adult approval of violence. *Aggressive Behavior,* 1975, *1*(2), 193-211.

RIGDON, J. D., & TAPIA, F. Children who are cruel to animals—a follow-up study. *Journal of Operative Psychiatry,* 1977, *8*(1), 27-36.

ROBIN, M., Ten BENSEL, R. W., QUIGLEY, J., & ANDERSON, R. K. A study of the relationship of childhood pet animals and the psycho-social development of adolescents. Proceedings Conference on the Human-Animal Bond, University of Pennsylvania Press, 1981.

SHANOK, S. S., MALANI, S. C., NINAN, O: P., GUGGENHEIM, P., WEINSTEIN, H. & LEWIS, D. O. A comparison of delinquent and nondelinquent adolescent psychiatric inpatients. *American Journal of Psychiatry,* 1983, *140*(5), 582-585.

TAPIA, F. Children who are cruel to animals. *Clinical Psychiatry and Human Development,* 1971, *2*(2), 70-71.

TAPIA, F., JEKEL, J., & DUMKE, H. R. Enuresis: An emotional symptom? *Journal of Nervous and Mental Disturbance,* 1960, *130,* 61-66.

Ten BENSEL, R. W. Historical perspectives of human values for animals and vulnerable people. Proceedings Conference on the Human-Animal Bond, University of Minnesota, 1983.

Ten BENSEL, R. W., WARD, D. A., KRUTTSCHNITT, C., QUIGLEY, J., & ANDERSON, R. K. Attitudes of violent criminals toward animals: A comparison with a control group. Proceedings Conference on the Human—Animal Bond, University of Minnesota, 1983.

THOMAS, K. *Man and the natural world.* New York: Pantheon Books, 1983.

WASHINGTON POST. Psychiatrist describes Wersick's upbringing. April 25, 1979.

WASHINGTON STAR. Police looking for friend of "Sam" suspect. August 15, 1977.

WAX, D. E., & HADDOX, V. G. Enuresis, firesetting, and animal cruelty in male adolescent delinquents: A triad predictive of violent behavior. *Journal of Psychiatric Law,* 1974, *2*(1), 45-72.

WELSH, R. Severe parental punishment and delinquency: A developmental theory. In Wertheimer and Rappoport (Eds.), *Psychology and the problems of today.* Illinois: Scott Foresman and Co., 1978.

BIOGRAPHICAL NOTES

STEPHEN R. KELLERT is a Associate Professor at the Yale University School of Forestry and Environmental Studies. For the past 10 years, he has conducted various studies on human perceptions and behavioral interactions with animals. He is also President of the Connecticut Audubon Society.

ALAN R. FELTHOUS is Associate Professor of Psychiatry and Chief of Forensic Service, Department of Psychiatry and Behavioral Sciences, University of Texas Medical Branch, Galveston, Texas. He was formerly Section Chief, C. F. Menninger Memorial Hospital in Topeka, Kansas. Professional interests include psychiatric consultations to prisons and jails, forensic consultations on psycholegal issues, and research on aggressive behaviors.

Childhood and Adolescent Characteristics of Pedophiles and Rapists

David Tingle,* George W. Barnard,** Lynn Robbins,***
Gustave Newman**** and David Hutchinson*****

In recent years there has been an upsurge of interest in sexual offenders. The apparent increase in the number of child molestation cases reported to the press has led to a greatly heightened public awareness of this problem and to the development of programs concerning themselves solely with "child sexual abuse." There have been considerable research data on the psychological aspects of the adult sexual offender and the sexual preference of paraphiliacs, but little is known about causative factors. Such research generally focuses on four specific areas of interest. Firstly, a few epidemiologic studies; secondly, Minnesota Multiphasic Personality Inventories (MMPIs) and other psychological tests; thirdly, self-reported questionnaires (the most sophisticated one being that developed by the Clarke Institute[1]); and finally, various penile tumescence measurements. Freund,[2] a pioneer in this area as early as 1963, was able to differentiate homosexuals from heterosexuals on the basis of erection responses to deviant or nondeviant slides as measured by a penile plethysmograph. Freund and his colleagues continue to refine and expand this technique. A similar method in the investigation of sexual choice is the penile circumference measurement. This increasingly popular device (initially described by Fisher et al. in 1965[3]) consists of an elastic tude placed around the penis and filled with either water, mercury, or graphite. Both these psychophysiologic methods are reliable predictors of sexual preference.

---

*Associate Professor and Chief, Adult & Adolescent Psychiatric Inpatient Service, Department of Psychiatry, University of Florida, Gainesville, FL 32610, U.S.A.

**Professor and Chief, Consultation-Liaison Service, Department of Psychiatry, University of Florida.

***Associate, Department of Psychiatry, University of Florida.

****Associate Professor, Department of Psychiatry, University of Florida.

*****Former Unit Treatment and Rehabilitation Director, North Florida Evaluation and Treatment Center, Gainesville, Florida.

Address all communications to: Dr. D. Tingle, Department of Psychiatry, College of Medicine, J. Hillis Miller Health Center, University of Florida, Gainesville, FL 32610, U.S.A.

The authors wish to acknowledge the assistance of Valerie Mercak on this paper.

[1]Langevin, R., editor (1985). *Erotic preference, gender identity, and aggression in men: New research studies* (pp. 287–341). New Jersey: Lawrence Erlbaum Assoc.

[2]Freund, K. (1963). A laboratory method of diagnosing predominance of homo- or hetero-erotic interest in the male. *Behavior Research and Therapy, 1*, 85–93.

[3]Fisher, C., Gross, J., & Zuch, J. (1965). Cycle of penile erections synchronous with dreaming (REM) sleep. *Archives of General Psychiatry, 12*, 29–45.

Reprinted from the *International Journal of Law and Psychiatry* 9 (1986): 103–16, with kind permission of Elsevier Science Ltd., Oxford, England.

The personality characteristics and attitudes of rapists have been extensively studied. In a comparison of the "needs systems" of 20 male rapists with a group of violent nonsex offenders, Scott[4] found that rapists have a higher need for abasement and dominance, and a lesser need for autonomy and nurturance. Rabkin,[5] using an epidemiologic technique, concluded that rapists tend to be under 30 years of age, poorly educated, unskilled, and disproportionately black. Few were found to be overtly mentally ill. More recently, Prentky et al.,[6] using data gleaned from 1600 "heterogeneous" rapists, categorized them into eight groupings on the basis of the relative contribution of sexual and aggressive drives to their offenses. (They thought these groupings might be useful for intervention, treatment, and forensic purposes.) Furthermore, various MMPI studies have been conducted in some detail on rapists. One such study by Armentrout and Hauer[7] studied 13 rapists of adults, 21 rapists of children, and 17 non-rapist sexual offenders and found the elevations of the psychopathic (4) and the schizophrenic (8) scales on the MMPI to be much higher in the rapists than in the non-rapists. Additionally, this 4–8 elevation is higher in the rapists of adults than in the rapists of children. Other studies by Huesmann et al.[8] generally confirm the elevation of the 4–8 profile. In a sophisticated study of rapists, nonviolent sex offenders, and nonsexual assaultive offenders, using normal controls, Langevin[9], confirmed this tendency to an elevation of the MMPI scales 4 and 8, and noticed, like other researchers, that the profiles of the rapists were very similar to the nonsexual assaultive groups, differing only in having a lower score on the "paranoid" scale. This study also involved the administration of the Clarke Sexual History Questionnaire for Males and the Clarke Parent-Child Relations Questionnaire, among others. On all parameters in this study, the rapists resembled the assaulters in personality and diagnosis. Both groups were "super heterosexuals" who have a higher than average frequency of conventional sexual outlets—their only discernable difference being in the commission of rape. Rapists engaged in a very wide range of sexual behaviors including exhibiting, peeping, obscene phone calls, and toucheurism—the so-called "courtship disorders." The study concluded that their violent history, abuse of alcohol, poor socialization as children, and higher sexual "drive" were major factors that predisposed them collectively to rape. Generally, rapists seem to be similar to other violent offenders with antisocial personality characteristics.

There is less research on personality characteristics and attitudes of pedophiles, who are often lumped with rapists on the assumption that they represent a more

[4]Scott, R. L. (1982). Analysis of the needs systems of twenty male rapists. *Psychological Reports 51*, 1119–1125.

[5]Rabkin, J. G. (1979). The epidemiology of forcible rape. *American Journal of Orthopsychiatry, 49*(4), 634–647.

[6]Prentky, R., Cohen, M., & Seghorn, T. (1985). Development of a rational taxonomy for the classification of rapists: The Massachusetts Treatment Center System. *Bulletin of the American Academy of Psychiatry and Law, 13*(1), 39–70.

[7]Armentrout, J. A., & Hauer, A. L. (1978). MMPIs of rapists of adults, rapists of children and nonrapist sex offenders. *Journal of Clinical Psychology, 34*(2), 330–332.

[8]Huesmann, L. R., Lefkowitz, M. M., & Eron, L. D. (1978). Sum of MMPI scales F, 4 and 8, as a measure of aggression. *Journal of Consulting and Clinical Psychology, 46*, 1071–1078.

[9]Langevin, X. *supra* note 1, at 21–33.

or less homogeneous group, even though Finkelhor[10] reports that the pedophile group has emerged as a separate entity over the past 10–12 years. Sociologically, he found that many pedophiles are relatives of their victims, and associated factors seem to be family isolation and a patriarchal family structure. Stepfathers and live-in boyfriends of the mothers seem more at risk to be child molesters. Gaffney et al.,[11] using charts of hospitalized patients (one of the rare studies not involving convicted offenders) separated them into pedophiles and other paraphiliacs with a control group of depressives. Eighteen and a half percent of these male paraphiliacs have family members with sexual deviancy as opposed to a sexual deviancy prevalence in the depressives of three percent. More interestingly, they "bred true" in that the families of pedophiles had pedophilia, as opposed to other sexual deviancies, as their prominent sexual disorder. Gaffney concluded that sexual deviancy, rather than being a continuum, includes at least two separate entities, namely, the pedophiles and "other paraphiliacs." Consequently, a genetic factor in pedophilia is suggested. In a recent review article, Araji and Finkelhor[12] examined the evidence to support four of the etiologic theories for pedophilia. The Emotional Congruence Theory views the pedophile's compelling attraction to children as being related to the adult's emotional needs being met by the immature psychosocial characteristics of the child. The Sexual Arousal Theory holds that child molesters display an atypical pattern of sexual arousal which is related to the early childhood sexual experiences with adults which pedophiles frequently claim to have had. The Theory of Blockage suggests that there is a block in the satisfaction of emotional and sexual needs of other adults so the individual turns to children for gratification. In support of this theory, there is some evidence that pedophiles have problems relating to adult females. Finally, disinhibition is said to remove normal inhibitions against sexual contact with children, with alcohol involvement having the most empirical support. For future research the authors suggest grouping the pedophiles into such categories as age of victim; preferred sex objects; enduringness of sexual interest in children; and incestuous, nonincestuous victim choice — incestuous pedophiles seem to be even more heterogenous than nonincestuous subjects. They recommend that future research be done on prisoner pedophiles, despite epidemiologic considerations, as they are the most accessible group. MMPIs have also been employed in pedophile studies. McCreary[13] tested two groups of child molesters, one with and one without previous arrests for child molestation. He found no typical personality profiles but rather a heterogeneous variety of personality factors, apparently more severe in repeat offenders. Although the pedophile has characteristically been described as shy and unassertive, the passivity of pedophiles is being questioned by Panton[14]

---

[10]Finkelhor, D. (1982). Sexual abuse: A sociological perspective. *Child Abuse and Neglect, 6*(1), 95–102.

[11]Gaffney, G. R., Lurie, S. F., & Berlin, F. S. (1984). Is there familial transmission of pedophilia? *Journal of Nervous and Mental Disorders, 172*(9), 546–548.

[12]Araji, S., Finkelhor, D. (1985). Explanations of pedophilia: Review of empirical research. *Bulletin of the American Academy of Psychiatry and Law, 13*(1), 17–37.

[13]McCreary, C. P. (1975). Personality differences among child molesters. *Journal of Personality Assessment 39*(6), 591–593.

[14]Panton, J. H. (1978). Personality differences appearing between rapists of adults, rapists of children and nonviolent sexual molesters of female children. *Research Communications in Psychology, Psychiatry & Behavior, 3*(4), 385–393.

who compared the MMPis of three groups of incarcerated offenders, 30 rapists of adults, 30 rapists of children, and 28 nonviolent pedophiles. The two rapist groups did not differ significantly from each other but the nonviolent pedophiles were very different, showing low self-esteem, anxiety, aversion to violence, inadequacy, and a fear of heterosexual failure. Armentrout and Hauer[15] found similar results in their MMPI study. Langevin[16], comparing heterosexual pedophiles with homosexual pedophiles and bisexual pedophiles together with a fourth group of controls, administered MMPIs, a section of the Clarke Sexual History Questionnaire, Clarke Parent-Child Relations Questionnaire and other tests. Overall, his three pedophile groups have less education, more psychotic scale elevations on the MMPI, and worse relationships with their mothers than the controls. Surprisingly, 22% of the heterosexual pedophiles were involved in serious violence, contrasting with the findings of earlier studies. Only the homosexual pedophile group had reduced frequency of sexual outlet with adult females, whereas the other pedophilic groups were average in this area. Overall, it would appear that studies of pedophiles do not show any strikingly consistent findings other than perhaps impairment in relationships with the mother.

Comparisons of the personality characteristics and attitudes of rapists with those of child molesters are less plentiful. Davidson[17] found that pedophiles and rapists share strong feelings of dependency and have passive aggressive types of personality with marked feelings of inferiority. Henn et al.,[18] comparing rapists with pedophiles, concluded that we are dealing with two distinct populations. Their rapists were younger, showed a higher prevalence of antisocial personality, and a tendency to repetitive violent crime. Pedophiles showed a much greater age range and were not antisocial or violent. They did show rather more diagnoses such as organic brain syndrome, mental retardation and schizophrenia than did the rapists. When Anderson et al.[19] gave 92 sex offenders MMPIs, they found that pedophiles could not be distinguished from other sex offenders by this test. Abel, Mittelman, and Becker,[20] using 411 paraphiliac outpatient volunteers, found that the 89 rapists attempted or completed 744 rapes on an average of 7.5 victims. The 232 child molesters had each attempted 238 child molestations and had completed 166 on 75.8 victims. They found that 16.8% of the child molesters were involved with rape, while 50.6% of their rapists were involved in child molestation. Although the victims of sexual assault are known to be frequently reluctant to notify the police or other agencies, the magnitude of these statistics is surprising. "Courtship disorders" were also very common in both groups. In an attempt to improve the validity of traditional clinical interviews, these investigators did psychophysiologic measurements following the sexual ques-

[15]*Supra* note 7.

[16]Langevin, X. *supra* note 1, at 143–155.

[17]Davidson, A. T. (1983). Sexual exploitation of children: A call to action. *Journal of the National Medical Association, 75*(10), 925–927.

[18]Henn, F. A., Herjanic, M., & Vanderpearl, R. H. (1976). Forensic psychiatry: Profiles of two types of sex offenders. *American Journal of Psychiatry, 133*(6), 694–696.

[19]Anderson, W. P., Kunce, J. T., & Rich, B. (1979). Sex offenders: Three personality types. *Journal of Clinical Psychology, 35*(3), 671–676.

[20]Abel, G. G., Mittelman, M. S., & Becker, J. V. (1985). Sexual offenders: Results of assessment and recommendations for treatment. In *Clinical criminology: Current concepts.* Toronto: M & M Graphics.

tionnaire interview on 24 consecutive referrals. In 70% of these cases, this assessment showed paraphiliac arousal not reported during the initial clinical interview. Of those individuals for whom discrepancies existed, 70% admitted to the additional paraphiliac interest. In light of these findings, the authors seriously question the reliability of histories from convicted paraphiliacs in a prison setting. The frequent multiplicity of sexual object arousal choice is demonstrated by Freund and Costell,[21] who used visual stimuli and a penile plethysmograph, and demonstrated that nondeviant males responded not only to adult women, but also to adolescent and young girls in decreasing order, indicating that deviant arousal may be a quantitative and not a qualitative difference. The reliability of penile tumescence measurements in differentiating rapists from other nonsex offenders is confirmed by Quincy et al.[22] using response to consenting sex and rape scenes. Penile tumescence measurements have even been proposed as a predictor for the potential for violence in pedophiles. Avery-Clark and Laws[23] separated 31 male pedophiles on the basis of their history into "more dangerous" and "less dangerous" groups. They then tested their penile erection response to audiotaped descriptions of sexual assaults varying in degrees of aggressiveness and on a pregenital-genital continuum. They found the more dangerous group were significantly more responsive to the aggressive stimuli than were the less dangerous abusers. Abel and associates,[24] measuring penile response to erotic stimuli with a variety of diagnostic groups including male pedophiles, found that the pedophiles responded similarly to both audio and video presentation stimuli, unlike the others. Predictably, the homosexual pedophiles showed equal arousal to young boys, "their paraphiliac choice", as they did to adult women. Sex offenders are lumped together in psychological, sociological, and descriptive studies and only in the last decade have the possible differences between them begun to emerge. These differences are often contradictory and fail to be replicated in subsequent studies. Psychophysiological determination of sexual preference is our most useful method of identifying potential paraphiliacs, but even this can apparently be faked on occasion (Laws & Holman[25]). Rapists seem to resemble other violent nonsex offenders in many areas but pedophiles are a very heterogeneous group, with disturbed maternal relationships as the only consistent finding. This study is an attempt to compare childhood and adolescent experiences of these two groups in a forensic treatment center setting and perhaps lend some credence to the notion of categorizing pedophiles separately.

[21]Freund, K., & Costell, R. (1970). The structure of erotic preference in the nondeviant male. *Behavior Research and Therapy, 8*, 15–20.

[22]Quinsey, V. L., Chaplin, T. C., & Varney, G. (1981). A comparison of rapists' and nonsex offenders' sexual preferences for mutually consenting sex, rape, and physical abuse of women. *Behavior Assessment, 3*, 127–135.

[23]Avery-Clark, C. A., & Laws, D. R. (1984). Differential erection response patterns of sexual child abusers to stimuli describing activities with children. *Behavior Therapy, 15*(1), 71–83.

[24]Abel, G. G., Blanchard, E. B., & Barlow, D. H. (1981). Measurement of sexual arousal in several paraphiliacs: The effects of stimulus modality, instructional set and stimulus content on the objective. *Behavior Research and Therapy, 19*(1), 25–33.

[25]Laws, D. R., & Holmen, M. L. (1978). Sexual response faking by pedophiles. *Criminal Justice and Behavior, 5*, 343–357.

Materials and Methods

The study was carried out at the North Florida Evaluation and Treatment Center (NFETC). This is a 200 bed forensic psychiatric facility located in north central Florida near Gainesville and served in part by faculty members of the University of Florida. Within this center, 62 beds are allocated to the diagnosis and treatment of mentally disordered sex offenders. These are men who were found guilty of committing a sexual offense and were sentenced to prison. While in prison, they requested a transfer to the forensic psychiatry program.

On arrival at NFETC each individual is given a 90 day evaluation, following which he may be accepted into the treatment program or sent back to prison. As part of the evaluation process, data are obtained from each individual covering a broad basis of factors that include socio-developmental patterns, education, employment, marital and military histories, and a physical and mental health history. A detailed structured interview is employed to minimize interviewer variation. The interview is done by a psychiatric resident.

Following the evaluation, the staff jointly makes the determination as to whether the individual would profit from the program. An individual accepted remains at the Center until, in the opinion of the staff, he has obtained maximum benefits or until he has completed treatment successfully. The average length of stay is around three years for those completing successfully.

The philosophical basis for the therapeutic approach at the NFETC is that a major personality reconstruction must take place before the sex offender can function benignly in society. This requires an emotional and intellectual commitment on the part of the offender, as he must change his view of himself and others and extensively alter his problem-solving patterns. To this end, early in the evaluation process, the sex offender must display a willingness to assess the person he is now, the process by which he arrived at this person and the dynamics of his involvement with his victim or victims. He must show a willingness to explore his past in great detail and to probe his relationships with other people.

The data for this study were obtained from 64 consecutive admissions to NFETC over a 21 month period. Of these, 21 were rapists and 43 were child molesters. Rapists were defined as those men who had been found guilty of a crime of sexual violence (sexual battery or attempted sexual battery); the child molesters were defined as those found guilty of a nonviolent sexual crime against minors under 16 years of age (lewd and lascivious behavior). It was not known whether there were any homosexual child molesters in our sample. Although some of the child victims were family members or relatives, none of them were actual daughters of the offenders.

The interviews were all completed within the first two–three weeks of their stay and, indeed, were a part of the intitial evaluation.

The data were computerized and subjected to statistical analysis using the Chi Square test for significance and Fisher's Exact Test. It should be noted that the use of multiple Chi Square Tests increases the likelihood of type I errors; i.e., false positive significant levels. This study will compare the two groups of offenders in terms of characteristics of family unit, relationships to family members and significant others outside the family, and problems with the educational system and the law.

Results

Social and demographic comparisons (Table 1). The rapist and child molester groups were similar in racial composition. The child molesters were significantly older than the rapists, they were also slightly better educated and, at the time of their arrest, more of the child molesters had an intact marriage.

Family and child parent relationships (Table 2). Differences emerged in several factors related to the childhood relationship with parents. First, while both groups came from broken homes, a significantly higher percentage (71.4%) of the rapists came from families with separated or divorced parents than did the child molesters (44.2%).

The role of the father of both the rapist and the child molester emerged as a relatively insignificant one in the home. While the child molesters reported a slightly greater degree of closeness to the father than the rapists, about 50% of both groups reported not being close at all.

Whereas the general pattern with both groups is characterized by a lack of fathering, the pattern of the child molester is characterized by a singular degree of closeness and attachment to the mother. Almost 83% of this group claimed to have had a close or very close relationship with their mother. Although over three-quarters of the child molesters reported this feeling of closeness, less than a quarter (23.3%) found her to have been a person to whom they could turn when troubled to discuss their problems.

The rapists had significantly more arguments with their mothers than the child molesters had. There is no difference between the two groups in the degree of

TABLE 1
Social Demographics

		Rapists (n = 21)	Child Molesters (n = 43)
Race			
White		81.0%	88.4%
Black		14.3%	7.0%
Hispanics		4.8%	4.6%
Age (mean)		26.0	31.4*
	(S.D.)	5.9	10.6
Education			
Less than high school degree		52.4%	39.5%
High school degree		38.1%	46.5%
AA or Bachelor's degree		9.5%	14.0%
Marital Status			
Married		9.5%	25.0%
Separated		0.0%	10.0%
Divorced		38.1%	22.5%
Single		52.4%	42.5%

*$p < .05$

TABLE 2
Family Characteristics

	Rapists ($n = 21$)	Child Molesters ($n = 43$)
Parents Separated/Divorced	71.4%	44.2%*
Abandoned by mother	14.3%	11.6%
Abandoned by father	14.3%	14.0%
Degree of closeness to father		
very close	5.3%	13.5%
close	36.8%	37.8%
not close	57.9%	48.6%
Degree of closeness to mother		
very close	40.0%	30.0%*
close	15.0%	52.5%
not close	45.0%	17.5%
Discussed plans or problems with father	19.1%	11.6%
Discussed plans or problems with mother	19.1%	23.3%
Neglected by father	47.6%	32.6%
Neglected by mother	28.6%	23.3%
Frequent arguments with father	23.8%	32.6%
Frequent arguments with mother	57.1%	27.9%*
Father was problem drinker	42.9%	25.6%
Mother was problem drinker	19.0%	11.6%

*$p < .05$

argumentation with the father. As previously mentioned, neither group felt close to their father.

There was a considerable degree of violence in the homes of both groups of future sex offenders (Table 3). About 40% of each group reported having been physically abused by their parents. The violence was not only directed toward them, but the parents displayed violence toward one another and toward other children in the household as well. Furthermore, the violence on the part of the parents of the rapists was extended toward others outside the home. In what may

TABLE 3
Violence in the Home

	Rapists ($n = 21$)	Child Molesters ($n = 43$)
Physically abused by parents	42.9%	39.5%
Parents showed violence toward one another	38.1%	20.9%
Parents showed violence toward other children in household	28.6%	23.3%
Parents showed violence toward others outside home	19.0%	4.7%
Ran away from home	66.7%	46.5%
In foster family or in institution for part of childhood	28.6%	18.6%

be considered a reaction to this family violence, over two-thirds of the rapists and almost half of the child molesters reported having run away from home during their youth. A societal response to this turmoil within the home was to place a sizeable number in foster homes or institutional care.

Sexual abuse in childhood (Table 4). Men from both of these sex offender groups reported having been victims of sexual abuse during their childhood. Thirty-eight percent of the rapists and 56% of the child molesters acknowledged that they had been sexually abused as children. This difference approaches but does not quite reach statistical significance.

The child molesters reported having been sexually abused for the first time at mean age 8.5 years while the rapists reported a slightly higher mean age of 9.2 years. While there are no significant differences in the type of abuse reported, it is noteworthy that over half of both groups indicated that the sexual contact consisted of more than simple fondling. Oral contact was the predominant mode followed by anal contact. We found that of those who had experienced sexual abuse in childhood, around two-thirds of the rapists and the child molesters had been abused by males only (Table 5). Thirteen percent of the child molesters had been sexually abused by females only, while no rapists had had only female abusers. Seventeen percent of child molesters and 38% of the rapists had been abused by both males and females.

The primary abusers of the rapists (50%) were friends, whereas the main abusers for the child molesters were relatives.

Conflict in the school (Table 6). The early development of problems with aggression in the rapists is exemplified by the fact that one-third of them had been expelled from elementary school. The difficulty for the rapists seems to start in the elementary school and continue through middle school into high school.

The rapists are statistically different from the child molesters in the proportion who experienced conflict with their teachers. Over half of the rapists and about one-quarter of the child molesters reported having had trouble getting along with their teachers. The two groups are similar in the amount of conflict they had with classmates.

Significantly more rapists reported engaging in contact sports in high school

TABLE 4
Sexual Abuse in Childhood

Incidence:		Mean Age When Sexually Abused
Rapists: 8 (38.1%)		9.2 (S.D. 3.54)
Child Molesters: 24 (55.8%)		8.5 (S.D. 4.93)

	Rapists (*n* = 8)	Child Molesters (*n* = 24)
TYPE:		
Oral	62.5%	62.5%
Anal	50.0%	45.8%
Fondling	38.1%	45.8%

TABLE 5
Identity of the Sexual Abuser

	Rapists (n = 8)	Child Molesters (n = 24)
Sex:		
Males only	63%	70%
Females only	0	13%
Both males and females	38%	17%
Relationship:		
Relatives only	12.5%	43.5%
Friends only	50%	13.0%
Strangers only	0	17.4%
Relative & Friend	25%	8.7%
Stranger & Friend	0	4.4%
Relative & Stranger	12.5%	4.4%
Relative, Friend & Stranger	0	8.7%

than child molesters (Table 7). While not statistically significant, a greater percentage of the rapists reported participation in music and arts in high school while a larger percentage of the child molesters took part in social clubs.

Antisocial behavior (Table 8). When one looks at the childhood patterns of both these groups of offenders, it can be seen that the interpersonal conflict in the home spills over into conflict with others outside the home. About three-quarters of the child molesters and almost 86% of the rapists reported having had no or few friends while growing up.

TABLE 6
Conflict in the School

	Rapists (n = 21)	Child Molesters (n = 43)
Expelled from elementary school	33.3%	4.7%*
Expelled from middle school	28.6%	16.3%
Expelled from high school	33.3%	32.6%
Expelled for:		
Fighting	38.1%	20.9%
Verbal offense	23.8%	16.3%
Smoking	23.8%	9.3%
Alcohol/drugs	14.3%	7.0%
Truancy	23.8%	18.6%
Had trouble getting along with:		
Teachers	57.1%	25.6%**
Classmates	28.6%	30.2%

*$p < .01$
**$p < .05$

TABLE 7
Extracurricular Activities

	Rapists (n = 21)	Child Molesters (n = 43)
Extracurricular activities in high school		
contact sports	61.9%	23.3%*
music/arts	47.6%	27.9%
social clubs	9.5%	18.6%

*p < .01

There are marked differences in the way in which aggression is handled by the two groups. This is seen by the greater involvement of the rapists in fighting in early childhood. The difference becomes statistically different in adolescence with over 38% of the rapists indicating they had fought often at this stage of their development and less than 10% of the child molesters acknowledging this past behavior. Both groups reported a marked decrease in the number of fights as young adults; however, the rapists were still more heavily involved in fights than the child molesters were when they were in the young adult stage (14.3% vs 2.3%). Significantly more of the rapists than the child molesters (57.1% vs 23.3%) had hurt someone badly in at least one fight. Over half of the rapists indicated that their fights had come about when they were under the influence of alcohol. This does not mean that they were aggressive only while under the influence of alcohol because the rapists show significantly higher levels of aggression than the child molesters in all facets of their lives.

This higher level of aggression in the rapists is seen by their high incidence of

TABLE 8
Early Aggression

	Rapists (n = 21)	Child Molesters (n = 43)
Had no or few friends while growing up	85.7%	74.4%
Often in fights as a child	33.3%	14.0%
Often in fights as an adolescent	38.1%	9.3%*
Often in fights as a young adult	14.3%	2.3%
Hurt someone badly in at least one fight	57.1%	23.3%*
Got into fights when under the influence of alcohol	52.4%	14.0%*
Set fire to buildings	19.0%	2.3%
Showed cruelty to animals	47.6%	27.9%
Destroyed property	57.1%	23.3%*
Age (mean) when stopped wetting the bed	8.07 yrs	7.29 yrs
Stole as a child	76.2%	74.4%
Had temper tantrums	47.6%	41.9%

*p < .01

fire setting, cruelty shown to animals and property destruction (Table 8). There is no statistical difference between the groups of sex offenders in percentage reporting childhood stealing and temper tantrums, or in mean age when they stopped wetting the bed.

Conflict with the law (Table 9). The rapist's problems with aggression are further reflected in his criminal history of charges of violence other than the one which led to his current incarceration. Over half of the rapists were arrested as juveniles as contrasted with about 40% of the child molesters. There is no significant difference in the two groups in the percentage charged with violent crimes until they are out of the juvenile justice system. In the adult court, however, the difference between the two groups is marked. Slightly over three-quarters of the rapists (76.2%) had been previously charged as an adult with a violent crime in contrast with 30.2% of the child molesters having been so charged.

When one looks at the degree of association of both the rapists and the child molesters with persons who have had problems with the law, one is struck by the number of other family members, especially brothers, who have been charged with a crime. As a teenager and as an adult, both the rapists and child molesters reported having close friends who had trouble with the law; indeed, 43% of the rapists reported that as an adult they had close friends who had been in trouble with the law.

Discussion

This study compares convicted rapists with convicted child molesters. Both groups had volunteered for a treatment program and had undergone the same selection process. Neither group may necessarily be representative of rapists and child molesters in general and, if this is the case, the differences we have found

TABLE 9
Criminal History

	Rapists (n = 21)	Child Molesters (n = 43)
Arrested as a juvenile	52.4%	39.5%
Charged with violent crime when less than 18	9.5%	14.0%
Charged with violent crime when 18 or over	76.2%	30.2%*
Family member charged with crime:		
Father	4.8%	16.3%
Mother	9.5%	4.7%
Brother	42.9%	32.6%
Sister	4.8%	7.0%
Close friends in trouble with law		
as a teenager	23.8%	18.6%
as an adult	42.9%	14.0%**

*$p < .001$
**$p < .05$

may not lend themselves to generalization. This is unlikely, however, as the bulk of our findings are concordant with studies already discussed. As we were looking for differences between the two groups we did not add nonsex offender controls. The possible inclusion of homosexual child molesters in our study might have adversely affected the homogeneity of this group.

The validity of self-reported data is always moot. This must be set against the selection process and motivation of our subjects which might tend to select out in favor of the truth, particularly as they had no indication that any particular response would be advantageous to them. Reinterviewing at a later date would have given us an estimate of the reliability of the data but was not feasible in this study.

The developmental differences between the rapists and child molesters were evident from their early youth. The high percentage (71.4%) of broken homes for the rapists would suggest disruption of family life with its ensuing instability and potential for friction. Conversely, although the claimed frequency (83%) of child molesters who felt close or very close to their mothers was very high, only about a quarter (23.3%) of them found her to be a person to whom they could turn when troubled to discuss their problems. This closeness may be more suggestive of a dependent relationship with the mother rather than a reciprocal relationship where problems could be discussed and an effort made to reach solutions. This speculation is further borne out by the fact that about one-fourth of both rapists and child molesters reported feeling neglected by their mothers.

The lack of closeness to father reported by both groups may reflect his absence from the home, but part of this may be due to the father being a problem drinker. About a quarter of the child molesters had fathers whom they considered to be problem drinkers. Alcoholism on the part of the mother was less of a factor for both groups studied.

A surprising finding was the lack of a significant difference between the two groups regarding sexual abuse in their childhood, although this may merely be a reflection of the relatively small numbers of individuals in both groups. Anecdotally, the primary therapists of the sex offenders report that it is common practice for the sex offenders to deny having been sexually abused in childhood during the initial stages of treatment, particularly in the case of rapists.

Overall, the data disclosed clearer developmental profiles for the rapists than for the child molesters. The rapists were significantly higher than the child molesters in their level of aggressive behavior displayed during childhood. They had more frequent arguments with their mothers, they had more trouble getting along with teachers and they were more frequently expelled from elementary school. Additionally, they were more likely to have seriously hurt their victims in fights, they more frequently set fire to buildings and destroyed property, and they were more likely to have participated in contact sports.

This paper is a descriptive exercise which suggests that the adult crime of rape is associated with early conflicts involving aggression, whereas the greater attachment to the mother in child molesters suggests early dependency conflicts. The issue of sexual motivation in rapists is not addressed.

Future studies might examine childhood and adolescent experiences in sexuality, aggression, and maternal relationships. Larger numbers of subjects are clearly desirable and a standardized test such as the Clarke Parent-Child Relations

Questionnaire[26] might be utilized. Hitherto unrecognized differences might be concealed by the existence of many subgroups within both rapists and child molesters. Criteria for such subgroups might involve the degree of violence used in the offense, recidivism, the frequency and nature of other offenses and other sexual characteristics and habits. The Clarke Sexual History Questionnaire might help identify some of these features and has the advantage of being comprehensive and well validated. Psychophysiologic testing of the subjects would not only confirm sexual object preference, but might help identify such subgroups for in-depth investigation. Studies currently underway incorporate these considerations and the results will be reported at a future date.

---

[26]Paitich D., & Langevin, R. (1976). The Clarke Parent-Child Relations Questionnaire. A clinically useful test for adults. *Journal of Consulting Clinical Psychology, 44*, 428–536.

Alan R. Felthous,[1] *M.D. and Stephen R. Kellert,*[2] *Ph.D.*

Psychosocial Aspects of Selecting Animal Species for Physical Abuse

Authorized Reprint from Journal of Forensic Sciences November 1987
Copyright American Society for Testing and Materials, 1916 Race Street, Philadelphia, PA 19103

REFERENCE: Felthous, A. R. and Kellert, S. R., **"Psychosocial Aspects of Selecting Animal Species for Physical Abuse,"** *Journal of Forensic Sciences,* JFSCA, Vol. 32, No. 6, Nov. 1987, pp. 1713–1723.

ABSTRACT: Identification of psychosocial factors in selecting animals for abuse is relevant to mankind's relationship to the world of animals and to the psychology of human aggression. A major study of animal abuse involving 152 male subjects resulted in the identification of 23 subjects who have histories of substantial animal abuse. In attempting to identify psychosocial factors that may affect recurrent abusers' choices of animals to mistreat, findings are presented under four thematic questions: (1) Are animals selected for abuse because they are perceived to be dangerous? (2) Is there a relationship between method of abuse and type of animal selected for cruelty? (3) Are some types of animals more likely than others to evoke predisposing attitudes and abusive behaviors? (4) What kind of relationships do abusers have with the animals they choose to mistreat?

KEYWORDS: psychiatry, animal abuse, human behavior

Psychosocial aspects of animal abuse have received little scientific inquiry. Childhood cruelty to animals has been suggested as a behavioral prodrome of violence against people, either as a single behavior [1] or as part of a triad, the other elements being persistent enuresis and firesetting [2–6]. Despite the burgeoning literature on childhood cruelty to animals as a signal of poorly controlled aggression, repeated literature searches by the authors failed to produce any articles on psychological factors involved in selecting particular kinds of animals for physical abuse. Yet the identification of such factors is relevant to mankind's relationship to the world of animals and to the psychology of human aggression. The purpose of this inquiry is to discuss findings from a major study of animal abuse that suggest psychosocial factors operative in selecting what types of animals individuals choose to mistreat physically.

Golden-haired marmosets are not likely to be targeted for abuse, simply because they do not exist in the United States except in zoos. A species that is well populated, lives in close proximity to people, and is easily subdued and captured will be more vulnerable to abuse than a species that is not so available to human hands and weapons. Differential availability, then, accounts for some of the variability in rates of abuse for different species.

Presented at the 37th Annual Meeting of the American Academy of Forensic Sciences, New Orleans, LA, 10–15 Feb. 1986. Received for publication 22 Dec. 1986; revised manuscript received 28 March 1987; accepted for publication 30 March 1987.

[1]Chief of forensic sciences and associate professor of psychiatry, Department of Psychiatry and Behavioral Sciences, The University of Texas Medical Branch, Galveston, TX.

[2]Associate professor, School of Forestry and Environmental Studies, Yale University, New Haven, CT.

Social attitudes about various species may also influence an individual's choice of an animal to abuse. Kellert and Berry preferred the following as factors that determine to what extent an animal is valued: aesthetic appeal of the animal; intelligence of the animal; phylogenetic relatedness to humans; size of the animal; economic value of the animal; perceived dangerousness to humans; likelihood of causing property damage; cultural and historical importance; relationship to human society (for example, pet, farm animal, game, pest); predatory tendencies; skin texture and morphological structure; and means of locomotion (for example, swimming, flying, walking, crawling) [7].

In a literature review and discussion of social attitudes toward different animals, Kellert postulated five factors that may influence valuation of an animal when socioeconomic interests compete with interests in animal preservation: (1) aesthetic value (for example, butterfly versus slug); (2) phylogenetic closeness to humans (for example, bear versus jelly fish); (3) presumed threat of the animal to human health and productivity (for example, cricket versus cockroach); (4) cultural and historical importance of the animal (for example, American bald eagle versus vulture); and (5) political and actual economic value of the species (for example, oysters versus starfish) [8].

Although an individual may be influenced by cultural attitudes to select a particular animal for abuse, he might just as well be directed by more idiosyncratic factors such as symbolic significance of the animal which is peculiar to him.

The present discussion is based largely on findings from a study of prisoners and nonprisoners, particularly findings of those subjects who gave histories of a pattern of substantial animal abuse in childhood and who were typically impulsively and recurrently aggressive to people [9,10]. One should not generalize and conclude that all abusers are inclined to select animal victims in the same way as these subjects. For example, different psychological mechanisms are operative in psychotically disturbed abusers [11]. Neither should one assume that attitudes of these abusers toward particular animals necessarily correspond to predominant cultural attitudes toward these same animals. Nonetheless, mention will be made where cultural attitudes and perceptions appear to be congruent with those of abusers.

After briefly describing the original study of animal abuse, we will organize this discussion around four unifying themes with the objective of identifying psychosocial factors that may influence an individual's choice of animal to abuse:

- Are animals selected for abuse or killing because they are a menace to people or because they have harmed or threatened the individual abuser?
- Is there a relationship between method of cruelty and type of animal chosen to abuse, and is an animal abused because of attributes that render it especially suitable to the type of abuse that the individual wants to perpetrate?
- Are some types of animals more likely than others to evoke predisposing attitudes and abusive behaviors?
- What kind of relationships do substantial abusers have with the animals they abuse?

Some overlap in observations and inferences made within the context of each thematic inquiry is unavoidable.

Method of Study

Since methodology was presented fully in an earlier report [9], it is merely summarized here. To obtain an ample sample of diffusely, recurrently aggressive subjects, the populations of two prisons were selected for study: The U.S. Penitentiary in Danbury, Connecticut, and the U.S. Penitentiary in Leavenworth, Kansas. Thirty-two aggressive prisoners, eighteen moderately aggressive prisoners, and fifty-two nonaggressive prisoners were included. In addition, fifty nonprisoner men were randomly selected in New Haven, Connecticut, and Topeka, Kansas [9].

Prison subjects, aggressive, moderately aggressive, and nonaggressive, tended to be in their 30s and most were of urban origin. All inmates were men. The nonprisoner subjects were randomly selected in urban, small town, and suburban areas in or near New Haven, Connecticut, and Topeka, Kansas. Adult males were selected to ensure a comparable nonprisoner sample [9].

A standardized interview schedule with over 440 closed and openended questions was administered to each subject. Subjects were asked about 16 specific types of animal cruelties in childhood and adolescence. Other activities inquired about were involvements with family pets, training animals, raising livestock, trapping, hunting, attending dog, cock or bull fights, and miscellaneous activities such as horseback riding. Subjects were asked about sexual play with animals, injury to the subject by an animal, and psychotic perceptions of animals. Subjects who acknowledged abusive behaviors were further asked what type or types of animals were abused, how old the subject was, how often he abused, what his motivation was, what the animal's resulting condition was, what his feelings about it afterwards were, if other people were involved, and over how many years he abused animals.

Levels of aggressiveness were based on scores on a ten-point scale that rated frequency and severity of aggressive physical behaviors and threats made by the subject while incarcerated. Ratings were done by prison counselors who knew and followed inmates. These ratings were not shared with interviewers until interviews were finished, and they were never shared with the subjects. In addition to ratings of observed and reported violent behaviors, self-reports of violent behaviors were included in the final assignment of level of aggressiveness.

The first report of this study demonstrated a statistically significant association between the recurrently aggressive prisoners and frequency of reported abuses in comparison with all other groups, prisoners and nonprisoners [9]. A second report, which presented descriptive accounts of the extent and quality of abusive behaviors, suggested an association between a prevalent pattern of abuse and the group of aggressive prisoners [10].

Twenty-three subjects gave histories of "substantial cruelty to animals" which was defined as a pattern of deliberately, repeatedly, and unnecessarily hurting vertebrate animals in a manner likely to cause serious injury. Sixteen of these belonged to the aggressive prisoner group, four to the nonaggressive prisoner sample, and three to the nonprisoner sample. Most of the nonaggressive prisoner subjects with a history of substantial abuse in childhood were also violent as adults, although not sufficiently violent to be so classified. Similarly the three nonprisoner subjects also had histories of dangerous assaults or fights. In comparison with nonaggressive prisoners and nonprisoner subjects, abusive aggressive subjects abused more animal species, typically including cats or dogs, and perpetrated a greater variety of cruel acts [10].

Dangerous Qualities of Animals

One might think that those animals that are manifestly harmful or dangerous to people would be singled out for abuse or extermination. A national attitudinal survey by Kellert and Berry found that the six most disliked animals are associated with injury or death [7]. Data from the present study indicated that men with a pattern of abusing animals in childhood did not preferentially select dangerous species. Even when subjects hated or despised a particular type of animal, dangerousness of the animal was not offered as a reason for their prejudice. Though one subject victimized water moccasins, the other two who killed snakes did not target venomous species. Horses, cows, pigs, rats, birds, small game, fish, frogs, salamanders, dogs, cats, lizards, snakes, and turtles were all abused, and these animals are not generally known for being dangerous to people.

A few of the many reported abusive acts were in response to an attack by the animal. Several subjects who were bitten by a dog struck the animal in swift retaliation. But these cases constituted only a tiny minority of abusive acts, and even these subjects did not develop a prejudice against dogs. Curiously, most subjects who acknowledged some fear of dogs in early childhood belonged to the aggressive group, whereas most subjects who had been bitten by a dog were nonaggressive prisoners or nonprisoners. Fear of dogs was not associated with having been bitten.

Even harmless creatures can be maligned. Features of the animal's behavior and anatomy can invite projections of malicious feelings onto the animal-victim [12]. The point to be made here is that animals were not selected for abuse simply because they were *known* to be dangerous to people or to the individual abuser.

Harmless vertebrate animals are handier, safer, and more plentiful than dangerous vertebrates. Differential opportunity is presumably an important factor. Most predators, for example, are by nature reclusive, solitary, and uncommon. More pertinent to the psychological understanding of victimizing nondangerous animals, we identified nine motivations for abuse, based largely on expressed statements of abusers: (1) to control an animal; (2) to retaliate against an animal; (3) to satisfy a prejudice against a species or breed; (4) to express aggression through an animal; (5) to enhance one's own aggressiveness; (6) to shock people for amusement; (7) to retaliate against another person; (8) to displace hostility from a person to an animal; and (9) nonspecific sadism. Each of these motivations was previously defined and illustrated with examples [9]. The point to be made here is that dangerousness of the animal was not needed for a subject to act on most of these motivations. For the recurrently aggressive subjects of this study, the objective of cruelty and gratuitous killing was not to create a safer world for people.

Methods of Abuse

Physical or behavioral attributes may lend an animal to a particular method of abuse. Sociocultural attitudes may also suggest suitability of an animal to a certain type of abuse. Considering the act together with the animal may help to identify psychosocial factors in the selection of animal victims.

Table 1 illustrates differential patterns of abuse for various animals. The table lists only those specific abuses that were reported by more than three subjects. Types of abuses re-

TABLE 1—*Animal abuse, category and method.*[a]

Method of Abuse	Category of Animal Abused						
	Large Farm Animals	Dogs	Cats	Small Pets	Small Wild Animals	Other	Total
1. Dismembered	0	0	0	0	7	1	8
2. Exploded	0	0	0	0	4	2	6
3. Cut or stabbed	0	0	0	0	5	0	5
4. Burned or electrocuted	1	0	3	0	5	0	9
5. Shot	0	3	1	0	8	2	14
6. Broke bones	0	1	3	0	0	2	6
7. Thrown from height	0	3	7	0	0	0	10
8. Beat	3	6	5	1	3	0	18
9. Stoned	0	4	3	0	4	0	11
10. Entered into fights	0	4	0	0	0	0	4
11. Other abuses	0	6	11	3	9	0	29
Total	4	27	33	4	45	7	

[a]This table illustrates that the vertebrates which were abused by the greatest variety of methods of cruelties were cats, dogs, and small, wild animals. Though numbers are too small for statistical analysis, the table suggests differential patterns of abuse for various classes of animals.

ported less frequently are aggregated under "other abuses." Likewise, only those classes of animals that were abused by more than one method and by more than two subjects are specified in the table. Animals not abused by more than one method and by more than two subjects are included collectively under "other." Figures under each category of animal represent the number of subjects who abused animals of this class by the methods indicated. In some cases a single subject contributed to several entries. The table does not reflect the numerous isolated acts done by subjects who did not report a pattern of recurrent, substantial abuse.

More subjects reported *beating, stoning,* and *shooting* than any other method of abuse. Cats, dogs, and small wild animals were abused by more subjects and in more ways in comparison with small pets and large farm animals. In the discussion that follows, a relationship is suggested between methods of abuse and types of animals selected for abuse.

Dismemberment involved only small animals with parts or extremities that could be easily removed: wings from birds, legs from rodents and amphibians, tails from lizards and snakes, heads from turtles, and testes from a raccoon. One subject excised hearts from tadpoles. The many subjects, aggressive and nonaggressive, who tore wings from insects are not included in the table of abuses to vertebrates. It is easier to dismember small animals in comparison with larger creatures such as dogs or horses.

All animals abused by dismemberment were wild. No subject admitted dismembering goldfish, gerbils, parakeets, or other small animals that are domesticated. Since dismemberment is one of the more severe cruelties, categorical selection of wild animals is remarkable.

Animals that were *exploded* were also small and wild: rodents, small game, and amphibians. Two subjects "caught" fish by detonating explosives in ponds. One subject put a cat in a microwave oven, but it was unclear whether he knew the result would be explosion of the animal. This abuse, therefore, was classified as "burning." Small, wild animals were also preferentially targeted for *indiscriminate shooting.*

Several factors may be operative in the selection of small, wild animals for dismemberment, explosion, and purposeless killing. Small, wild animals are not highly valued by society, they are owned by no one, and social prohibitions against their abuse are weak to nonexistent. The ability to empathize with animals that seem far removed from the world of people is not great, especially for individuals whose capacity to empathize is limited. This limited capacity to empathize with such animals may allow the expression of sadistic impulses among violence prone individuals.

Kellert previously proffered an explanation for the lack of moral consideration that is generally paid to invertebrates. This explanation may pertain to small, wild animals that are perceived to be useless:

> For most people, moral worth is based on presumptions regarding the animal's capacity for experiencing pain or thought . . . i.e., the animal as an individual capable of eliciting empathy. A moral perspective of animals is, thus, related to a concern for the creature's presumed ability to suffer. If the animal is not perceived as an experiencing being, most people feel little or no obligation to safeguard the welfare of these animals.[3]

Cruelty to small animals may represent an attempt to master feelings by an active, externalizing process. Small animals seem safe because their ability to counterattack is nil. By contrast, attempting to dismember an alligator would prove technically difficult and dangerous.

The small size of an animal may predispose it to differential treatment, because a small animal can creep, slither, crawl, or fly into a person's space without his awareness. A mouse

[3]S. R. Kellert, "Social and Perceptual Factors in Species Preservation," unpublished manuscript.

that skitters under doors and furniture, darting in and out of awareness, is more disarming than the same animal well illuminated and contained in a glass terrarium.

Animals that were *set on fire* were cats and small wild animals, including rodents. One subject burned snakes with an accelerant, but with this exception, animals that were set aflame were furry. The flammable nature of fur renders these animals physically suitable for burning. Fire is a weapon of destruction which has been used in the expression of prejudicial hatred, and cats and rodents were common objects of prejudice.

Breaking bones was another form of abuse whereby some animals were victimized more than others. One half of the subjects who fractured bones selected cats for this cruelty (three out of six). Cat bones are of an easily breakable size, not too small and not too large. One subject broke a dog's leg bone, presumably without foreknowledge that this would be the specific injury resulting from throwing a brick at the dog. Another subject "snapp(ed)" chickens' necks, not to leave them with broken or dislocated vertebrae, but to kill them. Conversely, broken bones were the end result intended for cats that were abused in this manner. Though numbers were small, cats seem to have been singled out for this cruelty.

Most of the animals *thrown from high elevations* were cats (70%; seven out of ten). Cats are small enough to be carried and thrown, but it is curious that no one admitted throwing a smaller species of animal from heights. Cats are known for their ability to reposition themselves in midair and land safely from a fall of a few yards. But dropping cats from water towers, bridges, and high buildings is tantamount to killing them. By now it should be appreciated that cats were disproportionately selected for several of the more extreme methods of cruelty. More will be said later of cruelty to cats.

In contrast to dismemberment, explosion, and burning involving predominantly wild animals, *beatings* were more commonly inflicted on domestic animals that were to some measure already under the subject's control. In the case of dogs, livestock, and equids, beatings served to gain more control over the animal. Dogs were beaten as an adjunct in training to exact obedience or to promote aggressiveness. Two bludgeoned snakes to death. Several beat cats, not to train or control, but to kill them.

Only three subjects *applied chemical irritants* to animals. One put dry ice on live fish to cause them to suffer. Two rubbed irritants on dogs' anuses to punish the animals for offensive behaviors. Together with the subject who repeatedly kicked his dog in the testicles, these subjects directed hurtful acts to "sexual" parts. Although the expressed motive was to punish their dog, the animal's misbehavior may also have provided an excuse for acting upon a sadistic impulse to hurt the dog's perineal area.

All four subjects who repeatedly entered animals in *fights* used their pet dogs for this form of entertainment. A few subjects tied cats' tails together, but there was a striking difference in the quality of the subjects' interest in dog fights compared with cat fights. Subjects who staged cat fights wanted to see the cats destroy one another. They did not hope for one cat to emerge the victor. Those who entered pet dogs in fights wanted very much to see their own dog win. They experienced vicarious pleasure and pride in their dog's aggressiveness and ultimate victory.

Attitudes Toward Particular Species

All 16 aggressive criminals who had histories of substantial animal cruelties in childhood abused cats or dogs. There were enough acts of cruelties against cats and dogs to permit some observations and inferences about attitudes toward these two species in particular. Cruelties to invertebrates, specifically plucking wings off insects, were even more common, reported by about one third of all 152 subjects interviewed. Many people do not regard invertebrates as sentient creatures, so they do not regard pulling off their wings to be nearly as cruel as dismembering vertebrates.

Cats

A greater variety of cruelties involved feline victims in comparison with all other types of animals. Fifteen different types of cruelties inflicted on cats were acknowledged by subjects who abused animals substantially. Most subjects who abused cats used several different methods. The number of different cruelties to cats by different subjects totalled thirty-three. Cats, more than any other species, were thrown from high places (70%). Cats comprised one third of the furry animals that were burned or electrocuted.

Breaking bones involved cats more than any other type of animal. One half of the subjects (50%) who reported breaking an animal's bones selected cats for this cruelty. The only animals to have their tails tied together were cats. Injuries inflicted upon cats were often severe and many cruelties resulted in death: beating, exploding in microwave oven, shooting for target practice, drowning, throwing into an incinerator. Other acts were likely lethal, although death was not explicitly mentioned as the animal's known resulting condition: setting on fire with an accelerant, running over with a car, throwing in front of moving cars, and throwing from bridges and high buildings. Merely totalling all types of cruelties perpetrated by all subjects would not provide the total number of cats that were severely abused or killed, because some subjects had abused cats by a specific method numerous times. A few estimated having killed about 50 cats.

The high incidence of cat abuse in the present study compares with results of an earlier study of 346 male patients admitted to an inpatient psychiatric service of a naval hospital [13]. All but 1 of the 18 subjects who had repeatedly tortured cats or dogs abused cats, and the number who had tortured cats was nearly triple the number who had tortured dogs. Although most studies of animal abuse in the literature involve small samples and do not systematically identify the types of animals victimized, the impression is that cat abuse is recorded more often than the abuse of any other species.

As was suggested above, physical features of cats render them suitable for some specific methods of abuse. Cats have long flexible tails that can be joined together. Fur burns. Their bones are easily broken. Cats are small enough to be carried about and dropped from heights. But physical features alone do not adequately explain the high incidence and severity of cat abuse or the considerable prejudice that abusers harbor against cats.

Cultural prejudice against cats appears to be prevalent. In a national survey, Kellert and Berry demonstrated that despite their commonality and affiliation with people, cats are not as widely appreciated as dogs, horses, robins, and other animals [7]. The marketability of books on black humor pertaining to cats would further suggest a cultural anti-cat prejudice. Popular superstitions regarding cats identify these creatures as having evil influences. Numerous phrases attest to negative attitudes against cats (for example, "cat o' nine tails," "there is more than one way to skin a cat," "enough room to swing a cat," "fighting like Kilkenny cats"). Our country's European heritage recalls an era when cats were burned by the thousands because they were believed to be witches' familiars and vessels of the devil [14,15].

The authors do not suggest that cats are loathed universally, or predominantly in the United States. Ancient Egyptians deified cats [14]. Today in the United States, cats are one of the commonest of indoor and outdoor pets. The bonding of many adults and children to domesticated felines is well known.

Despite the popularity of cats among many people, others hold an identifiable prejudice against cats. Presumably most people who dislike these animals do not act on their prejudice by deliberately injuring and killing cats. Results of the present study indicated that impulsively aggressive men disproportionately acknowledged cat hatred and cat cruelty.

Subjects who abused and killed cats typically admitted prejudice against these animals. They described cats as spooky or eerie. Indeed, cats, even though domesticated, seem inscrutable and are therefore suitable for projection of unacceptable feelings [13]. One subject likened his cat hatred to his prejudice against people of another race. Several subjects had mothers who hated cats and identified them as repositories for negative projections.

Although none of the subjects identified cats as symbolic of evil women, a "bad mother," or the female genitalia, the possibility of consciously or unconsciously associating cats with women ought to be considered in aggressive men whose sexual and aggressive impulses may be fused at a primitive level, poorly differentiated, and poorly modulated (see, for example, Ref *16*). Although empirical evidence is scant, Revitch suggested that cat hatred and abuse are associated with compulsive sexually motivated murderous attacks against women [*17,18*]. In the present study, the number of men who admitted rape was small, so an association between sexual assault and cat abuse was not established.

Finally, it should be noted that none of the 32 aggressive prisoners and none of the 23 subjects who substantially abused animals admitted having owned pet cats. Aggressive subjects in particular expressed no present or past positive emotional attachment to cats.

Dogs

Second only to cats, dogs were abused by more subjects, in more ways, and with greater frequency than any other vertebrate species. Like cats, dogs are rather commonplace and available, but here the comparison ends. Cruelties against dogs were not associated with prejudicial feelings against dogs. None of the subjects admitted a categorical hatred of dogs.

Stoning, beating, and entering in dog fights comprised most of the abuses to dogs. Injuries from stonings and beatings were seldom severe, and dogs entered into fights had a fair chance of prevailing. In comparison with dismemberments and explosions of small, wild animals and in comparison with the various abuses of cats, cruelties to dogs were less severe. Unlike cats, dogs were not beaten to death. Some dogs were killed in retaliation for an act that offended the subject, but none were killed because of a hatred or disdain for dogs in general.

Dogs were often abused in order to influence or control the pet's behavior. Dogs were beaten to shape their behavior and to maintain dominance. They were beaten and punished to extinguish undesirable behavior. Pet dogs were also beaten to foster an aggressive disposition, so they would attack people on command or ferociously battle other dogs. A few subjects beat equidae and livestock, expressedly to control their behavior, but with these exceptions, dogs were the only animals for which abuse was intended to control or train.

Dogs that were beaten, starved, or entered into dog fights were the subjects' own pets. Subjects identified with their pet dogs, especially the aggressive, vicious, and powerful qualities of their dogs. Several subjects used their dogs as instruments of aggression against people and other dogs. Thus, pet dogs often represented extensions of themselves. Subjects took pride in their dogs' triumphs in animal combat which enhanced the subjects' esteem in the eyes of peers. Even though they mistreated their dogs, they felt attached to them. They described their relationship with their dogs as special and exclusive. The loss of a pet dog in childhood was impactful, more upsetting for some subjects than the disruption of any human relationship.

Nature of Relationship with Abused Animals

Subjects who substantially abused animals regarded their animal victims as worthless objects, hated objects, or narcissistic objects. Interestingly, these attitudes towards animals compare with the relationships with people which have been described in individuals with an Antisocial Personality Disorder (APD). Although this study did not attempt to establish psychiatric diagnoses, many of the subjects probably had an APD, a disorder of character that is disproportionately represented in prison populations. In response to questions in interviews, subjects typically acknowledged extensive histories of antisocial and aggressive behaviors listed as criteria for APD in DSM III [*19*].

Animals regarded as worthless by abusive subjects included invertebrates, amphibians, and other small, wild animals. Such animals are commonly perceived as having little aesthetic appeal and no appreciable intelligence or sentience; they are popularly regarded as phylogenetically, morphologically, and affiliatively distant from humans. In other words, small, wild animals are perceived to have a number of the negative attributes offered by Kellert and Berry [*7*]. Several of the species or groups of animals tend to be devalued by many people. Some degree of childhood cruelty to invertebrates, for example, plucking insects' wings, may eventually prove to be common among children who do not progress to substantial abuse of higher forms of animal life. However, in the present study, abuses perpetrated on amphibians, reptiles, fish, birds, and small wild mammals were typically severe and motivated by nonspecific sadism [*9*]. These animals were callously abused solely for sadistic pleasure derived from the act.

Hated animal victims were objects of focused prejudice. Cats were disproportionately represented as hated objects, but a few subjects hated and abused snakes. One abused snapping turtles and one killed rats in order to satisfy a categorical prejudice. Abusive acts against objects of hatred, like abuses of worthless objects, tended to be brutal. Cultural attitudes may have played a role in identifying these animals as objects of prejudice. In a few cases, a parental figure, who reportedly hated the same animal, may have identified it as a repository for projection and object for abuse. Psychosocial dynamics of animal prejudice may be similar to those of racial and sexist perceptions attended by aggressive behaviors against people.

The third distinctive attitude towards animal-victims involved only subjects' pet dogs, objects of narcissistic attachment. Subjects used their dogs as weapons, instruments of aggression against people or other animals, usually other dogs. They identified with their dog's toughness and ferociousness. They took pride in their dog's aggressive behaviors. Abuses consisted of inhumane methods of fostering an aggressive disposition and entering dogs in bloody fights. Other abuses served to gain control over the pet and to shape its behavior.

Three subjects reported what appeared to have been an unstable triangular relationship between the subject, his father, and his large powerful dog. Each of these subjects enjoyed a positive attachment to his dog, but his relationship with his father was a mutually hostile one. And father was perceived to be especially hostile toward the subject's dog. Subjects deliberately promoted an aggressive disposition in their dog, so it could serve as an instrument of aggression. Eventually, the dog's aggressiveness became excessive, and father killed or got rid of the animal. The subject was left with an abiding resentment against his father for having taken away what the subject experienced to be a part of himself. A few of these subjects were emotionally moved in recalling this loss. Thus, their early bonding to a large, strong, aggressive dog was remarkable for men whose human relationships appeared to be shallow or hostile.

Conclusions

Data from a major study of childhood cruelty to animals in prisoners and nonprisoners indicate that not all species of animals are abused equally in numbers or severity. Patterns of abuse appear to bear some relationship to the type of animal. The selection of animal victims for substantial abuse is multidetermined; thus a few generalizations would not explain animal selection in every case.

Aggressive subjects who perpetrated substantial abuse did not typically select animals that are known to be harmful to people. Availability of animals and suitability for particular methods of abuse appeared to be factors in selection. Various species or groups of animals evoked different attitudes and patterns of abuse. Abused animals were regarded as worthless objects, objects of categorical, poorly explained prejudice, objects of frustration to be vengefully destroyed, or narcissistic objects admired for viciousness, but brutally controlled by the subject.

Subjects in this study who gave a history of substantial animal abuse in childhood and adolescence tended to show diffuse aggression, including violence towards people. Substantially abusive subjects typically abused a variety of animals, used a number of methods, and expressed different motivations. Identification of psychosocial factors that direct the vector of aggression against a particular species or group of animals can enhance dynamic understanding of aggression in recurrently, impulsively violent individuals. More speculatively, antisocial, nonpsychotic, violence prone individuals may act in part on cultural perceptions of animals. If empirical findings can substantiate this heuristic inference, the social problem of animal abuse can be regarded as both a manifestation of abnormal aggression of individuals and differential cultural attitudes toward various types of animals.

Acknowledgments

The study upon which this inquiry was based was initiated and sponsored by the World Society for the Protection of Animals and funded by the G. R. Dodge Foundation. Many thanks to John and Joyce Walsh and to Scott McVay for making this research possible and for their considerable help, encouragement, and support.

References

[1] Mead, M., "Cultural Factors in the Cause of Pathological Homicide," *Bulletin of the Menninger Clinic.* Vol. 28, 1964, pp. 11–22.

[2] Macdonald, J. M., "The Threat To Kill," *The American Journal of Psychiatry.* Vol. 120, 1963, pp. 125–130.

[3] Hellman, D. S. and Blackman, N., "Enuresis, Firesetting, and Cruelty to Animals: A Triad Predictive of Adult Crime," *The American Journal of Psychiatry.* Vol. 122, 1966, pp. 1431–1435.

[4] Wax, D. E. and Haddox, V. G., "Enuresis, Firesetting and Animal Cruelty: A Useful Danger Signal in Predicting Vulnerability of Adolescent Males of Assaultive Behavior," *Child Psychiatry and Human Development.* Vol. 4, 1974, pp. 151–156.

[5] Wax, D. E. and Haddox, V. G., "Sexual Aberrance in Male Adolescents Manifesting a Behavioral Triad Considered Predictive of Extreme Violence: Some Clinical Observations," *Journal of Forensic Sciences.* Vol. 4, No. 1, Jan. 1974, pp. 102–108.

[6] Felthous, A. R. and Bernard, H., "Enuresis, Firesetting and Cruelty to Animals: The Significance of Two Thirds of This Triad," *Journal of Forensic Sciences.* Vol. 24, No. 1, Jan. 1979, pp. 240–246.

[7] Kellert, S. R. and Berry, J. K., *Knowledge. Affection and Basic Attitudes Toward Animals in American Society.* National Technical Information Service PB-81-173106, Springfield, VA, 1980, p. 31.

[8] Kellert, S. R., "Affective, Cognitive, and Evaluative Perceptions of Animals," in *Behavior and the Natural Environment.* I. Altman and J. F. Wohlwill, Eds., Plenum, New York, 1983, pp. 241–267.

[9] Kellert, S. R. and Felthous, A. R., "Childhood Cruelty Toward Animals Among Criminals and Noncriminals," *Human Relations.* Vol. 38, 1985, pp. 1113–1129.

[10] Felthous, A. R. and Kellert, S. R., "Violence Against Animals and People: Is Aggression Against Living Creatures Generalized?," *The Bulletin of the American Academy of Psychiatry and the Law.* Vol. 14, No. 1, 1986, pp. 55–69.

[11] Felthous, A. R., "Psychotic Perceptions of Pet Animals in Defendants Accused of Violent Crimes," *Behavioral Sciences and the Law.* Vol. 2, No. 3, 1984, pp. 331–339.

[12] Felthous, A. R., "Aggression Against Cats, Dogs, and People," *Child Psychiatry and Human Development.* Vol. 10, No. 3, Spring 1980, pp. 169–177.

[13] Felthous, A. R., "Childhood Cruelty to Cats, Dogs and Other Animals," *The Bulletin of the American Academy of Psychiatry and the Law.* Vol. 9, No. 1, 1981, pp. 48–53.

[14] Dale-Green, P., *Cult of the Cat.* The Riverside Press, Boston, 1963, pp. 120–130, 137–177.

[15] Oldfield, M., *The Cat in the Mysteries of Magic and Religion.* Castle Books, New York, 1956.

[16] Revitch, E., "Sexually Motivated Burglaries," *The Bulletin of the American Academy of Psychiatry and the Law.* Vol. 6, No. 3, 1978, pp. 277–283.

[*17*] Revitch, E. and Schlesinger, L. B., "Murder: Evaluation, Classification, and Prediction," in *Violence: Perspectives on Murder and Aggression.* Jossey-Bass, San Francisco, 1978, pp. 138–164.

[*18*] Revitch, E., "Sex Murder and the Potential Sex Murderer," *Diseases of the Nervous System.* Vol. 26, No. 10, Oct. 1965, pp. 640–648.

[*19*] *Diagnostic and Statistical Manual of Mental Disorders.* 3rd ed., American Psychiatric Association, Washington, DC, 1980.

Address requests for reprints or additional information to
Alan R. Felthous, M.D.
The University of Texas Medical Branch, Galveston
Graves Bldg. 1.200, RT D29
Galveston, TX 77550

Serial Murderers: Four Case Histories

By Faith H. Leibman*

THE INCREASE in homicide in the United States, particularly in terms of serial murders, has raised many questions concerning the socioeconomic factors surrounding such crimes. Both society and those in the criminal justice system have begun to feel the need to answer long-held questions concerning serial murder. This is particularly true in light of the publicity given the family histories of perpetrators of homicide. This article will explore the psychological profiles of a selected group of serial murderers in order to determine the common emotional and environmental backgrounds of these individuals. Through analysis of these findings and further studies, it may be possible to develop criteria for early identification of persons with such tendencies and to develop early treatment programs for such individuals.

In order to view serial murder in perspective, one must first understand the underlying cause of murder generally, excluding felony murders and hired assassins. Additionally, one must consider the application of factors involved in homicides as a whole. Studies in the area of homicide seem to indicate that there are three primary psychological elements contributing to motivation for murder (Abrahamsen, 1973; Holmes, 1988): frustration, fear, and depression. It is frequently the intensity of these feelings, combined with the murderer's interactions with his environment, that bring about the desire—and oftentimes the compulsion—to murder. In brief, homicides occur as a result of an intense conflict emanating from a struggle between an internal need for self-preservation and the stresses pressuring the murderer from the external environment. The roots of this inner conflict are often found in the early childhood of those committing homicide. Studies support the findings that children as early as 1 or 2 years of age may be hurt by the rejection or criticism of others (Langwin, 1983). It is also clear that resentment brought about as a result of such rejection is frequently repressed by those who later commit murder. Repression often becomes a pattern of behavior leaving little need for release of anger. Upon reaching adulthood, the individual

who thus far has adequately repressed rage since childhood may find himself in situations where he is unable to suppress hostile feelings. In these circumstances, the ego-protective mechanisms, previously used successfully, fail, and the individual then acts out in a violent manner. This is particularly true when the person feels threatened or frustrated. Complicating this problem may be situations or people that predispose the murderer to frustrated or angry reactions.

The literature described three distinct types of murderers: ego disharmonious (or ego-dystonic), psychotic murderers, and ego-harmonious (ego-syntonic) (Abrahamsen; 1973, Holmes, 1988). Ego disharmonious murderers are those who experience a conflict between their ego and their super-ego or their conscience. This conflict leads to an altered state of consciousness or a dissociative reaction. The individual is then unable to control his aggressive behavior or feelings of hostility and comes to react violently or explosively.

The psychotic murderer is an individual who suffers from a mental illness such that he has had a complete break with reality.

The ego harmonious type of killing is carried out with little, if any, disruption of the functioning of the ego. The murder that takes place is rational and acceptable to the perpetrator on a conscious level.

In general, the primary characteristics of a murderer are as follows: "Helplessness, impotence, a nagging feeling of revenge (all carried over from childhood), an irrational hatred of others, suspiciousness, hypersensitivity to injustices or rejection, self-centeredness, an inability to withstand frustration, an overpowering feeling of frequent uncontrollable emotional outbursts, a need to retaliate, destroy or tear down by killing" (Abrahamsen, 1973).

Serial murder is best characterized as an ego-dystonic act, since the murderer frequently has, at least on a conscious level, disassociated himself from the killings. In fact, when confronted with evidence of their crimes, many serial murderers have difficulty believing that they are capable of such acts. A serial murder, unlike a mass murder, involves the killing of several people (usually) within the same area, during a fairly short period of time, at the hands of a single assailant. This type of murder is distinguished from a mass murder wherein a number of victims are killed at

*Ms. Leibman is a forensic psychologist with the Atlantic County Jail, as well as a professor, Department of Criminal Justice, Temple University. She wishes to thank her friend and mentor, Donald Fiscor, for his help and support.

Reprinted from *Federal Probation* 53 (1989): 41–45, with permission of the U.S. Administrative Office of State Courts, Probation and Pretrial Services.

one time, frequently in a "murder spree."

A review of the case histories of four serial murderers presented in the appendix indicates a certain commonality in their social and emotional development prior to commission of the act of murder:

- Cruel and extremely violent parenting.
- A rejection in childhood by the parents.
- A rejection by a member of the opposite sex in adulthood.
- Contact with the criminal justice system—adult and/or juvenile.
- Commitment to a mental health facility.
- Aberrant sexual patterns.
- A loner.

There is also a style and pattern to killings by serial murderers. The victims chosen are frequently similar physically. Additionally, the relationship between the perpetrator and victim is usually that of mere acquaintances, sometimes even strangers. Rarely are the victim and perpetrator closely related. At times the serial murderer is motivated to kill in an almost obsessive manner.

Serial murders have a number of characteristics in common. Firstly, most of the killers are between 25–35 years old. The victims of these homicides, however, may fall into any age bracket. Secondly, serial murderers' victims are almost always female, and their killers are almost always male. Thirdly, serial killings are generally intraracial, and victim and killer are Caucasian. Finally, as noted earlier, serial murderers usually exhibit an obsessive-compulsive pattern in their killings which tends to be repetitive in nature.

The profiles presented in the appendix show that the childhoods of the four serial murderers were marked by cruel and violent parenting in three of the four cases, with the fourth showing a pattern of extensive verbal abuse. Additionally, all four of the murderers discussed were significantly rejected in their childhood. Parental abuse and rejection were major themes in the lives of these serial murders. Bundy was rejected by his natural father who effectively "abandoned" him before he was born. His mother, though present throughout his childhood, did not offer the emotional support he needed. De Salvo was physically abused by his father, and his mother was unable to supply enough love and attention to make up for this abuse. Kemper's mother continuously belittled him and punished him with physical restraints (in the cellar, locked in his room, etc.) Brudos was the product of a hostile, angry, sometimes violent father and a mother who did not really want him.

All of the men discussed were not only abused or rejected but also were loners, unable to openly express anger towards those who caused them emotional pain. Bundy felt embarrassed and angry over his illegitimacy. De Salvo was unable to express his anger in a home where his father would have beaten him for such a display. Later he was unable to express his anger over his wife's denial of sex to him for fear of losing her. Kemper knew that a showing of anger in his home would cause even further rejection and punishment from his already caustic mother. Brudos feared that his wife would leave him if he continued to pressure her to perform unusual sexual acts.

Since all four men were loners, not only were they unable to vent their anger at the person who caused this hurt, they had no one else to whom they could express their feelings. Additionally, all four saw the expression of anger towards their mothers as being of life-threatening proportion since the blood bond of mother and child was the only bond that was permanent in their lives. Consequently, Bundy, De Salvo, Brudos, and Kemper repressed their rage from childhood until adulthood. In adulthood, however, the stresses of the outside environment, combined with their repressed rage, created a highly volatile situation. Essentially, the anger at their mothers repressed from childhood (which they were unable to vent directly) was displaced onto their victims.

Bundy's attacks on women began after his initial rejection by his girlfriend Marjorie, his failure to complete college, and then his later inability to be accepted to law school. De Salvo's murders began after the birth of a handicapped daughter and the total refusal of his wife to engage in sexual relations with him as well as her constant belittling of him. Kemper began killing women after he was sent against his will to his grandparents' home and at a time when he was unsuccessful in his attempts to make friends with anyone at school or near the isolated farm where his grandparents lived. Brudos started to commit acts of violence after he felt that he was "losing control" over his wife and upon her refusal to care for him both sexually and emotionally in the way he desired.

All four men began their killings when they felt that they were unable to control their environment. This feeling of lack of power, combined with repressed range from childhood and stoked by the seeds of rejection throughout adolescence (and, in some cases, young adulthood), created the circumstances that were ripe for murders.

It is clear that serial murderers begin to kill as a result of increasing feelings of rejection, frustration, anger, and powerlessness. The lack of friends to confide in and share hurt feelings with was a common element in the lives of Bundy, De Salvo, Kemper, and Brudos. Another feature they shared was a feeling of significant rejection by a woman emotionally close to them directly prior to the first homicide. This rejection was the propelling motive for the initial violent behavior. It also was the spark for Bundy, De Salvo, Kemper, and Brudos' future acts of violence. It appears, therefore, that the rejection by a woman in adulthood was the catalytic factor that returned them to the rejection in childhood (by their mother) and caused the pent-up emotions of a lifetime to be projected onto their victims.

In conclusion, there emerges a pattern of emotional history and behavior that is common to all of those in the group under study in this article.

It is extremely important for the protection of society that criminal justice researchers conduct further studies into the factors that make up the emotional history of serial killings, in an attempt to refine the criteria to be evaluated. Having such criteria will allow identification of potential serial killers and, hopefully, lead to their treatment before they emerge in deadly destruction.

REFERENCES

Abrahamsen, D. *The Murdering Mind*. New York: Harper & Row, 1973.

Bartholomew, A. Milte, K., and Galbally. "Sexual Murder: Psychopathology and Psychiatric Jurisprudential Considerations." *Australian and New Zealand Journal of Criminology, 8*, 1975, pp. 143-152.

Brittain, R. "The Sadistic Murderer." *Medicine, Science and the Law, 10*, 1976, pp. 198-207.

Cheney, M. *The Co-ed Killer*. New York: Walker & Co., 1976.

Danto, B., Bruhns, J., and Kutscher, A. *The Human Side of Homicide*. New York: Columbia University Press, 1982.

Feldman, M., Mallouh, K., and Lewis, D. "Filicidal Abuse in the Histories of 15 Condemned Murderers." *American Academy of Psychiatry and the Law Bulletin, 14*, 1986, pp. 345-352.

Frank, G. *The Boston Strangler*. New York: New American Library, 1966.

Holmes, R. and De Burger, J. *Serial Murder*. Newbury Park, CA: Sage Publications, 1988.

Kahn, M. "Murderers Who Plead Insanity: A Descriptive Factor—Analytic Study of Personality, Social and History Variables." *Genetic Psychology Monographs, 84*, 1971, pp. 275-360.

Langevin, R., Paitich, D., Orchard, B., Handy, L., and Russon, L. "Childhood and Family Background of Killers Seen for Psychiatric Assessment: A Controlled Study." *Bulletin of the American Academy of Psychiatry and Law, 11*, 1983, pp. 331-41.

Levin, J. and Fox, Jr. *Mass Murder: America's Growing Menace*. New York: Plenum Press, 1985.

Linedecker, C. *The Man Who Killed Boys*. New York: St. Martin's Press, 1980.

Lunde, D. *Murder and Madness*. New York: W.W. Norton, 1979.

MacDonald, J. *The Murderer And His Victim*. Springfield, IL: Charles C. Thomas, 1986.

Michaud, S. and Aynesworth, H. *The Only Living Witness*. New York: Simon and Shuster, 1983.

Palmer, S. *The Psychology of Murder*. New York: Thomas Y. Cromell Company, 1960.

Rule, A. *Lust Killer*. New York: New American Library, 1983.

Rule, A. *The Stranger Beside Me*. New York: New American Library, 1980.

Sullivan, T. and Maiken, P. *Killer Clown: The John Wayne Gacy Murders*. New York: Pinnacle Books, 1983.

Tanay, E. *The Murderers*. Indianapolis: Bobbs-Merrill, 1976.

Wille, W. *Citizens Who Commit Murder*. St. Louis: Warren H. Green, Inc., 1974.

Wolfgang, M. *Studies in Homicide*. New York: Harper & Row, 1967.

APPENDIX

Case History I — Theodore Bundy

Theodore Bundy was born in 1946 to a prim department store clerk and a sailor who disappeared as soon as Bundy's mother told him she was pregnant. Her shame over her situation caused her to travel in her seventh month to a home for unwed mothers in Burlington, Vermont. Bundy's mother returned to Philadelphia after his birth and remained there until he was 4 years old. At that time, Bundy and his mother went to Tacoma, Washington, to join a great uncle. Bundy was angry and confused over having to leave his grandfather who had cared for him during the first few years of his life. Bundy also was upset about his mother's decision to change his last name which she had done in order to deter strangers from asking embarrassing questions.

Within a short time, Bundy's mother married Johnnie Bundy. Ted Bundy saw his new stepfather as an interloper and was jealous of the time he spent with Bundy's mother. When Ted Bundy was 6 years old his mother had another child. Bundy began to feel deprived, initially because of the relationship between his great uncle Jack and his son John and also because of the attention shown by his parents to his new baby sister. Additionally, at some point in his early adolescence, Bundy found out that he was illegitimate. This caused Bundy to become furious at his mother for failing to tell him and angry at his stepfather whom he had never liked. His stepfather had a bad temper which escalated as Bundy became more openly defiant towards him.

Bundy remained a loner throughout his high school and early college years. He started college at his uncle's school, University of Puget Sound, and then transferred to the University of Washington in his sophomore year. While there he began to date a California socialite who was everything Ted Bundy was not. The summer after they started dating he enrolled at Stanford University, but was unable to keep up academically. He began to fail in his coursework, the only area in which he had consistently been successful. Eventually, his girlfriend, Marjorie, broke up with him. Bundy felt rejected and lonely. He tried transferring from the Chinese language program to the University of Washington's urban planning program but failed at that too.

He traveled over the country for a while and then settled into working as a busboy in a hotel dining room. He felt uncertain of himself and somewhat angry over the way things had turned out with both school and Marjorie. He made a friend at this point who was a thief and drug user, and the two of them began to break into houses and steal things. Shortly, after these burglaries took place, Bundy began to become involved in politics. He then started going to a college tavern in the neighborhood and one evening met a woman he could not get out of his mind. He dated this woman, Liz, for a few months but continually lied to her, building up a false reputation as a writer and law student. After 3 months passed, Bundy and Liz took out a marriage license and made plans for a ceremony. At the last minute Bundy tore up the marriage license, telling Liz that it was too soon to marry. The reality was that he felt that he could not tell her the truth about his status in life. He later confessed to his girlfriend, and she forgave him. They continued to date but Bundy began to threaten her and press her to have sex in unusual ways, including tying her up with pantyhose before they had sex. Academically, by this time Bundy had completed college at the University of Washington and had applied to the law school of the University of Puget Sound for acceptance. In July 1973 Bundy flew to California to see Marjorie, with whom he had kept in touch since their breakup. He maintained a facade with Liz and managed to keep up his relationship with Marjorie from Seattle. Marjorie flew to Seattle to see him at Christmas while Liz flew home to Utah. Bundy proposed to Marjorie, and she then flew back to California assuming they were to be married in the near future. When she did not hear from him for a month she called him, and he neither apologized nor explained. She then told him never to call her again. Shortly thereafter, Bundy's first victim was abducted. Other victims followed the January 1974 one, many sexually molested and brutally slain.

Case History II — Albert De Salvo

Albert De Salvo was raised in the Boston slums by an alcoholic and violent father. His father would often come home drunk with prostitutes and would hit his mother in front of these women. De Salvo's father would beat the children for no reason at all. On one occasion De Salvo's father smashed De Salvo across the back with a pipe. At some point in his youth, De Salvo was sold to a farmer in Maine for $9. The family lived in poverty and was constantly on welfare; the children frequently went without food. De Salvo's father began De Salvo's "criminal career" by teaching him how to steal at the age of 5. By the time De Salvo was 12 years old he had two arrests for breaking and entering and larceny. At that time he was convicted and sent to Lyman School for Delinquent Boys. Sexually, De Salvo began to experiment with neighborhood girls at the age of 10, and when he was 15 years old he was seduced by a married woman.

Upon his release from the Lyman School, he continued to commit property crimes, though on a wider scale. He particularly enjoyed breaking and entering homes where women were sleeping. Eventually De Salvo joined the Army and was sent to Germany. There he married a German girl who was quite innocent and scared of sex. De Salvo, on the other hand, apparently had an uncontrollable sex drive and pressured his wife constantly for sex. He was in love with his wife and her denial of sex caused him to feel rejected and degraded. At other times she would insult him in front of friends, causing him to feel hurt and betrayed. While in Germany he began to seduce and assault women though he was never charged with these crimes. Upon his return to America he continued to molest and rape women and was finally arrested and sent to a state hospital. In 1961, after his release from the state hospital, his wife rejected him totally, calling him "an animal" and refusing to have sex with him except when she desired it. It was then that he began his killings. In total, he was convicted of murdering 13 women, all of whose corpses he violated with an object or an obscene decoration or arranged as a dead body. In discussing his case with the police, De Salvo noted that if his wife had given him the sex he wanted and had not degraded him, he would not have had to prove he was a man through acts of violence.

Case History III — Edmund Kemper

Edmund Kemper III was born in 1948. By the time he was a year old his parents had separated. In 1957 his mother moved Kemper and his two sisters to Montana where she later remarried. A year and a half later her second husband left her. Two years later, Mrs. Kemper again remarried.

Mrs. Kemper's treatment of her son bordered on cruelty. She constantly punished and ridiculed him, trying to "make a man out of him." She often locked him in the cellar and berated him for failing to live up to her social ambitions. As early as age 10, Kemper began to kill family pets and had thoughts of killing family members, particularly an older sister whom his mother favored. He also began to follow women down the street fantasizing that they would love him. At the age of 13 he killed a family cat who appeared to favor his sister, decapitating the cat. As a result of this behavior his mother decided to send him (against his wishes) to live with his paternal grandparents. He remained angry at being forced to live on an isolated California ranch with his grandparents, particularly his grandmother who treated him in similar ways as his mother did. At the age of 14 he killed his grandmother by shooting her and then his grandfather when he returned from an errand. He was convicted on homicide charges and spent the next 4 years in a maximum-security mental hospital.

In 1969 he was released to his mother at the age of 21. His mother continued to engage in frequent verbal battles with him, belittling him for failing to reach the social level to which she had aspired for him. Kemper, nevertheless, went to great efforts to try to please his mother, struggling for her love, but always without success. He continued to feel inadequate particularly because of his inability to meet his mother's demands. Within a year of his release from the mental hospital he began murdering young female hitchhikers.

Case History IV — Jerome Brudos

Jerome Brudos was born on January 31, 1939. His mother had one other child, a boy who was a few years older than Brudos. Her real desire was for her second child to be a girl. As a result of this she never became attached to her younger son, favoring his older brother instead. Brudos' father was a man who was easily offended and became hostile if he thought he was being taken advantage of. He frequently was verbally abusive to Brudos.

Brudos first exhibited fetishist behavior when he was 5 years old. At that time, he found a pair of women's high-heeled shoes which he brought home and tried on. His mother became angry with him over the act and punished him by confining him to his room. Eventually, he was let out and ran to be consoled by a neighbor. This neighbor woman and another little girl in the neighborhood were Brudos' only "friends." Both were sickly. Eventually his little playmate died, and the neighbor woman became too sick to spend time with him. He felt that he could not trust women and wavered between depression and frustration. As he grew older he became more obsessed with women's shoes and tried to steal them whenever he could. These episodes caused his mother to become increasingly punitive and to offer more love and attention to his older brother. Mrs. Brudos was rigid, strong, and controlling, and Brudos could never seem to win her affection.

At the age of 16, Brudos broke into a neighbor's house and stole her underwear. He later offered to help her find it. Instead of doing so, when she arrived at his house he made her undress at knifepoint. He then took pictures of her and left. Following this incident, Brudos attempted to date normally but had no success due to his appearance and his awkwardness with girls. In 1956, however, he lured a 17-year-old girl into his car, beat her, and ordered her to strip off her clothes. As a result of this event, Brudos was committed to the Oregon State Hospital. Upon his release, he finished high school and joined the armed services.

Brudos had trouble meeting women and distrusted women generally. Eventually, he married a woman 6 years younger than he after she had become pregnant by him. Following the birth of their daughter, Brudos insisted his wife allow him to take nude pictures of her and requested other more sexually bizarre acts from her. In the beginning his wife acquiesced, but eventually she rebelled. Brudos began to think that his wife did not love him, and to relieve his depression over this he started to steal underwear and shoes again. Brudos became more frustrated when his wife refused to pose for him or have sex with him. Brudos' assaults on women then increased and eventually be began to rape and finally killed one woman in 1968. Brudos continued to murder three other women before being caught by the police in 1969. Brudos not only killed his victims, he frequently amputated their breasts and took pictures of their nude bodies once they were dead.

BY RANDALL LOCKWOOD, PH.D., AND ANN CHURCH

DEADLY SERIOUS

T HE HSUS HAS A LONG HISTORY OF WORKING CLOSELY WITH LOCAL, STATE, and federal law enforcement agencies to combat cruelty to animals. Many of these agencies have become acutely interested in the connection between animal cruelty and other forms of violent, antisocial behavior. They have found that the investigation and prosecution of crimes against animals is an important tool for identifying people who are, or may become, perpetrators of violent crimes against people.

Earlier this year Sen. William Cohen of Maine formally asked U.S. attorney general Janet Reno to accelerate the U.S. Department of Justice's research in this area. On June 6 The HSUS met with the staffs of Senator Cohen and Sen. Robert Smith of New Hampshire and with representatives of the FBI and the Justice Department. One participant was Supervisory Special Agent Alan Brantley of the FBI's Investigative Support Unit (ISU), also known as the Behavioral Science Unit. The ISU is responsible for providing information on the behavior of violent criminals to FBI field offices and law enforcement agencies worldwide. Special Agent Brantley served as a psychologist at a maximum-security prison in North Carolina before joining the FBI. He has interviewed and profiled numerous violent criminals and has direct knowledge of their animal-abuse histories. In his role as an ISU special agent, he shares that information with agents at the FBI Academy and law enforcement officers selected to attend the FBI's National Academy Program. When we asked Special Agent Brantley how many serial killers had a history of abusing animals, his response was, "The real question should be, how many have not?"

As law enforcement officials become more aware of the connection between animal abuse and human-directed violence, they become more supportive of strong anticruelty laws and their enforcement. We are encouraged by this development. We were granted permission to visit the FBI Academy, in Quantico, Virginia, to continue our discussion with Special Agent Brantley.

AN FBI

PERSPECTIVE

ON ANIMAL

CRUELTY

Reprinted from *Humane Society News* (Fall 1996), 1–4, with kind permission of the Humane Society of the United States.

"SOMETIMES VIOLENCE AGAINST ANIMALS IS SYMBOLIC. WE HAVE HAD CASES WHERE INDIVIDUALS HAD AN EARLY HISTORY OF TAKING STUFFED ANIMALS . . . AND CARVING THEM UP."

—Alan Brantley,
FBI Supervisory Special Agent

HSUS: What is the history of the Behavioral Science Unit/ISU?

BRANTLEY: The Behavioral Science Unit originated in the 1970s and is located at the FBI Academy. Its purpose is to teach behavioral sciences to FBI trainees and National Academy students. The instructors were often asked questions about violent criminals, such as, "What do you think causes a person to do something like this?" The instructors offered some ideas, and as the students went out and applied some of these ideas, it was seen that there might be some merit to using this knowledge in field operations. In the mid-1980s, the National Center for the Analysis of Violent Crime was founded with the primary mission of identifying and tracking serial killers, but it also was given the task of looking at any violent crime that was particularly vicious, unusual, or repetitive, including serial rape and child molestation. We now look at and provide operational assistance to law enforcement agencies and prosecutors worldwide who are confronted with any type of violent crime.

HSUS: You have said that the FBI takes the connection between animal cruelty and violent crime very seriously. How is this awareness applied on a daily basis?

BRANTLEY: A lot of what we do is called threat assessment. If we have a known subject, we want as much information as we can obtain from family members, co-workers, local police, and others, before we offer an opinion about this person's threat level and dangerousness. Something we believe is prominently displayed in the histories of people who are habitually violent is animal abuse. We look not only for a history of animal abuse, torment, or torture, but also for childhood or adolescent acts of violence toward other children and possibly adults and for a history of destructiveness to property.

Sometimes this violence against animals is symbolic. We have had cases where individuals had an early history of taking stuffed animals or even pictures of animals and carving them up. That is a risk indicator.

You can look at cruelty to animals and cruelty to humans as a continuum. We first see people begin to fantasize about these violent actions. If there is escalation along this continuum, we may see acting out against inanimate objects. This may also be manifest in the writings or drawings of the individual affected. The next phase is usually acting out against animals.

HSUS: When did the FBI first begin to see this connection?

BRANTLEY: We first quantified it when we did research in the late 1970s, interviewing thirty-six multiple murderers in prison. This kind of theme had already emerged in our work with violent criminals. We all believed this was an important factor, so we said, "Let's go and ask the offenders themselves and see what they have to say about it." By self report, 36 percent described killing and torturing animals as children and 46 percent said they did this as adolescents. We believe that the real figure was much higher, but that people might not have been willing to admit to it.

HSUS: You mean that people who commit multiple, brutal murders might be reluctant to admit to killing animals?

BRANTLEY: I believe that to be true in some cases. In the inmate population, it's one thing to be a big-time criminal and kill people—many inmates have no empathy or concern for human victims—but they might identify with animals. I've worked with prisoners who kept pets even though they weren't supposed to. They would consider someone else hurting their pet as reason enough to commit homicide. Also, within prisons, criminals usually don't want to talk about what they have done to animals or children for fear that other inmates may retaliate against them or that they may lose status among their peers.

HSUS: Where is violence against animals coming from? Are criminals witnessing it in others? Convicted serial killer Ted Bundy recounted being forced to watch his grandfather's animal abuse.

BRANTLEY: For the most part, in my experience, offenders who harm animals as children pretty much come up with this on their own. Quite often they will do this in the presence of others and teach it to others, but the ones with a rich history of violence are usually the instigators. Some children might follow along to be accepted, but the ones we need to worry about are the one or two dominant, influential children who initiate the cruelty.

HSUS: What components need to be present for you to think a child or adolescent is really in trouble?

BRANTLEY: You have to look at the quality of the act and at the frequency and severity. If a child kicks the dog when somebody's been aggressive toward him, that's one issue, but if it's a daily thing or if he has a pattern of tormenting and physically torturing the family dog or cat, that's another. I would look to see if the pattern is escalating. I look at any type of abuse of an animal as serious to begin with, unless I have other information that might explain it. It should not be dismissed. I've seen it too often develop into something more severe.

Some types of abuse, for example, against insects, seem to be fundamentally different. Our society doesn't consider insects attractive or worthy of affection. But our pets are friendly and affectionate and they often symbolically represent the qualities and characteristics of human beings. Violence against them indicates violence that may well escalate into violence against humans.

You also need to look at the bigger picture. What's going on at home? What other supports, if any, are in place? How is the child doing in school? Is he drinking or doing drugs?

HSUS: We are familiar with the "classic" cases of serial killers, like Jeffrey Dahmer, who had early histories of animal abuse (see the Summer 1986 *HSUS News*). Are there any recent cases you have worked on?

BRANTLEY: The Jason Massey case jumps out as being a prominent one. This was a case from 1993 in Texas. This individual, from an early age, started his career killing many dogs and cats. He finally graduated, at the age of 20, to beheading a thirteen-year-old girl and shooting her fourteen-year-old stepbrother to death.

He was convicted of murder. I was brought in for the sentencing phase to testify as to his dangerousness and future threat to the community. The prosecutors knew that he was a prolific killer of animals, and that he was saving the body parts of these animals. The prosecutor discovered a cooler full of animal remains that belonged to Massey and brought it to the courtroom for the sentencing hearing. It caused the jurors to react strongly, and ultimately the sentence was death.

HSUS: Mr. Massey had been institutionalized at his mother's request two years before the murders since she was aware of his diaries, which recorded his violent fantasies, and his animal killings, yet he was released. Do you think that mental health officials have been slower than law enforcement agencies in taking animal abuse seriously?

BRANTLEY: We've made this a part of a lot of our training for local police, and I think most police recognize that when they see animal mutilation or torture that they need to check it out; but police have to triage and prioritize their cases. We try to tell people that investigating animal cruelty and investigating homicides may not be mutually exclusive.

We are trying to do the same for mental health professionals. We offer training to forensic psychiatrists through a fellowship program and provide other training to the mental health community. I think psychiatrists are receptive to our message when we can give them examples and case studies demonstrating this connection. The word is getting out.

HSUS: Do you think more aggressive prosecution of animal-cruelty cases can help get some people into the legal system who might otherwise slip through?

BRANTLEY: I think that it is a legitimate way to deal with someone who poses a threat. Remember, Al Capone was finally imprisoned for income-tax evasion rather than for murder or racketeering—charges which could never be proven.

HSUS: Have you ever encountered a situation where extreme or repeated animal cruelty is the only warning sign you see in an individual, where there is no other violent behavior? Or does such abuse not occur in a vacuum?

BRANTLEY: I would agree with that last concept. But let's say that you do have a case of an individual who seems not to have had any other adjustment problems but is harming animals. What that says is that while, up to that point, there is no documented history of adjustment problems, there are adjustment problems now and there could be greater problems down the road. We have some kids who start early and move toward greater and greater levels of violence, some who get into it starting in adolescence, and some who are adults before they start to blossom into violent offenders.

HSUS: Do you find animal cruelty developing in those who have already begun killing people?

BRANTLEY: We know that certain types of offenders who have escalated to human victims will, at times, regress back to earlier offenses such as making obscene phone calls, stalking people, or killing animals. Rarely, if ever, do we see humans being killed as a precursor to the killing of animals.

HSUS: How would you respond to the argument that animal cruelty provides an outlet that prevents violent individuals from acting against people?

BRANTLEY: I would disagree with that. Animal cruelty is not as serious as killing human beings, we have to agree to that, but certainly it's moving in a very ominous direction. This is not a harmless venting of emotion in a healthy individual; this is a warning sign that this individual is not mentally healthy and needs some sort of intervention. Abusing animals does not dissipate those violent emotions; instead, it may fuel them.

HSUS: What problems do you have in trying to assess the dangerousness of a suspect or a known offender?

BRANTLEY: Getting background information is the main problem. People know this person has done these things, but there may be no record or we haven't found the right people to interview.

HSUS: That's one of the reasons why we have put an emphasis on stronger anticruelty laws and more aggressive enforcement—to get such information in the record.

BRANTLEY: A lot of times people who encounter this kind of behavior are looking for the best in people. We also see cases where people are quite frankly afraid to get involved, because if they are dealing

with a child or adult who seems to be bizarre or threatening, they are afraid that he or she may no longer kill animals but instead come after them. I've seen a lot of mental health professionals, law enforcement officers, and private citizens who don't want to get involved because they are afraid . . . and for good reason. There are very scary people out there doing scary things. That's largely why they are doing it and talking about it: they want to intimidate and shock and offend, sometimes regardless of the consequences.

HSUS: Is there hope for such an individual?

BRANTLEY: The earlier you can intervene, the better off you'll be. I like to be optimistic. I think in the vast majority of cases, especially if you get to them as children, you can intervene. People shouldn't discount animal abuse as a childish prank or childish experimentation.

HSUS: Have you ever seen any serial killers who have been rehabilitated?

BRANTLEY: I've seen no examples of it and no real efforts to even attempt it! Even if you had a program that might work, the potential consequences of being wrong and releasing someone like that greatly outweigh the benefits of attempting it, in my opinion.

HSUS: There is also a problem in trying to understand which acts against animals and others are associated with the escalation of violence, since police records, if they exist, are often unavailable or juvenile offenses are expunged. Sometimes only local humane societies or animal-control agencies have any record. The HSUS hopes to facilitate consolidating some of these records.

BRANTLEY: That would be great. If animal-cruelty investigators are aware of a case such as a sexual homicide in their community and they are also aware of any animal mutilation going on in the same area, I would encourage them to reach out to us. ∎

Randall Lockwood, Ph.D., is HSUS vice president, Training Initiatives.

Ann Church is HSUS deputy director, Government Affairs.

"THIS [ANIMAL CRUELTY] IS NOT A HARMLESS VENT-ING OF EMOTION IN A HEALTHY INDIVIDUAL; THIS IS A WARNING SIGN THAT THIS INDIVIDUAL . . . NEEDS SOME SORT OF INTERVENTION."

—Alan Brantley, FBI Supervisory Special Agent

The Humane Society of the United States
2100 L Street, NW, Washington, DC 20037

SECTION 6: DEVELOPMENTAL PSYCHOPATHOLOGY
The "Triad" and Conduct Disorder

Can we predict violent behavior? This is a question that fascinates and challenges lay and professional audiences alike. It is clear that if we were able to accurately gauge an individual's propensity for violence, this ability would facilitate prevention and intervention. Making such predictions is an inexact science but one to which considerable attention has been devoted. In this section we include samples of published work on the diagnosis of antisocial behavior and the ways that cruelty to animals has been used to inform such diagnoses.

The American Psychiatric Association began publishing its *Diagnostic and Statistical Manual of Mental Disorders* (*DSM*) in 1952 and has produced four additional versions over the past forty-five years. This manual has become a standard reference for psychiatrists, psychologists, and other mental-health professionals for diagnosing and categorizing psychological disorders. One of the categories included since the first edition addresses aggressive and destructive behavior in childhood and adolescence and has been variously labeled as "adjustment reaction" or, more recently, "conduct disorder."

The evolution of the *DSM* to include cruelty to animals as a symptom of psychological dysfunction reflects changes in the mental-health community's evaluation of the significance of animal maltreatment. Although the first edition and the subsequent 1968 edition mention "cruelty" and "destructiveness" as significant symptoms of adjustment or aggressive reactions of childhood, cruelty to animals is not specifically mentioned. The 1980 edition (*DSM-III*) introduced the label "conduct disorder" (CD) to identify children and adolescents who violated the rights of others as well as social norms or rules. Violent behavior against people was included as symptomatic, but, again, no mention was made of animal maltreatment. Physical cruelty to animals was finally included, among a variety of other antisocial acts, as a symptom of CD in the 1987 edition of the manual (*DSM-III-R*).

However, it was still unclear whether clinicians considered cruelty to animals as more comparable to the destruction of property (another CD symptom) or to physical cruelty to people. This issue was clarified in the latest edition (*DSM-IV,* 1994), a portion of which we have reprinted in this section, which includes a list of symptoms with the heading "Aggression to People and Animals." As a result, clinicians' attention is now explicitly directed to animal abuse, and its diagnostic relevance has been heightened.

The significance of CD as a disorder of childhood and adolescence stems from its relatively frequent incidence and prevalence. Since CD that emerges in early childhood and is left untreated means a poor prognosis for later childhood, adolescent, and adult mental health, early identification of CD is critical for effective intervention. In addition, a great deal of research is now available associating CD and other externalizing symptoms to histories of physical and sexual abuse and exposure to domestic violence (areas that have their own connections to animal maltreatment).

The study by Robert L. Spitzer, Mark Davies, and Russell A. Barkley illustrates a formal analysis of the various symptoms of CD and demonstrates that physical cruelty to animals is a quite reliable criterion for the clinical diagnosis of CD. Among the other symptoms of CD examined in this study is deliberate fire setting—another destructive behavior but one that has received greater research and therapeutic attention.

This leads us to the next set of articles, which examine a "triad" of behavioral symptoms considered to predict violent behavior—fire setting, cruelty to animals, and enuresis. The rationale behind such research is that a single symptom rarely predicts psychological dysfunction. Some psychologists and psychiatrists believe that this particular constellation of destructive symptoms (enuresis is sometimes tied to sadistic tendencies) might prove more valuable in diagnosing antisocial behavior than any of these symptoms alone. The paper by Daniel S. Hellman and Nathan Blackman attempts to make this case by examining a group of adolescent and adult prisoners undergoing psychiatric treatment. The triad was more common for prisoners convicted of aggressive crimes (45 percent of cases) than for those convicted of nonaggressive offenses (13 percent). The authors conclude that "It is the detection and early management of children in the throes of the triad that might well forestall a career of violent crime in the adult." The importance of the triad was confirmed in D. E. Wax and V. G. Haddox's case studies of male adolescents in custody at the California Youth Authority. Six individuals displayed the triad and had extensive histories of physically and sexually violent assaults on others. However, G. Adair Heath, Vaughn A. Hardesty, and Peter E. Goldfine's study of children seen in a psychiatric outpatient clinic suggests that the relation between elements of the triad is not straightforward and uniform. These authors used the *Child Behavior Checklist,* completed by parents, to determine the presence of the triad. This raises a critical research issue: although parents may be aware of a child's enuresis, cruelty to animals and fire setting may be performed secretively, away from home, and outside of parental awareness. Thus, the prevalence of certain symptoms may have been underestimated in this study. A similarly complex picture of the triad's diagnostic value is revealed in Alan R. Felthous and Bernard Yudowitz's research with assaultive and nonassaultive female offenders. Cruelty to animals, enuresis, and fire setting had frequencies of 36 percent, 45 percent, and 45 percent, respectively, among assaultive female offenders. The comparable percentages for nonassaultive females were 0 percent, 15 percent, and 23 percent.

We end this section with a paper by Blair Justice, Rita Justice, and Irvin A. Kraft that presents a more conservative perspective on the value of the triad in predicting violence in adults. These authors examined the childhood case histories of more than a thousand children who had been referred for learning and behavior problems; they later located fifty-seven of these children in the adult case files of the Texas Department of Correction and discovered that eight of the fifty-seven had been convicted of violent crimes. Justice, Justice, and Kraft found that childhood histories of fighting, tantrums, school problems and truancy, and interpersonal problems were more commonly associated with later violence than elements of the triad. Rather than arguing against the importance of the triad, however, they suggested that the "quartet" of symptoms they found should be used in conjunction with the triad to predict serious emotional disturbance. Focusing on cruelty to animals in isolation may not always have significant diagnostic value, but such cruelty may be embedded within a constellation of behavioral symptoms that can alert the clinician to a child's potential for severe antisocial behavior.

312.8 Conduct Disorder

Diagnostic Features

The essential feature of Conduct Disorder is a repetitive and persistent pattern of behavior in which the basic rights of others or major age-appropriate societal norms or rules are violated (Criterion A). These behaviors fall into four main groupings: aggressive conduct that causes or threatens physical harm to other people or animals (Criteria A1-A7), non-aggressive conduct that causes property loss or damage (Criteria A8-A9), deceitfulness or theft (Criteria A10-A12), and serious violations of rules (Criteria A13-A15). Three (or more) characteristic behaviors must have been present during the past 12 months, with at least one behavior present in the past 6 months. The disturbance in behavior causes clinically significant impairment in social, academic, or occupational functioning (Criterion B). Conduct Disorder may be diagnosed in individuals who are older than age 18 years, but only if the criteria for Antisocial Personality Disorder are not met (Criterion C). The behavior pattern is usually present in a variety of settings such as home, school, or the community. Because individuals with Conduct Disorder are likely to minimize their conduct problems, the clinician often must rely on additional informants. However, the informant's knowledge of the child's conduct problems may be limited by inadequate supervision or by the child's not having revealed them.

Children or adolescents with this disorder often initiate aggressive behavior and react aggressively to others. They may display bullying, threatening, or intimidating behavior (Criterion A1); initiate frequent physical fights (Criterion A2); use a weapon that can cause serious physical harm (e.g., a bat, brick, broken bottle, knife, or gun) (Criterion A3); be physically cruel to people (Criterion A4) or animals (Criterion A5); steal while confronting a victim (e.g., mugging, purse snatching, extortion, or armed robbery) (Criterion A6); or force someone into sexual activity (Criterion A7). Physical violence may take the form of rape, assault, or in rare cases, homicide.

Deliberate destruction of others' property is a characteristic feature of this disorder and may include deliberate fire setting with the intention of causing serious damage (Criterion A8) or deliberately destroying other people's property in other ways (e.g., smashing car windows, school vandalism) (Criterion A9).

Deceitfulness or theft is common and may include breaking into someone else's house, building, or car (Criterion A10); frequently lying or breaking promises to obtain goods or favors or to avoid debts or obligations (e.g., "conning" other people) (Criterion

Reprinted with permission from the American Psychiatric Association, *Diagnostic and Statistical Manual of Mental Disorders,* 4th ed. (Washington, D.C.: American Psychiatric Association, 1994).

A11); or stealing items of nontrivial value without confronting the victim (e.g., shoplifting, forgery) (Criterion A12).

Characteristically, there are also serious violations of rules (e.g., school, parental) by individuals with this disorder. Children with this disorder often have a pattern, beginning before age 13 years, of staying out late at night despite parental prohibitions (Criterion A13). There may be a pattern of running away from home overnight (Criterion A14). To be considered a symptom of Conduct Disorder, the running away must have occurred at least twice (or only once if the individual did not return for a lengthy period). Runaway episodes that occur as a direct consequence of physical or sexual abuse do not typically qualify for this criterion. Children with this disorder may often be truant from school, beginning prior to age 13 years (Criterion A15). In older individuals, this behavior is manifested by often being absent from work without good reason.

Subtypes

Two subtypes of Conduct Disorder are provided based on the age at onset of the disorder (i.e., Childhood-Onset Type and Adolescent-Onset Type). The subtypes differ in regard to the characteristic nature of the presenting conduct problems, developmental course and prognosis, and gender ratio. Both subtypes can occur in a mild, moderate, or severe form. In assessing the age at onset, information should preferably be obtained from the youth and from caregiver(s). Because many of the behaviors may be concealed, caregivers may underreport symptoms and overestimate the age at onset.

Childhood-Onset Type. This subtype is defined by the onset of at least one criterion characteristic of Conduct Disorder prior to age 10 years. Individuals with Childhood-Onset Type are usually male, frequently display physical aggression toward others, have disturbed peer relationships, may have had Oppositional Defiant Disorder during early childhood, and usually have symptoms that meet full criteria for Conduct Disorder prior to puberty. These individuals are more likely to have persistent Conduct Disorder and to develop adult Antisocial Personality Disorder than are those with Adolescent-Onset Type.

Adolescent-OnsetType. This subtype is defined by the absence of any criteria characteristic of Conduct Disorder prior to age 10 years. Compared with those with the Childhood-Onset Type, these individuals are less likely to display aggressive behaviors and tend to have more normative peer relationships (although they often display conduct problems in the company of others). These individuals are less likely to have persistent Conduct Disorder or to develop adult Antisocial Personality Disorder. The ratio of males to females with Conduct Disorder is lower for the Adolescent-Onset Type than for the Childhood-Onset Type.

Severity Specifiers

Mild. Few if any conduct problems in excess of those required to make the diagnosis are present, and conduct problems cause relatively minor harm to others (e.g., lying, truancy, staying out after dark without permission).

Moderate. The number of conduct problems and the effect on others are intermediate between "mild" and "severe" (e.g., stealing without confronting a victim, vandalism).

Severe. Many conduct problems in excess of those required to make the diagnosis are present, or conduct problems cause considerable harm to others (e.g., forced sex, physical cruelty, use of a weapon, stealing while confronting a victim, breaking and entering).

Associated Features and Disorders

Associated descriptive features and mental disorders. Individuals with Conduct Disorder may have little empathy and little concern for the feelings, wishes, and well-being of others. Especially in ambiguous situations, aggressive individuals with this disorder frequently misperceive the intentions of others as more hostile and threatening than is the case and respond with aggression that they then feel is reasonable and justified. They may be callous and lack appropriate feelings of guilt or remorse. It can be difficult to evaluate whether displayed remorse is genuine because these individuals learn that expressing guilt may reduce or prevent punishment. Individuals with this disorder may readily inform on their companions and try to blame others for their own misdeeds. Self-esteem is usually low, although the person may project an image of "toughness." Poor frustration tolerance, irritability, temper outbursts, and recklessness are frequent associated features. Accident rates appear to be higher in individuals with Conduct Disorder than in those without it.

Conduct Disorder is often associated with an early onset of sexual behavior, drinking, smoking, use of illegal substances, and reckless and risk-taking acts. Illegal drug use may increase the risk that Conduct Disorder will persist. Conduct Disorder behaviors may lead to school suspension or expulsion, problems in work adjustment, legal difficulties, sexually transmitted diseases, unplanned pregnancy, and physical injury from accidents or fights. These problems may preclude attendance in ordinary schools or living in a parental or foster home. Suicidal ideation, suicide attempts, and completed suicide occur at a higher than expected rate. Conduct Disorder may be associated with lower than average intelligence. Academic achievement, particularly in reading and other verbal skills, is often below the level expected on the basis of age and intelligence and may justify the additional diagnosis of a Learning or Communication Disorder. Attention-Deficit/Hyperactivity Disorder is common in children with Conduct Disorder. Conduct Disorder may also be associated with one or more of the following mental disorders: Learning Disorders, Anxiety Disorders, Mood Disorders, and Substance-Related Disorders. The following factors may predispose the individual to the development of Conduct Disorder: parental rejection and neglect, difficult infant temperament. inconsistent child-rearing practices with harsh discipline, physical or sexual abuse, lack of supervision, early institutional living, frequent changes of caregivers, large family size, association with a delinquent peer group, and certain kinds of familial psychopathology.

Associated laboratory findings. In some studies, lower heart rate and lower skin conductance have been noted in individuals with Conduct Disorder compared with those without the disorder. However, levels of physiological arousal are not diagnostic of the disorder.

Specific Culture, Age, and Gender Features

Concerns have been raised that the Conduct Disorder diagnosis may at times be misapplied to individuals in settings where patterns of undesirable behavior are sometimes viewed as protective (e.g., threatening, impoverished, high-crime). Consistent with the DSM-IV definition of mental disorder, the Conduct Disorder diagnosis should be applied only when the behavior in question is symptomatic of an underlying dysfunction within the individual and not simply a reaction to the immediate social context. Moreover, immigrant youth from war-ravaged countries who have a history of aggressive behaviors that may have been necessary for their survival in that context would not necessarily warrant a diagnosis of Conduct Disorder. It may be helpful for the clinician to consider the social and economic context in which the undesirable behaviors have occurred.

Symptoms of the disorder vary with age as the individual develops increased physical strength, cognitive abilities, and sexual maturity. Less severe behaviors (e.g., lying, shoplifting, physical fighting) tend to emerge first, whereas others (e.g., burglary) tend to emerge later. Typically, the most severe conduct problems (e.g., rape, theft while confronting a victim) tend to emerge last. However, there are wide differences among individuals, with some engaging in the more damaging behaviors at an early age.

Conduct Disorder, especially the Childhood-Onset Type, is much more common in males. Gender differences are also found in specific types of conduct problems. Males with a diagnosis of Conduct Disorder frequently exhibit fighting, stealing, vandalism, and school discipline problems. Females with a diagnosis of Conduct Disorder are more likely to exhibit lying, truancy, running away, substance use, and prostitution. Whereas confrontational aggression is more often displayed by males, females tend to use more nonconfrontational behaviors.

Prevalence

The prevalence of Conduct Disorder appears to have increased over the last decades and may be higher in urban than in rural settings. Rates vary widely depending on the nature of the population sampled and methods of ascertainment: for males under age 18 years, rates range from 6% to 16%; for females, rates range from 2% to 9%. Conduct Disorder is one of the most frequently diagnosed conditions in outpatient and inpatient mental health facilities for children.

Course

The onset of Conduct Disorder may occur as early as age 5-6 years but usually in late childhood or early adolescence. Onset is rare after age 16 years. The course of Conduct Disorder is variable. In a majority of individuals, the disorder remits by adulthood. However, a substantial proportion continue to show behaviors in adulthood that meet criteria for Antisocial Personality Disorder. Many individuals with Conduct Disorder, particularly those with Adolescent-Onset Type and those with few and milder symptoms, achieve adequate social and occupational adjustment as adults. Early onset predicts a worse prognosis and an increased risk in adult life for Antisocial Personality Disorder and Substance-Related Disorders. Individuals with Conduct Disorder are at risk for later Mood or Anxiety Disorders, Somatoform Disorders, and Substance-Related Disorders.

Familial Pattern

Estimates from twin and adoption studies show that Conduct Disorder has both genetic and environmental components. The risk for Conduct Disorder is increased in children with a biological or adoptive parent with Antisocial Personality Disorder or a sibling with Conduct Disorder. The disorder also appears to be more common in children of biological parents with Alcohol Dependence, Mood Disorders, or Schizophrenia or biological parents who have a history of Attention-Deficit/Hyperactivity Disorder or Conduct Disorder.

Differential Diagnosis

Although **Oppositional Defiant Disorder** includes some of the features observed in Conduct Disorder (e.g., disobedience and opposition to authority figures), it doe:s not include the persistent pattern of the more serious forms of behavior in which either the basic rights of others or age-appropriate societal norms or rules are violated. When the individual's pattern of behavior meets the criteria for both Conduct Disorder and Oppositional Defiant Disorder, the diagnosis of Conduct Disorder takes precedence and Oppositional Defiant Disorder is not diagnosed.

Although children with **Attention-Deficit/Hyperactivity Disorder** often exhibit hyperactive and impulsive behavior that may be disruptive, this behavior does not by itself violate age-appropriate societal norms and therefore does not usually meet criteria for Conduct Disorder. When criteria are met for both Attention-Deficit/Hyperactivity Disorder and Conduct Disorder, both diagnoses should be given.

Irritability and conduct problems often occur in children or adolescents having a **Manic Episode.** These can usually be distinguished from the pattern of conduct problems seen in Conduct Disorder based on the episodic course and accompanying symptoms characteristic of a Manic Episode. If criteria for both are met, diagnoses of both Conduct Disorder and Bipolar I Disorder can be given.

The diagnosis of **Adjustment Disorder** (With Disturbance of Conduct or With Mixed Disturbance of Emotions and Conduct) should be considered if clinically significant conduct problems that do not meet the criteria for another specific disorder develop in clear association with the onset of a psychosocial stressor. Isolated conduct problems that do not meet criteria for Conduct Disorder or Adjustment Disorder may be coded as **Child or Adolescent Antisocial Behavior** (see "Other Conditions That May Be a Focus of Clinical Attention," p. 684). Conduct Disorder is diagnosed only if the conduct problems represent a repetitive and persistent pattern that is associated with impairment in social, academic, or occupational functioning.

For individuals over age 18 years, a diagnosis of Conduct Disorder can be given only if the criteria are not also met for **Antisocial Personality Disorder.** The diagnosis of Antisocial Personality Disorder cannot be given to individuals under age 18 years.

Diagnostic criteria for 312.8 Conduct Disorder

A.   A repetitive and persistent pattern of behavior in which the basic rights of others or major age-appropriate societal norms or rules are violated, as manifested by the presence of three (or more) of the following criteria in the past 12 months, with at least one criterion present in the past 6 months:

Aggression to people and animals

(1)   often bullies, threatens, or intimidates others

(2)   often initiates physical fights

(3)   has used a weapon that can cause serious physical harm to others (e.g., a bat, brick, broken bottle, knife, gun)

(4) has been physically cruel to people

(5) has been physically cruel to animals

(6) has stolen while confronting a victim (e.g., mugging, purse snatching, extortion, armed robbery)

(7) has forced someone into sexual activity

Destruction of property

(8) has deliberately engaged in fire setting with the intention of causing serious damage

(9) has deliberately destroyed others' property (other than by fire setting)

Deceitfulness or theft

(10) has broken into someone else's house, building, or car

(11) often lies to obtain goods or favors or to avoid obligations (i-e., "cons" others)

(12) has stolen items of nontrivial value without confronting a victim (e.g., shoplifting, but without breaking and entering; forgery)

Serious violations of rules

(13) often stays out at night despite parental prohibitions, beginning before age 13 years

(14) has run away from home overnight at least twice while living in parental or parental surrogate home (or once without returning for a lengthy period)

(15) is often truant from school, beginning before age 13 years

B. The disturbance in behavior causes clinically significant impairment in social, academic, or occupational functioning.

C. If the individual is age 18 years or older, criteria are not met for Antisocial Personality Disorder.

Specify type based on age at onset:

Childhood-Onset Type: onset of at least one criterion characteristic of Conduct Disorder prior to age 10 years

Adolescent-OnsetType: absence of any criteria characteristic of Conduct Disorder prior to age 10 years

Specify severity:

Mild: few if any conduct problems in excess of those required to make the diagnosis **and** conduct problems cause only minor harm to others

Moderate: number of conduct problems and effect on others intermediate between "mild" and "severe"

Severe: many conduct problems in excess of those required to make the diagnosis **or** conduct problems cause considerable harm to others

The *DSM-III-R* Field Trial of Disruptive Behavior Disorders

ROBERT L. SPITZER, M.D., MARK DAVIES, M.P.H., AND RUSSELL A. BARKLEY, PH.D.

Abstract. The members of the *DSM-III-R* Advisory Committee responsible for the diagnostic criteria for the disruptive behavior disorders (attention deficit hyperactivity disorder, oppositional defiant disorder, and conduct disorder) were able to reach agreement on potential items to be included in the final diagnostic criteria. However, there was considerable disagreement about the relative utility of different items for the three disorders and no agreement on how many items should be required from a final list of discriminating items to establish each of the diagnoses. This article describes the method and results of a national field trial of the proposed criteria. Using as a standard the diagnosis of these disorders made by expert clinicians with experience with these disorders, the diagnostic criteria that were finally included in *DSM-III-R* demonstrated high sensitivity, specificity, and internal consistency. *J. Am. Acad. Child Adolesc. Psychiatry*, 1990, 29, 5:690–697. **Key Words:** disruptive, attention deficit, oppositional, conduct, field trial.

The rationale for the development of the items for the diagnostic criteria for the disruptive behavior disorders, attention deficit hyperactivity disorder (ADHD), oppositional defiant disorder (ODD) and conduct disorder (CD) is described by Barkley et al. (unpublished manuscript). The members of the *DSM-III-R* Advisory Committee responsible for the diagnostic criteria for these disorders were able to reach agreement on potential items to be included in the final diagnostic criteria. They were also able to reach agreement, in the case of ADHD, on the value of abandoning the grouping of the component items under three separate rubrics (inattention, impulsivity, hyperactivity) and instead to treat the items polythetically, consistent with a general trend in *DSM-III-R* towards a polythetic format for diagnostic criteria. However, there was considerable disagreement within the Advisory Committee about the relative utility of different items for the three disorders and no agreement on how many items should be required from a final list of discriminating items to establish each of the diagnoses.

In order to provide am empirical basis for resolving these issues, a national field trial of the proposed items sets was conducted in early 1985. The field trial was designed to answer the following questions:

1. Which items in the proposed criteria sets for the disruptive behavior disorders have sufficient discriminating power to be included in the final item sets?

2. What is the internal consistency of the three item sets? This addresses the issue of the extent to which the criteria for each of the three disorders are representative of its particular domain of psychopathology.

3. What threshold (minimum number of items) for making the diagnosis should be selected to maximize its sensitivity and specificity, using a clinical diagnosis made without ref-

erence to the diagnostic criteria as the validity criterion? This addresses the descriptive validity of the diagnoses, that is, the extent to which the clinical features of the disorders are unique to them.

4. Is the prevalence of the disorders, diagnosed clinically without using the *DSM-III-R* diagnostic criteria, similar to the prevalence based on the final *DSM-III-R* criteria?

5. What is the level of agreement between clinical diagnoses made without using the *DSM-III-R* diagnostic criteria and diagnoses based on the final *DSM-III-R* criteria?

6. Is the pattern of comorbidity of the disruptive behavior disorders similar with diagnoses made clinically and diagnoses made with the *DSM-III-R* criteria?

7. Is there empirical support for the *DSM-III-R* convention that CD preempts a diagnosis of ODD? In other words, does the pattern of psychopathology indicate a Guttman type (1) of relationship between CD and ODD in which the majority of cases of CD also exhibit the defining symptoms of ODD?

Method

Clinical facilities that evaluated large numbers of children who received diagnoses of one or more of the disruptive behavior disorders were recruited for the field trial. Table 1 lists the 10 field trial sites with demographic and diagnostic data for each site. (Note: This list is correct. Because of clerical error, the listing in Appendix F of *DSM-III-R* is incorrect.) In all, 550 children were evaluated by 72 clinicians. As can be seen, the average age of the subjects is similar across sites as is the usual preponderance of male subjects in child psychiatry clinics.

Each facility was asked to evaluate at least 50 subjects from all consecutive referrals until at least 10 cases had been evaluated for each of the following five groups: ADHD, ODD, CD, other mental disorders (e.g., specific developmental, major depression, overanxious disorder), and no mental disorder. Cases with a diagnosis of a pervasive developmental disorder were excluded, since this diagnosis precludes the diagnosis of ADHD. If a case had a diagnosis from more than one of the five groups, the same case would go towards filling the cells of each of the appropriate diagnoses.

The clinicians were asked to make a diagnosis ''as you ordinarily do in clinical practice'' and without consulting the

Accepted January 8, 1990.

Dr. Spitzer and Mr. Davies are from the New York State Psychiatric Institute and the Department of Psychiatry, Columbia University. Dr. Barkley is from the Department of Psychiatry, University of Massachusetts Medical Center, Worchester, MA.

The authors thank Dr. William E. Pelham for his many helpful comments in reviewing the initial manuscript.

0890-8567/90/2905-0690$02.00/0© 1990 by the American Academy of Child and Adolescent Psychiatry.

TABLE 1. *Field Trial Sites[a], Demographic Data, and Diagnoses[b]*

Site and (No. of Interviewer)	N	Mean Age	Male %	ADHD %	ODD %	CD %	Other %
1. Western Psychiatric Institute and Clinic, University of Pittsburgh School of Medicine, Pittsburgh, PA (23)	85	10.2	65	33	27	32	42
2. Department of Pediatrics and Child Study Center, Yale University School of Medicine, New Haven, CT (6)	83	8.2	64	43	20	8	53
3. Division of Child Psychiatry, New York State Psychiatric Institute, and Babies Hospital, Columbia-Presbyterian Medical Center, New York (6)	80	9.6	75	70	22	10	49
4. Child Study Center, Summer Treatment Program, Dept. of Psychology, Florida State University, Tallahassee, FL (1)	59	8.6	80	83	44	24	35
5. Department of Pediatrics, Child Development Center, University of California, Irvine, CA (2)	54	8.3	94	96	43	26	20
6. Division of Child Psychiatry, Washington University School of Medicine, St. Louis, MO (3)	49	9.6	71	29	24	26	51
7. Center for Children, Youth & Families, Dept. of Psychiatry, University of Vermont, Burlington, VT (2)	44	8.6	59	36	11	18	59
8. Neuropsychology Clinic, Medical College of Wisconsin, Milwaukee, WI (3)	44	8.8	77	68	18	20	62
9. Department of Child Psychiatry University of California, Los Angeles, CA (24)	38	11.2	72	42	13	55	32
10. Child Psychiatry Branch, National Institute of Mental Health, Bethesda, MD (2)	14	8.0	100	100	21	64	0
Total (72)	550	9.2	73	56	26	24	44

[a]The coordinators for the sites were: 1. Anthony Costello, M.D., 2. Bennet A. Shaywitz, M.D., 3. William Chambers, M.D., 4. William Pelham, Ph.D., 5. James Swanson, M.D., 6. Felton Earls, M.D., 7. Thomas Achenbach, Ph.D., 8. Russell A. Barkley, Ph.D., 9. Dennis Cantwell, M.D. and 10. Judith Rapoport, M.D.

[b]ADHD = Attention deficit hyperactivity disorder, ODD = oppositional defiant disorder, CD = conduct disorder, Other = nondisruptive diagnosis (e.g., anxiety disorder, mental retardation) and no mental disorder.

ratings that the clinician made on the proposed *DSM-III-R* diagnostic criteria for the disorder. In making this "clinical" diagnosis, the clinicians were encouraged to consider factors that were not in *DSM-III* or the *DSM-III-R* proposed criteria, such as response to treatment, family history, symptoms of the disorder that are not in these item lists, and laboratory measures of attentional disturbance.

The diagnostic assessment was predominantly based on a clinical interview of the parent (95%) and the child (72%). Less frequently, the assessment made use of a structured interview with the child (30%), parent (38%), school records (37%), and psychometric tests or lab measures (42%). At the time of evaluation, 12% of the children were receiving a psychotropic drug. The quality and completeness of the information was judged by the raters to be "good" or "excellent" in 82% of the cases.

Following the evaluation, the clinician completed a symptom check list that listed all of the items proposed for the diagnostic criteria for the three disruptive behavior disorders. The items were not identified with their corresponding diagnoses but, presumably, most of the clinicians realized to which diagnoses they referred. Each item was rated as present, absent, or no information.

For purposes of data analysis, different rules were ruled to handle missing information about the diagnostic criteria. For calculating sensitivity and specificity of individual diagnostic criteria, all cases were considered valid that had information on the particular item (Tables 3, 5, and 7). Thus, a case for which the clinician did not have sufficient information to

make a judgment that the item was either present or absent (not an uncommon occurrence in the real world of clinical assessment), was not included in this data analysis. For calculating the psychometric descriptors of the *DSM-III-R* diagnoses at different thresholds, a valid case had to contain information on all of the diagnostic, criteria (Tables 4, 6, and 8). In calculating agreement between clinical and *DSM-III-R* diagnoses, a valid case had to have valid information for both diagnoses (Table 9). For calculating the comorbidity of clinical and *DSM-III-R* diagnoses, valid diagnoses had to be available for all clinical and *DSM-III-R* diagnoses. Because of these rules for handling missing information, the number of subjects reported in the various tables vary. Table 1, which reports the clinical diagnoses (no missing information), has the largest NS, whereas, Table 10, which has the most restrictive definition of a valid case, has the smallest NS.

Results

As expected, there was a high degree of comorbidity within the group of disruptive behavior disorders. As can be seen in Table 2, which presents the comorbidity of the clinical diagnoses, most of the cases with a diagnosis of a disruptive behavior disorder also had another mental disorder. Over half of the cases of ADHD also had a diagnosis of either ODD or CD. Similarly, over half of the cases of CD also had a diagnosis of ADHD, and over half of the cases of ODD also had a diagnosis of ADHD. Although the degree of comorbidity may represent referral biases to the particular clinics that were involved, the results suggest that each of these disruptive

TABLE 2. *Comorbidity of Clinical Diagnoses*

	N	%
Attention deficit hyperactivity disorder (ADHD) (*N* = 311)		
ADHD only	109	35
ADHD and ODD (with or without nondisruptive diagnosis)	94	30
ADHD and CD (with or without nondisruptive diagnosis)	71	23
ADHD and nondisruptive mental disorder	37	12
Oppositional defiant disorder (ODD) (*N* = 140)		
ODD only	29	21
ODD and ADHD (with or without nondisruptive diagnosis)	94	67
ODD and nondisruptive mental disorder	17	12
Conduct disorder (CD) (*N* = 130)		
Conduct disorder (CD) only	45	35
CD and ADHD (with or without nondisruptive diagnosis)	71	55
CD and nondisruptive mental disorder	14	11
Nondisruptive mental disorder only (*N* = 104)		
No mental disorder (*N* = 30)		
Total	550	100

TABLE 3. *Sensitivity, Specificity, and Odds Ratio for Proposed Criteria for Clinical Diagnosis of Attention Deficit Hyperactivity Disorder*

Criterion (Abbreviated)	Sensitivity (*N* = 291–310)	Specificity (*N* = 222–236)	Odds Ratio
1. Fidgets or squirms	91	54	11.85
2. Difficulty remaining seated	85	65	10.67
3. Easily distracted	91	50	10.59
4. Difficulty awaiting turn	82	79	9.18
5. Blurts out answers to questions	65	83	9.03
6. Difficulty following instructions	85	61	8.92
7. Difficulty sustaining attention	86	57	8.12
8. Shifts between uncompleted tasks	84	59	7.56
9. Difficulty playing quietly	64	79	6.65
10. Talks excessively	73	68	5.70
11. Interrupts or intrudes on others	74	66	5.59
12. Doesn't listen	85	44	4.52
13. Loses things	66	69	4.37
14. Physically dangerous activities	47	79	3.35
Extremely messy or sloppy[a]	54	70	2.81

[a] Item not included in final item set.

TABLE 4. *Sensitivity, Specificity, Positive Predictive Value (PPV), Negative Predictive Value (NPV), and Total Predictive Value (TPV) of Attention Deficit Hyperactivity Disorder Criteria by Different Thresholds for Making the Diagnosis (ADHD, N = 260; NonADHD, N = 291)*

Threshold (Minimum No. of Symptoms)	Sensitivity	Specificity	PPV	NPV	TPV
5	95	53	73	88	77
6	91	61	76	83	78
7	87	71	80	80	80
8	85	80	85	79	83
9	76	83	86	72	79
10	69	91	91	68	78
11	60	94	93	63	74

disorders (particularly ODD) are usually seen in association with another disruptive behavior disorder.

ADHD. The sensitivity, specificity, and odds ratio for the proposed criteria for ADHD were calculated, using the clinical diagnosis of ADHD as the criterion. This data is presented in Table 3 with the items ordered, as in the *DSM-III-R* manual, by the magnitude of the odds ratio (odds of the item in cases diagnosed ADHD divided by the odds of non-ADHD cases). Generally, the odds ratios are quite high, indicating that the items have considerable discriminating power. On the basis of this analysis, the item, "Often extremely messy or sloppy" was dropped because of its comparatively low odds ratio.

The odds ratios indicate that clinicians gave more weight to the items, "Fidgets or squirms" and "Difficulty remaining seated"—symptoms of overactivity—than they gave to items describing inattentiveness and impulsivity. The item with the best combination of sensitivity and specificity was an item with face-validity for tapping impulsivity—"Difficulty awaiting turns in games or group situations." Also of interest, the items with face-validity for assessing inattention all had low specificity (e.g., "Doesn't listen," "Easily distracted," and "Difficulty following instructions").

The internal consistency of the item set was very high, 0.90. Using the fourteen items, Table 4 presents the psychometric properties of the items set by different thresholds for making the diagnosis, as can be seen, requiring at least eight of the 14 items maximizes the total predictive value and yields sensitivity and specificity above 0.80. Therefore, the *DSM-III-R* criteria for ADHD require at least eight of the 14 items.

ODD. Table 5 presents the sensitivity, specificity, and odds ratio for the proposed criteria for ODD, again using the clinical diagnosis of ODD as the criterion. Cases with a clinical diagnosis of CD were excluded from the analysis as these cases would be expected to have a large number of the

items for ODD. As with ADHD, the odds ratios are quite high, indicating that the items have considerable discriminating power.

The item, "Bullies or is mean to other children (other than physically cruel)" had a reasonably high odds ratio. However, it was deleted from the final ODD *DSM-III-R* item set because it seemed to describe behavior that was closer to the underlying construct of CD than to the construct of ODD, and it was as correlated with the clinical diagnosis of CD as with

TABLE 5. *Sensitivity, Specificity, and Odds Ratio for Proposed Criteria for Clinical Diagnosis of Oppositional Defiant Disorder*[a]

Criterion (Abbreviated)	Sensitivity (N = 136–139)	Specificity (N = 268–278)	Odds Ratio
1. Loses temper	87	59	9.61
2. Argues with adults	86	59	9.22
3. Actively defies requests or rules	84	62	8.15
4. Deliberately annoys other people	77	69	7.30
5. Blames others for his mistakes	73	65	5.09
Bullies or is mean to other children[b]	48	86	5.40
6. Touchy or easily annoyed	73	61	4.16
7. Angry or resentful	67	68	4.34
8. Spiteful or vindictive	44	89	6.06
9. Swears or uses obscene language	36	87	3.78

[a] Cases with a clinical diagnosis of conduct disorder have been excluded from the analysis as these cases would be expected to have a large number of the items for oppositional defiant disorder.
[b] Item not included in final item set.

the clinical diagnosis of ODD.

The internal consistency of the total item set was high, 0.85. Using the nine items, Table 6 presents the psychometric properties of the full item set by different thresholds for making the diagnosis. As can be seen, requiring at least five of the nine items maximizes the total predictive value and yields sensitivity and specificity of approximately 80. Therefore, the *DSM-III-R* criteria for ODD require at least five of the nine items.

TABLE 6. *Sensitivity, Specificity, Positive Predictive Value (PPV), Negative Predictive Value (NPV), and Total Predictive Value (TPV) of Oppositional Defiant Disorder Criteria[a] by Different Thresholds for Making the Diagnosis (ODD, N = 130, NonODD, N = 249)*

Threshold (Minimum No. of Symptoms)	Sensitivity	Specificity	PPV	NPV	TPV
2	96	40	45	95	59
3	93	59	54	94	71
4	88	70	61	92	76
5	80	79	67	88	79
6	67	86	72	83	80
7	51	92	77	78	78
8	33	96	80	73	74

[a]Cases with a clinical diagnosis of conduct disorder have been excluded from the analysis as these cases would be expected to have a large number of the items for oppositional defiant disorder.

CD. The sensitivity, specificity, and odds ratio for the proposed criteria from CD are presented in Table 7. Interestingly, the item, ''often lies,'' is the item with the best combination of both sensitivity and specificity. Although all of the

TABLE 7. *Sensitivity, Specificity, and Odds Ratio for Proposed Criteria for Clinical Diagnosis of Conduct Disorder*

Criterion (Abbreviated)	Sensitivity (N = 112–130)	Specificity (N = 386–408)	Odds Ratio
Unusually early sexual activity[a]	13	99	14.97
1. Stolen without confrontation	43	94	11.34
2. Runaway from home at least twice	18	98	10.85
3. Often lies	80	72	10.23
Early use of tobacco or drugs[a]	19	97	8.63
4. Deliberately set fires	35	93	7.37
5. Truant	24	95	6.20
6. Broken into someone's house or car	9	98	6.22
7. Deliberately destroyed property	51	86	6.12
8. Physically cruel to animals	23	94	5.07
9. Forced someone to have sex	5	99	4.93
Borrows without permission[a]	40	86	4.25
10. Used a weapon in fights	16	95	3.76
Cheats in games[a]	40	85	3.72
11. Initiates physical fights	53	77	3.84
12. Stolen with confrontation	1	100	3.17
13. Physically cruel to other people	16	94	3.14

[a] Item not included in final item set.

items had considerable discriminating power, four items were eliminated. The items describing unusually early sexually activity and use of tobacco or drugs were dropped because they did not describe behavior that was inherently antisocial, even though the behaviors are risk factors for the diagnosis. The items describing borrowing without permission and cheating in games were eliminated because of the high frequency with which such symptoms are also commonly seen in OD and ADHD.

The internal consistency of the total item set was acceptable, 0.73, although lower than ADHS and ODD. Using the 13 final *DSM-III-R* items, Table 8 presents the psychometric properties of the full item set by different thresholds for making the diagnosis. A threshold of at least three items was chosen as this maximized the total predictive value (0.85) and yields a sensitivity of 0.71 and a specificity of 0.90.

Prevalence of disorder by method of diagnosis. The prevalence of the three disorders, by clinical diagnosis and by *DSM-III-R* criteria, was calculated for each site and for the total sample (Table 9). This was done in order to determine if, for some sites, there are statistically significant discrepancies between the prevalence of the disorders according to whether the diagnosis was clinical or based on the *DSM-III-R*

TABLE 8. *Sensitivity, Specificity, Positive Predictive Value (PPV), Negative, Predictive Value (NPV), and Total Predictive Value (TPV) of Conduct Disorder Criteria by Different Thresholds for Making the Diagnosis (CD, N = 113, NonCD, N = 372)*

Threshold (Minimum No. of Symptoms)	Sensitivity	Specificity	PPV	NPV	TPV
1	97	54	39	99	64
2	90	73	50	96	77
3	71	90	68	91	85
4	50	95	74	86	84
5	30	97	76	82	81
6	12	99	74	79	79

TABLE 10. *Comorbidity of Clinical and DSM-III-R Diagnoses*

	Clinical		DSM-III-R		
	N	%	N	%	p <
ADHD alone	106	26	80	19	0.01
ODD alone	32	8	46	11	0.06
CD alone	39	9	27	7	0.05
ADHD and ODD	75	18	75	18	NS
ADHD and CD	59	14	78	19	0.01
Neither ADHD, ODD, or CD	103	25	108	26	NS
Total	414	100	414	100	

criteria. Although for some sites the prevalence of the disorders differs markedly according to whether the diagnosis was clinical or based on the *DSM-III-R* criteria, when the total sample is examined, the prevalences are virtually identical for ADHD and CD, and differ only slightly for ODD ($p <$ NS).

Agreement between clinical diagnosis and DSM-III-R diagnosis. Table 9 also presents the kappa agreement between the clinical diagnosis and the *DSM-III-R* diagnosis for each site and for the total sample. There is considerable variability across the sites and for the total sample the agreement is only fair for ADHD and CD, and poor for ODD.

Psychometric properties of item sets by age and sex. The sensitivity, specificity, and total predictive value were calculated for three age groups (2 to 7, 8 to 11, and older) and by sex. The only systematic effect of age was slightly decreased sensitivity in the older children for ADHD (0.92, 0.82, and 0.72, respectively, $p < 0.05$) and a corresponding increase in specificity (0.74, 0.77, and 0.89, respectively, $p < 0.10$). There were no differences between the sexes.

Comorbidity. The comorbidity of the three disruptive behavior disorders with other disorders was examined for the clinical diagnoses and for diagnoses based on the *DSM-III-R* criteria (Table 10). (Because of the hierarchical rule of CD excluding a diagnosis of ODD, comorbidity for these disorders involves examining association with ADHD and with nondisruptive disorders.) There was a slight, but statistically significant, tendency for the *DSM-III-R* diagnoses to be associated with greater comorbidity; conversely, clinicians were more likely to give a single diagnosis of a disruptive behavior disorder.

DSM-III-R hierarchic relationship of CD to ODD. There were 113 cases that met the criteria for CD and had no missing information regarding the presence or absence of all of the ODD items. Of these, only 18 (16%) did not also have at least five of the nine ODD items. Thus, the pattern of psychopathology between CD and ODD approximates a Guttman type of scaling, which is implicit in the *DSM-III-R* convention that CD preempts a diagnosis of ODD.

TABLE 9. *Prevalence of Disruptive Behavior Disorders by Clinical Diagnosis and Diagnosis Made by DSM-III-R Criteria[a] and Agreement (Kappa) between Clinical Diagnosis and Diagnosis Made by DSM-III-R Criteria*

	ADHD			ODD			CD		
Site[c]	Clinical %	DSM-III-R %	K	Clinical %	DSM-III-R[a] %	K	Clinical %	DSM-III-R %	K
1. Western Psychiatric Institute	33	50	0.67	40	28	0.35	29	24	0.34
2. Yale	48	61	0.49	24	42	0.28	10	18	0.33
3. Columbia	71	43	0.41	28	31	0.76	9	2	0.27
4. Florida State University	82	82	1.00	58	42	0.61	23	30	0.82
5. University of California-Irvine	96	79	0.28	56	46	0.49	26	40	0.71
6. Washington University	30	43	0.52	34	46	0.18	24	24	0.76
7. University of Vermont	39	41	0.44	14	5	0.22	18	34	0.37
8. Medical College of Wisconsin	66	66	0.89	21	26	0.19	20	11	0.67
9. University of California- Los Angeles	28	24	0.73	25	38	0.71	56	41	0.57
10. National Institute of Mental Health	100	93	0.00[b]	60	60	1.00	67	58	0.82
Total (unweighted)	58	57	0.64	34	35	0.47	23	24	0.60

[a] If the subject was positive for the CD algorithm, the diagnosis of ODD by algorithm was not considered.

[b] There was no variability in the clinical diagnosis of ADHD as the diagnosis was given to all 14 cases.

[c] See Table 1 for site location.

Discussion

The results of this field trial of the proposed criteria for the disruptive behavior disorders are historically significant in that this is the first attempt by a DSM committee of the American Psychiatric Association to empirically establish the discriminating power of item pools and cutoff scores for the classification of common childhood psychiatric disorders. Previous committees responsible for developing the diagnostic manual have been criticized for their heavy reliance on committee consensus without testing the soundness of these decisions against more empirical approaches to developing classification schemes (Quay, 1986). This field trial therefore represents a significant step forward in the effort to combine the merits of both expert committee consensus with empirical validation in establishing a taxonomy of child behavioral disorders. In general, despite the limitations of the field trial, the results support the success of this approach and should serve as the basis for additional refinement of these criteria and item pools in developing *DSM-IV*.

In developing the *DSM-III-R* criteria, the committee made use of previously validated item pools from behavior rating scales. This, along with a shift in the item format to a polythetic or dimensional approach (rather than the categorical approach used in *DSM-III*), greatly enhanced the likelihood that the criteria sets would have high discriminating power. The use of a large sample of children of varying ages drawn from a wide range of geographic and socioeconomic areas suggests that the results can be generalized, despite the possibility that individual facilities might have considerable referral bias. The inclusion of mixed cases as well as normal children and those with other psychiatric disorders, instead of or in addition to these three disruptive behavior disorders, provided for a better test of the discriminating power of these items, rather than relying on exclusively pure cases of these three disorders.

The findings with respect to the degree of comorbidity among the three disorders, based on the clinical diagnoses made by field trial clinicians, are quite consistent with previous studies employing other means of classification. Using teacher ratings, Loney and Milich (1982) found that 46% of children rated as significantly aggressive were also rated as significantly hyperactive, while McGee et al. (1984) reported a 69% overlap between these dimensions based on both parent and teacher ratings. Aggression in these studies represents a similar item pool to that used to establish ODD and CD in the present field trial. These percentages are very close to the 55% to 67% overlap found in this study between ODD/CD and ADHD. However, Munir et al. (1987) evaluated the comorbidity of ADD with CD and oppositional disorder (OD) using the older *DSM-III* criteria for these disorders, and found 36% of ADHD children to also have CD and 59% to also have OD. The authors' percentages (23% and 30%, respectively) of co-occurrence of ODD and CD with ADHD are lower probably due to their instructions to clinicians to consider relying on more than simply the *DSM-III* criteria, such as rating scales, family history, and laboratory findings, in reaching their clinical diagnoses. Furthermore, Munir et al. (1987) relied on a single clinic site in a tertiary care facility within a large metropolitan area

(Boston) for their subjects, leaving open the possibility that their findings may be skewed as a result; whereas, the present trial relied on multiple sites across diverse geographic settings.

The discriminating power (odds ratios) of the final item sets and their internal consistency was quite high for all three disorders. The findings for internal consistency are comparable to those usually reported for dimensions of rating scales believed to reflect these same childhood disorders (Achenbach and Edelbrock, 1983; Barkley, 1988). This should hardly be surprising given that the item pools of behavior rating scales served as one basis for the selection of items for these *DSM-III-R* diagnoses. Nevertheless, this reliance on empirically established item pools as at least one consideration in item selection, not to mention prior research on these disorders, anchors the present diagnostic criteria much more firmly in the scientific literature. It also permits some application, albeit indirectly, of the substantial research literature (Achenbach and Edelbrock, 1978; Hinshaw, 1987; Barkley, 1988) that exists on the validation of these item pools in considering the validity of these diagnostic categories.

The kappa coefficients of agreement between the clinicians diagnoses and diagnoses based on the new *DSM-III-R* cutoff scores were relatively modest. However, this is not surprising since the clinicians were instructed to not limit their diagnostic decision to the information contained in the item list. Hence, these coefficients do not reflect interrater agreement that could be achieved when both raters are using the identical item pool and sources of information. Even past research on the interrater agreement, using diagnostic criteria from the *DSM-III* (American Psychiatric Association, Appendix F, 1980; Strober et al., 1981; Werry et al., 1983; Cantwell, 1988) where both judges employed the same criteria, found agreements ranging from 0.39 to 1.00 with mean agreements of 0.68 for ADD, 0.60 for CD, and 0.59 for OD—agreements very close to the 0.60 found here for both ADHD and CD. The authors' finding of 0.40 for the ODD category probably reflects the considerably different item pool and more stringent cutoff score used in the new *DSM-III-R* criteria, as compared to the old *DSM-III* items for OD on which many of the clinicians probably relied. It is therefore quite likely that future studies of the interjudge agreement of the new *DSM-III-R* criteria will be at least equal to or better than those found for *DSM-III*, especially when they become incorporated into standardized, structured psychiatric interviews, and certainly better than in the present study between clinicians' judgments and the new *DSM-III-R* criteria.

An important finding in the present trial deals with the decision in the *DSM-III-R* for a diagnosis of CD to preempt the diagnosis of ODD. The authors' finding that as many as 84% of children with CD also have the symptomatic features of ODD supports this decision and is consistent with previous theoretical and empirical papers that propose that CD most often evolves along with or is a later developmental stage of ODD (see McMahon and Wells, 1989, for a review). Even so, more research is required on that small percentage of children who develop CD in the absence of ODD as this may provide findings fruitful to additional refinement of the CD diagnosis, perhaps into subtypes, in future revisions of the DSM.

There are several limitations of the present field trial which must be considered in interpreting these results. First, the criterion used for determining the validity of the new criteria was individual, clinical judgment rather than some objective or consensus standard. In addition, no consistent standard for reaching such diagnostic judgments was applied across sites or within sites. At first glance, this would seem to introduce an intolerable degree of heterogeneity in the diagnostic criterion against which one is attempting to validate a new set of criteria. However, this heterogeneity was probably limited by several actors: (1) the reliance by most clinicians on the *DSM-III* criteria for these disorders; (2) substantial familiarity of the judges with the new item pools being tested; (3) some similarity between the new item pools and those used in *DSM-III*; (4) reliance on similar rating scales and cutoff points across at least half or more of the sites; and (5) the use of expert clinicians who are quite familiar with each others' views and likely share a common conceptualization of the symptom constructs that comprise each disorder.

Furthermore, it is not clear what other standard could have been used across sites other than clinical judgment in validating the new item lists and cutoff scores. No completely objective and validated laboratory measure exists for establishing the presence of any of these behavioral disorders—if it did, the need for new diagnostic criteria would be moot. Strict reliance on a more quantitative, dimensional standard, such as a parent or teacher rating scale, as some have suggested (Achenbach, 1980; Quay, 1986), is fraught with its own limitations (Cantwell, 1988). Parent and teacher ratings are equally subjective (Barkley, 1988) and often have limited item coverage for the rarer childhood disorders. Certainly, the statistical methods used in their construction involve some arbitrary decisions of their own and can lead to quite discrepant results when different statistical methods are used. Moreover, the contamination resulting from a reliance on these statistical methods, as both the validation criterion and as a source for the item lists, would have assured artificially high levels of agreement between them. The previous findings that the *DSM-III* diagnostic criteria set forth in structured psychiatric interviews showed reasonable convergence with diagnoses made by this more statistical approach, based on rating scales (Edelbrock and Costello, 1988), is reassuring and implies that the convergence between the statistical approach and the new *DSM-III-R* criteria would be even higher since these scales served as a source for the current item list. Until more objective methods of establishing the presence of symptoms of a disorder are developed, standardized, and validated, the present approach seemed to be the best available method for testing these new item pools.

Another limitation of this trial was its reliance on children presenting primarily to child psychiatry/psychology clinics. Referrals to such centers are known to have different types, degrees, and comorbidities of problems than children presenting to primary care centers (e.g., schools and primary care physicians), or than children detected as statistically deviant in epidemiological surveys of communities. The authors'

inclusion of at least two pediatric clinics may have helped to attenuate this problem somewhat. However, it is also not clear that building a taxonomy of childhood behavior disorders, intended for clinical applications yet based entirely on epidemiological samples, is any more satisfactory than the present approach.

The authors' findings also suggest several directions for the *DSM-IV* committee to pursue. First, it seems important that subsequent revisions of these criteria build upon this initial effort at an empirical basis for diagnosis rather than completely scrapping them and beginning anew. It is highly unlikely that such a new attempt could achieve much better sensitivity and specificity of the item pool as the present effort has unless some radical theoretical reformulation of these disorders occurs in the interim. It would seem more prudent to attempt to refine these item lists and cutoff scores, adding new items shown in research to have higher discriminating power or providing greater detail or content clarification of the present items.

Second, it seems probable that the cutoff scores derived here should vary to some degree depending upon the age groups of children to which they are applied. Preschool and adolescent subjects were not as well represented in the trial sample, making the cutoff scores for each disorder most appropriate for children 6 to 12 years of age. It is quite likely that a somewhat higher cutoff score may be necessary for preschool age children when a lower one may be needed for adolescents, at least for the ADHD and ODD criteria, in view of the well-known developmental changes that occur in the prevalence of these items across these wide age ranges (Achenbach and Edelbrock, 1981). The authors' finding that the sensitivity for the ADHD cutoff score diminished significantly with age implies that such an adjustment may be necessary. A recent follow-up study of ADHD and normal children into adolescents by Barkley et al. (1990) suggests that a cutoff score of 6 to 14 may be more sensitive for children 13 and older, while the cutoff scores for ODD and CD may require little or no revision.

Finally, the utility of smaller item sets for achieving reliable and valid diagnoses of these disorders should be explored. This would greatly aid in the convenience of applying these criteria in clinical situations as well as in developing structured interviews of reasonable length to be widely adopted for clinical and research purposes.

References

Achenbach, T. (1980), DSM-III in light of empirical research on the classification of child psychopathology. *J. Am. Acad. Child Psychiatry*, 19:395–412.
—Edelbrock, C. S. (1983), *Manual for the Child Behavior Checklist and Revised Child Behavior and Revised Child Behavior Profile*. Burlington, VT: University Associates in Psychiatry.
——(1981), Behavioral problems and competencies reported by parents of normal and disturbed children aged four through sixteen. *Monog. Soc. Res. Child Dev.* 46:1–81.
——(1978), The classification of child psychopathology: a review and analysis of empirical efforts. *Psychol. Bull.* 85:1275–1301.
American Psychiatric Association (1980), *Diagnostic and Statistical Manual for Mental Disorders, Third Edition*. Washington, DC: APA.
Barkley, R. A. (1988), Child behavior rating scales and checklists. In: *Assessment and Diagnosis in Child Psychopathology*, eds. M. Rutter, A. Tuma & I. Lann. New York: Guilford Press, pp. 113–155.

—Fischer, M., Edelbrock, C. S. & Smallish, L. (1990), The adolescent outcome of hyperactive children diagnosed by research criteria: I. an 8-year prospective follow-up study. *J. Am. Acad. Child Adolesc. Psychiatry,* 29: 546–557.

Cantwell, D. P. (1988), DSM-III studies. In: *Assessment and Diagnosis in Child Psychopathology,* eds. M. Rutter, A. Tuma & I. Lann. New York: Guilford Press, pp. 3–36.

Edelbrock, C. S. & Costello, A. J. (1988), Convergence between statistically derived behavior problem syndromes and child psychiatric diagnoses. *J. Abnorm. Child Psychol.* 16:219–232.

Hinshaw, S. P. (1987), On the distinction between attention deficits/hyperactivity and conduct problems/aggression in child psychopathology. *Psychol. Bull.* 101:443–463.

Loney, J. & Milich, R. (1982), Hyperactivity, inattention, and aggression in clinical practice. In: *Advances in Developmental and Behavioral Pediatrics,* eds. D. Routh & M. Wolraich. Greenwich, CT: JAI Press, pp. 113–147.

McGee, R., Williams, S. & Silva, P. A. (1984), Behavioral and developmental characteristics of aggressive, hyperactive, and aggressive-hyperactive boys. *J. Am. Acad. Child Psychiatry,* 23:270–279.

McMahon, R. J. & Wells, K. C. (1989), Conduct disorders. In: *Treatment of Childhood Disorders,* eds. E. Mash & R. Barkley. New York: Guilford Press, pp. 73–134.

Munir, K., Biederman, J. & Knee, D. (1987), Psychiatric comorbidity in patients with Attention Deficit Disorder: a controlled study. *J. Am. Acad. Child Adolesc. Psychiatry,* 26:844–848.

Quay, H. C. (1986), A critical analysis of DSM-III as a taxonomy of psychopathology in childhood and adolescence. In: *Contemporary Directions in Psychopathlogy: Toward A DSM-IV,* T. Millon & G. L. Klerman. New York: Guilford Press, pp. 151–165.

Strober, M., Green, J. & Carlson, G. (1981), Reliability of psychiatric diagnosis in hospitalized adolescents—interrater agreement using DSM-III. *Arch. Gen. Psychiatry,* 38:141–145.

Werry, J. S., Methven, R. J., Fitzpatrick, J. & Dixon, H. (1983), The interrater reliability of DSM-III in children. *J. Abnorm. Child Psychol.* 11:341–354.

ENURESIS, FIRESETTING AND CRUELTY TO ANIMALS: A TRIAD PREDICTIVE OF ADULT CRIME

DANIEL S. HELLMAN, M.D. AND NATHAN BLACKMAN, M.D.

The frustrations of an ever-changing, complex society have created tensions and a tendency to explosive aggressiveness of increasing intensity alarming to our rapidly expanding urban society. The importance of predictive factors and early detection or prevention of criminal behavior is paramount. The purpose of this study is to determine if enuresis, firesetting and cruelty to animals in childhood are significantly related to aggressive violent crimes in the adult.

A strong relationship exists between parental loss or rejection and the evolution of personality disorders and mental illness(7, 9, 17, 18, 22). This loss or rejection of a parent causes not only primary separation anxiety but also aggression, the function of which is to achieve reunion(5). This aggression has been observed in the Rorschach tests of rejected children(21); and the aggressive outbursts of adults who murder are associated with a history of maternal or paternal deprivation(3, 4).

Salfield(20) has noted that enuretic children appear to have great difficulty in controlling their expression of love and aggression. Enuresis, itself, is considered to have a sadistic significance with the act of urinating being equivalent to phantasies of damaging and destroying(8), and Coriat(6) has emphasized its direct association with hate. A relationship between enuresis and parental rejection has been suggested by Berman(2). He believes that because of the child's intense hostility towards the mother, whom he feels he has lost as a love object, sphincter control on mother's terms may be repudiated.

If, therefore, enuresis is an overt demonstration of hostility in retaliation for parental rejection, then one would expect to observe its incidence in delinquent and acting-out children. Thus, Michaels(15) has reported several studies relating persistent enuresis with juvenile delinquency and psychopathic personality. Glueck and Glueck(10) noted that 28.2% of the delinquents in their study had enuresis as opposed to only 13.6% in their control group. Hirsh(11) reported that of 367 delinquent boys 31.9% were enuretic and 94.9% of those who were enuretic persisted in this trait beyond 11 years of age. A relationship between enuresis and adolescent stealing has also been described(1).

Enuresis has also been noted to be intimately associated with firesetting. Michaels and Steinberg(16) noted that boys who are delinquent and have a history of persistent enuresis often show pyromaniac tendencies. Lewis and Yarnell(12) also observed the incidence of enuresis with firesetters. Firesetting has also been found to be an integral trait in Japanese children who show other aggressive acting-out and delinquent behavior(19).

The final factor, that of cruelty to animals, has been observed by Margaret Mead in a variety of cultures. She suggests that the torturing or killing of "good animals" by the child may be a precursor to more violent acts as an adult(14). MacDonald has reported a clinical impression that the triad of enuresis, firesetting and cruelty to animals is an unfavorable prognostic sign in those who threaten homicide(13).

This research was conducted at the Malcolm Bliss Mental Health Center, St. Louis, Mo., and was supported in part by Public Health Service grant MH-5804 from the National Institute of Mental Health.

Dr. Hellman's current address is 643 Sixth Avenue South, Suite 105, St. Petersburg, Fla.

This paper was accepted for publication in November 1964.

METHODOLOGY

This study was conducted at an acute intensive psychiatric treatment center serving the St. Louis area. The Social Maladjustment Unit functions as the equivalent of a court clinic, but its philosophy is that of a multidisciplinal team study of the offense as well as the offender in terms of interpreting him to the community and contributing to his eventual disposition through legal or medical channels.

Patients are referred to this unit by the various courts, parole offices and city jails. All referrals receive an inpatient evaluation for 3 to 4 weeks consisting of routine laboratory studies and intensive physical, social and psychiatric examinations, and in most cases this includes also an EEG and a complete battery of psychological tests. Independent intensive interviews are conducted by a resident in psychiatry, by the director and a senior consultant to the unit. A formal staffing conference is held at the end of this time and there is concurrence of diagnosis and treatment planning.

Eighty-four prisoners served as subjects for this study and included all consecutive admissions to the Social Maladjustment Unit from September 1963 to July 1964. These prisoners were divided into 2 groups. The first group consisted of persons charged with aggressive, violent crimes against the person. These included murder, serious assaults, armed robbery and forcible rape. The second group consisted of persons charged with misdemeanors and relatively nonaggressive felonies such as burglary, child molestation, stealing, car theft and forgery.

The report as to the presence of the triad was elicited as part of the intensive psychiatric examination that all subjects are exposed to. Very frequently a social history would confirm the presence or absence of enuresis whereas the history of firesetting and cruelty to animals was not always obtainable through this source, as the relatives were unknowing of these acts.

Enuresis is defined as unintentional voiding of urine, usually occurring during sleep and persisting in the individual past the age of 5 years.

Firesetting is defined as setting particular objects on fire as a child. Typical examples of this symptom are setting fire to a shed or car, collecting refuse and combustible materials in order to build bonfires, homemade bombs, homemade flame throwers out of lighter fluid cans and the like.

Cruelty to animals was positive if the subject reported killing or torturing dogs, cats, pets or baby animals. Examples are pouring kerosene or gasoline on an animal and setting fire to it, tying a dog and cat together at their tails and then hanging the rope over a branch to watch them kill each other, injecting animals with various fluids, and the like.

RESULTS

As is shown in Table 1, of 84 prisoners 31 were charged with aggressive crimes against the person and 53 were charged with misdemeanors and minor felonies. Twenty-one had a positive triad of enuresis, firesetting and cruelty to animals and two-thirds of these were charged with aggressive crimes. A partial triad (one or two of the traits) occurred in 17 patients and 56% of these had committed aggressive crimes. Thus of 31 patients charged with aggres-

TABLE 1
Characteristics of the Sample

	N	RACE		MARITAL			$\bar{X}$ AGE	$\bar{X}$ EDUC.	$\bar{X}$ I.Q.	$\bar{X}$ FELONY CONVICTIONS
		W	N	M	S	SEP. OR DIV.				
Aggressive crimes	31	15	16	11	10	10	33.9	8.4	88	1.6
Nonaggressive crimes	53	25	28	12	31	10	30.2	8.1	89	0.8
Total	84	40	44	23	41	20	31.5	8.2	89	1.1

sive crimes 23 or 74% had a history of triad or part of the triad. Of the 53 nonaggressive crime subjects only 7 had a positive triad and 8 a part of the triad. The association of the triad or a part of the triad to aggressive crimes was significant to the .001 level ($\chi^2 = 16.63$). The probability of each trait occurring in the presence of any other trait was also significant ($p = .001$).

Table 2 shows that the age range was

TABLE 2
Triad Related to Crime

	AGGRESSIVE CRIMES	NONAGGRESSIVE CRIMES	P
Triad Positive	14	7	<.001
Enuresis	21	15	<.001
Firesetting	16	8	<.001
Cruelty to animals	16	9	<.001
Triad Negative	8	46	<.001

from 15 to 66 years old with a mean age of 31.5. The mean age for aggressive criminals was 33.9 and for nonaggressive subjects 30.2. Thus age and type of crime was not significant. The mean age of those subjects with the triad or part of the triad, however, was 26.6 years whereas the mean age of those negative for the triad was 35.6 ($\chi^2 = 3.83$, $p = .05$).

There were 40 white males and 44 Negro males. Thirty-eight were married and 46 were single, widowed or divorced. No correlation was found between the triad and race or marital status. There was also no relation between the triad and whether the subject was the youngest or oldest in the family. Ninety-five percent of the subjects had a history of parental loss or deprivation.

The mean Full Scale I.Q. for 62 of the subjects was 89. There was no relationship between I.Q. and the type of crime or between I.Q. and the triad.

Of the 84 subjects, 45 were diagnosed as character disorders, 15 as psychotic and 19 as mentally deficient or organic (see Table 3). There was no relationship between diagnostic category and type of crime or between diagnosis and the presence of the triad.

ILLUSTRATIVE CASES

Case 1: Albert was a 15-year-old male charged

TABLE 3
Diagnoses

	N	AGGRESSIVE CRIMES	NON-AGGRESSIVE CRIMES
Personality disorders	45	15	30
Organic brain disorders	15	7	6
Psychotic disorder	13	5	10
Mental deficiency	6	2	4
Psychoneurotic disorder	5	2	3

with murder first degree and assault with intent to rob with malice. He was the second of 3 children. Enuresis occurred until age 8 and persisted as occasional rare bedwetting to the present. As a child he was constantly building small fires in ashtrays and wastebaskets and played with matches. At the age of 12 he obtained a rifle and thoroughly enjoyed shooting birds, dogs, cats and other animals. Since the age of 8 or 9 he has liked to stick pins and needles in his sisters' dolls.

The boy's father was a sociopath who had served time in prison, was twice dishonorably discharged from the Army and had committed acts of oral sodomy on both of his daughters. The patient repeatedly gave instances where his mother had shown marked favoritism towards his 2 sisters. She often told him he would grow up to be a thief, a bum and a sexual pervert like his father.

He began stealing money from his parents at age 9 and shortly thereafter committed burglaries. On one occasion he caught his older sister in the bathroom and threw knives at the door. Shortly before the present homicide he began snatching purses from older women at the point of a butcher knife. Psychologicals revealed a Full Scale I.Q. of 104.

Case 2: Billy was a 20-year-old male, the oldest of 5 children. He stated that he felt his parents had always hated him because he had less intelligence than his brothers and sisters. (His I.Q. was 76.) His father frequently beat him and he was always the scapegoat in the home. Enuresis persisted until age 17. As a boy he remembers pouring lighter fluid on some curtains at home and setting them on fire. He also once set his cousin's car on fire. On many occasions he would catch pigeons and wring their necks or would scratch cats and rub turpentine into their wounds.

During his teens he committed burglaries and robberies and began using narcotics at age 16. Prior to his admission to the hospital the patient and 2 of his friends first robbed a middle-aged man, then tied him up and beat him to death.

Case 3: Clarence was a 39-year-old, married male charged with first degree robbery. His parents and siblings continually made fun of him. He was enuretic until age 14. As a boy he would pour gasoline on dogs and cats and set them on fire. He deliberately set a barn on fire and has burned various other properties. He has served 3 prison terms for assault with intent to kill and 2 armed robberies. Intellectual functioning is in the borderline defective range.

DISCUSSION

The plight of the child faced by either rejection or ambivalence from his parents may express itself in various forms of aggressive acting-out behavior. As the child grows and matures under this continuous frustration of rejection he may adopt various defenses. Such defenses include withdrawal, denial, submission, etc. If, however, he continues to revolt, to react more aggressively, he sets up a pattern of hostile behavior and projects this upon the environment. At this point he no longer is just seeking attention, albeit in bad acts; nor is he just evolving anger and creating havoc with the expectation and even the promise to expect punishment. For these children, aggression has assumed a primary importance and they retaliate with violent means against a hostile and rejecting society. Enuresis has been considered to be related to aggression and phantasies of destruction. Thus if some children develop a pattern of aggressive behavior one would expect enuresis to persist through childhood. In this study 33 of 36 subjects had enuresis past age 8 years and in 70% this trait persisted into their teens.

Enuresis is accompanied by other forms of acting-out behavior; two particularly severe forms occur in firesetting and cruelty to animals. From phantasies of destruction through the act of voiding, the child proceeds to the active destruction of fire with its magical omnipotence and then to direct violence against good animals—animals which are accepted by adult figures whereas the child was not.

The consequence of this childhood pattern will continue to be one of violent aggressive behavior towards society. Thus in the group under study 74% of those committing violent, aggressive crimes had a history of the triad or part of the triad as compared with its presence in only 28% of those committing no violent antisocial acts. There is also a background of previous assaults, rapes and burglaries in about 75% of these.

In our series, age and type of crime showed no relationship but those subjects giving a positive history of the triad were significantly younger than those with a negative triad. Thus aggressive crimes against the person and the presence of the triad are not significantly related just because of age. Rather it may be postulated that younger individuals are better able to remember the problems and escapades of childhood than are the elder population. A man in his early twenties may more easily recall setting a neighbor's shed on fire or injecting a cat with turpentine than a man in his forties or fifties.

The triad is proposed as a pathognomonic sign, as an alert to both the parents and the community that the child is seriously troubled; that if this readiness to project and elicit fear or pain, to be violent and destructive, is not alleviated nor remedies found for it, this pattern of hostile behavior may well lead to adult aggressive antisocial behavior.

The prevention of serious criminal acts in adults will ultimately be accomplished not merely through punishment or withdrawal of freedom of the perpetrators of violence. It will be accomplished by the community's response to the cries of the desperate, to the feelings of anxiety in those in whom the triad of firesetting, enuresis and cruelty to animals has served notice of a desperate apprehensiveness, of a pattern of creating threat and hurts as a means of coping with hostile surges. It is the detection and early management of children in the throes of the triad that might well forestall a career of violent crime in the adult.

SUMMARY

A study of 84 prisoners shows that out of the 31 charged with aggressive crimes against the person, three-fourths had the triad of enuresis, firesetting and cruelty to animals whereas in the 53 subjects accused of a nonaggressive crime only 15 had either the triad or a partial triad. It is postulated that the presence of the triad in the child may be of pathognomonic importance in predicting violent antisocial behavior. The relationship of the triad with early rejection or severe deprivation by parental figures is discussed. The importance of early detection of the triad and serious attention toward resolving the tensions that precipitated it is stressed.

REFERENCES

1. Bachet, M. : Sur la Frequence de l'Enuresie chez les Enfants et Adolescents Auteurs de Vols, Arch. Franc. Pediat. (Paris) 85:296-299, 1948.
2. Berman, S.: Antisocial Character Disorder : Its Etiology and Relationship to Delinquency, Amer. J. Orthopsychiat. 29:612-621, 1959.
3. Blackman, N., Weiss, J. M., and Lamberti, J. W. : The Sudden Murderer. III. Clues to Preventive Interaction, Arch. Gen. Psychiat. 8:289-294, 1963.
4. Blackman, N., and Hellman, D. S. : The Masque of Adequacy, symposium of the Medical Correctional Association and the Manhattan College Institute for Forensic Research, in press.
5. Bowlby, J.: Childhood Mourning and Its Implications for Psychiatry, Amer. J. Psychiat. 118:481-498, 1961.
6. Coriat, I. H. : The Character Traits of Urethral Erotism, Psychoanal. Rev. 11: 426-434, 1924.
7. Earle, A. M., and Earle, B. V. : Early Maternal Deprivation and Later Psychiatric Illness, Amer. J. Orthopsychiat. 31:181-186, 1961.
8. Fenichel, O. : The Psychoanalytic Theory of Neurosis. New York : W. W. Norton and Co., 1945.
9. Field, M. : Maternal Attitudes Found in Twenty-Five Cases of Children with Primary Behavior Disorder, Amer. J. Orthopsychiat. 10:293-311, 1940.
10. Glueck, S., and Glueck, E. T. : Unraveling Juvenile Delinquency. New York : Commonwealth Fund, 1950.
11. Hirsh, N. D. M. : Dynamic Causes of Juvenile Crime. Cambridge, Mass. : Sci-Art Publications, 1937.
12. Lewis, N. D. C., and Yarnell, H. : Pathological Firesetting. New York : Nerv. Ment. Dis. Mono. no. 82, 1951.
13. MacDonald, J. : The Threat to Kill, Amer. J. Psychiat. 120:125-130, 1963.
14. Mead, M. : Cultural Factors in the Cause and Prevention of Pathological Homicide, Bull. Menninger Clin. 28:11-22, 1964.
15. Michaels, J. J. : Disorders of Character. Springfield, Ill. : Charles C. Thomas, 1955.
16. Michaels, J. J., and Steinberg, A. : Persistent Enuresis and Juvenile Delinquency, Brit. J. Delinq. 3:114-120, 1952.
17. Partridge, G. E. : A Study of Fifty Cases of Psychopathic Personality, Amer. J. Psychiat. 84:953-973, 1928.
18. Rabinovitch, R. D. : *in* A Differential Study of Psychopathic Behavior in Infants and Children ; Round Table, 1951, Amer. J. Orthopsychiat. 22:230-236, 1952.
19. Sakamoto, M. : A Dynamic Psychopathology of Firesetting in Schizophrenic Children, Osaka City Med. J. 6:56-59, 1960.
20. Salfield, D. J. : Enuresis : Addenda After Two-and-a-Half Years, Z. Kinderpsychiat. 23:107-111, 1956.
21. Schactel, A. H., and Levi, M. B. : Character Structure of Day Nursery Children in Wartime as Seen Through the Rorschach, Amer. J. Orthopsychiat. 15:213-222, 1942.
22. Szurek, S. A. : Notes on the Genesis of Psychopathic Personality, Psychiatry 5: 581-586, 1942.

Sexual Aberrance in Male Adolescents Manifesting a Behavioral Triad Considered Predictive of Extreme Violence: Some Clinical Observations

> He who lights a fire during the day will wet his bed
> that night. (German and Mexican-Spanish proverb)

The wisdom of the proverb makers continues to pique our interest as the subtle inter-relationship among the triad of enuresis, fire-setting, and animal cruelty is observed. Elsewhere the authors have reviewed the literature on these behaviors and new clinical evidence concerning the validity and meaning of this predictor is offered [1]. The present paper is limited to a discussion of sexually aberrant behavior, particularly from a developmental point of view, in six male adolescents who manifest the triad.

Considering the biophysiological needs of the human organism, clinical observers (particularly following the discoveries of Sigmund Freud) have commonly described human behavior in terms of a set of interlocking need systems [2]. Currently the essential needs are thought to include: (1) nutrient intake, (2) oxygen intake, (3) water intake, (4) waste elimination, (5) temperature reuglation, and (6) periods of sleep. Simply put, failure of regulation or delivery in any one of these need systems results in disease and eventual death. The human infant, considered to be most vulnerable during the first few months and possibly years of life, is incapable of meeting his own needs. Hence, he must depend upon others for survival. In our western culture this dependent condition seems to continue through late adolescence and, in many instances, into early adulthood.

Returning to the interlocking system of vital needs, we may note in early infancy that a gradient of tension, with its low point describing moderate discomfort and its high point describing imminent collapse of the organism, can be projected to describe the relationship between need gratification, tension discharge, and biological survival. As a need remains unmet, tension in the form of physical discomfort increases. Associated with this gradient are the numerous "feeling states" or emotions in their rawest forms. Biology and psychology are thus inextricably intertwined and the discharge of tension (that is, the experience of need fulfillment) is a powerful influence upon behavior. Whether we can

Presented at the 25th Annual Meeting of the American Academy of Forensic Sciences, Las Vegas, Nev., 21 Feb. 1973. Received for publication 3 April 1973; accepted for publication 31 May 1973.

[1] Formerly senior research psychologist, Reiss-Davis Child Study Center, Los Angeles, Calif. (at the time of this study), and presently a member of the faculty of the Department of Psychiatry, University of Michigan Medical School, Ann Arbor, Mich.

[2] Assistant professor of psychiatry, University of Southern California School of Medicine, Institute of Psychiatry, Law and Behavioral Science, Los Angeles, Calif.

safely argue that all behavior is determined by this system is difficult to say. The homeostatic and pleasure principles familiar to students of psychoanalytic thought are briefly described herein.

Our point is not to raise a psychoanalytic debate, but rather to offer foundation to the notion that man's sexuality is evident in a variety of forms. This fact may be all too evident to judges and lawyers familiar with cases involving sexual perversion. The essential model for sexual discharge is a state of arousal, followed by a heightening of tension and then by a release from that tension to a more quiescent state. This is the model for the discharge of tensions in other areas as well, as noted above. In the infant, for the most part, typical genital sexual expression does not predominate, although male infants do achieve erections either spontaneously or from penile contact with objects, and infant females do explore the outer labia and sometimes, spontaneously, the vagina as well. Infantile sexuality is viewed as assuming a number of forms (that is, polymorphous), and relates to a variety of cutaneous experiences, particularly around the various orifices of the body.

This view of polymorphous infantile sexuality becomes quite important when clinical examples of sexual perversion and related aberrant sexual behavior are discussed. As noted, the variety of experiences sought in the expression of perverse sexual activities varies greatly in number and type [3]. However, the aim (that is, reduction of the tension associated with sexual excitement) remains a constant in such activities.

In reviewing our data, we noted that each of the six subjects in the study demonstrated marked sexual deviation as well as the atypical development in this area. At the time this discovery appeared to be serendipitous, but we have presently come to accept this as another graphic element of disturbance in the personality formations of these young men.

Methodology

The six cases described in this study were observed by the authors in their service as clinical consultants to the California Youth Authority. Although such referrals are preselected to a significant degree (that is, declared delinquent under the California Welfare and Institutions Code, §602; demonstrated significant psychological symptoms so as to merit a psychiatric evaluation), there was no further active selection of cases for this study by the authors. A total of 46 cases was referred to the authors and seen during a six-month period of time. Of these, six adolescents demonstrated the triad of enuresis, fire-setting, and excessive cruelty to animals. Four additional cases were considered to exhibit the triad but complete documentation of one or more of the components was not possible; therefore, these cases were not included in this study. Although the authors believed that many youth authority subjects possessed the triad under consideration, denial of one or more of the symptoms by the subject was considered sufficient for exclusion. Each subject was seen individually in psychiatric evaluation and subsequent referral for psychological testing. The following case vignettes are developed from the psychiatric evaluation, psychological testing, and review of all available supporting materials.

Each case is not presented in its entirety. Rather, there is a brief sketch of the essential developmental and judicial data, followed by a discussion of the aberrant sexual material.

Case Presentations

Case 1

Ted M., a 17-year-old of Mexican-American Indian background has documented police involvement from the ninth year. Complaints have included petty theft, incorrigibility, multiple runaway episodes, grand theft (auto), and burglary. Serious assaultive behavior was first documented in his early teens, and when Ted was 14 one of his victims was hospitalized for several weeks. Assaultive aggressiveness has continued and has become more severe despite treatment efforts. The product of a chaotic and disorganized family with an alcoholic father and an infrequently present mother, Ted is fourth in a sibship of five, each of whom has been involved in a serious asocial act ranging from murder to assault with a deadly weapon. Ted's disorganized behavior has resulted in a state hospitalization, during which he was diagnosed as experiencing a schizophrenic reaction of the chronic undifferentiated type.

His atypical sexual behavior has primarily involved exhibitionism. He has appeared before the authorities several times following episodes of indecent exposure. He is unable to describe or to discuss the circumstances leading to the expression of such impulsive behavior. In addition to these episodes, he has been involved in some rather provocative sadistic activity including attempts to brand the letters "MF" on a younger lad's chest. When recounting this incident, however, Ted reported having experienced sensations of excitement and then release. Notably, the psychologist remarks that Ted's performance on projective tests indicates marked confusion in the area of sexual identification.

Case 2

Harry H. is a 13-year-old caucasian with a history of violent, dangerous acts causing referrals to police authorities in his ninth year and commitment at the age of 13. This boy has attempted to murder, on separate occasions, a foster father and a natural brother, the former with a gun and the latter by stabbing with a knife. Numerous observers have described Harry as having experienced severe deprivation and overt rejection in the early years of life. Though he has been diagnosed as experiencing an adjustment reaction of early adolescence, his extreme unsocialized aggressive behavior, considered with his developmental history, would suggest the presence of more malignant psychopathology. Notably, Harry was the passive victim of numerous overt sexual assaults in childhood. Thus, it is not surprising that the boy's aggression very much pervades his attempts at sexual expression. Natural and foster parents describe him as engaging in "unusual sexual practices" otherwise unspecified. While a ward of the youth authority, Harry has been reported to be the frequent active participant in group sexual activities, including performing fellatio on his peers.

Case 3

Phillip D., a 20-year-old caucasian, was first detained by authorities as a runaway in his 12th year. He was a known petty thief during his early teens. By mid-adolescence he was judged guilty of two separate charges of forcible rape, and in the later teens answered to two separate charges of arson as well as a charge of property destruction. In his 20th year he was charged with carrying a concealed weapon and discharging a pistol near a residence. A summary of psychological and psychiatric evaluations describes Phillip as having a personality disorder of the schizoid type. He is currently viewed as a decompensating borderline psychotic who, under stress, will fulminate in overt psychosis.

Phillip's history reveals tenuous control of impulses, particularly those of a sexual nature, throughout development. In the early teens he was reported to have left obscene notes for females of his acquaintance. Some five years following the episodes of attempted rape for which he was charged, this young man was involved in the sexual molestation of small neighborhood girls. At that time his interest appeared to be in coercing the youngsters into exhibiting their genitalia to him. During the current psychiatric evaluation

Phillip reports that, although married, he has avoided intercourse with his young wife. His reasons for genital sexual abstinence were unclear at the time of the study.

Case 4

Charles L., a 16-year-old caucasian, was referred for assault with a deadly weapon with the intent to commit murder (two counts). Little historic material is available on his family or his development, and he reports moderate to heavy use of dangerous drugs, including barbiturates, amphetamines, and alcohol. Psychiatric and psychological examiners have diagosed Charles as psychotic, most likely of the paranoid schizophrenic type. Within the ideation distinguishing him as paranoid are numerous fantasies of attack and assault on his person by others, as well as an associated blurring and confusion of his masculine sexual identification.

Case 5

Richard R., an 18½-year-old Mexican-American, was first detained by the police in his 14th year for burglary. At age 17, he was committed to the youth authority for exhibiting a firearm in a threatening manner. A parole violation involved possession of a loaded shotgun and resulted in his return to an institution. He has a history of drug involvement with associated violent, antisocial behavior dating back to his 14th year. Development marked by severe physical and emotional deprivation has resulted in psychotic vulnerability. At present the psychiatric diagnosis involves personality disorder, asocial type, with borderline (paranoid) features. Richard's highly conflicted personality formation involves features of masculine protest, as evidenced by a compulsive fascination with firearms, weapons, and other such symbolic materials. Psychological and psychiatric examiners have found evidence of specific difficulties in the area of sexual identification and homosexual (latent) concerns.

Case 6

Vern L., a 13-year old caucasian with a documented history of violent acts dating back to the eighth year, was most recently referred for battery (one count). The product of a chaotic household, this boy has responded to his mother's asocial and sadistic tendencies by performing similar acts. Himself the witness and possible participant in his mother's perverse sexual escapades, Vern now performs sadistically with other youngsters, particularly younger boys. His most recent offense was burning a seven-year-old child (male) with lighted cigarettes. Vern's performance on psychological tests indicates that he pictures himself as "an invulnerable seductive but punitive tormentor of females." On occasion he overtly described himself as being similar to his mother in sexual terms, that is, in terms of interest and activity. On one occasion, he was alleged to have set fire to a hut in which he and his mother were locked, and in another instance he attempted to set fire to a man whom he did not like.

Discussion

What continues to appear to be most striking in the case material is the degree to which sexual impulse expression is plastic and therefore may mold to a variety of forms. Granted that each of our subjects is deeply disturbed and all are products of chaotic households and victims of irregular child-rearing approaches; considered together, these cases illustrate the very essence of sexual aberrance. Hence, we would prefer to focus our discussion on the various modes of deviation illustrated by these cases, rather than to discuss each case in terms of the forms of psychopathology which it demonstrates.

Fusion of Sexual and Aggressive Impulse

All of the cases which we have presented illustrate a degree of fusion of sexual and aggressive material. Essentially, aggressive, assaultive, abusive activity and some form of sexual expression become inseparable for such individuals. Current psychological theory concerning the differentiation and regulation of impulses and drives acknowledges that in infancy and early childhood the urgency of the basic vital needs predominates, and only after the human organism develops ways of securing these needs do the more distinct sexual and aggressive areas emerge independently. They are at first seen as commingled, however, and it is not unusual to observe in late infancy or early childhood the expression of affection mixed with some obvious piece of aggression such as biting, hitting, pushing, or even rather violent hugging. In many of our subjects this fusion has continued into adolescence or even early adulthood. Perhaps the clearest demonstration of this occurs in the material presented by the forcible rapist. Phillip clearly demonstrates this fusion, both in his avowed sexual abstinence toward his wife and his numerous attempts at forcible rape. It would appear that the tender, nonaggressive aspects of sexual expression are unavailable to him. In some sense his partner must be his victim or he is unable to participate with her. Sexuality and violent aggression must be present in the sense that he must act upon both impulses in order to receive gratification.

Turning of the Passive Experience into an Active One

A number of our subjects had been brutalized or assaulted sexually in childhood. Harry and Vern, in particular, had been the passive participants in sexual attacks by others. One might assume that Ted may also have experienced similar attacks. These young men were active participants in sadistic attacks upon younger and presumably weaker individuals. Noted in their materials are at least two instances of attempts to burn or to brand others by means of lighted cigarettes. In addition to the delight taken in inflicting pain and injury upon others, each seemed to be turning what was at one time passively experienced (that is, being burned) into activity (that is, inflicting burns upon someone else). The psychological mechanism involved in such a reversal of roles is usually termed "identification with the aggressor." In such a role reversal the individual finds a means of mastering feelings of incompetence, anger, and frustration by becoming very much like the obvious object of the original discomfort.

Problems in Sexual Identification

Each of our subjects demonstrates, to some extent, instability in this sense of adequacy as a male. Psychological test reports on many of our subjects repeatedly emphasize a blurring or a confusion of the subject's identity in this area. Essentially this means that the process by which one learns to express sexuality in terms of behavior socioculturally appropriate to one's biological gender has not occurred. We are quite familiar with the biochemical basis for the human organism's bisexuality or, more correctly, polysexuality. Studies in the area of embryology, endocrinology, and even recent advances in the study of human sexual response and development underscore this fact. Hence, much of what is accepted as masculine or feminine (that is, gender specific) is socioculturally determined and therefore is influenced as much by social learning as by chemistry. Failure in this learning process occurs for a variety of reasons, including poor "teachers," "teachers" or role models who are indeed *too* adroit, hormone imbalance, failure in emotional development, or neurotic conflicts regarding aspects of identification and consequent sexual expression. Without in-depth study of the individual, determination of the precise cause of difficulties in the area of gender identification is quite difficult. We do know, however, that the more severely disturbed or psychotic the patient, the more infantile and therefore polymorphous the sexual expression will be. Similarly, the greater the deviation from the nuclear family environment, the higher the vulnerability to deviation from the norm of acceptable gender-associated behavior. We believe it is clear that our subjects demonstrated blurring and confusion in this area for a variety of reasons, and in at least two instances aggressive assaultive behavior and preoccupation with armaments and weaponry are determined by the individual's need to assert what he believes to be active, aggressive masculinity.

Polymorphous Perverse Behavior

We have already made much of the point that (infantile) sexuality is polymorphous. Sexual perversion is defined psychologically according to developmental criteria. Typically many forms of sexual activities are commonly observed and considered to be age-appropriate in infancy and early childhood. However, when these activities are carried on from an earlier stage into the later stages of development, and are maintained as the individual's principal mode of sexual activity and source of release, the very same behaviors are considered perverse. Several examples of perversion occur in our case materials. The exhibitionistic and voyeuristic activities of Ted and Phillip clearly demonstrate this developmental trend. Consistent with his severe psychotic disturbance, Ted derives much pleasure from exhibiting himself and thus being seen by others. This pleasure is thought to be akin to the elation which is observed in small children or infants when they are observed, particularly by the parents and principally by the mother. We are all too familiar with the devastating results on successful personality formation when the child has not thought himself to be highly regarded by the parents. Ted's "showing off" seems to be directly related to this line of development. Phillip, on the other hand, shows a higher level of concern or curiosity, manifested in his compulsion to observe the genitalia of little girls. Since his difficulties illustrate the broadest range of aberrant behavior in our sample, we cannot at this time be sure whether his curiosity relates to the usual concerns which young boys have about the failure of girls to be equipped genitally in the same way as they are, or whether he has less fear of retaliation for his sexual and aggressive wishes at the hands of young children in contrast to peers or adults. Phillip also appears to be driven to confront others with obscene language. This behavior is termed *coprolalia* and may become an extreme compulsion for some individuals. Again this behavior is not uncommon but rather to be anticipated in young children who begin to discover "dirty language." In some children, the demonstration of this repertoire becomes very important, much to the annoyance of those who must listen.

Conclusion

We believe that the German and Mexican-Spanish proverb carries an additional connotation. We have in the past understood this to suggest a consistently observed relationship between fire-setting and enuresis. However, in the light of this discussion it may have a more universal application concerning elements of excitement and subsequent regressive loss of control. We have attempted to illustrate the developmentally regressive aspects of sexual aberrance principally by examination of such material observed in six cases of violently aggressively adolescent and young adult males. In the discussion, we have illustrated both the range and scope of human sexuality and its expression, particularly in those areas considered by society to be deviant. The implications of this psychologic-psychiatric point of view for legal-judicial action and penal correctional treatment of such offenders is clearly a topic for future presentations and discussion. We hope that this article may provide a beginning stimulus for such further consideration.

References

[1] Haddox, V. and Wax, D., "Enuresis, Fire-Setting, and Animal Cruelty in Male Adolescent Delinquents: Clinical Manifestations of a Triad Predictive of Violent Sexual Behavior," Unpublished manuscript, 1973.
[2] Fenichel, O., *The Psychoanalytic Theory of Neurosis*, W. W. Norton, New York, 1945.
[3] Freud, S., *Three Essays on the Theory of Sexuality*, standard ed., Vol. 7, Hogarth Press, London, 1953, pp. 125–245.
[4] Hellman, D. S. and Blackman, N., "Enuresis, Fire-Setting and Cruelty to Animals: A Triad Predictive of Adult Crime," *American Journal of Psychiatry*, Vol. 122, 1966, pp. 1431–35.

University of Michigan Medical Center
Children's Psychiatric Hospital
Ann Arbor, Mich. 48104

Firesetting, Enuresis, and Animal Cruelty

G. Adair Heath, Vaughn A. Hardesty,
and Peter E. Goldfine
Maine Medical Center
Portland, Maine

Firesetting, enuresis and cruelty to animals was studied in 204 consecutive admissions to a general child psychiatric clinic. Children exhibiting these behaviors were compared on demographic variables and clinical measures of adjustment in the areas of competence, total pathology, externalizing (conduct problems) and internalizing (emotional problems). Findings indicate a complex interrelationship, with enuresis and cruelty to animals being related to, and interacting with, only a portion of the total firesetting population. Enuresis was significantly associated with non-cruel firesetters and cruelty to animals was significantly associated with non-enuretic firesetters. The implications of these findings for our understanding of the etiology, current adjustment status and prognosis for firesetters in a child psychiatric population is discussed.

Many authors have discussed and investigated the relationship between firesetting, enuresis and animal cruelty. Freud (1905/1953) noted that it was common to warn children that playing with fire would lead them to wet the bed. As a result of his work with his famous patient, Dora, and his analysis of the Prometheus myth, he proposed a link between enuresis, sexual problems and firesetting. This relationship was maintained in the analytic literature, but given a somewhat different direction by later authors who pointed to the importance of aggression in firesetting and bedwetting. (Fenichel, 1945; Grinstein, 1952; Klein, 1932).

It was not until 1940, however, that firesetting was actually studied in children (Lewis and Yarnell, 1951; Yarnell, 1940). In these and other studies, the rate of enuresis was determined for selected samples of firesetters (See Table 1).

Other authors have pointed to a relationship between enuresis, firesetting and aggression. Michaels (1955), in examining the relationship between enuresis and juvenile delinquency, found no significant association between enuresis and firesetting. Michaels and Steinberg (1952) examined the relationship between persistent enuresis and juvenile delinquency, and found that 15.8% of the enuretic delinquents had engaged in firesetting while only 4.9% of the non-enuretic delinquents had done so.

The historical relationship between cruelty to animals and firesetting is somewhat less clear. Mead (1964) has pointed out that each culture places a taboo on certain forms of cruelty and killing. She felt that the torturing and killing of animals in a forbidden way might prove an important diagnostic sign for the motiveless type of killer. Bender (1959) was the first to point out that firesetting, along with other symptoms, was a significant factor in those children and adolescents who have killed. MacDonald (1963) noted that the presence of firesetting, enuresis and cruelty to animals was an unfavorable prognostic sign in those who threatened homicide. Helman and Blackman (1966) sought to determine whether firesetting, enuresis and cruelty to animals were predictive of aggressive adult crimes. In a retrospective study, they compared adult prisoners charged with aggressive crimes with a second group of prisoners charged with nonaggressive crimes. Seventy-four percent of the prisoners charged with aggressive crimes had a history of the symptom triad or a part of the triad, while only 28% of the nonaggressive group exhibited the triad or a part of the triad. This was a statistically significant difference. Similarly, MacDonald (1968), in an attempt to determine potential predictors of homicide, compared the rates of a number of factors, including firesetting, cruelty to animals and enuresis in three matched groups: convicted murderers, hospital patients who had made homicidal threats and hospital patients who had no history of homicidal behavior or threats. Statistical analysis of the data did not support the usefulness of firesetting, enuresis, or cruelty to animals as predictors of homicidal behavior.

Wax and Haddox (1974) investigated the relationship between the triad of persistent enuresis, firesetting and cruelty to animals, and violent behavior in six incarcerated adolescent males who were considered the most assaultive and dangerous within the California Youth Authority. The authors considered the triad to be a useful danger signal in predicting assaultive behavior in adolescents.

Sendi and Blomgren (1975) used independent raters to make a comparison between three groups of ado-

Reprint requests should be addressed to:
G. Adair Heath
Maine Medical Center
22 Bramhall Street
Portland, ME 04102

Reprinted from the *Journal of Child and Adolescent Psychotherapy* 1 (1984): 97–100, with kind permission of Williams & Wilkins, Waverly.

lescent patients: ten who committed homicide, ten who threatened or attempted homicide, and ten hospitalized controls. The authors found approximately equal rates for individual items of the triad in the three groups. No patient of any group had all three behaviors of the triad. They concluded that neither the items of the triad nor the triad itself was useful in predicting homicidal behavior or homicidal threats or attempts. Finally, Kuhnley, Hendren and Quinlan (1982) compared juvenile firesetters and nonfiresetters who were psychiatric inpatients and found the firesetters to be cruel to animals more often, but no difference was observed with regard to enuresis.

While there has been much speculation regarding the relationship between firesetting, enuresis and cruelty to animals, most of the actual research conducted has suffered from methodological deficiencies, including clinical case studies or retrospective studies with questionable methodology. This study is an attempt to present empirical data on the relationship between childhood firesetting, enuresis and cruelty to animals in a child psychiatric outpatient population.

Method

Subjects

Subjects for the study were 204 consecutive outpatient admissions to a child psychiatric clinic in a medium-sized northeastern city. The subjects ranged in age from four to sixteen years, and there were 130 boys and 74 girls in the sample.

Procedure

Children were identified as enuretic, cruel to animals, and/or firesetting by parental identification on the Child Behavior Checklist (CBCL) (Achenbach and Edelbrock, 1978). These items are rated zero for absent, one for occasional and two for frequent. In addition, only children six years and older were classified as enuretic, since this cut-off would most likely include only those children having persistent enuresis, which has been reputedly linked to firesetting. Children rated as setting fires on the CBCL must also have set a fire within the past year which actually caused damage to, for instance, a rug, grass or struc-

TABLE 1

Firesetting Studies: Reporting Rates for Enuresis

Investigators	Number of Children	Rate of Enuresis	Population
Lewis & Yarnell (1951)	238	9%	Mixed psychiatric and nonpsychiatric sample in which some cases were not included
Yarnell (1940)	69	15%	Mixed inpatient and outpatient psychiatric sample
Kaufman et al (1961)	30	46%	Residential treatment sample of all male psychiatric patients
Nurcombe (1964)	21	57%	Predominantly outpatient psychiatric sample of males
Vandersall & Weiner (1970)	20	20%	Outpatient psychiatric sample

TABLE 2

Relationship Between Firesetting, Enuresis and Cruelty to Animals

	Firesetters	Non-Firesetters	χ^2	df	p
Enuresis	8 (28.6%)	21 (15.7%)	2.6223	1	N.S.
Cruelty to animals	8 (28.6%)	20 (14.9%)	2.1376	1	N.S.
Enuresis, excluding cruel children	7 (35%)	15 (13%)	4.4308	1	<0.05
Enuresis, in cruel children only	1 (12.5%)	6 (30%)	0.23	1	N.S.
Cruelty to animals, excluding enuretic children	7 (35%)	14 (12.4%)	4.9437	1	<0.05
Cruelty to animals in enuretic child only	1 (12.5%)	6 (28.6%)	0.175	1	N.S.

ture, in order to be classified as a firesetter. These definitions resulted in 32 children being identified as firesetters, 29 as enuretic and 28 as cruel to animals.

Clinical information was gained from the clinic charts, a family information sheet and the CBCL. This instrument has norms for referred and nonreferred populations of different age groups and sexes. It provides a measure for each child on competency and psychopathology scales. The competency scale is made up of three subscales: actvity, social, and school functioning. The psychopathology scale consists of 118 items which load on factors like depression, delinquency or aggression. These factors, in turn, load on second-order factors of internalizing (overcontrolled or emotional problems) or externalizing (undercontrolled or conduct problems). All items sum to make a total pathology score. These measures were used as dependent measures in the analysis.

Results

Analysis revealed that firesetting was not significantly associated with enuresis or cruelty to animals. The combination of enuresis and cruelty to animals in a single individual was equally infreqent in the firesetting and nonfiresetting populations (3% and 4%, respectively). However, by controlling for enuresis and cruelty to animals, significant associations were found for the nonenuretic firesetting with cruelty to animals and for non-cruel firesetters with enuresis. (See Table 2).

In order to ascertain if the presence of enuresis and cruelty to animals separately or together has any effect on the current adjustment status of the firesetters, a series of analyses of variance were performed. A three-way analysis of variance (firesetting by enuresis by cruelty to animals) showed no significant interactions with socioeconomic status (SES), externalizing, internalizing or activity as dependent measures.

A two-way analysis of variance (firesetting by enuresis) revealed no significant effects. However, a two-way analysis of variance (firesetting by cruelty to animals) showed that cruel children were significantly more externalizing [$F(1,193) = 16.655$, $p<0.001$] and significantly more internalizing [$F(1,193) = 7.257$, $p<0.008$] than non-cruel children.

Discussion

The findings of the current study show no significant overall association of enuresis and cruelty to animals to firesetting. However, a significant association is noted for enuresis with the non-cruel firesetters. Likewise, there is a significant association of cruelty to animals with the non-enuretic firesetters. The small sample size did not permit meaningful break-

down of the analysis for sex, SES, and age with regard to the relationship to the above variables. The rates of 17.9% enuresis and 17.3% cruelty to animals in the total population appear to be consistent with Achenbach and Edelbrock's (1981) data on a referred population. The 28.6% rate of enuresis in the firesetting population is not significantly higher than in the non-firesetting population. This rate is also consistent with the 20% rate found in the one comparable outpatient study of Vandersall and Weiner (1970).

This study, in addition to its primary aim of providing empirical data on the relationship of firesetting to cruelty to animals and enuresis, provides some demographic data on the symptom of cruelty to animals in a child psychiatric population. Our study found no significant association between cruelty to animals and SES, age and sex. Achenbach and Edelbrock (1981) in their standardization of the Child Behavior Checklist, on a much larger referred and nonreferred population, reported that cruelty to animals provides a small effect (about 5% of total variance) in the differences between referred and nonreferred children. Furthermore, the authors reported that clinical status (referred versus non-referred), male gender, younger age and clinical status-gender interaction accounted for 5%, less than 1%, 1% and less than 1% of the variance, respectively, of the cruelty-to-animals score.

Because numerous studies have been conducted on the demography of enuresis in general and child psychiatric populations, analysis of the association of enuresis with age, sex and SES was not conducted. Previous studies have shown bedwetting in referred and nonreferred populations to be higher in younger age groups, to fall rapidly with age and to be slightly greater represented in the lower SES groups. Some studies have indicated that boys are more enuretic than girls (Anders and Freeman, 1979). Again, Achenbach and Edelbrock's (1981) standardization data on the Child Behavior Checklist indicate no significant sex difference.

While the present study shows that enuresis and cruelty to animals do not appear to be significant factors with respect to the current adjustment of firesetters, the question about the prognostic significance of enuresis and cruelty to animals for firesetters cannot be answered from this cross sectional data. If enuresis is an important indicator of a constitutional tendency towards lack of controls, as Michaels (1955) postulates, the symptoms of firesetting, enuresis and cruelty to animals are merely tips of the iceberg of a more important, but ill-defined, constitutional vulnerability. Thus, in the individuals with this vulnerability, cruelty to animals, enuresis and firesetting may be indicative of a significant problem but probably not "pathognomonic" of later adult violence, as Hellman and Blackman state (1966). As pointed out in other studies which attempt to relate individual characteristics with behavioral outcomes, situational or environmental factors appear to be more significant than individual traits in predicting future behavior (Monahan, 1981).

Further study of the internalizing, cruel-to-animals, firesetting subgroup is planned with the aid of Edelbrock and Achenbach's (1980) profile type program for use with the Child Behavior Checklist. A study of the relationship of cruelty to animals and enuresis to the follow-up status of firesetters is also planned. Finally, because most firesetters are not brought to mental health agencies (Winget and Whitman, 1973), these results should not be overgeneralized to other firesetting populations.

References

Achenbach, T. M., & Edelbrock, C. S. (1978). The classification of child psychopathology: A review and analysis of empirical efforts. *Psychological Bulletin, 85,* 1275-1301.

Achenbach, T. M., & Edelbrock, C. S. (1981). Behavioral problems and competencies reported by parents of normal and disturbed children age four-sixteen. *Monographs of the Society for Research in Child Development, 46,* 1-82.

Anders, T. F., & Freeman, E. D. (1979). Enuresis. In J. D. Noshpitz (Ed.), *Basic handbook of child psychiatry: Vol. 2. Disturbances of development* (pp. 546-555). New York: Basic Books.

Bender, L. (1959). Children and adolescents who have killed. *American Journal of Psychiatry, 116,* 510-513.

Edelbrock, C. S., & Achenbach, T. M. (1980). A typology of child behavior profile patterns: Distribution and correlates for disturbed children aged six-sixteen. *Journal of Abnormal Psychology, 8,* 441-470.

Fenichel, O. (1945). *The psychoanalytic theory of neurosis.* New York: W. W. Norton.

Freud, S. (1953). Fragment of an analysis of a case of hysteria. *Standard Edition* (Vol. 7, pp. 64-92). London: Hogarth Press. (Original work published 1905).

Grinstein, A. (1952). Stages in the development of control of fire. *International Journal of Psychoanalysis, 33,* 416-420.

Hellman, D. S., & Blackman, N. (1966). Enuresis, firesetting, and cruelty-to-animals: A triad predictive of adult crime. *American Journal of Psychiatry, 122,* 1431-1435.

Kaufman, I., Heims, L. W., & Reiser, D. D. (1961). A re-evaluation of the psychodynamics of firesetting. *American Journal of Orthopsychiatry, 22,* 63-72.

Klein, M. (1932). *Psychoanalysis of children.* London: Hogarth Press.

Kuhnley, E. J., Hendren, R. L., & Quinlan, D. M. (1982). Firesetting by children. *Journal of the American Academy of Child Psychiatry, 21,* 560-563.

Lewis, N. D. C., & Yarnell, H. (1951). Pathological firesetting (pyromania). *Nervous and Mental Disease Monograph, 82,* 8-26.

MacDonald, J. (1963). The threat to kill. *American Journal of Psychiatry, 120,* 125-130.

MacDonald, J. (1968). *Homicidal threats.* Springfield: C. C. Thomas.

Mead, M. (1964). Cultural factors in the cause and prevention of pathological homicide. *Bulletin: Menniger Clinic, 28,* 11-22.

Michaels, J. J. (1955). *Disorders of character.* Springfield: C. C. Thomas.

Michaels, J. J., & Steinberg, A. (1952). Persistent enuresis and juvenile delinquency. *British Journal of Delinquency, 3,* 114-123.

Monahan, J. (1981). *The clinical prediction of violent behavior: Crime and delinquency issues* (DHHS Publication No. ADM 81-921). Washington, D. C.: U. S. Government Printing Office.

Nurcombe, B. (1964). Children who set fires. *Medical Journal of Australia, 1,* 579-584.

Sendi, I. B., & Blomgren, P. G. (1975). A comparative study of predictive criteria in the predisposition of homicidal adolescents. *American Journal of Psychiatry, 132,* 423-427.

Vandersall, J. A., & Weiner, J. M. (1970). Children who set fires. *Archives of General Psychiatry, 22,* 62-71.

Wax, D. E., & Haddox, V. G. (1974). Enuresis, firesetting, and animal cruelty: A useful danger signal in predicting vulnerability of adolescent males to assaultive behavior. *Child Psychiatry and Human Development, 4,* 151-156.

Winget, C. N., & Whitman, R. M. (1973). Coping with problems: Attitudes toward children who set fires. *American Journal of Psychiatry, 130,* 442-445.

Dr. Heath is Director of Child Psychiatry at Maine Medical Center and Associate Clinical Professor of Psychiatry at the University of Vermont School of Medicine. At the Maine Medical Center, he directs the Child Psychiatric Clinic Program, the Therapeutic Nursery Program for preschoolers and is involved in the teaching of child psychiatry residents and medical students.

Approaching a Comparative Typology of Assaultive Female Offenders

Alan R. Felthous and Bernard Yudowitz

THIS TWO-PART STUDY explores the potential for assaultive behavior in females. The first part compares assaultive and nonassaultive female offenders for the presence of specific historical variables, and finds several significant differences. In the second part, the total female offender sample is compared with a male offender sample for presence of the same variables. The nearly equal incidence of several variables in both samples, such as persistent enuresis and firesetting, suggests a need for reassessment of some traditional theoretical formulations.

While considerable research has been devoted to the study of male offenders, the study of female offenders has been neglected. Both fiction and technical literature tend to present sociopathy as a deviant form of maleness. The corresponding stereotype for the deviant female seems to be the hysterical seductress. Actually, though fewer in absolute numbers, the majority of female offenders are committed for the same offenses as men: drunkenness, vagrancy, disorderly conduct, larceny-theft, and assault (Mattick, 1974). Assault, in particular, is commonly regarded as masculine behavior. The increase in personal violence committed by females in recent years invites reexamination of the importance of sex identification in these and other crimes.

If sociopathy is considered a male disorder, then behavior associated with sociopathy can also be regarded as sex linked. J. J. Michaels (1955) made this kind of association in attaching diagnostic importance to the quadrad of maleness, psychopathy, persistent enuresis, and firesetting. Males may indeed be more likely than females to demonstrate these three elements, but to include maleness in this typology, at least on a conceptual level, excludes females. This sexual dichotomy can result in overlooking significant sociopathic elements in females and an unreasonable double standard for treatment or punishment.

Freud's theory of the relationship between fire, urination, and phallus supports this sort of sexual dichotomy. In a footnote to his discussion on the importance to mankind of gaining control over fire, as one of the first steps toward civilization, Freud implied that the psychodynamic connection between urination and one's attitude toward fire is determined by the presence or absence of phallic anatomy.

It is as though primal man had the habit, when he came in contact with fire, of satisfying an

From McLean Hospital, Institute of Law and Psychiatry, Belmont, Mass. For reprints, see address at end of paper.

Alan R. Felthous, MD, is a staff psychiatrist at the Naval Regional Medical Center, Oakland, Calif.

Bernard Yudowitz, MD, LLB, is Director of the Institute of Law and Psychiatry at McLean Hospital, Belmont, Mass.

The authors are grateful to Mollie C. Grob, ACSW, and Judith Singer, PhD., for their assistance in the preparation of this paper.

Reprinted from *Psychiatry* 40 (1977): 270–76, with kind permission of the Guilford Press.

infantile desire connected with it, by putting it out with a stream of his urine . . . . Putting out a fire by micturating . . . was therefore a kind of sexual act with a male, an enjoyment of sexual potency in a homosexual competition . . . . Further, it is as though woman had been appointed guardian of the fire which was held captive on the domestic hearth, because her anatomy made it impossible for her to yield to the temptation of this desire [1930, p. 90 n.]

If phallic anatomy predetermines an individual's psychodynamic and behavioral destiny, it might follow that firesetting and enuresis are male-linked behaviors. And what of the relationship between maleness and other factors which have been associated with violent behavior?

This study intends to explore the relative importance of biological sex, sex-related cultural factors, and asexual constitutional and psychodynamic factors in the genesis of assaultive potential. In order to do this, two questions about female offenders will be asked: Can certain measurable variables serve to differentiate assaultive female offenders from nonassaultive ones? And is there a sexual differential for variables which may be associated with assaultive behavior?

Hypothetically, some historical variables may be specific indicators or antecedents of poor control over aggressive impulses; these variables ought to lack sexual specificity. Other variables which are associated with violence are cultural in origin and may or may not be related to sex. Identification of signs of assaultive potential in females and determination of the relative significance of each sign could eventually lead to the development of a useful typology distinguishing assaultive female offenders from nonassaultive offenders.

METHOD

The study sample consisted of 31 female and 19 male offenders. The female offenders were inmates at the Massachusetts Correctional Institution at Framingham; 25 of them were evaluated in succession shortly after they entered the facility; 2 had returned from escape status; the others had just been admitted and were awaiting classification. Six of the 31 subjects were referred for psychiatric evaluation because an emotional disorder was suspected.

The 19 male offenders were inmates of the Middlesex County House of Correction in Billerica, Massachusetts. Three subjects were referred for suspected emotional problems, but the other 16 had just arrived and were awaiting classification.

Evaluations for this study included administration of a multiple choice questionnaire, a psychiatric interview, and review of the subject's record. The questionnaire contained 11 demographic items and 27 items that were hypothetically related to assaultive behavior. Included in these 27 items were signs of childhood psychopathology (such as school truancy and deficient or improper parenting), habits (such as carrying weapons), and interests (such as favored sports).

Each item of the questionnaire was framed so that the response could be judged deviant or nondeviant. For example, the possible responses to the item on age of persistent enuresis were: under 6, 6 to 9, 10 to 14, and 15 or older. Under 6 years was considered nondeviant while all other age groups were deviant. The percentage of deviant responses for each item could then be determined for each sample, based on the total number of replies to the item rather than the number of subjects in the sample.

The questionnaire was administered at the beginning of the interview in order to minimize the influence the interview might have on responses. Subjects were invited to ask about any items which seemed unclear. Several subjects asked that the questions be read to them, as comprehension of print was more difficult for them.

In order to identify assaultive and nonassaultive female examples, individual offender charts were examined, with particular attention given to the verified court record, the probation record, the FBI record, the intake conviction data form, and the administrative chronology. Some charts did not have all of these documents. The documented history of a *conviction* of a crime of personal violence (assault and battery, assault with a deadly weapon, manslaughter or murder) was the criterion for assignment to the assaultive group. Assignment to the nonassaultive group was based on an absence of known *charges* which involve personal violence. Seven of the females studied were not assigned to either group because of ambiguities. Armed robbery, for instance, was considered an ambiguous charge or conviction, because although there was a risk of serious injury to someone, the specific objective was acquiring money.

Since the male subjects were included in the study for comparison with the total female sample, they were not divided into assaultive and nonassaultive groups.

RESULTS

Demographic data showed that the majority of male offenders and both assaultive and nonassaultive female offenders were young, single, urban adults who were relatively uneducated and were unemployed. The females ranged in age from 18 to 39, with 52% in the 20–24 age group; 67% did not complete high school; 68% of the subjects and 67% of their fathers had worked at skilled or unskilled jobs, but only 57% of the subjects had held a job for four consecutive weeks in the two years prior to incarceration. Racially, the total female sample consisted of 21 whites (68%) and 10 blacks (32%). All but 2 of the female subjects (94%) came from urban communities; 64% were single; 61% were repeat offenders. There were no significant demographic differences between the assaultive and nonassaultive subgroups.

The ages of the male subjects ranged from 18 to 60. Like the female subjects, most (53%) fell within the 20–24 group; 78% did not graduate from high school. Reflecting the cultural-sexual differential in employment, males showed a higher rate of employment (84%) than the female subjects. However, presumably in contrast to employment patterns in the noncriminal population, 26% of the male subjects had not held a job for four consecutive weeks in the two years prior to conviction. Racially, 18 subjects were white, and one black. In comparison to female subjects, although most of the males came from a city, 42% lived in nonurban areas (32%, small town; 10%, suburb). Much like the females, 63% of the males were single. While most males (63%), like the majority of female subjects (64%), said they adhered to the Catholic faith, it should be added that most subjects of both sexes came from the Boston area, which has a large Catholic population.

The percentage of deviant responses to each item in the assaultive female sample ($N = 11$) was compared with the corresponding percentage of deviant responses in the nonassaultive female sample ($N = 13$); subtraction yielded the differential percentage for each item. Items were then ranked in ascending order of the differential percentages (Table 1). The chi-square test showed that histories of physically injurious paternal punishments ($p < .02$) and cruelty to animals ($p < .02$) were significantly associated with convictions for crimes of personal violence. There was also a trend for parental alcoholism to be associated with the assaultive sample ($p < .10$). Other variables which showed an increased incidence (more than 20%) in the assaultive sample included persistent enuresis, severe childhood headaches, deviant paternal punishments (i.e., neglectful permissiveness or physical brutality), physically injurious maternal punishments, early abandonment by one or both parents, destructive firesetting, and poor peer relationships in childhood. The history of carrying a deadly weapon and preference for detective movies was found in well over 50% of both assaultive and nonassaultive subjects, and there was no substantial differential percentage for either variable.

Of those items which showed a greater percentage of deviant responses in the nonassaultive sample (Table 2), the differential percentage was at least 20% for four items: tripping false fire alarms, frequent childhood temper tantrums, childhood fights with injury, and school truancy. A history of turning in false fire alarms was significantly associated with the nonassaultive sample ($p < .01$). Childhood temper tantrums and fights in which the subject injured her opponent showed a similar associative trend ($p < .10$ for both items). Deviant responses for all childhood fights, including those in which the other child was not injured, showed no significant discrepancy between the assaultive and nonassaultive groups.

Two of the 6 subjects who were referred for presumed emotional disturbances fell into the assaultive group. Although the "referred subgroup" was too small for meaningful comment, it is interesting to note that a disproportionate number showed a history of enuresis (4) and firesetting (3). Both of the assaultive females

had continued to wet the bed well beyond 10 years of age, and each had set fire to a house or building.

Comparison of the total male and female samples by application of the chi-square test showed that the male offenders had a significantly higher incidence of poor grades in elementary school ($p < .05$), carrying deadly weapons ($p < .05$), and unjustified punishments by their mothers ($p < .01$). Male subjects also revealed a trend toward a higher incidence of violent childhood temper tantrums ($p < .10$) and childhood head injury with loss of consciousness ($p < .10$). The differential percentage for all five variables was greater than 20% (Table 3).

Female offenders (Table 4) showed a significantly higher incidence of physically injurious punishments by their fathers ($p < .001$), deviant paternal punishments ($p < .02$), frequent childhood temper tantrums ($p < .01$), and preference for detective movies ($p < .01$). There was also a

Table 1

ITEMS OF HIGHER INCIDENCE IN ASSAULTIVE FEMALES*

Item	Assaultive Females	Nonassaultive Females	Differential Percentage
Injurious paternal punishments	56%	8%	48%
Parental alcoholism	70	31	39
Cruelty to animals	36	0	36
Persistent enuresis	45	15	30
Childhood headaches	45	15	30
Neglectful or brutal paternal discipline	67	39	28
Injurious maternal punishments	33	8	25
Early parental abandonment	55	31	24
Firesetting	45	23	22
Poor peer relations	36	15	21

* Items for which deviant responses were at least 20% greater for assaultive females are tabulated.

Table 2

ITEMS OF HIGHER INCIDENCE IN NONASSAULTIVE FEMALES*

Item	Assaultive Females	Nonassaultive Females	Differential Percentage
False fire alarms	0%	77%	77%
Frequent temper tantrums	64	92	28
Fights with injury	0	23	23
School truancy	64	85	21

* Items for which deviant responses were at least 20% greater for nonassaultive females are tabulated.

Table 3

ITEMS OF HIGHER INCIDENCE IN MALES*

Item	Males	Females	Differential Percentage
Unjustified maternal punishments	42%	10%	32%
Carried a deadly weapon	74	45	29
Violent temper tantrums	58	32	26
Childhood head injury	32	10	22
Poor school work	26	6	20

* Items for which deviant responses were at least 20% greater for male offenders are tabulated.

Table 4

ITEMS OF HIGHER INCIDENCE IN FEMALES*

Item	Females	Males	Differential Percentage
Injurious paternal punishments	59%	5%	54%
Neglectful or brutal paternal discipline	72	42	30
Frequent temper tantrums	81	52	29
Early parental abandonment	45	21	24
Preference for detective movies	61	37	24

* Items for which deviant responses were at least 20% greater for female offenders are tabulated.

trend for the females to have a higher incidence of abandonment by one or both parents before the age of 10 ($p < .10$).

There was an appreciable percentage of deviant responses to a number of other items for both the male and female samples, but the sexual differential for these items was rather small. Childhood temper tantrums and school truancy occurred in well over 50% of the subjects in each of the four samples (male offenders, female offenders, assaultive females, and nonassaultive females).

DISCUSSION

Three items of higher incidence in the assaultive female sample than in the nonassaultive sample belong to the familiar symptom-triad of enuresis, firesetting, and cruelty to animals. Our data suggest that these three elements may carry significance, but not pathognomicity, as indicators of assaultive potential in females. Although enuresis, firesetting, cruelty to animals, and violent behavior may occur less commonly in females than in males,

the presence of these items can be expected to convey comparable significance in both male and female subjects.

If future research corroborates these findings, Freud's fire-urine-phallus theory may have to be reformulated in order to account for such empirical findings in females. A structural explanation, independent of sex, seems to offer the clearest understanding of the higher incidence of elements of the symptom-triad in the assaultive sample.

All three of these behaviors can be regarded as signs of poor control over aggressive impulses. These behaviors do not seem to be directly affected by cultural factors, in contrast to drug abuse, for example, wherein there is a strong interactive process between subcultural contextual factors and individual psychic determinants. Behaviors of the symptom-triad may occur in the context of considerable pregenital ego pathology characterized by poor integrative functions and primitive defense mechanisms, such as denial and projection, which do not effectively modulate aggressive impulses. In addition to a structurally defective ego, the superego is stymied in development. It is the ego pathology with diffusely inadequate control of aggressive impulses which is primarily responsible for the overt physical expression of aggressive impulses. This is not to say that only impulsive individuals with ego pathology are capable of physical assaults: individuals with fairly intact egos can be quite assaultive, even homicidal. In our judgment, however, those who fit the former description are more likely to show *greater variety* of aggressive and impulsive behaviors, including the elements of the symptom-triad.

Michaels (1959, 1965) has discussed quite thoroughly the ego defects in the impulsive personality disorder, and we need not elaborate them here. It should be stressed, however, that this structural theory of aggressive impulsivity is, in its essential elements, relatively unaffected by sex. Although males may have a higher constitutional titer of aggressive drive, the female potential for aggressive impulsivity, given an equal quantity of aggression and similar ego defects, is similar to that of males.

Returning to our comparative data on the assaultive and nonassaultive female groups, the evidence for inadequate parental care raises some interesting etiological considerations. Specifically, the assaultive sample showed a higher incidence of deviant and physically injurious parental punishments and parental alcoholism. Climent and Ervin (1972) also found a higher incidence of alcoholism in the fathers ($p < .01$) and mothers ($p < .05$) of violent subjects ($N = 40$; 6 females) compared to nonassaultive subjects ($N = 40$; 9 females). These observations may reflect a hereditary factor in ego defects marked by aggressive impulsivity. Reference can be made to Schulsinger's (1972) twin adoption study. Having defined psychopathy as a consistent pattern of impulse-ridden or acting-out behavior lasting beyond the age of 19, Schulsinger found that psychopaths who had been separated from their biological parents were almost twice as likely to have biological relatives with psychopathy than were the nonpsychopathic adopted twins.

The impact of parental neglect and brutality during the formative years cannot be overlooked. In addition to the global adverse effect of neglect and brutality on ego development, more specific effects occur. Brutality fosters resentment and, at the same time, inculcates assaultiveness as a defense (identification with the aggressor) and coping mechanism. Brutality causes the child to perceive himself as evil and his world as threatening. Neglect leads to a poor self-image, inability to feel love and compassion, retarded development of defensive and adaptive mechanisms, and the underdevelopment of cognitive skills.

In addition to the aforementioned variables, the sample of assaultive female offenders had a higher incidence of severe headaches in childhood. Climent and Ervin also reported significantly more headaches in violent offenders than in a nonviolent control group.

In comparing the total male and total female samples, the relative lack of significant discrepancy in the incidence of some items is as interesting as some of the sexual disparities. Persistent enuresis, firesetting in childhood, and torturing animals were of nearly equal incidence in both samples (though the male sample had a higher incidence of killing animals). This is consistent with the conclusion that the elements of the symptom-triad, when present, are no more or less significant for males than for females.

Childhood temper tantrums and school truancy, apparently significant as general indicators of social maladaptiveness, were high in all four groups, and were not significantly disparate in the male and female groups. Inability to adapt to the structure and demands of a school system precedes failure to conform to legal norms of society; this appears to be equally true for both male and female offenders.

Conclusion

The findings of this preliminary study suggest that injurious paternal punishments and cruelty to animals are significant as correlates of assaultive behavior in female offenders. Other variables indicate a more general social maladaptiveness in both male and female subjects. The typology of the aggressive, impulsive personality disorder observed in males appears to be equally applicable to impulsively assaultive females.

Further research is necessary to establish more firmly the relative significance of each variable and clustering of variables as signs of impulsive-assaultive potential. More signs will undoubtedly arise, filling out the profile. A promising study in further unraveling the nature of impulsive aggressivity would be a systematic comparison of assaultive males and assaultive females. As the sexual components, biologically and culturally determined, become better delineated, the genesis and anatomy of potential for assault will come into clearer focus.

Alan R. Felthous, MD
142-A Barbers Point Road
NAS-Alameda, Calif. 94501

REFERENCES

Climent, C. E., and Ervin, F. R. "Historical Data in the Evaluation of Violent Subjects," *Arch. Gen. Psychiatry* (1972) 27:621–624.

Freud, S. "Civilization and its Discontents (1930)," *Stand. Ed. Complete Psychol. Works,* Vol. 21; Hogarth, 1961.

Mattick, H. W. "The Contemporary Jails of the United States: An Unknown and Neglected Area of Justice," in D. Glaser (Ed.), *Handbook of Criminology;* Rand McNally, 1974.

Michaels, J. J. *Disorders of Character;* Charles C Thomas, 1955.

Michaels, J. J. "Character Structures and Character Disorders," in S. Arieti (Ed.), *American Handbook of Psychiatry,* Vol. 1; Basic Books, 1959.

Michaels, J. J., and Stiver, L. "The Impulsive Psychopathic Character According to the Diagnostic Profile," *Psychoanal. Study of Child* (1965) 20:124–141.

Schulsinger, F. "Psychopathy: Hereditary and Environment," *Int. J. Mental Health* (1972) 1:190–206.

Early-Warning Signs of Violence: Is a Triad Enough?

BY BLAIR JUSTICE, PH.D., RITA JUSTICE, PH.D., AND IRVIN A. KRAFT, M.D.

While noting that a triad of childhood symptoms—enuresis, firesetting, and cruelty to animals—has been accepted as predictive of violence in adulthood, the authors believe that other symptoms may serve as even more useful predictors. On the basis of a literature search, interviews with many persons who had had contact with troubled youth, and in-depth interviews with eight convicts who had shown behavior problems as children, they identified four symptoms—fighting, temper tantrums, school problems and truancy, and interpersonal difficulties—as early-warning signs that may indicate serious emotional disturbance which is likely to result in violent behavior.

VIOLENCE IS NOT NEW to our society, either as a reality or as a subject for research concern (1). For at least 15 years researchers and clinicians in many fields have sought understanding and predictors of the violence-prone individual (2–4). In the field of psychiatry a triad of childhood symptoms—enuresis, firesetting, and cruelty to animals—has had fairly widespread acceptance as being predictive of individual violence in adulthood. The purpose of this study is to examine the sufficiency of this triad.

Firesetting, enuresis, and cruelty to animals have been associated with violent aggression both as individual symptoms and as symptoms appearing conjointly (5–7). What seems to have been ignored in much of the literature is the fact that although these predictive symptoms do appear, other symptoms correlate with this triad and emerge as even more useful childhood predictors of later violence (2, 4, 8, 9). The diversity of symptoms listed in the literature as childhood predictors of adult violence is so great that we set about determining if a consensus—or even synthesis—exists.

METHOD

The first step in identifying early-warning signs of vio-

Dr. Blair Justice is Professor of Social Psychology, School of Public Health, University of Texas at Houston, and Project Director, Project for the Prevention of Individual Violence; Dr. Rita Justice is Research Psychologist, Southwest Center for Urban Research, Houston, Tex., and Assistant Director, Project for the Prevention of Individual Violence; and Dr. Kraft is Associate Professor of Psychiatry and Pediatrics, Baylor College of Medicine, Houston, Tex., and Director, Texas Institute of Child Psychiatry. Address reprint requests to Dr. Blair Justice, P.O. Box 20186, Houston, Tex. 77025.

lence was to find out what signs or symptoms were already being identified as predictors. A systematic analysis of the literature between 1950 and 1971 in the fields of psychiatry, psychology, sociology, medicine, criminology, behavioral science, and law was conducted. A total of 1,500 references on individual violence was found in 237 journals; 188 of these contained references to predictors of violence. The content of these 188 references was analyzed for frequency of mention of symptoms or behavior patterns.

In addition to analyzing the literature, we conducted 779 tape-recorded interviews with people in 25 professions having contact with troubled youth. A total of 264 of those interviewed were in health professions, including physicians (23 persons), mental health personnel, nurses, and health educators. The interviewees were asked open-ended questions on what they thought were predictive symptoms of violent behavior. The responses were recorded by trained collators and analyzed by computer.

A final source of information was 1,055 case studies of schoolchildren that had been worked up between 1955 and 1958. At the time the case histories (or "social histories") were taken, the children were having learning or behavior problems in the classroom, or both. The social histories were taken by visiting teachers under the supervision of one of us (I.A.K.), who was the consulting psychiatrist for the school district. The names of these 1,055 children were checked against the files of the Texas Department of Correction (TDC), and 57 were located.[1] Of the 57, eight had been convicted of violent offenses. These eight were interviewed in depth to assess the presence or absence of early indicators of violent behavior.

RESULTS

Using the information gathered from the literature survey, the 779 interviews, and the case studies of the eight follow-up interviews, four early-warning signs or behavior patterns were identified.

As table 1 indicates, fighting was the most commonly cited early predictor of potential violence; it appeared as a symptom in all the follow-up case histories. Temper tantrums, school problems and truancy, and inability to

[1] These 57 people were under the jurisdiction of TDC on January 1, 1971, when the search was made. Some others may have been under the jurisdiction of TDC and released, but accessible TDC records did not reflect this information.

Reprinted from the *American Journal of Psychiatry* 131 (1974): 457–59. Copyright 1974 by the American Psychiatric Association. Reprinted by permission.

TABLE 1
Prevalence of Childhood Behaviors Predictive of Adult Violence

Behavior	Number of Citations in the Literature*	Percent of Interviewees Citing the Behavior (N = 799)**	Number of Citations in Follow-Up Case Histories (N = 8)
Fighting	83	15.5	8
Temper tantrums	50	9.8	6
Inability to get along with others	28	12.5	6
School problems and truancy	24	11.0	8
Bedwetting	25	0.3	0
Cruelty to animals	9	3.8	4
Firesetting	2	0.8	1

*Some publications (N = 188) cited more than one behavior.
**The behavior was cited in response to the question, "What do you feel are early-warning signals in the behavior of a person who might commit an act of violent crime?"

get along with others ranked behind fighting as predictors.

In only one category, number of citations in the literature, did bedwetting rank higher than any of the four behaviors mentioned above. In the other two categories bedwetting appeared infrequently. Cruelty to animals and firesetting were seldom mentioned in articles and interviews, and only cruelty to animals appeared fairly often as a symptom in the follow-up case histories.

These behaviors—fighting, school problems and truancy, temper tantrums, and inability to get along with others—are manifested by all children at some time; but when they appear together, excessively, or at inappropriate ages, the four behaviors indicate a strong possibility of violent behavior in adulthood.

The identification of these four behavior patterns as predictors of violence does not mean that other predictors are invalid. Enuresis, firesetting, and cruelty to animals, as well as many other symptoms, were listed as predictors of violent behavior. However, fighting, temper tantrums, "aloneness," and truancy and school failure appeared more frequently.

CASE REPORTS

The following case history summaries were taken from the eight follow-up interviews conducted with inmates who had shown signs of disturbance as children.

Case 1. Donald, aged 19, was serving a life sentence for murder with malice and theft. When interviewed by the visiting teacher at age 10 he was inattentive in school, lied, was involved in fights two or three times a week, was a bully, and was having moderate to severe difficulty in reading, spelling, and arithme-

tic. He had few friends and spent most of his idle time watching television or wandering around alone. At age 10 he began skipping school and dropped out in the seventh grade. He began stealing (taking candy bars) at age six.

Case 2. At age 25, Larry was confined to maximum security in prison because of an "overall history of instability." At the time of the interview he was serving a ten-year sentence for burglary with an intent to commit theft, preceded by 13 years of multiple offenses of various types, ranging from assault to murder.

At age 12 Larry had been listless, daydreamed, and had severe staring spells. In regard to school he played truant, lied, and had severe learning problems in reading, spelling, and math. Larry also fought, threw temper tantrums, had few friends, and burned cats. He was not enuretic.

Case 3. Gilbert was first arrested at age 11 for vandalism; he had destroyed some park benches. Three years later he was arrested for aggravated assault after threatening another youth with a pocketknife. At age 20 he was serving a six-year term for auto theft. Gilbert first came to the attention of school authorities at age seven because of his chronic truancy. He was inattentive in class and had severe learning problems in reading, spelling, and math.

Gilbert remembered that his first fight occurred when he was 10 years old. He had temper tantrums "once in a while" through adolescence, had few friends, and reported that as a kid he would "throw cats as far as he could." There was no report of enuresis or firesetting.

Case 4. At age 18 Richard was serving a life sentence for rape and robbery by assault. By age 14, when Richard was interviewed by the visiting teacher, he had a juvenile probation department record for breaking and entering and car theft. In school he was seclusive, inactive, inattentive, tired, had staring spells, and he stole, lied, and fought.

Richard recalled having few friends and remembered hurting an animal only once—a dog that was trying to bite him. Neither enuresis nor firesetting was reported.

DISCUSSION

As already noted, the early-warning signs of violence defined in this study are behavior patterns that appear in every child at some time. How, then, is it possible to be certain that a child exhibiting these behaviors will later commit violence? It is not.

These warning signs do not pinpoint a specific individual who is certain to commit an act of violence. Rather, the early-warning signs are behavior patterns designed to serve as an "alert." This "alerting" approach is similar to that of the American Cancer Society with its list of seven warning signs. It is clear that no one sign means a person has cancer, but its presence should be a source of concern and should stimulate follow-up action. Similarly, the behaviors that represent the early-warning signs of potential violence should stimulate action.

The four early-warning signs identified in this study—fighting, temper tantrums, school problems and truancy, and inability to get along with others—seem to appear more frequently in violent persons than do firesetting, bedwetting, and cruelty to animals. The triad has not been found incorrect in predicting adult violence; that was not the purpose of the study described here. However, the triad does appear to have more limited breadth in diagnosis than do the four early-warning signs. Neither the triad nor the "quartet" offers infallible diagnostic tools, but both, particularly taken in conjunction, are indicators of serious emotional disturbance that is likely to result in violent behavior.

REFERENCES

1. Graham HD, Gurr TR: The History of Violence in America. New York, Bantam Books, 1969
2. Glueck S, Glueck E: Predicting Delinquency and Crime. Cambridge, Mass, Harvard University Press, 1960
3. Bender L: Children and adolescents who have killed. Am J Psychiatry 116:510–513, 1959
4. Abrahamsen D: The Psychology of Crime. New York, Columbia University Press, 1960, pp 74–75
5. Hellman DS, Blackman N: Enuresis, firesetting, and cruelty to animals: a triad predictive of adult crime. Am J Psychiatry 122:1431–1435, 1966
6. Michaels JJ: Enuresis in murderous aggressive children and adolescents. Arch Gen Psychiatry 5:490–493, 1961
7. Shaw CR: The Psychiatric Disorders of Childhood. New York, Appleton-Century-Crofts, 1966, pp 299–302
8. Bender L: Aggression, Hostility, and Anxiety in Children. Springfield, Ill, Charles C Thomas, 1960
9. Robins LN: Deviant Children Grow Up. Baltimore, Williams & Wilkins Co, 1966

SECTION 7: CHILD ABUSE, ELDER ABUSE, AND DOMESTIC VIOLENCE

The first two articles reprinted in this section address the confluence of child abuse, domestic violence, and animal maltreatment by directly assessing the extent of overlap between these differing forms of aggression and cruelty. Frank R. Ascione's essay reports on a sample of women who had been battered by their partners and reported their partners' threatening to or actually hurting or killing one of their pets. The high prevalence of animal abuse in this sample (and in a follow-up study by Ascione) suggests another area for animal-welfare concern and the need for helping women find safety for their animals as well as for themselves and their children. Ascione also found that children in these families display significant cruelty to animals. Living in a violent family environment may lead some children to vent their own fear and anger on those more vulnerable than they are.

This last point could also apply to a classic study in this field, by Elizabeth DeViney, Jeffery Dickert, and Randall Lockwood, the only study whose primary purpose was examining the relation between child abuse and the abuse and neglect of pets. The hallmarks of this research include a focus on families who had received formal social-service designation as "abusive" of their children and the measurement of abuse and/or neglect of the pets residing in these homes. Again, the high degree of overlap between child abuse, especially physical abuse, and maltreatment of pets is alarming.

The empirical data provided by these two studies serve to highlight the importance of more practical and applied issues in child and animal welfare, which are addressed in the paper by Lynn Loar and Kenneth White. Their article notes similarities and some ironic differences in the quality of care that our society provides for children and for animals. These two advocates describe how their respective work in animal welfare and child welfare has come together in the formation of a community coalition to reduce violence in all its forms.

The interrelations between different forms of violence to people and to animals receives thoughtful attention in the paper by Carol J. Adams. Writing from the perspective of feminist and environmental philosophies, Adams reflects on the association between the maltreatment of animals and various areas of interpersonal abuse and maltreatment: partner battering, marital rape, pornography, child sexual abuse, serial homicide, and sexual harassment. Her analyses suggest a number of areas ripe for empirical study and lead us to note a relatively unstudied aspect of the link between animal and human maltreatment, the abuse of the elderly. Barbara Rosen's article summarizes what we do know about the connection between animal cruelty and elder abuse, but nearly all of this information is anecdotal. Our knowledge of the dynamics of child abuse and neglect and domestic violence has relevance here, but elder abuse is worthy of serious study in its own right.

The last four articles deal with a controversial area in the abuse literature—ritualistic abuse of children and adults. The articles by F. Jonker and P. Jonker-Bakker and by Walter C. Young and his colleagues describe case studies in Holland and the United States where child and adult victims have related experiences of ritualistic abuse, often involving acts of cruelty toward animals. The controversial nature of this topic is addressed from a psychiatric research perspective in the article by Frank W. Putnam and from a law-enforcement perspective in Kenneth V. Lanning's article. All of these commentaries suggest caution in the conduct and reporting of research on this topic and yet remain sensitive to the traumatic experiences victims of ritualized abuse may have undergone.

Battered Women's Reports of Their Partners' and Their Children's Cruelty to Animals

Frank R. Ascione

ABSTRACT. Anecdotal reports of cruelty to pet animals in families where partner battering occurs are common but there exist few empirical data on this issue. Determining the forms and prevalence of such cruelty is important since abuse of pets may be a method batterers use to control their partners, may be related to batterers' lethality, and may result in children in such families being exposed to multiple forms of violence, a significant risk for mental health problems. Thirty-eight women seeking shelter at a safe house for battered partners voluntarily completed surveys about pet ownership and violence to pets. Of the women reporting current or past pet ownership, 71% reported that their partner had threatened and/or actually hurt or killed one or more of their pets. Actual (as distinct from threatened) harm to pets represented the majority (57%) of reports. Fifty-eight percent of the full sample of women had children and 32% of these women reported that one or more of their children had hurt or killed pet animals; in 71% of these cases, the women had also

Frank Ascione, PhD, is Professor in the Department of Psychology and Adjunct Professor in the Department of Family and Human Development at Utah State University. His current work focuses on clinical and applied research on the relations between child maltreatment, domestic violence, and cruelty to animals.

Address correspondence to: Frank Ascione, PhD, Professor, Department of Psychology, Utah State University, Logan, UT 84322-2810.

The assistance of Kathy Monson and Heather Hoffman in the conduct of this study is greatly appreciated. Thanks also to Karen Ranson for professional secretarial services.

Based on papers presented at the 4th International Conference on Family Violence, Durham, New Hampshire, July 24, 1995 and the National Conference on Children Exposed to Family Violence, Austin, Texas, June 8, 1996.

Journal of Emotional Abuse, Vol. 1(1) 1998

reported animal abuse (threatened or actual) by their partner. This study represents one of the first empirical analyses of the prevalence of animal maltreatment in a sample of battered women. The high prevalence rate of batterers' threatened or actual harm of animals and the relatively high rate of animal abuse reported for the children in this sample are relevant for future research and policy analyses. *[Article copies available for a fee from The Haworth Document Delivery Service: 1-800-342-9678. E-mail address: getinfo@haworth.com]*

KEYWORDS. Animal abuse, emotional abuse, domestic violence, pet abuse, batterers, lethality, children

Pets were terribly important to her; they were her only source of comfort and affection. One afternoon, Billy said he had had it with her damn cats and started screaming that he was going to kill them. Kim didn't take it too seriously. (Browne, 1987, p. 154)

. . . Aubrey got angry with the family dog for straying outside their yard. He loaded one of his nine guns, then shot and killed it. The kids began to sob, devastated. He grabbed (one child's) hair . . . slapped another of the kids, then began crying himself. Joyce tried to comfort them all. But her feelings of anger were mixed with genuine terror: in a moment of rage, she knew, Aubrey could kill any one of them and cry about it afterward. (Walker, 1989, pp. 20-21)

These examples associating partner abuse with cruelty to animals and, in one case, child maltreatment are but two of the many anecdotal references to the abuse of animals in the literature on domestic violence (Adams, 1994). Following an analysis of existing research and policy issues relevant for understanding the relation between domestic violence and animal maltreatment, the results of a small-scale descriptive study of the prevalence of animal cruelty experiences in a shelter sample of battered women are reported. Implications for future research and for the well-being of women and children experiencing family violence are then discussed.

INTRODUCTION AND BACKGROUND

In an earlier paper (Ascione, 1993), existing research on childhood cruelty to animals, its relation to various forms of family and community violence, and its significance as a symptom of Conduct Disorder are reviewed. The clearest evidence of this relationship is found in studies of the effects of physical and sexual abuse on children. Relatively less information is available on the effects of exposure to domestic violence on children's relations with pets and other animals. *Adult* partner cruelty to animals has been described anecdotally (e.g., Dutton, 1992; Gelles & Straus, 1988; Walker, 1979), and includes references to partners torturing or killing animals and forcing women to engage in bestiality. In one of the rare empirical studies including examination of the domestic violence/animal maltreatment relation, Renzetti (1992) found that 38% of women, with pets in abusive lesbian relationships reported maltreatment of pets by their partners. The effects of partner animal abuse on the women whose animals are hurt or killed and the effects of witnessing both parent *and* pet abuse on children's mental health warrant more focused research attention.

Partners' Abuse of Animals

Information about the forms and prevalence of cruelty to animals in families experiencing domestic violence is not easily culled from existing research. One reason is the inconsistency, across studies, in whether questions about animal maltreatment are included in assessments. In some cases, data about animal abuse may be incorporated, explicitly or implicitly, under more general categories of abuse. For example, in Walker's (1984) interviews with battered women, bestiality was mentioned as an example of "unusual sex acts" the women were asked to perform by their partners. In the group of women who had experienced relationships with battering and non-battering partners, this experience was reported by 41% and 5%, respectively. Walker also reported that, when with a batterer, 16% of the women reported directing their own anger at their "children or pets"; when with a non-batterer, the figure was 3%. In a similar vein, cruelty to animals may be implicit in measures of psychological maltreatment. Brassard, Hart, and Hardy's (1993) categories of "Terrorizing" (including ". . . threats directed toward loved ones or objects . . .") and "Exploiting/Corrupting" (including ". . modeling antisocial acts . . .") are examples.

Occasionally, specific items related to animal maltreatment appear in domestic violence questionnaires or checklists. Renzetti's (1992) study is one example. Another is Dutton's (1992) "Abusive Behavior Observation Checklist" in which being "required to be involved with an animal in a sexual way" is an item under the "unwanted sexual behavior" category (p. 160) and "abused your/his/her family pets" is listed under "Psychological Abuse–Intimidation" (p. 161).

Domestic violence and cruelty to animals are, at times, examined together in discussions of assessing partner dangerousness or lethality (Campbell, 1995). One assessment, proposed by Straus (1993) to facilitate identification of "high risk violence," includes the item, "threats or actual killing or injuring a pet." However, another dangerousness assessment inventory does not mention animal maltreatment in any form (Stuart & Campbell, 1989).

Children's Abuse of Animals

The literature on the effects of exposure to domestic violence on children's mental health has been recently reviewed by Jaffe and Sudermann (1995) who note the complexity and variability of such effects from one study to another. Cruelty to animals as a childhood reaction to exposure to domestic violence has not been directly explored. Suggestive information, however, can be derived from studies of children of battered women in which externalizing problems and/or conduct disorder symptoms are examined [since the 1987 revision, both the Diagnostic and Statistical Manual of Mental Disorders (3rd edition revised) and the Diagnostic and Statistical Manual of Mental Disorders (4th edition) (American Psychiatric Association 1987, 1994) include physical cruelty to animals as a symptom of Conduct Disorder].

One recent study that included a sample of both sheltered and community battered women and their 6-12 year old children found that domestic violence was related to ". . . children's general psychopathology . . ." (McCloskey, Figueredo, & Koss, 1995). The authors report that women's partners' hurting or killing pets did load (albeit, at a low level) on a factor labeled, "escalated aggression," a factor that included other severe forms of threatened or actual interpersonal aggression. Other studies have also found a relationship between observing domestic violence and externalizing psychological symptoms both in preschool-age children at a shelter or residing at home (Fantuzzo et al., 1991) and in an older (8-12 year old) sample of Israeli children living at home (Sternberg et al., 1993). However, it is unclear how often externalizing symptomatology manifests itself in the form of cruelty to animals since reports rarely describe, understandably, results for individual items on assessment inventories. It should also be noted that in Sternberg et al.'s study, and in a similar study with a shelter sample (O'Keefe, 1995), child outcomes may vary depending on whether the child was physically abused in addition to being exposed to partner abuse.

Given the recent upsurge in concern with the deleterious effects of community or neighborhood violence on children (e.g., Taylor, Zuckerman, Harik, and Groves, 1994), it is appropriate that greater attention be given to violence that is perhaps even less escapable for children: violence among family members in one's home. This issue is receiving cross-cultural and international attention (Levinson, 1989; Patrignani & Villé, 1995). However, examination of the confluence of partner abuse, child abuse, and the maltreatment of animals is in its infancy. Greater attention is being given, at a national policy level, to the overlap between partner abuse of women and child maltreatment (Ascione, 1995; Dykstra, 1995; Koss et al., 1994; Schecter & Edelson, 1995), and between the abuse of children and violence toward animals (American Humane Association, 1995; Deviney, Dickert, & Lockwood, 1983). The associations among all three types of domestic violence (which may also include sibling abuse: Suh & Abel, 1990; Wiehe, 1990; and elder abuse: Rosen, 1995) are only beginning to be explored (e.g., Arkow, 1995). For example, physical, emotional, and sexual abuse have been noted by Wiehe and Herring (1991) as components of sibling abuse. In the area of emotional abuse, these authors explicitly include the torture or destruction of a pet as one form of psychological maltreatment. One can only speculate if siblings, in some cases, may abuse animals as a result of observing similar abuse performed by batterers.

RESEARCH OBJECTIVES

The objectives of the present study included determining: (1) the prevalence of pet ownership in a sample of women entering a shelter for battered partners in northern Utah,[1] (2) the prevalence of threatened and/or actual harm to pets by the women's partners, and (3) evidence for animal maltreatment by the women's children. In addition to quantitative information, qualitative information on the types of animal maltreatment described were examined. Ways that information about cruelty to animals could assist professionals who serve families experiencing domestic violence and who address animal welfare are also examined.

METHOD

Sample

Thirty-eight women seeking in-house services (as distinct from crisis telephone services) at a shelter for battered partners in northern Utah agreed to be interviewed by shelter staff about their experiences with maltreatment of pets (in a 1990 report, Rollins and Oheneba-Sakyi found

Utah spouse abuse prevalence to be comparable to national estimates). The women ranged in age from 20 to 51 years (mean age = 30.2) and reported the following marital status: married–57%, separated–3%, divorced–8% and single–32%. This was the first visit to the shelter for 54% of the women; the remaining women reported an average of 1.9 prior visits (range 1-6). For the 58% of women with children, the mean number of children was 2.8 (range 1-8) and their ages ranged from 8 months to 20 years.

Procedures

Women were interviewed by shelter personnel within a few days of their entry into the shelter and after the initial crisis circumstances had subsided. It was stressed that participation was confidential (only shelter staff would know participants' identities) and voluntary, and that decisions to agree to or refuse participation would not affect shelter services. None of the women approached declined participation.

The interview used an early version of the *Battered Partner Shelter Survey (BPSS)–Pet Maltreatment Assessment* (Ascione & Weber, 1995). Given the stress associated with entering a shelter, the number of questions was kept to a minimum. Interviewers did report, however, that many of the women were appreciative that someone had finally asked them about concerns they had for their pets.

The BPSS included the following questions:

- Do you now have a pet animal or animals?
    If yes, what kinds?
- Have you had a pet animal or animals in the past 12 months?
    If yes, what kinds?
- Has your partner ever hurt or killed one of your pets?
    If yes, describe.
- Has your partner ever threatened to hurt or kill one of your pets? If yes, describe.
- Have you ever hurt or killed one of your pets?
    If yes, describe.
    (if client has children)
- Have any of your children ever hurt or killed one of your pets?
    If yes, describe.
- Did concern over your pet's welfare keep you from coming to this shelter sooner than now?
    If yes, explain.

Completed BPSS forms were coded by shelter staff and then provided to the author for tabulation and analysis. Shelter staff also provided aggregate information on participants' marital status, presence and number of children, and women's reports of prior visits to the shelter.

RESULTS

Seventy-four percent of the women reported current pet ownership or pet ownership in the 12 months prior to the women's entry into the shelter. Of these women, 68% owned more than one pet. Dogs and cats were most common; one woman reported horses as pets, and fish, birds, chickens, rabbits, and a goat were also mentioned.

Nearly three-quarters (71%) of the women with pets reported that their male partner had threatened to hurt or kill and/or had actually hurt or killed one or more of their pets. Examples of the former included threats to put a kitten in a blender, bury a cat up to its head and "mow" it, starve a dog, and shoot and kill a cat. Actual harm or killing of animals was reported by 57% of the women with pets and included acts of omission (e.g., neglecting to feed or allow veterinary care) but most often acts of violence. Examples reported included slapping, shaking, throwing, or shooting dogs and cats, drowning a cat in a bathtub, and pouring lighter fluid on a kitten and igniting it.

Of the women with pets, two (7%) reported that they had hurt or killed one of their own pets. Both incidents were described as accidental (stepping on a kitten and running over a dog chasing the woman's car). In one case, there was also partner cruelty to animals, in the other there was none.

Twenty-two women had children and 32% (N = 7) of these women reported that one of their children (three girls and four boys) had hurt or killed a pet or pets. Behaviors ranged from sitting on a kitten and throwing a kitten against the wall to cutting a dog's fur and tail, pulling a kitten's head out of its socket, and sodomizing a cat. For 5 of these 7 cases (71%), the mother had also reported that her partner had threatened to or actually hurt or killed pets.

Eighteen percent of the women with pets reported that concern for their animals' welfare had prevented them from coming to the shelter sooner. Their concerns included worries for the animals' safety, fear of relinquishing pets to find affordable housing, placing pets with neighbors, and abandoning a pet to keep it away from the partner.

DISCUSSION

Although this study did not include comparison samples of non-battered women or battered women who are not currently in shelters, the substantial rate of partner cruelty to animals is clearly a cause for concern. Caution must be exercised in generalizing from this study's small sample to state and national samples; however, extrapolation of this study's findings may help estimate the scope of the potential problem. For example, 3 million is a conservative estimate of the number of U.S. women assaulted by their male partners each year (see Browne, 1993). If half of these women have pets (again, a conservative estimate [Ascione, 1992]), 71% partner cruelty to animals represents hundreds of thousands of families where pet victimization, actual or threatened, is part of the landscape of terror to which some women are exposed. Using the most recent Utah state statistics, over a thousand women in Utah alone may experience partner abuse of their pets. Abuse may include either threats or actual harm or both. Threats may be considered a less significant problem; however, Edleson and Brygger (1986) note that interventions for male batterers may reduce the frequency of abusive acts to a greater degree than threats of abuse. The latter may be more disturbing to some women.

There is some evidence that the results obtained in the present study are not unique to this particular sample of women. Arkow (1996) recently noted two surveys, one conducted in Colorado and the other in Wisconsin, in which 24% and 80%, respectively, of women seeking domestic violence assistance reported animal abuse by their partner.

Two women in the present sample admitted to hurting or killing their own pets, both described as accidental incidents. As noted earlier, Walker (1984) reported that some battered women admit to directing their anger at their children or pets and the fact that some batterers may hold women's pets hostage (Walker, 1989) may lead women to abandon their animals rather than leave them home as prey for batterers. These abandonments are understandable since shelters for battered women may not accept pets and alternative animal care may be financially difficult for a woman to arrange if she is seeking shelter for herself and her children. Programs to address this need are beginning to emerge, such as a collaborative effort in Loudoun County, Virginia among Loudoun Abused Women's Shelter, Loudoun County Animal Care and Control, the Humane Society of Loudoun County, and privately owned boarding kennels.[2] In cases where an animal has already been hurt or killed, women (and their children) may be experiencing unresolved grief about pet loss that may need to be acknowledged and addressed by shelter staff or counselors.

A number of practical and policy issues are raised when implementing programs to board animals of women who enter shelters (health, space, and animal/child management issues usually preclude allowing pets in such facilities). First, domestic violence shelter staff need to be trained about the potential significance of separation from pets and animal cruelty as additional emotional stressors for their clients, both women and children. Intake forms should include items related to women's experience of animal abuse and these items should also be added to the list of questions asked by crisis telephone line workers. Second, information about animal abuse may be valuable in developing safety plans for women who remain at home with their abusers and for those women planning to return home after a shelter stay. Third, if a woman places her pet for boarding, animal shelters need to develop policies ensuring the confidentiality of such placements and methods to deal with a batterer who attempts to claim a pet (in some cases, as a method of further coercing or intimidating his partner).

The reported prevalence of cruelty to animals by children in this sample is further cause for concern and is comparable to levels reported for mental health clinic samples of children, assessed with the Child Behavior Checklist (CBCL) and its variants (Achenbach & Edelbrock, 1981; Achenbach, Howell, Quay, & Conners, 1991), and to data from a sample of children who had been sexually abused (William Friedrich, April, 1992, personal communication). Friedrich noted that in a sample of 2-12 year olds who were substantiated victims of sexual abuse, 35% of the boys and 27% of the girls were reported to be cruel to animals on the CBCL (figures for a comparison group of nonabused boys and girls were 5% and 3%, respectively). In another report (Deviney et al., 1983), 26% of children who were physically or sexually abused and/or neglected displayed animal maltreatment. Although causal relations cannot be determined given the present study's descriptive strategy, children observing their parents' abuse of animals (along with other forms of violent and destructive behavior) may foster imitative cruelty. Educating battered women about the significance of children's cruelty to animals as a potential symptom of psychological distress may be warranted since some women may believe such behavior is cathartic. As one of our participants said, "We were all concerned about the cat and the dog but I figured it was better that the animals were dealing with his hostility instead of the kids or myself, the spouse."

IMPLICATIONS

Information about children's cruelty to animals may be relevant for interventions for children exposed to domestic violence. In some cases (e.g., Peled & Davis, 1995), therapy may involve asking children to identify with an animal to assist children in expressing emotions. Some children may also identify with animals as symbols of vengeance against a battering parent (e.g., Silvern & Kaersvang, 1989). Children may also identify themselves or their battered parent with a pet the children themselves have harmed. Therapists may be advised to routinely obtain information about cruelty to animals prior to using animal-related exercises. Furthermore, information about children's positive relations with and concern for their pets and other animals was not assessed in the present study but could also serve therapeutic ends (see Figure 1 where a 9 year old child has drawn himself cowering behind a couch as his mother and beloved pet bird are threatened by an abusive stepfather).

Legal Implications

The potential for cruelty to animals to be an indicator of the capacity for interpersonal violence has, in part, led to some states increasing their criminal penalties for severe animal maltreatment (one recent example is the State of Washington's 1994 revised cruelty-to-animals law). Increased penalties, including incarceration, for such cruelty can help remove violent individuals from the family and community and place them in settings where there is the potential for receiving therapy. In 1995, an Everett, Washington man received a one-year sentence (in addition to four years for intimidating a witness) after pleading guilty to first-degree animal cruelty for burning his partner's kitten in a kitchen oven ("Man gets 5 years in cat-torture case," 1995). He had also been charged with raping his partner (the witness he intimidated) but these charges were dropped in a plea bargain (the rape charge was dropped because the woman refused to press charges). As noted by one prosecutor, "We must, as prosecutors, recognize that it is unacceptable to excuse and ignore acts of cruelty toward animals. Anyone who can commit such cruelty is in desperate need of incarceration, counseling or other immediate attention. We cannot afford to accept such violence, nor will the public let us" (Ritter, 1996, p. 33).

Case Example

A vivid example of the confluence of spouse battering, child abuse (emotional and physical), and cruelty to animals is provided in recent reports of a murder trial in Salt Lake City. "Peggy Sue Brown was acquitted Thursday of fatally shooting her husband–the first time a defendant has used battered women's syndrome as a defense in a Utah murder case" (Hunt, 1996b, p. B1). "Brown testified she killed her husband after he beat, raped and locked her in a closet for days without food or water during their seven-year marriage. She said Bradley Brown, 23, had made

her a virtual prisoner in their home. He also beat and terrorized their young children" (p. B8). One of Ms. Brown's children testified that Mr. Brown had on one occasion kicked her one year old brother into a wall.

The level of terror Mr. Brown apparently instilled in his family members is illustrated by another incident noted during the trial. "(He) hung a pet rabbit in the garage and summoned his wife. When she came with the baby on her shoulder, her husband began skinning the animal alive. Then he held the boy next to the screaming rabbit. 'See how easy it would be?' Bradley said" (Hunt, 1996a, p. B3).

Recommendations

In addition to the relatively small and volunteer sample, this study has a number of limitations that should be addressed in future research. First, we relied solely on women's reports of their partners', own, and children's behavior regarding the treatment of animals. Sternberg et al. (1993) have cautioned that interreporter agreement about child problems, for example, between family members experiencing domestic violence, may be low. Edleson and Brygger (1986) found that partners in battering relationships may not agree on levels of different forms of violence a batterer perpetrates. In their sample of battered men who had undergone intervention, women and men's exact agreement, at intake, on the men's actions or threats against pets was 24%. Clearly, multisource assessments are needed in this area.

Second, sample size precluded examination of differential effects based on children's gender and age, issues Jaffe and Sudermann (1995) urged more thorough study. The present study also did not assess the levels of violence these women experienced and to which their children may have been exposed.

Third, there was no attempt to rate severity of partner cruelty to animals. More empirical information is needed about the forms, severity, and chronicity of partner cruelty to animals and its value for risk assessment (Straus, 1993), and the development of typologies of batterers (Holtzworth-Munroe & Stuart, 1994). We have developed a protocol for assessing the animal cruelty performed by children and adolescents (Ascione, Thompson, & Black, in press) which may be applicable to adults who abuse animals.

Finally, we do not yet understand how the dimensions of partner and/or child cruelty to animals differ for families where the mother seeks shelter or decides to remain at home. Do children's relations with pets differ in these circumstances? For example, Fantuzzo et al. (1991) note how the shelter experience often entails separating children from buffers in their home environment (e.g., toys, peers). Separation from beloved pets, who may be significant sources of psychological support and attachment, may be an unaddressed issue for both the child and the battered parent.

NOTES

1. In 1992, Utah state agencies provided shelter for 1,634 women and 2,047 children (Utah Domestic Violence Advisory Council, 1994). In 1995, the figures were 1,974 and 2,722, respectively (Diane Stuart, personal communication, January 25, 1996).

2. For information on this program, contact the Director, Loudoun County Department of Animal Care and Control, Rt. 1, Box 985, Waterford, VA 22190/TEL 703 777-0406.

REFERENCES

Achenbach, T. M., & Edelbrock, C. S. (1981). Behavioral problems and competencies reported by parents of normal and disturbed children aged four through sixteen. *Monographs of the Society for Research in Child Development, 46*(1, Serial No. 188).

Achenbach, T. M., Howell, C. T., Quay, H. C., & Conners, C. K. (1991). National survey of problems and competencies among four to sixteen-year-olds. *Monographs of the Society for Research in Child Development, 56* (Serial No. 225).

Adams, C. (1994). Bringing peace home: A feminist philosophical perspective on the abuse of women, children, and pet animals. *Hypatia, 9*(2), 63-84.

American Humane Association. (1995). Children's Division Policy Statements—Violence toward children and animals. *Protecting Children, 11*(1), 14d.

American Psychiatric Association. (1987). *Diagnostic and statistical manual of mental disorders* (3rd ed. rev.). Washington, DC: Author.

American Psychiatric Association. (1994). *Diagnostic and statistical manual of mental disorders* (4th ed.). Washington, DC: Author.

Arkow, P. (1995). *Breaking the cycles of violence*. Alameda, CA: The Latham Foundation.

Arkow, P. (1996). The relationships between animal abuse and other forms of family violence. *Family Violence and Sexual Assault Bulletin, 12*, 29-34.

Ascione, F. R. (1992). Enhancing children's attitudes about the humane treatment of animals: Generalization to human-directed empathy. *Anthrozoös, 5*, 176-191.

Ascione, F. R. (1993). Children who are cruel to animals: A review of research and implications for developmental psychopathology. *Anthrozoös, 6*(4), 226-246.

Ascione, F. R. (1995, October). A call for collaboration between child abuse and domestic violence advocates. *Child Protection Leader*. Englewood, CO: American Humane Association.

Ascione, F. R., Thompson, T. M., & Black, T. (in press). Childhood cruelty to animals: Assessing cruelty dimensions and motivations. *Anthrozoös*.

Ascione, F. R., & Weber, C. (1995). Battered partner shelter survey (BPSS). Logan: Utah State University.

Brassard, M. R., Hart, S. N., & Hardy, D. B. (1993). The Psychological Maltreatment Rating Scales. *Child Abuse & Neglect, 17*, 715-729.

Browne, A. (1987). *When battered women kill*. New York: Free Press.

Browne, A. (1993). Violence against women by male partners: Prevalence, outcomes, and policy implications. *American Psychologist, 48*, 1077-1087.

Campbell, J. C. (1995). Prediction of homicide of and by battered women. In J. C. Campbell (Ed.), *Assessing dangerousness: Violence by sexual offenders, batterers, and child abusers* (pp. 96-113). Thousand Oaks, CA: Sage.

Deviney, E., Dickert, J., & Lockwood, R. (1983). The care of pets within child abusing families. *International Journal for the Study of Animal Problems, 4*, 321-329.

Dutton, M. A. (1992). *Empowering and healing the battered woman*. New York: Springer.

Dykstra, C. (1995). Domestic violence and child abuse: Related links in the chain of violence. *Protecting Children, 11*(3), 3-5.

Edleson, J. L., & Brygger, M. P. (1986). Gender differences in reporting of battering incidents. *Family Relations, 35*, 377-382.

Fantuzzo, J. W., DePaola, L. M., Labert, L., Martino, T., Anderson, G., & Sutton, S. (1991). Effects of interparental violence on the psychological adjustment and competencies of young children. *Journal of Consulting and Clinical Psychology, 59*(2), 258-265.

Gelles, R. J., & Straus, M. A. (1988). *Intimate violence*. New York: Simon and Schuster.

Holtzworth-Munroe, A., & Stuart, G. L. (1994). Typologies of male batterers: Three subtypes and the differences among them. *Psychological Bulletin, 116*(1), 476-497.

Hunt, S. (1996a, November 13). Battered women's syndrome? *Salt Lake Tribune*, p. B3.

Hunt, S. (1996b, November 15). Battered wife is acquitted of murder. *Salt Lake Tribune*, p. B1.

Jaffe, P. G., & Sudermann, M. (1995). Child witnesses of woman abuse: Research and community responses. In S. M. Stith & M. A. Straus (Eds.), *Understanding partner violence* (p. 213-222). Minneapolis: National Council on Family Relations.

Koss, M. P., Goodman, L. A., Browne, A., Fitzgerald, L. F., Keita, G. P., & Russo, N. F. (1994). *No safe haven: Male violence against women at home, at work, and in the community*. Washington, DC: American Psychological Association.

Levinson, D. (1989). *Family violence in cross-cultural perspective*. Newbury Park, CA: Sage.

Man gets five years in cat-torture case. (1995, April 20). *The Seattle Times*, p. B2.

McCloskey, L. A., Figueredo, A. J., & Koss, M. P. (1995). The effects of systemic family violence on children's mental health. *Child Development, 66*, 1239-1261.

O'Keefe, M. (1995). Predictors of child abuse in maritally violent families. *Journal of Interpersonal Violence, 10*(1), 3-25.

Patrignani, A., & Villé, R. (1995). *Violence in the family: An international bibliography with literature review.* Rome, Italy: United Nation's Interregional Crime and Justice Research Institute.

Peled, E., & Davis, D. (1995). *Groupwork with children of battered woman.* Thousand Oaks, CA: Sage.

Renzetti, C. M. (1992). *Violent betrayal: Partner abuse in lesbian relationships.* Newbury Park, CA: Sage.

Ritter, A. W., Jr. (1996). The cycle of violence often begins with violence toward animals. *The Prosecutor, 30,* 31-33.

Rollins, B. C., & Oheneba-Sakyi, Y. (1990). Physical violence in Utah households. *Journal of Family Violence, 5,* 301-309.

Rosen, B. (1995). Watch for pet abuse—it might save your client's life. *Shepard's Elder Care/Law Newsletter, 5*(No. 5), 1-7.

Schecter, S., & Edleson, J. L. (1995). In the best interest of women and children: A call for collaboration between child welfare and domestic violence constituencies. *Protecting Children, 11*(3), 6-11.

Silvern, L., & Kaersvang, L., (1989). The traumatized children of violent marriages. *Child Welfare, 68,* 421-436.

Sternberg, K. J., Lamb, M. E., Greenbaum, C., Cicchetti, D., Dawud, S., Cortes, R. M., Krispin, O., & Lorey, F. (1993). Effects of domestic violence on children's behavior problems and depression. *Developmental Psychology, 29*(1), 44-52.

Straus, M. A. (1993). Identifying offenders in criminal justice research on domestic assault. *American Behavioral Scientist, 36,* 587-600.

Stuart, E. P., & Campbell, J. C. (1989). Assessment of patterns of dangerousness with battered women. *Issues in Mental Health Nursing, 10,* 245-260.

Suh, E. K., & Abel, E. M. (1990). The impact of spousal violence on the children of the abused. *Journal of Independent Social Work, 4,* 27-34.

Taylor, L., Zuckerman, B., Harik, V., & Groves. B. M. (1994). Witnessing violence by young children and their mothers. *Developmental and Behavioral Pediatrics, 15*(2), 120-123.

Utah Domestic Violence Advisory Council. (1994). *Five year state master plan for the prevention of and services for domestic violence.* Salt Lake City: Utah State Department of Human Services.

Walker, L. E. (1979). *The battered woman.* New York: Harper and Row.

Walker, L. E. (1984). *The battered woman syndrome.* New York: Springer Publishing.

Walker, L. E. (1989). *Terrifying love.* New York: Harper and Row.

Wiehe, V. R. (1990). *Sibling abuse.* Lexington, MA: Lexington Books.

Wiehe, V. R., & Herring, T. (1991). *Perilous rivalry: When siblings become abusive.* Lexington, MA: Lexington Books.

The Care of Pets
Within Child Abusing Families

Elizabeth DeViney, Jeffery Dickert,
and Randall Lockwood

Drs. DeViney and Dickert are with the Family Enrichment Program, Morristown Memorial Hospital, Morristown, New Jersey. Dr. Lockwood is with the Department of Psychology, State University of New York, Stony Brook, NY 11794. (Send requests for reprints to Dr. Lockwood.)

The treatment of animals was surveyed in 53 families in which child abuse had occurred. Patterns of pet ownership, attitudes towards pets and quality of veterinary care did not differ greatly from comparable data from the general public. However, abuse of pets by a family member had taken place in 60 percent of the families. The families in which animal abuse was indicated tended to have younger pets, lower levels of veterinary care and more conflicts over care than non-abusive families in the study. There were several parallels between the treatment of pets and the treatment of animals within child-abusing families, suggesting that animal abuse may be a potential indicator of other family problems. These findings also suggest that it may be helpful to review the role of pets in these families as part of the therapeutic process.

The belief that one's treatment of animals is closely associated with the treatment of fellow humans has a long history. Several philosophers have suggested this connection, even without accepting the concept of intrinsic rights of animals. In the thirteenth century Saint Thomas Aquinas, in *Summa Contra Gentiles*, followed his defense of exploitation of animals with the observation that:

> "...if any passages of Holy Writ seem to forbid us to be cruel to dumb animals, for instance to kill a bird with its young, this is...to remove man's thoughts from being cruel to other men, and lest through being cruel to other animals one becomes cruel to human beings..." (Regan and Singer, 1976, p. 59).

Immanuel Kant echoed these same sentiments 500 years later, suggesting that the only justification for kindness to animals was that it encouraged humane feelings towards mankind. In his essay on "Duties to Animals and Spirits" he wrote:

> "...Our duties towards animals are merely indirect duties towards humanity. Animal nature has analogies to human nature, and by doing our duties to animals in respect of manifestations of human nature, we indirectly do our duties to humanity." (Regan and Singer, 1976, p. 122).

In "Metaphysical Principles of the Doctrine of Virtue" he came to a similar conclusion regarding cruelty to animals:

> "...cruelty to animals is contrary to man's duty to himself, because it deadens in him the feeling of sympathy for their sufferings, and thus a natural tendency that is very useful to morality in relation to other human beings is weakened." (Regan and Singer, 1976, p. 125).

Reprinted from the *International Journal for the Study of Animal Problems* 4 (1983): 321–29, with kind permission of the Humane Society of the United States.

Writers sympathetic to the notion of animal rights have also proposed an association between kindness and cruelty to animal and man. Schopenhauer, in critique of Kant, proposed that:

"Boundless compassion for all living beings is the firmest and surest guarantee of pure moral conduct, and needs no casuistry. Whoever is inspired by it will assuredly injure no one, will wrong no one, and will encroach on no one's rights...The moral incentive advanced by me as the genuine is further confirmed by the fact that the animals are also taken under its protection." (Regan and Singer, 1976, pp. 125–126).

The simplest statement of this belief is Albert Schweitzer's comment that

"the ethics of reverence for life makes no distinction between higher and lower, more precious and less precious lives" (1965, p. 47).

There have been few attempts to systematically study the relationship between the treatment of animals and humans by specific individuals. Mead (1964) found evidence that, in a variety of cultures, torturing or killing of animals by a child may precede more violent acts by that individual as an adult. Several studies have focused on the frequent association between criminal violence in adulthood and persistent enuresis, fire-setting and animal abuse during childhood (MacDonald, 1963; Hellman and Blackman, 1966; Wax and Haddox, 1974: Felthous and Bernard, 1979).

Felthous (1980) suggested that physical abuse of a child may result in the child abusing animals and exhibiting other aggressive behavior against people which may persist into adulthood. Fucini (1978) indicated that violence against pets may be an indicator of other forms of family violence. Hutton (1981) reported that of 23 families in a British community known to the RSPCA for reasons of animal abuse or neglect, 82 percent were known to local social service agencies and were described by these agencies as having "children at risk" or signs of neglect and physical violence.

Beck (1981, p. 232) specifically suggests that:

"animal abuse has long been overlooked as an indicator, monitor, and even precursor to the antisocial behaviors people inflict on each other, including child abuse and neglect, spouse beating, rape, and homicide."

The present study was undertaken in an attempt to determine the extent to which pets are included in the patterns of abuse and neglect seen in abusive families. We see this as a first step in clarifying the role that pets play within the home of these families and in identifying possible ways of using information about the human/animal bond in the understanding and treatment of family violence.

Method

The sample consisted of fifty-three families involved with the New Jersey Division of Youth and Family Services for reasons of child abuse as defined by New Jersey Statute 9:6–1 of the Protective Custody Law. Under this law, an abused or neglected child is defined as any child under 18 years of age:

"whose parent or guardian inflicts or allows to be inflicted upon the child physical injury through other than accidental means which results, or potentially could result, in a substantial risk of death, a serious or prolonged disfigurement, or impairment or loss of function of any bodily organ;"

"whose physical, mental or emotional condition has been impaired because of the failure of his or her

parent or guardian to provide adequate food, clothing, shelter, education, medical or surgical care;"

"against whom a sex act has been committed by a person responsible for his or her care or by someone else permitted to commit such an act by the person responsible for the child's care; or"

"who has been willfully abandoned by his or her parent or guardian."

The sample was chosen from a pool of 200 such families on the basis of pet-ownership and availability for the study. A comprehensive interview schedule containing 55 questions was developed in consultation with several humane societies and experts on animal care. Questions dealt with demographic variables, pet care and attitudes toward pets, as well as general information on pets owned by the family over the last 10 years. A staff member of the Family Enrichment Program interviewed one adult or teenager in each household. The interviews took place in the family's homes. In each case they were conducted by a staff member currently working with the family who had observed interactions with pets at first hand. This approach allowed us to detect discrepancies between how the families stated they treated their

pets and the actual treatment observed.

Description of the Sample

The average age of adult respondents to the interview was 33.25 years. Three respondents were between 12 and 14. The families in this sample had an average of 2.7 children under the age of 18, with a mean age of 8.2 years.

The pattern of pet ownership in this sample was similar to that described in a variety of surveys of pet-owners (Table 1). The number of dogs owned by dog-owners was somewhat higher than in other studies (Table 2), but was within the typical range.

The majority of interviewees reported a positive attitude toward their pets. Sixty-seven percent reported that they had pets for companionship while 17 percent said that the main purpose was protection. Eighty-one percent indicated that they would feel sad or hurt if they lost or had to give up their pets. Three people specifically stated that they would feel like they had lost a child if anything happened to their pets and two mentioned that they would kill anyone who would try to harm their animals. The remaining 19 percent said they would be unconcerned or even happy if anything happened to their pets.

TABLE 1. Present Pet-Ownership in Pet-Owning Families

		This Survey	Franti et al. (1980)	Kellert (1980)	Griffiths & Brenner (1977)
	DOG	69	77	69	73
%	CAT	53	53	27*	42
OWNING	BOTH	28	33	NR	15
	EITHER	94	97	96	NR
	OTHER	6	3	4	NR

NR = not reported
*Kellert (1980) reported on only one pet/household (thus totals = 100%), so cat owners who also own dogs are not reported.

TABLE 2 Number of Pets Owned by Pet-Owners		
Study	**# Dogs/Dog-owning Household**	**# Cats/Cat-owning Household**
This Survey	1.84	1.89
Franti et al. (1980)	1.2–1.5*	1.4–2.1*
Griffiths & Brenner (1977)	1.24	1.95
Lockwood (1979)	1.96	2.11
Schneider & Vaida (1975)	1.2	1.4
Franti & Kraus (1974)	1.5	1.5

*Range across different communities surveyed

Most people spoke favorably of their pet's personality and behavior, using such descriptions as "happy", "loving", "friendly" and "playful". Only 9 percent used adjectives such as "nasty" or "nervous". One client, who admitted to brutally beating his cat regularly, described the animal as "very affectionate and cute and very playful".

In 36 percent of the families the children were described as having a "good", "loving" or "playful" relationship with pets in the family. In 26 percent of the families the children were reported to hit, kick, pester or annoy a pet. Six percent of the interviewees indicated that the children ignored or neglected the pets.

Care of Pets

Responses to questions on feeding, exercise and basic care did not differ noticeably from acceptable standards, but the socially acceptable replies were generally obvious. These questions yielded contradictions between the client's replies and the case workers' observations in 17 percent of the sample. For example:

"Mrs. G. said she gave the two dogs water three to four times daily. However, the animals never had food or water available to them (during the interviewer's visits) even on the hottest summer days."

Most people reported that they fed their animals commercial food one or two times a day and 90 percent indicated that water was continuously available or was given at least daily. There were a few unusual responses such as "he does not take water often — once a month" and "I give him water whenever he pants."

Table 3 gives the proportion of pet-owners who reportedly made use of veterinarians in our sample and in stratified samples in a variety of U.S. communities. The use of veterinary services among dog owners fell below the lowest rate reported for the general population. Use of such services among cat owners did not differ noticeably from that reported elsewhere. Use of veterinary services is closely associated with occupation and family income (Dorn, 1970; Franti et al., 1980). Within the population from which our sample was drawn, 21 percent are non-working, 37 percent are laborers and 14 percent service workers. Thus lower use of veterinary services may be explained by the tendency toward lower socio-economic status in our study group and among families with child abuse in general.

Fifty percent of the dog owners in our sample reported that their animals had been vaccinated. This is not inconsistent with the report that 60 percent had seen a veterinarian. However, 81 per-

	Dog-Owners	Cat-Owners
TABLE 3 Proportion of Pet-Owners Utilizing Veterinary Services		
This Survey	60%	66%
Franti *et al.* (1980)	74–91%	40–63%
Dorn (1970)	61–91%	65–78%

cent of the cat owners reported that their animals had been vaccinated, despite the fact that only two-thirds had reportedly been to veterinarians. This difference may be explained by the fact that several owners reportedly made use of free vaccination programs in some areas.

The reported incidence of spayed female dogs in our sample (27 percent) is slightly lower than the 32–36 percent rates reported in three separate demographic studies (Griffiths and Brenner, 1977; Heussner et al., 1978; Franti et al., 1980). The proportion of neutered cats owned by people in our sample (16 percent) was half the 33–34 percent value reported in those surveys.

Incidence of Animal Abuse

We defined animal abuse according to criteria stated by Leavitt (1978). Meeting one of these was sufficient for classifying a family as exhibiting animal abuse. The criteria were:

1. Observable or reported pain or suffering due to inflicted pain beyond forms of discipline commonly accepted in our society.

2. Causing the death of an animal in an inhumane manner.

3. Abandoning an animal in an environment which is not natural to it or in which it is incapable of surviving.

4. Failing to provide care as indicated by poor sanitary conditions, lack of proper nutrition, lack of shelter or inhumane confinement.

Twenty-five percent of the inter-

viewees affirmed that they or a member of their household had injured their pets at some time. In an additional 38 percent of the families the case worker observed animal abuse or neglect first hand which was either underreported or not reported in the interview.

Thirty-four percent of the interviewees gave indications that some of the pets they had previously owned had been either abused or neglected. This was inferred from reports of the manner in which pets had died, were lost, or disposed of. For example:

"Cat was shot by husband."

"Husband dropped off dog in the woods."

"Dog was let loose on the highway."

Kicking or punching small animals was the mildest treatment to be considered abuse in this survey. Other abusive actions included hitting the pet with a hard object (excluding sticks or newspaper), throwing hard objects at the pet or other acts that clearly endangered the animal's life.

In all, 60 percent of the families (N = 32) were identified as having had at least one family member who had met at least one of the criteria for abuse to a family pet. Thirty-six percent met the first criterion (pain and suffering), 6 percent met the second (inhumane death), 13 percent met the third (abandoning) and 25 percent met the fourth (neglect). Twenty percent of the families met two or more of the criteria. In the majority of cases falling into categories 1 and 2, one or both parents were the major source of abuse to the animals. In only 14 percent of these cases were the children the sole abusers of animals. Of 31 cases in which the identity of the abused animal was clear, 18 (58 percent) involved dogs, 10 (32 percent) involved cats, 1 (13 percent) involved both dogs and cats and 2 (6 percent) involved birds.

The interviewers commented favorably on the treatment and care of pets in only 5 of the 53 families (9 percent). Specific comments included:

"Takes obvious pride in her horse, she is a responsible owner."

"Pets are compassionately cared for."

"(The cat) is a very loved pet of this household. He gets more than adequate care and is the source of great amusement to the family."

Comparison of Pet-Abusers With Non-Abusers

Interview responses and field reports for the 32 families in which animal abuse had been reported were compared with those of the remaining 21 families in which no animal abuse had been indicated. There were no significant differences between these groups with respect to pet ownership and reasons given for owning pets. There were no differences in the use of positive adjectives in descriptions of the pets' personality.

The abusive and non-abusive groups showed differences with respect to their pets (Table 4). In general the abusive group had more younger pets and fewer pets over 2 years of age than their non-abusive counterparts or the general population. However, due to the small sample size these differences were not statistically significant. A high proportion of young animals in a population usually indicates high mortality and rapid turnover. This suggests that the abusive group did not have their pets for as long as the non-abusive group. The number of families that reported having pets that were lost, hit by a car, or ran away was not significantly different for the abusive and non-abusive groups.

We hypothesized that conflict over the care of a pet might be related to the incidence of animal abuse. There was evidence of disagreement over the feeding of pets. Forty-four percent of the abusive group and only 16 percent of the non-abusive group reported that the person who was supposed to feed the animal and the person who actually fed the pet were different ($x^2 = 4.19$, df = 1, p < .05). Viewed another way, 82 percent of those cases in which there was conflict over the feeding of the pet involved families in which animal abuse was reported.

Among dog and cat owners in the abusive group, 45 percent reported that they had never taken the animal to a veterinarian, compared to 29 percent in the non-abusive group. This difference was in the expected direction but was not statistically significant ($x^2 = 1.14$, df = 1, p < .2). In the non-abusive group, 88 percent reported that their dog or cat had received vaccinations compared to only 61 percent in the abusive group. As indicated earlier, these figures may represent exaggerations in a socially acceptable direction but the difference is significant ($x^2 = 3.86$, df = 1, p < .05). The two groups did not differ with respect to the proportion of dogs or cats that were spayed (all p > .5).

Some incidents of animal abuse may be due to an inability to control the animal. Twenty-two percent of the abusive group perceived their pets as not being well-behaved, compared to 6 percent in the non-abusive group. Although this difference was not significant ($x^2 = 2.3$, df = 1, p > .1), it suggests that pets that are abused tend to be or become behavior problems. It is possible that the abusive group had pets that were more aggressive or more difficult to control. This is sup-

TABLE 4 Age Distribution of Dogs and Cats

	DOGS		
	< 1 yr. old	1–2 yrs. old	> 2 yrs. old
with abusive owners (29)	31%	24%	45%
non–abusive owners (13)	15%	23%	62%
general pop.[1] (335)	18%	24%	58%

	CATS		
	< 1 yr. old	1–2 yrs. old	> 2 yrs. old
with abusive owners (17)	24%	47%	29%
non–abusive owners (13)	8%	38%	54%
general pop.[1]	17%	43%	40%

1. from Franti *et al.* (1980)

ported by the fact that 69 percent of the families with animal abuse reported that a family pet had injured a person, compared to only 6 percent of the families in the non–abusive group ($x^2 = 4.4$, df $= 1$, p $< .05$).

The abusive group differed from the non–abusive group with respect to the forms of discipline they employed with the pet (which was not used as a criterion to differentiate the two groups). Physical means (spanking with stick, hands or newspaper) were reportedly used by 88 percent of the non–abusive owners ($x^2 = 5.33$, df $= 1$, p $< .05$).

Comparisons of Form of Pet and Child Abuse

All of the families were involved with the Division of Youth and Family Services for reason of child abuse. It was possible to determine the form of abuse in 48 of the 53 cases. In 40% (N $= 19$) the children were physically abused. In 10% (N $= 5$) there was sexual abuse and

in 58% (N $= 28$) the children were in a neglectful home situation. In 4% of the cases (N $= 2$) there was risk of abuse due to psychiatric illness. In our sample of pet-owning child-abusers, 88% of the families in which physical abuse took place also had animals that were abused. In those cases where physical abuse of children was not present, animal abuse was seen in only 34% ($x^2 = 12.07$, df $= 1$, p $< .001$). Neither sexual abuse of children nor neglect differentiated the animal abuse from animal non–abuse groups.

Conclusions and Implications for Further Research

The families in this survey had all shown some impairment of their capacity to provide care for children. A large proportion also showed a breakdown in their capacity to care for pets. This findings lends empirical support to the belief that a battered pet may be a sign that other types of violence are occurring in the family (Fucini, 1978). It also lends considerable weight to the warning offered by Van Leeuwen (1981, p. 182):

> *"It would be sad...if in analogy to child abuse there persisted a reluctance to recognize the existence of animal abuse among the so-called accidental injuries brought to the veterinarian's attention. Greater awareness of animal abuse may lead veterinarians to initiate mental health intervention for the abusing family in addition to treating the animal."*

The relationship between animal abuse and child abuse is not a simple one. As with child abuse, most cases of mistreatment involved either long-term neglect or relatively few instances of clearly detectable harm (Cohen and Sussman, 1975). Repeated injury was not usually indicated. Abusers of animals and children alike often report deep affection for their victims, but we also found that 50 percent of the animal abusers with more than one pet tended to split them into "good" and "bad" pets, a theme that is common in cases of child abuse (Wasserman, 1967). Only 13 percent of the non-abusive group made such a distinction.

There are several parallels between the possible origins of violence to animals and to children. Some family violence may be seen in terms of "scapegoating" of an innocent and powerless victim by a recipient of violence. This could explain the involvement of children in animal abuse in 37 percent of the households in which pet abuse was reported. Another common theme in disturbed families is "triangling" in which aggression is directed against one family member indirectly through actions against a third (Minuchin, 1974). Since many family members have close bonds to pets, these animals can become the targets of abuse intended to hurt a person. This pattern has been reported by Robin *et al.* (1981) who found that a high proportion of delinquent adolescents had owned pets to

which they were closely attached but which had been killed by a parent or guardian.

Child abuse may also originate, in part, from a lack of familiarity with the needs of children or unrealistic expectations about their abilities. This was clearly a factor in several of the instances of animal abuse and neglect. Additional problems with both children and animals may come from unfamiliarity with effective ways of using reinforcement to achieve desired changes in behavior. Finally, family conflicts over responsibility for basic care of both children and animals may generate additional tensions that lead to abusive behaviors.

For reasons of confidentiality, we were unable to assess the relationship between particular patterns of child abuse and animal abuse in the families in this survey. We are currently conducting an intensive analysis of the involvement of pets in the family dynamics in a small number of families in which child abuse has occurred.

Even in families with child abuse, many members express great love and concern for animals. With clearer understanding of the role of pets within these families it should be possible to integrate the family's feelings and actions toward their pets into the therapeutic process as a tool for understanding both the healthy and unhealthy processes that are taking place. Ultimately the objective of those who work to prevent child abuse is the same as that of those who seek to prevent mistreatment of animals — to foster an ethic which appreciates the sensitivity of all life.

Acknowledgments

This study was supported by a grant from the Geraldine R. Dodge Foundation. We wish to thank the staff of the Division of Youth and Family Services and the Family Enrichment Program at Morristown Memorial Hospital for their assistance in conducting the interviews.

References

Beck, A.M. (1981) Guidelines for planning pets in urban areas. In Bruce Fogle (ed.) *Interrelations between People and Pets*. Springfield, Ill.: C.C. Thomas. pp. 231–240.

Cohen, S.J. and Sussman, A. (1975) The incidence of child abuse in the U.S. *Child Welfare 54*:432–443.

Dorn, C.R. (1970) Veterinary medical services: Utilization by dog and cat owners. *JAVMA 156*:321–327.

Felthous, A.R. (1980) Aggression against cats, dogs and people. *Child Psych. and Human Development 10*:169–177.

Felthous, A.R. and Bernard, H. (1979) Enuresis, firesetting and cruelty to animals: The significance of two-thirds of this triad. *J Forensic Sci 24*:240–246.

Franti, C.E. and Kraus, J.F. (1975) Aspects of pet ownership in Yolo County, California. *JAVMA 164*:166–171.

Franti, C.E., Kraus, J.F., Borhani, N.O., Johnson, S.L. and Tucker, S.D. (1980) Pet ownership in rural northern California (El Dorado County). *JAVMA 176*:143–149.

Fucini, S. (1978) The abuser: first a dog then a child? *American Humane 5*:14–15.

Griffiths, A.O. and Brenner, A. (1977) Survey of cat and dog ownership in Champaign County, Illinois, 1976. *JAVMA 170*:1333–1340.

Helman, D.S. and Blackman, N. (1966) Enuresis, firesetting and cruelty to animals: A triad perspective of adult crime. *Am J Psychiatry 122*:1431–1435.

Hutton, J.S. (1981) Animal abuse as a diagnostic approach in social work: A pilot study. Paper presented at International Conference on the Human/ Companion Animal Bond, Philadelphia, PA.

Kellert, S.R. (1980) American attitudes toward and knowledge of animals: An update. *Int J Stud Anim Prob 1*:87–119.

Leavitt, E.S. (1978) *Animals and Their Legal Rights*. Washington, D.C.: Animal Welfare Institute.

Lockwood, R. (1979) Reader survey of *Pet News Magazine*. *Pet News* Nov/Dec.

MacDonald, J.M. (1963) The threat to kill. *Am J Psychiatry 120*:125–130.

Mead, M. (1964) Cultural factors in the cause and prevention of pathological homicide. *Bulletin of the Menninger Clinic 28*:11–22.

Minuchin, S. (1974) *Families and Family Therapy*. Cambridge, MA: Harvard University Press.

Regan, T. and Singer, P. (eds.) (1976) Animal Rights and Human Obligations. New Jersey: Prentice-Hall.

Schneider, R. and Vaida, M.L. (1975) Survey of canine and feline populations: Alameda and Contra Costa Counties, California, 1970. *JAVMA 166*:481–486.

Robin, M., ten Bensel, R., Quigley, J., and Anderson, R. (1981) A study of the relationship of childhood pet animals and the psycho-social development of adolescents. Paper presented at International Conference on the Human/Companion Animal Bond, Philadelphia, PA.

Schweitzer, A. (1965) *The Teaching of Reverence for Life*. N.Y.: Holt.

Van Leeuwen, J. (1981) A child psychiatrist's perspective on children and their companion animals. In Bruce Fogle (ed.) *Interrelations between People and Pets*. Springfield, Ill.: C.C. Thomas. pp. 175–194.

Wasserman, S. (1967) The abused parent of the abused child. *Children 15*(5): 175–179.

Wax, D.E. and Haddox, V.G. (1974) Enuresis, fire-setting and animal cruelty: A useful danger signal in predicting vulnerability of adolescent males to assaultive behavior. *Child Psychiatry and Human Development 14*:151–156.

Connections Drawn Between Child and Animal Victims of Violence

Dr. Lynn Loar and Kenneth White

Reprinted from:The Latham Letter

Balanced perspectives on humane and related environmental issues
Published by the Latham Foundation, Alameda, California 94501
Volume III, Number 3, Summer 1992.

"If only it were all so simple! If only there were evil people somewhere insidiously committing evil deeds, and it were necessary only to separate them from the rest of us and destroy them. But the line dividing good and evil cuts through the heart of every human being. And who is willing to destroy a piece of his own heart?"

—Alexander Solzhenitsyn

Introduction

We met late in the Fall of 1990, both invited to join a panel discussion at the annual national meeting of the Humane Society of the United States. At our first meeting we immediately established that we both view our practical work as advocates for voiceless victims from the same philosophical starting point: that is, whether child or animal or, for that matter, dependent adult becomes victim, violence in itself is the problem. Cruelty and violence are the issue; the species of the victim is to a large degree determined by environment, opportunity and coincidence. Furthermore, cruelty and violence are tolerated, if not encouraged, by society.

Out of this meeting and the talk we gave at that first conference, our two agencies have joined to create the Humane Coalition Against Violence. The role of the coalition has been, essentially, educational. We have conducted a number of training seminars for child welfare workers, Animal Control and State Humane Officers, social workers, veterinarians and police inspectors. We have also acted as a resource for legislators considering a number of proposed modifications to state and local laws.

When the editor of the LATHAM LETTER approached each of us to author an introductory article on the topic of violence from our individual perspectives, we both readily accepted. As we considered the task, however, we came to see how interesting it might be for each of us to "stretch" to the other's course; for the social worker to speak about animals, and for the animal welfare worker to speak about children. Considering the nature of the topic as well as of the journal, we further agreed that these articles would best be written from a very personal perspective and purposely not intended as scholarly research papers.

Lynn Loar has worked in the field of social work for 10 years and currently is the Educational Coordinator for the San Francisco Child Abuse Council. This private non-profit organization's mandate is to advocate for children in those areas ignored or badly served by the "official system." Their programs include training for professionals who work with abused and neglected children, public awareness campaigns, and the development of model programs to address gaps in services. Examples include a pilot treatment program for sex offenders incarcerated in San Quentin Prison, an interdisciplinary developmental play therapy group, a drama and movement program for sexually abused children and a physical and recreational therapy program for toddlers who were prenatally exposed to drugs. Her article, "Upsetting Comparisons," describes the professional care available to her dog at a time of failing health and compares this to the level of medical care typically provided to a child removed from a family in crisis.

Kenneth White has worked in the field of animal welfare for 14 years and currently is the Deputy Director for the San Francisco Department of Animal Care and Control. This municipal government agency is responsible for the care of San Francisco's stray, abandoned, neglected and mistreated companion animals and wildlife, as well as for the enforcement of all local and state animal welfare and anti-cruelty laws. His article, "Watching Ralph Smile," is a personal remembrance of watching one child find something simple and extraordinary.

We both hope you find these articles of interest.

Upsetting Comparisons

Lynn Loar, Ph.D.

I am a social worker in the Bay Area, one of many working with abused and neglected children. Until recently I was also a pet owner; my dog died at age 14 of cancer. During her lifetime, I lived in North Carolina, Virginia, Washington DC, Maryland and California. In each location, I found excellent veterinary services for her, all of which charged affordable fees, provided extended hours during the week as well as weekend appointments in convenient locations, and rarely kept me waiting more than five or ten minutes for any scheduled appointment. Emergency care was swift and effective; inquiries and phone calls were promptly returned, and informative and practical advice was routinely given.

When I moved to California some seven years ago, I began using the services of a nearby veterinarian on the recommendation of several friends. Three years after he began to care for my dog, he surgically removed a small malignant growth from her mouth. Because of his specific knowledge of her health and the excellence of the care he provided, I continued to take my dog to him for treatment even after I moved 30 miles away two years later.

However, when the cancer began to grow into the dog's lungs, I became concerned about having to drive for an hour while she was experiencing difficulty breathing. A veterinary practice in my new locale advertised the availability of house calls, so I set up an appointment. A veterinarian and her assistant came (on time) to my home, took an extensive medical history, did a very thorough exam (mostly with the dog lounging on the couch and enjoying the attention—indeed, apologies were proffered to the dog when she was required to stand after repeated efforts to slide the stethoscope under her belly had failed), reviewed current medications, and explained their rationale for the house-call practice, namely that aging dogs and cats should be able to die at home in familiar settings rather than spend their last few hours in the stressful and unpleasant atmosphere of a veterinary office. I was encouraged to keep in touch, call for advice, and was presented with a bill for $60.00.

When my dog's health began to fail—on a Friday afternoon—my long-time veterinarian said in a telephone call that the dog might have a treatable infection perhaps due to her two years on prednisone, or the cancer might have filled her lungs. Blood work and a urine test were needed to determine the severity of the problem. I next called the veterinarian with the house-call practice who—although she was no longer on the house-call rotation—offered to stop at my home on her way to work at 8:30 Saturday morning to collect urine and blood samples. She said she would do the urine test herself upon arrival at her office and would send the blood sample to the lab in the noon run, with results available on Monday. Based on protein she found in the urine, my dog was started on antibiotics late Saturday morning. The treatment would be reassessed once the results of the blood test were available. My bill for the home visit, tests and medicine came to $100.00. I made an appointment for Monday afternoon with my primary veterinarian. By the time I arrived, both doctors had been faxed copies of the lab report and had conferred with each other about possibilities for treatment.

While I am glad I was able to provide this

quality of care for my beloved dog, I do not understand why so much less is available to the children I work with. The fact that this caliber of veterinary care is readily obtainable to the average uninsured consumer in so many states suggests that it is certainly possible to provide comparable care at reasonable cost to our children. Let me contrast the experience of providing care for my dog with attempting to seek medical care for abused and neglected children as a social worker with Child Protective Services in an affluent suburban county in the Bay Area.

Adequate medical care, unfortunately, is the exception rather than the rule for our nation's impoverished and uninsured children. Indeed, at least one-fifth of Caucasian and more than one-third of minority children grow up in poverty in our affluent nation. New immigrants, many of whom arrive in ill health, experience deprivation at substantially higher rates.

When a social worker must remove a child from his or her home, it is usually due to an emergency that endangers the child, abandonment by the parent(s), incapacity to care for the child by the parent(s) due to psychiatric dysfunction or drug or alcohol abuse, or ongoing sexual abuse in which the abusing adult has access to the child and the non-offending parent is unable or unwilling to protect the child. In the midst of this family crisis a social worker, who is usually a stranger to the child, has to remove the child from his/her home, take the child to the county hospital for a medical examination and then on to a foster home or ency shelter.

experience and that of my colleagues, waits of an hour or two in the hospital for a cursory physical exam (or grueling one if sexual abuse is involved) are not unusual, even though the social worker notifies the hospital ahead of time that the child is arriving. In addition, although most facilities have a special pediatric waiting room, the often-longer wait at the hospital pharmacy for a prescription (many poorly cared-for children have an untreated ear, throat or lung infection or similar illness) does not, and often exposes children to severely injured and disturbed patients while they wait in the hallway. The medicine must be obtained at the hospital pharmacy as the Medi-Cal paperwork has not been processed yet. Children entering placement are thus usually forced to endure four to six hours of transition from a crisis to placement with strangers.

In one case, I removed two small boys whose mother had overdosed on drugs and was taken by ambulance to the emergency room. The boys and I were waiting (for what turned out to be three hours) for medicine for their ear infections, when they noticed their own mother on a stretcher in the hallway, and overheard contemptuous talk about her and her drug habit by two hospital staff members.

Conscientious foster parents take the newly arrived child to their own pediatrician as soon as the child has made an initial adjustment to their home. Never have I seen records faxed from the former pediatrician, health center or hospital. In fact, it is rarely possible to get basic information on the child's medical history within a week or two. Enrollment in school in the foster parent's neighborhood is frequently delayed when proof of current immunizations is not immediately forthcoming from the former pediatrician or health center. In frustration, social workers or foster parents often make what should be an unnecessary trip to that doctor's office to obtain the records so that the child can enter school.

Not only is a child's health potentially compromised by the difficulty in obtaining information promptly, but also the child's safety. Even in Silicon Valley, computerized case records are a dream of a better funded future. Records are still handwritten, and filed by clerks; they are often inaccessible after hours or in emergencies. If a family has moved across county lines, records may be stored in several counties and not be recorded in the central registry in Sacramento (both due to Sacramento's backlog and the counties'). Unless the social worker knows the former county of residence and can prevail on an overworked stranger to pull an old record, the vital information of the severity of prior incidents of abuse or neglect will be unobtainable when the initial decision to remove the child or allow him/her to remain at home must be made.

Through my recent work with the San Francisco Department of Animal Care and Control, I have come to learn how successful humane workers can be in dealing with abusive and negligent adults. Indeed, they are often more able to resolve their cases than are child welfare and other social workers in similar situations. Rather than bemoan a society that appears to value its dogs and cats above its children, or fall into destructive infighting so common among helping professionals these days due to budgetary shortfalls and decreasing resources, I would hope my colleagues would look to our animal welfare counterparts as teachers. We need to learn how they have become so good at their work, and ask their assistance in a combined struggle against violence and neglect affecting any living creature.

Watching Ralph Smile

Kenneth White

It's been a bad week, a very bad week. The week began with a cat thrown from a third story window by an "angry" owner. (Hopefully, the cat will heal under our care and, hopefully, the legal system will work cooperatively with us in prosecuting the accused in a felony case of cruelty against animals.) This week's midpoint brought us an abandoned dog whose leather collar was so tight around the flesh of his neck that it had to be surgically removed, exposing a one-inch gouge of rotting tissue and maggots circling his throat. This week ended with a request for assistance from San Francisco Police Officers arresting someone who had settled an argument by using a shotgun. In his apartment they found three animals: a small black kitten dying of neglect, a live rattlesnake whose head had been taped to the bottom of a filthy cage, and a species of arboreal tarantula in a cage furnished with a plastic replica of a human skull.

It's also been a week which predicts that an annual horror is just on the horizon. For most people, the approach of spring is a time for joy; for animal welfare professionals, however, it is the beginning of "kitten season." Throughout the months of "kitten season," we will see somewhere between 30 and 50 kittens brought to our doors every single day. Most of them will be too young to be away from their mothers and many of them will be sick. Even for those healthy, friendly cats, the mathematics work against them—there are simply more animals brought in than there are homes. At this writing, still in winter, several newborn litters have arrived already and the seasonal increase in the number of animals which must be humanely killed is frighteningly close at hand.

As always, there have also been victories this week, each one precious. Twenty-nine lost dogs were returned to their homes and 32 more previously lost, abandoned, neglected or mistreated examples of "man's best friend" were placed with new and caring families. During this week the Department of Animal Care and Control was also able to reunite five lost cats with their anxious caretakers and find homes for 34 more.* But the heavy weight of this week has made it hard for me to take much solace in its high points. At these times I reach back for a very special memory, one which reminds me why I came to work in this field and, frankly, to help me keep going.

In 1977, fresh from graduate school, I was hired as a teaching assistant in a small special education school for adolescent boys. My students were all from very poor inner-city families. All were years behind academically, some barely able to read or write. Many of them had been abused, physically as well as emotionally, and were now in foster care. Depending upon the situation, all could be violent.

Ralph was in many ways the toughest of the bunch. At age 13, he already had his "male bravado pose" firmly in place. His walk was cool, his talk was cool, and his face rarely revealed his thoughts or emotions. On one typically drizzly San Francisco spring day, the teacher and I decided to reward Ralph's unusually cooperative recent behavior with a trip to the beach. One-on-one trips to the beach, me and a kid for the afternoon school session running along the sand looking for shells and rocks, had become a school favorite. This was the first time Ralph was to be given the opportunity.

We drove by my house for our other companion, Hamish, my big black and brown and very goofy dog, hopped inside the camper shell on the back of my pick-up truck ready for the five-minute drive to the beach. He, too, loved these trips.

I was startled to learn during our brief drive that Ralph, a native San Franciscan, had never been to the beach which begins where our City ends. Living at home with his mother along with several other children, Ralph had never seen the Pacific Ocean even though he had spent his entire life just a few minutes from it. He responded to my surprise with a couple of typically sarcastic comments about sand, dirt and water. In reality, this lack of parent interaction was, of course, entirely insignificant in comparison to the real neglect and abuse which made up most of his early life at home.

In San Francisco, one drives right up to this nation's paved Western border, parks and then walks down a few steps onto a narrow beach. At the top of the stairs Ralph became mute and his mouth opened wide. Surprisingly, he grabbed my hand and held on tightly as we walked down the steps onto the sand. Hamish, of course, went nuts, dashing back and forth, barking, and running in and out of the water. But Ralph just stared.

Ralph stared at the water so hard and so long that I began to get worried. And, then, without saying a word he started to walk. Like a magnet, the Pacific pulled him straight on. Slowly he walked towards and then into the water. I grabbed him back out as his ankles got soaked and carried him back onto the sand. Then, still without saying a word, he repeated this sleepwalker's stride into the ocean again.

Halfway to the water on Ralph's third strange trip, Hamish, either curious or concerned by this unusual human behavior, interceded in the not-so-subtle manner peculiar to big dogs. He literally threw himself into Ralph, knocking them both down onto the sand. Legs and arms

and sand exploded for a second and then everything got very still. Ralph first looked about, and then suddenly burst out with the first real laugh I had ever heard from him. He laughed and laughed and laughed while Hamish pranced about wagging his tail, barking at the air and then licking his young friend.

The rest of the afternoon was wonderful, although Ralph never could put into words what he had felt or thought during those first strange minutes. For the rest of the day, we were three friends enjoying each other and the world around us.

For an afternoon, 15 years ago, I saw Ralph smile. I saw a small, frightened and neglected child enjoy a walk along the beach with a dog. I saw them run and fall and run again. It is Ralph's smile that reminds me why I came to work in this field of people and other animals. After a week like this one, it is Ralph's smile that helps keep me going.

The San Francisco Department of Animal Care and Control's Animal Shelter houses approximately 16,000 animals each year. In 1991, a total of 2,115 cats were either reunited with their owners or adopted into new homes and 6,496 were put to death; 2,149 dogs were either reunited with their owners or adopted into new homes and 1,476 were put to death; 1,750 "other" animals, including native wildlife, exotic animals and other domestic pets were either returned to their native habitats, reunited with their owners or adopted while 2,235 were put to death.

The Shape of Cruelty

Kenneth White

If cruelty were an object—a thing in and of itself—what shape would it have? How would one recognize it? Certainly not a simple shape. For example, not a line making causal connections between stimulus and response, environment and behavior; nor a circle narrowly and obviously defining itself, distinct from everything outside its circumference.

Writing about the link between abuse to children and abuse to animals, Dr. Randall Lockwood of the Humane Society of the United States eloquently coins the terms "The Tangled Web" as a way of illustrating the interconnectedness of his subject.* For our purpose, I prefer to think of children's drawings I've seen of single cell animals observed under a microscope: many limbed amorphous creatures reaching out in every direction, crossing themselves, difficult to describe.

Whatever its shape, cruelty has no beginnings and no endings. If Adolph Hitler and Idi Amin are deep in the center of cruelty's shape, where do we place the person who spanks his/her child, or the individual who enjoys gratuitous and explicit violence against women in film? We know where to place Dwayne Wright,

arrested by the Pennsylvania SPCA for pouring lye onto six dogs "just to see the dogs suffer" according to their investigative report, but where do we fit the factory farm owner or even the diner sitting down to a meal of steak and lobster? Cruelty has no beginnings or endings but it surely touches us all, both as victims and as perpetrators.

This tangled web or this many-limbed and fluid creature has, of late, been the topic of study to look at the inter-connectedness of violence against animals and children. Consider the following, just a few examples of many:

- Albert DeSalvo, better known as the "Boston Strangler" who savagely killed 13 women in the early 1960's, had as a child trapped dogs and cats in orange crates and shot arrows into the boxes.

- Carrol Edward Cole, executed in 1985 as one of this country's most prolific mass murderers. His first recorded act of violence as a child was to strangle a cat.

- Ted Bundy, executed in 1989 for one of as many as 50 murders, claimed that he spent much of his childhood with his grandfather torturing animals. Evidence also links Bundy to graves filled with animal bones in Utah.

After review of the literature available, I offer the following:

- that a number of victims of child abuse will look for victims of their own, whether while still children or as adults, and that certainly a small animal makes a convenient target;

- the link between abuse of animals as a child and violent behavior as an adult is frighteningly well documented;

- that violence against animals can be seen as a predictor or even a training ground for future violent acts against people.

Although the question may appear ridiculous to many of us, if some myopic individual wants to know why we are so worried about animals when children are suffering, it is fair to answer that although the victims are different the phenomena are inseparable. To dismiss concern for either children or animals only hurts the promise of a better future for both.

Author's Note: Dr. Lockwood's "Training Key #392" developed for the International Association of Chiefs of Police and his article "The Tangled Web" (co-authored with Guy Hodge and published in HSUS' Summer 1986 "Humane Society News") are two vital documents on the subject of violence against animals and people. I owe a great deal to Dr. Lockwood's thoughts on this topic, expressed both in writing and in personal communication.—KW

History of the Humane Coalition Against Violence

Although recognition of horrible realities can initially paralyze one, it is these beliefs which led Dr. Lynn Loar of the San Francisco Child Abuse Council and Kenneth White of the San Francisco Department of Animal Care and Control to form the Humane Coalition Against Violence (HCAV). Working cooperatively with other professionals from both animal welfare and child protective services, we present the following chronology of some of our activities, in part as an example of what is possible for other communities.

October 1990: HCAV forms the basis of a workshop on the topic "Violence: Its Human and Animal Victims" at the annual national conference of the Humane Society of the United States.

December 1990: HCAV speaker delivers the keynote address to a meeting of the California Animal Control Directors' Association.

February 1991: HCAV author publishes a guide for animal welfare workers on how to assess and report suspicions of child abuse and neglect, in the professional journal CHAIN ("California Humane Action and Information Network").

April 1991: HCAV joins the faculty of the California State Humane Officers Training Academy for animal welfare and anti-cruelty law enforcement professionals.

July 1991: HCAV presents a basic course on how to assess and report suspicions of child abuse and neglect for San Francisco Bay Area State Humane and Animal Control Officers.

August 1991: HCAV meets with the San Francisco Department of Social Services Emergency Response Unit Program Manager to develop a protocol for cases involving neglected or abused children and animals.

August 1991: HCAV contributes to an article entitled "Is There A Difference Between Animal Abuse and Child Abuse?" published in the professional journal ANIMAL WARDS.

September 1991: HCAV conducts training for the San Francisco Police Department Juvenile Division.

November 1991: HCAV meets with representatives of the Children's Advocacy Institute and the Humane Society of the United States to formulate a legislative agenda with the expectation of adding Animal Control and State Humane Officers to the list of mandated reporters of suspected child abuse and neglect.

January 1992: At the invitation of the Latham Foundation, HCAV speakers open the second day of a California conference on animal issues held at the University of California at Davis.

January 1992: HCAV meets with the legislative aide to a member of the San Francisco Board of Supervisors to discuss model legislation.

February 1992: HCAV conducts a workshop at a statewide conference sponsored by the California Consortium for the Prevention of Child Abuse.

March 1992: HCAV addresses the California Veterinary Medical Association House of Delegates.

March 1992: HCAV addresses the Public Safety Committee of the California State Assembly on behalf of a bill proposed by Assemblyman Jack O'Connell which would add Animal Control and State Humane Officers to the list of mandated reports of suspected child abuse.

April 1992: HCAV addresses the State Humane Association.

Scheduled in the near future: The Humane Coalition Against Violence will also be featured presenters on the topic of cruelty against children and animals at conferences sponsored by the American Humane Association, the California Animal Control Directors' Association, the Humane Society of the United States, and the Latham Foundation.

Bringing Peace Home: A Feminist Philosophical Perspective on the Abuse of Women, Children, and Pet Animals

CAROL J. ADAMS

In this essay, I connect the sexual victimization of women, children, and pet animals with the violence manifest in a patriarchal culture. After discussing these connections, I demonstrate the importance of taking seriously these connections because of their implications for conceptual analysis, epistemology, and political, environmental, and applied philosophy. My goal is to broaden our understanding of issues relevant to creating peace and to provide some suggestions about what must be included in any adequate feminist peace politics.

I. INTRODUCTION

I have been a vegetarian since 1974. In 1978, I started a hotline for battered women in rural upstate New York where I lived at that time. Because my vegetarianism was motivated by a concern for animals, I began to notice that animals—as well as the batterer's female sexual partner—were often victimized by violent men. For instance, one day a woman whom we had been helping to leave her violent husband called to report what had happened when he returned the children after his visitation was over. The children, the husband, and the wife were all sitting in his pickup truck in the driveway. Something occurred that enraged him. Simultaneously, the family dog appeared in the driveway. He plunged the truck forward so that it ran over the dog. He then threw the truck in reverse and backed over the dog. He repeated this forward-backward motion many times. Then he got out of the truck, grabbed his shotgun, and, in front of his devastated family, shot the dog several times.

Empirical evidence indicates that acts of sexual exploitation, including physical battering of sex partners, often involve violence against other animals as well. Drawing on a model provided by Karen J. Warren (Warren 1992,

Warren forthcoming) I will make explicit the variety of connections between sexual violence and injury to animals which I will call the woman-animal abuse connections. I will then demonstrate the importance to feminist philosophy of taking seriously these empirical connections because of their implications for conceptual analysis, epistemology, political philosophy, environmental philosophy, and applied philosophy. In doing this, I hope to set a standard and provide a set of suggestions about what must be included in any adequate feminist peace politics. It is not my goal in what follows to use the examples of the abuse of animals solely to illustrate how women and children are made to suffer. Then I would recapitulate on a philosophical level what the abuser actually does, using animals instrumentally. Instead, I seek to broaden the reader's worldview about what counts as "feminist peace issues" to include concern about the connections between abuse of animals and women.

This essay takes Elizabeth Spelman's (1982) implicit understanding that somatophobia—hostility to the body—is symptomatic of sexism, racism, classism, *and* speciesism, and demonstrates how hostility to despised and disenfranchised bodies, that is, those of animals, children, women, and nondominant men, becomes interwoven. To avoid somatophobia, feminist philosophy must take the connections between abuse of animals and abuse of women seriously.

II. Terminology

Several terms which feature in my argument deserve attention up front. I will use the conventional term "pet" to describe animals who are a part of a household.[1] Those involved in the movement to free animals from human oppression prefer the term "companion animal." While I find this term helpful, the word "pet" suggests some commonalities between sexualized behavior and animals: the term "pet" also connotes sexual activity, specifically, fondling and caressing.

Battering is a component or kind of sexual violation, since it occurs against one's sexual partner. Catharine MacKinnon's insights on this matter are helpful: battering "is sexually done to women. Not only in where it is done— over half of the incidents are in the bedroom. Or the surrounding events— precipitating sexual jealousy. . . . If women as gender female are defined as sexual beings, and violence is eroticized, then men violating women has a sexual component" (MacKinnon 1987, 92).[2]

One might suggest that the violence examined in this essay is really "male violence." But the minute we widen the scope of inquiry to include the other animals, we must proceed with sensitivity to the way language may be inaccurate. The anthropocentric presumption that "male" and "female" can be used interchangeably with "men" and "women" is erroneous. What is actually being discussed is human-male violence. While in what follows I am vigilant in using the adjective human to qualify male, I will abide with convention in discussing animal abuse, allowing that meaning to exclude human animals. Moreover, personally and philosophically I find the use of the pronoun "its" disturbing when used to refer to nonhuman animals. However, again, for the purpose of continuity of narratives when providing the empirical information, I will not intercede with [sic]s when "its" is used.

III. EMPIRICAL EVIDENCE

Karen J. Warren argues that understanding the empirical connections between women and nature improves our understanding of the subordination of women while also establishing the practical significance of ecofeminist philosophy (Warren 1992). Empirical connections that reveal connections between the abuse of animals and the abuse of women expose another layer of intentional infliction of suffering by violent men, another way of comprehending the phenomenology of sexual violation. I am concerned about what this control and terror means for women and our subordination, *and* for animals and their subordination.

Testimony from survivors and their advocates indicate two significant configurations in which sexually violent men harm women, children, and animals. There is a threat or actual killing of an animal, usually a pet, as a way of establishing or maintaining control over women and children who are being sexually victimized. And, there is a use of animals in sexually violating women or children, or the use of animals to gain some sort of sexual gratification. Of concern is a third way in which sexual exploitation influences behavior toward animals: anecdotal evidence suggests that child victims of sexual abuse injure animals. These configurations will be discussed under the specific forms that the sexual exploitation takes: battering, marital rape, pornography, child sexual abuse, ritual abuse, serial killing, and sexual harassment. Taken together, this evidence, as we will see, has striking implications for feminist philosophical considerations.

Battering is one form of human male sexual violence that victimizes women, children, and animals. Threats and abuse (often fatal) of pets by a woman's sexual partner occur in his attempts to establish control. As with other forms of battering, the killing of a pet is "done to show control and domination" (Ganley [1981] 1985, 16). Lenore Walker points out, "As a way to terrorize and control their women, batterers have even been known to hold pets hostage" (Walker 1989, 76). According to guides on identifying a batterer, the following are warning signs: he hunts; he own guns; he has threatened, harmed or killed a pet (Statman 1990). "Abusers are often cruel to animals. Many kill them for sport, and this should not be minimized. Anyone who beats a dog or other pets should be considered a potential batterer" (Pope-Lance and Engelsman 1987, 40). Bonnie Burstow, a radical feminist and therapist warns that the killing of a pet by a human male heterosexual partner is one of the signs that "the woman is in an imminently life-threatening situation and immediate action is called for" (Burstow 1992, 149). For instance, one man slashed two pet cats to death and then threatened to turn the butcher knife on his wife and her dog (*Dallas Times Herald*, June 15, 1991). In another incident, Molly, after a brutal battering by her husband that lasted several hours, "realized he was laughing. Molly had seen him beat a dog like that once, slowly until it died. She remembered that he had laughed then, too." Shortly after that, Molly killed her husband in self-defense (Browne 1987, 133; see also Walker 1989, 20-21).

Diana Russell describes an incident that occurred in California: "[Michael] Lowe casually pumped a shot into the dog. The sheepdog ran under the family's truck, cowering in pain as Lowe went back into the house and returned with a .30-.30 Winchester rifle. He called to the animal and made her sit in front of him as he fired five more shots, killing the family pet [in front of the family]. Three months later he did the same to his wife. Then he killed himself" (Russell [1982] 1990, 296). Anne Ganley, a psychologist who has pioneered in victim-based counseling for batterers, identifies "the destruction of property and/or pets" as one of four forms of battering (along with physical, sexual, and psychological battering). She observes that: "typically, the offender and the victim do not identify the destruction of property/pets as part of the battering; yet it is. The offender's purpose in destroying the property/pets is the same as in his physically attacking his partner. He is simply attacking another object to accomplish his battering of her. Sometimes we minimize the seriousness of this form of battering by saying that at least it is better than hitting her. Unfortunately, it often has the same psychological impact on the victim as a physical attack" (Ganley [1981] 1985, 15). (And we need to remember that pet battering *does* injure someone.)

Angela Browne found that many of the women she interviewed who had killed their husbands in self-defense frequently reported destruction of animals: "These incidents often seemed to the women a representation of their own death" (Browne 1987, 157). The killing of pets often resulted in the loss of a battered woman's last hope.

> The kitten was sitting in the yard. Billy got his rifle, walked up to it, and shot it. Then he hunted down the other two cats and shot them. Kim was hysterical—following him around, tugging on him, jumping up and down and screaming. She begged him not to kill the cats, and after he had, she begged him not to leave them there. So he picked them up and threw them over the fence. After Billy went to sleep that night, Kim crept out, found the cats, and buried them. Then she laid down in the field and cried. (Browne 1987, 153-54)

When the husband destroys a pet, he may be destroying the woman's only source of comfort and affection.[3]

A little-studied form of battering involves the use of animals for humiliation and sexual exploitation by batterers and/or marital rapists. This is the second form of sexual violence victimizing women and animals. Batterers and *marital rapists* (and the two groups are neither mutually exclusive nor completely inclusive of each other) may train dogs to "have sex with" their wives (Russell [1982] 1990, xii) or force their wives to have sex with a dog: "He would tie me up and force me to have intercourse with our family dog. . . . He would get on top of me, holding the dog, and he would like hump the dog, while the dog had its penis inside me" (Walker 1979, 120). The batterer's/rapist's control is amplified by requiring humiliating acts of his victim. Linda Marchiano ("Linda Lovelace") threatened by her batterer, Chuck, with death, was subjected to sex with a dog ("Lovelace" 1980, 105-13; see also 206): "Now I felt totally defeated. There were no greater humiliations left for me" (113). She explained, "From then on if I didn't do something he wanted, he'd bring me a pet, a dog" (112). As with the preceding cases, the threat or actual use of a pet to intimidate, coerce, control, or violate a woman is a form of sexual control or mastery over women by men.

A third linking of violence against women, children, and animals to human male sexual violence is *pornography*. One genre of pornography features sexual activity "between" humans and animals. (I qualify this term since I believe this activity to be coercive.) Bears, snakes, and dogs—to name just a few of the species of animals incorporated into pornographic films—are shown in a variety of sexual and sexualized positions with women. Linda "Lovelace's" sexual violation with a dog was filmed and became a popular pornographic loop. This loop—often cited by reporters and others in response to *Ordeal* ["Many who have seen *Deep Throat* or another, even sleazier film in which her co-star was a dog, will argue that Linda Lovelace liked what she was doing, and liked it a lot." ("Lovelace" 1986, 141, quoting Chip Visci of the Detroit *Free Press*)]—depicts what Marchiano considers "the worst moment of my life" ("Lovelace" 1986, 194). There is some evidence that some viewers of pornography have attempted to duplicate such scenes in abusing their partners (see Russell 1984, 126).

My fourth case-in-point concerns *child sexual abuse*. The testimony of survivors of child sexual abuse reveal that threats and abuse of their pets were often used to establish control over them, while also ensuring their silence, by forcing them to decide between their victimization or the pet's death. Sylvia Fraser poignantly describes the dilemma this threat by her father-rapist presented to her as a child:

> Desperation makes me bold. At last I say the won't-love-me
> words: "I'm going to tell my mommy on you!"

My father needs a permanent seal for my lips, one that will murder all defiance. "If you say once more that you're going to tell, I'm sending that cat of yours to the pound for gassing!"

"I'll . . . I'll . . . I'll . . ."

The air swooshes out of me as if I have been punched. My heart is broken. My resistance is broken. Smoky's life is in my hands. This is no longer a game, however desperate. Our bargain is sealed in blood. (Fraser 1987, 11-12)

This type of threat is not restricted to father-daughter rape. Alice Vachss, formerly a prosecutor of sex crimes, reports on this phenomenon in *Sex Crimes*: children "are threatened with huge, child-oriented consequences if they tell. The molester kills a kitten and says the same thing will happen to the child" (Vachss 1993, 465). One chilling case example involved a two-and-a-half-year-old girl whose abuser claimed to have killed the pet rabbit, cooked it, and forced her to eat it, warning her that if she reported the abuse, the rabbit's fate would be hers (see Faller 1990, 196).

Besides physical abuse of animals by child sexual abusers, there is the sexual use of animals by some child sexual abusers. In these cases, the sexual use of animals seems to enhance or expand or extend the abuse of the genuinely powerless and unsuspecting victim. For instance, one colleague reported a case in which a veterinarian, upon discovering that the dog had a sexually transmitted disease, made a referral that resulted in the discovery that the father was also sexually abusing his two pre-adolescent daughters. And there are others cases (see Faller 1990, 56-57).

A child may injure animals or pets or "stuffed animals" as a sign or signal or expression that something is very wrong. Abuse of animals is recognized in the most recent revision of the *Diagnostic and Statistical Manual of Mental Disorders of the American Psychiatric Association* (DSMRIII 1987) as one of the symptoms indicative of Conduct Disorder (see Ascione 1993). A pre-adolescent boy who had been brutally raped by his father described how he would tie a firecracker around a cat and watch as it exploded. Brohl reports that "an adult survivor tearfully related that when she was seven years old she drowned her cat" (Brohl 1991, 24). While Ascione cautions that "much of the information on the relation between sexual abuse of children and children's cruelty toward animals is derived from retrospective research," he is also able to provide some information drawn from a more reliable methodology:

William Friedrich (April, 1992, personal communication) has generously provided data from a large-scale study of *substantiated* cases of sexual abuse in children 2-12 years of age. Most of these children had been victimized within twelve months of data collection that included administration of the Child Behavior Checklist (Achenbach 1988). Parental reports of cruelty to animals were 35% for abused boys and 27% for abused girls; the percentages were 5% for nonabused boys and 3% for nonabused girls, a highly significant difference based on clinical status.(Ascione 1993, 238-39)

Though the existence of *ritual abuse* continues to be debated in the social science literature and in the popular press, mutilated animals have been found in various parts of the country, and victims and some perpetrators describe the central role that killing animals has in ritual abuse (see for instance Raschke 1990, 39-41, 61, and passim). Consequently, reports of ritual abuse indicate a fifth pattern of patriarchal violence against women and other disenfranchised adults, children, and animals in which all aspects of abuse of animals is evident (see Hudson 1991, Anonymous 1992, Gould 1992, Young 1992, Smith 1993). To review, there are threats, abuse, torture, and killing of pets and other animals to establish control. Additionally, there is the use of animals for humiliation and further sexual exploitation. For instance, Elizabeth Rose reports forced sexual contact with animals as one aspect of ritual abuse (Rose 1993, 44). Last, injury to animals is one way that a child signals that something is wrong. Psychologists who have worked with survivors of ritual abuse indicate that, along with several other specific actions, physical symptoms, and preoccupations, harming animals or describing animals that have been hurt can be a warning sign that a child has been a victim of ritual abuse.

A sixth linking of violence against women, children, nondominant men, and animals to human male sexual violence is the *killing of animals by serial murderers* and other murderers who rape and mutilate. Serial killers share some common features: they are likely to report their crimes, are almost always male and usually younger than 35, and "the earliest acting out of sadistic impulses often occurs in the early teens in the form of torturing and killing animals such as cats and dogs" (Lunde 1976, 53). For instance, as a child, serial killer Jeffrey Dahmer searched the neighborhood for roadkills that he kept in a toolshed; kept the bones of racoons, dogs, cats, ground-hogs, squirrels, and chipmunks inside formaldehyde-filled pickle jars; kept an animal graveyard with skulls on top of crosses; and collected stuffed owls, rabbits, and small birds. According to one psychologist, David Silber, "His behavior didn't change. The objects changed" (quoted in Dvorchak 1991). Cruelty to animals in childhood was one of the significant differences in behavioral indicators between sexual murderers who were themselves abused before they became abusers and murderers without such a history (see Ressler et al. 1986).

Last, *sexual harassment* often includes pornographic material involving explicit depictions of human-animal sexual activity or reference to this material. Since an adequate discussion of sexual harassment takes me beyond the scope of the essay, I mention it here only to be sure it is included in the patterns of ways human male sexual violence has operated to subordinate women, children, and animals in interconnected ways. According to the testimony of their victims, sexual harassers incorporate this pornography that depicts animals with women into their victimization activities. Moreover, again according to victims and akin to Marchiano's experience, it is this aspect of sexual harassment that is the most humiliating. For instance, during the hearings to review the nomination of Clarence Thomas to the Supreme Court, held in October 1991 before the Senate Judiciary Committee, we heard from Anita Hill of Thomas's references to pornography: "I think the one that was the most embarrassing was his discussion of pornography involving these women with large breasts and engaged in a variety of sex with different people or animals. That was the thing that embarrassed me the most and made me feel the most humiliated" (Phelps and Winternitz 1993, 315).

IV. PHILOSOPHICAL IMPLICATIONS OF THE EMPIRICAL EVIDENCE

We have seen how animals are victims, too, through a variety of acts of sexual violence and exploitation. Truly this material on the connection between abuse of women, children and nondominant men and abuse of animals is painful to encounter. But only by taking this material seriously can we expand our knowledge about sexual violation and recognize its implications for feminist philosophy. In this section, I will show the importance of the connections of abuse of women and animals for feminist philosophy by examining the specific areas of conceptual analysis, epistemology, political philosophy, environmental philosophy, and applied philosophy.

V. CONCEPTUAL ANALYSIS

The empirical evidence cited above details a shocking hostility to the bodies of disenfranchised others—women, children, nondominant men, and animals. As Elizabeth Spelman recognized when she proposed the concept of somatophobia (hostility to the body), one of the important reasons for feminists to recognize somatophobia is to see the context for women's oppression and the relationship it has with other forms of oppression. Clearly, women's oppression is interwoven with that of animals, so that women and animals are both trapped by the control exercised over their own *and* each other's bodies (i.e., women and children who stay silent because of abusers' threats to their pets; pets who are killed to establish a climate of terror).

Spelman believes that it is important for feminists to recognize the legacy of the soul/body distinction and its use in denigrating women, children, animals, and "the natural," who are guilty by association with one another and with the bodily (Spelman 1982, 120, 127). The problem is not only that women are equated with animals' bodies, for instance in pornography, but also that *animals are equated with their bodies*. The soul/body split that concerns Spelman and that she identifies as a part of Western philosophical tradition is acutely evident in notions of animals having no soul, and in our current secular period, of animals having no consciousness, undergirding the instrumental ontology of animals as usable.

Spelman recognized that somatophobia is enacted in relationships such as men to women, masters to slaves, fathers to children, humans to animals (127); now we see that it is actually often enacted in relationships such as men to women *and* animals, fathers to children *and* animals. The connections between the abuse of women and the abuse of animals make explicit that somatophobia applies to species as well as gender, race, and class interactions. It also requires that we rethink philosophical arguments which rely on anthropocentric notions of harm from sexual objectification (see, for instance, LeMoncheck 1985, esp. 14-21).

The testimony of Anita Hill about the humiliating experience of hearing about pornography that included women with animals illuminates Spelman's formulation of somatophobia, particularly the insights that it applies to gender, race, class, and species, and that oppression is interwoven. Consider, for instance, Kimberlé Crenshaw's brilliant article on how feminist and antiracist narratives are structured in such a way as to exclude understanding the experience of a black woman such as Anita Hill. Crenshaw describes the working of interwoven oppressions of race and sex in the racializing of sexual harassment: "While black women share with white women the experience of being objectified as 'cunts,' 'beavers,' or 'pieces,' for them those insults are many times prefaced with 'black' or 'nigger' or 'jungle' " (Crenshaw 1992, 412). The sexual aggression experienced by women of color will often simultaneously represent their subordinate racial status.

In her discussion of the representation of African American women in pornography and the way such representation enabled the pornographic treatment of white women, Patricia Hill Collins ties together the racialization of sexual aggression against black women with the racist view that equated black women with animals:

> within the mind/body, culture/nature, male/female opposi-
> tional dichotomies in Western social thought, objects occupy
> an uncertain interim position. As objects white women become
> creations of culture—in this case, the mind of white men—
> using the materials of nature—in this case, uncontrolled female

sexuality. In contrast, as animals Black women receive no such redeeming dose of culture and remain open to the type of exploitation visited on nature overall. Race becomes the distinguishing feature in determining the type of objectification women will encounter. Whiteness as symbolic of both civilization and culture is used to separate objects from animals. . . . The treatment of all women in contemporary pornography has strong ties to the portrayal of Black women as animals. . . . This linking of animals and white women within pornography becomes feasible when grounded in the earlier denigration of Black women as animals. (Collins 1990, 170-71, 172)

As Collins points out, race and gender have been inscribed *onto* species: the pre-existing division upon which pornography imposes its images is of animals—beasts, bodies not redeemed by souls—and animal nature, the notion that there is some pure, unmediated bodily sexuality that is not socially constructed. Sander Gilman writes that Buffon, for instance, "stated that this animallike sexual appetite went so far as to lead black women to copulate with apes" (see Gilman 1985, 212). Pornography that features black women and animals together may function specifically as a racializing of both sex and species hierarchies. In fact, it appears that women of color are more likely to be used in pornography that shows bestiality (see Mayall and Russell 1992). Thus, sexual harassment of women of color by reference to such pornography will carry an added dimension to its demeaning and controlling message. In other words, given the association of black women's bodies and bestiality, Anita Hill may have experienced a specific form of racialized sexual harassment. Only by including animals within the lens of feminist philosophy can the extent and effect of somatophobia in a culture be made visible.

VI. EPISTEMOLOGICAL ISSUES

If something is invisible we do not have access to it for knowledge. Much of the sexual victimization of women, children, and animals takes place in such a way as to be invisible to most people. In addition, there is the general invisibility of culturally accepted forms of animal abuse, such as flesh eating, hunting, animal experimentation.[4] What will overcome the invisibility of animal abuse and of the connection between abuse of animals and abuse of women? A relational epistemology helps overcome this culturally structured invisibility. To the person who has a relational epistemology, who has significant relationships with animals, *and* who values these interactive relationships, animal abuse will be less invisible. A relational epistemology also means that a woman experiencing abuse does not isolate her experience, but empathetically may see one's experience as like, rather then radically different from, another's.

As a feminist speaker in the national animal rights movement, I have been approached by many sexual abuse survivors throughout the country who tell of how they made connections between their own sexual abuse and the use and abuse of animals. In 1990, one woman told me how the experience of being choked by her abusive husband transformed her relationship with animals. Suddenly she realized that just as her husband claimed to love her yet was trying to kill her, she claimed to love animals yet she ate them. She survived his attack, left the marriage and became active in vegetarian and animal rights activities in her community. A relational epistemology, in itself, does not automatically result in concern for animals. Aspects of animals' lives and their experience of oppression may remain invisible because of a dominant metaphysics that views animals instrumentally and accepts a value hierarchy. But if one starts to extend out a relational epistemology, this value hierarchy breaks down a little more and a metaphysical shift may occur.[5]

Second-person relationships provide the foundation for such a metaphysical shift. The concept of second persons, introduced by Annette Baier and amplified by Lorraine Code, recognizes that our knowledge is never atomistically individualistic or "self-made." Instead we become persons through our dependence upon other persons from whom we "acquire the essential arts of personhood" (Baier, qtd. in Code 1991, 82). In other words, lives begin in communality and interdependence; thus in our acquisition of knowledge, "persons are essentially second persons" (Code 1991, 85). The connections between the abuse of animals and the abuse of women suggests that second-person relationships exist between humans and animals as well as between humans and humans. Women and children victimized by abusers reveal intense second-person relationships with animals as well as humans. Otherwise how could control be so inexorably established by the brutalization of pets? How else could they see their death prefigured in the death of the pet?

This second-person relationship can serve as a catalyst to change one's metaphysical stance vis-à-vis the other animals. As happened with the woman being choked by her husband, she suddenly recognized through second-person relations that she had accepted a value hierarchy that failed to protect or value animals. As Code explains: "Imposing meaning on someone else's existence from a position removed from it and ignorant of, or indifferent to, its specificities is at the furthest remove from second-person relations in their normative dimension" (Code 1991, 86). Second-person relations enable second-person thinking, from which the metaphysical shift evolves. With second-person thinking "knowledge claims are forms of address, speech acts, moments in a dialogue that assume and rely on the participation of (an) other subject(s)" (Code 1991, 121). Significantly, for the battered woman and many others, these other subjects are/include animals.

A relational epistemology paves the way for a metaphysical shift because it acknowledges the value of relationships, and of thinking relationally. Given this position, it is harder to say that our relationships are only with human beings, because many of us have significant relationships with animals. Thus seeing ourselves as born into relationships rather than as atomistic, self-made individuals allows for an important metaphysical shift too: no longer seeing humans as radically other than nonhuman life forms, no longer erecting a boundary between the presumably "self-made human" and the presumably "nature-made animal." Someone who has a relational epistemology is in a position to see what the dominant culture in its metaphysics has constructed as invisible and acceptable; the relational epistemology disables the functioning of somatophobia and its undergirding of animal oppression. This metaphysical shift involves valuing animals as other than objects or bodies and repudiating a subject-object relationship premised on domination rather than respect. It acknowledges that animals have a biography not just a biology (Regan 1983), and that what is required is an anthropology, not an ethology, of animals (Noske 1989).

Feminist philosophers may distrust "animal rights" activism because "animal rights" philosophy is not based on a relational epistemology. However what may be going on is that many animal rights activists (80 percent of whom are estimated to be women) join the animal rights movement based on a relational epistemology that enables a metaphysical shift that repudiates somatophobia. However, in the absence of a well-developed and popularized defense of animals based on a relational epistemology, they seek for a way to verbalize that which has not been bridged—their knowledge stance with an activist language. Rights (and interest) language has so far gained currency in the animal advocacy movement as the appropriate activist language. The result is that because the animal rights movement has been thought to have been begotten in the image of its "fathers" (Tom Regan and Peter Singer), feminist philosophy may have misread what is happening epistemologically.

VII. POLITICAL PHILOSOPHY

The gender-specific public/private distinction is a conceptually flawed one. Historically, in Western culture, female-gender-identified traits have been associated with the private ("domestic," "home") sphere, while male-gender-identified traits have been associated with the public ("civic," "political") sphere. The private sphere is, for women, "the distinctive sphere of intimate violation and abuse, neither free nor particularly personal" (MacKinnon 1989, 168). Pateman argues further that the subordination of women in the private sphere, ("the sexual contract") is what enables the construction of modern political theory ("the social contract"). Not only does the public/private distinction inscribe sexual difference and domination, it keeps invisible the empirical connections between human male sexual violence and violence toward women, children, and animals which this essay identifies. This prevents feminist philosophy from recognizing the importance of ecofeminist insights into what Karen Warren calls "women-nature connections" as being at the heart of feminist philosophy.

If we review the features of an oppressive conceptual framework that Warren has identified (1987, 1990), the way that the public/private distinction operates in the abuse of women and animals will become clearer. Among the features of an oppressive conceptual framework is value-hierarchical thinking or "up-down thinking" that places higher value, status, or prestige on what is up rather than what is down. Abuse enacts a value hierarchy—through abusive behavior a person establishes control, becoming "up" rather than "down"—while originating in value hierarchies: those who are "down" in terms of (public) status—women, children, nondominant men, and animals are more likely to be victimized.

Warren also identifies value dualisms as part of an oppressive conceptual framework. Disjunctive pairs such as human/animal, male/female, adult/child, white/"non-white" are seen as oppositional rather than as complementary, and exclusive rather than inclusive. Higher value is accorded the first item in each dyad. Until recently, violence in the "private" home was not closely scrutinized by the public sphere (women, children, and animals having less value than men, adults, and humans). Feminist peace politics seeks to change this. As Sara Ruddick observes, "As there is no sharp division between the violences of domestic, civic, and military life, there is also no sharp division between the practices and thinking of private and public peace" (Ruddick 1993, 118). It is essential for feminist peace politics to recognize the human/animal dualism central to public/private distinctions. From Aristotle on, the conception of "manhood"—the public, civic man—depended heavily on seeing women not merely as "lesser humans than men but less-than-human": "it was precisely the sharpness of the Athenian conception of manhood that bore with it a necessary degradation and oppression of women, a denial of the status of 'human' to women" (see Brown 1988, 56). Thus, women were devalued through association with devalued animals. While we have progressed from this theoretical equation of women with animals, we have not eliminated the value dualism that undergirded such public/private separations, the value dualism by which biology determines who is "mind" and who is "body." We have just removed the human species from this debate. Whereas biology is no longer acceptable for determining human value, it remains acceptable for determining animals' less-than-human value. The role of biology as a central determining factor in the perpetuation of the human/animal dualism is similar to and interrelated with the way that privacy perpetuates the male/female dualism: that is, "biology" and "privacy" provide alibis for abuse.[5]

Finally, the "glue that holds it all together" (Warren, correspondence July 1993) is a logic of domination: "a value-hierarchical way of thinking which explains, justifies, and maintains the subordination of an 'inferior' group by a 'superior' group on the grounds of the (alleged) inferiority or superiority of the respective group" (Warren 1987, 6). The idea of the private/public division protects the private domain from being the focus of certain ethical and philosophical concerns, concerns such as justice, that are often presumed to pertain only to the public realm (Okin 1989). This private/public division functions as a part of the logic of domination: the "I-have-a-right-to-do-what-I-want-in-my-own-home" patriarchal justification for abusive behavior against those constructed as "inferior"—adult female partners, children, and animals.

Through the operation of value hierarchies, value dualisms, and the logic of domination, the public/private distinction has functioned historically within patriarchal oppressive contexts to keep human male sexual violence toward women, children, and pets out of the higher status "political" areas and in the inferior, out-of-police-concern private arena. This is to the detriment of women, children, pets, and the entire culture.

VIII. Environmental Philosophy

One could argue that environmental abuse is a form of somatophobia, that abuse of the earth is an expression of the hatred of the earth's body. For this reason alone environmental philosophy should be attentive to the conceptual issues raised by the connection between the abuse of animals and the abuse of women. In addition, and very specifically, information about the association between guns, hunting, and battering suggests that any environmental philosophy that defends hunting or offers a hunting model must be re-evaluated.[7] Environmental and ecofeminist philosophers who appeal to a hunting model of any culture need to rethink the implications of applying it to the dominant Western cultures where battering is the major cause of injury to adult women, and hunting and owning guns is implicated in this battering. In fact, some advocates for battered women argue that battering incidents increase just prior to hunting season. Moreover, at least one batterer's program requires batterers to relinquish all their guns and firearms in order to participate in the program (see Stordeur and Stille, 1989).

IX. Applied Philosophy

Several areas of applied philosophy are affected by these empirical connections between human male sexual violence toward women, children, and animals. In what follows I touch on a few of these areas.

A. PUBLIC POLICY

Public policy. Because of Health Department regulations, shelters for battered women cannot generally allow pets in the shelters. The movement to protect battered women needs to establish relationships with local veterinarians and animal advocates so that pets can be sheltered. Shelters need to inquire: "Do you have a pet that lives with you? Are you afraid to leave the animal? Do you need shelter for your pet?"[8]

Training humane workers and animal control officers to check for child abuse when following up on animal abuse has begun in some places, such as Florida, Ohio, Washington, D.C., and parts of California. But humane workers and animal control officers should also be trained about woman-battering since injury to pets occurs not only in relationship to child abuse and neglect but also in cases of battering. Veterinarians, too, need to be trained along these lines, and the question of mandatory reporting of animal abuse needs to be addressed by the veterinary profession. But I am in no way advocating that a woman's decisions about whether to remain or leave should be overridden by intervention by these professionals. Instead, their role as allies should be established. And information about pet injury as itself being a form of battering needs to be publicized.

Homeless shelters and battered women's shelters are often offered surplus animal flesh from hunters. In fact, hunters, including the well-known celebrity bow-hunter Ted Nugent, often organize giveaways to these shelters. (We should be reminded that battered women make up about 40 percent of homeless people [see Zorza 1991]). But given the association of hunting and violence against humans, and batterer programs that require batterers to stop using any guns, accepting flesh from hunters to feed battered women and other homeless individuals presents ethical problems. (I know of at least one battered women's shelter that refused to accept flesh from hunters and of some animal activist and vegetarian organizations who adopt a battered women's shelter at which they periodically serve vegetarian meals.)

B. BIOMEDICAL ETHICS

The relationship between being a survivor of child sexual abuse and anorexia (which is receiving more attention, see Root 1991, and Sloan and Leichner 1986) needs more exploration by those sensitive to the ethical legitimacy of vegetarian claims. One private-practice dietitian and counselor observed that "the animalistic nature of meat and dairy might seem particularly disgusting to patients recovering from sexual abuse" (Krizmanic 1992, 58). This is, in fact, one of the symptom clusters associated with ritual abuse survivors: "Did the child suddenly develop an eating disorder, e.g. refuse meat, catsup, spaghetti, tomatoes?" (Hudson 1991, 32; see also Gould 1992, 214). I have argued elsewhere that young girls might have a problem with food while also being vegetarians for ethical reasons (see Adams 1990, 159-62). In one location in Los Angeles, 90 percent of the anorexics being counseled were vegetarian (with 50 percent considered to have good reasons for their vegetarianism, i.e., they are not doing it solely to diet or restrict their fat intake because of "obsessive" concern for calories), while another program in Indiana estimated that 25 percent of "patients" at its program were vegetarian. Interestingly, "some dietitians and counselors insist that eating meat is integral to recovery" (Krizmanic 1992, 59). Rather than having their motives for vegetarianism pathologized, anorexic young women could benefit from a recognition that a relational epistemology may have catalyzed a metaphysical shift regarding "meat" animals.

C. PHILOSOPHICAL PSYCHOLOGY

Some programs offer healing to survivors of sexual victimization, including formerly battered women, through "animal-assisted therapy." Alice Vachss describes the comforting presence of a dog she brought to work at the sex crimes prosecutors' offices; some child victims only testified on videotape with the dog present: "With Sheba there to make her feel safe enough, the little girl was able to tell what had been done to her" (Vachss 1993, 172). A social worker at a battered women's shelter in Boston told Jay McDaniel, "The more my clients learn to trust animals and the Earth . . . the more they begin to trust themselves. And the more they trust themselves, the better they can free themselves from exploitive relationships" (McDaniel 1992, 1).

X. CONCLUSION: IMPLICATIONS FOR FEMINIST PEACE POLITICS

The connections between the abuse of animals and the abuse of women have important implications for a feminist peace politics. In conclusion I sketch some of the variety of ways of integrating the woman-animal abuse connections into evolving feminist peace politics and philosophy.

The connections between the abuse of animals and the abuse of women call attention to the effect of war and patriarchal militarism on relations between humans and animals and on the lives of animals. Like abusers, occupying forces may kill animals as an expression of control, to instill terror, and to ensure compliance. I have been told such stories: in one case, in the 1970s, after capturing the adult men in a household, the occupying military force very deliberately shot the pet canary in the assembled presence of the family. Just as with battery, such actions are reminders of how mastery is both instilled and exhibited. In addition, the destruction of animals, like rape, is a part of wartime actions (see, for instance, Brownmiller 1975, 39). Moreover, as Ascione reports (drawing on the work of Jonathan Randal and Nora Boustany), anecdotal evidence suggests that "children exposed to chronic war-time violence display violent and cruel behavior toward animals" (Ascione 1993, 232).

Sexualized violence takes on new dimensions in the light of the connections between the abuse of animals and the abuse of women. "The sadistic murderer derives sexual pleasure from the killing and mutilation or abuse of his victim. . . . The act of killing itself produces very powerful sexual arousal in these individuals" (Lunde 1976, 53, 56).[9] Thus, sex-crime offenders might relive their crime through animal surrogates. Arthur Gary Bishop, a child molester and murderer of five boys, relived his first murder by buying and killing as many as twenty puppies. (Most frequently the movement is in the other direction.) After doing an extensive literature review of children who are cruel to animals, Frank Ascione queries "What is the effect on the child who sexually abuses an animal and that animal dies (Such as boys having intercourse with chickens)?" (conversation, September 1993). That the sadistic attacks on horses, often involving sexual mutilation, that have occurred in southern England since the mid-80s are called "horse-ripping" suggests the sexualizing of animal abuse (see Doniger 1993, 25).

Making animal abuse visible expands feminist peace politics. Instead of the glorification of anonymous death in massive numbers that we encounter in heroic war writings, the connections between the abuse of animals and the abuse of women remind us of the specific embodiedness and agonizing painfulness of every single death. In the place of unnamed troops, there are named individuals, including animals. These names remind us that all victims—the pets as well as the troops—have a biography. In addition, we now see that biologisms, and the racism such biologisms give rise to, are involved in attitudes toward "animals" and "the enemy" (see Kappeler, forthcoming). The militaristic identity, like the abuser's control, is dependent on others as objects, rather than subjects. Moreover, it has been observed that "women are more likely to be permanently injured, scarred, or even killed by their husbands in societies in which animals are treated cruelly" (Levinson 1989, 45, cited in Ascione 1993). Finally, our growing understanding of the commodification of bodies in conjunction with militarism (Enloe 1989) can benefit from insights into the commodification of animals' bodies (Noske 1989). Dismantling somatophobia involves respecting the bodily integrity of all who have been equated with bodies.

In response to the conceptual connections between women and animals, feminism has often attempted theoretically to sever these connections (e.g., Wollstonecraft [1792] 1967, Beauvoir [1953] 1974). Clearly, in the light of the connections between the abuse of animals and the abuse of women, this theoretical response is inadequate because it presumes the acceptability of the human/animal value dualism while moving women from the disempowered side of the dyad to the dominating side. Any adequate feminist peace politics will be nonanthropocentric, rejecting value dualisms that are oppositional and hierarchical, such as the human/animal dualism.

In her discussion of feminism and militarism, bell hooks refers to "cultures of war, cultures of peace" (hooks 1989, 97). We have seen how the connections between the abuse of women and the abuse of animals both enact and occur within cultures of war. It remains for feminists to define clearly and specifically how animals will be included in cultures of peace.

NOTES

Thanks to Karen J. Warren for encouraging me to explore the philosophical implications of this subject and for her attentive readings of previous versions of this essay, as well as Duane Cady, the reviewers for *Hypatia*, and Frank Ascione, Bruce Buchanan, Jane Caputi, Kathleen Carlin, Pat Davis, Josephine Donovan, Leigh Nachman Hofheimer, Jennifer Manlowe, Drorah O'Donnell Setel, Ken Shapiro, Marjorie Procter-Smith, and Nancy Tuana for valuable discussions and promptings. Thanks also to Greta Gaard and Melinda Vadas, careful critics of an earlier draft, and DeLora Frederickson and Pam Willhoite, valued colleagues involved both in the movement against violence against women and Feminists for Animal Rights.

1. Just how humans should relate to other animals in any intimate way, that is, the feminist implications of "pet" keeping and whether domestication of animals is consistent with a nonhierarchical feminist theory, is beyond the scope of this paper, but see in general Noske (1989), Tuan (1984), Serpell (1986), and Mason (1993).

2. I am uncomfortable with term "battered woman" although it is one that the movement against violence against women has itself adopted. I agree with Sarah Hoagland (1988) that the term elides the agency of the batterer, while also ascribing an unchanging status to his victim. However, because it is the commonly adopted term, and is used by the scholars and activists from whom I draw my empirical data, I will use the term in this essay.

3. These same acts of battering occur in some lesbian relationships. While human male violence is responsible for most of the damage to women and the other animals in cases of battering, a patriarchal, hierarchical culture will find expressions of this form of violence in some women's same-sex relationships. Where there is an acceptance of a patriarchal value hierarchy, some will wish to establish control (and be on top in terms of the hierarchy) through violence: "38% of the respondents who had pets reported that their partners had abused the animals" (Renzetti 1992, 21). These acts of battering are considered violent and coercive behavior (see Hart 1986, 188). The battered lesbian whose partner injures or destroys a pet faces a double burden: overcoming the invisibility or trivializing of lesbian battering and the invisibility or trivializing of abuse to animals.

4. I do not argue for these claims here, for ecofeminist or feminist defenses of vegetarianism, or for the interconnections between human male sexual violence and flesh eating. I do so elsewhere (Adams 1990, 1991, 1993). Furthermore, whether or not one accepts such arguments does not directly affect the argument of this piece. My point here is simply to show that eating, hunting, and dissecting animals certainly belong on the table for discussion of interconnecting forms of violence which are relevant to any feminist peace politics or any (eco)feminist analysis of violence.

5. This discussion of epistemological issues was worked out with the supportive insights and patient prodding of Nancy Tuana.

6. Challenges to the ways by which we draw the line between "human" and "animal" can be found in Haraway (1992), Birke (1991 a&b), Midgley (1979, 1983), and Noske (1989) among others.

7. See for instance Foster, et al. (1989) on the presence of a firearm in the home as one of the factors present in battering relationships that end in homicide.

8. I acknowledge the logistical problem this issue presents, and the concern that women might abandon the animals, not because of cruelty or insensitivity, but because they are overwhelmed with reshaping their own lives and feel that the animals are safer removed from the batterer's presence. Still, I believe it is an important step to make in protecting women and animals. I am indebted to DeLora Frederickson and Pam Willhoite for their advocacy of this program. For information on setting up such a program (developed for a workshop that DeLora and I gave at the 1993 Texas Council on Family Violence Conference), please send a stamped (52 cent) self-addressed envelope to me at 814 Grinnell Dr., Richardson, TX 75081.

9. Jane Caputi (1987) challenges Lunde's assertion that this occurs only in rare individuals, she sees it instead as constitutive of "the age of sex crime."

REFERENCES

Achenbach, T. M. 1988. *Child behavior checklist (for ages 2-3, for ages 4-16)*. Burlington, Vermont: Center for Children, Youth, and Families.

Adams, Carol. 1990. *The sexual politics of meat: A feminist-vegetarian critical theory*. New York: Continuum.

———. 1991. Ecofeminism and the eating of animals. *Hypatia* 6(1): 125-45.

———. 1993. The feminist traffic in animals. In *Ecofeminism: Woman, animal, nature*, ed. Greta Gaard. Philadelphia: Temple University Press.

American Psychiatric Association (1987). *Diagnostic and statistical manual of mental disorders*. 3rd ed. rev. Washington, D.C.: American Psychiatric Association.

Anonymous. 1992. *Ritual abuse: A broad overview*. Baltimore, Md: Survivors of Incest Anonymous, P.O. Box 21817.

Ascione, Frank R. 1993. Children who are cruel to animals: A review of research and implications for developmental psychopathology. *Anthrozoos* 6(4): ??-??.

Baier, Annette. 1985. Cartesian persons. In *Postures of the mind: Essays on mind and morals*. Minneapolis: University of Minnesota Press.

Birke, Lynda. 1991. Science, feminism and animal natures I: Extending the boundaries. *Women's Studies International Forum* 14(5): 443-50.

———. 1991b. Science, feminism and animal natures II: Feminist critiques and the place of animals in science. *Women's Studies International Forum* 14(5): 451-58.

Brohl, Kathryn. 1991. *Pockets of craziness: Examining suspected incest*. Lexington, MA: Lexington Books.

Brown, Wendy. 1988. *Manhood and politics: A feminist reading in political theory*. Totowa, N.J.: Rowman and Littlefield.

Browne, Angela. 1987. *When battered women kill*. New York: Free Press.

Brownmiller, Susan. 1975. *Against our will: Men, women and rape*. New York: Simon and Schuster.

Burstow, Bonnie. 1992. *Radical feminist therapy: Working in the context of violence*. Newbury Park, CA: Sage.

Caputi, Jane. 1987. *The age of sex crime*. Bowling Green, OH: Bowling Green State University Popular Press.

Code, Lorraine. 1991. *What can she know? Feminist theory and the construction of knowledge*. Ithaca: Cornell University Press.

Collins, Patricia Hill. 1990. *Black feminist thought: Knowledge consciousness and the politics of empowerment*. Boston: Unwin Hyman.

Crenshaw, Kimberlé. 1992. Whose story is it anyway? Feminist and antiracist appropriations of Anita Hill. In *Race-ing justice, engendering power: Essays on Anita Hill, Clarence Thomas and the construction of social reality*, ed. Toni Morrison. New York: Pantheon Books.

de Beauvoir, Simone. [1953] 1974. *The second sex*. Trans. and ed. H. M. Parshley. New York: Vintage.

Doniger, Wendy. 1993. Diary. *London Review of Books*. 23 September: 25.

Dvorchak, Robert. 1991. Dahmer's troubled childhood offers clues but no simple answers. *Dallas Times Herald* August 11.

Enloe, Cynthia. 1989. *Bananas, beaches and bases: Making sense of international politics*. Berkeley: University of California Press.

Faller, Kathleen Coulborn. 1990. *Understanding child sexual maltreatment*. Newbury Park, CA: Sage.

Foster, Lynne A., Christine Mann Veale, and Catherine Ingram Fogel. 1989. Factors present when battered women kill. *Issues in Mental Health Nursing* 10: 273-84.

Fraser, Sylvia. 1987. *My father's house: A memoir of incest and of healing*. New York: Harper and Row.

Ganley, Anne L. [1981] 1985. *Court-mandated counseling for men who batter: A three-day workshop for mental health professionals*. Washington, D.C.: Center for Women Policy Studies.

Gilman, Sander L. 1985. Black bodies, white bodies: Toward an iconography of female sexuality in late nineteenth-century art, medicine, and literature. *Critical Inquiry* 12: 204-42.

Gould, Catherine. 1992. Diagnosis and treatment of ritually abused children. In *Out of darkness: Exploring satanism and ritual abuse*. See Sakheim and Devine 1992.

Haraway, Donna. 1992. Otherworldly conversations; terran topics; local terms. *Science as Culture* 3(14): 64-98.

Hart, Barbara. 1986. Lesbian battering: an examination. In *Naming the violence: Speaking out about lesbian battering*. See Lobel 1986.

Hoagland, Sarah Lucia. 1988. *Lesbian ethics: Toward new values*. Palo Alto: Institute for Lesbian Studies.

hooks, bell. 1989. Feminism and militarism: A comment. In *Talking back*. Boston: South End Press.

Hudson, Pamela S. 1991. *Ritual child abuse: Discovery, diagnosis and treatment*. Saratoga, CA: R & E Publishers.

Kappeler, Susanne. forthcoming. Animal conservationism and human conservationism. In *Animals and women: Feminist theoretical explorations*, ed. Carol J. Adams, Josephine Donovan, and Susanne Kappeler.

Krizmanic, Judy. 1992. Perfect obsession: Can vegetarianism cover up an eating disorder? *Vegetarian Times* (June): 52-60.

Levinson, David. 1989. *Family violence in cross-cultural perspective.* Newbury Park, CA: Sage.

LeMoncheck, Linda. 1985. *Dehumanizing women: Treating persons as sex objects.* Totowa, N.J.: Rowman & Allanheld.

Lobel, Kerry. 1986. *Naming the violence: Speaking out about lesbian battering.* Seattle: Seal Press.

"Lovelace," Linda, [Linda Marchiano]. With Mike McGrady. 1980. *Ordeal.* New York: Berkeley Books.

————. 1986. *Out of bondage.* Secaucus, N.J.: Lyle Stuart Inc.

Lunde, Donald T. 1976. *Murder and madness.* San Francisco: San Francisco Book Co.

MacKinnon, Catharine A. 1987. *Feminism unmodified.* Cambridge: Harvard University Press.

————. 1989. *Toward a feminist theory of the state.* Cambridge: Harvard University Press.

McDaniel, Jay. 1992. Green grace. *Earth ethics: Evolving values for an earth community* 3(4): 1-4.

Mason, Jim. 1993. *An unnatural order: Uncovering the roots of our domination of nature and each other.* New York: Simon and Schuster.

Mayall, Alice and Diane E. H. Russell. 1992. Racism in pornography. In *Making violence sexy,* ed. Diana E. H. Russell. New York: Teachers College.

Midgley, Mary. 1979. *Beast and man: The roots of human nature.* Ithaca: Cornell University Press.

————. 1983. *Animals and why they matter.* Athens: University of Georgia Press.

Noske, Barbara. 1989. *Humans and other animals: Beyond the boundaries of anthropology.* Winchester, MA: Unwin Human.

Okin, Susan Moller. 1989. *Justice, gender, and the family.* New York: Basic Books.

Pateman, Carole. 1988. *The sexual contract.* Stanford: Stanford University Press.

Phelps, Timothy M., and Helen Winternitz. 1993. *Capitol games: The inside story of Clarence Thomas, Anita Hill and a supreme court nomination.* New York: Harper Perennial.

Pope-Lance, Deborah J., and Joan Chamberlain Engelsman. 1987. *A guide for clergy on the problems of domestic violence.* Trenton: New Jersey Department of Community Affairs Division on Women.

Randal, Jonathan and Nora Boustany. 1990. Children of war in Lebanon. In *Betrayal: A report on violence toward children in today's world,* ed. Caroline Moorehead. New York: Doubleday.

Raschke, Carl A. 1990. *Painted black: from drug killings to heavy metal—the alarming true story of how satanism is terrorizing our communities.* New York: Harper and Row.

Regan, Tom. 1983. *The case for animal rights.* Berkeley: University of California Press.

Renzetti, Claire M. 1992. *Violent betrayal: Partner abuse in lesbian relationships.* Newbury Park, CA: Sage.

Ressler, Robert K., Ann W. Burgess, Carol R. Hartman, John E. Douglas, and Arlene McCormack. 1986. Murderers who rape and mutilate. *Journal of Interpersonal Violence* 1(3): 273-87.

Root, Maria P. 1991. Persistent, disordered eating as a gender-specific, post-traumatic stress response to sexual assault. *Psychotherapy* 28(1): 96-102.

Rose, Elizabeth S. 1993. Surviving the unbelievable: A firstperson account of cult ritual abuse. *Ms* (January/February): 404-450.

Ruddick, Sara. 1993. Notes toward a feminist peace politics. In *Gendering war talk,* ed. Miriam Cooke and Angela Woollacott. Princeton: Princeton University Press.

Russell, Diana E. H. 1984. *Sexual exploitation: Rape, child sexual abuse, and workplace harassment.* Newbury Park, CA: Sage.

———. [1982] 1990. *Rape in marriage: Expanded and revised edition with a new introduction.* Bloomington: Indiana University Press.

Sakheim, David K. and Susan E. Devine. 1992. *Out of darkness: Exploring satanism and ritual abuse.* New York: Lexington Books.

Serpell, James. 1986. *In the company of animals: A study of human-animal relationships.* New York: Basil Blackwell.

Sloan, G., and P. Leichner. 1986. Is there a relationship between sexual abuse or incest and eating disorders? *Canadian Journal of Psychiatry* 31(7): 656-60.

Smith, Margaret. 1993. *Ritual abuse: What it is. Why it happens. How to help.* San Francisco: Harper San Francisco.

Spelman, Elizabeth V. 1982. Woman as body: Ancient and contemporary views. *Feminist Studies* 8(1): 109-131.

Statman, Jan Berliner. 1990. Life doesn't have to be like this: How to spot a batterer before an abusive relationship begins. In *The battered woman's survival guide: Breaking the cycle.* Dallas: Taylor Publishing Co.

Stordeur, Richard A. and Richard Stille. 1989. *Ending men's violence against their partners: One road to peace.* Newbury Park, CA: Sage.

Tuan, Yi-Fu. 1984. *Dominance and affection: The making of pets.* New Haven: Yale University Press.

Vachss, Alice. 1993. *Sex crimes.* New York: Random House.

Walker, Lenore. 1979. *The battered woman.* New York: Harper and Row.

———. 1989. *Terrifying love: Why battered women kill and how society responds.* New York: Harper & Row.

Warren, Karen J. 1987. Feminism and ecology: Making connections. *Environmental Ethics* 9(1): 3-20.

———. 1990. The power and the promise of ecological feminism. *Environmental Ethics* 12(3): 125-46.

———. 1992. Women, nature, and technology: An ecofeminist philosophical perspective. *Research in Philosophy and Technology* 13: 13-29.

———. Forthcoming. *Ecofeminism: Multidisciplinary perspectives.* Bloomington: Indiana University Press.

Wollstonecraft, Mary. [1792] 1967. *A vindication of the rights of woman.* ed. Charles W. Hagelman, Jr. New York: W. W. Norton.

Young, Walter C. 1992. Recognition and treatment of survivors reporting ritual abuse. See Sakheim and Devine 1992.

Zorza, Joan. 1991. Woman-battering: A major cause of homelessness. *Clearinghouse Review* (special issue): 421-29.

Watch for Pet Abuse —
It Might Save Your Client's Life

"*Something's wrong with the dog next door. He's screaming in pain.*" *Barbara Fabricant hangs up the phone, quickly pins on her California humane officer badge and rushes to the dog's house.*

"Can I see your dog?" She flies through the house to the yard, and carries the shrieking dog, whose legs all are broken, to her car. She re-enters the house and hears whimpering from inside a closet. "Another dog!" Fabricant groans — but this time it's an old man with bruises all over his arms.

The little man whines, "Every day my son orders me to sign over the house to him. When I refuse, he punches me." Today the old man's son slammed the dog against a concrete wall.

"If it weren't for that dog, I would have never found out about the old man," says Fabricant, who has investigated animal cruelty cases for 25 years. "Elder and animal abuse go together so often that when I see one I automatically look for the other."

"If everyone did this, fewer elders and animals would be abused," says Dr. Frank Ascione, psychology professor at Utah State University in Logan, UT. Ascione lectures internationally about the connection between animal abuse and child abuse. He says, "Study after study show that all too often, people who abuse animals will abuse humans, too." For example, most violent, imprisoned criminals abused animals when they were children. Of 23 British families who abused animals, 83 percent endangered their children, too. Of 53 American families who abused their children, 60 percent abused their pets, too.

Psychiatrist Alan Felthous studied 18 patients who'd repeatedly tortured dogs and cats. All were highly aggressive toward other people. One even had murdered a boy. When the Utah Division of Youth Corrections interviewed teen-age hellions, 21 percent admitted they'd tormented animals in the past year.

About one in 20 elders is abused, some experts say. Half our homes have pets — so you have many abused elders living with pets who are likely abused, too. "Pets are often the most visible victims," says Dr. Randall Lockwood, a psychologist at the Humane Society of the United States.

Most often, it's neighbors who report the bony dog chained to the tree, or the singed cat perched on the fence. "Elders, on the other hand, are often the most *hidden* victims. While the kids go off to school, mom goes to the market and dad goes to work, the elder could be locked in the basement and no one outside the family would even know. We should keep an eye out for the most visible victims — pets. They can lead us to the hidden victims, the elders."

Ascione says, "If you see a beaten dog, suspect there might be an equally bruised elder. And if you find out an elder's being starved by their son or daughter, suspect the cat might be starving, too. Lawyers, veterinarians, social workers, doctors and anyone else who deals with elders or animals should be on the watch for both kinds of abuse."

Grandmas and Pets
Sink in the Same Boat

It's no surprise that the same brutes pick on elders and animals. Pets and grandmas get bloodied, neglected and raped for the same reasons: greed, anger, frustration and ignorance.

"My friend's son is starving her and her dog," the hysterical telephone voice urges. "Hurry, before the dog dies."

Barbara Fabricant races to the house. "He locks me in this room, and won't take me to the doctor," an emaciated old woman moans. "He's trying to slowly kill me so he can get all my money."

The old woman is more worried about her dog than about herself. He's the only comfort she has left.

Reprinted from *Shepard's ElderCare/Law Newsletter* 5 (July 1995): 1–9. Copyright 1995 by Shepard's McGraw/Hill, transferred to Thomson Legal Publishing 1996. Reprinted with permission.

340

> **Most often, it's neighbors who report the bony dog chained to the tree, or the singed cat perched on the fence. "Elders, on the other hand, are often the most hidden victims. While the kids go off to school, mom goes to the market and dad goes to work, the elder could be locked in the basement and no one outside the family would even know.**

Greedy people are willing to torment an elderly parent — or the parent's pet — to get a pay-off. In a study of 204 abuse cases, most of the adult children depended on mom or pop to pay the bills. Fabricant reports, "About five elders have actually told me, 'I want an attorney, so I can take my son out of my will. He's abusing my pet so I'll die and he'll inherit."

Some people will lash into an elder or animal, even though they don't have a penny to gain. "These abusers are mentally sick," Ascione says. Psychologists compared 46 families who abused elders with 251 families who didn't. The abusers were much more likely to have been arrested, hospitalized for a psychiatric disorder or involved in violent behavior outside their family.

Researchers asked 1,653 professionals, "What most often causes the elder abuse you see?" The number one answer: "Alcohol and drug abuse."

"My neighbor's dog keeps crying. Please investigate," the telephone voice pleads.

Barbara Fabricant finds the dog shackled to a two-meter chain, standing in 65 centimeters of water, in heavy rain. "My dog used to sleep with me," an old woman wails. "But my son moved in and won't let my dog in the house. He's doing this to torture me."

"Some people may abuse animals because they want to shock their elderly parents," Ascione says. "Others are punishing the parent for beating *them* up when they were children. People have also tortured pets to 'get back at' the animals: 'He chewed up my favorite couch.' 'He didn't obey me.' 'He bit me.'"

"Dump Your Anger" is often the name of the game: Daddy beats little Tommy, who then kicks the dog. Tommy grows up and lashes into Daddy, who is now as helpless as the dog was.

"Some children see their father beat their mother, or starve the cat, and then learn to behave that way themselves," Ascione explains. "Studies show that when parents hit a dog with a stick, for example, their children copy that behavior. Some parents even reward children for abusing animals. Fortunately, a recent study shows only 30 to 40 percent of children in abusive homes grow up to be abusers."

"Hey, it's not all my fault!" some abusers gripe. "*You* try feeding a grouchy old lady who refuses to eat, and calls you a creep for trying. *You* try living with a dog who barks when you're trying to sleep."

Ascione says, "The burden of caring for elders or pets can push some people over the edge into abuse. One man, for example, recently buried puppies alive because he didn't want the burden of caring for them."

Some people get frustrated because they can't control their headstrong old mother, or their feisty young kitten. So they lash out brutally.

But sometimes these "bad" elders and pets are only bad because the abuser doesn't understand their needs. "An elder or cat might be urinating all over the bed," Ascione says. "Rather than consult a doctor or veterinarian to find out the reason, some people will punish the elder or cat instead."

Lockwood shares, "I've seen dogs and 5-year-olds beaten in the same household. But the abusers are not always sadistic. Often they're just immature. They merely need to be taught how to housebreak a dog or toilet-train a child."

Lockwood says if you lock up such people, they'll be out in 30 days, beating animals and people again. Ascione agrees we should educate people more about caring for elders and pets. "Animal control should help people choose the right size dog, and advise them how to discipline their pets."

Elders and pets have one more strike against them: prejudice. First-year medical students, for example, seemed to show their ageism: 48 percent prefer to serve younger patients; only 4 percent prefer elders. Meanwhile, we don't need studies to uncover species prejudice: Almost everyone will say, when asked, that animals are inferior to people.

It's easier to abuse an old lady or a rabbit if you look down on them.

Silent Victims

Most elders and animals suffer silently. The police rarely find out about their singed tails, broken legs, parched throats or raped bodies. Pets can't call the police, and many abused elders are afraid to. Maybe their adult child will punish them for complaining — beat them even harder, or refuse to take care of them.

Some elders feel embarrassed, and don't want to bring shame on the family. Others are too sick to call the police, or don't know where to get help.

Fabricant recalls, "One old woman would feed stray cats. Her son would empty the cats' food bowls into the trash, right in front of his mother. Then he'd put the cats in a carton and leave them in Box Canyon, which is full of coyotes. 'Your cats are now coyote food,' he'd taunt.

"Many old women feed strays, and become terribly emotionally involved with them. They're afraid to complain about their abusers, because the authorities will find out they have too many cats." Fabricant actually has seen animal regulators ignore the abuse, and instead say, "Ma'am, you're only allowed three cats."

So elders rarely complain, and pets, of course, never do. "Even though the elder or dog looks suspiciously bruised or bloody, some abusers can hop from doctor to doctor, or from vet to vet, so that no one doctor or vet catches on," Ascione says.

Abusers often lie: "My dog got cut on a barbed wire fence." "My mother fell down the stairs."

Ascione says, "Health professionals need to protect elders and animals more. People in the community need to help out more, too." Many people believe an animal is the owner's property and they don't have the right to interfere. Or they'll see an elder being abused, but don't want to "meddle in the family's affairs."

"That son abused his mother when he fed her cats to coyotes," Fabricant says. "When you mentally abuse an elder, you can hurt her as much as if you beat her. The son could have caused his mother to have a stroke, for example."

Many elders have lost their spouses and many of their friends. Often their pets are their main contacts with the outside world, their main companions to hug.

"If someone beats the elder's dog, or doesn't give the dog enough food, water or veterinary care, they're abusing the elder, too," Lockwood says.

> *Most elders and animals suffer silently. The police rarely find out about their singed tails, broken legs, parched throats or raped bodies. Pets can't call the police, and many abused elders are afraid to. Maybe their adult child will punish them for complaining — beat them even harder, or refuse to take care of them.*

John knows his grandpa is afraid of Rex, the attack pit bull chained in the front yard. But John wants Rex and his grandpa to live near the front of the house. John's selling crack in the rear rooms. Rex keeps snoopers away, and Grandpa gives the place a wholesome "family" smell.

"I've heard of sons and grandsons endangering elders this way," Lockwood says. If you see a dangerous-looking dog, and an elder in the front room, he suggests you investigate.

Lockwood says people have abused children and women, then threatened them, "I'll hurt your pet if you tell anyone." Sometimes the abuser actually will kill the pet. "I think people have probably hurt elders' pets for the same reason," he says.

How to Know a Red Light When You See One

As an elder care professional, you are in an excellent position to spot dangerous situations.

Red Light #1: When you walk in, the dog hides under the table. Ten minutes later it comes out trembling. The owner tries to pet the dog, but it darts away.

"Many animals act scared simply because they haven't been socialized enough," Lockwood says. Some breeds are naturally nervous or withdrawn. Other animals may be frightened because they were abused in a previous home. "So a frightened animal isn't necessarily going to lead you to an elder abuser," Lockwood says. But you should comment anyway: "Gee, he seems real shy."

Abusers often volunteer: "Yeah, whenever he gets out of line, I like to loosen a few teeth." (Don't blurt out, "Has anyone abused this dog?" or the abuser may clam up.)

Red Light #2: The dog's ribs are showing. You look in the food dish and see only bread crumbs.

"If you see a malnourished animal, or a lot of low-quality food, that could mean the elder's malnourished too," Lockwood says. "Someone may even be taking the elder's money, forcing him to eat pet food." The pet could be skinny because it's old or sick, but you should still comment (nonjudgmentally): "Oh, poor dog. What happened to it?"

Someone reported to Lockwood, "My neighbor's dog is tied without food or water." Lockwood rushed over and found a grandmother badly needing food and medical care. "This is the animal abuse we humane workers are most likely to see: a dog tied in the backyard, for example, without food or water."

What if the starved pet is locked away in a closet? (Fabricant has found pets in cupboards, too.) Lockwood says professionals dealing with family abuse should ask routinely, "Are there animals in the home? Have they been hurt, injured or abandoned? Are they at risk now?

Do they seem adequately cared for?" Those kinds of questions should be on the behavioral checklists you use to assess violence.

Scan for emotional abuse, too. Is the dog tied up alone in the yard all the time, without companionship? Are the pet mice kept in a cage the cats (their natural predators) paw at?

Red Light #3: The horse has open wounds, large tumors or another disorder, or is limping.

Ask, "Oh, poor horse. What happened to him?" Lockwood says, "If a pet isn't getting adequate care, that's a warning sign this is not a nurturing household. Or maybe the household doesn't have the resources to care for dependents — pets or elders."

People complained to Fabricant, "Our neighbor's horses are thin. One's dead from bloat." Fabricant found the elderly horse owner in a wheel chair. "I've had one stroke," he complained, "and my son is starving my horses to make me have another stroke. He wants to inherit my ranch."

Red Light #4: The elder says, "My cat disappeared last week."

Ask, "Why do you think the cat disappeared?" The elder might blurt out, "My son has always hated that cat. I don't know what happened to the cat."

Lockwood says, "That's a red flag telling you to investigate further."

He advises lawyers, CPAs, insurance professionals and anyone else who visits elders' homes to listen attentively. If you see an elder frowning, ask, "Why are you sad?" The elder might say, "My bird died today."

Then ask, "What happened to your bird?" The elder might say, "I think my daughter hit him too hard." Or "My bird was sick a long time, and nobody would give me any money to get him to a vet."

Elders who withdraw into their own world have to get out eventually and walk the dog, or buy pet food. "Often pets keep elders plugged into the real world," Lockwood says. Social workers and others who want to learn how their clients feel can use the pet as a launching pad.

Red Light #5: You see many animals treated badly.

Lockwood says, "I've seen elders living at puppy mills: 60 dogs in chicken-wire pens, so the owner can make a few bucks on the side." When you see someone exploiting animals, maybe they're exploiting the elder, too.

Or maybe you've got an "animal collector." Lockwood says this is often "a sweet little old lady who apologizes, 'The house is a little messy,' and when you enter it's covered in cat feces." Collectors might have 50 or so cats. The animals are sick, the place is deteriorating and the collector is in denial.

Lockwood has found elders who are so fleabitten or infested with animal-borne disease that they need medical care. "Often, if they don't have resources to care for their animals, they don't have resources for themselves, either."

What Else Can You Do?

✔   *Know your animal welfare counterpart.* You service elders in your town, region or state. Who services the animals there? Ascione says, "Social welfare officials and animal officials sometimes are working on the same case and don't even know it." Lockwood says one often meets the other on the way out the client's door!

At least know who you can call if you suspect animal abuse. Lockwood urges professionals to organize "humane coalitions against violence." You might meet once a month for breakfast, for example, to get to know each other and share your experiences.

> *"A frightened animal isn't necessarily going to lead you to an elder abuser," Lockwood says. But you should comment anyway: "Gee, he seems real shy." Abusers often volunteer: "Yeah, whenever he gets out of line, I like to loosen a few teeth. . . ." If you see a malnourished animal, or a lot of low-quality food, that could mean the elder's malnourished, too.*

✔ *Cross-train.* Lockwood holds workshops around the country on the link between human and animal abuse. "At one workshop," he says, "a phone company supervisor said his phone installers were reporting many horror stories. They wanted to know who to report the abuse to."

Lockwood says a phone installer should know what legal protection is available if he or she reports finding an elder tied to a dirty bed. "Many people don't realize their states require them to report human abuse."

Lockwood feels every state should require people to report elder and animal abuse. "So far, no one has to report animal abuse, except Colorado veterinarians."

✔ *Tell your colleagues about the elder-animal link.* Write articles for trade publications. Give lectures.

✔ *Use humane societies as a resource.* Do you want to hold a workshop? Lockwood can facilitate it, or at least help you organize it. He can also put you in touch with humane workers with whom you can form a local coalition.

"I can send you information on your local animal cruelty laws," he says. "If you want to write or speak on the elder-animal link, I can send you information." Lockwood also can help you write questions on animal cruelty for your intake questionnaires.

Help Grandparents And Pets

"Many people say, 'Animals are not as important as people. So why bother helping animals while we have all these abused elders to tend to?' " Ascione says. "But a dog who painfully shies away from her owner or who has suspicious welts all over her back can be the perfect clue to lead you to an elderly father who's whimpering in a closet.

"If you hear an elder scream and you know he has a pet, call an elder protection agency *and* an animal welfare agency." If your elderly neighbor's dog starts to look neglected, ring the doorbell and check on your neighbor.

"It's not a matter of who's more important," Ascione says. "We need to protect both elders *and* animals, because both are often tangled up with each other in the same web of abuse." ❖

Barbara Rosen is a journalist in Ashland, OR.

> *You can call Lockwood at (301) 258-3030, or write him at the Humane Society of the United States, 2100 L Street NW, Washington DC 20037.*
>
> *Your local humane society also can inform you of animal cruelty laws and refer you to humane workers with whom you can network.*

Stop Animal Abusers — Before They Abuse Elders

*H*ow did the lawyer blunder? In New York a 12-year-old-boy strangled a neighbor's cat with a hose clamp. No one punished him. A year later, he strangled a 4-year-old child.

The cat's owners had contacted a lawyer. How had the lawyer goofed?

"Most lawyers and other professionals don't realize how much a person who abuses an animal is at risk for abusing a person," says Dr. Randall Lockwood, a psychologist at the Humane Society of the United States. "This should be part of the training for judges, police, teachers — everyone who deals with families."

Studies show that many people abusers started out as children who abuse animals. Take, for example, 28 rapist-murderers in one study: Thirty-six percent were cruel to animals when they were children. In another study of inmates, 48 percent of the rapists and 30 percent of the child molesters admitted cruelty to animals as children.

Little Albert DeSalvo, who became "the Boston strangler," trapped dogs and cats in orange crates and shot arrows into the boxes. Little Ted Bundy, later a serial killer, admitted spending much of his childhood torturing animals.

"I'm not saying everyone who pulls wings off a butterfly will be a serial killer," Lockwood admits. "But children and adults who abuse animals are statistically at risk and should be taken seriously."

Yet even when someone clearly violates the law — sets a cat on fire, for example — lawyers and judges often ignore it. "We don't have the resources to investigate every human offense," they complain. "How can we handle the cat burnings too?"

Lockwood feels courts should prosecute cat burners, or give them adequate counseling, diversions, etc., because they are at risk.

Let's go back to the lawyer those bereaving cat owners contacted. When they asked him to help prosecute the boy who strangled their cat, he said they didn't stand a chance. It was only a cat.

If the lawyer had armed himself with statistics from the Humane Society of the United States, he might have bolstered his case.

And what about the lawyer who stepped in when the cat killer strangled the child the following year? She could have used the same data to make the case against the murderer. The boy strangled a cat; didn't this indicate something about how dangerous he might be to people?

"Lawyers can introduce this data in plea bargains, custody agreements, and so forth," Lockwood says. "If lawyers want to document the poor care an elder is getting, then why not bring up the poor care the pets are getting?" Maybe the front door's always open; dogs run out in the street and have gotten hit by cars. Or there's broken glass on the porch that cats get cut on.

Lockwood would like to see felony-level penalties for juveniles and adults who abuse animals. "Putting everyone in jail isn't the solution. But when animal abuse is a felony, it's easier to investigate cases and require counseling, diversions, and so forth."

Teach Children to Care About Animals

"*E*very school should require humane education," Lockwood says. "And we should put children who come from violent homes into programs like Green Chimneys, where they learn to treat animals kindly."

He's seen about six adolescent animal abusers turn around dramatically after judges sentenced them to work in animal shelters.

"The adolescents bathed and trained the animals, helped adopt them out and helped give them veterinary care. It was a chance for the teens to undo the wrongs they'd done."

One teen had nearly killed a dog by dragging it behind his car. Lockwood says, "We gave him a camera and sent him out with cruelty investigators. He saw stuff that turned his stomach. We also made him hold animals while they were being euthanized." The boy rescued and helped rehabilitate a dog hit by a train.

Lockwood recalls, "He ended up writing me and the judge, saying this changed his life. It's been three years, and he has no other offenses."

Should we wait until people mangle or kill an animal before we act? Lockwood says no. "If a 10-year-old keeps pulling a cat's tail even after a warning, start asking questions. Why is she doing it? Is she saying, 'I want Daddy's attention,' or 'I want Mommy to set more limits for me,' or 'I'm feeling really bad about something that happened to me, and I want to make something else feel that bad?' You might also try to find out where the child learned to yank the cat's tail."

Why should you, an elder care professional, be worrying about a cat's tail? Picture the little girl 50 years from now, caring for her elderly mother. — *BR*

EXPERIENCES WITH RITUALIST CHILD SEXUAL ABUSE: A CASE STUDY FROM THE NETHERLANDS

F. JONKER AND P. JONKER-BAKKER

General practitioners, Oude Pekela, The Netherlands

Adapted for English publication by Jane Gray, M.D., Kempe National Center, Denver, CO

IN MAY 1987, cases of child sexual abuse came to light in Oude Pekela, an industrial Dutch village of 8,000 in northeastern Holland. The purpose of this communication is to (1) describe the children's stories, behaviors, and physical findings; (2) relate the community's reactions; and (3) propose suggestions for improving evaluations of ritualistic child sexual abuse.

CHILDREN'S STORIES, BEHAVIORS, PHYSICAL FINDINGS

A 4-year-old boy with anal bleeding presented to a general practice office in Oude Pekela during May 1987. The initial evaluation revealed no clear cause for the anal bleeding. Over the next few days the child told a story of sexual abuse, including a history of sticks being inserted into his anus, and mentioned a friend who had also been involved. The two sets of parents collaborated and subsequently contacted the police. When the index child was again seen medically because of persistent anal bleeding, the mother told us about his story of sexual abuse and her contact with the police.

Law enforcement interviews began immediately. When the two boys implicated 25 other children, 17 officers were assigned to the police investigation team, but that number was involved for a short time. Only a few members of the criminal investigation team had experience interviewing child witnesses, and they had little awareness or any knowledge of "ritual crimes." The total investigation time lasted 18 months but did not produce any incriminating evidence such as admissions by the offenders, photographs, or videotapes although children reported being involved in filming activities. During this time 98 children, 4–11 years of age, were interviewed. There was no possibility of all the children knowing each other, as they lived in different areas and attended different schools. Younger children (3–6) were implicated early, but eventually cases of older victims became known. Usable information was provided by 62 of the children, and 48 children gave clear statements of sexual victimization.

During the interviews, the children told of events consistent with large scale ritualistic abuse. They described watching a videotape and seeing their friends on the screen, a tactic

---

Presented at the 3rd International Conference on Incest and Related Problems at the Institute of Education of London University, August 1989.

probably used to overcome the children's resistance and fear. Then parties were held, and the children were instructed to undress. They remembered sitting on the floor naked, being forced to lick the genitals and breasts of adults, and walking around in circles with little leather belts tied around their penises. They also told of swimming in pools where their heads were dunked under water, of being washed with colored shampoo, and of rubbing paint on each other. They spoke of having feces rubbed on them, being urinated on, being forced to remove feces from the anus of an adult, and than having to eat the feces and drink urine and semen. Twigs and other small objects, such as plastic toys, were inserted into penises, vaginas and rectums. The children were forced to have genital and oral-genital contact with adults and each other. Many children of both sexes and all age groups reported seeing animals; some were real, and others were adults dressed as animals, i.e., bears, lions, crocodiles, etc. Dogs were set loose on them and became "wolves."

The children told of being beaten with belts which had hooks on them, punched in the stomach, tied to poles while knives and stones were thrown at them, and of being locked in closets and cages. Some children spoke of a rope being tightened around their neck until their "eyes rolled around in their heads."

The children also talked of more bizarre events, such as being in a church and having to lie naked on a table. They said that they saw Caucasian and black babies strapped into cradles. Then they were forced to cut the babies loose and carve a cross on their backs. They also saw a dead baby in a plastic bag, and told of a black baby whom they were forced to hit with sticks. However, they were told that hitting this baby wasn't bad because "black babies don't have a heart or blood anyway." When interviewers asked the children, "Wasn't the black baby a doll?" they replied, "No, have you ever seen a doll crawl or heard one cry?" The children said they had played with dolls on certain occasions, but that these dolls were without heads. It was clear the children could distinguish between dolls and human infants.

A number of children spoke of a brown-skinned, deformed child who was about 6 years old. A yellow cross was placed on the child's chest, after which the chest was cut open; something reddish brown was taken out and placed in a little box. The children spoke of similar happenings with white babies and animals. These events all took place in a dark shed with lighted candles. The children were forced to wear long white robes and assist with killings by beating the victims with shovels. Then the remains were thrown into deep pits.

They told of an elderly couple who did not look European, who were murdered too. The children said they couldn't always understand the adults, as they spoke a strange sounding language and reported that the leader was called "master." The adults threatened the victims not to talk about their experiences lest their parents would be killed, their home set on fire, or they would experience what was done to a kitten, which the children had seen killed by a circular saw.

COMMUNITY REACTIONS

The children told of these events early in the interviewing process, but adults had difficulty believing them. The police and some parents thought the stories were fantasies and ignored them. The children then felt they were not being believed and stopped talking about these events. The authorities elected not to make these stories known to the public. However, several parents wrote down the stories their children told them at confidential times (bedtime), and months later substantiating details were related by other children.

Unfortunately, the interviews and physical examinations of the children were not done systematically. Often several policemen interviewed the same child. Interviews were done in the home, and subsequent interviewing took place also in the schools. Our experience was that the children were less reticent to talk at school to the teacher since they had been threatened if they told their parents. Some police inquiries were superficial: Not all the children thought to be involved were interviewed; some were interviewed individually and others in groups. Problems with the police investigation may have stemmed, in part, from their initial disbelief, leading to a delay in consultation with experts in the fields of police inquiry and child psychiatry.

After six weeks of nonproductive police inquiry and partially due to pressure by the media, the Justice Department consulted a child psychiatrist. Differences of opinion between the physicians, criminal investigators, and the public prosecutor developed, which compounded the problem. The Justice Department had requested that the child psychiatrist only determine whether something had actually happened to the children. He interviewed the children at school or the police station, either individually or in groups. The children's statements were consistent in detail; and when interviewed in groups, the children often corrected each other or added more information. His conclusion was that something had happened beginning in August 1986 and reached its peak during Easter vacation of April 1987. His interviews revealed that children of both sexes, between the ages of 3 and 12, were coaxed or forced, either singularly or in groups, into buildings in the area of Oude Pekela. They were then engaged in "games" which culminated in sexual activities. The smaller children were usually kept together in groups during the abuse, while the older children were abused in groups and/or individually. Many of the children were abducted more than once, in different groups, by different adults (both men and women) who approached the children in different cars or on bicycles and then brought the children to different buildings. Sometimes the abductors were dressed as clowns. Often the children were abducted under the influence of drugs put in candy, lemonade, and ice cream; by pills, injections, or black balloons placed over their mouths.

Parents were not kept informed by the authorities of the progress of the investigation. They heard contradictory reports in the press and began to feel they were not being taken seriously by the police or local government. Therefore, in January 1988, an anonymous group of parents wrote a letter outlining their children's experiences and distributed it throughout the community. This disclosure resulted in community upheaval, and within two days the police arrested two possible offenders. However, the suspects were subsequently released because of lack of evidence. The next week a meeting was held to explain the circumstances of the investigation to the infuriated parents. The atmosphere of the meeting was tense and hostile as the parents were unable to accept the fact that the police had no results from their investigations. The parents decided they had no confidence in the police or local government, reproached them for their lack of interest, and refused to give them any more information.

Then the Minister of Justice himself decided to go to the village and speak with the parties separately in order to pacify parents and restore confidence. After his visit, the parents again gave information to police, but a feeling of trust that the childrens' disclosures would be dealt with was never restored.

Survey

The authors attempted to acquire more objective data by undertaking a survey of the parents of 90 of the children 6–8 weeks after the first disclosures. The survey studied children's behavioral changes which had become apparent to their parents. The information gathered from the survey is not reported using scientific criteria nor analyzed statistically but rather is presented as behavioral changes worthy of clinical note. It should also be stated that the number of older children in the survey was relatively low inasmuch as older children did not disclose until later because of shame, confusion, and fear. Moreover by the time of the survey, police activities had already been reduced, and many of the older victims had not yet been discovered. Also it was impossible to contact the parents of all children thought to be involved.

The questionnaire surveyed 63 families having a total of 90 children (49 males and 41 females); 66 of these children had been interviewed by the police. Ages ranged from 3–10, with 65% of the children 5 years old or younger. Of the parents surveyed, 87% were certain that their children had been involved; 12% felt involvement was a possibility; and none felt that their children definitely were not involved. However, the police felt that of the 66 they interviewed, 48% were certainly involved; 39% had a definite possibility of involvement; 9% were only possibly involved; and 3% were definitely not involved. The reason for police interviewing only a part of the children was that to their opinion more interviewing would not bring fresh and useful information.

Behaviors surveyed included sleep disturbances, enuresis, sexualized behaviors, swearing, aggression, isolation and anxiety. While a few children exhibited some of these behaviors before the abuse, most of these behaviors began or were aggravated during the abuse (sleep disturbances, enuresis, aggression and anxiety); others (sexualized behaviors, including masturbation and tongue kissing, swearing, and isolation) were noticed after the child's involvement was recognized. A few children showed a decrease in symptomatology or displayed them equally throughout the study period. Although every parent at first had found plausible explanations for physical abnormalities, by the time of the survey they remembered signs/symptoms from the phase when sexual abuse was ongoing but involvement not yet recognized. In both sexes the most common physical signs and symptoms noted by the parents were bruises in abnormal places and unusual sleepiness, possibly due to the drugs. The next most common signs noted were inflamed genitalia and pain on urination or defecation, complaints of itching inflamed anal areas (more common in boys), and stained underwear (more common in girls).

Even though many parents, physicians, social workers, police officers, and members of the general public believed that the children's stories were true, there was still a large number of people who ascribed the stories to the children's fantasies. This disbelief had negative influence on the children and their parents. The controversy surrounding the events in Oude Pekela made great demands on many parents, leaving them little time or energy to come to terms with what had happened to their children and to support them. The Dutch police remain unconvinced. Even the concerned public prosecutor has said, "Just because it happens in the States, doesn't mean that it happens here." There seemed to be little knowledge of occultism and no eagerness to learn.

SUGGESTIONS FOR IMPROVING EVALUATIONS

The professionals who were involved have reassessed the evaluation process in order to clarify issues and propose suggestions to improve assessments in large scale ritualistic sexual abuse.

Child sexual abuse victims are often fearful and confused. Therefore, professionals who interview or examine them must approach them with openness, understanding, and compassion. This attitude helps the child feel that he or she is being taken seriously. Experiments show that children are not more suggestible than adults. It is therefore more likely that because of that fear and confusion, a child will falsely deny the matter than falsely accuse. One can also experience, as we have done in Oude Pekela, that a child after telling an entire story will then say: "I made it all up." The pressure and fear have then became too much for the child. The effect ritualistic abuse has had on the child must always be kept in mind.

Interviewers of sexually abused children must not reject a child's story, no matter how impossible or bizarre it seems. When a child is ready to talk, it is essential to allow time for the child to elaborate while the interviewer maintains a nondirective attitude. In addition, it is important for the interviewer to note how the child tells the story, what the child is actually saying, when he is expressing feelings, and what constitutes the real details. During the Oude Pekela interviews, a discrepancy was sometimes noted between the expected affect of the children and the events, especially with the terrible facts. When the use of drugs became apparent, the reasons for this discrepancy became clear. Impairment of the senses by drugs also hindered the children's ability to identify abductors and locate sites.

The interviewer must understand the child's vocabulary and his/her meaning of the words, being careful to record the child's exact statements and not translate or interpret. The interviewer also needs to observe and record the child's affect while he/she tells the story. Smaller children of Oude Pekela spoke of scary animals in the form of lions. When the older children spoke of lions, they did not show fear because they had seen zippers on the paws of the lions and understood that the lions were adults wearing costumes.

Older children were more reticent to tell what had happened to them. The interviewer must recognize that children with previously identified problems, or from a broken home, are more inclined to be influenced by earlier traumas when answering questions than a child from a well-functioning family. The parents were also subject to feelings of shame, so that within entire families few members might be aware or able to talk of the child's involvement.

It was also learned that children were not as capable as adults in arranging events in chronologic order and did not spontaneously report the totality of events, but over time they were able to elaborate. The children often recalled entire events when they could associate them within their own experiences, i.e., seeing certain streets or kinds of cars helped them remember. Therefore, it is important to conduct several interviews during the evaluation process. At first we were not aware of the satanic rituals; we heard many things from the children which we could not understand, and ascribed them to the children's fantasies. Repeated interviews over time clarified these issues.

Even though a child is fearful, one has to give serious consideration to the interviewing of the child. Some Oude Pekela children became less fearful after telling of their experiences; thus some of the interviews with the child psychiatrist became therapeutic as well as diagnostic. After visits with the psychiatrist, some children became more relaxed, especially when they told of a traumatic but heretofore concealed experience and they did not meet with the disapproval they had expected.

An essential part of any investigation of children is involvement of the parents. However, the evaluators need to determine whether the relationship between the parents and child is good and if the parents are capable of participation. Needless to say, parents must also be interviewed with sensitivity and empathy. They should be asked to write down the child's story word for word, record when he or she says it, what the child's emotional state seems to be, and whether the disclosure is influenced by external factors.

The difference in reactions between mothers and fathers was striking. The fathers were furious for a short period, even wanting to kill the possible offenders. Then they wished to hear nothing more about it, and later some denied the situation. The mothers were sad for the child and concerned about the child's future. Frequently the marital relationship became tense with each partner having little understanding of the other's feelings. Couples spoke of loss of libido and even feelings of disgust towards sexuality. Not infrequently parents would remark, "We would like to have another baby who is still pure and not so damaged."

All children suspected of being victimized should undergo a standardized and complete physical examination by a medical practitioner experienced in the field of child sexual abuse.

Not all of the children in Oude Pekela were physically examined, and no child examined showed permanent physical damage.

In summary, the literature indicated that ritualistic child sexual abuse is not rare. Finkelhor (1988) found signs of ritual abuse in 13% of cases involving sexually abused children in daycare centers in the United States. Other cases of ritualistic abuse have been reported in Canada and England. Case reports indicate babies are sacrificed during satanic rites, with blood playing an important role in this context. Mutilation of animals is commonly used as a threat to ensure the child's compliance with secrecy. In some cults sacrifices are preferably made between Palm Sunday and Easter.

It is important for child abuse professionals to be aware that the most bizarre stories may indicate the possibility of satanic rituals. The Oude Pekela affair received much attention, outrage, and denial in the press. Parents were depicted as being subject to mass hysteria and fanatic porno hunters. Since then, other cases of multiple child sexual abuse by nonrelatives have come to light, but the level of public concern has clearly diminished. The public appears to have become accustomed to the phenomenon. Large scale sexual abuse of children and child pornography threatens to become a part of organized crime with its financial gains, all at the expense of children.

Acknowledgement—The authors are most grateful to Professor G. Mik, child psychiatrist consulted by the Minister of Justice regarding the Oude Pekela investigation, for his useful comments.

REFERENCE

Finkelhor, D., Williams, L., & Burns, N. (1988). *Nursery crimes: Sexual abuse in daycare*. London: Sage.

PATIENTS REPORTING RITUAL ABUSE IN CHILDHOOD: A CLINICAL SYNDROME. REPORT OF 37 CASES

WALTER C. YOUNG

The National Center for the Treatment of Dissociative Disorders, Denver, CO

ROBERTA G. SACHS AND BENNETT G. BRAUN

Dissociative Disorders Program, Rush North Shore Medical Center, Rush-Presbyterian-
St. Luke's Medical Center, Chicago, IL

RUTH T. WATKINS

School of Professional Psychology, University of Denver, Denver, CO

Abstract—Thirty-seven adult dissociative disorder patients who reported ritual abuse in childhood by satanic cults are described. Patients came from a variety of separate clinical settings and geographical locations and reported a number of similar abuses. The most frequently reported types of ritual abuse are outlined, and a clinical syndrome is presented which includes dissociative states with satanic overtones, severe post-traumatic stress disorder, survivor guilt, bizarre self abuse, unusual fears, sexualization of sadistic impulses, indoctrinated beliefs, and substance abuse. Questions relating to issues of reliability, credibility and verfiability are addressed in depth, and the findings and implications are discussed.

Key Words—Ritual abuse, Satanic cults, Dissociation.

INTRODUCTION

OVER THE PAST several years, the authors have evaluated and treated increasing numbers of patients who report ritual abuse by satanic cults during childhood. The reports were initially met with disbelief, and a search of the professional literature revealed only a few references which related specifically to the ritual abuse of children by satanic cults. Reports of abuse in connection with satanic rituals have been included in descriptions of the types of childhood abuses reported by multiple personalities (Braun, 1986; Kluft, 1988; Putnam, 1989). Other authors have described ritual abuse and some of the consequences for adult and child survivors (Gould, 1987; Kelley, 1988; Terr, 1988). Hill and Goodwin (1989) noted the similarities between current patient reports and historical descriptions of satanic rituals.

Reprinted from *Child Abuse and Neglect* 15 (1991): 181–89, with kind permission of Elsevier Science Ltd., Oxford, England.

This paper describes a group of adults with similar psychopathology who report having been abused in childhood during the rituals of satanic cults. Satanic cults are specifically defined here as, and limited to, intrafamilial, transgenerational groups that engage in explicit satanic worship which includes the following criminal practices: ritual torture, sacrificial murder, deviant sexual activity, and ceremonial cannibalism. The authors have specifically chosen the word "ritual," rather than "ritualistic," to describe satanic abuse. This is to emphasize that these patients are reporting abuse which occurred in connection with specific satanic rituals and to avoid any implication that the abuse was "ritual-like."

A report is presented of 37 cases that displayed a number of symptoms thought to reflect a clinical syndrome. The most frequently reported types of ritual abuse and psychiatric sequelae are outlined and followed by illustrative clinical vignettes. Questions relating to issues of reliability, credibility, and verifiability are then addressed in depth and the findings and implications discussed.

METHOD

Thirty-seven patients, ranging in age from 18 to 47 years, were evaluated over a period of two years (1986–1988) following referral for treatment of dissociative disorders. Evaluation consisted of psychological assessment and ongoing clinical interviews, so that data collection began when patients entered treatment and continued as it progressed. Thirty patients (27 females and 3 males) were diagnosed and treated as inpatients. They were admitted to five separate wards in four separate hospitals across the country. Seven patients (six female and one male) were treated as outpatients. Patients were included in the study if they carried a DSM-III-R (1987) diagnosis of multiple personality disorder (MPD) or dissociative disorder not otherwise specified (NOS), and if they reported ritual abuse associated with satanic worship. Patients were excluded if they left treatment before six months had elapsed or there was otherwise insufficient documentation in their medical records. The predominance of female MPD patients is consistent with gender incidence differences reported elsewhere in the literature (Putnam, 1989).

The patients treated on the inpatient wards attended some group activities and group psychotherapy together. There were also opportunities for informal interactions. However, the authors believe that there was minimal discussion between patients of their reports of satanic abuse, as patients tended to be secretive about this information and reluctant to share.

Most of the information and reports of childhood ritual abuse emerged gradually over the course of treatment. Patients typically presented with some memories of abuse at home, but nearly complete dissociation for the ritual abuse. At times, intrusive images of cult abuse arose unexpectedly while patients were in the process of working through memories of familial abuse. Reports occurred spontaneously as patients abreacted, dreamed, or experienced flashbacks of people wearing robes in rituals. Reports also occurred in dissociated states and during hypnotic interviews. In general, those related during dissociated states, hypnosis and abreactions appeared in a piecemeal fashion. They often appeared to be combinations of a number of memories that had been condensed and lacked a clear sequencing of events. The reports were elaborated as treatment progressed and patients could focus in greater detail on material that was deeply repressed. Additional information was obtained from patient journals, artwork and, in a few cases, through a review of clinical records subsequent to discharge from the treatment facility.

Table 1. Percentage of 37 Patients Reporting 10 Ritual Abuses in Childhood

Abuse Reported	# Patients	% Patients
1. Sexual abuse	37	100
2. Witnessing and receiving physical abuse/torture	37	100
3. Witnessing animal mutilation/killings	37	100
4. Death threats	37	100
5. Forced drug usage	36	97
6. Witnessing and forced participation in human adult and infant sacrifice	31	83
7. Forced cannibalism	30	81
8. Marriage to satan	26	78[a]
9. Buried alive in coffins or graves	27	72
10. Forced impregnation and sacrifice of own child	20	60[a]

Total # patients = 37. Total female patients = 33. Total male patients = 4.
Note. Records gathered from discharged patients may not have documented the data of some abuses, so that the table may reflect a lower than actual level of positive findings.
[a] Percentages based on 33 female patients.

Report of 37 Cases

Ritual abuse. All patients reported abusive rituals during satanic worship, but reported some differences such as the color of robes worn by cult members, types of cult-related symbols and instruments, or details of rituals. The ritual abuses most frequently reported included forced drug usage, sexual abuse, witnessing and receiving physical abuse/torture, witnessing animal mutilation and killings, being buried alive in coffins or graves, death threats, witnessing and forced participation in infant "sacrifice" and adult murder, "marriage" to satan, forced impregnation and sacrifice of own child, and forced cannibalism. Table 1 lists these ritual abuses and the percentages of patients reporting them.

Patients often had a difficult time relating memories of ritual abuse which they had been told to keep secret. Communication of this material was typically accompanied by marked internal opposition, and often followed by self-destructive behaviors. Table 1 reflects the numbers of patients reporting these abuses at the end of the study.

The clinical syndrome. The clinical syndrome presented here represents a set of symptoms or psychiatric sequelae exhibited by the majority of the study population. These included unusual fears, survivor guilt, indoctrinated beliefs, substance abuse, severe post-traumatic stress disorder, bizarre self-abuse, sexualization of sadistic impulses, and dissociative states with satanic overtones (see Table 2).

Table 2. Percentage of 37 Patients Displaying 8 Psychiatric Sequelae from Reported Ritual Abuse in Childhood

Sequelae	# Patients	% Patients
1. Severe post-traumatic stress disorder[a]	37	100
2. Dissociative states with satanic overtones	37	100
3. Survivor guilt	36	97
4. Indoctrinated beliefs	35	94
5. Unusual fears	34	91
6. Sexualization of sadistic impulses	32	86
7. Bizarre self-abuse	31	83
8. Substance abuse	23	62

[a] Met requirements for DSM-III-R.

PTSD symptoms were prominent, with high levels of anxiety and panic, easy triggering by external stimuli, flashbacks, nightmares and intrusive images. These symptoms alternated with states of withdrawal, feelings of numbness, or shifts into dissociated functional states or alter personalities.

Other symptoms common to the study population included hearing internal voices or conversations, experiencing a sense of being controlled by inner forces, and periods of amnesia. These were related to the underlying dissociative disorder and were not symptoms of psychosis.

Clinical vignettes.

Vignette #1. A. was a 30-year-old female admitted for the evaluation and treatment of multiple personality disorder. Prior to hospitalization, A. had been recalling memories of incest and sexual abuse as a child. As these memories were uncovered, A.'s level of functioning began to drop, and she became increasingly suicidal. She was hospitalized, presenting an acute danger to herself.

A. displayed symptoms of anxiety and depression upon admission. Mental status examination and psychological testing revealed no evidence of a thought disorder or psychosis. Post-traumatic stress disorder was indicated when test stimuli triggered intrusive memories and flashbacks. Prior psychiatric history included several brief hospitalizations over the last ten years for suicide attempts and unexplained self-lacerations. A. had previous diagnoses of psychotic delusional depression, bipolar disorder, borderline personality disorder, and schizophrenia. Medical history included permanent sterility as a result of pelvic inflammatory disease at age 15.

Shortly after admission, one of A.'s child personality alters drew a picture which depicted a ceremonial altar, people wearing robes, and a number of satanic symbols. The child alter described the drawing as a ritual in which an infant was apparently sacrificed. Following this dissociative episode, A. reported that a satanic-like alter was now determined to punish the child alter for "telling secrets." A. subsequently carved inverted crosses upon her forearm, describing anesthesia and relief at the sight of her own blood.

Over the course of treatment, further reports emerged of ritual abuse occurring between the ages of 3–16 years. A. experienced abreactions in which she appeared to be reliving memories of abuse and indoctrination that included torture, electrical shock, and a mock operation where she was told that a bomb was placed inside her body that would explode if she ever told secrets or did not obey the dictums of her cult. A. also experienced abreactions where she appeared to be giving birth. She reported the memory of a serial rape by male cult members when she was 13 years old, resulting in pregnancy. After premature induction of labor, A. reported that she was forced to assist in her infant's sacrifice. It was this event which had been represented by the earlier drawing. A. recalled two more pregnancies which were terminated by forced abortions. The fetuses were reportedly dismembered, and body parts and fluids consumed during the rituals which followed.

A. experienced a major depressive episode and severe survivor guilt as memories of ritual abuse surfaced. She became confused over whether she was a victim of a criminal satanic cult or a perpetrator of unspeakable crimes. On several occasions A. was found masturbating in a dissociated state while using a doll to reenact the killing of an infant. She experienced flashbacks in which she pictured her father and paternal grandmother dressed in robes during rituals. She was terrified of any gifts or correspondence received from family members, as she felt they were meant to convey an order of silence. A. was observed to be particularly anxious and prone to flashbacks on both Christian and satanic holidays.

Vignette #2. B. was a 38-year-old female admitted for the treatment of multiple personality disorder. Her symptoms included a long history of significant substance abuse, depressive episodes, unusual fears, suicidal gestures, dissociation, and self-mutilating behaviors. The latter included several bizarre forms of self-abuse such as carving triple 6s on her leg. Psychiatric history consisted of numerous hospitalizations since the age of 16 years, and a variety of diagnoses including schizophrenia, schizoaffective disorder, and borderline personality disorder with psychotic features. Mental status examination and extensive psychological testing revealed no evidence of a thought disorder or psychosis. B. dissociated on several occasions during the testing, displaying an alter personality which was clearly different in presentation. Medical history included complaints of migraine headaches since grade school and periodic consultations for unusual somatic disturbances which could not be diagnosed. Examination revealed extensive scarring as a result of self-inflicted lacerations and cigarette burns on her forearms and legs.

B. presented two systems of dissociative states. One system appeared to be identified primarily with familial abuse, while the other appeared to be identified with cult functions and roles. For example, one alter personality's sole responsibility was reportedly to mutilate animals in sacrifices at specific times during satanic rituals. Other alters, with names such as "Natas" and "Keeper" reportedly emerged at certain times to carry out other specific ritual-related tasks. B. reported the belief that she must kill herself at age 39 if she had failed to rejoin the satanic cults into which she had been initiated.

B. was a strict vegetarian who exhibited on several occasions an extreme phobic response to red meat. She also responded in a phobic manner when she underwent an EEG. B. later connected this specific fear to having undergone cult indoctrination involving the use of electric shock.

During hospitalization, B. made a serious suicide attempt in which she taped her mouth shut, put a bag over her head, and taped her hands behind her back so she could not easily be resuscitated if discovered. B. also exhibited bizarre sexualization of her sadistic impulses. In one instance, she was found to have inserted razor blades into her vagina while masturbating.

DISCUSSION

The clinical picture presented by patients who report ritual abuse in childhood raises key questions related to their reliability, verifiability, and credibility. The reliability of these reports depends upon the extent to which the patients reporting the information and the methods used to obtain the information can be trusted and relied upon. The availability and consistency of confirmatory data and hard evidence determines the verifiability. Both of these combine to influence the plausibility of these reports and, ultimately, their credibility. While all of the questions related specifically to these three issues cannot be answered definitively at this time, they need to be articulated for the purpose of future investigations.

Reliability

It is striking that the patient group reported many similar experiences despite coming from diverse areas, being treated in different locations, and having minimal contact with each other. Unfortunately, the present study does not rule out the possibility that these patients had read nonprofessional literature describing reports of satanic cult activity and ritual childhood abuse. They could have incorporated certain incidents from articles or books as "pseudo-memories," and retrieved them with the same conviction as real memories (American Medical Association, 1985; Orne, 1979, 1980; Pettinati, 1988). It is also possible that these patients have developed a powerful satanic metaphor for conveying and explaining other forms of severe abuse actually suffered during their childhoods.

Van Benschoten (1990) points out that reports cannot be accepted as literally accurate, but that the truth of reports are "inextricably woven together with threads of misperception, suggestion, illusion, dissociation, and induced trance phenomena, to form the complex web which becomes the survivor's memories" (p. 29).

There are additional problems related to patient reliability. Patients often reported being drugged during rituals, which could affect the reliability of their recall. Recall also could be influenced by deceptive cult practices designed to confuse initiates. Patients have reported that as older children they assisted in the deception of younger children: They had substituted dolls for real infants or, in one case, switched a pregnant woman with a female child who had been raped to demonstrate the power of satan to grow a woman and her baby almost instantaneously. If patients were very young at the time of abuse, the reports would contain distortions related to the stressful circumstances in which the memory was encoded and reflect their immature cognitive capacities.

Various internal misperceptions may also occur in dissociated states. Reported experiences may be real, distorted, or fabricated, or they may represent the confusion of real, fantasied, or misperceived elements. For example, one patient dissociated into a personality state who cut a pentagram on her forearm and marked her room with cult symbols. Later she had no idea what had happened, but another dissociated personality described a cult member who marked the wall and then cut her. This was experienced as a real external event by the second dissociated personality, who was unable to recognize that an internal interaction between dissociated states had been mistaken for a real event.

On the other hand, the development of multiple personality disorder and other dissociative disorders is known to follow prolonged abuse in childhood (Kluft, 1985a; Putnam, 1989; Spiegel, 1986). Further, a large percentage of abused children will use dissociative defenses (Emde, 1971; Fraiberg, 1982; Kluft, 1985a, 1985b; Young, 1988a, 1988b). Therefore, it is not surprising that if patients endured extensive and terrifying experiences of satanic ritual abuse in childhood, they would subsequently appear in clinical treatment settings presenting dissociative defenses.

With regard to methodology, the reliability of memories retrieved during hypnosis has been the subject of exhaustive study (Pettinati, 1988). While hypnosis has been found to enhance recall of repressed memories in amnesic patients, it may also result in the reporting of increased amounts of false information (American Medical Association, 1985; Orne, 1979, 1980). Patients in this study who integrated personality states during treatment became increasingly certain that their reports of ritual abuse reflected actual memories. The patients who remained fragmented were less inclined to be certain about what really happened. The patients often had difficulty reporting memories separately and sequentially, similar to the tendency of deeply hypnotized subjects to recall memories in a disconnected fashion. Unfortunately, a definitive statement about the authenticity of memories retrieved during hypnosis cannot presently be made, other than to note that memory may be both enhanced or fabricated during hypnosis. Only the independent verification of patient reports can absolutely determine their credibility.

Verifiability

Confirmatory data and hard evidence in support of the patient reports was difficult to secure. None of these cases were referred to law enforcement agencies for verification. Family members were not contacted for reasons of confidentiality and because patients typically reported the involvement of at least one family member in the satanic worship. The patients expressed fears of retaliation if cult members should learn that they were reporting cult activities.

In spite of these limitations, some corroborative evidence was obtained. Patient physical examinations revealed the following stigmata: one patient with a distorted nipple, one patient with scars on the back that were not likely self-inflicted, one patient who displayed a satanic tatoo on his scalp representing a mark of identification for a specific cult, and one patient with a breast scar that reportedly resulted from a satanic ritual. Softer, but still suggestive, physical evidence included three cases of endometriosis diagnosed prior to age 16 and one case of sterility with a report of pelvic inflammatory disease at age 15.

Corroborative evidence was also obtained when patient photographs of alleged cult members were shown to other patients from a similar geographic region. Four patients independently identified, by name and cult roles, the individuals in the photographs. Neither group of patients were in contact with each other during their treatment with the authors when these independent identifications were made.

One patient reported being forced to watch her mother strangle a newborn sibling while her father also observed. Later a cult ritual was held in which the infant was dismembered and consumed. The mother informed the rest of the family that the child had died from "crib" death shortly after birth. Independent verification was partially obtained from a brother who remembered the pregnancy and a "funeral" at home, but never saw the infant. Neither the hospital in which the infant was statedly born, nor the state's Bureau of Vital Statistics had any record of the infant's birth or death.

Other "soft" evidence was obtained from a patient's grade school records. These revealed a significant drop in school performance from age 7–10 years, the three years that this patient reported cult participation and ritual abuse. School performance improved at age 11 when the family moved to a new town and ended their satanic cult involvement.

Credibility

These reports of ritual abuse are incredible. If they are true, the abuse typically began at an early age and was dissociated from conscious memory until treatment began. The authors were initially reluctant to even entertain the question of the credibility of these reports. It became unavoidable after the recognition that similar reports of ritual abuse were being made by patients from a variety of geographic locations, all presenting a similar clinical syndrome. The establishment of credibility is critical, not only for treatment purposes, but for ethical considerations as well. For instance, it would be important in instituting reporting procedures for law enforcement and child protection agencies. It is particularly important to at least attempt to establish credibility if patients report ongoing cult involvement.

Hill and Goodwin (1989) discuss credibility as a key issue in the treatment of survivors of extreme childhood trauma and abuse. Following a survey of pre-Inquisition historical documents describing satanism and satanic practices, they compiled a list of 11 elements of satanic ritual: (1) secret nocturnal feasting around a special table or altar; (2) ritual orgiastic sex involving incest, homosexuality, and anal intercourse; (3) imitations and reversals of the Christian mass; (4) ritual use of blood, semen, urine, or excrement; (5) sacrifice of embryos and infants often using knives followed by cooking in a cauldron and/or ritual cannibalism; (6) ritual use of animals; (7) ritual use of torches, candles, and darkness; (8) chanting, especially of names of demons; (9) drinking a drug or potion; (10) dancing backward in a circle or other ritual use of the circle; and (11) dismemberment of corpses and extraction of the heart. While Hill and Goodwin do not suggest that this historical evidence constitutes proof that patients' reports of ritual abuse by satanic cults are true, they do suggest that as one possibility to be considered for further investigation. It is interesting to note how the elements they list correlate with the abuses reported by the study population.

Ganaway (1989) urges caution in validating reports of ritual abuse and suggests that reports of ritual abuse may serve as screens to cover abuse of a more "prosaic" sort.

In a comprehensive overview, Van Benschoten (1990) reviews the current thinking about ritual abuse. She states that such reports can neither be accepted at face value nor unequivocally denied and urges critical judgement to avoid denying overgeneralizing the issue.

Several authors have addressed the issue of coercion and indoctrination among cult devotees (Galanter, 1982; Maleson, 1981; Spero, 1982; Ungerleider & Wellisch, 1979). Clark (1979) studied a range of nonsatanic religious sects and cults across the country. He noted the behavioral conditioning involved in the indoctrination of cult members, as well as the harsh penalties threatened or imposed on some members, including death. Clark also reports the presence of dissociation as a central adaptive mechanism, and that some cult members reported the awareness of a "double personality" (p. 280). Morse and Morse (1987), in describing psychotherapy with victims from a variety of cults and sects, comment on the "pairing of sex and pain" (p. 565). They note that "all victims show symptomatology of post-traumatic stress disorder" (p. 566), and frequently displayed dissociative symptoms. They further describe "imposed pathology" (p. 566), similar to the indoctrinated beliefs described by the patients in this study, and state there is "always present an intense underlying fear of retribution from the group or the leader" (p. 568). The DSM-III-R (1987) notes that dissociative states may occur in people "who have been subjected to periods of prolonged and intense coercive persuasion (e.g., brainwashing, thought reform, or indoctrination while the captive of terrorists or cultists)" (p. 277). What may be unique to the current population is the entrenchment of these patients' defenses and their satanic overtones.

CONCLUSION

This paper presents a clinical syndrome found in 37 patients reporting ritual abuse in childhood by satanic cults. The patients came from a variety of separate clinical settings and geographical locations and reported a number of similar abuses at the hands of cult members. All presented a similar clinical syndrome marked by dissociative states with satanic overtones, severe post-traumatic stress disorder, bizarre self-abuse, unusual fears, sexualization of sadistic impulses, indoctrinated beliefs, substance abuse, and survivor guilt.

Questions relating to the reliability of the study methods, along with a lack of strong, independent verification of all reports of ritual abuse presented in this paper, prevent a definitive statement that the reports of ritual abuse are true. Therefore, it is only possible at this time to describe a clinical syndrome of patients who report ritual abuse during childhood at the hands of satanic cults.

While these 37 patients report ritual abuse by cults, there is no intention to suggest that all satanic groups engage in this behavior. The patients reported here describe involvement in satanic cult groups from the earliest years of childhood, and appear to represent a different group of patients than teenagers who voluntarily report a vicarious involvement with satanic activity and paraphernalia. The reports of these patients which match other current reports of children being ritually abused in day care settings (Finkelhor, Williams, & Burns, 1988; Gould, 1987; Moss, 1987) make it imperative that we at least listen seriously to these reports and make careful assessments. Independent verification of the validity of these reports requires the publication of case studies where documentation of satanic cult abuse can be made.

REFERENCES

American Medical Association: Council on Scientific Affairs. (1985). Scientific status of refreshing recollections by the use of hypnosis. *Journal of the American Medical Association, 253,* 1918–1923.

Braun, B. G. (1986). Issues in the psychotherapy of multiple personality disorder. In B. G. Braun (Ed.), *Treatment of multiple personality disorder* (pp. 1–28). Washington DC: American Psychiatric Association Press.

Clark, J. G. (1979). Cults. *Journal of the American Medical Association, 242,* 279–281.

Diagnostic and statistical manual of mental disorders (3rd ed., rev.). (1987). Washington, DC: American Psychiatric Association Press.

Emde, R. (1971). Stress and neonatal sleep. *Psychosomatic Medicine, 33,* 491–497.

Finkelhor, D., Williams, L., & Burns, N. (1988). *Sexual abuse in day care: A national study.* Durham, NH: University of NH Press.

Fraiberg, S. (1982). Pathological defenses in infancy. *Psychoanalytic Quarterly, 51,* 612–635.

Galanter, M. (1982). Charismatic religious sects and psychiatry: An overview. *American Journal of Psychiatry, 139,* 1539–1548.

Ganaway, G. K. (1989). Historical truth versus narrative truth: Clarifying the role of exogenous trauma in the etiology of multiple personality disorder and its variants. *Dissociation, 2,* 205–220.

Gould, C. (1987). Satanic ritualistic abuse: Child victims, adult survivors, system response. *California Psychologist, 22,* 1.

Hill, S., & Goodwin, J. (1989). Satanism: Similarities between patient accounts and pre-Inquisition historical sources. *Dissociation, 2*(1), 39–44.

Kelley, S. J. (1988). Ritualistic abuse of children: Dynamics and impact. *Cultic Studies Journal, 5,* 228–236.

Kluft, R. P. (Ed.). (1985a). *Childhood antecedents of multiple personality.* Washington, DC: American Psychiatric Association Press.

Kluft, R. P. (1985b). Multiple personality in childhood. *Psychiatric Clinics of North America, 7,* 121–134.

Kluft, R. P. (1988). On giving consultations to therapists treating MPD. *Dissociation*, 1(3), 23–29.

Maleson, F. G. (1981). Dilemmas in the evaluation and management of religious cultists. *American Journal of Psychiatry*, 138, 925–929.

Morse, J., & Morse, E. (1987). Toward a theory of therapy with cultic victims. *American Journal of Psychotherapy*, 16, 563–570.

Moss, D. C. (1987). Are the children lying? *American Bar Association Journal*, 59, 59–62.

Orne, M. T. (1979). The use and misuse of hypnosis in court. *International Journal of Clinical and Experimental Hypnosis*, 27, 311–341.

Orne, M. T. (1980). On the construct of hypnosis: How its definition affects research and its clinical application. In G. Burrows & L. Dennerstein (Eds.), *Handbook of hypnosis & psychosomatic medicine*. Elsevier, North Holland: Biomedical Press.

Pettinati, H. M. (Ed.). (1988). *Hypnosis and memory*. New York: Guilford.

Putnam, F. W. (1989). *Diagnosis and treatment of multiple personality disorder*. New York: Guilford.

Spero, M. H. (1982). Psychotherapeutic procedure with religious cult devotees. *Journal of Nervous and Mental Disease*, 170, 332–344.

Spiegel, D. (1986). Dissociation, double binds, and post-traumatic stress in multiple personality disorder. In B. G. Braun (Ed.), *Treatment of multiple personality disorder* (pp. 61–77). Washington, DC: American Psychiatric Association Press.

Terr, L. (1988). What happens to early memories of trauma? *American Academy of Child and Adolescent Psychiatry*, 27, 96–104.

Ungerleider, J. T., & Wellisch, D. K. (1979). Coercive persuasion (brainwashing), religious cults and deprogramming. *American Journal of Psychiatry*, 136, 279–282.

Van Benschoten, S. C. (1990). Multiple personality disorder and satanic ritual abuse: The issue of credibility. *Dissociation*, 3, 22–30.

Young, W. C. (1988a). Observation on fantasy in the formation of multiple personality disorder. *Dissociation*, 1(3), 13–20.

Young, W. C. (1988b). Psychodynamics and dissociation: All that switches isn't split. *Dissociation*, 1(1), 33–37.

Résumé—Trente-sept patients adultes présentant des troubles dissociatifs et ayant subi des sévices rituels par des sectes sataniques au cours de leur enfance sont décrits. Les patients tout en provenant de sites cliniques et géographiques variés ont rapporté un nombre similaire d'abus. Les types d'abus rituels les plus fréquemment décrits sont analysés. Un syndrome clinique est présenté, comprenant des états dissociatifs à tendances sataniques, des états de tension post-tramatique très sévères une culpabilité du survivant, des automutilations bizarres, des peurs insolites, une sexualisation des pulsions sadiques, des croyances endoctrinées et de la toxicomanie. Les questions liées à la fiabilité, la crédibilité sont analysées en profondeur et les données et les implications sont discutées.

Resumen—Se describen treinta y siete adultos con trastornos disociativos que reportaron abuso ritual en la niñez por parte de cultos satánicos. Los pacientes vinieron de diferentes tipos de clínicas y localidades y reportaron un número de abusos similares. Se describen los tipos de abuso ritual reportados con mayor frecuencia, y se presenta un síndrome clínico que incluye estados disociativos con aspectos satánicos, trastornos severos de stress post-traumáticos, sentimientos de culpa del sobreviviente, auto-abuso bizarro, miedos extraños, sexualización de los impulsos sádicos, creencias por adoctrinamiento, y abuso de sustancias. Se analizan a fondo los problemas de fiabilidad, credibilidad y verificabilidad, y se comentan los resultados y sus implicaciones.

COMMENTARY

THE SATANIC RITUAL ABUSE CONTROVERSY

FRANK W. PUTNAM

Laboratory of Developmental Psychology, National Institute of Mental Health, Bethesda, MD

THE ISSUES RAISED by the papers of Jonker and Jonker-Bakker and Young and colleagues are representative of a major controversy dividing the child abuse community, the alleged existence of a vast international, multigenerational, conspiracy practicing religious worship of satan through sex and death rituals involving torture, incest, perverted sex, animal and human sacrifice, cannibalism, and necrophilia. In addition to suffering rape, bizarre tortures and being forced to participate in victimizing others, alleged victims of satanic ritual abuse (SRA) are often reported to have been "brainwashed" with the aid of hypnosis and drugs and implanted with suggestions to kill themselves or commit other acts on command. These "triggers" allegedly can be activated by covert cues embedded in prosaic objects, e.g., flowers or greeting cards, in a manner strikingly reminiscent of scenes from the "The Manchurian Candidate," a famous movie about "brainwashing" during the Korean War.

Although a few articles alleging SRA activities have been published in clinical journals, most of the information now circulating in the therapist, child protective service, and police communities is derived from workshops, seminars, symposia, and lectures delivered at trainings and professional meetings. As Mulhern has documented in a systematic study of the teaching techniques used by lecturers on SRA, many of these training sessions use a set of proselytizing strategies employed by organizations seeking to convert individuals to a specific belief system (Mulhern, 1991). In the past three years, scores of professional workshops on the diagnosis and treatment of SRA have been held in the United States and Canada. Some of the same presenters have participated in similar trainings and clinical consultations in England and Holland.

Despite the widespread dissemination of information on alleged SRA activities and the increasingly frequent diagnosis of SRA in patients with dissociative disorders, there is a complete absence of independent evidence corroborating the existence of such cults or their alleged activities such as human sacrifice, cannibalism, and sex and death orgies. Despite hundreds of investigations in the United States by local police departments and the Federal Bureau of Investigation, there has never been a single documented case of satanic murder, human sacrifice, or cannibalism (Lanning, 1989b). Similarly, the police in Holland and England, despite intensive investigations, have failed to find any evidence substantiating allegations of SRA. This disturbing failure to establish any credible independent verification of the

Reprinted from *Child Abuse and Neglect* 15 (1991): 175–79, with kind permission of Elsevier Science Ltd., Oxford, England.

existence of satanic ritual abusive activities has led many in the child abuse community to urge extreme caution in accepting allegations of SRA as established fact.

The papers considered here represent two major perspectives on the SRA problem, the allegations made by adults who report that they experienced SRA in childhood (Young et al.) and the allegations of children who report being recently involved in SRA (Jonker and Jonker-Bakker). It is commonly asserted in SRA trainings that the allegations of adult and children SRA victims are very similar, supporting claims that satanic cults are multigenerational. In actual fact, there are often major discrepancies between adult and child descriptions of SRA activities suggesting that these two sets of allegations may derive, in part, from separate sources and that they are not simply transgenerational equivalents. As Young et al. note, there is general agreement in the child abuse community that teenage use of satanic symbols and themes in heavy metal/punk rock music and culture is not directly related to the SRA allegations made by children or adults.

In evaluating reports of SRA it is important to note the underlying beliefs of the authors. The Jonker and Jonker-Bakker paper begins, "In May 1987, cases of child sexual abuse came to light in Oude Pekela . . . (p. 191)." Throughout this paper the authors express a firm and unwavering conviction that these acts did in fact happen and were accurately described by the children, although parents and the police expressed disbelief and ultimately the case was closed for lack of evidence. Young et al. (1991) seemingly adopt a more neutral position, although they indicate that their initial disbelief rapidly gave way to an increasing acceptance of the possibility of SRA, a shift paralleled by many of their patients who became ". . . increasingly certain that their reports of ritual abuse reflected actual memories" (p. 186). Most SRA workshops proceed from the strongly held conviction that SRA activities are real and constitute a major threat to our society.

Both papers state that their purpose is to convey to clinicians information on a set of symptoms and behaviors that constitute evidence for a specific SRA syndrome. Neither paper, however, contains a comparison group; consequently it is impossible to ascertain the specificity of these suggested sequelae. Based on Table 2, with the exception of the vaguely described "dissociative states with satanic overtones," the Young et al. (1991) sample would be symptomatically indistinguishable from any of the published series of MPD patients (e.g., Coons, Bowman, & Milstein, 1988; Putnam, Guroff, Silberman, Barban, & Post, 1986; Ross, Norton, & Wozney, 1989). Similarly, the list of behaviors noted by Jonker and Jonker-Bakker (sleep disturbances, enuresis, sexualized behaviors, swearing, aggression, isolation, and anxiety, p. 194) are indistinguishable from the effects of many types of stress and trauma in children and in no way constitute the specification of a unique SRA syndrome.

It is surprising how little actual data is contained in either paper. Although they refer to a survey of 90 children, the Jonker and Jonker-Bakker paper is entirely descriptive relying on quotations for documentation, several of which are clearly not first hand from the children, e.g., "Some children spoke of a rope being tightened around their neck until their 'eyes rolled around in *their heads*'" (italics added, p. 192). Repeatedly the Jonker and Jonker-Bakker paper implies that many or all of the children reported a similar experience, but never once actually gives the percentage of children responding positively or negatively. In the case of the adults, Young et al. were in an excellent position to gather a great deal of additional information, as well as detailed medical workups and photographic documentation of the physical findings that they cite as corroborative evidence. In the future, reviewers must require higher standards of data collection, documentation, and analysis to support claims of SRA syndromic specificity.

The only source of information on alleged SRA experiences for both papers are the memories of the alleged victims. Young et al. discuss a few of the many problems that patients with dissociative disorders have in remembering traumatic events. In addition to profound effects of trauma on recall, many of the memories of alleged satanic ritual abuse were uncovered with the use of hypnosis. Both laboratory and forensic investigations have shown a number of serious problems with the accuracy and validity of memories recovered through hypnotic techniques (Perry, Laurence, D'Eon, Tallant, 1988).

The principle argument that both papers use to advance the validity of their allegations is that these reports were made independently and yet are highly similar in detail. Nowhere, however, is there a systematic analysis of the actual degree of similarity of these allegations. Young et al. stress the geographic separation of their patients and claim that when their patients were in contact with each other, e.g., as patients on a unit specializing in the treatment of dissociative disorders, they were reluctant to reveal details to each other. Jonker and Jonker-Bakker state "There was no possibility of all the children knowing each other . . . (p. 191)." These assertions represent a naive and simplistic model of contagion, based on the idea that individuals must be in direct contact with each other to share common information. Studies of the sociometric patterns of rumor contagion have demonstrated that rumors, urban-legends, and other folk tales can be rapidly disseminated throughout our society and are shared in common by large numbers of people who have never directly met each other. The child abuse community is particularly susceptible to such a rumor process as there are multiple, interconnected communication/education networks shared by therapists and patients alike. In addition, there is massive media dissemination of material on the satanic through dramatic autobiographical accounts, sensational talk-shows, and news reports of alleged cases, not to mention the numerous movies and television programs that feature occult and demonic themes. Contagion and contamination are very real and powerful processes that can account for a large degree of apparent similarity in SRA allegations.

Using a strategy commonly observed in SRA seminars and lectures, Young et al. seek to link the allegations of their patients with accounts of satanic practices described in historical sources. In particular, they cite Hill and Goodwin (1989) as listing 11 elements of satanic ritual derived from pre-Inquisitional accounts. The article by Hill and Goodwin has been previously criticized as a highly selective reading of historical sources (Noll, 1989). Distinguished medieval scholars, including Cohn (1975) and Russell (1972) do not find any evidence that satanic cults, witches' covens, or black masses ever existed in those times. Rather it appears that these elements, which permeate many SRA workshop descriptions of satanism, first appeared as part of 18th and 19th century occult revivals, popular among the upper class in Europe and the United States (Cohn, 1975). However, allegations of ritual murder of infants, blood drinking, cannibalism, and other abominations have frequently been made by majority groups against minorities and were invoked by Hitler against the Jews and Gypsies. Indeed, in a few SRA seminars, one can detect an underlying antisemitic theme that is reminiscent of the Blood Libel.

The picture of the alleged satanic cults that emerges from the two papers is not readily believable. On the one hand, they are said to be highly organized, multigenerational, international groups with membership turnover (e.g., the Young et al. subject whose family left the cult when she turned 11 (p. 186) that practice highly codified religious rituals. On the other hand they are depicted as evil incarnate participating in violent cannibal rape orgies, which incredibly leave absolutely no trace of the blood and gore spilled. Equally incredibly, in the case of the Jonker and Jonker-Bakker paper, they were able to repeatedly lure large numbers of children away from their normal play or school activities, drug them, and force them to participate in painful and disgusting rituals without anyone ever noticing that the children were missing or without the children protesting to their parents or teachers. Such total child crowd control is incomprehensible to anyone who has ever tried to herd a group of children through a museum or zoo.

One must ask how can such large scale, violent, and bloody activities escape detection in every single instance where they have been alleged to have occurred? Authorities on criminal conspiracies note that the larger a conspiracy is and the longer that it is in operation, the more difficult it is to keep it a secret, particularly if members can leave the organization. Studies of real cults, e.g., Hare Krishna, Children of God, People's Temple, have shown that when such groups engage in violent or criminal behavior they often implode and disintegrate in rapid order. How do the satanists avoid this fate?

The most frightening image emerging from these two papers is not the alleged satanic conspiracy, but the actual massive social disorder that occurred in Oude Pekela, Holland. Jonker and Jonker-Bakker describe a community turned against itself, filled with fear, anger, and distrust. Ultimately, the national government had to intervene to restore some measure of confidence in the local authorities. Similar breakdowns in public trust of the police and social service agencies have occurred in connection with allegations of SRA activities in the United States and England. This is the most destructive legacy of such a witch hunt. The Jonker and Jonker-Bakker paper is particularly inflammatory in this regard, repeatedly stating or implying, without specifying any actual evidence, that the police were, at best, incompetent, unqualified, and neglectful. In the future, unsubstantiated charges of police or government incompetence or neglect in the handling of SRA investigations should not be published in professional journals as they only serve to erode public and professional trust in the law enforcement community. A loss of confidence in the police or a fracture in the crucial working alliance between the police and child protective services would be catastrophic for the safety and well-being of children at risk for abuse and neglect.

What then are we to make of the allegations contained in the two papers and the larger SRA controversy dividing the child abuse community? Like the now discredited "Missing Children Movement" of the early 1980s, which once alleged that tens to hundreds of thousands of children were being kidnapped and murdered each year, there may be a very small kernel of truth here, e.g., the U.S. Department of Justice now estimates that there are 52–158 children kidnapped and murdered by strangers each year, the majority being between 14–17 years of age (Lanning, 1989a). There is no evidence, however, to support claims that hundreds to tens of thousands of babies and children are being sacrificed or abused in satanic rituals.

The explanation for these claims probably lies in a complex set of dynamics operating in the larger child abuse community. Ganaway has discussed some of the psychological issues that appear involved in the confabulation of satanic allegations by adults (Ganaway, 1989). The material generated by the children is particularly susceptible to being influenced and/or misinterpreted by interviewers primed by SRA workshops to read evidence of satanic abuse into every nonspecific symptom of stress and trauma. The labyrinthine communication/rumor networks of the child abuse community, crisscrossing an array of disparate professions and disciplines, rapidly and uncritically transmits SRA allegations generating a false impression of menace and extracting a common denominator profile that is mistaken for evidence of similarity.

There is obviously more at work here than these elements, but this process can be studied and understood and a better approximation of the truth distilled. It is important to acknowledge that there is, in fact, a serious controversy within the child abuse community about the existence of SRA. It is important that we in the field seek to resolve this issue in an objective and scientific manner. Critiques and claims should focus on the nature, quality, and interpretation of the data rather than on the personalities involved. We must not permit disagreements on this subject to disrupt working relationships, to pit discipline against discipline, or to destroy the hard won credibility of child abuse victims, adult or child. There is a great deal at stake here.

REFERENCES

Cohn, N. (1975). *Europe's inner demons: An enquiry inspired by the great witch hunt.* New York: Basic Books.

Coons, P. M., Bowman, E. S., Milstein V. (1988). Multiple personality disorder: A clinical investigation of 50 cases. *Journal of Nervous and Mental Disease,* **176,** 519–527.

Ganaway, G. (1989). Historical truth versus narrative truth: Clarifying the role of exogenous trauma in the etiology of multiple personality disorder and its variants. *Dissociation,* 2, 205–220.

Hill, S., & Goodwin, J. (1989). Satanism: Similarities between patient accounts and preinquisition historical sources. *Dissociation,* 2, 39–44.

Lanning, K. V. (1989a).*Child sex rings: A behavioral analysis for criminal justice professionals handling cases of child sexual exploitation.* Washington, DC: National Center for Missing and Exploited Children.

Lanning, K. V. (1989b, October). Satanic, occult, ritualistic crime: A law-enforcement perspective. *Police Chief,* pp. 1–11.

Mulhern, S. A. (1991). Satanism and psychotherapy: A rumor in search of an inquisition. In J. T. Richardson, J. Best, & D. Bromley (Eds.), *The satanism scare.* Paris: Aldine de Gruyter.

Noll, R. (1989). Satanism, UFO abductions, historians and clinicians: Those who do not remember the past. *Dissociation,* 2, 251–253.

Perry, C. W., Laurence, J. R., D'Eon, J., Tallant, B. (1988). Hypnotic age regression techniques in the elicitation of memories: Applied uses and abuses. In H. Pettinati (Ed.), *Hypnosis and memory.* New York: Guilford Press.

Putnam, F. W., Guroff, J. J., Silberman, E. K., Barban, L., Post, R. M. (1986). The clinical phenomenology of multiple personality disorder: Review of 100 cases. *Journal of Clinical Psychiatry,* **47,** 285–293.

Ross, C. A., Norton, G. R., Wozney, K. (1989). Multiple personality disorder: An analysis of 236 cases. *Canadian Journal of Psychiatry,* **34,** 413–418.

Russell, J. B. (1972). *Witchcraft in the middle ages.* Ithaca, NY: Cornell University Press.

RITUAL ABUSE: A LAW ENFORCEMENT VIEW OR PERSPECTIVE

KENNETH V. LANNING

Behavioral Science Instruction and Research Unit
FBI Academy
Quantico, VA

ONE OF THE BASIC PROBLEMS of discussing or publishing articles about "ritualistic" abuse of children is how to precisely define it. After eight years of trying I have given up and prefer not to use the term. It is confusing, misleading, and counterproductive. The use of the word satanic is almost as confusing and certainly more emotional. I prefer the term multidimensional child sex ring.

Not all ritualistic activity is spiritually motivated. Not all spiritually motivated ritualistic activity is satanic. In fact, most spiritually or religiously based abuse of children has nothing to do with satanism. Most child abuse that could be termed "ritualistic" by various definitions is more likely to be physical and psychological than sexual in nature. Not all ritualistic activity with a child is abuse or a crime.

When a victim describes and investigation corroborates what sounds like ritualistic activity, several possibilities must be considered. The ritualistic activity may be part of the excessive religiosity of mentally disturbed, even psychotic offenders. It may be a misunderstood part of sexual ritualism. The ritualistic activity may be incidental to any real abuse. The offenders may be deliberately engaging in ritualistic activity with a child as part of child abuse and exploitation. The motivation, however, may not be to indoctrinate the child into a belief system, but to lower the inhibitions of control, manipulate, or confuse the child. To open the Pandora's box of labeling child abuse as "ritualistic" means to apply the definition to all acts by all spiritual belief systems.

There are many valid perspectives from which to assess and evaluate allegations of child sexual abuse. Parents may choose to believe simply because their children make the claims. The level of proof necessary may be minimal because the consequences of believing are within the family.

A therapist may choose to believe simply because his/her professional assessment is that the patient believes the victimization and describes it so vividly. The level of

Reprinted from *Child Abuse and Neglect* 15 (1991): 171–73, with kind permission of Elsevier Science Ltd., Oxford, England.

proof necessary may be no more than therapeutic evaluation because the consequences are between the therapist and patient. No independent corroboration may be required.

A social worker must have more real, tangible evidence of abuse in order to take protective action and initiate legal proceedings. The level of proof necessary must be higher because the consequences (denial of visitation, foster care) are greater.

The law enforcement officer deals with the criminal justice system. The levels of proof necessary are reasonable suspicion, probable cause, and beyond a reasonable doubt, because the consequences (criminal investigation, search and seizure, arrest, incarceration) are so great. The level of proof for taking action on allegations of criminal acts must be more than simply that someone alleged it and it is possible. This in no way denies the validity and importance of the parental, therapeutic, social welfare, or any other perspective of these allegations.

When, however, therapists and other professionals begin to conduct training, publish articles, and communicate through the media, the consequences become greater, and therefore the level of proof must be greater. The amount of corroboration necessary to act upon allegations of abuse is dependent upon consequences of such action. We need to be concerned about the dissemination and publication of unsubstantiated allegations of bizarre sexual abuse. Information needs to be disseminated to encourage communication and research about the phenomena. The risks, however, of intervenor and victim "contagion" and public hysteria are potential negative aspects of such dissemination.

Because of the highly emotional and religious nature of this topic, there is a greater possibility that dissemination of information will result in a kind of self-fulfilling prophecy. If such extreme allegations are going to be disseminated to the general public, they must be presented in the context of being assessed and evaluated from a professional perspective. Since most therapists do not have a staff of investigators, the assessment and evaluation of such allegations are areas where law enforcement and other professionals (anthropologists, folklorists, sociologists, etc.) may be of some assistance to each other in validating these cases individually and in general.

In 1983 when I first began to hear victims' stories of bizarre cults and human sacrifice, I tended to believe them. I had been dealing with bizarre deviant behavior for many years and had long since realized that almost anything is possible. The idea that there are a few cunning, secretive individuals in positions of power somewhere in this country regularly killing a few people as part of some ritual or ceremony and getting away with it is certainly within the realm of possibility. But the number of alleged cases began to grow and grow. We now have hundreds of victims alleging that thousands of offenders are murdering tens of thousands of people, and there is little or no corroborative evidence. The very reason many experts cite for believing these allegations (i.e., many victims, who never met each other, reporting the same events) is the primary reason I began to question some aspects of these allegations.

Any professional evaluating victims' allegations of ritualistic abuse cannot ignore the lack of physical evidence (no bodies or physical evidence left by violent murders), the difficulty in successfully committing a large-scale conspiracy crime (the more people involved in any crime conspiracy, the harder it is to get away with it), and human nature (intragroup conflicts resulting in individual self-serving disclosures are likely to occur in any group involved in organized kidnapping, baby breeding, and human sacrifice). There are alternative explanations for why people who never met each other can tell the same story. It is interesting to note that, without having met each other, the hundreds of people who claim to have been abducted by aliens from outer space also tell stories and give descriptions of the aliens that are similar to each other. This is not to imply that allegations of child abuse are in the same category as allegations of abductions by aliens from outer space. It is intended only to illustrate that individuals who never met each other can sometimes describe similar events without necessarily have experienced them.

Why then are victims describing things that don't SEEM to be true? This is the great controversy and crucial question of these cases. Some of what victims of ritualistic abuse allege is physically impossible (victim cut up and put back together, severe injuries with no scars); some is possible but improbable (human sacrifice, cannibalism, vampirism); some is possible and probable (child pornography, clever manipulation of victims); and some is corroborated (medical evidence of vaginal or anal trauma, offender confessions). The principal criteria for many professionals' acceptance of these allegations by victims is simple: Is it possible? If what the victim describes is impossible, they look for alternative explanations (e.g. misperception, offender trickery, or symbolic meaning). If what the victim describes is possible, they accept it. Perhaps, however, whatever causes a victim to allege something impossible is the same or similar to what causes a victim to allege something possible but improbable.

There are many possible alternative answers to the question of why victims are alleging things that don't seem to be true. No attempt will be made to discuss them here. The first step, however, in finding the answers to this question is to admit the possibility that *some* of what the victims describe may not have happened. Many experts seem unwilling to even consider this. There is a middle ground - a continuum of possible activity. Some of what the victims allege may be true and accurate, some may be misperceived or distorted, some may be symbolic, and some may be "contaminated" or false. The problem, however, is to determine which is which. I believe that the majority of victims alleging ritualistic abuse are, in fact, victims of some form of abuse. Most of these victims are also probably not lying and have come to believe that which they are alleging actually happened.

Law enforcement has the obvious problem of attempting to determine what actually happened for criminal justice purposes. Therapists, however, might also be interested in what really happened in order to properly evaluate and treat their patients. How and when to confront patients with skepticism is a difficult and sensitive problem for therapists.

Until hard evidence is obtained and corroborated, the public should not be frightened into believing that babies are being bred and eaten, that 50,000 missing children are being murdered in human sacrifices, or that satanists are taking over America's day care centers. No one can prove with absolute certainly that such activity has NOT occurred. The burden of proof, however, as it would be in a criminal prosecution, is on those who claim that it has occurred. The explanation that the satanists are too organized and law enforcement is too incompetent only goes so far in explaining the lack of evidence. For at least eight years, American law enforcement has been aggressively investigating the allegations of victims of ritualistic abuse. There is little or no evidence for the portion of their allegations that deals with large-scale baby breeding, human sacrifice, and organized satanic conspiracies. Now it is up to mental health professionals, not law enforcement, to explain why victims are alleging things that don't seem to be true. Mental health professionals must begin to accept the possibility that some of what these victims are alleging just didn't happen and that this area desperately needs study and research by rational, objective social scientists.

If the guilty are to be successfully prosecuted, if the innocent are to be exonerated, and if the victims are to be protected and treated, better methods to evaluate and explain allegations of ritualistic "child abuse" must be developed or identified. Until this is done, the controversy will continue to cast a shadow over and fuel the backlash against the validity and reality of child sexual abuse.

SECTION 8: MEASUREMENT AND REPORTING

One of the frequent laments heard from people concerned with the link between animal maltreatment and interpersonal violence is the absence of state and national data on the incidence and prevalence of cruelty to animals. Unlike the field of child abuse and neglect, which has made great strides in reporting and maintaining yearly statistics, the field of animal welfare in the United States is just beginning to grapple with this issue.

In this section, the readings address issues concerning the reporting of animal maltreatment, primarily from the vantage point of the researcher. However, policy implications also emerge, as with the issue of human and animal welfare agencies sharing case information so that families displaying propensities to violence can be identified. The readings also illustrate psychologists', sociologists', veterinarians', ethicists', and social workers' convergence of interest in the link.

The article by Alan E. Kazdin and Karen Esveldt-Dawson introduces the Interview for Antisocial Behavior (IAB), an instrument for measuring a variety of forms of antisocial, aggressive, and destructive behaviors, including cruelty to animals, in children and adolescents. The advantages of such a scale include its specific focus on antisocial behavior (other checklists are often broader in scope and too lengthy for some purposes), its measurement of the duration and severity of antisocial activity, and its potential for both parental/guardian reporting on youth and youth self-reporting. This last advantage is important, since cruelty to animals may often be performed covertly. It should be noted that the IAB has been found to discriminate conduct-disordered youth from those without this disorder.

Frank R. Ascione, Teresa M. Thompson, and Tracy Black also introduce an instrument, the CAAI, which is designed to facilitate interviewing parents and youth about animal treatment, both positive and negative. The CAAI, although lengthy to administer, yields detailed information about the nature of children's maltreatment of animals, mal-

treatment they have either witnessed or performed, and their positive behavior toward animals. This information helps clinicians and researchers understand the motivations underlying the maltreatment of animals and may facilitate the development of intervention strategies for some youthful offenders or youth with psychological impairments.

Researchers might consider using the IAB and CAAI in tandem, with the IAB administered as an initial screen for cruelty to animals, and then, in cases where cruelty is present, the CAAI could be administered to create a more detailed picture of a child's behavior with animals.

In the next selection, Hannelie Vermeulen and Johannes S. J. Odendaal offer a sociological typology for categorizing various forms of physical and mental abuse of animals. The categories they describe are capable of objective definition and could form a checklist for both researchers and animal-welfare workers. This typology, or others that may emerge, could provide standardized reporting like that in the field of child abuse and neglect. Tracking new and existing cases of animal maltreatment would allow us to pinpoint the scope of the problem and to determine possible changes or stability in the incidence of animal abuse. Such tracking would also be critical in gauging the success of programs and policies aimed at reducing animal maltreatment.

If tracking of animal maltreatment is to become more common, professionals who deal directly with animal welfare issues will need to be convinced of the appropriateness and value of such tracking. Phil Arkow makes a case for veterinary medical professionals to report incidents of animal maltreatment that come to their attention. Arkow's paper reviews some of the obstacles to veterinarians' involvement (some of which are reminiscent of pediatricians' initial reluctance to report child abuse and neglect) and the benefits that could accrue from their professional involvement in addressing animal maltreatment. Bernard

Rollin's paper endorses much of what Arkow has to say on this issue and even suggests a legal mandate for veterinarians to report the abuse of animals.

Finally, a social-work perspective is provided by James S. Hutton, whose work gives us a taste of the benefits of tracking cruelty to animals in a more systematic fashion. Working with information from the files of the Royal Society for the Prevention of Cruelty to Animals in England, he was able to examine the overlap between cases of animal abuse and neglect and families' involvement with probation and social services. Although this was a small case study in a circumscribed geographical area, Hutton's research illustrates what "could be" if reporting and tracking animal maltreatment were taken more seriously.

The Interview for Antisocial Behavior: Psychometric Characteristics and Concurrent Validity with Child Psychiatric Inpatients

Alan E. Kazdin[1,2] and Karen Esveldt-Dawson[1]

The present study evaluated psychometric features and correlates of the Interview for Antisocial Behavior (IAB), a new measure designed to assess antisocial child behavior. Parents of 264 psychiatric inpatients (ages 6–13 years) completed the measure to evaluate antisocial behavior of their children. The investigation evaluated the relation of IAB scores to clinically derived diagnoses and to aggression and externalizing behaviors, as measured by different raters (parents, teachers), across different settings (home, school, hospital), and with different assessment methods (rating scales, behavioral role-play test). The results indicated that the IAB showed acceptable levels of internal consistency. A priori scores (severity, duration, total antisocial behavior) and factor analytically derived scales (Arguing/Fighting, Covert Antisocial Behaviors, Self-Injury) distinguished children with a DSM III diagnosis of conduct disorder, and scores on the IAB were more consistently related to other measures of aggression and externalizing behavior than to measures of internalizing behavior or overall severity of dysfunction. The implications of the results for use of the measure, particularly in relation to evaluation of the overt–covert dimension of antisocial behavior, are discussed.

KEY WORDS: antisocial behavior; conduct disorder; children.

Completion of this research was facilitated by a Research Scientist Development Award (MH00353) and by grants (MH35408, MH39642) from the National Institute of Mental Health and the Rivendell Foundation.

[1]Western Psychiatric Institute & Clinic, University of Pittsburgh School of Medicine, Pittsburgh, Pennsylvania 15213.

[2]To whom correspondence should be addressed at Department of Psychiatry, Western Psychiatric Institute and Clinic, 3811 O'Hara Street, University of Pittsburgh School of Medicine, Pittsburgh, Pennsylvania 15213.

Reprinted from the *Journal of Psychopathology and Behavioral Assessment* 8 (1986): 289–303, with kind permission of Plenum Publishing Corporation.

INTRODUCTION

Antisocial behavior in children encompasses aggressive acts, vandalism, theft, lying, firesetting, and a number of other behaviors that reflect major social rule violations. The significance of antisocial behaviors as a clinical problem is underscored by several characteristics including their relatively high prevalence and high rate of clinical referrals, stability and poor prognosis, and transmission within families across generations (see Kazdin, in press). Although the constellation of antisocial behaviors is widely recognized, there remain major questions about the dysfunction, its diagnosis, and its treatment.

The paucity of standardized measures of antisocial child behavior available for widespread use has partially impeded research. Several measures specifically devoted to antisocial behavior have been developed for adolescents (e.g., Curtiss *et al.*, 1983; Elliott & Ageton, 1980; Huesmann, Lefkowitz, & Eron, 1978; Kulik, Stein, & Sarbin, 1968). Because of the increased likelihood of adjudication and incarceration among adolescents, measures for this age group often sample delinquent and criminal acts (e.g., auto theft, sexual assault, substance abuse). The measures are less relevant for young children given the low base rates of these behaviors.

A few scales have been developed for child conduct problems (see Kazdin, 1986). As a notable example, the Eyberg Child Behavior Inventory (Eyberg & Robinson, 1983) measures conduct problems in the home. Although some clearly antisocial behaviors are included (e.g., stealing), the measure emphasizes several mildly bothersome behaviors (e.g., poor table manners, whining). Other measures have been developed for more severe antisocial child behavior at home, at school, and in hospitals (see Atkeson & Forehand, 1981; Kazdin, in press) but few have been standardized for widespread use.

There is a need to develop measures of antisocial behavior for clinically referred children who show behaviors that are embraced by the diagnosis of conduct disorder. Alternative characteristics would be desirable to include in such measures. To begin with, a broad range of symptoms should be sampled. Major rule violations (e.g., stealing) are often accompanied by less severe problems as well (e.g., disobedience, arguing with others) (Quay, 1979). Also, different dimensions relevant to antisocial behaviors should be covered. For example, overt and covert behaviors (e.g., tantrums, firesetting) (Loeber & Schmaling, 1985a) and aggressive and delinquent types of behaviors (e.g., fighting, stealing) (Gersten, Langner, Eisenberg, Simcha-Fagan, & McCarthy, 1976) should be included. The severity and duration of antisocial acts are also critical because these characteristics, along with the diversity of symptoms, have important prognostic implications (Kazdin, in press).

The present investigation examined the Interview for Antisocial Behavior, a parent-completed measure designed to assess antisocial behavior of their children. A parent-completed version was selected because parents are considered to be the most knowledgeable informants for children, to have access to a broad and protracted sample of behaviors, and to have a major role in clinical referral and treatment (Achenbach & Edelbrock, 1983). The purpose of the investigation was to evaluate the internal consistency and concurrent validity of the scale. Validity was examined by evaluating the relation of IAB scores to clinically derived diagnoses and to aggressive and externalizing behaviors, as assessed by different raters (parents, teachers), among different settings (home, school, hospital), and with different assessment methods (rating scales, behavioral role-play test).

METHOD

Subjects

The subjects consisted of 264 children (65 girls and 199 boys) and their mothers or maternal guardian. The children were all inpatients of a psychiatric facility where children are hospitalized for 2 to 3 months. The facility houses 22 children (ages 5–13 years) at any one time. The children are admitted for acute disorders including highly aggressive and destructive behavior, suicidal or homicidal ideation or behavior, psychotic episodes, and deteriorating family conditions. To be included, children were required to be at least 6 years old, to have a full-scale WISC-R IQ of 70 or above, to have no evidence of neurological impairment, uncontrolled seizures, or dementia, and to be receiving no psychotropic medication. The children ranged in age from 6 to 13 years (M = 10.1 years) and in full-scale IQ from 70 to 133 (M = 95.3). Two hundred four (77%) children were white: 60 (23%) were black.

Diagnoses of the children were based on DSM III criteria (American Psychiatric Association, 1980) and were obtained from direct interviews with the children and their parent(s) immediately before admission and psychiatric evaluation after the child had been admitted. Diagnoses were reached without reference to or use of the measures included in the present project. On the basis of the above sources of information, two staff members independently completed diagnoses for each child. Agreement on the principal Axis I diagnosis was relatively high (kappa = .72). In cases of disagreements, the case was discussed to reach a consensus on the appropriate diagnosis. Principal Axis I diagnoses included conduct disorder (*n* = 115), attention deficit disorder (*n* = 30), major depression (*n* = 28), adjustment disorder (*n* =

19), anxiety disorder ($n = 14$), psychosis ($n = 3$), and other mental disorders ($n = 55$).

The children's mothers or maternal figures ranged in age from 23 to 67 years (M = 34.1) and included biological mothers (84%), step-, foster, or adoptive mothers (12%), and other female relatives or guardians (4%). Family social class, calculated by the Hollingshead and Redlich (1958) two-factor index, yielded the following breakdown: Classes V (9%), IV (44%), III (31%), II (11%), and I (5%). The estimated monthly income for families ranged from $0 to $500 to more than $2,500 (median range = $500 to $1000); 39% of the families were on social assistance.

Assessment

Several measures were included because they encompassed aggressive and externalizing behaviors and were expected to correlate with the Interview for Antisocial Behavior. Assessments were administered to each child, parent, and teacher in the community in whose class the child was enrolled immediately prior to hospitalization. Assessments administered to the parent were completed within the first week to 10 days of the child's admission. Children completed a role-play test within the first 2 weeks of their admission. The measure of school behavior was mailed to the classroom teacher at the onset of the child's admission.

Parent-Completed Measures. Several measures were administered to the children's mothers to reflect a wide range of deviant and prosocial behaviors. The primary measure was the *Interview for Antisocial Behavior* (IAB), a structured interview designed to measure antisocial behaviors in children.[3] The measure is presented to the parent of the referred child and includes 30 items that pertain to a broad range of aggressive and antisocial behaviors (e.g., fighting, arguing, stealing, lying, and truancy). The items were selected from referral symptoms of conduct disorder patients seen for inpatient or outpatient treatment and from symptoms included in the DSM III diagnosis of conduct disorder. The item content is presented in Table I.

For each item, the parent is asked to rate the degree of the problem (severity) on a 5-point scale (1 = none at all, 5 = very much). If the behavior or problem is present (rating > 1 on the 5-point scale), the duration of the problem is rated on a 3-point scale [1 = recent or new problem (6 months or less), 2 = long time (more than 6 months), 3 = always]. Separate scores are available for severity and duration. A total antisocial behavior score (range, 30 to 240) across all items can be obtained by summing the severity and duration scores.

---

[3]Copies of the Interview for Antisocial Behavior are available upon request.

Table I. The Interview for Antisocial Behavior: Items and Item–Total Score Correlations, Factors and Loadings of Items, and Differences (ANOVAs) Comparing Youths with and Without a Diagnosis of Conduct Disorder (CD)

Factor/item	Item–total score r	Factor loading	CD vs. non-CD
Factor 1: Arguing/fighting			[F(1,256)]
1. Temper tantrums	.56***	.62	6.79*
2. Teasing others	.59***	.53	12.80***
3. Using obscene language	.59***	.49	15.55***
4. Talking back to parents	.56***	.61	6.77**
5. Respecting authority	.45***	.48	12.65***
6. A negative attitude (saying no often)	.61***	.58	<1
7. Controlling his/her behavior	.48***	.49	7.70**
8. Moving around a lot and yelling	.61***	.58	15.14***
15. Being cruel, bullying, or being mean to others	.69***	.62	22.62***
23. Getting into many fights	.65***	.67	40.09***
24. Getting along with other children	.43***	.44	<1
25. Punching, kicking, or biting others	.71***	.69	23.13***
26. Verbally threatening others	.64***	.64	23.89***
27. Getting mad all of a sudden	.67***	.70	7.92**
28. Starting arguments	.72***	.77	12.61***
29. Fighting with brothers & sisters	.43***	.35	3.30
30. Not being able to take turns or wait	.61***	.58	11.73***
Factor 2: Covert Antisocial Behaviors			
9. Breaking into cars, stores, etc.	.27***	.50	5.18*
10. Breaking windows of buildings, cars, etc.	.30***	.39	9.85***
11. Stealing from stores	.38***	.51	17.92***
12. Stealing from parents or friends	.54***	.62	35.35***
13. Setting fires	.32***	.48	27.83***
14. Being cruel to animals	.46***	.45	8.44**
19. Breaking things that belong to him	.60***	.52	7.64**
20. Breaking things that belong to family or friends	.67***	.54	18.14***
21. Cutting up things such as seats on buses	.37***	.43	<1
22. Writing on cars, walls, etc.	.43***	.58	6.03*
Factor 3: Self-Injury			
16. Stating (s)he wishes to be dead	.22***	.86	14.03***
17. Thinking about or trying to end his/her life	.20***	.93	20.34***
18. Trying to harm his(her)self	.30***	.63	5.81*

*p < .05.
**p < .01.
***p < .001.

The Children's Hostility Inventory (CHI) is a paper-and-pencil measure designed to measure different facets of child hostility and aggression. The instrument is completed by the parent, who answers 38 true–false items about the child. The scale has been derived from the Buss-Durkee Hostility Inventory for adults (Buss & Durkee, 1957). Items comprise several subscales including assaultiveness, indirect hostility, irritability, negativism, resentment, suspicion, and verbal hostility. A sum of these scales yields a total hostility score.[4] These scales encompass direct expression of aggressive acts as well as cognitive and perceptual processes reflecting hostile reactions to others. It was predicted that the IAB would be related to CHI scores.

The children's mothers also completed the Child Behavior Checklist (CBCL) (Achenbach & Edelbrock, 1983). The measure includes 118 items scored on a 0- to 2-point scale to cover multiple symptom areas that have been derived through factor analyses completed separately for boys and girls in different age groups (e.g., 6–11, 12–16 years old). Of interest for present purposes were the broad-band scales measuring internalizing, externalizing, and total behavior problems. These scales are available for all age and gender groups. Their inclusion was based on the prediction that IAB scores would correlate more highly with externalizing scores (outward directed symptoms) of the CBCL than with internalizing (inward directed) symptoms or total behavioral problems. The CBCL also includes three a priori social competence scales: activity scale (child participation in social activities), social scale (how well the child gets along with others), and school scale (how well the child is doing at school). Children high in antisocial behavior on the IAB would be expected to show more extreme externalizing scores, to show relatively poor social relations, and to be performing less well at school.

Teacher-Completed Measures. To evaluate performance at school, the children's teachers completed the School Behavior Checklist (SBCL-Form A2; Miller, 1977). The measure includes 96 true–false items reflecting behavioral characteristics that are rated by teachers. Factor analyses have yielded six scales that include low need achievement, aggression, anxiety, academic disability, hostile isolation, and extraversion. For present purposes, the following three scales were selected: aggression, anxiety, and total disability. The total disability scale reflects a summary of behavioral symptoms, includes the six subscales, and is designed to measure overall dysfunction. The IAB was expected to correlate more highly with the aggression scale of the SBCL than with the anxiety or total disability scale.

Child-Completed Measure. To provide a measure of overt behavior, a Behavioral Role-Play Test was administered individually to the child. This measure was administered only to a subsample ($n = 75$, or 28.4%) of the children because administration to the entire sample would be prohibitive. These children did not differ from the remainder of the sample in subject and demographic variables. The role-play measure focused specifically on

---

[4]The adult and child versions of the Hostility Inventory also include a guilt scale. This scale is not conceived as a type of hostility or aggression on a priori grounds and was excluded from the present analyses.

aggressive behavior rather than social skills (e.g., eye contact, giving help, sharing, providing compliments). Two parallel forms of the role-play measure were developed. One form was administered to each child so that half received each version of the measure. Each version included 10 situations that required the child to respond overtly in the situation. The situations included being teased by peers, being mildly provoked or accused by an adult, expressing anger, and others.[5] The situations were presented individually by a narrator, who first described the situation. The child was told to think about the situation and to imagine it going on. The situation was then presented a second time, at which point the child was to respond as he/she would if it really were happening. A typical scene was, "Imagine you're playing a game on the playground and someone on the other team shoves you hard because he's very angry that your team is winning. He says 'cheater!' to you."

The child's responses to the role-play test were all videotaped for subsequent scoring by research assistants naive to the purposes of the study, other assessment information, and diagnoses of the children. Role-play responses were scored along several dimensions. Of primary interest were categories of aggressive expression that included aggressive facial expression (looking angry or threatening, sneering), aggressive motor behavior (making physical gestures as a threat, clinching a fist, moving toward the assessor with an intent to harm or throw something), aggressive verbal content (verbal responses expressive of threats, dislike, or agreeing to engage in aggressive acts), and aggressive intonation (angry or provocative tone of speech). The final measure was an overall rating of aggressiveness and was made separately based on a global evaluation of the child's response to each situation. Each of the responses was scored separately for the 10 situations completed by the child. The response was scored on a 1- to 5-point rating scale for the degree of aggressiveness for that characteristic (e.g., motor behavior). A child's score for each response code was obtained by summing across 10 situations.

Raters included four independent study students who received approximately 20 hr of training before data collection began. The reliability of the role-play performance was evaluated by having two observers independently score the same videotapes of children. Independence of scoring was assured by having the tapes evaluated by the observers at entirely different times. Pairs of assessors independently scored the tapes of 46 (61.3%) of the 75 children to examine agreement. Pearson product–moment correlations were computed for total scores for each of the response categories for two observers. The correlations between observers were as follows: facial expression ($r = .71$), motor responses ($r = .89$), content ($r = .85$), intonation ($r = .78$), and overall rating of aggression ($r = .96$).

---

[5]Role-play situations and the scoring procedures can be obtained from the author.

To reduce the number of role-play variables and to minimize redundancies, selected categories were combined. Aggressive facial and motor responses were moderately correlated ($r = .76$, $p < .001$) and were summed to yield a single measure referred to as nonverbal aggression. Similarly, aggressive intonation and content ($r = .66$, $p < .001$) were summed to yield a single variable referred to as verbal aggression. Thus, for the data analyses, three role-play measures included nonverbal aggression, verbal aggression, and overall aggression rating.

RESULTS

Preliminary Analyses

To evaluate the influence of subject and demographic variables on performance on the Interview for Antisocial Behavior, two separate analyses of variance were completed for subject and demographic characteristics of children (age, sex, race, IQ) and their mothers (age, race, Hollingshead class, welfare status). Continuous variables (e.g., age) were analyzed by using median splits. Significant overall effects were obtained for total IAB score as a function of child sex and race [$F(1,262) = 6.83$, $p < .01$, and $F = 6.24$, $p < .02$, respectively]. Boys were higher in antisocial behavior than girls (M's = 115.4 and 103.3, respectively); white children were higher in antisocial behavior than black children (M's = 115.1 and 103.2, respectively). No other effects were obtained as a function of subject and demographic variables.

Internal Consistency

An examination of the internal consistency of the IAB yielded a coefficient alpha of .91 and a Spearman–Brown coefficient of .87. These statistics suggest an acceptable level of internal consistency. An examination of the individual item–total score correlations (Table I) reveals a relatively consistent pattern across items. Individual correlations are in the moderate range and significant for all of the items. The mean item–total correlation, averaged by Fisher's z' transformation, is $r = .51$ ($p < .001$).

To examine the internal structure of the scale further, factor analysis was conducted utilizing a principal-components solution with Varimax rotation. Three factors were extracted based on a scree test. These factors exceeded eigenvalues of 2.0. Loadings of $\geq .35$ were used to select items that defined individual factors. Table I presents the items, grouped by factors, along with their factor loadings. The initial factor included 17 items that reflect Arguing/Fighting. The items with the highest loading are starting arguments, getting mad all of a sudden, and punching, kicking, and biting others (items 28, 27, 25). The second factor included 10 items that reflect Covert Antisocial Behaviors. The items with the highest loading are stealing from parents and writing on cars (items 12, 22). The third and final factor included three items pertaining to Self-Injury and reflect thoughts or attempts to end one's life (items 16, 17, 18).[6]

Diagnosis of Conduct Disorder

Individual Items. An initial question related to the validity of the IAB is the extent to which the measure distinguishes children who have received a primary or secondary diagnosis of conduct disorder ($n = 156$) from those who did not ($n = 108$). To examine if individual items discriminated diagnostic groups, a MANOVA was completed comparing conduct- and non-conduct-disordered children across the 30 IAB items. A significant overall effect ($F = 3.70$, $p < .001$) was followed with analyses of the individual items.

As evident in Table I, conduct- and non-conduct-disordered children differed significantly on all but four items. A few of the findings warrant special comment. First, the items that discriminate best were getting into many fights, stealing from parents and friends, and setting fires (items 23, 12, 13). Second, the items that were no different between conduct-disordered and non-conduct-disordered children were a negative attitude (saying no often), cutting up things such as seats on buses, not getting along with others, and fighting with brothers and sisters (items 6, 21, 24, 29). Third, for three items, conduct-disorder children were significantly *lower* than non-conduct-disorder children. These items include wishing to be dead, thinking about ending one's life, and trying to harm oneself (items 16, 17, 18) and comprise the third factor obtained from the factor analysis noted previously.

Summary Scores. It is likely that the actual value and use of the scale would derive from the scores obtained from summing the items, thereby permitting a wider range of scores to differentiate conduct- and non-conduct-disordered youth. The IAB yields scores for severity and duration; these scores

---

[6]To examine the replicability of the factor structure within the present study, the total sample ($N = 264$) was divided randomly into two groups. Factor analyses were completed with the separate samples to identify three factors that emerged. The results from the separate samples were consistent with the overall analysis. For the first factor (Arguing/Fighting), 16 of the 17 items of the overall analysis loaded ($\geq .35$) on this factor. The differences were for items 14 and 29, which did not consistently load on the factor in each of the subgroup analyses. For the second factor (Covert Antisocial Behaviors), 8 of the 10 items from the overall analysis loaded on both of the subgroup analyses. Items 10 and 14 were different in the subanalyses. For the third factor (Self-Injury), the three items that defined the dimension were identical in each subgroup analysis and the overall analysis.

were moderately correlated with each other ($r = .64$, $p < .001$). One-way analyses of variance revealed that conduct-disordered youths were significantly higher than those without such a diagnosis for severity and duration of antisocial behavior [F's $(1,256) = 27.56$ and 16.41, respectively; both $p < .001$] and, of course, on total antisocial behavior ($F = 27.07$, $p < .001$). Separate scores were also computed for the three factors. Conduct-disordered youths attained significantly higher scores for Arguing/Fighting [$F(1,256) = 24.50$, $p < .001$] and Covert Antisocial Behaviors ($F = 35.14$, $p < .001$) and lower scores for Self-Injury ($F = 14.71$, $p < .001$) than non-conduct-disordered youths.

Antisocial Behavior and Related Constructs

To examine the relations of antisocial behavior to other measures, children who received scores above and below the median (median $= 113.5$) in their total IAB scores were delineated, respectively, as high- and low-antisocial youths. The means, standard deviations, and group differences on each of the measures are presented in Table II. MANOVAs were completed separately for parent (CBCL, CHI) and teacher (SBCL) measures and revealed significant overall effects for level of antisocial behavior ($F = 14.82$, $p < .001$; $F = 15.66$, $p < .001$; $F = 3.94$, $p = .01$).

Univariate analyses of variance (Table II) revealed that children high in antisocial behavior were significantly higher on CBCL internalizing, externalizing, and total behavior problem scales and lower on the social scale. Thus, youths high in antisocial behavior evinced more symptoms and less prosocial behavior than their less antisocial peers. On the CHI, high-antisocial youths showed significantly higher deviant behavior on all of the hostility subscales. On the SBCL, high-antisocial youths were scored by their teachers as higher in aggression at school but not higher in anxiety or overall behavioral problems. Finally, for the subsample of children who received the role-play test, high-antisocial youths were seen as showing higher nonverbal aggression (facial expressions and motor movements) and higher overall ratings of aggression.

The relations of antisocial behavior to other measures of functioning completed by parents and teachers and the children's role-play performance were examined by computing Pearson product–moment correlations. To control for familywise error rates, given the number of correlations computed, alpha was corrected using the Bonferroni adjustment. For an alpha of .05, the adjustment required a correlation of $p < .004$ for significance. The correlations between performance on the IAB and other measures are presented in Table III.

Significant correlations of the IAB and externalizing behavior (CBCL), total hostility (CHI), aggression (SBCL), and nonverbal aggression (role play)

Table II. Means and Standard Deviations on All Measures for the Total Sample and Separately for Children with Low or High Scores (Median Split) on the Interview for Antisocial Behavior

Measure	Total sample (N = 264) M	Total sample (N = 264) SD	Antisocial behavior Low M	Antisocial behavior High M	F test
Child Behavior Checklist					(df = 1,252)
Internalizing	72.6	10.5	70.7	74.6	9.20**
Externalizing	76.1	9.2	71.6	80.7	82.06***
Total Behavior Problem	76.3	9.1	72.6	80.0	50.65***
Activities	45.0	11.3	44.8	45.2	<1
Social	32.4	13.5	35.4	29.2	13.02***
School Performance	35.2	12.3	36.1	34.2	1.23
Children's Hostility Inventory					
Assaultiveness	4.0	1.5	3.2	4.7	67.95***
Indirect Hostility	4.0	1.1	3.5	4.5	55.39***
Irritability	4.5	1.4	4.0	5.0	38.38***
Negativism	2.4	0.8	2.1	2.6	26.35***
Resentment	2.3	1.3	1.9	2.7	27.28***
Suspicion	1.9	1.2	1.8	2.1	4.00*
Verbal Hostility	4.7	1.4	4.2	5.2	46.34***
Total Hostility	23.7	5.6	20.7	26.7	100.29***
School Behavior Checklist					
Anxiety	59.6	12.5	61.2	58.0	2.73
Aggression	75.6	15.0	72.2	78.8	7.94**
Total Disability	70.3	11.4	69.1	71.4	1.64
Behavioral Role-Play Test					(df = 1,73)
Nonverbal Aggression	36.9	3.9	38.2	35.3	10.15***
Verbal Aggression	31.0	4.8	30.4	31.4	<1
Overall Aggression	29.7	9.6	32.0	27.2	4.79*

*p < .05.
**p < .01.
***p < .001.

support the construct validity of the measure. Some evidence for discriminant validity might be drawn from the relatively lower correlations of IAB scores with internalizing behavior (CBCL) and anxiety (SBCL). Yet the high correlation of the IAB with total behavior problems on the CBCL raises questions about the specificity of the measure and/or the contribution of antisocial behavior to overall levels of deviance.

DISCUSSION

The goal of the present investigation was to evaluate the Interview for Aggression. The results indicated that the measure demonstrated acceptable levels of internal consistency, as reflected in significant item–total score correlations and coefficients of reliability; a priori scale scores (severity, duration, total) and factor analytically derived scores (Arguing/Fighting, Covert Antisocial Behaviors, Self-Injury) distinguished children independently

Table III. Correlations of the Interview for Antisocial Behavior with Other Measures

Measure	Total IAB score
Child Behavior Checklist	
Internalizing	.29**
Externalizing	.69**
Total Behavior Problem	.56**
Activities	−.02
Social	−.29**
School Performance	−.09
Children's Hostility Inventory	
Total Hostility	.68**
School Behavior Checklist	
Anxiety	−.15*
Aggression	.29**
Total Disability	.13*
Behavioral Role-Play Test	
Nonverbal Aggression	.36**
Verbal Aggression	.07
Overall Aggression	.16

*$p < .05$.
**$p < .001$. The Bonferroni corrected alpha level for $p = .05$ given the number of correlations computed is $p = .0038$. These correlations met this level.

diagnosed as conduct disorder; and IAB scores were related to other measures of aggression and externalizing behavior across different settings (home, school, hospital) and different assessment methods (parent and teacher ratings, behavioral role-play test).

Analyses of individual items revealed low to high item–total score correlations that were consistently positive and significant. Yet not all of the individual items discriminated conduct disorder and nonconduct disorder youths. The four items that were not significantly different (items 6, 21, 24, 29) were in the predicted direction and loaded on the two major factors. The differences favoring conduct-disordered youths on each of these items and their significant item–total score correlations suggest that they contribute to the total score in differentiating antisocial behavior and perhaps should be retained.

Of greater significance in evaluating the scale were the three items related to self-injury (items 16, 17, 18). For these items, conduct-disordered youths were significantly lower than non-conduct-disordered youths. The items comprised a single factor. The direction of the differences suggests that antisocial youths are less likely to think about or to engage in self-directed aggression. Indeed, the latter behaviors are more characteristic of internalizing disorders such as depression (see Kazdin, French, Unis, Esveldt-Dawson, & Sherick, 1983). For a scale of antisocial behaviors, the data lobby for excluding the three self-injury items. Needless to say, inward directed symptoms may be very important to assess in the evaluation of antisocial behavior. The presence of antisocial symptoms such as anxiety may have important diagnostic and treatment implications (see Jesness, 1971; Jesness & Wedge, 1984). Yet the IAB is not proposed as a measure to supplant broader scales that assess the full spectrum of symptoms. Other measures that accomplish this broader goal remain essential for comprehensive diagnostic and assessment purposes.

Of greater interest than the individual items are the specific factors that emerged from the analyses. The first two factors (Arguing/Fighting and Covert Antisocial Behaviors) closely parallel the overt–covert behavior dimension for delineating antisocial youths (Loeber, 1985; Loeber & Schmaling, 1985a). Overt antisocial behavior consists of those acts that are confrontive such as fighting, arguing, and temper tantrums. Covert antisocial behaviors consist of concealed acts such as stealing and firesetting. Evidence suggests that overt, covert, and mixed patterns of antisocial behaviors are associated with different long-term prognoses, responses to treatment, and family interaction patterns (see Kazdin, in press; Loeber & Schmaling, 1985b; Patterson, 1982). As yet, however, no standard measure is available to assess these different patterns of behaviors. Whether the IAB will be useful in this regard requires further study.

There are several limitations of the present study that must be borne in mind when evaluating the Interview for Antisocial Behavior and interpreting the results. First, a number of antisocial behaviors were not included in the measure. Behaviors such as substance abuse, sexual assault, auto theft, and others, often included in measures of antisocial behavior in adolescent and adult samples (e.g., Elliott & Ageton, 1980; Kulik *et al.,* 1968), were excluded because of the low base rates of these behaviors among antisocial youths in the age range of interest. It still might be useful to include such symptoms because of their significance when they do occur. Second, the study did not include a sample of normal (nonreferred) or outpatient samples. These other samples are important because inpatient cases may suffer extreme conditions (e.g., diffuse psychopathology, parent and family dysfunction) that may influence the generality of the results. Third, interpretation of the results for the IAB must take into account the fact that the information was based on parent reports. Considerable research has shown that parental reports of deviance in their children may be influenced by their own symptoms (especially depression and anxiety), as well as marital discord, parent self-esteem, and reported stress in the home (e.g., Griest & Wells, 1983; Mash & Johnston, 1983). The influence of these factors on IAB scores was not evaluated in the present study.

Further work on the measure is needed along several fronts. Data on the stability of performance over time (test–retest reliability), the performance of nonreferred samples, and the longitudinal study of overt and covert behaviors are three areas that would evaluate the utility of the measure. These areas are currently being pursued in light of the promising preliminary results regarding characteristics of the scale with severely disturbed inpatient children.

ACKNOWLEDGMENTS

The author is grateful to Debra Colbus, Antoinette Rodgers, Todd Siegel, and members of the clinical-research team of the Child Psychiatric Treatment Service.

REFERENCES

Achenbach, T. M., & Edelbrock, C. S. (1983). *Manual for the Child Behavior Checklist and Revised Child Behavior Profile.* Burlington, VT: University Associates in Psychiatry.

American Psychiatric Association (1980). *Diagnostic and statistical manual of mental disorders* (3rd ed.). Washington, DC: American Psychiatric Association.

Atkeson, B. M., & Forehand, R. (1981). Conduct disorders. In E. J. Mash & L. G. Terdal (Eds.), *Behavioral assessment of childhood disorders* (pp. 185-219). New York: Guilford.

Buss, A. H., & Durkee, A. (1957). An inventory for assessing different kinds of hostility. *Journal of Consulting Psychology, 21,* 343-349.

Curtiss, G., Rosenthal, R. H., Marohn, R. C., Ostrov, E. Offer D., & Trujillo, J. (1983). Measuring delinquent behavior in inpatient treatment settings: Revision and validation of the Adolescent Antisocial Behavior Checklist. *Journal of the American Academy of Child Psychiatry, 22,* 459-466.

Elliott, D. S., & Ageton, S. S. (1980). Reconciling race and class differences in self-reported and official estimates of delinquency. *American Sociological Review, 45,* 95-110.

Eyberg, S. M., & Robinson, E. A. (1983). Conduct problem behavior: Standardization of a behavioral rating scale with adolescents. *Journal of Clinical Child Psychology, 12,* 347-354.

Gersten, J. C., Langner, T. S., Eisenberg, J. G., Simcha-Fagan, D., & McCarthy, E. D. (1976). Stability in change in types of behavioral disturbances of children and adolescents. *Journal of Abnormal Child Psychology, 4,* 111-127.

Griest, D. L., & Wells, K. C. (1983). Behavioral family therapy with conduct disorders in children. *Behavior Therapy, 14,* 37-53.

Hollingshead, A. B., & Redlich, F. C. (1958). *Social class and mental illness.* New York: Wiley.

Huesmann, L. R., Lefkowitz, M. M., & Eron, L. D. (1978). Sum of MMPI Scales F, 4, and 9 as a measure of aggression. *Journal of Consulting and Clinical Psychology, 46,* 1071-1078.

Jesness, C. F. (1971). Comparative effectiveness of two institutional treatment programs for delinquents. *Child Care Quarterly, 1,* 119-130.

Jesness, C. F., & Wedge, R. F. (1984). Validity of a revised Jesness Inventory I-Level classification with delinquents. *Journal of Consulting and Clinical Psychology, 52,* 997-1010.

Kazdin, A. E. (in press). *Conduct disorders in childhood and adolescence.* Beverly Hills, CA: Sage.

Kazdin, A. E., French, N. H., Unis, A. S., Esveldt-Dawson, K., & Sherick, R. B. (1983). Hopelessness, depression and suicidal intent among psychiatrically disturbed inpatient children. *Journal of Consulting and Clinical Psychology, 51,* 504-510.

Kulik, J. A., Stein, K. B., & Sarbin, T. R. (1968). Dimensions and patterns of adolescent antisocial behavior. *Journal of Consulting and Clinical Psychology, 32,* 375-382.

Loeber, R. (1985). Patterns and development of antisocial child behavior. In G. J. Whitehurst (Ed.), *Annals of child development* (Vol. 2). New York: JAI Press.

Loeber, R., & Schmaling, K. B. (1985a). Empirical evidence for overt and covert patterns of antisocial conduct problems: A meta-analysis. *Journal of Abnormal Child Psychology, 13,* 337-352.

Loeber, R., & Schmaling, K. B. (1985b). The utility of differentiating between mixed and pure forms of antisocial child behavior. *Journal of Abnormal Child Psychology, 13,* 315-335.

Mash, E. J., & Johnston, C. (1983). Parental perceptions of child behavior problems, parenting self-esteem, and mothers' reported stress in younger and older hyperactive and normal children. *Journal of Consulting and Clinical Psychology, 51,* 86-99.

Miller, L. C. (1977). *School Behavior Checklist manual.* Los Angeles: Western Psychological Services.

Patterson, G. R. (1982). *Coercive family process.* Eugene, OR: Castalia.

Quay, H. C. (1979). Classification. In H. C. Quay & J. S. Werry (Eds.), *Psychopathological disorders of childhood* (2nd ed.). New York: Wiley.

Childhood Cruelty to Animals: Assessing Cruelty Dimensions and Motivations

Frank R. Ascione, PhD,
Teresa M. Thompson, and Tracy Black

ABSTRACT

Preventing and treating childhood cruelty to animals will require a) qualitative, as well as quantitative, assessment methods and b) specification of the varied motivations for such behavior. Although some information is available about the prevalence and frequency of animal maltreatment in samples of children and adolescents, especially those diagnosed with Conduct Disorder, other dimensions of such maltreatment (e.g., severity, chronicity) are only beginning to be explored.

We describe the research and development process leading to construction of a semi-structured interview, the Children and Animals (Cruelty to Animals) Assessment Instrument (CAAI), for use with children over four years of age and their parents, to obtain information on animal maltreatment. The CAAI was field-tested with a community and clinical sample of twenty children and included children in day treatment and residential programs for emotionally disturbed youth, incarcerated adolescents, and children accompanying their mothers to shelters for battered women.

The dimensions of cruelty to animals scorable using the CAAI include: SEVERITY (degree of intentional pain/injury caused), FREQUENCY (number of separate acts), DURATION (period of time over which cruelty occurred), RECENCY (most current acts), DIVERSITY ACROSS AND WITHIN CATEGORIES (number of types and number of animals within a type that were abused), ANIMAL SENTIENCE LEVEL, COVERT (related to child's attempts to conceal cruelty), ISOLATE (individual versus group cruelty), and EMPATHY (indications of remorse or concern for the injured animal). A method is described for converting these ratings to numerical scores in which higher scores indicate more severe, problematic cruelty. Varied motivations for children's cruelty to animals are discussed including curiosity and peer reinforcement, modification of mood state, imitation of adult cruelty, and using animals as an "implement" of self-injury. The need for the CAAI is especially critical for assessment since we often found discrepancies between parent reports on one-item cruelty-to-animals assessments (e.g., Child Behavior Checklist) and CAAI results.

Department of Psychology, Utah State University, Logan, Utah 84322-2810

*Based on a paper presented at the 7th International Conference on Human-Animal Interactions, Geneva, Switzerland, September 8, 1995. CAAI development was facilitated by a grant from the Geraldine R. Dodge Foundation, the Humane Society of the United States, the American Humane Association, the Massachusetts Society for the Prevention of Cruelty to Animals, and the American Society for the Prevention of Cruelty to Animals. We thank Ms. Karen Ranson for her professional assistance during the course of this project and the variety of agencies who cooperated. Finally, we thank the parents and children who shared their experiences. Request reprints from: Frank R. Ascione, Department of Psychology, Utah State University, Logan, Utah 84322-2810, E-mail: FRANKA@fs1.ed.usu.edu.

OVERVIEW

The relation between childhood cruelty to animals and both concurrent and future violent behavior has received limited but increasing research attention (Ascione, 1993; Felthous & Kellert, 1987). Preventing and treating childhood cruelty to animals will require a) qualitative, as well as quantitative, assessment methods and b) specification of the varied motivations for such behavior. Although some information is available about the prevalence of animal maltreatment in samples of children and adolescents (e.g., Achenbach & Edelbrock, 1981; Achenbach, Howell, Quay, & Conners, 1991), other dimensions of animal maltreatment (e.g., severity, chronicity, involvement in sexual abuse) are only beginning to be explored. The significance of cruelty to animals as a symptom relevant for assessing children's mental health status has been formally acknowledged in the last two revisions (1987 - DSM-IIIR and 1994 - DSM-IV) of the Diagnostic and Statistical Manual of Mental Disorders (American Psychiatric Association, 1994), specifically with reference to Conduct Disorder.

We describe the construction and field-testing of a semi-structured interview, the Children and Animals [Cruelty to Animals] Assessment Instrument (CAAI), for use with children over four years of age and their parents, to obtain information on animal maltreatment. The CAAI was field-tested with a community and clinical sample of twenty children (mean age=10.4 yrs; 85% Caucasian, 10% Spanish surname, 5% African-American). Seventy-five percent of the participants were boys and 65% of the parents reported having a family pet. The clinical sample included children in day treatment and residential programs for emotionally disturbed youth, incarcerated adolescents, and children accompanying their mothers to shelters for battered women. All sources of participants were located in northern Utah.

CAAI CONSTRUCTION AND FIELD-TESTING

The basic format of the CAAI was developed after careful consideration of other assessments of aggression and antisocial behavior in children. One critical consideration was designing an instrument that could be used with adults (specifically, parents/guardians) and with children. Because of this, a format that would list and describe increasingly cruel and destructive acts was judged inappropriate and very likely unethical for use with children from non-clinical samples.

A semi-structured interview format was selected since we would be assessing children with verbal skills who could respond to simply-worded questions about their current and past behavior with animals. Interview questions were organized to assess witnessing and performing cruelty and kindness toward animals in four categories (farm, wild, pet, and stray). Each set of questions (see Appendix A for samples) was designed to stand alone since other researchers might only wish to use parts of the CAAI (e.g., a study focusing on children's observation of violence to animals; a

study of parents' description of their children's kindness to pet animals). The remainder of this report focuses on the portion of the CAAI related to cruelty to animals.

The dimensions of cruelty that could be assessed using the CAAI included the following: SEVERITY (based on the degree of intentional pain and injury caused to an animal as well as sexual abuse of an animal), FREQUENCY (the number of separate acts of cruelty noted in the assessment results), DURATION (the period of time over which the cruel acts occurred), RECENCY (based on the most current act(s) of cruelty performed), DIVERSITY/ACROSS CATEGORIES (the number of different categories of animals harmed), DIVERSITY/WITHIN CATEGORY (the number of individual animals harmed), SENTIENCE (the level of sentience for the animal that was harmed), COVERT (the child's attempts to conceal cruel behavior), ISOLATE (whether the cruelty occurred alone or with other children and/or adults present), and EMPATHY (the degree of the child's remorse for cruel acts or concern for animals' welfare).

As part of our field testing, we also administered the Child Behavior Checklist (CBCL-- Achenbach & Edelbrock, 1981) and examined the Aggressive Behavior subscale as well as Item #15, "cruel to animals." One purpose of this administration was to examine informally relations between the CAAI and a standardized measure of child and adolescent problem behaviors. CBCL information was available for 18 of the 20 participants. We found that 44% of the sample's scores on the Aggressive Behavior subscale fell into the Borderline Clinical or Clinical ranges. In addition, 56% of the sample received a score of 1 ("Somewhat or Sometimes True") or 2 ("Very True or Often True") on Item #15.

Following approval of the project by Utah State University's Human Subjects review board, we solicited voluntary participation from parents/guardians and youth from a variety of clinical sources as well as from the community. We described the nature of the interview to adults and youth and secured informed consent before proceeding. Participants were assured confidentiality (except in cases where a youth might reveal intent to engage in self-injury or injury to others - parents/guardians would be informed in such cases).

We provided animal-related toys and books, during interviews with youth, that proved effective in maintaining the interest of even the youngest participants. Toys and books were especially valuable with younger children to clarify different types of animals and to assist children in identifying animals with which they were personally familiar but for which they might not have ready labels. Some "acting out" and play behaviors that occurred spontaneously suggest that the materials could be used in assessing preverbal children in future research. (A protocol for administering the CAAI is available from the first author.)

DEVELOPMENT OF A QUANTITATIVE CAAI CRUELTY RATING

Written records of interviews with parents/guardians and youth were typed and then used as the basis for testing a preliminary version of a quantitative cruelty rating system (see Appendix B). The aforementioned cruelty dimensions were each assigned numerical ratings of 1, 2, or 3 with higher ratings designed to reflect more severe, problematic cruelty. The ratings were based on definitions of each dimension as well as numerous examples, with inclusion and exclusion rules, to guide assigning scores of 1, 2, or 3. Scores based on this rating system could range from 0 (no instances of cruelty to animals) to 30 (severe, chronic, and recent cruelty towards a variety of animals with the youth displaying no empathy).

In our sample, we found total scores ranging from 0 to 27. Most of the ratings fell into the 10-20 range suggesting that future research with larger samples of children examine clinical cut-off scores for separating cruelty into mild, moderate, and severe categories.

QUALITATIVE ANALYSIS

In addition to its potential for quantitative scoring, the CAAI yielded rich information for qualitative analysis and raised questions about the reliability of single-item assessments of cruelty to animals.

First, information from the CAAI was valuable for exploring the varied motivations children may have for engaging in cruelty to animals. The motivations include curiosity and exploration, especially by younger children, who may not yet have internalized values regarding the kind treatment of animals, peer reinforcement for cruel behavior (for example, in cases where a gang may require animal cruelty as part of its initiation rites), using cruelty to animals (including sexual abuse of animals) as a means of changing one's current mood to a more excited one, imitating, either consciously or not, the witnessed cruelty to animals performed by others, and using cruelty to animals as a means of self-injury (as in the case of one child who agitated the family cat until the cat clawed the child's arms). It should be emphasized that these motivations were derived by focusing on the cruelty dimensions of the CAAI; examining the kindness dimensions, as well, suggests that destructive and gentle behaviors may coexist in children's repertoires, making analysis of the cruelty phenomenon more challenging.

Second, use of the CAAI revealed that checklists including only one brief item on cruelty to animals may sometimes provide misleading information or fail to capture the level of cruelty that some children display toward animals. For example, we found that, in some cases, children failed to mention obvious acts of cruelty their parents had noted and, in other cases, the reverse was true. The value of multimethod (checklist and interview) and multiple informant (parent and child) approaches to assessment was reinforced by our experiences. In one case, a parent gave her child a rating of 1 on the cruel to animals Child Behavior Checklist (CBCL) item (Achenbach & Edelbrock, 1981). The parent then proceeded to describe, during the CAAI interview, a longstanding pattern of vicious, lethal animal cruelty her child engaged in. Parents clearly may differ in the reference point they use for judging their children's behavior toward animals--what is considered "cruel" in one family may be acceptable discipline in another family (Thompson & Ascione, 1995). In another case, the parent was unaware of her child's cruelty since it occurred covertly. Relying solely on parental report would have yielded a distorted picture of this child's behavior with animals.

LIMITATIONS/FUTURE DIRECTIONS

• Preliminary analyses of interrater reliability (computed as the percent of identical scores for two independent raters) in scoring the cruelty dimensions suggest that agreement ranges from adequate to good. Some dimensions yielded excellent agreement between raters (e.g., for RECENCY, 83% exact agreement) while others were marginal (e.g., ISOLATE, 60% exact agreement). This suggests a need for further elaboration of the scoring criteria and expansion of sections of the CAAI to probe more extensively about certain cruelty dimensions.

• In future research, it would be valuable to obtain information on levels of <u>interpersonal</u> violence that a youth has witnessed and/or engaged in within the family context (e.g., wife battering, sibling abuse). Our current protocol did not allow us to ask questions of this nature due to the added ethical, confidentiality, and reporting requirement issues.

• The CAAI was designed for research use and its potentially lengthy administration time (depending on the number of incidents described and the detail in reporting) may limit its value in non-research settings (e.g., use by law enforcement, animal control). We are currently working on a checklist-format version of the CAAI that would tap the same dimensions of cruelty (and provide for listings of motivations for cruelty) but assess them in a more efficient manner. This version would be most applicable in cases where animal maltreatment is already suspected or verified and the issue is one of determining the severity of the cruelty and potential psychopathology of the perpetrator.

• Future research should also focus more intensely on developmental analysis of cruelty to animals. The relatively small sample size in this study precluded examination of age-related factors in cruelty to animals and developmental changes in such behavior. Are there patterns of age-related changes in the form that animal maltreatment takes for individual children? If these patterns can be identified, would this information facilitate the design of intervention efforts?

REFERENCES

Achenbach, T. M., & Edelbrock, C. S. (1981). Behavioral problems and competencies reported by parents of normal and disturbed children aged four through sixteen. *Monographs of the Society for Research in Child Development, 46*(1, Serial No. 188).

Achenbach, T. M., Howell, C. T., Quay, H. C., & Conners, C. K. (1991). National survey of problems and competencies among four to sixteen-year-olds. *Monographs of the Society for Research in Child Development, 56* (Serial No. 225).

American Psychiatric Association (1994). *Diagnostic and Statistical Manual of Mental Disorders* (4th ed.). Washington, DC: Author.

Ascione, F. R. (1993). Children who are cruel to animals: A review of research and implications for developmental psychopathology. *Anthrozoös, 6*(4), 226-246.

Felthous, A. R., & Kellert, S. R. (1987). Childhood cruelty to animals and later aggression against people: A review. *American Journal of Psychiatry, 144,* 710-717.

Thompson, T., & Ascione, F. R. (1995, April). *Childhood cruelty to animals: In the eye of the beholder?* Paper presented at the biennial meeting of the Society for Research in Child Development, Indianapolis, IN.

APPENDIX A
CAAI Sample Sections
Children and Animals Assessment Instrument (CAAI) - Youth Form
[Perform - Cruelty items for Pet Animals][1]

----

[1]The complete CAAI has separate sections for questions about PERFORMING or WITNESSING KINDNESS or CRUELTY to FARM, WILD, PET, and STRAY animals. There are parallel YOUTH and PARENT forms of the CAAI. In the parent form, respondents are asked about <u>their children's</u> experiences and activities. The CAAI Youth and Parent forms including all sections are available from the first author.

PPC#1. How many pet animals can you name?

PPC#2. What kinds of pet animals do people have in this part of [name of state]?
[prompt to name insect, reptile/amphibian, fish, bird, mammal]

PPC#3. Which of **these** kinds of pet animals have you seen in your neighborhood?
[prompt about species mentioned in question PPC#2]

PPC#4. Sometimes, kids and grownups treat pet animals in ways that are not good or ways that are mean. Can you remember a time when you were mean to a pet animal or hurt a pet animal?
[probe if others involved]

PPC#5. When did this happen?

PPC#6. Did anyone else besides you see this happen? Who was that?

PPC#7. What sort of animal was it?

PPC#8. Who were the other people who were mean to the pet animal? [if applicable]
[probe regarding gender, age, relation to respondent]

PPC#9. What did you do that was mean?

PPC#10. How many times did you do this?

PPC#11. Can you think of a reason why you did this?

PPC#12. Where did this happen?

PPC#13. What did the pet animal do?

PPC#14. How did doing this make you feel?

PPC#15. Did you tell anyone about what you did?

PPC#16. What did they say or do after you told them?

PPC#17. Is there anything else you want to tell me about this?
Can you tell me about **another** time when {recycle to PPC#4 and following questions on additional sheet}

Children and Animals Assessment Instrument (CAAI) - Youth Form
[Witness-Cruelty items for Wild Animals]

WWC#1. How many animals can you name that **live in the wild?**

WWC#2. What wild animals live in this part of [name of state]?
[prompt to name insect, reptile/amphibian, fish, bird, mammal]

WWC#3. Which of **these** animals have you seen when **you** were out in the wild (for example, when you were walking along a field, near a lake, in the mountains)?
[prompt about species mentioned in question WWC#2]

WWC#4. Sometimes, kids and grownups treat wild animals in ways that are not good or ways that are mean. Can you remember a time when you saw someone being mean to a wild animal or hurting a wild animal?
[probe if more than one person involved]

WWC#5. When did this happen?

WWC#6. Did anyone else besides you see this happen? Who was that?

WWC#7. What sort of animal was it?

WWC#8. Who was the person who was mean to the wild animal?
[probe regarding gender, age, relation to respondent]

WWC#9. What did the person do that was mean?

WWC#10. How many times did the person do this?

WWC#11. Can you think of a reason why the person did this?

WWC#12. Where did this happen?

WWC#13. What did the wild animal do?

WWC#14. How did seeing this make you feel?

WWC#15. Did you tell anyone about what you saw?

WWC#16. What did they say or do after you told them?

WWC#17. Is there anything else you want to tell me about this?
Can you tell me about **another** time when {recycle to WWC#4 and following questions on additional sheet}

APPENDIX B
Cruelty Ratings Perform Cruelty Sections of CAAI

Rating Instructions for SEVERITY

Read through the narrative summaries of the interview with the child or adolescent.
[For SEVERITY ratings, pay special attention to responses to items # 4, 9, 13, 14, and 17, e.g., items 4 and 9 will provide information on general features of the behaviors, item 13 may suggest degree of distress to the animal, item 14 may suggest mitigating circumstances and information about the child's motivation, and item 17 may provide other relevant details omitted in earlier responses.]

SCORE A 0 IF: No instances of maltreatment of any kind are mentioned or only one case of minor, teasing, non-destructive, non-painful act is mentioned.

Examples: holds squirming kitten but releases it after 30-60 seconds, blows into dog's face, makes loud noise to scare sleeping pet, bangs on side of bird cage, chases ducks, withdraws food after providing it, throws rock into pond dispersing waterfowl but clearly not aiming to hit animals, trapping insect and preventing its return to wild (separate from killing what are considered to be insect pests), spraying birds in tree with garden hose at a distance.

If, for whatever reason, participant describes accepted hunting practices in this section, mark as "0/HUNT".

SCORE A 1 IF: More than one or repeated cases of behavior similar to examples described above.

It is assumed that the acts would not cause physical harm or damage or more than minimal discomfort, given the animal involved. Acts receiving this rating would be described as **ANNOYING, FRIGHTENING, INTERFERING, RESTRAINING.**

Use this level if unintentional neglect or developmentally related irresponsibility or lack of knowledge has harmed animal, even to the point that animal dies. If resulting harm is at level 2 or 3 as described below mark as "1+".

SCORE A 2 IF: One or more instances of acts of maltreatment that are presumed to result in pain or discomfort to the animal, perhaps accompanied by minor physical damage (e.g., scratch or superficial cut, loss of a feather, minor eye irritation, sprain) and what would be judged in some animals as significant fear and escape behavior. If applicable, acts in this category would result in distress vocalizations.

Examples: playing "catch" with an animal, tying animals legs together with string, pressing together animal's jaws, shoving animal away, throwing objects unlikely to cause more than minimal discomfort or damage (e.g., rubber ball at dog's head, sand at bird), twisting limbs, applying manual pressure assumed to be uncomfortable (e.g., pressing in on eyes, pinching tail or ear). Do **not** use this category if a weapon, instrument, heat, caustic agent, etc. is used to harm the animal (see below).

If behavior involves sexual activity with an animal (either with the animal as agent or as recipient) that is primarily touching or fondling and does not involve penetration with body parts or objects/instruments, scores as "2/S".

SCORE A 3 IF: One or more instances of maltreatment considered to result in significant pain or discomfort to an animal, perhaps accompanied by significant physical damage (e.g., deep cut, loss of part of limb or other external body part [piece of ear, wing]) or resulting in death. Acts that prolong suffering, that could be labeled torturing are included here. The maltreatment may be administered manually or through the use of instruments, weapons, extremes of temperature, interference with respiration, or use of caustic agents.

Examples: pouring flammable liquid on an animal and igniting it, immersing a mouse in boiling water, tying plastic around the head of a cat, using weapons on non-game animals, tying animal to railroad track to be run over, grabbing animal by body part (e.g., tail, back legs) and hitting animal against object or surface, PURPOSEFUL DEPRIVATION of food/water for significant periods of time.

Do not score if child gives credible self-defense rational for severe act e.g., strikes at "unprovoked", attacking dog with metal pipe, grabs and throws down to ground bird pecking at child's head.

If behavior involves sexual activity with an animal that includes penetration with body parts or instrument, or damage to animal's anal or genital area, score as "3/S".

****

If multiple instances of cruel acts varying in severity have been mentioned in the interview, enter the MOST SEVERE instance.

Rating Instructions for FREQUENCY

After completing the rating for severity, review instances where a RATING OF AT LEAST 1 was given. Count up the number of instances where ratings equal to or greater than 1 were assigned.

SCORE A 1 IF: One or two instances were noted.

SCORE A 2 IF: More than two but fewer than six instances were noted.

SCORE A 3 IF: Six or more instances were noted.

[Please note that with this preliminary rating system, frequency is being scored separate from severity. Later iterations may include a weighting procedure to control for opportunities for different levels of severity - e.g., one act of level three severity could equal three acts of level one severity. An algorithm for dealing with this issue remains to be developed.]

Rating Instructions for DURATION

This refers to the period of time within which the maltreatment incidents occurred not to how recent the events were (see RECENCY below).

Considering the instances recorded in the incident x incident records above,

SCORE A 1 IF: Acts of maltreatment occurred during a one month period.

SCORE A 2 IF: Acts of maltreatment occurred during a six month period.

SCORE A 3 IF: Acts of maltreatment occurred during a period longer than six months.

SCORE NI IF: There is not enough information to rate.

Rating Instructions for RECENCY

This relates to how recently acts of maltreatment receiving a SEVERITY rating of at least 1 have occurred.

SCORE A 1 IF: Acts of maltreatment occurred OVER one year ago.

SCORE A 2 IF: Acts of maltreatment occurred less than one year ago but longer than six months ago.

SCORE A 3 IF: Acts of maltreatment occurred within the past six months.

SCORE NI IF: There is not enough information to rate.

Rating Instructions for
DIVERSITY/ACROSS-CATEGORIES

Considering ALL of the instances recorded,

SCORE A 0 IF: No instances of cruelty to any kind of animal (farm, wild, stray, or pet).

SCORE A 1 IF: One of four TYPES of animal maltreated.

SCORE A 2 IF: Two of four TYPES of animal maltreated.

SCORE A 3 IF: Three or four of four TYPES of animal maltreated.

Rating Instructions for
DIVERSITY/WITHIN-CATEGORY

If DIVERSITY/CROSS-CATEGORIES received a "1" rating or higher, then score the number of individual animals maltreated (e.g., four different cats were abused, dozens of birds were burned).

SCORE A 1 IF: No more than two animals were maltreated within any one category (e.g., you would still rate a "1" if two pet cats, two wild deer, two calves, and one stray dog were maltreated).

SCORE A 2 IF: More than two but fewer than six animals were maltreated within any category.

SCORE A 3 IF: Six or more animals were maltreated within any category.

SCORE NI IF: Record does not have enough information for making decision about numbers within category.

Scoring Instructions for SENTIENCE

SCORE A 1 IF: Animal maltreated or killed is an invertebrate (e.g., worm, insect).

SCORE A 2 IF: Animal maltreated or killed is a cold-blooded vertebrate (e.g., fish, amphibian, reptile).

SCORE A 3 IF: Animal maltreated or killed is a warm-blooded vertebrate (e.g., bird, mammal).

If multiple maltreatments have been recorded, score sentience level FOR THE MOST SEVERE INSTANCE.

Scoring Instructions for COVERT

This category is related to the effort or lack of effort the individual displays to conceal the actions as they are performed. Make judgments on this category REGARDLESS OF WHETHER INDIVIDUAL REVEALS THE ACTIONS TO OTHERS AT SOME LATER TIME.

SCORE A 0 IF: Child performs act in front of others (who ARE participants).

SCORE A 1 IF: Child performs act in front of others (who ARE NOT participants).

SCORE A 2 IF: Child happens to be alone when act performed.

SCORE A 3 IF: Child purposely acts secretively or describes methods of concealing his or her actions.

If multiple maltreatments have been recorded, score covert level FOR THE MOST SEVERE INSTANCE.

Scoring instruction for ISOLATE

This category relates to mitigating effects of presence of other people. For example, child would be considered less responsible if adults are sanctioning the cruel behavior.

SCORE A 1 IF: Child is with one or more adults who are participants (possibly with peers present) when act occurs.

SCORE A 2 IF: Child is with one or more peers ONLY who are participants when act occurs.

SCORE A 3 IF: Child acts alone.

If multiple maltreatments have been recorded, score isolate level FOR THE MOST SEVERE INSTANCE.

Rating Instructions for EMPATHY

After reading the entire record or narrative (see, especially, responses to items #11, 14, and 17), and assuming that there is at least one incident of a severity rating of at least "1",
SCORE A 1 IF: Participant indicates verbally or displays some action displaying sensitivity to animal's distress. Use this rating level if child initiates attempt to make reparation for distress or damage caused.

SCORE A 2 IF: Participant vacillates between indication of caring and sensitivity to distress and callous, uncaring, sadistic attitude. Score here if caring is toward one class or species of animal and lack of caring, sensitivity is toward another class or species.

SCORE A 3 IF: Participant displays no evidence of caring but instead indicates delight in having caused distress, pain, death of the animal.

SCORE NI IF: There is not enough information on which to make a judgment about empathy.

PROPOSED TYPOLOGY OF COMPANION ANIMAL ABUSE

Hannelie Vermeulen and
Johannes S. J. Odendaal

Abstract. *Companion animal abuse is a universal phenomenon recorded since the earliest times. The lack of standardized definitions concerning companion animal abuse impedes research and reporting on the subject. In order to address this problem a typology of companion animal abuse is proposed for general application to identify the different types of abuse. Analysis of the records of the Society for the Prevention of Cruelty to Animals in South Africa indicated the usefulness of such a typology. Education based on the typology may contribute to the prevention of companion animal abuse.*

INTRODUCTION

Companion animal abuse traces back to the earliest times. It is a universal phenomenon and a considerable problem in the interaction between human beings and companion animals (Kellert and Felthous 1986). The seriousness thereof is often underestimated by the judicial system, the abuser, and society as a whole and not given necessary attention. This underestimation stems from incidents of abuse often being treated as isolated cases and not regarded as a serious, ongoing problem.

The lack of a standardized definition of companion animal abuse leads to a wide range of definitions being used and ultimately to discrepant research findings.

Cruelty/abuse is often defined using adjectives such as "deliberate," "malicious" and "repeated" (*Encyclopaedia Britannica* 1987; Felthous and Kellert 1986, 1987), which excludes many other forms of this phenomenon. In victimology the term "abuse" is preferred to "cruelty," for example, as in "child abuse" (Giovannoni 1979). To date, no references to the term "animal abuse" replacing the term "animal cruelty" have been identified. Following current victimological trends, as well as to lessen value judgment, the term "companion animal abuse" will be used in this article.

Several theories on human–animal interactions have been discussed by Kidd and Kidd (1987). Most of these focus on positive human–animal interaction. Existing behavior-based theories may explain specific types of abuse. For example, aggression theories such as that of Freud or Lorenz (Meyer 1982) may be applicable to assault, and Freudian explanations may be offered for bestiality (Jacobs 1992). However, there is no generally accepted theory explaining negative human–animal interaction on a continuum of behavior, including positive human–animal interactions.

This lack of theory constitutes a void in the explanation and understanding of the phenomenon, because the researcher has no theoretical base to argue from. In order to minimize this problem, a typology of companion animal abuse is advanced to identify the different types of abuse according to basic companion animal needs. The identification of the types would also point toward a continuum of negative behavior in contrast to the perception of abuse as a single act. A theory that could be expanded to include negative interaction is the attention-seeking theory for human–animal interaction (Odendaal 1990). This theory proposes that the positive side of human–animal interaction is

University of Pretoria, Department of Veterinary Ethology, Private Bag X04, Onderstepoort 0110, Republic of South Africa.

Reprinted from *Anthrozoös* 6 (1993): 248–57, with kind permission of the editors.

established by the need for attention in both human and companion animal to form a symbiotic social relationship. The lack of interest in animals by humans (or vice versa) is explained in terms of other sources of stimuli that fulfill the need for attention. On a continuum of behavior, the negative side of human–animal interaction could be added in the following way:

negative interaction—no interaction—
positive interaction.

Such a theory could be helpful in the explanation of the phenomenon in relation to other human–animal interaction studies.

No comprehensive statistics illustrating the abuse of companion animals are available in South Africa. The only related South African statistics are those published by the Society for the Prevention of Cruelty to Animals (SPCA) to illustrate their case loads. These statistics illustrate the actual amount of complaints received and followed up, but not the number of cases identified as abused or the type of abuse involved. Fragmented information on companion animal abuse may be an international problem.

DEFINITIONS

Before a typology is presented, definitions of certain key words for this study are given:

Companion Animal

A companion animal is defined as a dog, cat, or horse kept in the company of humans, inter alia, for social purposes, and subject to the following differentiating aspects: a personal name, personal care or control by humans, influence on the owner's lifestyle and the possibility of an

emotional relationship. Part of the definition was taken from Tromp (1988).

Companion Animal Abuse

Companion animal abuse is defined as the intentional, malicious, or irresponsible, as well as unintentional or ignorant, infliction of physiological and/or psychological pain, suffering, deprivation, and the death of a companion animal by humans. The abuse is based on harmful effects caused by the lack of the fulfillment of basic companion animal needs for their health and well-being. The abuse is thus independent of human intention or ignorance, socially sanctioned or socially rejected norms, and covers both single and repeated incidents (*Encyclopaedia Britannica* 1987; Kellert 1986, 1987).

A Typology for Abuse

A typology is the study of categorizing types of abuse. The basic requirements for a typology include uniformity, mutual exclusiveness, simplicity, meaningfulness, universality, measurableness, completeness and pragmatism (Pretorius 1986).

To comply with the requirements for uniformity, type of victimization was chosen to identify the different abuses. Mutual exclusiveness was obtained by the identification of types that could occur on their own as single acts. However, it is possible for more than one type to show elements of other identified types but to still exclude each other per definition. Because a specific abuse can fit the description of only one category, the typology may also be regarded as simplistic, keeping in mind that complexity may arise when more than one type of abuse occurs simultaneously. The typology may be regarded as meaningful, universal, and measurable as it is based on the science of companion animal ethology. It can also be accepted as complete because of the portrayal of the continuum of abusive behavior. The differentiations will lend practicality to the application of the typology. This would comply with the requirement of pragmatism.

A TYPOLOGY OF COMPANION ANIMAL ABUSE

Several victimological typologies, dating from that proposed by Mendelsohn (Galaway and Hudson 1981) to that of Fattah (Fattah 1989), were studied as a guideline for the construction of a typology on companion animal abuse. Fattah's typology of child abuse proved most helpful for the construction of this typology, since child and companion animal abuse resemble each other in some instances. Both victims are, for example, often biologically or mentally weaker than the abuser and not in the position to make a choice or avoid the circumstances or the consequences thereof. The three major categories of physical abuse of children, namely active maltreatment, passive neglect, and commercial exploitation, as well as the two major categories of mental abuse, namely active and passive abuse, are applicable to companion animals, but not without major refinement of the classification. The third classification of child abuse, namely sexual abuse, was included under the category of physical companion animal abuse, because of its physical nature. Here it is identified as active maltreatment (bestiality). Mental abuse, although applicable to both victims, differs in appearance. It is more common in human victims, and also easier identifiable, because human–human interaction is easier to interpret than human–animal interaction. The child can, for example, be interviewed or tested by using role play, whereas only the reaction of the companion animal, which might be misleading, can be tested. Overall, it is a category difficult to record and evaluate, because it leaves few or no perceptible traces.

The differences between the proposed typology and that of Fattah are most probably due to the difference in social standing between human and companion animal, as well as the difference in ability and usability. For example, children might be commercially exploited by using them as drug carriers, while the animal is more prone to acts such as indiscriminate breeding or experimentation. Abuse can be intentional or nonintentional, indicated by the effect on the victim and not the behavior of the abuser.

The types of abuse will be briefly defined where it is applied to actual reported cases.

APPLICATION OF THE TYPOLOGY ON SPCA RECORDS IN SOUTH AFRICA

By using two large convenient samples, the applicability of the typology to the phenomenon of companion animal abuse will be evaluated.

Caseloads of Four SPCAs

To evaluate the practical application of the typology, the caseloads of four SPCAs in the Pretoria-Witwatersrand area (the most densely populated area in the country), namely Silverton, Verwoerdburg, Randburg, and Johannesburg, were analyzed. These are privileged as well as less privileged areas and range from intercity to rural, reflecting different types of socioeconomic and cultural classes. A total of 1,863 cases ranging over a period of one year, from March 1, 1991, to February 29, 1992,

Table 1. Typology of Companion Animal Abuse

Physical abuse intentional or nonintentional	Active maltreatment	Assault Burning Poisoning Shooting Mutilation Drowning Suffocation Abandonment Restriction of movement Incorrect methods of training Inbreeding Trapping Transportation Fireworks Bestiality
	Passive neglect or ignorance	Lack of food and water Lack of shelter Lack of veterinary care Lack of sanitation General neglect
	Commercial exploitation	Labor Fights Indiscriminate breeding Sport Experimentation
Mental abuse intentional or nonintentional	Active maltreatment	Instillation of fear, anguish, and anxiety Isolation
	Passive neglect	Deprivation of love and affection Lack of recreational stimuli

were recorded and typified. The period of one year was decided upon to include possible fluctuation due to seasonal related issues as well as vacation periods.

Dogs were most commonly reported (79.8%), with cats (8.3%) and horses (2.3%) next. The remaining 9.6% included cattle, sheep, donkeys, birds, wild animals, and smaller animals such as rabbits, hamsters, and fish. The higher figure for dogs is

explained by the fact that restriction, which is the major type of abuse with the highest incidence rate, is most applicable to dogs.

An analysis of the abusers was also made to differentiate between institutionalized and noninstitutionalized abuse. The majority of reported cases involved private persons (92.0%), followed by pet shops (4.0%) and security firms (2.8%). The re-

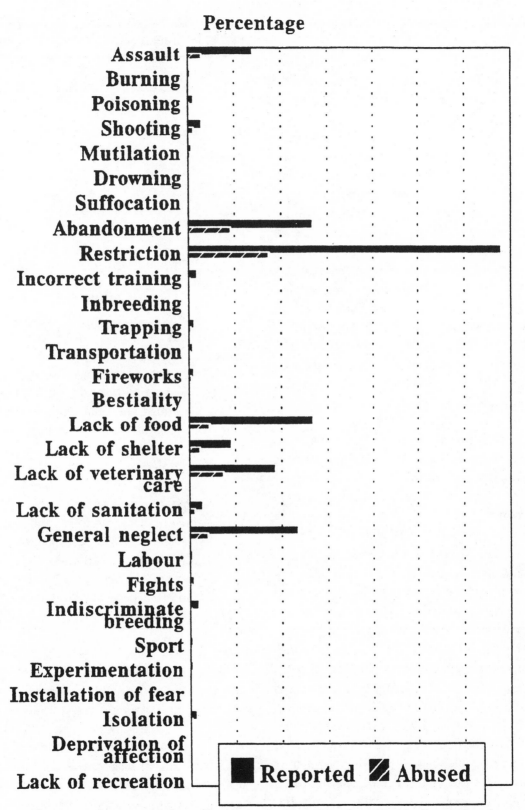

Figure 1. The Practical Application of a Typology for Companion Animal Abuse (*n* = 1863)

maining 1.2% was made up by other institutions such as riding schools, grooming parlors, and circuses. These proportions seem to be consistent with the number of animals under their respective control and are thus of no special significance.

Of the reported cases of companion animal abuse, 25.1% proved to involve maltreatment according to SPCA officials, 3.4% of abusers were charged, and 9.7% of the animals were confiscated. The discrepancy between alleged and proved abuse may be ascribed to several factors, including individual interpretation of the law, differentiation between SPCA guidelines, personal standards, societal values, as well as the interpretation and identification of the phenomenon of companion animal abuse. Another problem related to the high discrepancy between reported and identified cases of abuse is the difficulty of positive identification without physical symptoms or injuries. Fewer than half of the abused cases involved confiscation, because most of the problems could be solved by educating the persons involved or by supplying correct material where necessary. The animal is only confiscated when there is a very small possibility of improving its situation, after the owner was warned but did not respond, when the animal is in pain or abandoned, or when the owner signs it off voluntarily. This is due to the small possibility of rehoming abused animals. During the financial year of 1991/1992, only 38% of dogs, 19% of cats, and 36% of other animals were rehomed by all the South African SPCAs (SPCA 1992).

All the alleged companion animal abusers were not charged, because the SPCA follows a policy of education rather than prosecution. Although several of the cases might hold up in court legally, charges are

Table 2. Companion Animal Abuse at 4 SPCAs in South Africa

Action	Number	%
Not charged	1,151	61.8
Abused	468	25.1
Confiscated	181	9.7
Changed	63	3.4
Total	1,863	100.0

usually only laid in the most severe cases, be it intentional or unintentional. This is done in order to enable the SPCA to utilize its funds and manpower more effectively. Some cases of abuse can also not be prosecuted because the person(s) involved are not identifiable. The fact that the SPCA acts differently on different forms of abuse, for example, educate, warn, or prosecute, does not qualify some types as less abusive, but rather points to a flexible implementation of policy.

The major areas of reported abuse were restriction of movement (34.9% reported, 9.1% abused), lack of food and water (13.3% reported, 2.2% abused), abandonment (13.3% reported, 4.6% abused), general neglect (11.6% reported, 2% abused), lack of veterinary care (9.2% reported, 3.7% abused), and assault (6.9% reported, 1.5% abused).

Restriction of movement constitutes abuse when animals are confined to short leashes/tethers or small areas/enclosures, which do not allow sufficient freedom of movement or enough/regular exercise. Flesh wounds, strangulations, and amputations may manifest because of incorrect use of methods or materials. Secondary forms of abuse, for example, lack of shelter, food, water, and sanitation, may also accompany this primary abuse.

Lack of food and water is identified when animals have no access to either of the two. Depending on the period of deprivation, the animal may suffer from dehydration, hunger, starvation, or death. This abuse may be caused by neglect or ignorance.

Abandonment is suffered by many animals who no longer fit the lifestyle, temporarily or permanently, of the owner. Starvation, neglect, and proneness to physical injury are secondary forms of abuse accompanying abandonment. Objectification as well as behavior problems of the animal may be contributing factors to abandonment.

General neglect is a passive act easily recognizable by physical signs such as listlessness, paleness, weakness, emaciation, dirtiness, external parasites, eye discharges, and in the case of long-haired animals, a matted coat. Long-haired breeds, animals living in endemic parasitic areas, animals belonging to the elderly, sickly or excessively busy person, as well as to some members of lower socioeconomic classes, might be more prone to this abuse because of the difficulty in identifying the needs of the animal or spending enough time with it.

Lack of veterinary care ranges from wounds to fractures to untreated illnesses/diseases. Some animals are deprived of veterinary care because of uncaringness of the owner or fear of detection of abuse, and others are deprived of professional care because of the owners treating the animals themselves in order to save on financial cost or because of transportation problems. However, animals are also deprived of veterinary care through ignorance and unavailability of services, including the lack of preventative medicine such as vaccinations, parasite control, and inadequate nutrition.

Assault includes beating animals, throw-ing them from heights, or harming them in any way that may lead to visible injuries such as bruises, abrasions, visceral injuries, ocular damage, neurological and head injuries, or death. The injuries could also be invisible to the naked eye. This abuse may take place under several circumstances such as revenge against either the animal or the owner, discipline that may turn into abuse when overreaction takes place because of, for example, stress, predisposition, or with intent to get rid of unwanted animals, as when a bitch is in heat.

Although statistics reflect no cases of sexual animal abuse (bestiality), it does occur and SPCA hospitals researched have treated three known incidents (Lunn 1992). The South African Narcotics Bureau has also followed up on pornographic material containing animal scenes that were produced in South Africa (SANAB 1992). No incidents of abuse in sport were positively identified from SPCA files during the period of study. This might be due to the fact that good care is exercised in the animal's treatment because of its monetary value. Since dog fights are outlawed, fights are difficult to trace because of problems with identification and penetration of private circles. In 1986 a rodeo was stopped by court order after an application by the SPCA.

Only nine reported cases of mental abuse were positively identified. This might be due to the difficulty of the detection. The public might also not be aware of this abuse, and the inspectors do not necessarily check for symptoms thereof. However, several reports mention aspects of this type of abuse, without identifying it. For example, some dogs are described as being extremely nervous, as urinating when a hand is lifted, as howling and yelping when confronted, or as reacting overly submissively.

Many of the identified forms of abuse

described in the typology, such as inbreeding, drowning, suffocation, and deprivation of recreational stimuli, were not identified in the SPCA records. This does not prove their nonexistence, but rather suggests the possibility of silent crimes that take place undetected and unreported (dark figures). The possibility of these crimes was pointed out during personal interviews with animal welfare personnel (Lunn 1992).

Several other forms of abuse, such as lack of shelter and sanitation, incorrect methods of training, intentional shooting, poisoning, burning, mutilation, isolation, indiscriminate breeding, trapping, fireworks, transportation, and fights were also detected, but on a much smaller scale. This might be due to the difficulty in tracing or detecting these abuses, because of definitional variations and interpretations, as well as societal and cultural views and differences.

The forms of abuse identified in the typology but not discussed may be described as follows: Burning takes place with either hot water or fire, and poisoning includes both deliberate poisoning with, for example, organic phosphates, as well as accidental poisoning due to poisonous products left lying around or used indiscriminately (e.g., warferin). Shooting with bows and arrows, crossbows, airguns, other guns, revolvers, or catapults is also the cause of suffering and death among companion animals. Mutilation causes physical pain and discomfort and wounds and scar tissue are often visible. Drowning causes the death of the animal from inhalation of water into the lungs and suffocation due to a shortage of oxygen. This may occur during attempts to get rid of unwanted litters. Abandonment takes place when the animal is temporarily or permanently left without adequate care or intention of resuming care again. Incorrect

methods of training include, for example, beating or jerking around of the animal in a way that may cause physical or psychological harm. Inbreeding may constitute abuse when anatomical abnormalities and physiological disfunctions are caused by recessive genes, when closely related animals are interbred to strengthen specific positive or fashionable characteristics. Trapping often takes place with steel jaw or cage traps on farms. Transportation abuses take place when the animal is transported unprotected, which renders it vulnerable to injury, or when overloading, for example, of horses takes place. The explosion of fireworks may cause physical injury, stress, anxiety, anguish, and bewilderment, and bestiality is defined as attempted sexual intercourse or other sexual fulfillment.

Lack of shelter occurs when animals are left unprotected against nature's elements, and lack of sanitation becomes an abuse when companion animals are confined to areas without regular cleaning. Labor-related abuses take place when animals are overworked or ill-equipped to perform their duties, and fights constitute abuse when animals are instigated to fight each other and thus cause physical injury to each other. Indiscriminate breeding takes place when bitches are mated to maximize profits without consideration to the animal's condition or health, and sport abuse occurs when animals are pushed to deliver their utmost without consideration for their health and optimum performance. Any discomfort, pain or death suffered by an animal because of unethical experimentation is also considered abuse.

Instillation of fear, anguish, and anxiety constitutes abuse when the animal is suppressed in a tyrannical manner that leads to mental or physical symptoms. Isolation may be considered abusive when animals are confined without animal or human contact for extensive periods. This may result in behavior problems. Deprivation of love and affection takes place when no attention is paid to the animal or where a total lack of concern for its need for affection exists. Lack of recreational stimuli also constitutes abuse when the animal is left for extensive periods without anything to occupy itself with or without necessary exercise.

Because of an administrative problem, the data for February was not available at the Silverton SPCA and was thus not taken into account. Incidents of abuse were hightest in January and April (>9%), whereas May and June proved to have the lowest incident rates (<7%). The low rates occur during colder weather that keeps people more indoors, which might again keep them from noticing the abuse. The weather also keeps animals off the streets, which decreases their proneness to abuse. The peaks in April and January occur during vacation periods, when the abuse rate may increase because of improper organizing of care and protection of companion animals.

Spot checks by Johannesburg SPCA

The typology was also used in the analysis of 6,603 spot checks that were conducted by the Johannesburg SPCA in less privileged areas with a low report rate. These spot checks covered a period of four months, ranging from July, 1991, to October, 1991. To conduct these spot checks, inspectors were sent to specific areas where all residential dwellings were checked for animals and possible abuse. This information reflected households with animals and species of animals involved.

According to the spot checks, 40% of the households owned animals, and in 23% of these cases, abuse was identified by the inspectors. Of these cases, 89.8% involved dogs, 4.8% cats, and 5.4% both species. These spot checks confirmed the data of the official SPCA records. The major problem, restriction of movement, amounted to 84% of the problems experienced. Lack of food and water, shelter, sanitation, and veterinary care, and general neglect were the other problems reported. Other types of abuse were not recorded.

DISCUSSION

Abuse of companion animals is not a phenomenon that occurs in isolation. Several factors work together to create this negative end result. Possible factors enhancing companion animal abuse include:

- A companion animal is usually biologically and/or mentally weaker than human beings and not in a position to defend itself.

- An extreme leader–follower relationship between human and animal may contribute to harsh training for dominance.

- The dependency of companion animals on care and affection of human beings makes them vulnerable to the lack of or negative human attention.

- By objectification animals are regarded as property, to be treated only according to the owner's discretion.

- The low social standing of animals prohibits strong lay action in the form of social disapproval and report, as well as strong judicial action because of insufficient funds, manpower, and low prioritizing.

- Companion animals are available as a third party for assault to defuse anger between people in the same household.

This is an example of displaced aggression.

Companion animal abuse includes personal, cultural, environmental, and social elements. Because of the influence of these factors, as well as the fact that abuse takes place on a continuum from less severe to very severe actions, which may be intentional or unintentional, companion animal abuse is a complex phenomenon to deal with in a practical way. This could be the main reason why effective punitive treatment of the abuser rarely takes place.

Abuse prevention is based on thorough knowledge of companion animal needs as applied to the handling, transport, training, breeding, behavior, feeding, keeping, and care of companion animals, together with creating an awareness of the necessity to act on abuse and to report it. An approach that takes the human–animal interaction into account with regard to predisposing and triggering human and environmental factors, should be adopted. Preventive action of companion animal abuse should thus focus on education about the basic needs of and care for companion animals in a human environment.

Further research on the subject and refinement of the issues discussed could be helpful in the construction of a model that will be generally accepted for practical application and as a theoretical base. Research should pay attention to the completeness of the typology, as well as the identification of the different types of abuse. A classification system where multiple abuse as well as secondary abuses can be typified should be researched in order to address the full complexity of the issue.

REFERENCES

Encyclopaedia Britannica, 15th ed. 1987. *Micropaedia*. Ed. Goetz, P. W. 15th ed, Vol. 1, Animals, Cruelty to, 420.

Fattah, E. A. 1989. The child as victim: Victimological aspects of child abuse. In *The plight of crime victims*, ed. E. A. Fattah. London: Macmillan Press, 185–6.

Felthous, A. R., and S. R. Kellert. 1986. Childhood cruelty towards animals among criminals and non-criminals. In *The human–pet relationship*, pp. 71–82. Vienna: IEMT.

———. 1987. Childhood cruelty towards animals and later aggression against people: A review. *American Journal of Psychiatry* 144:711.

Galaway, B., and J. Hudson. 1981. *Perspectives on crime victims*. St. Louis: C. V. Mosby, 17.

Giovannoni, J. M. 1979. *Defining Child Abuse*. New York: Macmillan, 1–30.

Jacobs, M. 1992. *Sigmund Freud*. London: Sage Publications, 44.

Kidd, A. H., and R. M. Kidd. 1987. Seeking a theory of the human–animal companion bond. *Anthrozoös* 1:140–5.

Lunn, L. 1992. Veterinarian at the Johannesburg SPCA. Personal communication.

Meyer, W. F. 1982. Psychological theories of violence. In *Crimes of violence in South Africa*, ed. J. Van der Westhuizen. Pretoria, South Africa: Unisa Publishers, 84–9.

Odendaal, J. S. J. 1990. *Fundamentele gedragspatrone in die rehabilitasierol van geselskapsdiere (Fundamental behavior patterns in the rehabilitation role of companion animals)*. Rehabilitation in South-Africa 34(2):145–51.

Pretorius, R. 1986. *Die slagoffer-oortreder-sisteem van verhoudinge in misdaad (The victim-abuser-system of relationships in crime)*. In *Viktimologie*, ed. C. H. Cilliers. Pretoria, South Africa: HAUM, 31–2.

SANAB 1992. South African Narcotics Bureau. Personal communication.

SPCA 1992. Federal Council of the Society for the Prevention of Cruelty to Animals of South Africa. *Annual Report for 1991/1992*.

Tromp, G. 1988. *Het dier als vriend: Een sociologisch perspektief (The animal as friend: A sociological perspective)*. In *Dier of Ding. Objektivering van Dieren*, ed. M. B. H. Visser, and F. J. Grommers. Wagenen, Holland: Pudoc, 76.

The correlations between cruelty to animals and child abuse and the implications for veterinary medicine

Phil Arkow

Introduction

Historically, prevention of cruelty to animals has been closely linked, both philosophically and programmatically, with prevention of child abuse. Animal welfare and child protective organizations came into being concurrently in North America during the latter third of the 19th Century, as social justice reformers extended paternalistic concern to slaves, prison and asylum inmates, children, women, and animals. The humane movement was integral in this pattern, beginning with the Royal Society for the Prevention of Cruelty to Animals (RSPCA) in England in 1824 and spreading with the American SPCA in New York (1866), the Canadian SPCA in Montréal (1869), and the Ontario SPCA in Toronto (1873) (1). The historic 1874 "Mary Ellen" case in New York saw child abuse first prosecuted, using animal protection laws. It is not unrealistic to suggest that early veterinary medicine, grounded in both medicine and agriculture, was also part of this paradigm in which caring for less fortunate creatures became socially acceptable. The United States Veterinary Medical Association, which became the American Veterinary Medical Association (AVMA) in 1898, was organized in 1863, and 40 veterinary colleges (many now defunct) were chartered between 1852–1918.

Over the next century, humane organizations proliferated with many assuming both child and animal protective services; 307 of 539 (56.9%) humane societies surveyed in 1922 protected both (2). Even today, the American Humane Association remains the umbrella organization for both types of agencies, although no local humane societies still protect both children and animals. The objectives of both groups are identical: to foster an ethic which cares for the less fortunate.

Though both groups were social service agencies with limited law enforcement powers, advocates for the disenfranchised, preventative in orientation, and placing much faith in community education, child protection pulled ahead of animal welfare in public recognition. Over the years, children were no longer considered property, but today animals still are. This distinction was epitomized following Dr. C. Henry Kempe's seminal identification of the Battered Child Syndrome in 1962 (3). By 1967, all state legislatures had enacted statutes under which professionals, including, health care providers, educators, and law enforcement officials, were mandated to report suspected child abuse and neglect to social services authorities with assurances of immunity from civil or criminal liability. Today, every U.S. county has a department of child protection, every U.S. state has mandatory reporting, and accreditation and training for caseworkers are in place. By contrast, the humane movement has failed to adopt the child protection model, although an increasingly more professional network of municipal animal control facilities has been spun off; animal control, however, is rarely mandated, enforcement is haphazard and inconsistently localized, and training is sporadic and primarily voluntary. A further distinction is that a goal of animal welfare is *removal* of animals from cruel situations; a goal of child protection is *restoring* the child to the family.

Yet many opportunities for linkages still exist. It is not uncommon for humane officers to observe children in neglect; similarly, child abuse caseworkers routinely see neglected animals. Research in Bucks County, Pennsylvania, in 1980 confirmed suspicions that dysfunctional families may abuse both animals and children. Of 87 families surveyed, eight (9.1%) had been in contact with both the SPCA and children's social services agency, and some similarities in family behaviors were noted (4).

Research also found compelling evidence confirming intuitions that cruelty to animals, when perpetrated by children, might be a predictor of future antisocial behavior. Research documented: correlations between cruelty to animals, arson, and bedwetting among violent criminals; high levels of people-directed aggression among psychiatric patients who had tortured dogs and cats; and high incidences of early acts of cruelty to animals among aggressive criminals. A triad of symptoms, closely associating cruelty to animals, physical abuse by one or both parents, and violence toward people, was largely ignored by courts and social ser-

The Humane Society of the Pikes Peak Region, 633 South 8th Street, Colorado Springs, Colorado 80905

Phil Arkow is the Director of Education and Publicity for the Humane Society of the Pikes Peak Region in Colorado Springs, Colorado. He currently serves on the American Veterinary medical Association's Animal Welfare Committee, is on the Board of Directors of the Delta Society, and was one of the coordinators of the American Human Association's national task force on violence to children and animals.

This article was presented at the Canadian Veterinary Medical Association's Annual Convention July 4–8, 1992 in St. John's, Newfoundland. It has been edited, but not peer-reviewed.

Cet article est le compte-rendu d'une conférence donnée au congrès annuel de l'Association canadienne des vétérinaires, qui s'est tenu du 4 au 8 juillet, 1992 à St. John's (Terre-Neuve). L'article a été édité mais n'a pas été révisé par les pairs.

À nos lecteurs francophones
L'équipe éditoriale de la Revue exprime ses regrets devant l'impossibilité de traduire cet article.

Reprinted from the *Canadian Veterinary Journal* 33 (1992): 518–21, with kind permission of the Canadian Veterinary Medical Association.

vice agencies (5). Not until 1987 did the American Psychiatric Association's Diagnostic and Statistical Manual of Mental Disorders [DSM-III-R] include cruelty to animals among diagnostic criteria for conduct disorder (6).

Spectacular anecdotal incidents among serial killers enhanced this research. Mass murderer Theodore Bundy claimed he had spent his early years with a grandfather who assaulted people and tormented animals; circumstantial evidence linked him to animal graves. Albert DeSalvo, the "Boston Strangler," in his youth shot arrows into dogs and cats trapped in orange crates. David Berkowitz, New York's "Son of Sam," had shot a neighbor's Labrador retriever. Carroll Edward Cole, executed in 1985 for five of the 35 murders of which he was accused, said his first act of violence as a child was to strangle a puppy. James Huberty, who killed 21 at a McDonald's restaurant in San Ysidro, California, had been accused of shooting his neighbor's dog with an airgun. Earl Shriner, serving a one hundred and thirty-four and one-half year sentence for sexually mutilating a seven-year-old boy in Tacoma, Washington, had a juvenile history of stringing up cats, sticking firecrackers up the anuses of dogs, and slaughtering chickens. In 1975, neighbors photographed the skulls of animals impaled in the yard of Jeffrey Dahmer, imprisoned this year for the dismembering of 17 men in Milwaukee. None of these early incidents were reported to authorities.

Other anecdotes describe adults killing animals to punish or threaten children, often to obtain their acquiescence to satanic cults or sexual abuse; these incidents may later manifest in multiple personality disorder.

These reports come during heightened awareness of community violence, particularly in inner cities. Humane educators wonder how to teach kindness to animals to children who fear going to school because of drive-by random shootings. With pets present in more than 50% of households, cruelty to animals should now be considered another form of family violence, similar to abuse against children, spouses, elders, and other vulnerable members of society. Veterinary observation of an animal's condition may provide key insights into the psychological, emotional, and social patterns of the human caregiver.

Why people abuse animals

If cruelty to animals is morally reprehensible to both the humane ethic and the veterinary creed and potentially indicative of future violence, it is incumbent for all concerned with animal well-being to understand the roots of animal cruelty and to take preventative measures. Stephen R. Kellert and Alan Felthous (7) have uncovered nine distinct motives for cruelty to animals:

1. To control the animal, eliminating presumably undesirable characteristics.
2. To retaliate against a presumed wrong by the animal.
3. To satisfy a prejudice against a species or breed.
4. To instill violent tendencies in the animal to cause it to attack others.
5. To enhance one's own aggressiveness, impressing others with one's capacity for violence.
6. To shock people for amusement.
7. To retaliate against another person, exacting revenge through the victim's animals.
8. Displacement of hostility from a person to an animal, particularly in violent families where physically abused children abuse animals to "get even" for the beatings.
9. Nonspecific sadism, without any particular provocation, to derive pleasure from causing suffering.

Veterinary practitioners may see the results of dysfunctional family violence directed against animals. In one study of 53 New Jersey pet-owning families involved with physical/sexual child abuse or neglect, researchers found that levels of basic pet care, the use of veterinary services, and rates of pet sterilization did not differ noticeably from acceptable standards. Yet 13 (25%) of the families affirmed that a member of their household had injured their pets at some time. Caseworkers observed unreported animal abuse in an additional 20 (38%) of the families. In 47 (88%) of the families in which physical child abuse took place, animal abuse also occurred. Many abused animals, accompanied by children, will visit veterinarians. Clearly, the potential for veterinary involvement with abuse cases is widespread (8).

Opportunities for veterinary involvement

Veterinarians will likely see patients and clients exhibiting symptoms of abuse or neglect and may significantly improve the health of the individual or family, as well as that of the animal. "A considerable number of problems involving the emotional well-being of people come to the attention of veterinarians which would otherwise go unnoticed...due to the inherently emotional nature of the relationship of pets to humans and the fact that problems involving human relationships may become apparent in the context of animal-man interaction where they would not be clearly visible otherwise," wrote psychiatrist Michael McCulloch (9), who calculated in 1976 that small-animal practitioners in the United States see 55 million pets and 100 million people annually.

McCulloch suggested that veterinarians, though not specially trained as mental health counselors, have professional obligations to both human clients and animal patients which, at times, require evaluating problems confronting the human caregivers. Since practitioners often rely on humans to provide a pertinent clinical history, veterinarians are necessarily drawn into human emotional health and patterns of animal care in the home environment. Veterinarians regularly confront relationships which are unhealthy for the animal, the owner, or both. Veterinarians who encounter human or animal abuse victims may feel compelled to offer guidance on how the dynamics of the problem affect the well-being of the animal or make a referral to a physician, counselor, or appropriate social service agency. Although data are lacking, it is strongly suspected that such referrals are relatively uncommon (9). To make such a referral risks compromising the doctor-client relationship, which may not necessarily have the same priorities as the dotor-patient relationship, an ethical dilemma which has largely gone undiscussed.

Discussion of this ethical dilemma raises uncomfortable questions. What are veterinarians' legal responsibilities and moral obligations to report suspected child abuse to appropriate authorities? "The fundamental problem of veterinary medicine is... does the veterinarian have primary obligation to the animal or to the owner?" asked Bernard Rollin (10). He cited a California child abuse law which requires all medical professionals, including veterinarians, to report suspected child abuse, "thereby acknowledging a special social obligation of veterinarians in virtue, presumably, of their medical knowledge." Similarly, should veterinarians be required to report suspected animal abuse? "As of 1987, there is no legal duty to report animal cruelty cases to any authority except, in many states, in cases of staged animal fights. However, when veterinarians see animals that have been or are being mistreated, they have a deep moral duty to intervene in the animal's behalf."

To investigate these issues, I surveyed American legislative officials as to whether veterinarians are included among "health professionals" generally mandated to report suspected child abuse to county authorities. I also inquired whether humane and animal control officers are included among "peace officers" or "law enforcement officers" mandated to make such reports, and whether any of these groups is mandated to report suspected animal abuse.

While results are extremely informal and legal opinions by attorneys-general will be required, the responses were provocative. Disputing Rollins' finding, an attorney in the California Office of Child Abuse Prevention said veterinarians would not be included because the child would not be observed "in his or her professional capacity or within the scope of his or her employment." A similar response was received from Pennsylvania. In 15 American states, for the purposes of reporting suspected child abuse, veterinarians are apparently not considered "health professionals", "health practitioners", "medical professionals", practitioners of the "healing arts", "other person providing medical services licensed or certified in the state", or "any other health care provider". Only Colorado provides statutory authority mandating veterinarians who have reasonable cause to know or suspect that a child has been subjected to abuse or neglect, or who has observed the child being subjected to circumstances or conditions which would reasonably result in abuse or neglect, to immediately report the information, with immunity from civil or criminal liability, to the local department of social services or law enforcement agency.

No state officials consider humane agents or animal control officers "police or peace officers." Minnesota is apparently the only state in which veterinarians are obligated to report suspected cruelty to animals.

However, the Internal Revenue Service ruled in May 1991 that veterinary medicine is within the "field of health" and that veterinarians are "similar health care professionals" in a category including physicians, nurses, and dentists (11). How this definition will affect mandatory reporting remains to be seen.

There is a long tradition of veterinarians protecting public health through employment in food inspection, zoönoses control, comparative medical research, education, and human health and environmental agencies. Veterinary contributions to the emotional well-being of people has become increasingly recognized in recent years through a variety of human animal bond programs, such as, animal-assisted therapy and pet loss counseling. The public is predisposed to perceive veterinarians as community caregivers in health delivery systems.

Community involvement is encouraged by professional standards. The AVMA Principles of Veterinary Medical Ethics (12) notes that "the responsibilities of the veterinary profession extend not only to the patient but also to society. The health of the community as well as the patient deserves the veterinarian's interest."

Concerns about liability or loss of business from mandatory reporting laws have been minimal in human medicine. American Veterinary Medical Association ethics provide safeguards: "The ethical ideals of the veterinary profession imply that a doctor of veterinary medicine and the veterinarian's staff will protect the personal privacy of clients, unless the veterinarian is required, by law, to reveal the confidences or unless it becomes necessary in order to protect the health and welfare of the individual, the animals, and/or others whose health and welfare may be endangered" (12).

Why should veterinarians care about child abuse?

Beyond the veterinary creed of caregiving, several other aspects of the relationship between cruelty to animals and to children compel the veterinary profession to take leadership roles in exploring the complex constellation of abusive people-animal interactions:

- Public perception of the profession. Numerous surveys indicate the public is generally predisposed to consider veterinarians as benevolent members of the health care system and pets as significant members of the family.

- Increased cooperation with other community health care and animal welfare organizations. Independently, local coalitions against violence have formed in several cities where animal care and control centers work with child protection departments, exchanging investigation information and cross-training caseworkers to expand limited resources. Veterinarians, with professional expertise and medical training, can be instrumental in these coalitions.

- Enhanced opportunities to work symbiotically with the humane movement. Divisive single issues (such as spay clinics or laboratory research) distract veterinarians and the humane field from recognizing more significant concerns in which both have common interests. Respectful disagreement on some issues should not interfere with cooperation in matters on which there is agreement.

It is intriguing to speculate on what might occur were veterinarians mandatory reporters of suspected child abuse. Perhaps veterinarians would be perceived to be more in parity with physicians, dentists, and others in health care. Perhaps scientific orientation would generate research to test the intuitive, but undocumented, axioms of animal welfare which suggest that a child's treatment of animals will direct lifelong patterns toward human beings.

The danger is to do nothing in the face of emerging empirical support for these intuitive beliefs. "It would be sad...if in analogy to child abuse there persisted a reluctance to recognize the existence of animal abuse brought to the veterinarian's attention. Greater awareness of animal abuse may lead veterinarians to initiate mental health intervention for the abusing family in addition to treating the animal" (13).

Recommendations for the veterinary profession

1. Take reports of cruelty to animals seriously. In addition to immediate concern for the animals' welfare, battered pets are frequently symptomatic of other family dysfunctions and violence which, if unresolved, may lead to greater problems later. An animal-related incident may be the first point of prevention and intervention for social service networks.
2. Do not be afraid to become involved. Generally, any individual may report suspected child abuse to appropriate youth services or law enforcement authorities in good faith with full immunity from civil or criminal liability. Additionally, veterinarians should consider themselves to have a higher professional and moral obligation to report such suspicions, and should work for legislation to mandate their inclusion among other health professionals already integrated into the reporting system.
3. Participate and take leadership in community coalitions against violence. Veterinarians are excellently positioned to work with humane, animal control, social service, child protection, and criminal justice agencies to explore innovative strategies that protect the vulnerable and teach nurturing skills to those who most desperately need them.
4. Become aware of various roles which pets play for individuals and families seen in practice. Treat each case in the context of a complex constellation of human animal interactions, and recognize the potential for affecting human caregivers.
5. Clarify and articulate your personal responsibilities to both patients and clients, so as to mitigate inevitable ethical dilemmas and avoid sending out mixed messages to your clientele and the general public.

Conclusion

Cruelty to animals is a crime and should be treated as such. It is also symptomatic of disturbed individuals and dysfunctional families, and a predictor of future violence. Early intervention may prevent more serious incidents directed against animals and people. Referrals for counseling, social service intervention, and, in more serious cases, criminal prosecution may not only be warranted but incumbent upon the veterinarian who has taken a healing oath. Court-ordered community service for animal abusers may involve work in animal shelters or veterinary hospitals. Child abuse victims may find solace and healing in the veterinary or shelter environment. Humane education may combat the desensitizing effects of a widespread web of violence, particularly in highly urbanized areas where children are deprived of regular contact with animals (14). The evolution of more benign relationships in human society — what the President of the United States calls a "kinder and gentler nation" — might be enhanced by our mutual and cooperative promotion of a more positive and nurturing ethic between children and animals, and by the integration of veterinary medicine into the existing social service and health care systems.

References

1. Fairholme EG, Pain W. A Century of Work for Animals: The History of the R.S.P.C.A., 1824–1924. New York: EP Dutton, 1924: 226.
2. Shultz WJ. The Humane Movement in the United States, 1910–1922. New York: Columbia University Press, 1924: 14.
3. Kempe CH, Silverman FN, Steele BF, Droegemueller W, Silver HK. The battered child syndrome. J Am Med Assoc 1962; 181: 17–24.
4. Walker JR. A Study on the Relationship of Child Abuse and Pet Abuse (professional project). Philadelphia: University of Pennsylvania, School of Social Work, 1980, 24.
5. Lockwood R. The tangled web of animal abuse: the links between cruelty to animals and human violence. Washington, DC: Humane Society of the United States. The Humane Society News 1986 Summer: 10–15.
6. American Psychiatric Association: Diagnostic and Statistical Manual of Mental Disorders, 3rd ed. rev. Washington, DC: American Psychiatric Association, 1987: 53–56.
7. Kellert SR, Felthous AR. Childhood cruelty toward animals among criminals and noncriminals. Hum Relations 1985; 38: 1113–1129.
8. DeViney E, Dickert J, Lockwood R. The care of pets within child abusing families. Int J Study Anim Probl 1983; 4: 321–329.
9. McCulloch M. Contributions to mental health. In: Anderson RK, Fenderson DA, Schuman LM, Long E, Byrne JP, Strauman S, eds. A Description of the Responsibilities of Veterinarians as They Relate Directly to Human Health. Minneapolis: University of Minnesota School of Public Health, Contract No. 231-76-0202, Report June 1976 for U.S. Department of Health, Education and Welfare, Public Health Service, Bureau of Health Manpower, Division of Associated Health Professions: 9-1 – 9-20.
10. Rollin BE. Veterinary and animal ethics. In: Wilson JF, ed. Law and Ethics of the Veterinary Profession. Yardley, Pennsylvania: Priority Press, 1988: 24–49.
11. Service corporations: DVMs included in health. Washington DC: American Veterinary Medical Association: Washington Veterinary News 1991; 15 (5, May): 1.
12. American Veterinary Medical Association. Principles of veterinary medical ethics, 1990 revision. In: LaFrana J, ed. American Veterinary Medical Association Directory. Schaumburg, Illinois: American Veterinary Medical Association, 1992: 536–540.
13. Van Leeuwen J. A child psychiatrist's perspective on children and their companion animals. In: Fogle B, ed. Interrelations Between People and Pets. Springfield, Illinois: CC Thomas, 1981: 175–194.
14. Bustad LK, Hines L. Concern for children. In: Bustad LK, ed. Compassion: Our Last Great Hope. Renton, Washington: Delta Society, 1990: 57–60.

Ethical question of the month — April 1994
Question de déontologie du mois — avril 1994

Medical doctors are required to report cases of child abuse. **Should veterinarians be required to report cases of animal abuse?** *(Submitted by Ken Ross, Napanee, Ontario)*

On demande aux médecins de signaler les cas d'enfants maltraités. **Devrait-on demander aux médecins vétérinaires de signaler les cas d'animaux maltraités?** *(Soumis par Ken Ross, Napanee, Ontario)*

An ethicist's commentary on whether veterinarians should report cruelty

Concern about cruelty to animals is as old as recorded human thought. It can be found in the Old Testament, in classical philosophy, and in various strains of Eastern thought. Beginning in Britain in the early nineteenth century, concerns about cruelty to animals were codified in anticruelty laws, and one can find virtually no civilized society that does not include such legislation in its legal system.

Sources of social and philosophical concern about cruelty to animals have been twofold: First, there is a direct concern for the suffering of animals as conscious beings. This is specifically expressed in the ancient rabbinic tradition of Judaism, as the concept of "Tsaar Baalai Chayim" — literally, the "suffering of living things." Second, and of great historical importance, there is the notion that those who are cruel to animals are likely to "graduate" to people, and thus such behavior must be disallowed. This was the position of Saint Thomas Aquinas and is, in fact, official Roman Catholic theological doctrine (Aquinas believed that animals, lacking immortal souls, were in and of themselves not of moral concern, but that cruel behavior tended to spread). One can also find elements of this argument, historically, in judicial decisions interpreting the anticruelty laws in the United States.

Contemporary social ethics seem to embody both of these traditional concerns. First, as I have indicated in earlier columns and in other writings, society is in the process of developing an expanded ethic for the treatment of animals, which even addresses animal suffering that is not the result of cruelty, such as that arising out of research, testing, and industrialized agriculture. In such a milieu, there is, *a fortiori*, greater concern with the sort of wanton actions addressed by the cruelty laws. Second, contemporary research has confirmed the intuition connecting animal abuse with human abuse(1). It is now known that most of our recent, prominent serial killers had histories of cruelty to animals. Of particular interest is the close connection that has been established between the abuse of animals and the abuse of children.

Interestingly enough, for much of our history–indeed, well into the nineteenth century and, in some ways, even today–children enjoyed a moral status somewhat similar to animals; both were, in essence, property. It is ironic that, in the United States, laws against cruelty to animals were promulgated prior to laws forbidding cruelty to children; indeed, the first case of child abuse was prosecuted using the animal cruelty laws! The fact that, to this day, the American Humane Association has both an animal protection division and a child protection division bespeaks this close historical connection.

Conceptually, it is not hard to speculate about the connection between child abuse and animal abuse. Both children and animals are totally dependent, totally vulnerable, totally helpless, and totally innocent. The sort of coward, bully, or psychopath drawn to gratuitously hurting one would surely be equally drawn to harming the other, since the ease of victimization is manifested in both groups. Indeed, a recent article in the *Journal of the American Veterinary Medical Association* has explicitly spelled out the connection between the two forms of abuse, with special reference to the responsibility of veterinarians(2).

In the face of our discussion, the conclusion is evident: Yes, veterinarians should be obliged to report suspected animal abuse, for two excellent reasons. First, veterinarians need to be at the forefront of response to the new social concern about animals. I have argued for fifteen years that veterinarians are the rational, natural advocates for animals in society and, furthermore, that society expects them to fill this role. If they do not act against cruelty to animals, when even the traditional social ethic for animals condemned cruelty and codified that condemnation in law, how can they possibly be credible in responding to new and growing social ethical concerns about other areas of animal use not motivated by cruelty, from agriculture to zoos? Second, as health care professionals with an obligation to public health and welfare, they must act to ferret out those individuals likely to move from animal abuse to human abuse, particularly child abuse. Finally, they owe it to themselves to do it. Veterinarians see a great deal of animal abuse, much of it not the result of cruelty but rather a product of ignorance, greed, stupidity, etc. Often they have little power to prevent the problems that demoralize their professional

Reprinted from the *Canadian Veterinary Journal* 35 (1994): 408–9, with kind permission of the Canadian Veterinary Medical Association.

life; for example, the constant requests for euthanizing healthy animals. This is a very stressful situation, which can erode job satisfaction and lead to physical and mental health problems. In cases of overt cruelty, at least, they can be empowered to address the situation. Exercise of such empowerment must surely be an effective tool against the ravages of what, elsewhere, I have called "moral stress"–the discord between one's primary reason for entering veterinary medicine, that is, concern for animal well-being, and one's inability to stop many of the practices that go counter to animal well-being.

At the Colorado State University Veterinary Teaching Hospital, there has long been a policy requiring that every clinician who suspects cruelty must report the case to the director of the hospital, who then takes responsibility for reporting the case to the authorities.

Finally, such reporting should be legally mandated, so that there is no dilemma for the veterinarian–he or she should be obliged to report, by the ethic of social consensus, and thus is not betraying any confidence.

I thank Dr. Tim Blackwell for discussion and valuable suggestions.

Bernard Rollin, PhD

References

1. Kellert S, Felthous A. Childhood cruelty toward animals among criminals and non-criminals. Hum Relations 1985; 38: 1113–1129.
2. Arkow P. Child abuse, animal abuse, and the veterinarian. J Am Vet Med Assoc 1994; 204: 1004–1006.

James S. Hutton

40

Animal Abuse as a Diagnostic Approach in Social Work: A Pilot Study

Many people would readily agree that the companion animal is "part" of the family unit. The upsurge of interest in recent years has seemingly concentrated on the beneficial and therapeutic aspects of the human–companion animal bond. A recent article by Dr. Alan Felthous (1980) explores some of the relationships between childhood cruelty to animals and assaultive behavior directed at humans. Most subjects in his "animal cruelty" group had histories compatible with a higher level of aggressiveness against people, along with a significantly higher incidence of paternal neglect and/or abuse than normals. Doreen Hutchinson (1980) cited cases in which the companion animal has not been therapeutic, and she comments pertinently on the family circumstances that contributed to this condition. Roger Mugford (1981) also implies in his work that families sometimes need professional help and guidance to overcome mutual problems with their companion animals.

This study was based on the assumption that the companion animal takes its place as an integral part of the dynamics of family life and could therefore act as a diagnostic indicator of multiple varieties of "abuse" within families.

Reprinted from *New Perspectives on Our Lives with Companion Animals,* edited by Aaron Katcher and Alan Beck (Philadelphia: University of Pennsylvania Press, 1983), 444–47, with kind permission of the University of Pennsylvania Press.

METHOD

DESIGN

Free-ranging interviews were used to obtain primary data on subjects known to local RSPCA representatives during 1980. Starting with the names and addresses obtained from this primary source, I used a range of secondary sources to gather information about these families (including personal, family, and business networks as well as direct and indirect interviews). The design specifically reflected a desire to keep broadly within the perceived scope of established routines of information gathering within social services departments (that is, cheap, easy, relevant, and confidential). The geographical area covered was coincident with that serviced by one social service department area team. The two sets of data were then analyzed to see if subjects on the RSPCA list were known to local social services and probation officers and whether the descriptions given of the family were similar. Records were then scored for type of abuse identifiable within the family. Other data were noted because this was an exploratory study.

PROCEDURE

RSPCA representatives covering the geographical area of a local authority social services team were asked to give information relating to cases of animal abuse and neglect which had come to their notice during the year 1980. Index cards were supplied with headings for basic information; free-ranging interviews were then necessary, as were some trips to obtain the information to complete the cards; other investigations were also undertaken to establish basics (such as reference to the electoral register for names and addresses and, when necessary, establishing the identity of the individuals concerned, particularly when families had recently moved).

The second stage involved a complex investigation into each of the referrals to see if they were known to the local authority statutory services and if so, how and what was known. This information was obtained through a vast range of local contacts and information-gathering sources as well as via straightforward interviewing, a technique made easier because the author was born and raised in the community. The third stage was to check this information with whatever information was available by discussion with case workers and by referring to files within the probation and social services departments.

RESULTS

From a total of 43 original referrals, 20 were omitted from the study; 6 were not known to either probation or social services departments, 6 were not traceable by the methods employed, and 6 were duplications resulting from the same subjects being referred by more than one reference source. Of the twenty-three families with a history of animal abuse, 82.6 percent (19) were known to social services and 60.8 percent (14) were known to probation. Descriptions of the family in "general" terms appeared similar in 87 percent (20) of the cases seen by both probation and social services. Similarities between the description of family dynamics in social service reports and the referrals for animal abuse occurred in 69.6 percent (16) of cases.

Considering specific forms of abuse, 34.8 percent (8) involved children at risk; 43.4 percent (10) could be broadly classed as inadequate families; 21.7 percent (5) involved physical violence; 21.7 percent (5) concerned neglect; 30.4 percent (7) could not usefully be categorized. Of the cases reported to the RSPCA, 52.1 percent (12) involved dog(s); 21.7 percent (5) cat(s), and 26.1 percent (6) dog(s) and cat(s).

In the sample 91.3 percent (21) of cases had low incomes; 65.2 percent (15) were unemployed; 30.4 percent (7) were single parents; 69.6 percent (15) could have been described as "broken homes." When looking at housing we find only 8.7 percent (2) were owner-occupiers; 65.2 percent (15) were in adequate council or tied accommodation; and 26.1 percent (6) were in substandard housing. Moreover, 56.5 percent (13) of cases referred in this study had moved during the period under investigation.

DISCUSSION

Results from this study appear to suggest that referrals from the RSPCA involving animal abuse could also be families known to the probation and local authority social services departments. In such cases, descriptions given of the family tend to be similar both at a general level and more specifically in the "types" of abuse manifested within the family. This evidence suggests that animal abuse may be symptomatic of similar dynamics within the larger family group.

Any significance of the high mobility of the sample (56.5 percent of referrals) would need a much closer examination than is possible here. It may simply be a quirk of this particular group, or it could indicate that stresses within a family which may result in abuse are increased at times of instability such as are created when a family moves from one home to another.

The analysis of socioeconomic factors indicates the importance of viewing a family not simply as a collection of individuals being subjected only to the dynamics and pressures within that group, but also as an integral part of society, being subjectd to all the sociological pressures of a "total" environment.

As an initial exploration, the study was intended to generate hypotheses for further research. In any further studies it could be useful to: concentrate on specific categories of abuse such as cases involving violence. "Abuse" was never properly defined in this study and included violence, sexual abuse, neglect, and other miscellaneous categories. Larger samples should be taken from different catchment areas. Information from social services and probation should be used without the lengthy process of prior examination of community sources so more time and effort could be concentrated on those who are not known (but perhaps ought to have been known) to the agencies. The perspective of family dynamics should be studied, followed by identification of the role(s) of the companion animal in relation to other participants in the family group.

CONCLUSIONS

This pilot study has been encouraging in that the results tentatively indicate that information obtained from the RSPCA relating to animal abuse could act as an external reflection of similar phenomena within the "family" group. If the results are sound, the study of companion animals in the family might prove to be a useful addition to the diagnostic tools of the so-called "caring" professions such as social work.

My sincere thanks and gratitude to Alisdair Macdonald and Andrew Yoxall for their encouragement and guidance in my first attempt at serious study in this field. Gratitude must also be expressed to the RSPCA, probation, social services, and all the individuals who contributed so willingly to the study. Last, a word of thanks to Peter Messent and Pedigree Petfoods whose unobtrusive support were invaluable.

SECTION 9: THE HUMAN-ANIMAL BOND

Our final selections deal with several dimensions of the mistreatment of animals in the larger context of our complex relationships with animals. Companion animals are found in a majority of American households, and numerous studies (cited in Robin and ten Bensel, included in section 2) demonstrate how they are often treated as family members. At the same time millions of animals are consumed for food and may be seen primarily as commodities. How do our often conflicting relationships with animals influence our perception of abuse and neglect of these creatures?

The first selection, by Bruce Roscoe, Shirley Haney, and Karen L. Peterson, attempts to assess attitudes toward animals within the context of cruelty. They build on earlier observations that members of the community at large tend to be more critical of harmful acts to children than are professionals who routinely deal with people who mistreat children. This raises the question of how exposure to violence influences those who work to oppose it. In presenting various scenarios of abuse and neglect of animals or children to adolescents, they report that child maltreatment is generally viewed more harshly than animal maltreatment and that abuse is seen as more serious than neglect. Although these findings may seem unremarkable, they contradict reports from the press and social-service agencies that animal cruelty cases elicit greater public outcry than comparable child abuse and neglect cases.

This review offers a start on reconciling some of these inconsistencies in our attitudes toward child and animal abuse. They note that certain acts, such as ignoring illness and hitting with a stick or hands, are seen as equally harmful whether the victim is an animal or a child. Other mistreatment that is best characterized as psychological abuse or neglect, such as screaming at the victim, teasing with food, or constantly ignoring him or her, are seen as significantly more serious in the case of children. This reflects the fact that none of our existing animal-cruelty laws have categories of psychological abuse paralleling those recognized in the definition of child abuse. As more attention is drawn to the interconnections between cruelty to animals and to children, it will become increasingly important to understand and reconcile society's differing and often inconsistent attitudes to these problems.

The contribution from John E. Schowalter, while contemporary, takes an approach to animal cruelty closer to that of Ferenczi than to that of Felthous, Kellert, Ressler, and others. He emphasizes a psychoanalytic evaluation of individual case histories. The value of this article is its attention to the many different ways in which children involve animals in the psychodynamics of their interactions with family and peers. The case histories he presents demonstrate the diversity of roles that animals play for children—as they are loved, cared for, grieved over, threatened, hurt, or envied. Perhaps most significant for our subject is Schowalter's realization that having pets in the family creates "a natural laboratory for learning that might makes right." Like many of the other authors in this volume, Schowalter recognizes the significance of a child's ability to exercise power and control over animals, especially pets, and the problems that can emerge from improper application of that power.

The final contribution, from Temple Grandin, explores the issue of cruelty within a system where animals are intended to be killed—livestock slaughter. It is a fitting parallel to Locke's essay, where he noted that butchers of his era were not permitted to serve on juries, presumably in the belief that their profession may have led them to become too hardened to pain and suffering.

Grandin does not focus on the individual psychology of people employed within the livestock and slaughter trade but rather on institutional variables that can lead to animal cruelty. She documents cruelty or rough handling in nearly a third of the facilities studied and notes a correlation between the incidence of abuse and the overall physical quality of the plants. Of particular relevance to the ecology of violence is her observation that the key to humane handling was having a manager who enforced a strict code of conduct and was willing to take action against animal abusers. This was more important than geographical area or employees' cultural backgrounds in predicting abuse. Also significant is her observation that half of the livestock markets with evidence of cruel handling allowed young children to abuse animals. She offers a pragmatic solution to the complex issue of animal cruelty within the context of society's use of animals: pressure to change must combine the power of legal actions against cruelty with documentation of economic incentives for humane treatment.

CHILD/PET MALTREATMENT: ADOLESCENTS' RATINGS OF PARENT AND OWNER BEHAVIORS

Bruce Roscoe, Shirley Haney and Karen L. Peterson

ABSTRACT

This study investigated adolescents' ratings of various forms of child and pet maltreatment. Participants ($N = 614$) rated the seriousness of 20 vignettes (10 focusing on abuse; 10 focusing on neglect) on the potential harm each had to a child's or pet's welfare. Two instruments were administered. Half the adolescents completed the child maltreatment instrument first, while the rest completed the pet maltreatment instrument. Six weeks later all participants were administered the alternative instrument. Surveys were identical except that in one the victim was a three-year-old child and in the other it was a one-year-old pet dog. Results indicated adolescents were: (1) highly critical of parental and owner acts which constitute maltreatment, (2) more disapproving of abusive than neglectful acts, (3) less tolerant of inappropriate actions directed toward a child than toward a pet, and (4) more tolerant of the use of physical force toward a child if they had at some time been the person primarily responsible for the care of a pet.

Since the early 1960s, when professionals became concerned with the occurrence of child abuse, numerous individuals have attempted to identify and define acts which constitute child maltreatment. The orientation of these writers has included perspectives from the fields of psychology (Kempe & Helfer, 1972; Steele & Pollock, 1968), sociology (Gelles, 1973; Gil, 1975), and human ecology (Belsky, 1980; Garbarino, 1977). The perspective maintained by Giovannoni and Becerra (1979) is that child abuse and neglect are acts which become unacceptable when a sufficient number of the members of a social group define them as deviant from society's norms, thus defining maltreatment as social deviance.

Utilizing this model, Giovannoni and Becerra (1979) investigated the opinions of the people they viewed as primarily responsible for defining maltreatment, i.e., professionals who may deal with children who are mistreated (police officers, social workers, pediatricians, and lawyers) and people in the general society. The results of their study indicated that community members are more critical in their ratings

The authors wish to acknowledge the contributions of Jeremiah S. Strouse for his review and comments on early drafts of this paper.

Reprint requests to Bruce Roscoe, Ph.D., Associate Professor, Individual and Family Studies, Central Michigan University, Mount Pleasant, Michigan 48859.

Reprinted from *Adolescence* 21 (1986): 807–14, with kind permission of Libra Publishers, Inc.

of the potential harm done to children by various acts of inappropriate child rearing (e.g., banging child against wall, engaging in mutual masturbation with child, keeping child out of school, failing to provide health care for child) than are professionals who routinely deal with individuals who mistreat children.

In an elaboration of Giovannoni and Becerra's (1979) work, Roscoe (in press) queried later adolescents (17- to 21-year-olds) concerning their ratings of the same parental behaviors. Results indicated that adolescents as a group were more severe in their assessment of the same parental behaviors. This was explained in terms of two typical characteristics of adolescents: idealism (Elkind, 1975) and lack of experience in the role of child caregiver (Rice, 1984). In order to better understand the mediating role which being responsible for the care of a dependent person or pet may play in adolescents' ratings, the present study was undertaken. Realizing that relatively few adolescents have ever been the person primarily responsible for the care of a child, the responsibility for care of a pet was substituted as the discriminating factor. In keeping with previous findings, it was hypothesized that adolescents who had been responsible for the care of a pet would be more tolerant of parental and owner behaviors which could be potentially harmful to the recipient of such treatment.

The purpose of the present study was to further explore later adolescents' attitudes toward various forms of child and animal maltreatment. Of primary interest were the following questions: (1) How threatening to a child's well-being would adolescents rate specific acts of child neglect and child abuse? (2) Overall, would acts of abuse be viewed as more harmful than acts of neglect? (3) Would identical acts of maltreatment be rated more severely if the victim was a preschool-aged child or a one-year-old pet dog? (4) Would adolescents' ratings differ on the basis of their age, sex, and previous experience as the person primarily responsible for the care of a child or pet? Based on their assumed limited role as a primary caretaker of a child and greater likelihood of caring for a pet, it was thought that examination of these two groups would be informative in suggesting what value adolescents placed on high dependency, their view of the appropriate use of force toward persons in such a position, and the mediating effect caring for a dependent animal may have on acceptance of specific child-rearing techniques.

METHOD

Participants in the present study were 614 unmarried, later adolescents (387 females, 227 males), ranging in age from 18 to 22 years (*M*

= 18.95, *SD* = 0.7), enrolled in a central Midwestern university. Data were gathered by means of two paper-and-pencil instruments, each consisting of 20 brief vignettes: 10 presenting acts of neglect and 10 presenting acts of abuse. These vignettes were taken from a survey by Giovannoni and Becerra (1979) which was designed to assess attitudes toward parental maltreatment. Instruments were administered to participants in regular classroom settings. In keeping with Giovannoni and Becerra's protocol, subjects were asked to rate each vignette regarding how serious the maltreatment was from the perspective of the victim's welfare (in this case child or pet). Each vignette was rated on a scale from one to nine, with higher numbers assigned to incidents which were believed to be very serious and low numbers assigned to acts which were not so serious. Completion of the instrument was anonymous and took approximately 12 minutes.

The two instruments utilized were identical with two exceptions: (1) on one instrument subjects were directed to rate the seriousness of potential harm caused by parental acts, as described in the vignettes, to the well-being of a three-year-old child; on the second instrument subjects were to rate the seriousness of the act to a one-year-old pet house dog; (2) vignettes were altered so that one presented parental treatment of a child and the second that of an owner of a dog (e.g., form one: the parents hit their child in the head; form two: the owners hit their dog in the head). Approximately half the participants (324) received the child maltreatment survey first while the others (290) completed the pet maltreatment survey first. Six weeks after completion of the first survey, subjects were administered the alternative form of the instrument. At no time were the groups informed that they would complete a second survey at a later date. Test-retest reliability of the instruments, with a seven-week time lag, was .87 for the child maltreatment survey and .82 for the pet survey.

RESULTS

Analyses of the neglect and abuse vignettes concerning child and pet maltreatment indicated that both groups of items were highly correlated with one another and with summary maltreatment scores. Table 1 presents the correlation coefficients and levels of significance between each vignette and the summary scores. Seven of the 10 neglect items were correlated at a significance level of .05 or better with the summary neglect score, and 7 of the 10 abuse items had similar levels of significance to the summary abuse score. These high levels of association helped confirm the assumption that the vignettes reliably delineated the neglect and abuse constructs.

Table 1

<u>Correlation of Vignettes to Summary Neglect and Abuse Scores</u>

<u>Vignette</u>	<u>Summary Neglect Score</u>	<u>Summary Abuse Score</u>
Neglect		
1. Fail to feed for 24 hours	.859*	-.035
2. Fail to provide medical care	.691*	.139
3. Fail to clean child/pet	.669*	-.016
4. Ignore	.593**	-.242
5. Fail to give prescribed medication	.398	.373
6. Ignore illness	.645*	.277
7. Fail to wash	.796*	-.190
8. Send outside into inclement weather	.035	-.378
9. Leave in hazardous room	.372	.179
10. Fail to keep medical appointment	.456**	.396
Abuse		
11. Hit with hands	-.311	.759*
12. Burn with cigarette	.501	.401
13. Hit with a leather strap	-.543**	.587*
14. Serve alcohol to child/pet	.009	.128
15. Hit in head	.175	.645*
16. Immerse in tub of hot water	-.100	.537**
17. Constantly scream at	.253	.660*
18. Strike with wooden stick	-.029	.589**
19. Tease with food	.547**	.401
20. Bang against wall	.014	.623*

*p<.01, two-tailed. **p<.05, two-tailed.

Ratings of all vignettes (separately, combined, and by demographic groupings) indicated that later adolescents viewed each behavior as potentially quite harmful to a child's or pet's well-being (see Table 2). The average rating for vignettes describing acts of child maltreatment was 7.76 (range 6.0 to 8.7), while that for acts of animal maltreatment was 7.1 (range 5.3 to 8.5). Such scores reflect an assessment of these behaviors as seriously detrimental to optimal development. Regardless of the order in which participants completed the instruments, child maltreatment was viewed more harshly than was animal maltreatment, and acts of abuse were rated more harmful than those of neglect.

Table 2

Mean Ratings of Neglect and Abuse Vignettes

Vignette	Child		Pet		
	Mean	SD	Mean	SD	F Value
Neglect					
1. Fail to feed for 24 hours	8.3	1.1	6.9	1.9	2.6*
2. Fail to provide medical care	7.8	1.4	6.8	2.0	1.8*
3. Fail to clean child/pet	7.2	1.7	5.8	2.0	1.38**
4. Ignore	7.6	1.6	6.3	2.1	1.89*
5. Fail to give prescribed medication	8.6	1.4	7.7	1.7	1.40**
6. Ignore illness	8.1	1.2	7.9	1.3	1.22
7. Fail to wash	7.8	1.5	6.2	2.1	1.94*
8. Send outside into inclement weather	7.8	1.3	7.5	1.7	1.67*
9. Leave in hazardous room	7.7	1.4	7.0	1.9	1.78*
10. Fail to keep medical appointment	7.2	1.6	6.3	1.9	1.41**
Summary Neglect Score	7.7	1.1	6.8	1.4	8.71*
Abuse					
11. Hit with hands	6.0	2.2	5.3	2.2	1.04
12. Burn with cigarette	8.7	0.7	8.5	1.0	2.20*
13. Hit with a leather strap	7.8	1.6	7.9	1.6	1.08
14. Serve alcohol to child/pet	7.2	1.8	6.8	2.0	1.20
15. Hit in head	8.4	1.1	7.7	1.6	2.09*
16. Immerse in tub of hot water	8.4	1.1	8.1	1.4	1.59*
17. Constantly scream at	7.1	1.7	6.3	1.9	1.27**
18. Strike with wooden stick	8.0	1.5	7.8	1.5	1.07
19. Tease with food	8.1	1.2	6.9	1.9	2.51*
20. Bang against wall	8.6	0.8	8.5	1.1	1.69*
Summary Abuse Score	7.83	0.9	7.4	1.1	1.56*

*p<.01, two-tailed. **p<.05, two-tailed

Table 2 presents the ratings accorded the individual neglect and abuse vignettes relative to the specific victim, i.e., child or pet. Clearly, adolescents deemed the behavior/treatment as being less appropriate when directed toward a child than toward a pet. Of the 20 items presented, 9 of the 10 neglect, and 6 of the 10 abuse behaviors yielded statistically higher scores when the recipient of the treatment was a child. Adolescents obviously rated children as being more vulnerable than pets to the inappropriate treatment. The 5 items on which significant differences did not occur were: ignoring a child's/pet's illness, hitting with hands, hitting with a leather strap, giving alcohol to the child/pet, and striking with a wooden stick. Only one behavior, hitting with a leather strap, received a more severe rating for pet than child maltreatment (7.9 versus 7.8), and this difference is more likely spurious than real.

When data were examined in relation to specific characteristics and experiences, few noticeable differences were found. Later adolescents were more similar than dissimilar to one another regardless of age, as significant differences did not result between ratings when participants were grouped on this variable. Analyses of data on the basis of subjects' sex, however, revealed that females rated 17 of the 20 parent/owner actions as significantly more harmful than did males. Differences between the sexes on all but three of the vignettes achieved a significance level equal to at least .01. The three items on which no significant differences occurred were: not providing medical care ($F(3, 601) = 1.49$, $p < .48$), not keeping child/pet clean ($F(3, 601) = 1.37$, $p < .53$), and not giving child/pet prescribed medication ($F(3, 601) = 3.21$, $p < .07$).

As research by Giovannoni and Becerra (1979) and Roscoe (in press) has shown, previous experience in working with and caring for children is related to the ratings given to maltreatment vignettes. Thus, data were examined after grouping on the variable of subjects' prior experience as a caretaker of a child or pet. Three hundred one (49%) of the participants reported they had such responsibility at some time in their lives (4% had been responsible for a child's care, and 45% for that of a pet). Data analysis on this factor produced significant differences on seven items. On each of these, individuals who had never been primarily responsible for child or pet care rated the following behaviors as significantly more harmful to a child: ignoring ($F(3, 604) = 4.50$, $p < .03$), hitting with hands ($F(3, 605) = 3.64$, $p < .05$), hitting with a leather strap ($F(3, 605) = 14.18$, $p < .001$), hitting in the head ($F(3, 605) = 18.25$, $p < .001$), screaming ($F(3, 604) = 16.77$, $p < .001$), striking with a wooden stick ($F(3, 604) = 8.99$, $p < .003$), and teasing with food ($F(3, 604) = 13.37$, $p < .001$). It appears that individuals who have cared for a child or pet were more likely to view these child-rearing behaviors as less detrimental to a child's development than were individuals who had not had such experiences. No significant differences were found between groups regarding their ratings of maltreatment toward a pet.

DISCUSSION

Consistent with earlier findings (Giovannoni & Becerra, 1979; Roscoe, in press), results from the present study indicated that later adolescents were highly critical of parental acts which may constitute child maltreatment. Ratings on all vignettes were in the direction of being perceived as constituting a serious threat to a child's development. In addition, when compared to ratings of pet maltreatment (which also were perceived as highly detrimental), adolescents were significantly more disapproving on 15 of 20 behaviors when they were directed toward a child. These findings suggest that adolescents are aware of, and sensitive to, the potential vulnerability of highly dependent beings.

A further outcome of the study, again supporting other work, was that parent/owner actions which constituted abuse were assessed as more serious than were acts of neglect. Such findings were expected, as society is more disapproving of child abuse regardless of the fact that neglect is responsible for more children's deaths annually (American Humane Association, 1983), and is of greater cost in terms of financial dependency on society and later problems to the individual (Williams, 1980).

Perhaps the most important discovery was the finding that adolescents who had been responsible for the care of a pet gave significantly less harmful ratings to acts of physical force used against a child (i.e., hitting with hands, hitting with a leather strap, hitting in the head, and striking with a wooden stick). That is, adolescents who had cared for pets were more likely to see the use of physical force against a child as being appropriate than were their counterparts who had not been responsible for the care of a pet. Previous research (Giovannoni & Becerra, 1979) has shown that adults who worked with children displayed greater tolerance for harsh parental treatment of children. Results from the present study suggest that adolescents who care for pets are also more lenient toward parental acts of child abuse. It is possible that attitudes which adolescents develop while caring for a pet are to some extent generalized to the care of a child.

Overall, results indicate that adolescents are for the most part disapproving of parental and owner actions which constitute potential harm to those in their care. There are two important points to be drawn from this study. First, adolescents' high disapproval of the actions in the vignettes may reflect inappropriate standards regarding parenthood and unrealistic expectations for themselves as parents. It may be of value for parent education classes and family life education programs to help adolescents, prior to parenthood, to better understand the demands which accompany. raising children and provide alternative means of handling such demands. Second, education programs should ensure that students use appropriate strategies when caring for their pets and are selective in making generalizations from appropriate pet care to the care of children. With direction and guidance, parent and family life education programs can assist adolescents in developing realistic expectations for themselves as parents, and understanding the vulnerability and dependency of the children in their care.

REFERENCES

American Humane Association. *Annual report 1981: Highlights of official child abuse reporting.* Denver, CO: American Humane Association, 1983.

Belsky, J. Child maltreatment: An ecological integration. *American Psychologist,* 1980, *35,* 320–335.

Elkind, D. Recent research on cognitive development in adolescence. In S. E. Dragastin & G. H. Edler, Jr. (Eds.), *Adolescence in the life cycle.* New York: John Wiley and Sons, 1975.

Garbarino, J. The human ecology of child maltreatment: A conceptual model for research. *Journal of Marriage and the Family,* 1977, *39,* 721–735.

Gelles, R. J. Child abuse as psychopathology: A sociological critique and reformulation. *American Journal of Orthopsychiatry,* 1973, *43,* 611–621.

Gil, D. G. Unraveling child abuse. *American Journal of Orthopsychiatry,* 1975, *45,* 346–356.

Giovannoni, J. M., & Becerra, R. M. *Defining child abuse.* New York: Free Press, 1979.

Kempe, C. H., & Helfer, R. E. (Eds.). *Helping the battered child and his family.* Philadelphia: J. B. Lippincott, 1972.

Rice, F. P. *The adolescent: Development, relationships, and culture* (4th ed.). Boston: Allyn and Bacon, 1984.

Roscoe, B. Defining child maltreatment: Ratings of parental behaviors. *Adolescence,* in press.

Steele, B. F., & Pollock, C. B. A psychiatric study of parents who abuse infants and small children. In R. E. Helfer & C. H. Kempe (Eds.), *The battered child.* Chicago: University of Chicago Press, 1968.

Williams, G. J. Child abuse and neglect: Problems of definition and incidence. In G. J. Williams & J. Money (Eds.), *Traumatic abuse and neglect of children at home.* Baltimore: Johns Hopkins University Press, 1980.

CLINICAL EXPERIENCE

The Use and Abuse of Pets

JOHN E. SCHOWALTER, M.D.

Animals commonly influence children's behavior and development. Children involve animals in their use of such defense mechanisms as displacement, projection, splitting, and identification. These same mechanisms may also be used to deal with their experiences with animals. Therapists are encouraged to inquire into children's associations with animals as a means of more thoroughly understanding their patients.
Journal of the American Academy of Child Psychiatry, 22, 1:68–72, 1983.

A pet is "any animal that is domesticated or tamed and kept as a favorite, or treated with indulgence and fondness" (Murray, 1909). Almost all creatures, great and small, have been used as pets, but the magnitude of pet popularity is suggested by the number of dogs and cats in this country, estimated at 41,000,000 and 23,000,000, respectively (McWhirter, 1981). It is a rare child who reaches maturity without having had a pet. Given the ubiquity of pets, one cannot help but be surprised and puzzled by the sparse literature on how pets affect the mental life and development of children. Loney (1971) discussed the use of a canine therapist. Levinson (1969) has written most on the use of pets in therapy.

In this paper, I will summarize the various ways I have noticed animals to be used by children and their families. Data are drawn from general observations, clinical work with children, and the relatively scant literature that is available. I hope to show that a therapist's inquiry into a child's experience with pets is always indicated and will frequently reveal a source of powerful feelings and significant interactions.

Some General Meanings of Animals

Our ancestors' and our children's view of animals is different from ours as 20th century adults. For our ancestors, animals were not only endowed with human-like feelings and intelligence, but were often elevated to the status of gods. Probably aided by the fact that they were incapable of talking back and therefore unable to disillusion their worshippers, animals were endowed with a wide range of powers. As Frazer (1935) points out in *The Golden Bough*, the primitive worship of animals was common, because the animal was revered on account of some benefit, positive or negative, which the savage hoped to receive from it. Benefit could come either in the positive shape of protection, advice, and help which the animal afforded, or in the negative shape of abstinence from injuries which were in the power of the animal to inflict. Some of these same powers are sometimes attributed by 20th century children to their pets, and by so doing, commonly bring forth a complex mixture of feelings of awe, love, fear, and hate.

Jelliffe and Brink (1917) have described how animals are often thought to represent the baser sexual and aggressive instincts which the child tries to tame as he or she matures. They also point out how often in mythology gods take the form of animals in order to obtain sexual experiences. It is of historical interest that in the psychoanalytic literature the two earliest treatments of children, Little Hans (Freud, 1909) and Little Chanticleer (Ferenczi, 1913), involved youngsters who used animals (horses and fowl) as displacements of sexual interests leading to subsequent fears. Watson and Raynor (1920) used Little Albert to show how conditioning could cause animal fears, and indeed, numerous investigators have found that animals are among the most common phobias of young children (Angelino et al., 1956; Bauer, 1976; Marks, 1969).

Perhaps because of a natural fear of animals (and the primitive instincts which they represent), there is for most children great satisfaction in having an animal tamed and rendered harmless and subserviant. In fact, the camaraderie between children and pets is usually even greater than that between adults and pets. However, the adult tendency to anthropomorphize pets has been amply documented as well. Americans spend 4 billion dollars a year on pet food, 7 of 15 trade paperbacks on the January 3, 1982, *New York*

Dr. Schowalter is Chief of Child Psychiatry and Professor of Pediatrics and Psychiatry at the Yale Child Study Center (333 Cedar St., New Haven, CT 06510), where reprints may be requested.

This work was supported in part by a grant awarded by The Office of Maternal Child Health of HEW; The Connecticut Department of Health; and NIMH-Psychiatry Education Branch, Grant MH 05442-32.

This paper was presented at the Annual Meeting of the American Academy of Child Psychiatry, Washington, D.C., October 1982.

Times' best seller list were cartoon books about pets, and Szasz (1968) has detailed the popularity of pet fashions, pet cosmetics, pet mental health centers, pet pension plans, and pet cemeteries.

As we know from Piaget's (1929) work, all children go through a stage of development when it is natural to ascribe human traits to animals, and this explains the constant demand for children's books that depict animals as acting like humans. The substitution of animals for people in projective tests, such as the Children's Apperception Test (CAT) and the Blacky Picture Test, demonstrates the realization of psychologists that the use of animals provides some conforting distance for children, but poses no real barrier to identification or understanding. To obtain a relatively undefended and accurate portrayal of a child's view of him or herself and the immediate family members, some clinicians ask the patient to name the animal that seems most like each of them. Indeed, Freud (1913) made specific comment about the closeness children feel with animals when he stated, "children have no scruples over allowing animals to rank as their full equals. Uninhibited as they are in the avowal of their bodily needs, they no doubt feel themselves more akin to animals than to their elders, who may well be a puzzle to them" (p. 127).

Animals and Children

The clinical material will be presented in terms of psychoanalytic structural theory. Few of the examples belong in one category, and of course other theoretical constructs could be used.

Drive Derivatives

As already noted, animals often seem to represent the sexual and aggressive drives the young child is trying to master. Animals may be seen as the child's "old self" that has been or should be reformed. That parents allow the pet to do things that they do not allow the child to do can puzzle some children and anger others.

A 4-year-old child was brought for psychiatric evaluation because he had begun soiling his pants, and on two occasions left feces on the floor. During the evaluation, it was learned that the family had recently acquired a puppy, as yet not house-broken. In the child's play, this puppy always had a prominent role, and the boy was soon able to say directly how much he envied and resented the attention the puppy received from "going" on the newspapers laid out for it. Although not entirely conscious, it became clear that the boy's regression was a direct identification with the new pet. The parents were made aware of the meaning that the arrival of the pet and its incontinence had for their son and were helped to link for the boy

how his being a good example could help with the dog's training. The boy, therefore, became praised for the dog's continued success. In brief psychotherapy with the boy, the pleasure of soiling was acknowledged but so were the potential pleasures associated with being in control of his body and with getting more attention from his parents by helping the dog attain better control. Pride and an identification with the role of a parent prevailed, and in a month the boy and dog were retrained and trained.

Perhaps the most fascinating aspects of animals for many children are their sex organs and the fact that sex acts can be observed. Sex education is taught in many nursery schools and day care centers by having hamsters, guinea pig, rabbits or other small animals kept so the children can follow the pregnancy, birth, and mother-infant interaction. Interesting as these events are, it should not be surprising that children are often even more excited by observing intercourse. In my experience, by mid-grammar school most children have seen animals copulate. When this question is brought up in therapy naturally, either at the time that sex or their pet is being discussed, many patients can reveal what they have witnessed and what are their associations to the experience. Animals other than pets are also observed. One 12-year-old boy who was a morning newspaper carrier would watch worms copulating in the grass and on the sidewalk as he delivered the papers. He commented that there was "gooey stuff" between the worms and he would scare the couples into separating. The shame and pleasure produced by this voyeurism led to multiple associations with his parents' sex life and the ejaculations that had recently begun accompanying his masturbation. A 16-year-old mentioned that he and his dog had watched two squirrels making love in a tree. One squirrel fell off the limb, was stunned upon hitting the ground, and was killed by the dog. The boy gave the rather flippant moral that "it's not safe to make love in a tree," but seemed quite shaken with witnessing such a stark example of love and death. It was assumed that these were real events, but whether real or fabricated, they touched important psychodynamic issues for each patient.

The awareness of aggression as part of animal sexuality is a subject that often concerns children. This, at times, raises fears they have about their parents or themselves getting hurt by being sexual. It seems possible from the comments of a few patients that animal sex can stimulate anxiety about anal intercourse, and whether or not the patient noticed that female animals do not have a penis and testicles is often a useful way for the child psychiatrist to initiate a discussion of anatomical differences in the two sexes.

Probably common among children, but rarely

brought up in therapy, is sexual experimentation with animals. Karl Menninger (1951) has noted the ubiquity of societal condemnation of bestiality from the Hittite Code through the Talmud and Old Testament. In my experience, when sex with animals has occurred, the child has either fondled the genitals of the animal ("to see what would happen"), attempted to masturbate (usually unsuccessfully) against the animal, or had the animal (usually a dog) lick the patient's genitals. On the few occasions when a child has confessed to this behavior, the child usually revealed a wish to learn more about sexual anatomy, generally that of the other gender. Occasionally, with questioning, it also became clear that the animal represented a displacement of a loved one. This may or may not be a family member. In one case which I supervised, a sixth-grade boy fondled the male dog of a girl upon whom he had a crush. Usually, however, the displacement is not so conscious or obvious. In another case, a college student recalled in psychoanalysis that at age 13 he enticed the family dog, a male, to lick his penis. For months after the experience he had trouble urinating in public, did not want to pet male dogs, and feared that his action confirmed that he was homosexual. Only later in the treatment did it come to light that it was generally believed to be his mother's dog, and oedipal wishes and fears were also present.

Actual sexual intercouse between minors and animals undoubtably takes place, but scientific documentation is scanty. At the mid-century, Kinsey et al. (1948) estimated that approximately 8% of the males in the United States had had sexual contact with animals, and Ford and Beach (1951) have shown that in those cultures studied, bestiality is almost always more frequent and is considered normal in minors more often than in adults.

The child's aggressive as well as sexual drive often finds an outlet with animals. Pets are useful objects on which to try out the full range of emotions. Already noted is that children often fear animals, and a common parental warning is that an animal will hurt you if you do not act toward it in the right way.

On the other hand, a pet may be treated as an inanimate toy. A pet may represent for the child a figure which is lower on the family totem pole, and no matter how put-upon or demeaned one feels, it is still often possible to kick the dog. Some children seek out experiences with animals that will enhance their own feeling of superiority in strength and/or intelligence. At times this can become a natural laboratory for learning that might makes right. This behavior is often found to represent identification with the aggressor, usually a parent. For example, it is fairly common for middle-class children to capture bees and butterflies in jars. While this endeavor may also satisfy scientific

curiosity, more often than not the specimens are not studied, but die in captivity. Cruelty to animals has been suggested as a predictor of later delinquency, but the strength of this correlation is debated (Sendi and Blombren, 1975).

One boy in psychoanalysis who felt very deprived by his mother almost starved to death a dog she had given him. This happened twice. The fact that not only the boy but the mother seemed unaware that the dog was starving provided information for important interpretations.

Superego Derivatives

Menninger (1951) believed that the kindness which humans usually show animals is frequently based on reaction formation. Identification with the trusting and relatively helpless position of domesticated or small animals is certainly common. Children often feel as if they are parents to their pet. The anguish that people feel about cruelty toward animals often outstrips their feelings about what happens to humans. The classic example is antivivisectionists who condemn animal suffering as a means to prevent human suffering. At a less lofty level, a film critic recently reassured readers that no animals were employed in the spectacular stunts for which a movie was notorious, but did confess it was "irrational, no doubt, to fret more about endangered horses than about the endangered human beings who were the stunt men" (Powell, 1981).

Children are usually very sensitive to the misuse of pets, whether misused by themselves or others. One 10-year-old patient was distressed after reading about a dog who died when during the summer it was kept in a car with the windows rolled up. For this particular patient, associations led to the wish for the grisly demise of his younger brother. "I shuddered," he said, "when I read that the blood could boil in a dog trapped in a car on a hot day." The accuracy of the report notwithstanding, it became clear the shudder came primarily from guilt secondary to his own wishes. Drowned kittens, crippled dogs and other examples of woe to animals routinely bring strong feelings of sadness and remorse from children. A dog may be mourned more than a grandparent, but Mahon and Simpson (1977) have shown how the death of an animal is also often mourned so greatly because the event reawakens or allows discharge of feelings earlier felt but not expressed toward significant persons.

A dilemma commonly occurs when a member of the family becomes allergic to a pet. A decision must often be made whether a pet must go or the allergic person must suffer. Regardless of the decision, the outcome usually demands a choice between pet and family member or pet and discomfort. When the pet must go, there will be anger and mourning. If it is the child who is allergic, there will often be a feeling of guilt about what will happen to the exiled animal and concern about receiving the blame of the rest of the family. If another member of the family is the one who is allergic, there is often resentment and sometimes remorse for feeling resentment. When keeping the pet is approved medically, many allergic children are more comfortable putting up with some discomfort. At times, however, this decision is made by parents rather than by the affected child. On these occasions, there is usually insult to the child's self-esteem as well as to the immunological system.

Ego Derivatives

Pets are remarkably facile objects for displacements, especially for family members and for projections of the child's feelings toward him or herself. Animals can be used as symbolic representations even by young children who may not yet have the capacity to form coherent internal representations. Perhaps it is the ambiguity of seeming like a human and part of the family and yet not being human that helps facilitate this use of an animal. Two other traits that make an animal so ideal for trial actions are its constancy and the fact that it cannot talk back. Mark Twain once commented that the difference between a man and a dog is that "if you pick up a starving dog and make him prosperous, he won't bite you." This characteristic is especially important for children, who often feel at quite a disadvantage in the world of adults and often in need of an unequivocal friend. A child with a pet is never alone. A pet is a sounding board. It is guaranteed to listen sympathetically and never disagree or give bad advice.

A child's pet is also something warm that is always available for getting close to. In fact, it is not essential that the pet be warm, and a rather bizarre situation that helped me realize the importance of pets involved a fish. A 5-year-old boy was brought for psychiatric evaluation because he was developing a chapped hand from stroking his pet goldfish with his right forefinger. Tom was an only child who had always been insecure and was immature socially. Because of this, his entry into kindergarten had been delayed and he was spending an extra year in nursery school. The nursery school had an aquarium with a variety of fish, and, since the boy seemed to enjoy them, his otherwise rather inattentive parents bought him a male and female goldfish. He gave them the same names as the two goldfish at his school, but became especially attached to the female, Kathy. He could tell them apart because of Kathy's white markings. Although at first quite alarmed, the fish soon became accustomed to being petted up to 8 or 10 times a day. The boy's need to

feel close to the fish and take care of them as he wanted to be taken care of became clear in the evaluation. He was really quite maternal. He fed the fish and helped clean the tank. I learned that Kathy was also the name of a student teacher of whom the boy was fond. Petting the fish helped him feel both caring and cared for. A discussion of these psychodynamics with the boy and his agreement that they sounded right did not, however, decrease the fish petting to any substantial degree. His parents talked to Tom about other, land dwelling, pets. He said he would like a dog, and they bought one. They also spent more time with him themselves. Although the fish remained, Tom turned his attention to the newly acquired male beagle puppy. In therapy that extended for 4 months, the care he gave the dog and the more parental care he was receiving were discussed. At a 3-year follow-up, Tom was appropriately close to the dog and this closeness had seemed to aid him in becoming socially more outgoing and successful. The goldfish were still alive, but largely ignored by him.

Pets often become parent surrogates. Large pets especially tend to lend a feeling of strength through identification. Pets seem to be particularly important for only children and for children whose parents are not with them much. One thinks of Nana, the dog babysitter in "Peter Pan." In real life too, dogs are often used as babysitters.

One 12-year-old girl of separated parents impressed me with another use of pet constancy when she said her dog would never divorce her. Buying a child a pet around the time of a divorce is often an intuitive step which helps the child to form a new, firm attachment when another is breaking up. The feelings of loss and abandonment can be compounded when a parent who is leaving the house at the time of separation demands to take a pet that is also important to the children. A recommendation by the child psychiatrist that this not happen is an example of primary prevention.

There are many ways through their interactions with animals that children can feel more in control. A mother once told me of how this happened with her 8-year-old son, David. He was a shy boy with little self-confidence. One day David noticed a crow flying around the neighborhood, cawing and swooping down as though he was at least partially tamed. The boy bought some birdseed, called the crow and threw down handfuls of seed. The bird obviously had been tamed earlier and soon came when David called. This experience provided David with feelings of power and control, and an important sense of confidence. David's mother noted that the spectacle of the crow coming at David's bidding also impressed the neighborhood children and caused them to become more friendly.

Some of the examples given here are unusual, but

every person who had pets as a child or who has inquired about them with children is aware of the more common examples of how pets can enhance a child's sense of mastery, security and control. These include the cat that will come to the child but not to others, the dog that is waiting eagerly when one comes home from school, and the birth, feeding, and death of any pet as it goes through the life cycle. These common interactions with pets are not only usually reassuring, but provide the opportunity for support and a wide range of trial actions that usually make dealing with the other vicissitudes of life a little more easy.

At times, however, children become almost exclusively interested in animals. An idiosyncratic example of this would be the goldfish-petting boy described above, while more common examples include nursery and primary school-aged boys who are dinosaur fanatics (Schowalter, 1979) or pre- and early adolescent girls who are horse fanatics. When an interest in animals precludes an appropriate quantity or quality of contact with humans, psychiatric evaluation is indicated.

Conclusion

Children frequently use animals for displacements and projections of relatively unambivalent feelings. The inquiry of patients about their experiences with animals is often a very fruitful approach for understanding their wishes, fears, and displaced feelings.

References

ANGELINO, H., DOLLINS, J. & MECH, E. V. (1956), Trends in the "fears and worries" of school children. *J. Genet. Psychol.*, 89:263–267.

BAUER, D. H. (1976), An exploratory study of developmental changes in children's fears. *J. Child Psychol. Psychiat.*, 17:69–74.

FERENCZI, S. (1913), A little chanticleer. In: *Contributions to Psycho-Analysis.* Boston: Richard G. Badger, pp. 204–213, 1916.

FORD, C. S. & BEACH, F. A. (1951), *Patterns of Sexual Behavior.* New York: Harper.

FRAZER, J. G. (1935), *The Golden Bough; A Study in Magic and Religion, Vol. V,* Ed. 3. New York: Macmillan.

FREUD, S. (1909), Analysis of a Phobia in a Five-Year-Old Boy. *Standard Edition*, 10:5–147. London: Hogarth Press, 1955.

—— (1913), Totem and Taboo. *Standard Edition*, 13:1–161. London: Hogarth Press, 1953.

JELLIFFE, S. E. & BRINK, L. (1917), The role of animals in the unconscious, with some remarks on theriomorphic symbolism as seen in Ovid. *Psychoanal. Rev.*, 4:253–271.

KINSEY, A. C., POMEROY, W. B. & MARTIN, C. E. (1948), *Sexual Behavior in the Human Male.* Philadelphia: W. B. Saunders.

LEVINSON, B. M. (1969). *Pet-Oriented Child Psychotherapy.* Springfield: Charles C Thomas.

LONEY, J. (1971), The canine therapist in a residential children's setting. *This Journal*, 10:518–523.

McWHIRTER, N., ed. (1981), *Guiness Book of World Records* Ed. 19. New York: Bantam Books.

MARKS, I. M. (1969), *Fears and Phobias.* New York: Academic Press.

MAHON E. & SIMPSON, D. (1977), The painted guinea pig. *The Psychoanalytic Study of the Child*, 32:283–303.

MENNINGER, K. A. (1951), Totemic aspects of contemporary attitudes toward animals. In: *Psychoanalysis and Culture*, ed. G. B. Wilbur & W. Muensterberger. New York: International Universities Press, pp. 42–74.

MURRAY, J. A. H., ED. (1909), *A New English Dictionary on Historical Principles, Vol. VII.* Oxford: University of Oxford.

PIAGET, J. (1929), *The Child's Conception of the World.* New York: Harcourt, Brace.

POWELL, D. (1981), Hollywood Houdinis. *Punch, Vol. 280*, No. 7814 (Jan. 14), p. 67.

SCHOWALTER, J. E. (1979), When dinosaurs return. *Children Today*, 8:2–5 (May-June).

SENDI, I. B. & BLOMBREN, P. G. (1975), A comparative study of predictive criteria in the predisposition of homicidal adolescents. *Amer. J. Psychiat.*, 132:423–427.

SZASZ, K. (1968), *Petishism.* New York: Rinehart & Winston.

WATSON, J. B. & RAYNOR, R. (1920), Conditioned emotional reactions. *J. Exper. Psychol.*, 3:1–14.

BEHAVIOR OF SLAUGHTER PLANT AND AUCTION EMPLOYEES TOWARD THE ANIMALS

Temple Grandin

Abstract. *Abuses of animals at auctions and slaughter plants occur often. Commonly observed abuses include the dragging of crippled animals, hitting, and excessive prodding of animals. In both auctions and slaughter plants, employees are under pressure to maintain a steady flow of animals to the auction ring or slaughter lines. In both types of facilities large numbers of animals must be moved rapidly. The purpose of this study was to determine the behavior of people handling livestock in these types of facilities. Observations of the behavior of slaughter plant managers were also made to gain a better understanding of how management behavior affects employee behavior.*

SURVEY A—LIVESTOCK MARKETS

In 1984, an investigator was hired to make unannounced visits on sale day at 51 livestock markets in 11 southeastern states. His itinerary was objectively predetermined by a person who had no knowledge of the conditions in the markets. Ten percent of the markets on the published lists were visited in each state.

Twenty-one percent of the surveyed markets had excellent handling and 32% had either rough handling or acts of cruelty (Table 1). When the condition of the market facilities was evaluated, it was found that 35% had excellent, well-maintained facilities and 28% had dirty, broken-down, or poorly designed facilities (Table

Grandin Livestock Handling Systems, Inc., Suite 3, 1401 Silver Street, Urbana, IL 61801

2). Markets that had good facilities tended to have a lower incidence of rough handling (Table 3). The quality of the facilities had little effect on the incidences of overt cruelty nor on the incidence of rough handling due to poor management. Thirty-three percent had no water troughs or feeding facilities.

The size of the market was not related to handling practices, but markets that specialized in one species had a tendency to have better handling. Both the "excellent handling" markets as well as the "not acceptable handling" markets preferred battery-operated electric prods. This indicates that the important factor in handling is how a driving aid is used rather than what is used—a good handler will often tap an animal with the prod instead of shocking it. There was a tendency for handling to be more abusive when electric prods connected to an overhead wire were used. This type of prod will give a less localized shock compared to a battery prod.

SURVEY B—SLAUGHTER PLANT EMPLOYEE BEHAVIOR

Twenty-five federally inspected U.S. and Canadian slaughter plants were visited. More than two days were spent in each plant observing the behavior of employees who killed and handled the livestock. The visits were made by the author between 1975 and 1987. Plants were rated as belonging to one of three categories—1. Acts of deliberate cruelty occurring on a regular basis. 2. Rough handling occurring as a routine practice, and 3. Good to excellent employee behavior. The condition of plant equipment and facilities was not included in this rating even if they contributed to handling problems. This was strictly an employee behavior survey. Of the 25 plants, 8 (32%) were in category 1, 3 (12%) were in category 2, and 14 (56%) were in category 3. Twelve plants were surveyed before 1982 and 13 after 1982. The incidence of cruelty and abuse dropped from 67% during 1975–1982 to 23% in 1982–1987.

Reprinted from *Anthrozoös* 1 (1988): 205–13, with kind permission of the editors.

Table 1. Handling Ratings for Southeastern Livestock Markets

Category	Description	%
Excellent handling	Animals were moved quietly with a minimum of prodding. Care was taken to avoid slamming gates on animals, and they were never kicked or hit with solid objects	21%
Acceptable handling	Handling practices did not fall into the excellent or one of the not acceptable categories	47%
Not acceptable—rough handling	Many animals were handled roughly by more than one person, and management did not attempt to stop the abuse. A rough-handling rating was given if any one of the following abuses was observed as a routine practice: constant prodding with an electric prod when the animals had no space to move, slamming gates on animals, overcrowding and causing animals to pile up, hitting animals with sticks or other objects, and constant whipping of animals with whips	20%
Not acceptable—cruelty	Animals were dragged, thrown, or picked up by the tail or ears. This rating was also given if the majority of the employees handled most animals roughly and appeared to have no regard for them	12%

Source: Grandin, 1985.

Table 2. Facilities Ratings for Southeastern Livestock Markets

Category	Description	%
Excellent	All pens and chutes were clean and well-maintained with a minimum of sharp protrusions that could injure animals. Facilities also had to have adequate lighting to be placed in this category. A market with a good pen layout design was also placed in this category	35%
Acceptable	The majority of the pens and chutes were well-maintained and clean. A market with a few broken boards or muddy pens was placed in this category	37%
Dirty or needed major repairs	Many of the pens had broken fences or gates and there was a need for major repairs. A market was also placed in this category if it was littered with trash, or chutes showed no evidence of being cleaned out on a regular basis	22%
Design unsatisfactory	This rating was given if a design defect caused a serious handling problem that increased the amount of rough handling and was likely to cause injuries to animals	6%

Source: Grandin, 1985.

Table 3. Relationship Between Handling and Quality of Facilities

	Handling	
Facilities	Excellent/Acceptable	Not Acceptable/Cruelty
Excellent/Acceptable	28 (76%)	9 (24%)
Not Acceptable	7 (50%)	7 (50%)

$(X^2 = 3.11; p = 0.08)$

Factors Influencing the Abuse and Cruelty Incidence

Operations identified as having humane handling had a manager who enforced a strict code of conduct. If an employee abused an animal he was either fired or transferred away from the animals. Slaughter plants that had cruelty problems tended to have lax management in the livestock department. In four instances, slaughter plants markedly improved their handling rating after hiring a new manager. In one instance, handling got worse. Management enforcement of a strict code of conduct had a greater influence on employee behavior than the regional location of the plant or employee cultural background.

The size of the slaughter plant or livestock market was not found to be related to the incidence of bad employee behavior resulting in rough handling or cruelty. However, poorly maintained or poorly designed facilities correlated with an increased incidence of rough handling and livestock accidents. Gentle handling is impossible if animals constantly balk, fall down on slick floors, or become jammed in chutes. Facilities should be well-lighted and kept clean. It is also easier to encourage good employee attitudes in pleasant surroundings.

Good facilities, however, do *not* guarantee good handling. The two worst incidents of deliberate animal cruelty witnessed occurred in slaughter plants that had new, well-designed facilities. One man took pleasure in shooting the eyes out of cattle before he killed them. In the other plant, a man stabbed a meat hook deep into a live hog's shoulder and dragged it like a hay bale. One of these plants had lax management and never disciplined employees for

cruelty, while the other only gave a reprimand for stabbing the hog. In neither of these cases did managementpunish employees severely for cruelty.

Personal observations indicate that the incidence of rough handling tends to be lower in midwestern and more northern areas with an estimated incidence of rough handling for all types of livestock operations at 10%–15%. In the southern U.S. rough handling appears to be higher, probably due to a more widespread "macho" attitude. Kellert (1978, 1980) has also observed regional differences in attitudes toward animals. In Europe there was less interest in animal welfare in southern countries (Curtis and Guither, 1983). There appears to be a correlation between climate and handling. In Australia, there is a greater concern for animals in the cooler, southern parts. In the tropical north handling is more often very rough according to personal observations and discussions. There is a trend for slaughter plant managers in Scandinavian countries and in Canada to be more concerned about humane handling than are U.S. managers. Slaughter plants in Holland and Sweden are very civilized. The employees are concerned about animal welfare and the management is concerned about the welfare of the employees. By contrast, the slaughter houses are dreadful in Mexico. There is an impression that societies that treat people humanely also tend to treat animals humanely.

In the surveyed slaughter plants, approximately 4% of the employees directly involved with livestock committed acts of deliberate cruelty. These people appeared to enjoy watching an animal suffer. If a plant or feedlot has a cruelty problem, usually only one or two people are involved in the worst incidents. On the other hand, rough handling tends to become widespread in poorly managed operations. In some poorly managed plants and auctions over half the employees engaged in rough treatment of animals.

Abuse and Cruelty by Children

A disturbing finding in the livestock market survey was that half the markets rated as having cruel handling allowed young children to abuse animals. At one sale, a young seven- to eight-year-old boy continually hit feeder pigs on the nose in the auction ring. None of the adults sitting around the ring made any attempt to stop it. At another sale teenage boys appeared to enjoy hitting cattle with boards. Three or four different instances of children tormenting calves with an electric prod have been observed this year. Children who enjoy abusing animals may be more likely to engage in cruelty or aggressive behavior as adults (Felthous and Kellert, 1987). Leyton (1987) reports that serial killers Albert DeSalvo (The Boston Strangler) and Edmund Kemper, who cooked part of his victim in a macaroni casserole, both tortured cats when they were children. One slaughter plant employee handled cattle roughly and teased them; he stated that when he was a child he was forced to kill his pet steer. He said, "I could never love another beef again." His behavior was similar to the taunting of animals prior to sacrifice in the ancient bear cults. Serpell (1986) states that taunting the victim helps distance the killers emotionally from an animal they had tenderly reared. This employee, however, never committed an extreme act of cruelty such as the ones described previously.

Factors that Correlate with Improved Animal Handling

The two major factors that motivate managers to improve handling in slaughter plants are legal sanctions and economic incentives. Most of the handling improvements observed during 1982–1987 can be attributed to legal sanctions and economic incentives. In 1978, the jurisdiction of the Humane Slaughter Act was extended to

handling. In later years a greater percentage of the meat was sold on a carcass basis instead of on a live-weight basis. Ownership changes hands only *after* slaughter in a carcass-based system, and the seller has to pay for bruises.

Sellers exert strong pressure on plant management to improve handling and to take steps to improve handling at their feedlots. Cattle sold on a live-weight basis had almost twice as many discountable bruises (Grandin, 1981). Rough handling doubles the amount of bruising.

Within the last five years many pork plants have also started to export to Japan. The Japanese reject poor-quality pork. Reducing stress and excitement in the stunning chute will improve pork quality (Grandin, 1986). When a plant starts exporting to Japan, management usually takes immediate steps to improve handling, because they see the Japanese grader rejecting over 50% of their pork. Six of the plants visited during 1982–1987 exported pork to Japan. These plants all had good handling. Four non-exporting hog plants were also surveyed. Three of these plants had either rough handling or incidents of cruelty.

Personal observations indicate that severe rough handling, abuse, and neglect on farms, ranches, markets, and feedlots have remained at a steady 10%–15% of operations for the last ten years over the entire United States. They have not shown the improvement that has occurred in slaughter plants. Even though rough handling causes great economic losses it continues, because the market is segmented. The attitude of some market people is, "I don't care if they get shipping fever—that's the feedlot's problem." The abuses will continue unless there is a direct economic incentive or animal welfare pressure leads to legal sanctions. Approximately 25% of all operations have truly excellent handling.

PSYCHOLOGY OF SLAUGHTER PLANT MANAGERS

Michael Lesy (1987) in his book, *The Forbidden Zone*, describes a dreadful plant with a wisecracking, foul-mouthed manager. The manager tells endless dirty jokes. This type of manager is in a minority. The most common management psychology is simply denial of the reality of killing. Managers will use words such as "dispatching" and "processing" to avoid this reality.

Over the years the author has made many observations of the behavior of slaughter plant managers. In large plants with corporate offices in a distant city, management tends to deny the reality of killing. The few times they visit the plant they tend to avoid the kill area. Even managers who have their offices on the plant grounds sometimes have this attitude. One manager told the author that he would not expand the stockyard because he did not want to see it from his office window. He wanted his plant to look like a "food factory."

The meat-packaging room, coolers, and the dressing line where the carcass is cut up are often much better designed and maintained than are the stockyards and kill chute. Several plants had stockyards that were falling apart and neglected while the rest of the plant was new and modern. Management attitudes are further reflected by the fact that livestock handling and kill-chute jobs are often the lowest-paid jobs on the line.

This attitude makes no sense economically. Bruises cost the meat industry $46 million per year, and meat-quality problems due to animal stress cost even more (Livestock Conservation Institute, 1983; Grandin, 1986). Improving handling can increase Japanese acceptance of pork loins by 10%–25% (Grandin, 1986). Well-designed chutes and stockyards and good handling practices will reduce bruises and stress-related meat quality problems (Grandin, 1982, 1982a, b, 1981, 1980a; Kilgour, 1971). The actual cost of livestock accounts for at least half the operating costs of a slaughter plant.

The author has also worked with managers and engineers who really care about animals but who also avoid visiting the kill area because it upsets them. Managers who care about livestock often raise their own livestock or have had previous experiences working with animals. These managers will enforce a strict code of conduct. They appear to be motivated by a genuine caring for the animals. One engineering manager who raised cattle made unauthorized expenditures to improve the humaneness of slaughter equipment. A feedlot owner, newly in the slaughter business, built his new office looking out toward the plant

stockyards. From his office he could watch and ensure that employees did not abuse the animals. He seldom went inside the slaughter area. Managers promoted from the livestock-buying department are usually more concerned about animal treatment than managers promoted from other departments. A manager's background affects his attitudes. One of the best-managed and most humane slaughter plants in the United States is owned and run by a Mennonite family. Hard work and good values transformed a small business into a company with almost $400 million in annual sales. The managers have an attitude of humaneness toward both animals and employees and have state-of-the-art equipment throughout the plant. They are proud of their operation, which is one of the few plants that still conduct public tours. While the big corporations attempt to cover up what they are doing, this company is proud of its excellent operation. Another plant with excellent humane handling had many Mormons in high management positions.

PSYCHOLOGY OF SLAUGHTER PLANT EMPLOYEES

Herzog and McGee (1983), in a study of college-student attitudes to slaughter, found that when college students first visited a slaughter plant, the killing of the animals bothered them more than gutting the carcass. Owens et al. (1981) did a study on the psychology of euthanasia technicians who kill surplus dogs and cats at the animal shelters. They found that the technicians often felt guilty, but they felt that they were performing a needed service. One technician commented, "I would rather euthanize the animals myself than leave it to someone who does not know what they are doing." Slaughter plant employees have made similar statements. Several said that they took the kill-chute job to prevent sadistic people from doing it.

Some technicians adopt the mechanical attitude suggested by Owens' study (Owens et al., 1981): "permeating most responses was the theme of protecting oneself from the full impact of the act by isolating one's feelings from the act. Some accomplished this by talking about euthanasia formally or intellectually." The meat industry also has euphemisms for killing, such as "dispatching." Animal-shelter personnel have euphemisms for killing, such as PTS, "put them to sleep," (Arkow, 1985).

The people who actually do the killing in slaughter plants have three different approaches to their jobs. These are the mechanical approach, the sadistic approach, and the sacred ritual approach. These approaches usually are observed only in the people who actually do the killing or who drive the animal up the chute.

Mechanical Approach

The mechanical attitude is most common. The person doing the killing approaches his job as if he was stapling boxes moving along a conveyer belt. He has no emotions about his act. Most people who have the mechanical attitude kill the animals efficiently and painlessly. Employees who use the mechanical approach will chitchat about the weather and gossip while they kill hundreds of animals per day. The animals have become a commodity. A consulting engineer who raised cattle and designed a system for electrocuting hogs stated, "Hogs are just a commodity but I can't stand to watch cattle killed." He used the mechanical approach for hogs only.

Some slaughter plant employees who have humanely killed animals for many years act as if the animals were inanimate objects. They do not talk to animals, call them names, or get angry at them. A person who has fully accepted the mechanical attitude no longer has any emotions about the job. Serpell (1986) states that people who kill animals regularly become progressively desensitized. The first few killings are upsetting, but then the person becomes habituated, and the killing act becomes a reflex without emotion. Slaughter plant employees often comment that they were upset when they first started their jobs.

Sadistic Approach

The second approach is sadistic. The person starts to enjoy killing and will sometimes do extremely cruel things and torment the animals on purpose. A typical comment from a person with sadistic tendencies is, "They are just animals and it does not really hurt them." "It is going to die in five minutes so it does not matter how I treat it." The above statements are examples of devaluation of the subject according to social-psychology terminology. By devaluing the animal, the person justifies in his mind the cruel things he does to it.

This concept was graphically illustrated by a series of experiments with people during the 1960s and early 70s. The first experiments were conducted by Milgram (1963) and Elms and Milgram (1966). Human subjects were instructed by an experimenter to give progressively bigger electrical shocks to another subject when he made mistakes on a learning task. The highest shock level was labeled 450 volts, "Danger Severe Shock." Sixty-five percent of normal American males obeyed the experimenter's orders and administered the highest shock levels. The entire shocking procedure was fake, but the subject believed he was giving real shocks.

Subjects who obeyed and administered the highest shock level tended to devalue the other subject. A typical comment was, "The good scientist deserved to be followed while the stupid, excitable learner deserved to be given a lesson" (Elms and Milgram, 1966).

A similar study was designed by Zimbardo (1972), who placed college students in a simulated prison. Half the students were "guards" and half were "prisoners." One-third of the student guards treated the prisoners in a sadistic manner. Zimbardo concluded that normal people can be turned into sadists.

Fromm (1973) notes that two-thirds of the student guards did not turn into sadists and questions how they might be distinguished from the other third who did. In the Milgram experiments, many of the obedient subjects had emotional conflict and were nervous and upset when they pushed the shock buttons. On the other hand, some of the obedient subjects were calm and deliberate. Fromm suggests that the subjects who did not experience conflict may turn into sadists.

Sacred Ritual Approach

The third approach is to make the act of killing a sacred ritual. Many different societies have slaughter ceremonies. The American Indians showed respect for the deer and elk they ate. As a sign of respect the bones from these animals were not thrown to the dogs (Frazer, 1922). Serpell (1986) also describes slaughter ceremonies practiced by the ancient Greeks, Egyptians, Phoenicians, Babylonians, Hebrews, and Romans. Judaism attaches great seriousness to the act of taking life. One reason for the many laws detailing the precise manner in which animals are killed for food is to maintain controls on the act itself (Grandin, 1980b). A ritual serves to place controls on the act of killing and prevents it from getting out of control.

The *shochet* (ritual slaughterman) must be moral; otherwise he would be degraded by his work (Lesy, 1987). Grunwald (1955) stated that the person performing *shechitah* (slaughter) should think about the act of taking an animal's life:

> A man may kill an animal but he should always remember that the animal is a living creature and that taking life from the animal involves responsibility (Levinger, 1979).

Islam has similar controls. The slaughterman must have a clear mind. "The act of slaughter (Al-Dhabh) starts by pronouncing the name of Allah, the Creator (this is symbolic to take his permission and in order to make the slaughterman accountable and responsible and give compassion and mercy to the animal during this act)" (Katme, 1986).

The builders of high-speed automated pig-killing equipment in Holland appear to have similar feelings. The Machinefabriek, G. NIHJUIS B.V., in Winterswijk, Holland, named their most highly automated equipment "Walhalla." In Nordic mythology, Walhalla is the paradise for warriors who died gloriously in battle (Davidson, 1972). Richard Selzer (1987), a surgeon, after a visit to a slaughter plant describes his view of an ideally designed slaughter house that definitely falls in the sacred ritual category. He describes an atrium built from columns with carved cattle heads, a labyrinthine, serpentine loading ramp, and workers reciting prayers.

Promoting a humane attitude toward animals is extremely important. These words were written by a blind girl when she visited a slaughter plant and reached over the side of the chute and touched an animal:

> *The Stairway to Heaven—is dedicated to those people who desire to learn the meaning of life and not to fear death. We, through respect for these animals, can come to respect our fellow man as well (Tester, 1974).*

Signs with the above message have been placed over the kill chute in some plants to help improve employee attitudes.

Slaughter rituals usually occur among the people who actually perform animal killing. When animals are killed by hunting dogs or by traps there is no slaughter ritual (Serpell, 1986). The blame for the animal's death is shifted to the dogs. Burkert (cited by Serpell, 1986) states that sacrificial customs are elaborate exercises in blame-shifting. The priests are directly responsible for the animal's death, but theirs is a sacred duty and therefore forgivable. The gods are blamed instead, because they demanded the sacrifice.

Rituals also serve a beneficial function by placing controls on the act of killing, and they also help prevent the devaluation and detachment that leads to the mechanical approach or to sadism. For over 12 years the author has designed and operated the equipment used to kill animals in commercial slaughter plants. To prevent herself from degenerating into mechanical "box stapling" she uses the sacred ritual approach. A ritual can be simple and still be effective in controlling behavior and promoting respect for animals. The act of killing is controlled by an act of submission similar to a submissive wolf exposing its throat to a dominant wolf. The author's own ritual is to face the plant and bow her head down when first approaching it. She has also written "Stairway to Heaven" or "Valhalla" on some of the drawings for new systems. The braces and supports on one slaughtering system were designed utilizing the Greek Golden Mean and a mathematical sequence which determines the behavior of many things in nature. Humans do not really know what happens after death. A ritual act of submission before one kills an animal acknowledges the unknown that haunts all people.

The ritual also serves a very practical function of controlling bad behavior. The author has observed Kosher slaughter in 13 different U.S. slaughter plants with a total of over 20 days observation time. Even though plant employees sometimes abused the animals, a *shochet* was never observed taunting, teasing, or deliberately abusing an animal. This observation illustrates the power of the ritual to control behavior. Some Kosher plants have cruel, dangerous methods for restraining the animal, which would have a tendency to encourage cruel behavior. Sixty-one percent of the Kosher plants engaged in cruel, dangerous live hoisting, and 23% had employees who abused animals. The *shochets* never engaged in abuse even though their working environment was often worse than that of most non-kosher plants. A total of 19 different *shochets* were observed actually killing animals.

Plant Case Study

The mechanical approach is the most common. In one large beef slaughter plant the author observed ten regular employees driving livestock, stunning, shackling, and bleeding cattle every week for three years. Seven employees utilized the mechanical approach, two were sadistic, and one worked hard to treat the animals with kindness. The plant manager cared deeply about humane treatment of animals, but he was unable to fire the sadistic employees because his superiors wished to avoid union problems. The people engaged in shackling, in hoisting of stunned animals, and in bleeding all had the mechanical attitude. The two sadists worked as a stunner operator and as a cattle driver. This pattern appeared in other plants. Shacklers and bleeders of stunned animals seldom engaged in cruelty. The stunned animal is either clinically dead or at least appears dead when it reaches their stations. Shacklers who hoisted fully conscious animals for ritual slaughter were often observed abusing animals. People do not torment or act sadistically toward dead animals or animals that appear dead.

CONCLUSION

It is important to rotate the employees who do the killing, bleeding, shackling, and driving. Nobody should kill animals all the time. Several plant managers and supervisors state that rotation helps prevent employees from becoming sadistic.

The author has worked many full shifts driving livestock and operating the kill chute at slaughter plants. Rotation every few hours between the kill chute and driving cattle up the chute made it easier to maintain a humane attitude. It is also easier to maintain a good attitude in plants with a slower line speed. At 1,000 hogs per hour it is almost impossible to handle the hogs properly. The constant pressure to keep up with the line leads to abuse. Maintaining respect for animals is much harder at 1,000 hogs per hour compared to 500 hogs per hour. Rotation of employees is even more essential on a high-speed line. One of the worst aspects of a high-speed line is the noise and confusion. Designing equipment to reduce noise would reduce stress on employees and animals.

The three types of approaches (Mechanical, Sadistic, and Sacred Ritual) have been repeatedly observed in over 150 slaughter plants. These three categories only apply to the people who actually do the killing and people who work in the kill-chute area. For managers the most common attitude is simply denial of the reality of killing. Some good managers who really care about animals often become upset when they have to watch the kill chute, but they express their caring by enforcing a strict code of employee conduct and spending money on good equipment. The paradox is that it is difficult to care about animals but be involved in killing them.

REFERENCES

Arkow, P. 1985. The Humane Society and the Human Animal Bond: Reflections on the Broken Bond. *Veterinary Clinics of North America 15:* 455–466.

Curtis, S. E., and H. D. Guither. 1983. Animal Welfare: an International Perspective. *Beef Cattle Science Handbook,* ed. F. W. Baker *19:* 1187–1191.

Davidson, H. R. R. 1972. *Gods and Myths in Northern Europe.* London: Penguin Books.

Elms, A. C., and S. Milgram. 1966. Personality Characteristics Associated with Obedience and Disobedience Towards Authoritative Command. *Journal of Experimental Research into Personality 1:* 282–289.

Felthous, A. R., and S. R. Kellert. 1987. Childhood Cruelty to Animals and Later Aggression Against People: A Review. *American Journal of Psychiatry 144:* 710–717.

Frazer, J. G. 1963. *The Golden Bough,* vol. 1 (abridged ed.). New York: The Macmillan Co.

Fromm, E. 1973. *The Anatomy of Human Destructiveness*. New York: Holt, Rinehart and Winston.

Grandin, T. 1986. Good Pig Handling Improves Pork Quality. European Meeting of Meat Research Workers, Ghent, Belgium.

Grandin, T. 1985a. Treatment of Livestock in Southeast U.S. Markets. Proceedings Livestock Conservation Institute, 14–24. Commissioned by Humane Information Services.

Grandin. T. 1985b. Livestock Handling Needs Improvement. *Animal Nutrition and Health* Aug., 6–9.

Grandin, T. 1982a. Welfare Requirements of Handling Facilities. Commission of European Communities Seminar on Housing and Welfare, Aberdeen, Scotland, July 28–30, 1983.

Grandin, T. 1982b. Pig Behavior Studies Applied to Slaughter Plant Design. *Applied Animal Ethology 9:* 141–151.

Grandin, T. 1981. Bruises on Southwestern Feedlot Cattle. Paper presented at 73rd Annual Meeting American Society of Animal Science, July 26–29.

Grandin, T. 1980a. Observations of Cattle Behavior Applied to the Design of Cattle Handling Facilities. *Applied Animal Ethology 6:* 19–31.

Grandin, T. 1980b. Problems with Kosher Slaughter. *International Journal for the Study of Animal Problems 1(6):* 375–390.

Grunwald, J. J. 1955. *The Schochet and Schechita in Rabbinic Literature*. New York: Feldheim Publishers.

Herzog, H. A., and S. McGee. 1983. Psychological Aspects of Slaughter Reactions of College Students to Killing and Butchering Cattle and Hogs. *International Journal for the Study of Animal Problems 4(2):* 124–132.

Katme, A. M. 1986. An Up to Date Assessment of the Muslim Method of Slaughter. In *Humane Slaughter of Animals for Food*, 37–46. U.K.: Universities Federation for Animal Welfare.

Kellert,S. 1980. American Attitudes Toward, and Knowledge of Animals: An Update. *Internat'l Journal for the Study of Animal Problems 1(2):* 87–119.

Kellert, S. 1978. Policy Implications of a National Study of American Attitudes and Behavioral Relations to Animals. U.S. Fish and Wildlife Service, U.S. Dept. of Interior, Stock No. 024–101–00482–7. Washington, D.C.: U.S. Govt. Printing Office.

Kilgour, R. 91 Animal Handling in Works, Pertinent Behavior Studies, 9–12. 13th Meat Industry Res. Conf., Hamilton, New Zealand.

Lesy, M. 1987. *The Forbidden Zone*. New York: Farrar, Straus and Girout.

Levinger, I. M. 1979. Jewish Attitude towards Slaughter. *Animal Regulation Studies 2:* 103–109.

Leyton, E. 1987. *Compulsive Killers: The Story of Modern Multiple Murder*. New York: New York Univ. Press.

Livestock Conservation Institute. 1983. Only You Can Stop Bruising, a $46 Million Annual Drain on the Livestock Industry. Madison, WI.

Milgram, S. 1963. Behavioral Study of Obedience. *Journal of Abnormal and Social Psychology 2(1):* 19–26.

Owens, C. E., R. Davis, and B. H. Smith. 1981. The Psychology of Euthanizing Animals; the Emotional Components. *International Journal for the Study of Animal Problems 2(1):* 19–26.

Selzer, R. 1987. *Taking the World in for Repairs*. New York: William Morrow and Co.

Serpell, J. 1986. *In the Company of Animals*. New York: Basil Blackwell.

Shoshan, A. 1971. *Animals in Jewish Literature*. Shoshanim, Rehovat, Israel.

Tester, G. 1974. Cited in Temple Grandin, 1976. The Stairway to Heaven. *National Humane Review* Jan. 1976.

Zimbardo, P. 1972. Pathology of Imprisonment. *Trans-Action 9* (Apr.): 4–8.

CONCLUSION

CRUELTY TO ANIMALS AND HUMAN VIOLENCE: SOME UNASKED AND UNANSWERED QUESTIONS

During the last forty years, many of society's concerns have focused on the quality of our physical environment and the threats to the integrity and health of that environment. As we enter the next millennium it is becoming clear that societal concerns about the proliferation of violence will be the basis of the next "environmental movement." Research, debate, and discussion about the causes and cures of violence in American society are already part of the discourse of nearly every discipline, from philosophy to criminology to evolutionary biology.

Society is looking for new tools and resources to employ in the efforts to combat violence, by identifying real or potential perpetrators at an early stage and by defining actions that might prevent violent behavior. Closer examination of animal cruelty within the framework of family and societal violence offers an opportunity to explore violence outside of the traditional "nature-nurture" debate over the origins of aggression. Cruelty to animals represents an objectively definable behavior that occurs within a societal context. It represents a good measure of the interaction between the behavior an individual is intrinsically capable of performing and the behavior his/her environment has allowed or encouraged. The fact that the definition of animal cruelty is so strongly influenced by cultures and subcultures need not be a complication but rather an opportunity to try to unravel the many influences that can shape violent behavior.

Closer analysis of the connections between cruelty to animals and other forms of violence offers new opportunities for the study of violence and the hope for new insights and solutions. There are many unanswered and unasked questions in the study of animal cruelty and violence, and obstacles that need to be overcome in the search for answers.

THE ECOLOGY OF VIOLENCE AGAINST ANIMALS

Most good science must begin with natural history. Because animal cruelty has traditionally been seen as a minor crime, basic quantitative information as to the nature and extent of animal cruelty has been limited. Good criminological analysis can begin with a solid "victimology." Hannelie Vermeulen and Johannes S. J. Odendaal have provided important first steps in remedying this gap (see section 8). However, further progress will depend on standardized reporting and tracking of animal cruelty cases around the country. Many key questions remain:

- What is the true incidence and prevalence of various forms of animal abuse and neglect?
- How does this victimology vary for different kinds of animals (for example, by species, as well as other factors, such as owned vs. stray, wild vs. tame vs. domestic)?
- What are the demographic attributes of the offenders and the frequency and severity of their acts?
- How do these demographics (age, sex, culture, residence, family size and structure, and criminal history) interact with victimology? For example, how closely do the actions of female offenders resemble those of the far more prevalent male offenders?
- How does the victimology and offender profile of intentional abuse differ from that of neglect or passive abuse or abandonment? Are these differences relevant in predicting the likelihood of future involvement in violence?
- How frequent are instances of "emotional abuse" of animals? No state laws currently recognize this as a category of abuse, but case history studies of animal cruelty routinely reveal practices that, if applied to a human, would constitute abuse, such as exposing a victim to imminent attack by another animal without allowing actual physical harm.
- What are the trends in animal cruelty cases (frequency, severity, chronicity, offender demographics) within specific reporting areas? Can

we confirm anecdotal impressions that such cases are becoming more frequent, more severe, or more likely to involve younger perpetrators?

• What is the extent of overlap with records of other known violent offenses, particularly interpersonal violence, including child abuse and domestic violence?

THE DYNAMICS OF ANIMAL CRUELTY AND HUMAN VIOLENCE

If we are to use the connections between animal cruelty and other forms of violence in a meaningful way to predict and/or intervene in the progression of violence, we need a much clearer picture of the place of animal abuse in the patterns and progression of violence. Most of our understanding of this connection has come from retrospective analysis of individuals or families in which serious human violence has already taken place. Far more attention is needed to prospective research to identify normal vs. pathological pathways involving participation in or witnessing the mistreatment of animals. Several recent works have focused on the long-range effects of victimization by observation of violence and cruelty.[1] There is also greater need to identify perpetrators' and witnesses' perceptions of the impact that these incidents of animal cruelty had on their development.

• What are the underlying dynamics of the victimology? For example, the killing of a dog may have different significance if it is the killer's own dog, a parent's or sibling's dog, a stray dog, a newborn puppy, or an aggressive animal that has bitten the perpetrator. Similarly, the incident may have different significance if the offender is a six-year-old, a twelve-year-old, or an adult or if it is the first, third, or twentieth such incident.

• What is the perpetrator's perception of the underlying dynamics? Much can be learned from the justifications provided for aberrant behavior, even if these explanations may not reflect true motivations.

• What critical incidents may be related to the earliest expressions of violence, and what was the response of parents, peers, and siblings to these events?

• What is the trajectory of the development of interpersonal violence that incorporates animal cruelty? How often is animal abuse truly predictive of escalation, and how often is it one manifestation of other forms of ongoing violence or antisocial behavior (such as bullying)? If violence has already progressed to serious or lethal levels, how often do offenders "regress" to violence against animals?

• How important are frequency and severity of animal cruelty as indicators of cruelty that represent a true potential for progression rather than a stage of experimentation with power and control?

• How important is peer pressure or parental assent in the initiation and escalation of animal cruelty?

• What factors are present when animal cruelty stops or does not escalate to other forms of violence? If we recognize that many individuals might engage in some acts of intentional animal abuse without progressing to other antisocial acts, it becomes essential to identify the stabilizing influences (internal, familial, or societal) that have prevented such a progression, including parental response to early cruelty, intervention by school, social-service, or law-enforcement authorities, and mental-health interventions.

• What physiological correlates of animal cruelty might exist that relate to other possible correlates of antisocial behavior (such as thrill-seeking or low responsiveness to stressful situations)?

• What is the role of external influences (drugs, alcohol) in the initiation of violent incidents against animals and others? We do know that substance abuse is frequently a factor in both child abuse and domestic violence.

• What is the role of exposure to media violence against animals in promoting imitation or desensitization to such violence?

---

1. See J. Osofsky, ed., *Children in a Violent Society* (New York: Guilford Press, 1997); and L. A. Leavitt and N. A. Fox, eds., *The Psychological Effects of War and Violence on Children* (Hillsdale, N.J.: Lawrence Erlbaum Associates, 1993).

- How often is animal cruelty a component of violence within dating relationships?
- How does the real or symbolic sexual role of animals influence the form of abuse that might be perpetrated? How prevalent is the direct sexual abuse of animals among violent offenders? The sexual connotations of animal abuse have been largely unexplored but could be of great importance in establishing the predicative significance of such cruelty to both domestic violence and other serious crimes, such as serial rape and homicide.

SOCIETAL CONCERNS AND RESPONSES TO ANIMAL CRUELTY

A December 1996 survey of 1,008 American households conducted by Penn & Schoen, Inc., for the Humane Society of the United States found that 42 percent of respondents believed animal cruelty to be moderately to extremely serious as a problem in this country, compared with 61 percent responding in this way to "environmental issues" and 78 percent to "child abuse." Of those surveyed, 71 percent supported making animal abuse a felony, and 81 percent felt that the enforcement of animal cruelty laws should be strengthened.

When professionals responding to violence display little attention to animal cruelty issues, this is apparently not because they reject its importance but rather because they are unaware of its importance or because they are concerned with other issues deemed more pressing. And many professions are aware of, and concerned about, this connection but have yet to translate that awareness into any standardized record keeping, intake procedures, or policies. Additional information is needed in many areas:

- How familiar are professionals in different disciplines (such as law enforcers, teachers, school psychologists, physicians, veterinarians, clergy, and court officials) with the possible significance of animal cruelty to the individuals with whom they work? Veterinarians, in particular, often feel ill-prepared to address issues of suspected animal abuse and, in many ways, are

in a position similar to that of pediatricians a generation ago, who were just beginning to face the problem of responding to suspected child abuse.

- What is a baseline level of animal abuse or neglect in families or individuals that might be considered to be normal?
- What are the obstacles to responding to information regarding the mistreatment of animals? We need a systematic assessment of why cases involving violence and animals succeed or fail within the criminal justice system.
- What is the impact of animal cruelty on society at large? How does it affect witnesses and other concerned parties?
- What motivates the frequent outpouring of public concern in high-profile animal cruelty cases when concurrent crimes against people may be ignored?
- What is the societal impact of labeling someone as an animal abuser?

LAW-ENFORCEMENT RESPONSES TO ANIMAL CRUELTY

Society's response to animal cruelty is reflected in the laws that are enacted to respond to the problem and in the level of enforcement. As of July 1997, eighteen states have felony-level provisions within their animal cruelty codes, a dramatic rise from just a decade ago. This reflects both societal pressure to respond to animal cruelty and legislative willingness to accommodate this demand. It is difficult, however, to document law-enforcement response, since such cases are generally not yet tracked in any systematic way other than through local humane groups with enforcement authority. Much information is still needed.

- How many animal-abuse and -neglect cases are handled on a regional and national basis? What proportion are dealt with through education, diversion, or other alternative mechanisms? How are cases handled differently by the juvenile court system and by the adult courts? What does the inaccessibility of juvenile court records imply for the effective assessment of the predictive value of tracking animal cruelty?

- What are the outcomes of cases that clearly involve severe or repeated intentional abuse? How do these outcomes compare with those of violent crimes against people?
- What obstacles might prevent the prosecution of cases considered to be serious?
- How is awareness of the connections between animal cruelty and violence against people being integrated into law-enforcement's response to domestic violence and into community policing?

SOCIAL-SERVICE RESPONSES TO ANIMAL CRUELTY

Humane organizations have made significant inroads in alerting social-service agencies to regard animal cruelty as a form of family violence that can be both indicative and predictive of other violence. Although only California formally includes animal-control officers and state humane officers among mandated reporters of child abuse, many other communities are providing for the cross-training of animal-abuse and child-abuse investigators or are including humane society representatives in local coalitions against violence. Similarly, there is a growing sensitivity to animal-cruelty issues among those responding to the needs of women seeking shelter from domestic violence. To maximize the effectiveness of these bridges between animal- and human-welfare advocates, we need more information about these cooperative efforts.

- How frequently are child- or domestic-abuse reports filed by humane officers? What proportion are validated, and how does this compare with other mandated reporters? If few reports are being made by well-trained reporters, what are the obstacles to such reporting?
- How routine are inquiries about the abuse of pets in assessing the needs of women seeking shelter? How widespread are programs to respond to these needs? Do programs that provide for response to those needs increase the likelihood that an abuse victim will leave in the earlier stages of escalating violence? What obstacles exist to effectively structuring programs that meet the needs of pet-owning victims?
- How important is it to address issues of pet loss and separation in meeting the needs of women and children leaving a violent environment? Since pets in these households may be both sources of support and victims or scapegoats, these issues might be quite complex.

PREVENTION AND INTERVENTION

The core assumption of many of the efforts against violence is that earlier detection of predispositions for violence will give the best opportunity for meaningful intervention. However, the lack of any standardized programs for detection and intervention has left this concept essentially untested. Many questions remain unasked and unanswered.

- Does response to severe or repeated animal abuse identify offenders at an early enough stage for successful intervention? Is this more reliable than other measures of antisocial behavior?
- What types of animal-cruelty offenses constitute the most significant warnings that intervention is needed? Is it more productive to target at-risk groups rather than active offenders?
- What are the most significant objectives for individuals who are recipients of intervention (for example, self-esteem, communication skills, empathy, anger management)?
- Is pairing offenders or high-risk individuals with nonviolent or humane mentors more effective than formal instruction in nonviolent skills or humane attitudes?
- How important are opportunities for undoing harm or being confronted by victims in structuring effective interventions?
- Does community service or other restitutional activities have better long-term results than purely punitive interventions?
- How important is it for animals to be involved in prevention and intervention programs? Can nurturing and other prosocial skills be taught in other ways (such as gardening projects)?
- When is the use of animals in therapy inadvisable? Are there patterns of violent history that should not be addressed through animal-assisted therapy or animal-assisted activities?
- What are the best short- and long-term measures of successful intervention in dealing with animal-abusing populations?

• Do interventions aimed at reducing interpersonal violence also affect animal abuse indirectly?

Answers to many of these questions will require the cooperation of individuals and agencies from many different disciplines. They will also require a truly prospective approach, identifying individuals involved in animal cruelty at the earliest possible stage and tracking the influences that prevent or promote the escalation to other forms of violent behavior. Violence makes victims of us all, and all segments of the community that deal with health and safety, kindness and cruelty, people and animals, must constantly find ways to build the connections that will make it possible to end this victimization.

Understanding our complex relationships with animals is starting to provide us with an impressive range of new resources that facilitate our efforts against violence, cruelty, and victimization. Incorporating our understanding of these relationships into problems of violence in a sense unites our concerns for the damage to our physical and psychological environment. By seeing ourselves as a part of nature and not apart from it, we can gain personal strength and satisfaction. By seeing ourselves as connected to families and communities and not controlled by them, we can reduce the need for violence.

Index